PHILADELPHIA GENTLEMEN

E. Digby Baltzell was born in Philadelphia, studied at the University of Pennsylvania and at Columbia University, and has spent his entire teaching career at the University of Pennsylvania. America's foremost sociologist of the upper classes, Professor Baltzell is also the author of *The Protestant Establishment.*

E. Digby Baltzell

PHILADELPHIA GENTLEMEN

THE MAKING OF A NATIONAL UPPER CLASS

WITH A NEW AFTERWORD BY THE AUTHOR

Q

Quadrangle Paperbacks
Quadrangle Books / Chicago

Preface

THIS IS A STUDY of an American business aristocracy, of colonial stock and Protestant affiliations, and centered in the older metropolitan areas along the Eastern Seaboard. Although primarily a Proper Philadelphia story, with ancient roots in the city's golden age at the close of the eighteenth century, it is also an analysis of how fabulously wealthy, nineteenth-century family founders, in Boston, New York, and Philadelphia, supported various exclusive institutions which produced, in the course of the twentieth century, a national, upper-class way of life.

In this book, I have had to cope with the problem of combining the materials of economic and social history with the methods and point of view of sociology. The sociologist should always be scrupulously careful to protect the anonymity of the subjects of his investigations. However, as most of the people discussed in these pages are, or will be, historical figures of some repute, this has proved undesirable if not impossible. There is, for example, no point in protecting the anonymity of George Gordon Meade, The Proper Philadelphian who commanded the Union armies at the Battle of Gettysburg. But since it is not the function of social science to repeat gossip, I have limited myself almost entirely to sources previously published and discussed individual idiosyncrasies only when they illuminate the analysis of institutions, which are but the shadows of men both living and dead. At all events, in an age blessed with an institutional determinism—partly the result of our propensity for submerging the individual in scientific abstractions—it is a pleasure to present a study of institutions which concrete persons have created, preserved, and given tone to.

I have had to wander from sociology into both American and local Philadelphia history. For their patient reading of this historical material, I am especially indebted to Edwin Wolf II, curator of The Library Company of Philadelphia, and Nicholas B. Wainwright, Research Librarian of The Historical Society of Pennsylvania. Needless to say, any faults in fact or interpretation are my own.

I should like to thank Dr. Martin P. Chworowsky, Director of the A. M. Greenfield Center for Human Relations, for his confidence in my work and for providing me with an invaluable grant-in-aid which allowed me to take half-time off from my teaching duties in the spring of 1956.

To my good friends, Joan Younger Dickinson, Milton M. Gordon and Michael Lalli for their critical judgment of style and content, to Eleanor Freisn for her patience with the typewriter, to Fred Gruenberger for his deft translations of association tables from IBM cards, and to Martha Gordon for her cartography, go my thanks and appreciation.

For broadening my sociological point of view with a deeper appreciation of American civilization, I am grateful to Robert E. Spiller. A continuing association which began with his seminar in American Civilization in the Institute of Humanistic Studies for Executives at the University of Pennsylvania in the Spring of 1954 has been an invaluable inspiration to me.

Finally, I owe my interest in the fascinating study of human society to two great teachers: the late Carl Kelsey of the University of Pennsylvania, and Robert K. Merton of Columbia. All who have studied under Professor Merton will appreciate my large debt to him.

Above all, I should like to thank Robert S. Lynd, without whose constant faith and encouragement at critical periods in my early academic career, this book would never have been completed.

Ithan, Pennsylvania

Contents

Tables

PHILADELPHIA GENTLEMEN

CHAPTER I

Introduction

> But the fact is that not only property, but the two
> institutions of property and social stratification are
> in the same position of moral ambiguity. Both are
> necessary instruments of justice and order, and yet
> both are fruitful of injustice. Both have, no less than
> government, grown up organically in traditional civi-
> lizations in the sense that they were unconscious
> adaptations to the needs of justice and order. The
> revolts against both of them by both the radical
> Christians and the radical secular idealists of the
> seventeenth and eighteenth centuries tended to be
> indiscriminate.
>
> REINHOLD NIEBUHR

LEADERSHIP and some form of stratification are inherent in all
human social organization. From the time of Plato's utopian
Republic, and his pupil Aristotle's more realistic *Politics*, the "few"
and the "many," the "rulers" and the "ruled," and the "Classes" and
the "masses" have been staple terms in the language of social
thought. Only in that delightful land of *Oz* are there more generals
than privates, and surely Alice might have found a "classless
society," like un-wet water, only in *Wonderland*. Yet perhaps man
has always dreamed of a golden age, free of the inevitable inequalities of all historical class situations:

> When Adam delved and Eve span
> Who was then the Gentleman?

Although scientific realism is deified in our time, modern social
theory, from Rousseau through Marx to the present, betrays, nevertheless, a utopian tendency to measure the good society, often
equated with democracy, in terms of such sociological monstros-
ities as "majority leadership" or the "classless society." Robert
Michels, for instance, in his well-known study of European labor
movements, comes to the pessimistic conclusion that democracy
is impossible because of what he calls the "iron law of oligarchy."[1]
While Michels is certainly right about the inevitability of "minority

leadership," his conclusion, which assumes, falsely, the alternatives, oligarchy *or* democracy, leads only to confusion.

Granted, all complex societies—aristocratic, democratic, or totalitarian—are oligarchical in that the few rule the many. A less utopian, more empirical test of democracy is whether the inevitable "minority of leaders," or oligarchy, is both *accountable* to the rest of the population and drawn from *all social levels* and not solely from the ranks of a few privileged families. Parliamentary representation, the two-party system, and universal suffrage, for example, are important, if imperfect, means of securing accountability; the inheritance tax, the abolition of entail and primogeniture, and universal free education are all designed to mitigate the advantages of birth and to foster social mobility in an open class, rather than a classless society.[2]

In modern America, virtue and social mobility have become synonymous. Our vices are often perverted virtues, however, and too much social mobility, especially at the elite level, perhaps may weaken the traditional means of checking the power of leaders. If power and authority are the bricks and mortar of all social structures, an upper class, based on inherited wealth and position, is but the organic institutionalization of power and authority within a traditional circle of privileged families. The revolutionary vanguard and party elites in modern dictatorships, or "Café Society" in this age of lonely crowds and mass communications, are but other, and perhaps more mechanical, ways of organizing the consciousness of kind and primary group solidarity of a privileged leadership. Although "Café Society" or the party elite may certainly be more *democratic* in their criteria for membership in the inner circle, perhaps an hereditary upper class may prove to be a more effective mediating group in institutionalizing the *accountability* of authority. After more than a century of concentrated attack on the evils of hereditary wealth and property, the problem of the accountability of power in an atomistic mass society has arisen to challenge the assumptions of the Western intellectual world. Certainly the liberal tradition, firmly grounded in the eighteenth century intellectual's mistrust of all established institutions, has too often failed to realize that both the democratic and aristocratic social processes are, like Siamese twins, indivisibly bound together in all healthy societies. Such patrician traditions of leadership and accomplishment provided by the Roosevelt, Adams,

Lowell, or Taft families have undoubtedly enriched the egalitarian soil of American life.

This is the study of an hereditary upper class, based on business wealth and power, which has grown up in Philadelphia during the two hundred or more years since the city's founding by that eccentric Quaker aristocrat, William Penn, in 1682. It is not our intention to attack the evils of hereditary wealth and the long-established family traditions in Philadelphia. We are concerned with an historical analysis of the structure and function of upper-class institutions. While assuming the desirability of established institutions which create an upper class consciousness-of-kind and more or less primary group solidarity, we shall nevertheless often refer to the abuses of privilege and the all too human frailties which inevitably prevent the proper functioning of such institutions. Finally, in many ways, this is an analysis of the adequacy of American institutions in fostering, among the rich and the powerful, a sense of *noblesse oblige,* an old sociological concept which seems to have found no place in the literature of contemporary American social science.

Philadelphia has been chosen as the central focus of this analysis of American upper class institutions for several reasons: First, there was the need to study the problem of social stratification in a large metropolitan area. During the nineteen thirties and forties, American sociologists, with elaborate staffs trained in interviewing techniques, the filling out of schedules, and the operation of IBM machines, made numerous, painstaking investigations of the social systems in the small community.[3] Very little systematic research, however, has been done on the metropolitan class structure. Philadelphia, a major American city since colonial times, not only provides a particularly good laboratory for studying the structure of well-established, urban institutions; it also is a convenient starting point for an analysis of the development of a national upper class in America which cuts across local boundaries to include fashionable families in all the older urban centers from San Francisco to New York, Boston, Philadelphia, or Baltimore. A description of the development of this national, metropolitan upper class will be an important task of this book. Secondly, Philadelphia provides an excellent example of a business aristocracy which has too often placed the desire for material comfort and security above the duties of political and intellectual leadership. While this is an all too common characteristic of modern commercial upper classes in general, both in Europe and America, the gradual withdrawal of the Philadelphia gentleman away from public service and into the counting house is a concrete illustration of a secular trend in this country which began with the rise of great fortunes after the Civil War.

The Elite and the Upper Class. A systematic treatment of social stratification usually has to arrive at some specific number of class levels. It is important to realize, however, that one divides a community into as many class levels as one must for the purposes at hand. Class levels are logical concepts to be used for analytical purposes: to fail to realize this and to "discover" in any community three, six, or nine classes is to run the risk of reification (the taking as real that which is only conceptual).[4]

For the purposes of this book, then, we shall act *as if* there were two aspects of high class position, an *elite* and an *upper class.* The *elite* concept refers to those *individuals* who are the most successful and stand at the top of the *functional* class hierarchy. These individuals are leaders in their chosen occupations or professions; they are the final-decision-makers in the political, economic or military spheres as well as leaders in the law, engineering, medicine, education, religion and the arts. Regardless of social origin or family position, whether Negro, Gentile or Jew, all successful and productive men and women are included within our elite concept.

In any stable social structure, certain elite members and their families will quite naturally over the years tend to associate with one another in various primary group situations and thereby develop a consciousness-of-kind and distinctive style of life. From Middletown to Moscow, this is a universal social process. In their second study of Middletown, for instance, the Lynds found that "around the families of the now grown-up sons and sons-in-law of the X clan, with their model farms, fine houses, riding clubs, and airplanes, has developed a younger set that is somewhat more coherent, exclusive, and self-consciously upper class."[5] Similarly, in Moscow, Barrington Moore, Jr., finds "evidence of a cultural separation of the new holders of high status from the masses of the population. In their leisure time the intelligentsia mingle more with one another than with the uneducated. It requires no great insight to perceive that a Soviet executive or scientist would find the company of other executives and scientists more congenial than that of a peasant or manual laborer. In this way different habits of speech, manners, and dress are built up and transmitted from one generation to the next. In addition, the tendency for families of similar social station to live near each other in the same community leads to the choice of marriage partners from families with approximately the same background. All these forces are at work in the Soviet Union, and it is safe to predict that they will eventually result in the emergence of a class system resembling in many ways that in the United States. . . ."[6]

"Twenty years ago," the English expert on the Russians, Edward Hallett Carr, wrote in 1951, "a school was started in the Kremlin in Moscow for children of high party and Soviet officials. Nobody supposes that its function was to enable these children to start equal with other Russian children."[7]

The *upper class* concept, then, refers to a group of *families*, whose members are descendants of successful individuals (elite members) of one, two, three or more generations ago. These families are at the top of the *social class* hierarchy; they are brought up together, are friends, and are intermarried one with another; and, finally, they maintain a distinctive style of life and a kind of primary group solidarity which sets them apart from the rest of the population. As Dixon Wecter put it: "A group of families with a common background and racial origin becomes cohesive, and fortifies itself by the joint sharing of sports and social activities, by friendship and intermarriage. Rough and piratical grandfathers had seized their real estate, laid out their railroads, and provided for their trust funds. The second and third generation, relieved from the counting house and shop, now begin to travel, buy books and pictures, learn about horses and wine, and cultivate the art of charm."[8]

Although this book will be concerned primarily with an analysis of the growth and development of an American metropolitan upper class, we shall constantly stress the relationship between an upper-class way of life and the present and past accomplishment of the elite individuals who, in the long run, make this way of life possible. C. Wright Mills has stressed the importance of tracing the relationship between the upper class and the elite in the following passage: "Are the intermarriage chances, the flow of prestige, influenced by what happens in banks? What is the distribution of legal skill, by family, by firm? Are there overlaps between the boards of banks, the elders of churches, and the prestige of ministers? Are 'social circles' and religious affiliations subtly interwoven with financial interests?"[9] It is to be hoped that these questions asked by Mills will be partially answered in this book.

Who's Who and the *Social Register*: Elite and Upper-Class Indices

Who's Who in America, a listing of brief biographies of leading individuals in contemporary American life, and the *Social Register*, a listing of families of high social class position, will be used as indices respectively of an elite and upper class.[10] In 1940 separate volumes of the *Social Register* were issued for each of twelve large metropolitan areas in this country: New York, Chicago, Cincinnati-Dayton, Buffalo, Boston, Baltimore, Philadelphia, St. Louis, Pittsburgh, Cleveland, San Francisco, and Washington, D.C. Of the approximately 12,000 residents of these twelve cities who were listed in *Who's Who* in that year, about one-fourth were also listed in the *Social Register*. In other words, the members of the upper classes had considerable influence on the elite in these cities.

Chapter II will discuss the rise of a national upper class in America during the last decades of the nineteenth century, and how the *Social Register* was founded in response to the need for a formal listing of this new, inter-city plutocracy. The chapters which follow will be concerned primarily with the historical development and contemporary structure of the Philadelphia upper class and its influence in the local elite in 1940. The nature of this contemporary relationship between the elite and the upper class will be based on an analysis of the brief biographies of the 770 Philadelphians who were listed in the 1940 *Who's Who*. Of these 770 members of the city's elite, 226, or 29 per cent, were also members of the local upper class. Their *Who's Who* biographies show how the members of the upper class (the 226 listed in the *Social Register*) differed significantly, in occupation, place of residence, religious affiliation, education, and club membership, from the rest of the elite (the 544 not listed in the *Social Register*) who were drawn from a wide variety of social class and ethnic backgrounds.

Proper Philadelphia Institutions. After first establishing the nature of upper-class leadership in the Philadelphia business and banking community in 1940, we will devote the major part of this study to an intensive analysis of how the small, Proper Philadelphia world was set off from the rest of the community by a common historical tradition and institutional structure which, over the years, nourished the growth of a distinctive style of life and value system. (For convenience and variety, "Proper Philadelphia" as well as "Proper New York, Boston, or San Francisco" will be used interchangeably with the term "upper class.") In large part, this analysis will consist of an historical discussion of upper-class institutions: the family, the neighborhood, the church, the private school and university, and the social club.

The tap root of any upper class, that which nourishes each contemporary generation with a sense of tradition and historical continuity, is a small group of families whose members were born to that class, and whose ancestors have been 'to the manor born' for several generations. This institutional analysis, then, will begin with the history of when and how the founders of some sixty Proper Philadelphia families first rose to positions of wealth and power. We shall show how these family founders, a majority of whom were included in the *Dictionary of American Biography* (a convenient index of an historical elite), came to the fore in Philadelphia's cultural and economic life during three fairly distinct historical periods. First, there were the eighteenth-century merchants and statesmen who produced Proper Philadelphia's Golden Age; these first family founders were followed by the pre-Civil War founders of family manufacturing firms and investment banking houses; and, finally, there were the late nineteenth- and early twentieth-century entrepreneurs who founded newer, and often fabulously wealthy, family lines.

On the whole, the 'old' family clans were founded before the Civil War. Even in 1940, those of more recent wealth were still considered 'new.'[11] Continuity in change, however, is the mark of a healthy society. The descendants of these family founders, whether they were East India merchants, colonial statesmen, pioneering manufacturers, railroad executives, coal barons, or traction tycoons, have intermarried and been assimilated into the fairly homogeneous subcultural world of Proper Philadelphia. In addition to piling up great fortunes and founding family dynasties, these men also established various upper-class institutions which, in turn, structured this process of assimilation by providing ways and means for the old and new rich to play and learn and worship together. They built up the fashionable Victorian neighborhood around Rittenhouse Square after the Civil War, and then moved their families out to such secluded suburbs as Chestnut Hill, which was planned and developed almost single-handedly by one large landowner, and the Main Line, an early suburban preserve for Pennsylvania Railroad executives. While most of them were originally Quakers, Presbyterians, Lutherans, and even Baptists, they soon built fashionable Episcopal churches around the Square and out in the suburbs, where the vast majority of their more genteel descendants were to worship eventually. They founded local private schools for their children, and also the University of Pennsylvania which played an important role in preparing their descendants for useful careers in law and medicine. And, of course, they had their exclusive clubs; election to membership was the final mark of entrance into the brotherhood of Proper Philadelphia.

In the course of the twentieth century, as transportation improved and the national corporation serving a national market became the norm, the New England Episcopalian boarding schools and the more fashionable Eastern universities began to educate an inter-city and national upper class. These fashionable family-surrogates taught the sons of the new and old rich, whether from Boston, Baltimore, Philadelphia, or San Francisco, the subtle nuances of an upper-class way of life. After World War I, the old school tie, or the "Ivy Leaf" and "Porcellian Pig," became totem symbols of pedigreed associational status recognized all over America (at least within upper-class circles). Wherever possible, then, we shall stress the fact that Proper Philadelphia is part of a *national* upper class with a similar way of life, institutional structure, and value system.

Leadership, and the exercise and retention of power within a small and hereditary group of families, is the ultimate end and justification for an upper-class way of life. For this reason, anecdotes about the charming idiosyncrasies of Proper Philadelphia will be avoided in favor of institutional analysis.[12] Nor will the behavior patterns of the leisured classes enjoying their leisure along the Main Line be discussed in any detail. Too often, social criticism of the privileged classes has treated the member of the *Social Register* as superficial "socialites," irresponsibly outside the main stream of American life. Although this view may reinforce a hypocritical definition of democracy, it is nevertheless bad sociology; and it is not borne out in the Philadelphia *Social Register,* which listed, with certain ethnic exceptions, almost all the most powerful bankers and businessmen in the city in 1940.

Even more disturbing are the sophisticated critics of American society who reinforce this popular view of the 'leisure classes.' The highly entertaining, if often inaccurate, writings of the late Thorstein Veblen, for instance, inadvertently played down the facts of power by their very emphasis on the conspicuously consuming leisure-time activities of America's new plutocracy at the turn of the century.[13] Even the serious sociology of W. Lloyd Warner, in stressing the fact that the old family leaders in *Yankee City* were looked up to because they "knew how to act" or possessed an inherited good taste in furniture, may have confused a by-product with the basis of privilege.[14]

Perhaps Harvey Warren Zorbaugh, in *The Gold Coast and the Slum,* has succeeded in reinforcing the popular stereotype of the "socialite" more successfully than most serious sociologists.[15] In this early sociological classic, one of the few references to the *Social Register* in the literature of sociology occurs in the following paragraph:

> The "social game" is a constant competition among those who are "in" for distinction and pre-eminence; a constant struggle upon the part of those who are not "in" to break into the circles of those who are in. Perhaps as good a criterion as there is of social position, which is the goal in the "social game," is the *Social Register,* a thin blue book which one can own only by virtue of having one's name in, containing a complete list of Chicago's socially acceptable, with their universities, their clubs, their marriages, their connections, and their deaths. To have one's name in the *Social Register* "one must not be 'employed' [sic!]; one must make application; and one must be above reproach."[16]

Some people of course have always played the "social game," and they have not always, or only, been members of the upper class. But few of the Proper Philadelphians who built up family fortunes have had either the time or the inclination to play the game; nor, for the most part, have their socially secure descendants. Moreover, exclusive private schools, neighborhoods, and social clubs are not necessarily frivolous aspects of the "social game" but, rather, an important means of consolidating a continuity of particular and partial power in the serious world of affairs. Even that ubiquitous upper-class rite of passage—the debutante ritual—serves the latent function of containing family wealth and power within a small select circle; the democratic whims of romantic love often play havoc with class solidarity.

Recent American social science has suffered from an unfortunate "time-provincialism": sociology without history and psychology without biography has become the norm. Throughout our discussion of the development of Proper Philadelphia institutions, the changing economic and social conditions upon which they were ultimately based will be emphasized constantly. We shall show, first of all, how Penn's city was ruled by a small Quaker oligarchy during most of the eighteenth century, and how these devout Quaker grandees founded several prolific family lines which have continued to produce important leaders in the city for over two centuries. Eventually, however, the Indian Wars, the general increase in wealth, and the ideas of the Enlightenment, which infected so many scions of good Quaker families during their quest for education abroad, all combined to produce a new Anglican gentry during Philadelphia's Golden Age —the years following the Revolutionary War. Federalist and Anglican Proper Philadelphia was at that time the host to the New World's most sophisticated and talented leaders. A class of gentlemen, steeped in the classics as well as the political theory of Locke and Rousseau, reluctantly had taken the lead in rebellion against the British Empire, and subsequently wrote the new nation's constitution after lengthy deliberation on Philadelphia's Independence Square.

After the War of 1812, a new bourgeois ethic entered the genteel drawing rooms around Washington and Independence Squares; Proper Philadelphia was busy assimilating the pioneers of America's soon-to-be-predominant business class. These were the days of the founding of family firms, both in manufacturing and banking; the consolidation of coal-mining interests; and the founding of such Proper Philadelphia institutions as the Pennsylvania Railroad and the Philadelphia Club. By the close of the Civil War, these new businessmen had replaced the merchant-statesmen as typical Proper Philadelphians.

The half-century following the Civil War, of course, produced a fabulous plutocracy whose handsome mansions surrounded Rittenhouse Square. Although the "Protestant ethic" still spurred on the *parvenu*, Proper Philadelphia increasingly preferred the richness of the Anglican ritual, and, in many subtle ways, a rigid code of drawing-room manners gradually replaced the more ancient moral values. The capitalist-entrepreneur still dominated the family firm as well as the patriarchal household. As the century waned, however, the fashionable investment bankers were busy creating a corporate concentration which would, of course, eventually spell the end of the family firm and all it meant to family power and sense of responsibility.

The period between the two world wars marked the final stage of this upper class history. The advent of the income tax, and the federal centralization accelerated by World War I, paved the way for the final triumph of an inter-city aristocracy based on affiliation with fashionable boarding schools, universities and clubs rather than prominent family position alone. These economic trends paralleled the social and sexual revolution of the twenties: the emancipation of women, the decline of male and parental authority, combined with the final destruction of the "Protestant ethic" all served to weaken the power of the family.

The steady stream of immigrants from southern and eastern Europe who came to America between 1880 and 1918 were to eventually change the traditional ethnic composition of the elite; and especially the predominantly Anglo-Saxon upper-class position of leadership. As the descendants of these new immigrants would not, however, materially change the ethnic composition of American leadership until after World War II, this is another reason for focusing this study on the pre-war era.

There were other signs of change in the air by 1940; even though most of them waited for the close of World War II to assert themselves. This was, of course, the period of the gradual retreat of the *entrepreneur* in favor of the large corporation *employee;* the investment banker began to lose power and prestige as the large corporations, large insurance companies, and the federal government began to invade the money market; at the same time public relations, invented by that proper Princetonian, Ivy Lee, became the newest rage; clean-cut young men from fashionable universities went into advertising rather than Wall Street. The bank account and the trust fund, life blood of an upper class, were replaced by the expense account and elaborate corporation retirement plans. It was the beginning of the new corporate feudalism and atomistic society of rank (cradle-to-the-grave security for those who play the game); local ties and family prestige were to be replaced eventually by the coat of arms of the "company man," that new aristocratic nomad who would move from suburb to suburb, in city after city, especially in the early years of his marriage when, in a previous age, he would have been busy establishing himself in some local community.

Philadelphia has been going through a cultural, civic and political renaissance since the end of World War II. Perhaps this is one of the best reasons for concentrating on the pre-war period—when conservative gentlemen-bankers and businessmen were still in control of the city. Fashionable Philadelphians are still powerful today in many areas, and leadership in the new reform movements includes many Proper Philadelphians, but the new social forces asserting themselves in the city must eventually result in a new balance of power between the traditional upper class and other centers of influence. In the exciting decade of reform since the war, life in Philadelphia has changed, but it is still too soon for any objective assessment of the changes.

All this suggests that 1940, the eve of America's entry into the Second World War to save democracy, may definitely have marked the end of another era in the history of Proper Philadelphia. While the era may, in fact, have ended in 1929, in our rapidly changing society the top echelons of any elite usually remain in command beyond the historical period in which they made their way to the top. It must be borne in mind that the Philadelphians listed in *Who's Who* in 1940 made their way, on the whole, before, or just immediately after, World War I. The 1930's were indeed a new era on the national political scene, but in Philadelphia, the same business leaders remained at the helm all through the Depression. A depression usually consolidates the power of those in control at its beginning; modern war, on the other hand, is productive of new elites and new family founders. Thus, with the exception of a few references to the present for historical contrast, we shall center our discussion on Proper Philadelphia prior to World War II.

CHAPTER II

The American Metropolitan Upper Class and the Elite

> Unlimited political democracy in America, for instance, does not prevent the growth of a raw plutocracy, or even an aristocratic prestige group, which is slowly emerging. The growth of this "aristocracy" is culturally and historically as important as that of plutocracy, even though it usually goes unnoticed.
>
> MAX WEBER

THE history of Western Civilization has been, in many ways, the story of the rise and fall of great metropolitan centers: Athens and Rome in the ancient world, Constantinople in the age of transition, Paris, along with Naples, Venice, and Milan in the Renaissance, London in the eighteenth and nineteenth centuries, and, finally, New York in the twentieth, each in its day, marked the center of pomp and power in the western world over a span of twenty-five centuries. And in each city, at the zenith of its power, an aristocracy of wealth or an upper class emerged. The last years of the Republic in Rome, when the Senate was an aristocracy of wealth, and the "Gilded Age" in America when the Senate was known as the "Millionaires' Club" may be similar sociological periods.

In the same vein, American history is partly reflected in the rise of different cities to positions of affluence and power: Salem and Newport rose to prominence along with the merchant shipper of the eighteenth century. Atlanta, Charleston, Richmond, New Orleans, and Mobile were centers of affluence in those chivalrous days just before the Civil War when the planter aristocracy dominated the United States Senate. Within the last few decades, Los Angeles and Detroit manifest a modern opulence as they supply the demands of a mass culture for movement and entertainment. Not the least indicative of the trend of our times is the growth of the nation's capital as the result of the shift in power from Wall Street to the government bureaucracy.

In any complex civilization, social and economic power tends to gravitate toward the large metropolis; and centralization is especially characteristic of modern American society where the national corporation, mass producing for a nationwide market, has steadily absorbed or replaced the local firm. In their excellent sociological analysis of the first successful labor strike in *Yankee City's* long history, which occurred in 1935, Warner and Lunt carefully document this modern pattern of centralization:

Big City capitalism had superseded small town capitalism in the vertical structure of corporate enterprise which had extended on beyond Yankee City to the great metropolis. At the time of the strike the local men, although born and reared in Yankee City, were little more than the factory managers for the Big City capitalists since they occupied inferior positions in this vastly extended vertical structure. They were not in a position to take leadership; they were not in a position of great power where they were free to make the decisions which always characterized the lives of Choate, Weatherby, and Pierce.[1]

Choate, Weatherby, and Pierce, highly respected, upper-class leaders in a departed era of local autonomy and local pride, "had long since taken up their residence in the Elm Hill Cemetery" in *Yankee City.* By 1930 the local shoe factory was owned and controlled by a New York corporation which operated a number of factories as well as a chain of 110 shoe stores in 56 cities: "even the name of Yankee City is not known to those whose financial power often controls decisions of the utmost importance for the town."[2]

All over America, as the members of small town elites become less and less important in each decade of the twentieth century, the more enterprising (and socially ambitious) members of the local upper classes moved to the large city. Many descendants of former coal barons in Scranton, Hazelton, or Wilkes-Barre lived along Philadelphia's Main Line in 1940.

At the same time that the large cities were absorbing members of many small town elites and upper classes, a national, inter-city, metropolitan upper class was becoming a reality in America: for the first time, in the last part of the nineteenth and early twentieth centuries, the New England boarding schools and the fashionable eastern universities provided the sons of the new and old rich from many cities with a common experience and set of subcultural standards.

The purpose of this chapter then, is to show how the *Social Register* became an index of this new, inter-city upper class which emerged in the last part of the nineteenth century in America; and how, in certain of the older metropolitan areas in 1940, the members of this new upper class were, in turn, also members of the contemporary elite, those listed in *Who's Who in America*. In other words, this chapter will serve to place the more detailed study of the upper class and the elite in Philadelphia within a national, rather than local, context, both historically and structurally.

The Social Register: A National Upper-Class Index

Human society is an historical process wherein each generation sifts to the top particular individual types—warriors, prophets, priests, merchants, bankers, or bureaucrats—whose talents are needed in any given period; these individuals, in turn, and within limits, make the decisions which shape the course of history. Thus Brooks Adams saw the history of England as partly reflected in the circulation of elites, wherein the feudal warrior, whose power lay in men and spears, was replaced during the Reformation by the large landowners who ruled England from the time of Henry VIII to the Revolution of 1688; the rising merchant adventurers who finally won their rights in 1688 were soon replaced by the manufacturing men such as Watt and Boulton whose talents led them to power after the Industrial Revolution. And, finally, from the time of the defeat of that symbol of martial power on the hill at Waterloo, both the manufacturing and landowning elites were dominated by, and often in debt to, the money power of Lombard Street.[3] The English upper class, often called an aristocracy, centers in a group of families who are descendants of those successful individuals of the remote and recent past, and is of course alloyed with those new men with a talent for power in the modern bureaucratic period.

As in England, America has produced a procession of successful men who have risen to positions of wealth and power, and whose children and grandchildren have been brought up in a more or less money-insulated world, often called polite society. In each generation, however, the old-money world has remained aloof from the larger and more opulent world of the newly rich.

All families are equally old. Thousands of Americans apparently boast of the sacred blood of *Mayflower* passengers, and all of us go back to Adam and Eve! In the limited social class sense, "old families" are those whose ancestors were affluent in an earlier day than their "new family" emulators. Within America's Eastern upper class, for example, the "old families" are certainly not *Mayflower* descendants; rather they are the descendants of eighteenth and early nineteenth century merchants and manufacturers. Inherited wealth is always and everywhere the basis of gentility. "All through Boston history," writes Cleveland Amory, "when a family loses its financial stability, it has a way of beginning to disappear."[4]

After the Civil War, America's eastern seaboard, provincial and familial aristocracies were eventually replaced by an exclusive and competitive associational plutocracy, rooted in the "Gilded Age" and continuing to the present day. As with so much else in American life, the 1880's witnessed a turning point in the structure of the upper class. Edith Wharton portrays this transitional period in three novels—*The Age of Innocence, The House of Mirth,* and *The Custom of the Country.* The first novel, which opens "on a January evening in the early seventies," presents a small, intimate, and formal "Society" which is soon to surrender to the assault of the *parvenu* described in the other two novels.

After 1880, New York became the center of upper-class social life in America. For one thing, new fortunes of undreamed-of proportions were founded in this period. According to Charles A. Beard, while there were only three millionaires in the United States in 1861, thirty-six years later there were at least thirty-eight hundred.[5] From all parts of the American continent, barons of dry-goods, utilities, coal, oil, and railroads moved their wives and families to the great metropolis, built ostentatious Victorian mansions, entertained on the grand scale, and, where possible, moved into "Society." Even their literary hero, Mark Twain, a self-made man from Missouri, was "a candidate for gentility."[6]

At first there was the usual resistance to accepting these new rich families. But "by one process or another amalgamation was affected and new varnish softened by the must of age. As the landed gentlemen of England had on various occasions saved their houses from decay by discreet jointures with mercantile families, so many of the established families in Boston, New

York, Philadelphia, and Baltimore escaped the humiliation of poverty by judicious selections from the onrushing plutocracy."[7]

In the year 1887, amidst this incredible "Gilded Age," the *Social Register* was copyrighted by the Social Register Association; the first volume appeared for New York City in 1888.[8] There were less than two thousand families listed in this "record of society, comprising an accurate and careful list of its members, with their addresses, many of the maiden names of the married women, the club addresses of the men, officers of the leading clubs and social organizations, opera box holders, and other useful social information."[9] America's associational aristocracy was born with the advent of the *Social Register*. "Here at last," wrote Dixon Wecter, in his *Saga of American Society*, "unencumbered with advertisements of dressmakers and wine merchants, enhanced by large, clear type and a pleasant binding of orange and black—which if anything suggested the colors of America's most elegant university—was a convenient listing of one's friends and potential friends. It was an immediate triumph."[10]

The New York *Social Register* was soon followed by volumes for Boston and Philadelphia in 1890, Baltimore in 1892, Chicago in 1893, Washington, D.C. in 1900, St. Louis and Buffalo in 1903, Pittsburgh in 1904, San Francisco in 1906, and Cleveland and Cincinnati-Dayton in 1910. Volumes for all these twelve cities have been issued yearly down to the present and in substantially the same form as the original New York *Social Register*. Other volumes were issued for Providence, R.I. (1905-1926), Minneapolis-St. Paul (1907-1927), Seattle-Portland (1914-1921), Pasadena-Los Angeles (1914-1926), Detroit (1918-1927), and Richmond-Charleston-Savannah-Atlanta (1905-1927) but were discontinued because of lack of interest.[11]

It is interesting that the *Social Register* is privately owned and lists social status, as it were, for a profit. The *Social Register* is issued annually in November and is sent to all families listed within its pages. The annual charge for a subscription ranges from five to ten dollars per city volume. Potential members must make application and include written references from present members; the only exceptions are to be found in Washington, D.C., where the President, the Vice-President, the Supreme Court, the cabinet, various members of the diplomatic corps, and all United States Senators (not Representatives) are listed automatically. This last point is indicative of stratification in a bureaucratic social structure where, like the military services, social class follows functional position; the senator, like the naval officer, is automatically a "gentleman."[12]

What is the relationship between the families listed in the *Social Register* and the captains of industry and finance who came to power in the "Gilded Age"? In his *Lords of Creation,* Frederick Lewis Allen shows how ten ideal-typical examples of the American financial elite at the turn of the century alloyed their gold with the American upper classes. Of interest here is the fact that, of these ten men—J. Pierpont Morgan, George F. Baker, James Stillman, Edward H. Harriman, John D. Rockefeller, William Rockefeller, Henry Huddlestone Rogers, William K. Vanderbilt, James R. Keen, and Jacob H. Schiff—all save the last were listed in the *Social Register* as of 1905. Allen notes that the exclusion of Schiff was "presumably due to the fact that he was a Jew, and the Jews constituted a group somewhat apart; the fashionable clubs were almost exclusively gentile; and the *Social Register* was virtually a gentile register."[13] As it illustrates the dynamics of upper-class formation in America, it is of interest to observe that Jacob Schiff's grandson, who married George F. Baker's granddaughter, was listed in both the *Social Register* and *Who's Who* as of 1940.

Ferdinand Lundberg's *America's 60 Families* is a study of America's wealthiest families, the majority of whose fortunes were made between the Civil War and World War I.[14] Of these sixty consanguine family units, well over three-fourths have traceable descendants (the same given and surnames as the family founder) who are listed in the 1940 *Social Register.* These descendants are married one with another as well as with those of less spectacular wealth but higher social position: in the twentieth century, for instance, "blood" has been nicely alloyed with "gold" as Biddles, Roosevelts, and Peabodys have married Du Ponts, Dukes, or Fields.

Finally, Gustavus Myers' *History of the Great American Fortunes* is a useful volume for validating the *Social Register* as an index of an American upper class.[15] This well-known book is a study of the men who amassed great fortunes in America from colonial times to the present (1936). The names of these wealthy family-founders (taken from the index of Myers' book) have been carefully checked against the names of the families listed in the twelve *Social Registers* in 1940. Table 1 is a listing of the famous family-founders in Myers' book whose descendants are listed in the contemporary *Social Register*.

The distinguished historian, Samuel Eliot Morison, once facetiously remarked that he attached great significance to the fact that the founding of the Brookline Country Club, in a Boston suburb, in 1882, coincided with the closing of the frontier in America. Certainly, the closing of the frontier (1890), the formation of the United States Steel Company (1901), the founding of Groton School (1884), the opening of the new "millionaires' country club" at Tuxedo Park, New York (1885), the rule of Mrs. Astor and Ward McAlister (1880's and 1890's), the Bradley Martin ball (at the cost of $369,200 in 1897), and the first issue of the *Social Register* (1888) were important, and interdependent, variables in a social situation which foreshadowed a centralized America in the middle twentieth century.

A centralized elite and upper class quite naturally follows from a centralized economy. From the beginning, provincial aristocracies of birth and breeding have been characteristic of all the older eastern cities in America. The *Social Register,* on the other hand, was born in an age of centralization and lists a new, associational, inter-city, aristocracy. For the first time, upper-class associations other than the family played an important role in socializing the young. The New England boarding school and the fashionable Eastern university became upper-class surrogate families on almost a national scale. J. P. Morgan, the symbol of economic centralization in America, for example, joined his contemporaries as trustees and benefactors of these exclusive educational associations, where they all, in turn, sent their sons to be educated together. Of the eighty-seven family-founders listed in Table 1, no less than sixty-five had one or more descendants who had attended either Groton, St. Mark's, or St. Paul's schools in the period between 1890 and 1940.

Groton, which opened its doors in 1884 with the elder Morgan as an original trustee, was founded by Endicott Peabody, whose ancestors were great Salem merchants.[16] In the twentieth century its role as an upper-class family-surrogate on almost a national (and international) scale is indicated by the fact that its 192 boarding students in 1940 were residents of fifteen states, the District of Columbia, Bermuda, Brazil, China, England, Hungary, Ireland, and Venezuela.[17]

Table 1—Deceased Elite Individuals in American Economic Life with Descendants who
Are Listed in the 1940 Social Register; the Names Are Taken from the Index
of History of the Great American Fortunes, by Gustavus Myers

Deceased-Elite Individual	Period When Wealth Was Acquired	Occupation: Or the Way in Which Wealth Was Acquired*
Elite Individuals with Descendants Listed in the Philadelphia Social Register in 1940		
Baer, George F.	Late 19th Century	Railroads
Biddle, Nicholas	18th-19th Century	Finance
Cassatt, A. J.	Late 19th Century	Railroads
Cope, Thomas Pym	18th-19th Century	Merchant
Dolan, Thomas	Late 19th Century	Utilities
Drexel, Anthony	Late 19th Century	Finance
DuPont, Coleman	20th Century	Chemistry
Elkins, William L.	Late 19th Century	Utilities
Hopkins, Johns	Early 19th Century	Railroads
Knox, Philander	Late 19th Century	Law
Penrose, Boies	20th Century	Politics
Ridgway, Jacob	18th-19th Century	Merchant
Scott, Thomas	Late 19th Century	Railroads
Wanamaker, John	Late 19th Century	Merchant
Widener, P. A. B.	Late 19th Century	Utilities
Elite Individuals with Descendants Listed in the Boston Social Register in 1940		
Adams, Charles F	Late 19th Century	Railroads†
Aldrich, Nelson	Late 19th Century	Finance
Ames, Oakes	Late 19th Century	Railroads
Brooks, Peter C.	18th-19th Century	Merchant
Cabot, George	18th-19th Century	Merchant
Derby, Elias	18th-19th Century	Merchant
Peabody, Joseph	18th-19th Century	Merchant
Perkins, Thomas	18th-19th Century	Merchant
Thorndike, Israel	18th-19th Century	Merchant
Elite Individuals with Descendants Listed in the Chicago Social Register in 1940		
Armour, J. Ogden	Late 19th Century	Manufacturing
Field, Marshall	Late 19th Century	Merchant
Leiter, Marshall	Late 19th Century	Merchant
McCormick, Cyrus	Late 19th Century	Manufacturing
Palmer, Potter	Late 19th Century	Merchant
Patterson, Joseph M.	Late 19th Century	Publisher
Elite Individuals with Descendants Listed in the New York Social Register in 1940		
Astor, J. J.	Early 19th Century	Furs, Land
Baker, George F.	Late 19th Century	Finance
Beekman, Henry	18th-19th Century	Land
Belmont, August	Late 19th Century	Finance, Utilities

Table 1 (Continued)

Deceased-Elite Individual	Period When Wealth Was Acquired	Occupation: Or the Way in Which Wealth Was Acquired*
Blair, John I.	Late 19th Century	Railroads
Brevoort, Henry	18th-19th Century	Land
Brown, Alexander	Late 19th Century	Finance
Carnegie, Andrew	Late 19th Century	Manufacturing
Choate, Joseph	Late 19th Century	Law
Clews, Henry	Late 19th Century	Finance
Cravath, Paul D.	Late 19th Century	Law
Cromwell, W. Nelson	Late 19th Century	Law
Dodge, Cleveland	Late 19th Century	Copper
Duke, James B.	20th Century	Cigarettes
Flagler, H. M.	Late 19th Century	Oil
Ford, Henry	20th Century	Autos
Goelet, Peter	18th Century	Land
Gould, Jay	Late 19th Century	Railroads
Griswold family	18th-19th Century	Merchants
Harriman, E. H.	Late 19th Century	Railroads
Havemeyer, H. O.	Late 19th Century	Sugar
Hill, J. J.	Late 19th Century	Railroads
James, D. Willis	Late 19th Century	Copper
Ledyard, L. Cass	Late 19th Century	Law
Lee, Ivy	20th Century	Public Relations
Livingston, Robert	18th Century	Land
Lorillard, Pierre	Early 19th Century	Snuff, Land
Morgan, J. P.	Late 19th Century	Finance
Payne, O. H.	Late 19th Century	Oil
Perkins, George	Late 19th Century	Finance, Insurance
Phelps, John T.	Late 19th Century	Copper
Phillips, Adolphus	18th-19th Century	Merchant
Rhinelander, William C.	18th-19th Century	Land
Rockefeller, John D.	Late 19th Century	Oil
Rogers, H. H.	Late 19th Century	Oil, Finance
Roosevelt, James	18th-19th Century	Land
Ryan, T. Fortune	Late 19th Century	Utilities
Schermerhorn, Peter	18th Century	Land
Schiff, Jacob	Late 19th Century	Finance
Schley, Grant B.	Late 19th Century	Finance
Schuyler, Peter	18th-19th Century	Land
Stettinius, Edward	Late 19th Century	Matches, Finance
Stillman, James	Late 19th Century	Finance
Stokes, Thomas	Late 19th Century	Copper
Taylor, Moses	Early 19th Century	Railroads, Finance
Vanderbilt, Cornelius	Early 19th Century	Shipping, Railroads
Van Rensselaer, K.	18th Century	Land
Villard, Henry	Late 19th Century	Railroads
Whitney, William C.	Late 19th Century	Utilities

Table 1 (Continued)

Deceased-Elite Individual	Period When Wealth Was Acquired	Occupation: Or the Way in Which Wealth Was Acquired*
Elite Individuals with Descendants Listed in the Baltimore, Cincinnati, Pittsburgh, San Francisco, St. Louis, or Washington *Social Registers* in 1940		
Crocker, Charles	Early 19th Century	Railroads
Elkins, Stephen B.	Late 19th Century	Land
Frick, Henry Clay	Late 19th Century	Manufacturing
Garrett, John W.	Early 19th Century	Railroads
Longworth, Nicholas	18th-19th Century	Land
Mellon, Andrew	20th Century	Finance, Manufacturing
Mills, D. O.	Early 19th Century	Finance
Pulitzer, Joseph	Late 19th Century	Publisher

* The occupations listed are of necessity limited to the principal field of endeavor. There was much overlapping. While "land" is listed for only a few individuals, almost all of the great fortunes in this country profited from the ownership of urban real estate. Finally, several lawyers and politicians are listed because these men were prominent in their day and were listed in the index of Myers' book.

† While Charles Francis Adams (Jr.) was a prominent railroad executive, he was a man of inherited wealth. When Charles Francis Adams I, the father of Henry, Charles, and Brooks, married the daughter of Peter Chardon Brooks, one of Boston's first millionaire merchants, the Adams family became wealthy for the first time.

These boarding schools not only bring together the sons of the "old" and "new" rich from Boston, New York, and Philadelphia to be socialized in one homogeneous atmosphere (the school family); they also serve to drain off the sons of the local, small-town upper classes all over America. Thus in *Yankee City* a young lady of the "upper upper" class, according to an observer in the Warner team, confessed that she could not find a suitable marriage mate because "all the young men have left."[18] She goes on to describe how her brother, a graduate of St. Paul's and Harvard, had recently taken a job in a large New York law firm and was engaged to marry a New York girl, "a sister of one of his classmates at St. Paul's."[19]

In the middle of the twentieth century, symbols of membership in exclusive associations have replaced the family *arms* of an earlier day. The school, or college club, "tie" or "hatband" is now, as we have said, a status symbol recognized within the upper classes in all cities. Although it has received little attention from sociologists, this change to a uniform national upper-class structure, which of course parallels the well-documented trend towards a centralized economy, will be emphasized throughout the rest of this book.

Who's Who in America:
A National Elite Index

Who's Who is a nationally recognized listing of the brief biographies of the leading men and women in contemporary American life. As such it is a perfectly democratic index of high functional class position and has wide prestige. This elite index is a listing of individuals of national rather than local prestige: in 1940, for example, three artists and one clergyman were the only ones listed in *Who's Who* from Newburyport, Massachusetts (*Yankee City*), while two members of the Ball family and ten others composed the entire listing from Muncie, Indiana (*Middletown*).[20]

As an upper class is intimately connected with history, the validity of the *Social Register* as an upper-class index depends on the relationship of its members with past elites. But an elite has no group existence or history—only individual members have a past; elite members are making history while some of their heirs will become members of some future upper class. Thus the validity of an elite index such as *Who's Who* depends on the reputation of the volume and the careful and objective methods used in selecting those who are included each year. *Who's Who* has been published by the A. N. Marquis Company since 1897; today some fifteen researchers examine over 200,000 persons before selecting approximately 30,000 to be included within each volume; the publishers have a long-standing reputation for their integrity in not including any person attempting to bribe or flatter his way into this exclusive index; "not a single sketch in this book has been paid for—and none can be paid for."[21]

In response to a standard form sent to all those persons chosen to be included in the current issue, each completed biography in *Who's Who* lists the following information: name, occupation, date and place of birth, full name of both parents, education and degrees, marital status—including name of spouse, date of marriage, and the full names of any children—occupational career, military experience, directorships and trusteeships, honorary societies and associational memberships, fraternal organizations, religious and political affiliation, club memberships, publications, and finally, home and business addresses.

No index is perfect, nor any sociological classification as homogeneous as might be desired. As an elite index, *Who's Who* has certain weaknesses: in the first place, it is too heavily weighted with educators and churchmen in contrast to the organizing elites of business, government, and labor (only labor leaders on the national scene are likely to be listed in *Who's Who*); secondly, in the distribution of power in any large, urban community, one must always remain aware of the social power exercised by those persons, e.g., the political "boss," who are not strictly "respectable." *Who's Who* gives no clue to the extent of this power in America. And, finally, certain individuals are listed in *Who's Who* more because of their prestige and prominence than because of any real achievement in a functional sense.

Whatever its inadequacies, however, *Who's Who* is a universally recognized index of an American elite and as such, contains accurate information about a class of people which the social scientist would be unable to secure on his own. People in this category, as a rule, do not have either the time or the inclination to supply such data solely for the purposes of sociological analysis. Moreover, this index, the product of year-in and year-out research in many communities in America, may be used to compare (1) different types of communities, as well as (2) the same community at two different periods.

One of the important differences between *Who's Who* and the *Social Register* is the way in which new members are added from time to time. In the first place, new families are added to the *Social Register* as a result of their making a formal application to the Social Register Association in New York City. In other words, a family having personal and more or less intimate social relations (in business, church, school, club, or neighborhood activities) with the various members of certain families who are listed in the *Social Register* reaches a point where inclusion seems expedient. Someone already listed in the *Social Register,* presumably a friend of the new family, obtains an application blank which is filled out by the new family (usually by the wife) and returned to the Social Register Association in New York along with several endorsements by present Register members as to the social acceptability of the new family. There will be a nominal fee. The next issue of the *Social Register*, including all pertinent information on the new family, will arrive the following November. The new family might be listed somewhat as follows:

Doe, Mr. and Mrs. J. Furness III (Mary D. Bradford) R, RC, ME, Y'15
    Miss Mary Bradford—at Vassar
    Mr. John F. IV—at Yale   Phone 1235
Juniors Miss Sarah—at Foxcroft   "Boxwood"
    Mr. Bradford—at St. Paul's   Bryn Mawr, Pa.

Insight into the structure and values of the American upper classes may be obtained by a perusal of the family listings in any contemporary volume of the *Social Register*. The ideal-typical Mr. Doe of Philadelphia, for example, belongs to three clubs, the Rittenhouse (R), the Racquet (RC), and the Merion Cricket (ME). He graduated from Yale in 1915, is educating his children at fashionable boarding schools, and lives on the Main Line. The familistic values of this upper class are indicated by the use of family given names (Bradford, the son), the use of "III" or "IV" as a mark of family continuity, and the listing of the maiden name of the wife. The patriarchal nature of the upper-class family is shown by the fact that the college attended by the wife (if any) is *never* listed in the *Social Register*.

Upper-class membership is a family affair, and grows out of subjective, primary group relationships, but elite individuals are chosen on the more objective basis of individual achievement. One does not apply for membership in *Who's Who*, nor is there even a nominal charge for being included. The following standards have been established by the publishers for inclusion within this elite index

Except for names which are included in *Who's Who in America* for one or more of the arbitrary reasons designated below, the aim is to include the names, not necessarily of the best, but rather of the best known, men and women in all lines of useful and reputable achievement—names much in the public eye, not locally, but generally. The standards of admission divide the eligible into two classes: (1) those selected on account of special prominence in creditable lines of effort, making them the subjects of extensive interest, inquiry or discussion; and (2) those included arbitrarily on account of official position—civil, military, naval, religious, or educational.[22]

Who's Who in America and the *Social Register*— Elite and Upper-Class Indices and the Relationship between Them

It is important to be clearly aware of the fact that any index used in the social sciences is only a convenient tool which is constructed to approximate any given concept one desires to use for the purpose of abstract analysis. For example, just as the "intelligence quotient"—which can be measured—is only an approximation of that which we call "intelligence"—which cannot be measured— so *Who's Who* and the *Social Register* are nothing more nor less than the best available indices of an elite and an upper class. By their very nature, constructed indices are simplifications; nonetheless they are essential tools in scientific analysis. In other words, we are only too well aware of the fact that there are individuals and families listed in the *Social Register* who are not "really" upper-class members and those not listed who obviously are; similarly, there are individuals who are leaders in their occupational fields who are not listed in *Who's Who* and, in turn, some of those listed are not "really" of elite status. For the purposes of this book, however, it will be assumed that *Who's Who* lists an elite, and the *Social Register* an upper class, in certain large metropolitan areas in America.

The twelve metropolitan areas in the United States with *Social Registers* in 1940 are shown in Table 2: column 1 shows the number of conjugal family units listed in the *Social Register* in each city, and column 2 shows the proportion of those listed in *Who's Who* in each city who are also listed in the *Social Register*. The concentration of power and talent in these cities is indicated by the fact that, while their populations make up only approximately 20 per cent of the total population of the United States, 40 per cent of all those listed in *Who's Who* in the country reside in these twelve metropolitan areas. Furthermore, it is certainly plausible to assume that the elite members in these cities have a more pervasive influence on the American social structure as a whole than the 60 per cent who are listed in *Who's Who* from the rest of the country.

In 1940, there were approximately 38,000 conjugal family units listed in the *Social Register* (Table 2); in that year, the estimated number of families in the country as a whole was 34,948,666 [23] Thus about one-tenth of 1 per cent of the families in the country were members of this upper class which, in turn, contributed no less than 9 per cent of all those listed in *Who's Who* in that year (31,752 individuals listed in *Who's Who*, 2,879 of whom were also listed in the *Social Register*). More important, of the 12,530 residents of these twelve metropolitan areas who were listed in *Who's Who*, 2,879 or 23 per cent were also listed in the *Social Register* (Table 2).

Of the eighteen metropolitan areas in the United States which had populations of over half a million in 1940, the twelve listed in Table 2 are the oldest social structures (they were the twelve largest in the country as of the 1900 Census). Detroit and Los Angeles, on the other hand, have grown to their present size largely in the twentieth century. Since the automobile and motion picture elites are relatively "new," there is apparently no coherent upper class in these cities (Henry Ford II and his family are listed in the New York *Social Register*). Presumably, the age and size of a social structure together with the rate of social change are important

Table 2—The Number of Conjugal Family Units Listed in the Social Registers of Twelve Large Metropolitan Areas in America, in 1940, and the Proportion of Those Listed in Who's Who in these Cities Who Are Also Listed in the Social Register

Metropolitan Areas	CONJUGAL FAMILIES IN THE SOCIAL REGISTER IN 1940	INDIVIDUALS LISTED IN WHO'S WHO WHO ARE			
		Listed in the Social Register		Not Listed in the Social Register	
	No.	No.	%	No.	%
New York	13,200	1,040	(20)	4,085	(80)
Philadelphia	5,150*	226	(29)	544	(71)
Boston	3,675	240	(28)	608	(72)
Washington, D.C.	3,530	715	(30)	1,670	(70)
Chicago	2,130	151	(11)	1,194	(89)
Baltimore	1,935	87	(26)	243	(74)
St. Louis	1,925	77	(24)	239	(76)
San Francisco	1,775	87	(23)	297	(77)
Pittsburgh	1,635	76	(22)	277	(78)
Cincinnati	1,305†	61	(29)	151	(71)
Dayton		11	(17)	51	(83)
Buffalo	1,125	43	(37)	72	(63)
Cleveland	1,065	65	(20)	260	(80)
All Cities	38,450	2,879	(23)	9,691	(77)

* Upper-class families in Wilmington, Delaware, including forty-five Du Pont conjugal family units, are listed in the Philadelphia *Social Register*.
† One volume of the *Social Register* includes families from both Cincinnati and Dayton.

variables in determining the nature of the class system. For example, Chicago, a young and rapidly changing middle-western metropolis, has twice as many individuals listed in *Who's Who,* and less than half as many families listed in the *Social Register,* as Philadelphia, an old and conservative eastern seaboard city. The upper class in Chicago, in turn, has less influence on the elite than the upper class in Philadelphia (Table 2—in Chicago 11 per cent and in Philadelphia 29 per cent of the elite are also in the upper class).

CHAPTER III

The Philadelphia Upper Class
and the Elite in 1940

> It is only that by force of circumstances the cap-
> tain of industry, or in more accurate words the
> captain of solvency, has in recent times come to be
> the effectual spokesman and type-form of the kept
> classes as well as the keeper and dispenser of their
> keep; very much as the war lord of the barbarian
> raids, or the baron of the middle ages, or the prince
> of the era of state making, or the priesthood early
> and late in Christendom, have all and several, each
> in their time, place and degree, stood out as the
> spokesman and exempler of the kept classes,
>
> THORSTEIN VEBLEN

IT IS SAID that an experienced employer once compared the social
structures of New York, Boston, and Philadelphia by citing three
typical letters of introduction brought by young men seeking jobs
in his firm; the letters from each city read somewhat as follows:

The Bostonian: "Permit me to introduce Mr. Jones who graduated
with highest honors in the classics and political economy at Harvard,
and later took a degree at Berlin. He speaks and writes French and
German, and if you employ him, I am sure his learning will make his
services extremely valuable to you."

The New Yorker: "The bearer, Mr. Brown, is the young fellow who
took hold of Street & Company's Chicago branch a few years ago and
built it up to one hundred thousand a year. He also made a great hit
as Jackson & Company's representative in London. He's a hustler all
right and you'll make no mistake if you take him on."

The Philadelphian: "Sir, allow me to introduce Mr. Rittenhouse
Palmer Penn. His grandfather on his mother's side was a colonel in the
Revolution, and on his father's side he is connected with two of the
most exclusive families in our city. He is related by marriage to the
Philadelphia Lady who married Count Taugenichts, and his family has
always lived on Walnut Street. If you should see fit to employ him, I
feel certain that his very desirable social connections will render him
of great value to you."[1]

Philadelphia is a conservative city; social connections there are perhaps somewhat more important than elsewhere in America. In all stable societies, however, the elite is composed of both self-made men and aristocrats. This chapter is concerned with an analysis of the democratic (achieved) and aristocratic (ascribed) aspects of elite selection in Philadelphia. In other words, which occupational positions within the elite are held by upper-class members, and which are not? What is the pattern of upper-class control in the city?

Talcott Parsons has observed that "it is one of the striking features of our occupational system that status in it is to a high degree independent of status in *kinship* groups, the *neighborhood* and the *like,* in short what are sometimes called *primary group* relationships."[2] This is no doubt the case in wide areas of American society. Nevertheless, it may be true that the higher the functional position, the more important social connections or social class considerations become. A young man from an "old family" in *Yankee City,* for example, was given a job in a large New York law firm because "they could hire all the smart young . . . lawyers they wanted to do the dirty work, but they needed men of character [upper upper class] to take over when it was time for the older men to retire."[3] This suggests that some pattern underlies the wide variation in status ascription (upper-class origins) as between the different occupational categories within the Philadelphia elite (Table 3).

For analytical purposes, an elite may be broken down into three groups: (1) those who have a goal-integrating function (line or executive) which includes the men who decide the *ends* which the given social structure will strive to attain; (2) the technically equipped (staff or professional) whose function it is to provide the knowledge or *means* through which those ends are achieved; and (3) those who perform the intellectual function in any society. The intellectuals neither make the decisions which determine the immediate goals of the society, nor provide technical knowledge or means; rather they are primarily concerned with values, morals, and ideas, in the large sense, or the normative and creative aspects of social life. In short then, an elite is composed of organizers, technicians, and intellectuals.

Various occupational categories should fit into one or another of these three functional divisions of any elite. It is important to

Table 3—Philadelphians in Who's Who in 1940—Occupation as Related to Social Class

SOCIAL CLASS

Occupation	Social Register		Non Social Register		Who's Who Total		Per Cent of Each Occupation in Social Register
	No.	%	No.	%	No.	%	
Bankers	24	(11)	8	(1)	32	(4)	75
Lawyers	20	(9)	19	(4)	39	(5)	51
Engineers	10	(4)	12	(2)	22	(3)	45
Businessmen	53	(24)	72	(13)	125	(16)	42
Architects	10	(4)	14	(3)	24	(3)	42
Physicians	16	(7)	27	(5)	43	(6)	37
Museum Officials	5	(2)	9	(2)	14	(2)	35
Authors	14	(6)	30	(6)	44	(6)	32
Graphic Artists	8	(4)	31	(6)	39	(5)	21
Public Officials	7	(3)	26	(5)	33	(4)	21
Educators	31	(14)	147	(27)	178	(23)	16
Opinion*	7	(3)	46	(8)	53	(7)	13
Musical Artists	2	(1)	14	(3)	16	(2)	12
Church Officials	8	(4)	72	(13)	80	(10)	10
Retired Capitalists	3		0		3		
Philanthropists	1		2		3		
Social Workers	2	(4)	2	(2)	4	(4)	39
Librarians	0		5		5		
Other	5		8		13		
Total	226	(100)	544	(100)	770	(100)	29

* Public relations, advertising, radio, editors.

point out, however, that the same occupation will not necessarily fit into any given functional division in all social structures, nor in the same social structure at different historical periods. In the medieval period in the West for example, the priesthood tended to perform both the intellectual and the goal-integrating function; in the modern totalitarian state these two functions are ordinarily reserved for the party functionary: the priest is liquidated and the surviving intellectuals become mere technicians. In a liberal democratic society, on the other hand, the business and financial elite is primarily concerned with goal-integration, while the intellectual remains autonomous to a relatively high degree. As modern society, whether totalitarian or democratic, becomes increasingly bureaucratized, however, the salaried intellectual in both business and government—the commercial artist, the industrial psychologist or sociologist, and various other types of "research" and ideological functionaries—become part of the technical elite. In fact, the more centralized a society becomes, the more people are concerned with means ("red tape").

The most important task of elite analysis is that of determining the changing composition of the goal-integrating group. James Burnham, for instance, who focused on this problem in his *Managerial Revolution,* attempted to show how the professional manager was replacing the financier or owner as the dominant member of the goal-integrating elite in modern bureaucratic society.[4] As he did not determine whether or not these new managers were recruited from the same upper class as the financiers and owners, however, Burnham had a tendency to confuse the ruling *class* (goal-integrating elite dominated by upper-class members) with the ruling *elite* (which may or may not be dominated by the upper class). In other words, if the composition of the ruling elite changes from financiers to managers of the Burnham type, this is an important elite change; but if both the *new* managers and the *old* financiers are recruited from the *same* upper class, there has not been a corresponding change in the ruling *class.* As we use the term, then, a ruling class is one which contributes upper class members to the most important, goal-integrating elite positions.

An upper class may or may not be a ruling class (it is not in *Yankee City*). However, if it is not a ruling class, it will soon be replaced by a new upper class. This important relationship between the goal-integrating elite and the upper class is the central focus of our analysis in this chapter. We will of course be interested in other parts of the elite. But we emphasize here that an upper class remains the ruling class only so long as its members are in the key executive positions, even though the technical and intellectual positions may be open to achievement.

In order to analyze the relationship between the upper class and the elite in Philadelphia within the framework of the three functions discussed above, the occupations in Table 3 will be classified into five homogeneous functional elites and a sixth miscellaneous category composed of those who do not fit into the first five. These functional elites are classified as follows in Table 4: Goal-integrating function (*1*) *Business elite;* Potential goal-integrating function (*2*) *Opinion & Political elite;* Technical function (*3*) *Physicians and architects;* Intellectual function (*4*) *Church & education,* (*5*) *Artists & authors;* Unclassified functions (*6*) *Miscellaneous occupations.*

Table 4—Philadelphians in Who's Who in 1940—Functional Elites as Related to Social Class

Functional Elites	SOCIAL CLASS						Per Cent of Each Elite in Social Register
	Social Register		Non Social Register		Who's Who Total		
	No.	%	No.	%	No.	%	
Business*	107	(47)	111	(20)	218	(28)	49
Opinion & Political	14	(6)	72	(13)	86	(11)	16
Medicine & Architecture	26	(12)	41	(8)	67	(9)	39
Church & Education	39	(17)	219	(40)	258	(34)	15
Artists & Authors	24	(11)	75	(14)	99	(13)	24
Other Occupations†	16	(7)	26	(5)	42	(5)	38
Total	226	(100)	544	(100)	770	(100)	29

* Includes businessmen, lawyers, engineers, and bankers.
† All other occupations in Table 3 (in addition to "museum officials," those listed at the bottom of Table 3).

In Philadelphia in 1940, the goal-integrating function was performed by the business elite, which includes businessmen, bankers, lawyers, and engineers.* Although differing in technical training, all these men perform essentially similar elite functions: the exercise of power over other men in making the decisions which shape the ends of a predominantly business-oriented social structure.

On the other hand, the potential goal-integrating elite is composed of public officials and those individuals who have been placed within the rather broad occupational category we call "opinion"—public relations, advertising, radio, and publishing executives as well as others who are engaged in various forms of communication. The members of this elite, trained in the arts of propaganda and influencing the emotions of men, although serving the ends of the business elite in 1940, may be potential leaders in organizing the type of social structure which appears to be emerging in America along with such goals as "security" or "social welfare" in contradistinction to "profits" and a "sound economy."

The physicians and architects—high prestige professionals—are placed within one technical elite.

The intellectual function is broken down into two parts: the clergy and the educators are one elite; the artists and authors

---

* At first blush, one might expect engineers to be classified as part of the "technical" elite. At the level of *Who's Who*, however, the engineer is almost exclusively an executive. As one engineer in the 1940 *Who's Who* (president of one of the leading consulting firms in the city) put it: "I have been too busy to go into engineering details for over 20 years now."

another. In a rather broad sense, the former perform the normative function, and the latter the creative.

The rest of the occupations, in the sixth, "sponge" category, are too heterogeneous to be susceptible to systematic analysis.

The Goal-Integrating Elite: A Business and Financial Aristocracy. America is a business civilization: in the first three decades of the twentieth century at least, the goal-integrating elite centered in business with its apex in finance. In 1940 Proper Philadelphia was a business ruling class. As the late Russell Davenport of *Fortune* has said: "If there were any way of adding up the Philadelphia *Social Register,* so to speak, it would probably be found that the names listed in the *Register* would represent a more active control over finance and industry than those of any other city."[5]

Philadelphia, from the days of Robert Morris, Thomas Willing, and Nicholas Biddle, has been called the "cradle of American finance." For generations the first families of Philadelphia have been intimately connected with the financial community. The Philadelphia National Bank, for instance, was the oldest and largest commercial banking institution in the city in 1940. Founded in 1803 by a liberal group of young Jeffersonians in order to break the Philadelphia banking monopoly of the Federalists, its first president was George Clymer, a signer of the Declaration of Independence. Many descendants of both George Clymer and the other founders of the "Philadelphia Bank" are listed in the Philadelphia *Social Register* in 1940. Moreover, of the 277 Philadelphia gentlemen, including Biddles, Drinkers, Clarks, Wideners, Cookes and Duponts, who have served on the board of directors of this venerable Philadelphia institution between 1803 and 1940, no less than 82 have traceable descendants (a genealogist would surely find more) listed in the 1940 *Social Register.* Finally, in 1940, both the president of the Philadelphia National and ten out of thirteen members of the board were in the upper class (see Table 5).

In contrast to Parsons' hypothesis concerning the nature of the American social structure as a whole, Frederick Lewis Allen perhaps provides a more valid picture of the generation of gentlemen here studied:

For the sons of the fortunate, the path of least resistance led to a financial career. For example, of the 55 members of the Porcellian and A.D. clubs (the two most fashionable clubs at Harvard) in the classes of 1904, 1905, and 1906, no less than 25 were engaged in finance a few years after graduation, two more were engaged in finance but had left it, and another two were in closely allied occupations. The social connections of well groomed young men could be turned to good account in a brokerage or banking house.[6]

Upper-class Philadelphians follow the pattern described by Allen. In 1940 they were firmly in control of both commercial and investment banking in the city. The presidents of the four largest commercial banks and the two largest savings banks in the city, as well as over 80 per cent of the directors of all six of these institutions, were upper-class members (Table 5). It is perhaps significant that the Girard Trust Company is the only bank where the president and *all* the board of directors are listed in the *Social Register*. This Philadelphia institution, housed in an impressive temple in the Greek Revival tradition of architecture, and conveniently located opposite John Wanamaker's department store where Proper Philadelphia shops, is the most popular guardian of the many family trust funds which are so indispensable to an upper-class style of life.[7]

It is safe to say of the half-century after 1890 that the invest-

Table 5—Philadelphians In Who's Who in 1940—Directorships Reported in 10 Prestige Institutions as Related to Social Class

	SOCIAL CLASS		
	SOCIAL REGISTER	NON SOCIAL REGISTER	WHO'S WHO TOTAL
Prestige Institutions*	No. of Directorships†	No. of Directorships	No. of Directorships
Banks			
Phila. Saving Fund Soc.	14	2	16
Western Saving Fund Soc.	8	1	9
Penna. Co.‡	5	4	9
Phila. Nat'l Bank	10	3	13
Fidelity Phila. Trust Co.	8	1	9
Girard Trust Co.	9	0	9
Insurance			
Penn Mutual Life Ins. Co.	15	3	18
Insurance Co. of N. Am.	8	2	10
Penna. Railroad	9	1	10
Univ. of Penna.	14	5	19
Total Reported Directorships	100	22	122

* In 1940, the presidents of all these institutions were listed in the *Social Register.*
† Proportion of total directorships reported which were held by individuals in the *Social Register* —82 per cent. This table only includes directorships reported in the 1940 *Who's Who* biographies of the Philadelphia elite.
‡ The Pennsylvania Company for Insurance on Lives and Granting of Annuities.

ment banker stood at the apex of the business community. Drexel & Company, founded in 1837 and in partnership with J. P. Morgan since 1850, is the leading investment banking house in the city. Long dominated by E. T. Stotesbury, the firm is now in the hands of Edward Hopkinson, Jr., whose great-great-great-grandfather was a close friend of Benjamin Franklin, whose great-great-grandfather signed the Declaration of Independence, whose great-grandfather wrote *Hail Columbia*, and whose grandfather lived to be the oldest graduate of the University of Pennsylvania.

Since colonial times, when John Dickinson and Joseph Gallaway were leading members of the bar, the Philadelphia lawyer has always been a leader in both civic and business affairs in the city. In fact, many upper-class bankers received their early training in the legal profession. Dr. Thomas S. Gates, for instance, president of the University of Pennsylvania in 1940, and probably the most influential member of the upper class in that year, began his career in the late John C. Johnson's famous law firm before he became a banker and finally a Morgan partner. Similarly, Edward Hopkinson, Jr. was for sixteen years a member of one of the leading law firms in the city.

Although only half of the lawyers within the elite were also listed in the *Social Register*, the most important law firms in the city were dominated by the upper class. There were seven leading firms in 1940; six were upper-class firms (over 80 per cent of the partners, and all the senior partners, were listed in the *Social Register*), and the seventh was a very distinguished Jewish firm.

In American upper-class development, the family founder has usually been a businessman or merchant; the members of the second and third generations, if they are interested in power, become lawyers or bankers. Within this Philadelphia elite, although the presidents of the largest insurance companies and the Pennsylvania Railroad are upper-class members, on the whole, the top executive positions in industry are not held by upper-class members. Thus the new corporation managers, in Burnham's sense, are not necessarily drawn from the same upper class as the financiers. This does not mean that the upper class has not contributed more than its share of leaders in the business elite (49 per cent in Table 4); it does show, however, that the top managerial positions are more open to achievement than banking and law. However, in addition to financial and legal influence, the upper class is well represented in industry through the boards of directors of various corporations. Within the Philadelphia elite, the upper-class member is much more likely to list directorships in both industrial and financial concerns than are the other members of the elite: for example, of the 314 directorships in industry reported by all 770 Philadelphians listed in *Who's Who,* 174, or over half, were reported by the 107 upper-class members of the business elite; moreover, of the 213 directorships reported in financial institutions, 137 or 63 per cent were reported by upper-class members.

The Philadelphia upper class, then, is a *business* aristocracy: through banks, the law, and through directorships, a relatively small primary group passes on control from one generation to the next. We shall have more to say about this pattern of upper-class control in a later chapter.

The Circulation of Elites. In relatively stable periods of history, an upper class will always tend to be closely allied with the goal-integrating part of any contemporary elite. But in periods of rapid social change, where new and quite different talents are needed for leadership, the values and style of life of an upper class in one period often tend to inhibit its members from succeeding in a new type of function. Brooks Adams saw this clearly when he said, "Nothing is commoner than to find families who have been famous in one century sinking into obscurity in the next, not because the children have degenerated, but because fields of activity which afforded the ancestors full scope, have been closed to the offspring."[8]

The personal qualities which made the late Franklin D. Roosevelt a great political leader, for example, were the very qualities that the business upper class to which he belonged most distrusted. Any upper-class member who becomes a leader of an increasingly important functional elite which is, in turn, threatening the power of the elite on which the upper class has a firm hold will be considered a "traitor to his class." In point of fact this "traitor," and others like him, serve to perpetuate upper-class influence on the functional class system as a whole by the very fact that they hold important positions within the new avenues to power. In the transition period—the nineteen thirties in America and in the world—it was no accident that the political leaders who came from upper-class backgrounds tended to be Democrats rather than Republicans; they were deviants in a predominantly Republican and business-oriented subculture.

The *Social Register* came into existence in an age when J. P. Morgan was saving President Cleveland and the United States Government from financial embarrassment; when the United States Senate often was referred to as a "millionaires' club"; and when the financiers were the "Lords of Creation" and the ruling elite in America. A half century later, the upper class in Philadelphia was primarily a business and financial aristocracy in very much the same pattern.

In the meantime, in the western world, new problems had arisen and new talents were needed for leadership. Following World War I, and especially during the Depression, the "new men of power"—Mussolini, Stalin, Hitler, Huey Long, and Roosevelt, among others—were those who sought and, in many cases, obtained, by one means or another, control over the minds and imaginations of men who had lost confidence in the "cash nexus." New goals were in order, and new goal-integrating elites came to power. As with the aristocrats of landed or financial wealth of an earlier day, presumably the sons and grandsons of these "new men of power" will evolve into an upper class.

Within this context—the fundamental change in goals, especially on the national level—it is useful to think of the political and opinion elite as a *potential* goal-integrating elite. In contrast to the business elite, only a small proportion of this potentially powerful elite is drawn from the upper class (Table 4).

Philadelphia, of course, has not had a local political ruling class in modern times. In the first half of the twentieth century, for example, there was no mayor or leading municipal official from the upper class. While it is true that upper-class members have not been officials in the local government, it is probably equally true that the local Republican party has for years been run to suit the business interests of the upper class in the city. This may be changing today. In 1951, for example, the citizens of Philadelphia, led by Richardson Dilworth and Joseph Sill Clark, Jr. (member of an old banking family; see below), elected their first Democratic mayor in the twentieth century. Mayor Clark and District Attorney Dilworth are both members of the city's upper class. Presumably, as government and government taxes become more important in the lives of Philadelphians, upper-class members will be attracted to this governmental elite. This may in fact be a trend throughout America.

Proper Philadelphians have not as a rule been inclined to serve their national government in leadership positions. In contrast to the Lodges of Boston, the Tafts of Cincinnati, or the Roosevelts of New York, few upper-class Philadelphians (with the exception of several in the national government, mainly appointive positions under Roosevelt) have been of major political stature either locally or nationally. The one former United States Senator from the upper class, George Wharton Pepper, a Philadelphia lawyer, was appointed to the position after the death of Boies Penrose in 1921. Membership in the Philadelphia upper class, it would appear, has not been conducive to service in the governmental or political elite. As Peter Drucker observes, "the withdrawal of the gentlemen from the political arena into the counting house . . . has led to a split between the political ruling class and the social ruling class which has prevented any one group from becoming *the* ruling class."[9]

Those individuals within the occupational category of "opinion" (with the exception of publishers)—the public relations or advertising executive and others who deal in ideas and ideologies rather than stocks and bonds or balance sheets—are new men with new techniques and new values. Like the public officials, they are not well represented (13 per cent) in the *Social Register* as of 1940 (Table 4). As with the political elite, however, the social class origins of the opinion elites in America may be in the process of change. Although the generation of gentlemen analyzed in this book tended to follow financial careers, their sons and grandsons, personable young men with good connections, are avoiding banks and brokerage houses and are to be found increasingly in the fields of advertising, public relations, or publishing. The Madison Avenues of America are filled increasingly with young men from the best boarding schools and "Ivy League" universities, and, certainly, the Luce publications, which cater to the ambitions of the rising middle classes in America, betray a self-conscious propensity towards Anglophilia and the "old school tie" which reflects the upper-class origins and aspirations of its editorial staff. Perhaps the Alsop brothers, products of Groton and an old Connecticut mercantile family, mark this movement of the gentlemen in America into the new opinion elites.

The circulation of elites is inevitable in a dynamic society. A vigorous upper class provides the social structure with a healthy continuity and an organic cohesion only if its members, in each generation, seek out, and become leaders in, the new avenues of power. In an English novel dealing with the conflicts between the landed gentry and the rising banking elites after the Napoleonic Wars, a landed gentleman berates his nephew who is going into *banking*: "Not a trade? Of course it's a trade—if usury is a trade! And you think to be one of them, do you? To join them and be another Peel, or one of Pitt's moneybags. . . . And vote Radical and prate of Reform and scorn the land that bred you?"[10] A little over a hundred years later, many banking gentlemen along the Main Lines and Walnut Streets of America felt the same way about their "radical" sons going down to work for the New Deal in those hectic days of reform in the early thirties, or attempting to clean up municipal government in Philadelphia.

The position of the gentlemen businessmen within the Philadelphia elite in 1940 marked the end of an era. Brought up in a world of economic security which ended in 1929, these bourgeois aristocrats were still firmly in control of the business elite in 1940. It remains for their sons and grandsons, like the English gentleman's nephew, to make their way along new avenues of power and influence. Some are doing just that. Robert S. Lynd, who has always worked toward an understanding, rather than a pure description, of society, anticipates this trend in America when he suggests that the younger generation of the "X Family" in *Middletown,* "as financially independent men," would go into government service:[11] In August, 1953, William H. Ball ("X Family") represented the United States Government at the Cecil Rhodes Centennial Exhibition in Bulawayo, Central Africa.

High Prestige Technical Elite: Physicians and Architects. In the United States, medicine and architecture have been traditionally upper-class professions. While the Proper Philadelphian has tended to avoid government service, his sense of *noblesse oblige* has been channeled into the support of hospitals and medical schools; he has always taken the initiative in raising money and giving generously of his time in various executive capacities. The city is, of course, a treasure-house of good architecture. Many upper-class families look back with pride to well-known leaders in both professions: such physicians as Benjamin Rush, S. Weir Mitchell, many Norrises, and the Peppers of the University of Pennsylvania Medical School represent upper-class traditions at their proudest and best; while Owen Biddle, Benjamin Henry Latrobe, and Frank

Furness, leading architects in their day, all have descendants in the contemporary upper class.

As one might expect, almost 40 per cent of this elite were also listed in the *Social Register* (Table 4). This rather high proportion of physicians and architects from the upper class may be due to two things: first, the period of education and apprenticeship is long and costly for both professions; and, second, their paying clients tend to be from the wealthier classes.

Throughout history the architectural profession has been closely allied with the wealthier members of the community: "Recent researches have shown that the status of the medieval architect, for example, was similar to his present-day counterpart. He dined with the wealthy and noble clients, including the King's departmental heads; he dined also with the merchants, who paid him to design and supervise the building of their town and country houses, as well as the schools, churches, and other public buildings which they endowed."[12] Thus George Howe, the leading architect in this high prestige elite, was a graduate of Groton and Harvard and a member of the Philadelphia Club; his Philadelphia clients included Robert McLean, publisher of the *Evening Bulletin,* for whom he designed a beautiful private residence in the Penllyn area as well as the new *Bulletin* Building in the center of the city; perhaps his most well-known piece of architecture is the Philadelphia Savings Fund Society skyscraper, always mentioned as a classic of its kind in any discussion of American architecture (see "P.S.F.S." directorships in Table 5). Although George Howe was a transplanted New Englander, his partner in designing the "P.S.F.S." building was Arthur Ingersoll Meigs, an impeccable Proper Philadelphian, whose ancestors had been leading physicians in the city for four generations (See Table 9).

Like the architect's clients, the successful physician's patients are often well-to-do. The scientific treatment of disease is combined with an intimate contact with the patient. Thus successful physicians are not only drawn from the upper class but are very likely to be assimilated into it when not wholly "to the manor born."

Intellectual Elite: Church and Education. Due to the nature of *Who's Who,* this is the largest functional elite. Americans profess to regard the educator and churchman as persons of high prestige. But, while the middle classes value education, perhaps as a means of mobility rather than out of respect for learning, the American upper class has, by and large, very little veneration for the educator. Professors are welcome in the best homes in Europe, but this is not the case, as a rule, in this country.

Of course, the nature of the client, both in the case of the educator and the clergy, is important. While the Episcopalian minister, especially the rector of a fashionable church, would be listed in the *Social Register,* others who minister to all classes would not be so listed. Of the eighty church officials listed in *Who's Who,* eight —five Episcopalians and three Presbyterians—were also listed in the *Social Register.*

The same pattern prevails among educators. Eighteen of the thirty-one educators listed in both *Who's Who* and the *Social Register* (see Table 3) were teaching in the professional schools of law and medicine. As education has been democratized, except for a few fashionable universities and private schools, educators have been drawn increasingly from the middle classes. On the other hand, important administrative positions (goal-integration) in education continue to be held by upper-class members. Within this Philadelphia elite, for example, the president of the University of Pennsylvania, a former Morgan partner, and the deans of both the medical and law schools, are all listed in the *Social Register.*

The intellectuals—the ideologists and interpreters of each age— perform an important, if often intangible, function within the social structure, and their social class origins constitute an important aspect of any sociological analysis. The fact that the upper class in Philadelphia, and in the nation as a whole, has not produced many leading historians, political scientists, or economists may reflect the unstable character of our time. Or, perhaps, it may indicate that the upper classes have lost the ideological initiative in America since the turn of the century. One is reminded of Tocqueville's diagnosis of a former age: "An aristocracy in the days of its strength does not only conduct affairs; it still directs opinion, gives their tone to the writers and authority to ideas. In the eighteenth century the French nobility had entirely lost this part of its supremacy."[13] In England during the same period, on the other hand, Tocqueville observed that "the writers on government mingled with those who governed." Perhaps the social origins of Lord Keynes and Karl Marx are not unrelated to their interpretation of society, and especially the remedies they propose.

Intellectual Elite: Artists and Authors. Artists and authors are more likely to be listed in the *Social Register* than educators and churchmen. In our culture, only the most successful creative artists and authors are able to make a living out of their art; the less successful require some other source of income in order to have the leisure time for creative work. Thus the high proportion of upper-class persons within this elite may be an index of the usefulness of inherited wealth and leisure. This point is emphasized by the fact that a large proportion of this elite are female (over 70 per cent of the upper-class females in Philadelphia listed in *Who's Who* are either artists or authors).

Although Philadelphia's literary tradition suffers when compared with Boston's, its painting and sculpture, partially because of the Academy of the Fine Arts (the oldest of its kind in America and a very Proper Philadelphia tradition), may stand comparison with the state of these arts in any other American city. Within this elite in 1940, however, there are few major figures in either field, and most of the authors and artists are known only locally.

Mr. Marquand of Newburyport (*Yankee City*) has painted the classic portrait of the Proper Bostonian in *The Late George Apley;* there exists no comparable portrait of the Proper Philadelphian. The three better-known modern authors who have written about upper-class Philadelphia—Struthers Burt, Christopher Morley, and Philip Barry—were all more interested in story-telling than in documentary fiction. Morley and Barry, with *Kitty Foyle* and *The Philadelphia Story,* have received far more popular acclaim than Burt, whose *Along These Streets* is a less stereotyped and far more sensitive portrait of Proper Philadelphia; they have exploited the easy stereotypes about Main Line suburban society, but Burt was concerned with the city—the man's world of the exclusive men's club where a woman's name is never mentioned, the narrow Philadelphia streets, the conservative law firms, and the like.

All three of these authors were, of course, listed in *Who's Who* in 1940, but none was then a resident of Philadelphia. Barry, upper class in background and listed in the New York *Social Register,* obtained material for his well-known play during visits with friends along the Main Line; both Morley and Burt eventually became expatriate Philadelphians. Morley, the son of a professor of mathematics at Haverford College on the Main Line, was never a part of the local upper class; Struthers Burt, although a "Philadelphian, bone of the bone," divided his time between a Wyoming ranch and Southern Pines, North Carolina; true to tradition, this expatriate Proper Philadelphian was, nevertheless, listed in the Philadelphia *Social Register* where he gave his membership in both the Rittenhouse and Franklin Inn Clubs.

Other Elite Members. The individuals placed here could not be fitted into any of the other five elites. The three retired capitalists might well have been included within the business elite, but, as their wealth appeared to be inherited, and they were not active, they were placed within this last group; needless to say, they were all upper-class members.

In order to test an hypothesis, two interesting occupations—museum officials and librarians—were separated out for contrast in social class origins. Our hypothesis was that the museum official would tend to have a higher social class position than the librarians. This is borne out in Table 3. More than one-third of the museum officials are listed in the *Social Register;* no librarians are listed.

The museum official, or curator, is an interesting individual. Until recently, there has been no formal professional school for training the members of this rapidly developing profession; at present, the Fogg Museum and a few other institutions are filling this need for professional training. Previously, museum officials in Philadelphia, and elsewhere, have been upper-class members with a certain amount of leisure time and inherited wealth, and an interest in "culture"; some of them, of course, have had great talent and have done creative jobs; and some have not.

Changing Upper-Class Influence. Is there any indication that the influence of the upper class on the elite in Philadelphia is of increasing or decreasing importance? A possible clue to this changing class situation may be obtained from Table 6, where the 695 males who reported their date of birth in *Who's Who* are divided into two age groups—those sixty-five and over, and those under sixty-five, in 1940. The older men made their way in the first part of the century and were at their peak occupationally in the 1920's; those in the younger group, under fifty-five in 1930, would be expected to be leaders in their fields in the 1930's and 1940's.

On the whole, the older group of males are more likely to belong to the upper class than the younger group—34 per cent as against 27 per cent listed in the *Social Register.* Moreover, in each of the five major elites except the authors and artists, the older generation tends to have a higher proportion in the upper class. There may be two possible explanations for this difference between age groups. First, the upper class may be more influential among the older men because these men hold the more important positions within the functional class system; these top positions, in turn, are more likely to be held by men of advanced years. In other words, this age differential in upper-class membership may not indicate a trend toward the decreasing importance of the upper class, but may be due to age alone. At the same time, there are indications that the upper class is less influential today. For example, among the younger generation of men are included three presidents of manufacturing companies which are among the ten largest in Philadelphia, one of the leading publishers in the city, and the president of the largest advertising firm in the city; none of those men is listed in the *Social Register*. Certainly the evidence is not conclusive. There is some indication, however, that upper-class membership is less important in Philadelphia than it used to be, and that upper-class control over the elite may have reached its peak in the first three decades of the twentieth century. Other evidence on this point will be brought out in later chapters.

What of the artists and authors, the deviant case, since more of the younger generation belong to the upper class? It is an interesting and plausible hypothesis that, as an upper class becomes more exclusive and contains more and more third- and fourth-generation families, its members, descendants of the big men (the

Table 6—Philadelphians in Who's Who in 1940—Functional Elites as Related to Age Groups and Social Class*

	AGE COHORTS							
	65 & OVER				UNDER 65			
Functional Elites	Social Register		Non Social Register		Social Register		Non Social Register	
	No.	%	No.	%	No.	%	No.	%
Business	40	(52)	37	(48)	61	(47)	68	(53)
Opinion & Political	5	(18)	22	(82)	9	(17)	44	(83)
Medicine & Architecture	18	(53)	16	(47)	8	(29)	20	(71)
Church & Education	22	(22)	77	(78)	16	(11)	131	(89)
Artists & Authors	5	(18)	23	(82)	9	(24)	28	(76)
Other	4	(29)	10	(71)	9	(41)	13	(59)
All Elites	94	(34)	185	(66)	112	(27)	304	(73)

* This table includes the 695 males who reported their date of birth. This group of males will be used throughout this book in order to indicate trends over time.

conspicuously consuming "Robber Barons" of whom Veblen wrote), tend increasingly to question their position of privilege and thus enter the arts rather than follow their fathers into the world of affairs. If this be true, it may explain why more of the younger generation originate in the upper class.

CHAPTER IV

The Structure and Function of an Upper Class

> Men being no longer attached to one another by any tie of caste, of class, of corporation, of family, are only too much inclined to be preoccupied only with their private interests, ever too much drawn to think only of themselves and to retire into a narrow individualism, in which every public virtue is stifled. Despotism far from struggling against this tendency makes it irresistible.
>
> ALEXIS DE TOCQUEVILLE

ONE of the most useful tools employed by the social scientist in attempting to understand the ways of human behavior is the culture concept. Culture may be defined as the normative ways of thinking and behaving, and the types of artifacts, which the members of a society in any given area—tribe, nation, region, etc.—hand down from generation to generation. Culture, then, is the learned social heritage of any particular society. Thus many types of behavior (often equated with "human nature"), many of our likes and dislikes, many of our ideas of right and wrong, and most of our aesthetic standards are conditioned by our particular cultural heritage. The uninitiated person who looks at a new and strange art form and says, "I do not understand that but I know what I like," may actually mean, "I like what I know."

The culture concept was introduced into the literature of social science by the cultural anthropologist who had worked almost exclusively with small, pre-literate societies where all individuals were socialized in a common cultural heritage. In a large and complex society like the United States, however, while there is, in a sense, a national culture shared in different degrees by all Americans, and which differentiates them from Englishmen, Frenchmen, or Russians, there are subcultural differences between regions, religious groups, ethnic groups, and social classes. The social heritage of an upper-class Episcopalian from Boston will be quite different from that of an Irish Catholic from Brooklyn, yet the Brooklyn Dodgers, Coney Island, and Harvard College are all part of the American cultural heritage. As Cooley has said, human nature is formed in primary groups and the inevitable fact of living in a more or less primary group segment of any complex social structure results in the emergence of subcultural class levels. Georg Simmel emphasized this when he said: "In fact, almost all custom is custom of estate or class."

Language is always a basic clue to group differences in culture and tradition. Our American language testifies to our historic cultural ties to Great Britain, as well as our more ancient roots in the Greek and Roman civilizations. Within the national culture, there are subcultural differences in language and accent. Accent clearly distinguishes the Southerner from his countrymen in the Middle West or New England. At the same time, there is a subtle upper-class accent in America which cuts across regional differences. Although each accent betrays its regional origins, the speech patterns of a Proper Bostonian, New Yorker, Chicagoan, or San Franciscan all have something in common with the upper-class nasal twang of the Proper Philadelphian. This upper-class accent is a British modification of the ordinary American language and may be partly traced to the imported British "Nannie" who has raised the children of the eastern seaboard rich for several generations. In addition, the "Harvard accent" of the Proper Boston Anglophiles has set the tone in countless New England boarding schools.

Most Americans vent their snobbery by branding uncouth manners and speech patterns in others as "lower class"; within the upper class the derogatory epithet "middle class" is used to dismiss so-called inferiors. In addition to accent, word usage also differentiates the members of the upper class from the rest of the population. They avoid carefully certain common words and expressions which are standard speech among the middle classes. The Proper Philadelphian, Bostonian, or New Yorker, for instance, never refers to "living-room or bedroom suites," "davenports," "divans," or "drapes," and, unlike almost all Americans (and like his British cousins), he makes the "a" in "tomato" always short.[1] Such word usage is sure to betray one's middle-class origins (or embarrassment at upper-class pretensions). The few words listed in Table 7

Table 7—Class Language Usage in America as of 1940

UPPER CLASS (Usage or Silence)	MIDDLE CLASS (Upper-Class Taboos)
The Household	
The upper classes *live* in a *house,* employ *servants* to *wash* the *curtains* and clean the *furniture,* including a *sofa;* they use the *toilet,* the *porch, library,* or *playroom.*	The middle classes *reside* in a *home,* hire *help* or *domestics* to *launder* the *drapes* and clean the house *furnishings* which include a bedroom *suite* (like in suit) and a *davenport;* they use the *lavatory,* the *veranda, den,* or *rumpus room.*
At the Table	
delicious vegetables and *jam*	*delectable greens* and *preserves*
tomato (like in Otto)	*tomato* (as in potato)
At School	
private or *boarding school*	*prep* school
headmaster, rector, head masters	*principal*
	teachers
grades (1-6), *forms* (1-6)	*grades* (1-12)
good *marks*	good *grades*
At Church	
rector	*pastor*
Clothing	
long dress, evening dress	*formal, formal gown*
underwear	*lingerie*
dress, dress shop	*gown, gown shop*
dinner jacket, black tie	*tuxedo, formal*
white tie	*tails, tailcoat*
Money	
rich	*wealthy*
high (the price)	*dear* (the price)
cheap	*inexpensive*
In General	
Hello (silence)	*pleased to meet you*
what?	*pardon?*
enough, thank you	*sufficient,* thank you
my wife	the wife, the Mrs.
courting	*dating, keeping company, going steady*
guests, friends for dinner	*company* for dinner
girl, boy, friend	*girl-friend, boy-friend*
beaux	*steady date, date, steady*
RSVP	the favor of a reply is requested
a *dance*	a *formal*
a *party*	an *affair*
I feel *sick*	I feel *ill*

serve to subtly differentiate the members of the American upper class from the rest of the population.

Upper-Class Cultural Orientation. In a recent paper, Florence Rockwood Kluckhohn developed the concepts of *Dominant and Substitute Profiles of Cultural Orientations.*[2] According to Dr. Kluckhohn, there are basic human problems faced by all cultures. Each culture answers these problems, which may be stated in the form of basic questions, in a different way. Three of these questions are as follows: First, what is the significant time dimension? Second, what type of personality is to be most valued? And third, what is the dominant modality of relationship between man and man? The alternative answers to these three questions may be illustrated as follows:

	Dominant American Profile	Upper-Class Profile
Time Dimensions	Future	Past
Personality	Doing	Being
Relationships between Men	Individualistic	Lineal

Most segments of American society, especially the middle classes, stress the *future,* the *doing* type of personality, and *individualistic* relationships between men. On the other hand, the upper-class subculture tends to be, in Dr. Kluckhohn's terms, a *substitute profile.* Where the average American tends to stress the future and to disregard the past and many forms of traditionalism, the upper classes more or less revere the past, especially the past accomplishments of their ancestors. Where most Americans value the doer and idealize the engineer-entrepreneur, the older ideal of the well-rounded gentleman-amateur still exists as the upper-class ideal. At least in part, the American aristocrat still mistrusts the narrow specialist and professionalism. Perhaps this is because he can afford a liberal education in history, the arts, and literature. Most Americans on-the-move, cannot afford the time for "useless book learning" and the more ornamental aspects of education; they prefer business and engineering schools. As someone once said, "While the mediocre European is obsessed with history, the mediocre American is ignorant of it." The values of the American upper class lie somewhere between these two extremes. Finally, of course, kin and cousin as well as ancestors have always played an important role in maintaining upper-class cohesion. Whereas many middle-class Americans want to forget their ancestry and often have risen above their kith and kin, the Proper Philadelphian tends to be bound by the ties of family, sometimes to his own detriment.

At this point it is well to stress that these contrasting cultural profiles—between the upper class and the rest of the population—are a matter of emphasis only. They are not mutually exclusive, nor are they clearly defined differences. Later chapters, however, will refer to the very real differences in *tendency*. One more thing must be said. Although the lineal relationship is still strong among the Philadelphia upper class, other institutions—the school, college, and club—are gradually replacing the family as the primary status referent. Presumably this will eventually lead to a more individualistic and associational cultural profile. The modern Madison Avenue aristocrat, a product of the best schools and "Ivy" universities, who carefully lunches at The Racquet Club and buys his clothes at Brooks Brothers is certainly more future-oriented and less lineally secure than was his grandfather.

Upper-Class Social Organization. In Philadelphia certain members of the upper class date their family and traditions to colonial times. This relatively small group of families forms a subculture at the top of the social class system which is, in turn, set apart from the rest of the community by various exclusive associations and neighborhoods, and distinguished by symbolic behavior patterns, beliefs, and artifacts.

The members of this upper class, bound together by common interests and experiences, have many friends and relatives in common. The family idea is, of course, extremely important. A nucleus of "old families"—Pembertons, Norrises, Morrises, Biddles, Cadwaladers, and Ingersolls—are fused with families of newer wealth and social position such as Wideners, Dorrances, and Pews. Among the more prolific clans, where Christmas or anniversary dinners of a hundred relatives are not unusual, there is a great deal of "cousin, aunt, and uncle this and that." The patriarchal Philadelphia gentlemen want their wives to be intelligent but not necessarily well educated or career-minded; large households and gracious entertainment are often a chore to the bookish or vocationally ambitious spouse. Children are highly valued, but often only as many as can be educated privately. And in even the most impecunious families, the faithful maid, often of twenty years service or more, is valued above a new automobile or any kind of public entertainment. (The impecunious Brills of *Wickford Point,* who borrowed from the maid to buy some gin, have their spiritual cousins in Philadelphia.)

Family life centers in the justly famous suburbs along the Main Line and in Chestnut Hill. In each community there is the fashionable Episcopal church where the collection is passed each Sunday by some of the city's leading bankers and businessmen. Ever since Nicholas Biddle built his famous "Greek revival" mansion at Andalusia the Proper Philadelphian has built himself beautiful suburban houses in the Georgian, Norman, or Pennsylvania Colonial style, and collected furniture over the years in the Chippendale, Hepplewhite, or Sheraton tradition—"nobody has Grand Rapids."

Even the most socially secure families, for reasons suggested below, place a high value on belonging to the correct clubs and associations, and making an appearance at the fashionable balls, dancing assemblies, weddings, and funerals; and where their children are concerned, the right summer resorts, dancing classes, schools and colleges, and finally, their daughter's debut, are each and severally of vital importance.

In addition to the family, then, an intricate web of exclusive associations, each one serving as a kind of upper-class family surrogate, serves to perpetuate upper-class solidarity and tradition.

The Fishing Company of the State in Schuylkill, founded in 1732, is the oldest association of gentlemen in this country.[3] Originally a mock state within a state situated on the banks of the Schuylkill River, it is now located near Andalusia on the Delaware River. Its members are still called "citizens" and its officers include a Governor, a Secretary of State, a Sheriff, and a Coroner. With a membership limited to thirty, some three hundred Proper Philadelphians have had the privilege of "citizenship" in over two hundred years. "The Fish House," as it is usually called, is now a cooking club where many a gentleman has served a long apprenticeship as the chef's assistant.

While the "Fish House" meets during the summer, the younger but equally exclusive Rabbit, founded in 1866, meets during the winter months. Modeled after the older club, the Rabbit is more conveniently located along the Main Line. When one of its members died recently, an obituary in the local newspaper listed his membership in the Racquet Club rather than the Rabbit; his family, needless to say, was somewhat upset.

The Philadelphia Club, founded in 1834, is the oldest men's

club in America. A later chapter will be devoted to a discussion of the importance of both the Philadelphia Club and the younger Rittenhouse Club within the upper class.

Finally, from generation to generation, the members of Philadelphia's best families have served in the First City Troop. Founded in 1774, "The Troop" is older than any regiment in the United States Army.

Ritual is an important aspect of social cohesion. The role of these voluntary associations in maintaining a sense of upper-class cohesion was recently brought out when "The Troop" paid an old debt of hospitality:

> In order to repay the hospitality tendered by the State-in-Schuylkill in 1815 and again in 1915, the Troop invited the Governor and Citizens of the Schuylkill Fishing Company of the State-in-Schuylkill to attend the annual dinner at the Armory in honor of Washington's Birthday. In full dress uniform, the Troop rode to the Philadelphia Club where an escort to the Armory was furnished Governor John W. Geary and the Citizens. One hundred and thirty-two Troopers of all Rolls were present and on this happy occasion a joint toast was drunk to the memories of George Washington and Samuel Morris. Captain Morris, it need hardly be added, was the Troop's Revolutionary Commander, and, for many years, Governor of the State-in-Schuylkill.[4]

Gentlemen in Philadelphia wear distinctive types of clothes, usually in the Brooks Brothers tradition (made by selected local tailors), and various symbols of exclusive associational affiliation. The various totem symbols of class position—the club necktie and hatband, the little charm (Ivy Leaf or Porcellian Pig) on the watch chain, or the rosette ("The Troop") on the lapel—are as much as to say, in Max Weber's words, "I am a gentleman patented after investigation and probation and guaranteed by my membership."

It is no accident that Max Weber found the archtypical example of his "Protestant ethic" in Philadelphia's Benjamin Franklin. The Philadelphia gentleman is intimately connected with business, and the history of *The Philadelphia Contributionship for the Insurance of Houses for Loss by Fire* is a Proper Philadelphia story.[5]

The Philadelphia Contributionship, founded in 1752 by Benjamin Franklin, Israel Pemberton II ("King of the Quakers"), and others, is the oldest fire insurance company in America. Down through the years, its management has always remained in upper-class hands. Since 1842, for example, the highest executive office—Treasurer—has remained within the same family: James S. Smith

(1842-1859), Jas. Somers Smith (1859-1894), and J. Somers Smith (1894-1941). The directors, including eleven Morrises and five Biddles, have come from the city's first families from colonial times to the present. In 1940, all twelve of the board of directors were listed in the *Social Register.*

In 1894, a progressive group of young Philadelphia insurance men led by Clifford Pemberton, Jr. attempted to control the Contributionship's four million dollars in assets by electing a new board of directors. Nicholas Biddle Wainwright, an historian of Old Philadelphia, describes the situation as follows:

Any insurance office which was open only from 10 A.M. to 2 P.M. and which employed superannuated clerks, whose attitude toward customers was that of master to slave, needed a shaking up, they maintained. Freely admitting that the Old Board was composed of the most respectable gentlemen in the city, the new element protested that something other than hereditary position and wealth was desirable in the Director of an insurance company.[6]

The stockholders went to the polls on June 7, 1894.

This extraordinary scene was one on which the papers commented at length and with apparent relish—"Local 400 in Line" was a favorite caption. Mingled with the throng were many well-known people of the day—former Mayor Richard Vaux, George W. Biddle of legal fame, C. Stuart Patterson, Archbishop Ryan, John Cadwalader, E. T. Stotesbury of Drexel's, John Sailer, onetime minister to Italy, William Potter, John Story Jenks, and many others of equal note. Both sides of the street were lined with carriages and others continued to arrive, many bringing feeble octogenarians who tottered to the polls with the aid of anxious relatives. . . . For the first time in history, ladies attended the Contributionship's election and were accorded the courtesy due their sex by not being required to stand in line. Seats were provided for them inside the building and they were allowed to vote alternately with the line of men. Boldt's Restaurant, located in the nearby Bullitt Building, gratuitously served sandwiches for their refreshment.[7]

After two days of voting, the ballots were counted, and the Old Board "came through with flying colors." As Mr. Wainwright puts it:

Obviously the attacking faction had completely miscalculated its Philadelphia. It had called the Company a stodgy old affair, little realizing that Philadelphia liked it to be old-fashioned because it stood as a living memorial to the city's past. Unquestionably, the most serious flaw in the liberal's offensive was the appearance it gave of an attack on vested interests and conservative property management. To protect these twin guarantees to security, as they understood the term, birthright Philadelphians rose from sick beds or entrained from distant cities to rally to the defense of principles they held sacred.[8]

Although inherited wealth is almost an indispensable aspect of upper-class position, the gentleman of leisure, contrary to the stereotype popularized by Thorstein Veblen, is rare in Philadelphia. On the contrary, there is a traditional emphasis on the "Protestant ethic" of hard work and a mistrust, amounting almost to an incapacity, for leisure. Like Henry James, those more sensitive Philadelphians, yearning for the subtleties of aristocratic patterns of leisure, left the land of their birth, especially during the crass and booming twenties, and settled as permanent expatriates in Europe. The second-generation *parvenu* who participates in the strenuous, conspicuous leisure of which Veblen wrote so bitterly is in sharp contrast to the mores of the third- and fourth-generation gentlemen. (The "Society" sections of the local newspapers, for example, which are read apparently with avid interest by the local middle classes, tend to chronicle the leisure-time activities of the newly fashionable members of the upper class). The Proper Philadelphian walks where other Americans would ride, and rarely takes a taxi; he lives within his income and never spends principal; favors an automobile of any color as long as it is black (whitewall tires); talks a great deal about how little, rather than how much, he paid for this and that, and never mentions what he is worth. He is, in effect, affirming his faith in the "Spartan-Puritan" virtues.

The Philadelphia gentleman has always emulated his English counterpart in clothes, sporting activities, club ritual, etc. One gentleman in this study, for example, sent his shirts for many years to be laundered in London. In contrast, however, to the upper-class Englishman's traditional participation in government service, which the Proper Philadelphian both admires and envies, his need for a sense of service to the larger community, or diluted sense of *noblesse oblige,* is channeled into the support of private cultural and charitable institutions such as hospitals, libraries, art galleries, schools and colleges. Membership in the armed forces in time of war is highly valued, and informal pressure and tradition assures patriotic service among the younger generation: "more gentlemen should be in government," so the self-analysis goes, "yet 'we', 'our class' did well in the war." Indicative of a more patriotic age than our own, it is of interest that men who served in World War I had stars after their names in the 1920 *Social Register.*

In many ways this primary group of upper-class Philadelphians approximates the type of social organization which various sociologists have characterized by such terms as "status," "folk," or *Gemeinschaft*. In *The Lonely Crowd*, David Riesman is concerned with the relationship between social character and social organization.[9] According to his interesting and perceptive hypotheses, as social organization evolves from the simple, and rural "folk" society to complex, urban civilization, social character changes, in response to the social situation, from what he calls the "tradition directed" personality, to the "inner directed," and finally, to the "other directed" personality type. Presumably, the social character of upper-class members differs from that of the other social classes in America. Following Riesman, it is our hypothesis that, in contrast to the prevailing "inner" and "other" directedness of the contemporary American social character, the members of the upper class, even in 1940, still retained a blend of the "tradition" and "inner" directed social character.

Perhaps former Senator George Wharton Pepper's description of a visit to his old law firm reveals both the Proper Philadelphia social character, and the substitute *cultural profile* of *past* orientation, in Dr. Kluckhohn's theoretical scheme discussed above: (Both J. Rodman Paul and George Wharton Pepper were old family members of the Philadelphia elite in 1940—listed in both *Who's Who* and the *Social Register*.)

Fifty years after I had bid the Biddle office good-bye I paid a courtesy call on Mr. J. Rodman Paul who, as a partner in the old firm, had fed me my first ration of Blackstone and had conducted many of the office quizzes. There he sat in the modern suite into which in recent years the firm had moved. Around him were the furnishings of half a century before, including a familiar framed facsimile of Magna Charta. "Whatever happened to Morris?" I asked, referring to Mr. Biddle's clerk who in student days had seemed to us already an old man. "Nothing has happened to him," was the reply, "you will find him in an adjoining room." I gasped. "There were three stenographers in those days," I said, "Miss Shubert, Miss McGarry and Miss McNutt. What ever became of them?" "They are still with us," he said—and so they were.[10]

The social organization of the Proper Philadelphia family, neighborhood, church, school, college, and club will be discussed in detail in later chapters.

The Functions of an Upper Class

The culture and social organization of the upper class have been discussed in brief. The members of this intricate web of patriarchal families and exclusive voluntary associations live in a subcultural world, well-defined and insulated by money. Their common set of customs, mores, and values differentiate them from the rest of the population. What is the function of such an upper class in a large metropolitan society?

One group of socio-anthropologists, who have been influenced by Warner, define a social class in the following way:

A "Social Class" is the largest group of people whose members have intimate access to one another. A class is composed of families and social cliques. The interrelationships between these families and cliques, in such informal activities as dancing, visiting, receptions, teas, and larger informal affairs constitute the function of the social class.[11]

Modifications are necessary before this definition can be applied to class relationships in a large metropolitan area. First, in Philadelphia, although the upper class tends to approximate this definition, there is *no other class* in the city "whose members have intimate access to one another." In this sense, then, while there may be *an upper class* in the city, there is no middle or lower class as such, only middle and lower *classes*. Confusion derives from the fact that the "Warner group" have, by and large, defined their terms and drawn their conclusions from evidence found in pre-literate societies and small American communities. It is simply not true that the class structure in Philadelphia is like that of "Middletown" or "Yankee City," or, as W. Lloyd Warner puts it, that "the lives of ten thousand citizens of Jonesville express the basic values of 140,000,000 Americans . . . that Jonesville is in all Americans and all Americans are in Jonesville, for he that dwelleth in America dwelleth in Jonesville, and Jonesville in him."[12] This point of view may very well lead to confusion if the difference between the small community and the large metropolitan area is one of kind rather than degree. As two excellent critics of the "Warner School" have said:

In cities like Dallas, Seattle, or Buffalo the only class of people who know and rank one another are Warner's "upper-uppers," i.e., those who are known as "society." The other "five classes" are much too numerous to permit that degree of personal acquaintance, which alone would make a system of interlocking status evaluations feasible.[13]

If this difference between communities of different sizes is valid, the upper class in Philadelphia is the only one which may be spoken of, *qua* class, in terms of a subculture bound together by a common tradition and a consciousness of kind which approximates a primary group; this upper class is a "we" group in a sense not applicable to any other class in the city.

Second, it is inadequate and misleading to limit the role of the social class to the rather incidental functions of providing a milieu for "visiting, receptions, teas, and larger informal affairs." On the contrary, the four primary functions of an upper class are: (1) to maintain a continuity of control over important positions in the world of affairs; (2) to provide a primary group social organization within which the informal aspects of the normative order—the folkways and mores—may operate as effective agents of social control; (3) to provide an autonomous power in the community as a protection against totalitarian power; and, finally, (4) to provide a more or less primary group social world within which the younger generation is socialized.

Thus the debutante ritual is a *rite de passage* which functions to introduce the post-adolescent into the upper-class adult world, and to insure upper-class endogamy as a normative pattern of behavior, in order to keep important functional class positions within the upper class.

In the last analysis, power over other people is the indispensable mark of high social status, and the primary function of an upper class is the exercise of power. When Theodore Roosevelt made the well-known statement that he "intended to be one of the governing class" rather than merely a gentleman of "cultivated taste," he reflected his historical sense of the function of upper-class membership.[14]

An upper class must maintain the power of leadership in order to limit the power of individual leaders. In any complex society the problem of the individual abuse of power is a perennial one. Among other things, a sense of honor and morality, and even a sense of *noblesse oblige,* serve to check the abuses of power. With characteristic insight, Tocqueville saw the necessary relationship between honor and self-conscious class loyalty. "To comprise all my meaning in a single proposition," Tocqueville wrote, "the dissimilarities and inequalities of men give rise to the notion of honor: that notion is weakened in proportion as these differences are obliterated, and with them it would disappear."[15] Among American social scientists, perhaps Ralph Linton is most clearly aware of the need for upper-class normative sanctions:

The lack of a definite aristocratic culture which provides the members of this ruling group with common ideals and standards of behavior and thus integrates them into a conscious society is perhaps the most distinctive aspect of the modern condition. Exploiters and exploited have existed since the dawn of history, but the only parallel to the modern situation is that of Rome in the days of the late Republic. Here also power came to be vested in the hands of a group of self-made men who had no common standards and no feeling of responsibility to each other or to the state.[16]

In any large social structure, then, and especially at the elite level, men are limited in their choice of ways and means by the laws—both customary and written—for the *society as a whole,* but, on the other hand, at the level of informal control, only by the *norms and sanctions of their peers.* A man caught in an act of dishonesty or disloyalty fears, above all, the criticism of his class, club, or life-long friends. It is no accident that it was the conservatives in the Senate of the United States, "the most exclusive club in the world," who forced the vote in favor of censoring the junior Senator from Wisconsin because they felt he had violated the informal code of this historic club of American parliamentarians.

Thus the knowledge that a common, upper-class background implies a mutually understood code of conduct may, and often does, influence a bank president when he promotes to an important fiduciary position someone from his own subcultural milieu—school, college, or similar club membership. The British have long been aware of the normative function performed by primary groups, and, undoubtedly, the relatively high level of integrity in British government circles is partly due to a strong tradition of upper-class control of the government elite. Stanley Baldwin's statement to the Harrow association in 1923, for example, suggests this pervasive class loyalty in England (usually ridiculed by the Left): "When the call came to me to form a government, one of my first thoughts was that it should be a government of which Harrow should not be ashamed."[17] Perhaps the late Franklin D. Roosevelt felt a certain sense of security when appointing fellow-Grotonians to important positions in the American government. Robert Sherwood, in his study of Roosevelt and Hopkins, makes an important observation on the relationship between inherited position and the abuses of power: "Over and over in history we have exemplified, it seems to me, the principle that the men who inherit, or easily gain, their power are less likely to intensify it at the expense of society than those men who have struggled for it in the service of a burning ideal."[18]

Although possibly guilty of a somewhat conservative and narrow conception of the duties and obligations of wealth, the upper class in Philadelphia has, on the whole, fostered an atmosphere of integrity and honesty within the business community. The Pennsylvania Railroad, for example, has been controlled by the local upper class for over a century. Louis M. Hacker contrasts this upper-class institution with the railroads run by such *parvenu* buccaneers as Drew, Vanderbilt, or Hill: "The Pennsylvania system was built up to become the most important railroad and in fact one of the most outstanding business enterprises in the country. The fraud which made the history of many of the rails a byword in American economic life was unknown to its annals; the stock manipulation of the Vanderbilts never had their parallel in its steady growth."[19]

From Emile Durkheim to Elton Mayo and George Homans, the integrative and normative function of the small group segments of the total social structure has been considered the central problem of sociology. In the words of Durkheim, "a society made up of a boundless dust-heap of unrelated individuals whom an over-developed state tries to hem and hold in, is a true sociological monstrosity."[20] Contrary to much of the unwitting bias in modern social thought, it is conceivable that membership in, and loyalty to, well-integrated subcultural segments of the culture as a whole is a necessary prerequisite for a healthy society. Loyal and ethnocentric Texans, Californians, Jews, Catholics, or upper-class members may be better Americans, and even better world citizens, than isolated "ex-culturated" individuals who "rationally" see in all such parochial loyalties *nothing but* anachronistic tribalism or snobbery. The latter tend to focus only on the excluding and rejecting aspects of all group life. They too often forget that participation through time in any subcultural milieu implies a degree of ethnocentrism without which the informal normative sanctions of society would hardly be a factor in influencing human behavior.

The modern totalitarian dictatorship, for instance, must always obliterate the existing upper class before proceeding to appropri-

ate all available power in the community. After deliberately
destroying all loyalties to family, class, ethnic, and religious groups,
the state demands, by propaganda, force, and fraud, the first loyalty
of all its citizens. A wise sociologist, Robert A. Nisbet who has
recognized this to be the central sociological problem of our age,
describes as follows the need for autonomous centers of power
within the modern state:

> The real conflict in modern political history has not been, as is so
> often stated, between State and individual, but between State and
> social group. . . . What Maitland once called the "pulverizing and
> macadamizing tendency of modern history" has been one of the most
> vivid aspects of the social history of the modern West, and it has been
> inseparable from the momentous conflicts of jurisdiction between the
> political State and the social associations lying intermediate to it and
> the individual. The conflict between central political government and
> the authorities of guild, village community, class, and religious body
> has been, of all the conflicts of history, the most fateful. . . .[21]
> To create the conditions within which autonomous *individuals*
> could prosper, could be emancipated from the binding ties of kinship,
> class, and community, was the object of the older *laissez faire*. To create
> conditions within which *autonomous groups* may prosper must be, I
> believe, the prime objective of the new *laissez faire*.[22]

The lesson of history, then, is the fact that a strong and autonomous upper class (an intermediate power group) is one of the
important bulwarks of freedom against an all-inclusive totalitarian
power. A business aristocracy which hoards its privileges at the
expense of the exercise of power marks the decline of modern
liberal democracy in the West.

Finally, in addition to the functions of providing various checks
on the abuses of power, an upper class also provides a learning environment. In a sense, no one is brought up in the national culture; one lives, matures, and learns a style of life in the family,
the neighborhood, and the class. The fourth function, then, of
the upper-class subculture is to provide a learning environment.
As Americans do not often spend their whole lives within one
subcultural milieu, it is useful to think of the learning process
as having two aspects: (1) *socialization*—assimilating a subculture into which one is born; and (2) *acculturation*—learning a subculture other than the one into which one is born.
In America, the problems of the immigrant, especially those of
the second generation, have been widely discussed in the lit-

erature. This problem is largely one of acculturation and the resulting culture conflicts. Most Americans, perhaps to a lesser extent, are experiencing similar conflicts insofar as they are first- or second-generation members of various subcultures; the *parvenu* American from Italy or Poland differs in degree rather than in kind from the *parvenu aristocrat* on the "Main Lines" of this country. "When a man passes from one class to another," wrote William Graham Sumner, "his behavior shows the contrast between the mores in which he was bred and those in which he finds himself. Satirists have ridiculed the parvenu for centuries."

The sociologist conceives of the refugee German scientist as having been *socialized* in the German culture and *acculturated* into the American way of life; this adult refugee, retaining the marks of the culture of his birth, will never be wholly a part of the new culture in which he finds himself. On the other hand, his five-year-old son is neither a *socialized* German nor an *acculturated* American, but a blend of both. Like the ascribed and achieved aspects of any status, subcultural membership has both its socialized and acculturated aspects whenever mobility is involved.

In order to sharpen the analysis of the processes of learning an upper-class style of life, it is broken down into five stages in Diagram 1. These stages are: (a) *babyhood*—largely unconscious learning within the immediate family; (b) *childhood*—early school experience and neighborhood primary play groups; (c) *adolescence* —private day school, boarding school, controlled courting situations (e.g., dancing class and summer resorts); (d) *young adulthood*—college and debutante rituals; and, finally, (e) *adulthood*— functional career and income become important, along with club and associational membership.

The socialized and acculturated aspects of learning an upper-class style of life may and do vary all the way from the case of the child born into an old, upper-class family [a] whose values, behavior patterns, and basic assumptions are unconsciously acquired and taken for granted, to the newly arrived, successful executive who has only come to this way of life in advanced years [e] through achieving membership in the proper subcultural associational groups. The behavior patterns, values, and basic assumptions of the subculture are consciously and rationally acquired by the executive who, like the refugee scientist, is primarily an acculturated member of the upper class. But if this newly arrived executive has moved to the "right" neighborhood and sent his children to the proper private schools at an early age, they (the children) will be more or less socialized into the subculture [b or c]; their behavior, however, will be more self-conscious and their position less taken for granted than that of their peers who were born into an upper-class family [a]. Finally, the executive may have had college-age children by the time he discovered or could afford this learning milieu [d]. A fruitful study of subculture conflict might be made of adolescents and young adults whose parents have placed them in this marginal upper-class position.

It has been suggested, rather formally and with a certain amount of oversimplification, that the socialized and acculturated aspects of learning an upper-class style of life vary from one individual to another as they enter this learning process at various age levels. Several things should be said about this process of learning and living in a subculture. First, the subculture provides the setting for the creation of those emotional ties which bind together individuals who have had a common life experience and background. As Ralph Linton has said:

DIAGRAM 1

Upper Class Socialization

Socialized Aspect
(Ascribed Status)

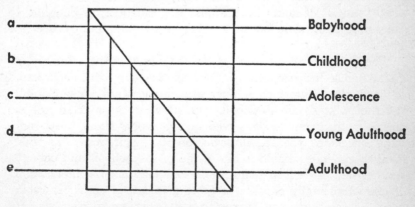

Acculturated Aspects
(Achieved Status)

The average individual in all societies feels a need for membership in some compact social unit larger than the family. He is unhappy and unsure of himself unless he feels that a number of other individuals share his particular ideas and habits and are his friends.[24]

These shared life experiences make for a closeness between men which is never replaced by any rational ties of interest. It follows, therefore, that the further individuals move out of the milieu into which they were born in order to achieve a higher status, the more rational and circumspect their lives become and the less emotionally secure they are. Perhaps it is just this aspect of modern American society, an isolated individualism symbolized by the high frequency of "contacts" as against "friends" in urban society, which results in so much emotional immaturity. As Linton wisely remarks: "Where there can be no rivalry in vital matters and no social climbing, snubbing becomes unnecessary and indeed meaningless. Membership in a rigidly organized society may deprive the individual of opportunities to exercise his particular gifts, but it gives him an emotional security which is almost unknown among ourselves."[25]

Why is there such a relatively high degree of insecurity, even among the supposedly secure members of the American upper classes? An answer to this important question suggests itself when one takes into account the increasing emphasis placed on the "right" schools, neighborhoods, dancing classes, colleges, and clubs among the urban upper classes; that is, the emphasis on institutions other than the family as status ascribing devices. As Cleveland Amory reports of familistic Boston: "If you send your daughter to the wrong dancing school at the age of six, you don't recover for three generations."[26]

The apparent paradox of the "old family social climber" in Philadelphia, for example, is often explained by the background of these "climbers" which is likely to include both the "right" family and the "wrong" neighborhood, education, etc. It is often just the most socially secure parents who do not worry about these snobbish aspects of the socialization process. Moreover, the "best" families may not be able to afford the proper schools and colleges, and, if they can afford them, their sons may not be intellectually or temperamentally capable of getting through. Again, Cleveland Amory observes that, at Harvard where no more than one-fifth of each class is selected for club membership, the "right" boarding school is more important than family position: "If the school is 'wrong' even 'right' ancestry is usually of no avail."[27] Many years ago, Max Weber noted that a student in America who was not admitted to any club was usually looked upon as a "sort of pariah." (One response to pariah status at Harvard was the founding of its newest, final club, the Delphic, by J. P. Morgan, in 1889.)

The difference here between the small town and the large metropolis is important. In *Yankee City*, for instance, to belong to a family which traces its ancestry back to eighteenth century ship owners may ascribe one a social position which is superior to one who descends from a mere sea captain. Lineage rivalry of this sort may seem rather absurd in any large metropolitan area where the fact of having graduated from Groton or Harvard will be a much more important aspect of one's ascribed social-class position; both of these are partly achievable.

J. P. Marquand, in *Point of No Return,* has given us a subtle analysis of the differences between the social structure of the small town and the big city. Charles Gray, for instance, experiences the inevitable conflicts due to the social class differences in a small town New England community where he and his *family* were not accepted by the "old family" parents of his fiancee. On the other hand, Marquand, with characteristic insight and irony, shows how, in Boston and New York, the fact of having graduated from Dartmouth rather than Harvard was the important ascription referent. Florence Kluckhohn indicates how *achieved* status may become *ascribed* in the following passage:

> The fact that an individual has achieved the status of being a graduate of Yale University in the Class of 1930, or any other such achieved status, is a most important point of ascription for future achievement. Viewing our social system as a whole, this—relatively speaking—is a far more important type of ascription referent than biological relatedness or membership in a kin group.[28]

A sophisticated sociology, then, must take into account the fact that such terms as "aristocracy," "old family," "lineage group," "gentleman," or "well bred"—survivals from an age of family continuity which is slowly dying—are less meaningful today, except in a relative sense. The contemporary "aristocrat" in Philadelphia and elsewhere does a great deal of talking about "new families" who are forever "buying their way into society" while conveniently forgetting how some ancestor of his did the same thing one or more generations ago. It is of interest here that the *Social Register* has increased in size in each decade of the first half-century of its existence (Table 8).

Table 8—The Increase in the Number of Family Units in the Philadelphia Social Register 1890-1940

	No. of Families in Social Register	No. of Families Added by Decades	Per Cent Increase by Decades
1890	135	....	....
1900	1939	1804	1,336
1910	3267	1328	68
1920	4275	1008	31
1930	4849	574	13
1940	5150	301	6

The first point to be made in interpreting Table 8 is that ascribed upper-class status in Philadelphia, in the first half of the twentieth century, has been achievable. Presumably, some of the increase in the size of the *Social Register* in this period has come from within the group, but, undoubtedly, a large part of the increase has been due to achieved membership from other parts of the social structure; there is, of course, no way of knowing how many of the new families came from other areas where they were members of the upper class and how many originated in lower subcultural levels both in Philadelphia and elsewhere. Secondly, although the Philadelphia *Social Register* has increased in size in each decade of the twentieth century, it has done so at a steadily decreasing rate. The inference here is that this upper class has developed into a more or less closed group over the years and that status within it is less and less achievable, or sought after.

What may be happening in Philadelphia and elsewhere in America is this: While the *parvenu* at the turn of the century was of colonial and northern European stock, and Protestant in religion, many of the present generation of successful men are non-Protestant, from the newer immigrant generations, and of southern and eastern European origins. In an excellent monograph by William Miller, who is attempting to correct the "rags-to-riches" stereotype held by so many historians,[29] there is a systematic analysis of 190 business leaders in America at the turn of the century. Miller discovered, among other things, that 73 per cent were of colonial stock, while the family origins of 82 per cent were traced to the British Empire. His findings clearly indicate that these leaders in American business, including the "new rich," did come from the favored ethnic groups. Thus, while the Yankee-British-Protestant *parvenu* may have desired, and been eligible for, *Social Register* status, the newer ethnic groups, although wealthy and equally successful, may not only be ineligible, but may not desire membership in this upper class. While the 1940 *Social Register* lists a few Irish Catholic families, there are many Irish Catholic, Italian, and Jewish families of high standing in the community and possessed of great wealth who are not, in this sense at least, in the upper class. More than at any other social class level, then, the upper class in America has many of the aspects of a caste.

CHAPTER V

Pre-Civil War First Family Founders

On the eve of the Civil War there had been many "seasoned clans" on the Eastern seaboard, some of them dating their origins back a hundred years or more, and boasting of ancestors who had served as preachers, judges, warriors, and statesmen in colonial times, in the heroic epoch of the Revolution, and in the momentous age of the new republic. Able to hold their own socially, if not politically, these select families had absorbed with facility the seepage of rising fortunes that gradually oozed into their ranks—until the flood of the new plutocracy descended upon them.

CHARLES A. BEARD

HISTORIC FAME and family fertility are the warp and woof of fashionable society. Contemporary "old family" prestige ultimately derives from the fact that one or more ancestors made a name (and money) for themselves and their children in the world of affairs of an earlier day. An analysis of the upper-class family structure is a necessary prerequisite for the discussion of the growth and development of fashionable neighborhoods, churches, schools, colleges, and social clubs, all of which will be covered in the chapters which follow. This chapter and the next two will be concerned with the relationship between Proper Philadelphia families and the economic, political, and intellectual history of the city.

In order to provide a framework for the systematic analysis of the development and structure of the Philadelphia upper class, from the eighteenth century to the present, approximately one hundred leading members of some sixty prominent Philadelphia families have been listed in Table 9. These particular families were chosen for two major reasons: distinguished past achievement and family continuity. Inclusion in the *Dictionary of American Biography*, the standard biographical reference in American history, was the primary measure of past achievement, while their descendants' inclusion in the 1940 *Who's Who* or *Social Register* provided the test of family continuity.

Almost all the families listed in Table 9 had one or more members listed in the *Dictionary of American Biography*.[1] The few exceptions to this rule were included because of local prominence and wealth even though no member of the family had achieved national distinction which, as far as the "DAB" is concerned, is largely a matter of prominence in public office. Thus many of the nineteenth-century family founders, such as Enoch W. Clark, who founded one of the city's leading banking houses, or George D. Rosengarten, a pioneer in the American chemical industry, preferred to remain in private life and avoided any kind of publicity while building up great fortunes. Other exceptions had to be made, of course, for the late nineteenth- and early twentieth-century family founders who were too recent to have attained a secure historical position, and who were, moreover, primarily money-makers rather than actual public servants. Surely it is safe to say, however, that most of these newer men—Clothier, Strawbridge, Pew, Stotesbury, Geist, Dorrance, and Kent—would have to be included in any list of prominent Philadelphians of their era. (See the next chapter.)

Table 9—Proper Philadelphia Families: Elite Members 1682-1940

Consanguine Family Historical Elite Members (DAB*) Contemporary Elite (1940 Who's Who)	Principal Occupation or Field of Enterprise
Norris Family (5 in DAB)	
Isaac (1671-1735)	Statesman; Penn's Representative
Isaac (1701-1766)	Leader Quaker Party of Pa.
Joseph Parker (1763-1841)	President Bank of Pa., Lawyer
George Washington (1808-1875)	Surgeon
William Fischer (1839-1901)	Opthalmologist
Charles C. (1940 Who's Who)	Physician
George Washington (1940 Who's Who)	Investment Banker
Pemberton Family (4 in DAB)	
*Israel (1684-1754)	Quaker Merchant Oligarchy
Israel (1715-1779)	King of Quakers; Merchant-Philanthropist
James (1723-1809)	Merchant, Philanthropist
John (1727-1795)	Quaker Preacher
John Clifford (1814-1881)	U. S. Army Mexican War; General Confederate Army in defense of Vicksburg.
Ralph (1940 Who's Who)	Physician

* All elite Philadelphians (except those with (*) before their names) were listed in the *Dictionary of American Biography* (DAB).

Table 9 (Continued)

Wharton Family (6 in DAB)

Samuel (1732-1800)	Merchant; Land Speculator
Thomas (1735-1778)	Statesman; President of Pa.
Robert (1757-1834)	Statesman; Mayor of Philadelphia
Thomas Isaac (1791-1856)	Lawyer, Author, Editor
Francis (1820-1889)	Lawyer, Episcopalian Clergyman
Joseph (1826-1909)	Ironmaster and Philanthropist

Morris Family (4 in DAB)

Anthony (1654-1721)	Brewer
Cadwalader (1741-1795)	Merchant, Statesman, Ironmaster
Anthony (1766-1860)	Merchant, Banker, State Senator
Caspar (1805-1884)	Physician, Philanthropist
Roland S. (1940 Who's Who)	Lawyer

Cadwalader Family (4 in DAB)

Thomas (1707-1779)	Physician, Landowner
John (1742-1786)	Merchant; General Continental Army
Lambert (1743-1823)	Merchant; Colonel Continental Army
John (1805-1879)	Judge, Lawyer

Biddle Family (4 in DAB)

Clement (1740-1814)	Merchant, Patriot
James (1783-1848)	Naval Hero
Nicholas (1750-1778)	Naval Hero
Nicholas (1786-1844)	Literature, President of Second Bank
A. J. Drexel (1940 Who's Who)	Author, Marine, Pugilist
A. J. Drexel, Jr. (1940 Who's Who)	Diplomat
George (1940 Who's Who)	Artist
Francis (1940 Who's Who)	Lawyer, New Dealer
Gertrude (1940 Who's Who)	Civic Leader
Clement M. (1940 Who's Who)	Merchant

Ingersoll Family (4 in DAB)

Jared (1722-1781)	His Majesty's Agent in Connecticut
Jared (1749-1822)	Lawyer, Statesman, Federalist
Charles Jared (1782-1862)	Lawyer, Jeffersonian Congressman
Edward (1817-1893)	Lawyer
R. Sturgis (1940 Who's Who)	Lawyer, Civic Leader
Jared (1940 Who's Who)	Businessman, Civic Leader

Coxe Family (3 in DAB)

Daniel (1673-1739)	Landowner; 1st Grand Master Masons
Tench (1755-1824)	Merchant, Political Economist
Eckley B. (1839-1895)	Engineer, Coal Operator

McKean Family (3 in DAB)

Thomas (1734-1817)	Statesman, Judge, Governor of Pa.
Joseph B. (1764-1826)	Lawyer, Judge
William Wister (1800-1865)	Naval Officer

Hopkinson Family (2 in DAB)

Francis (1737-1791)	Lawyer, Literature, Poet, Patriot
Joseph (1770-1842)	Jurist, Congressman, Author
Edward (1940 Who's Who)	Senior Drexel Partner

Table 9 (Continued)

Rush Family (4 in DAB)
  Benjamin (1745-1813)   Physician, Patriot, Humanitarian
  William (1756-1833)   First American Sculptor
  Richard (1780-1859)   Diplomat, Lawyer, Jeffersonian
  James (1786-1869)   Author, Physician, Philanthropist
    Benjamin (1940 Who's Who)   Chairman of the Board, Insurance
                                            Co. of North America

Chew Family (1 in DAB)
  Benjamin (1722-1810)   Chief Justice, Loyalist
    Oswald (1940 Who's Who)   Civic Leader

Willing Family (1 in DAB)
  Thomas (1731-1821)   Merchant; President 1st Bank of U. S.

White (William) Family (1 in DAB)
  William (1748-1836)   Bishop; Founder of Episcopal Church

Lewis (Mordecai) Family (None in DAB)
  *Mordecai Lewis (1748-1799)   Merchant
  †George T. Lewis (1817-1900)   Merchant; "Father of Penn Salt"

Drinker Family (None in DAB)
  *Henry (1743-1809)   Merchant, Ironmaster
  *Henry S. (1850-1937)   Mining Engineer, Pres. Lehigh Univ.
    Henry S. (1940 Who's Who)   Lawyer

Meade Family (5 in DAB)
  George (1741-1808)   Merchant
  Richard Worsam (1778-1828)   Merchant; U. S. Naval Agent, Spain
  Richard Worsam (1807-1870)   Naval Officer
  George Gordon (1815-1872)   Army Officer; Command Union Army
                                            at Gettysburg
  Richard Worsam (1837-1897)   Naval Officer; Made first Samoan treaty

Coates Family (1 in DAB)
  Samuel (1748-1830)   Merchant, Philanthropist
    George M. (1940 Who's Who)   Physician

Wetherill Family (2 in DAB)
  Samuel (1736-1816)   Chemist, Quaker Preacher
  Samuel (1821-1890)   Chemist

Roberts Family (2 in DAB)
  *John (1648-1724)   Landowner: "Pencoyd"; Prov. Assem.
  *Algernon (1751-1815)   Colonel Continental Army
  *Algernon Sidney (1798-1865)   Drugs, Coal, Railroads
  George Brooke (1833-1897)   President Pennsylvania Railroad
  Howard (1843-1900)   Sculptor
    Percival (1940 Who's Who)   Retired—Director U.S. Steel, Pa. Railroad

Penrose Family (3 in DAB)
  *Bartholomew (-1711)   Shipbuilder, Bristol, England, and Phila.
  Charles Bingham (1798-1857)   Lawyer, Politician
  Boies (1860-1921)   Lawyer, Senator
  Richard A. F. (1863-1931)   Geologist: Founder Amer. Soc. Econ., Geol.
    Charles (1940 Who's Who)   Engineer, Author

Table 9 (Continued)

Pepper Family (3 in DAB)
*George (1779-1846)   Brewer, Merchant
 George Seckel (1808-1890)   Lawyer, Philanthropist
 William (1810-1864)   Physician
 William Platt (1843-1898)   Physician, Provost Univ. of Penna.
  George Wharton (1940 Who's Who) Lawyer, Senator, Civic Leader
  William (1940 Who's Who)   Physician, Educator
  O. H. Perry (1940 Who's Who)   Physician, Educator

Lippincott Family (1 in DAB)
 Joshua B. (1813-1866)   Publisher
  Joseph Wharton (1940 Who's Who) Publisher

McMichael Family (1 in DAB)
 Morton (1807-1879)   Editor, Mayor of Philadelphia

Drexel Family (3 in DAB)
 Francis M. (1792-1863)   Investment Banker
 Anthony J. (1826-1893)   Investment Banker
 Joseph W. (1833-1888)   Investment Banker
  George W. Childs (1940 Who's Who) Banker, Philanthropist

Cooke Family (1 in DAB)
 Jay (1821-1905)   Banker, "Financier of Civil War"

Clark Family (None in DAB)
*Enoch W. (1802-1856)   Investment Banker

Brown Family (1 in DAB)
 John A. (1788-1872)   Banker, Philanthropist

Baird Family (1 in DAB)
 Matthew (1817-1877)   Baldwin Locomotive Works

Houston Family (1 in DAB)
 Henry Howard (1820-1895)   Railroads, Gold, Oil, Land
  Samuel F. (1940 Who's Who)   Shipping, Banker, Philanthropist

Harrison Family (1in DAB)
 Joseph, Jr. (1810-1874)   St. Petersburg-to-Moscow Railroad
  Leland (1940 Who's Who)   Ambassador to Switzerland

Lewis (S. Weir) Family (None in DAB)
*S. Weir (1819-1888)   China merchant, Banker
*John Frederick (1860-1932)   Lawyer, Real Estate Fortune

Disston Family (1 in DAB)
 Henry (1819-1878)   Founder Disston Saws

Wheeler Family (None in DAB)
*Charles (1827-1883)   Manufacturer, Ironmaster, Banker

White (S. S.) Family (1 in DAB)
 Samuel Stockton (1822-1879)   Founder S. S. White Dental Mfg. Co.

Table 9 (Continued)

Wood (Richard D.) Family (2 in DAB)
*Richard (1775-1822)   Merchant, Farmer
George B. (1797-1879)   Physician, Philanthropist
*Richard D. (1799-1869)   Merchant, Manufacturer, Banker
Horatio C. (1841-1920)   Physician, Scientist
    Horatio C. (1940 Who's Who)   Physician, Research

Wood (Alan) Family (None in DAB)
*Alan Wood (1800-1881)   Alan Wood Steel Company

Rosengarten Family (None in DAB)
*George David (1801-1890)   Rosengarten & Sons, eventually Merck

Lennig Family (None in DAB)
*Charles (1809-1891)   Charles Lennig & Co., leading Chemist

Meigs Family (5 in DAB)
Charles DeLucena (1792-1869)   Physician, Author
Montgomery C. (1816-1892)   Quartermaster-General Union Army
John Forsyth (1818-1882)   Physician
Arthur Vincent (1850-1912)   Physician, Author
William Montgomery (1852-1929)   Lawyer, Historian
    Arthur Ingersoll (1940 Who's Who)   Architect

Harrison Family (2 in DAB)
John (1773-1833)   Chemist
Charles C. (1844-1929)   Sugar Manf.; Provost Univ. of Penna.

Vaux Family (2 in DAB)
Roberts (1786-1836)   Merchant, Philanthropist, Penologist
Richard (1816-1895)   Mayor (Dem.); Penologist, Philan.

Borie Family (1 in DAB)
Adolph (1809-1880)   Merchant, Banker, Secretary Navy
    Charles Louis (1940 Who's Who)   Architect

Dallas Family (2 in DAB)
Alexander James (1759-1817)   Lawyer, Secretary of the Treasury
George Mifflin (1792-1864)   Lawyer, Mayor, Senator, Diplomat, Vice-President of the U. S.

Merrick Family (1 in DAB)
Samuel Vaughan (1801-1870)   Manufacturer, 1st Pres. Pa. RR
    J. Hartley (1940 Who's Who)   Educator, Civic Leader
    James Vaughan, 3rd (1940 Who's Who)   Educator, Head St. George's School

Lea Family (2 in DAB)
Isaac (1792-1886)   Publisher
Henry Charles (1825-1909)   Publisher, Philanthropist, Scholar

Mitchell Family (2 in DAB)
John Kearsley (1793-1858)   Physician
Silas Weir (1829-1914)   Physician, Novelist, Psychiatrist

Table 9 (Continued)

Jayne Family (1 in DAB)
  *David (1798-1886)   Patent Medicine King
  Horace Fort (1859-1913)   Physician
    Horace Howard Furness   Archeologist, Museum Director
    (1940 Who's Who)

Furness Family (3 in DAB)
  William (1802-1896)   Clergyman, Friend of Emerson
  Horace Howard (1833-1912)   Shakespearean Scholar, Philanthropist
  Horace Howard (1865-1930)   Shakespearean Scholar, Philanthropist

Weightman Family (1 in DAB)
  William (1813-1904)   Powers & Weightman, chemists

Taylor Family (1 in DAB)
  Frederick W. (1856-1915)   Father of Scientific Management

Scott Family (1 in DAB)
  Thomas A. (1823-1881)   President of Pennsylvania RR

Cassatt Family (1 in DAB)
  A. J. (1839-1906)   President of Pennsylvania RR

Widener Family (1 in DAB)
  Peter A. B. (1834-1915)   Traction Magnate
    Joseph E. (1940 Who's Who)   Art Connoisseur, Capitalist

Elkins Family (1 in DAB)
  William Lukens (1832-1903)   Traction Magnate
    William M. (1940 Who's Who)   Investment Banker

Dolan Family (1 in DAB)
  Thomas (1834-1914)   Textiles, Clothing Mfg., Traction

Strawbridge Family (None in DAB)
  *Justus C. (1838-1911)   Strawbridge & Clothier, Dept. Store
    Frederick H. (1940 Who's Who)   Retired Dept. Store Executive

Clothier Family (None in DAB)
  *Isaac H. (1837-1921)   Strawbridge & Clothier, Dept. Store
    Morris L. (1940 Who's Who)   Chm. Bd. Strw. & Cloth.
    William J. (1940 Who's Who)   Coal, Investment Banker

Wanamaker Family (1 in DAB)
  John (1838-1922)   John Wanamaker, Dept. Store

Converse Family (1 in DAB)
  John H. (1840-1910)   1st President of Baldwin Locomotives

McLean Family (1 in DAB)
  William Lippard (1852-1931)   Founder present *Evening Bulletin*
  Robert (1940 Who's Who)   President *Evening Bulletin*

Wister Family (None in DAB)
  *Owen (1860-1938)   Author, Lawyer

Table 9 (Continued)

Stotesbury Family (None in DAB)
  *Edward T. (1849-1938)   Senior Morgan Partner in Philadelphia

Dorrance Family (None in DAB)
  *John T. (1873-1930)   Founder Campbell Soup Company
    Arthur C. (1940 Who's Who)   Pres. Campbell Soup Company

Geist Family (None in DAB)
  *Clarence H. (1874-1938)   Utilities Magnate

Kent Family (None in DAB)
  *A. Atwater (1873-1949)   Founder Atwater Kent Radio
  (1940 Who's Who)

These families were not only leaders in the city's historical development; they were also prominent in the contemporary elite and upper class. For example, there were members of *all* these families listed in the 1940 *Social Register*, while one or more of the Norris, Pemberton, Morris, Biddle, Ingersoll, Chew, Drinker, Hopkinson, Rush, Wood, Pepper, Meigs, Lippincott, Merrick, Jayne, Widener, Drexel, Coates, Elkins, Clothier, Strawbridge, McLean, Pew, Dorrance, and Kent families were also listed in *Who's Who* in that same year. Of course, it must be remembered that many leading Philadelphians have not been included in Table 9 because of their family's lack of continuity. The families of such early aristocrats as Edward Shippen, James Logan, or William Bingham have died out, while such famous leaders as Benjamin Franklin, Stephen Girard, James Wilson, or the late Cyrus Curtis established no family line (except on the distaff side).

Within many of the older families we have added persons in Table 9 who were not listed in the "DAB." This was done in the interest of maintaining a sense of family continuity. For example, George Brooke Roberts, president of the Pennsylvania Railroad in the late nineteenth century, was not necessarily a family founder although he was the first of the Roberts line to attain national prominence. Thus the family goes back to John Roberts, who had originally settled on 1,000 acres of the "Welsh Tract," along what is now the Main Line, and built the farm house where George B. Roberts was born over a hundred years later. Similarly, Richard Wood, of Salem, New Jersey, father of George B. Wood and grandfather of Horatio C. Wood (also great-grandfather of Horatio C. Wood, a prominent physician listed in the 1940 *Who's Who*), was the first wealthy member of the Wood clan. At the same time,

Dr. George B. Wood's brother, Richard D. Wood, merchant, iron-master, and financial wizard, was included in the list because he was the real founder of the extremely large Wood fortune. In other words, if a family had at least one member listed in the "DAB," other contributors to the family's wealth and position were included in Table 9, even though they were not necessarily of national historical interest. Finally, this is by no means a complete list of "old family" Philadelphians (in the great family founding eighteenth century we have adhered strictly to the "DAB" criteria and thus left out many families of local prominence who were not listed in the "DAB"). Thus this is a basic list of families of both old and new wealth which were chosen in order to reflect a dynamic and historically relative use of the term "old family" or "Proper Philadelphia." For instance, John Wanamaker was newly rich at the turn of the century, while his great-grandson now represents, at least to the ordinary citizen if not to the die-hard antiquarian, the essence of family tradition in his position as vice-president of John Wanamaker's, Proper Philadelphia's favorite department store.

An historical discussion of Philadelphia's family founders will serve two purposes. First, by placing the origin of each family within the dynamic flow of economic and political events, we are able to emphasize the fact that "old family" is an historically relative term which in turn leads to an organic conception of the contemporary upper-class structure. It will emphasize once more the shallowness of such phrases as "lineage," "upper crust," or "society people," which are so often used without concrete historical analysis of the terms. Secondly, it is important to stress the fact that these family founders were not only money-makers; they were also founders of numerous cultural, civic, economic, and educational institutions in the city. Again and again, in the chapters which follow, the present structure of these institutions can best be analyzed by relating them to the men and families who have founded and dominated them over the generations.

Perhaps our age is all too prone to think in terms of abstractions such as "The Government," "The Corporation," or "The Ruling Class." After all, "an institution is but the lengthened shadow of one man," wrote Ralph Waldo Emerson, in the days when man was captain of his fate (or thought he was, which may be far more important) and before sociological (institutional) determinism became so fashionable among intellectuals. At any rate, institutions such as social clubs, neighborhoods, schools, and colleges do in fact partake of the character both of the men who founded them and those who run them through the years. A social club founded by the sons and grandsons of colonial patriots, for instance, presumably will be very different from one founded by new-rich businessmen desiring to consolidate their economic power after the Civil War.

Early Colonial Family Founders. Philadelphia was ruled by a small Quaker oligarchy during the late seventeenth and early eighteenth centuries.[2] A small group of men held most of the important positions, were related by marriage one with another, and made their fortunes over the seas, as daring merchants and traders, or inland with the Indians, whom they treated well from the very start. These early Quaker Grandees were a pious group who collected books and libraries and built fine formal gardens; their religion would not tolerate such worldly arts as painting and the theatre.

Israel Pemberton, Isaac Norris, and Anthony Morris were three leading Proper Philadelphia family founders in this early eighteenth-century period.[3] All three families have produced leaders in the city's economic, cultural and professional life for over two centuries. Thirteen members of these three families, for example, are included in the *Dictionary of American Biography,* and Charles C. Norris (physician), George Washington Norris (investment banker), Ralph Pemberton (physician), and Roland S. Morris (lawyer) are all listed in *Who's Who* in 1940. Just two years earlier, in 1938, Effingham Buckley Morris, president of the fashionable Girard Trust Company for over fifty-one years, died at his home in Ardmore on the Main Line.[4]

The first Isaac Norris was born in London and came to Philadelphia in 1693 where he became a leading merchant and landowner (Norristown, an industrial suburb of Philadelphia today, was part of the large Norris tract), and held many important governmental positions in the colony.[5] He had fourteen children, of whom Isaac II became the leading pacifist member of the Provincial Assembly and the "pride of Quaker historians."[6]

Israel Pemberton, whose father had migrated from Lancashire, England, in 1682, was born in the county of Bucks, just north of

Philadelphia. As a young man he came down to Philadelphia and became one of the city's wealthiest merchants. Israel Pemberton, his brother-in-law, James Logan, and Isaac Norris were the leading members of the Quaker oligarchy during the second quarter of the eighteenth century.

In *Meeting House and Counting House, The Quaker Merchants of Colonial Philadelphia 1682-1763,* Frederick B. Tolles describes the endogamous circle of early Quaker Grandees in Philadelphia as follows:

Thomas Lloyd, the most distinguished Friend of the first generation in Pennsylvania [no male heirs], was in a real sense the patriarch and progenitor of the Philadelphia Quaker aristocracy. . . . One of the few genuine patricians to be converted to Quakerism, this descendant of an ancient Welsh family came to Penn's colony in 1683, bringing a family coat of arms with fifteen quarterings. He played a prominent part in the early political life of the province, serving as President of the Council from 1684 to 1688 and as Deputy-Governor from 1691 to 1693. He was the acknowledged leader of the Conservative or Proprietary Party as opposed to the Popular Party of his distant cousin David Lloyd. After his death the tradition was ably carried on by his sons-in-law Isaac Norris, Richard Hill, Samuel Preston, and John Delavall. Richard Hill's second wife, Mary Stanbury, daughter of another Proprietary stalwart, later married Israel Pemberton, Jr., while a granddaughter of Thomas Lloyd married James Pemberton, thus carrying this family connection through the entire colonial period. The senior Israel Pemberton and James Logan, the two leading Philadelphia Quakers of the second quarter of the eighteenth century, married sisters; and the two daughters of James Logan became the wives of Isaac Norris II and John Smith [see Logan Pearsall Smith, Quaker aristocrat listed in *Who's Who* in 1940], both of whom bore leading parts in the religious, political, and mercantile life of Philadelphia around mid-century. It would be possible to go on almost indefinitely citing examples of close marriage bonds among families in the higher social ranges of Philadelphia Quakerism.[7]

Although not among the inner circle of Pembertons, Norrises, Lloyds, and Logans, Anthony Morris was Proper Philadelphia's most colorful and prolific family founder. Born in Old Gravel Lane, London, in 1654, he was converted to Quakerism, married and the father of four children before coming to America in 1682.[8] Landing in Burlington, New Jersey, he purchased 200 acres of land there but eventually came down to Philadelphia in 1687 where he became a prosperous merchant before founding one of the first breweries in the city (which, of course, prospered with the large influx of Germans who eventually arrived in Penn's city). Anthony Morris had seven children by his first wife who died in 1688. He had three children by his second wife, who had been married three times previously, and five children by his last wife, the widow of Governor Coddington of Rhode Island.[9] Prolific and prosperous down through the years, the Morris family, as we shall see, have been leaders in almost every Proper Philadelphia institution for over two hundred years.

Proper Philadelphia and the Founding of the New Republic. Proper Philadelphia's Golden Age spanned the last twenty-five years of the eighteenth century. This was also the city's most prolific First Family founding era. Many of the inner circle of Proper Philadelphians in the middle of the twentieth century, men who dominate the Philadelphia Club, the First City Troop, and the ancient Assembly Balls, as well as the banks, had prominent ancestors during the Revolutionary period. Rare is the First Family in Philadelphia whose members have ever again contributed so much to the nation, or to the world. In the last part of the eighteenth century, in sharp contrast to the twentieth, the members of the city's upper class were also leaders of a national elite—in statesmanship, in business, finance, and military affairs, as well as in law and medicine. Of the families listed in Table 9, members of the Wharton, Morris, Cadwalader, Biddle, Ingersoll, Coxe, McKean, Hopkinson, Chew, Willing, Rush, and White families played prominent roles during the Revolution and the founding of the new republic. The seeds of revolution and independence, for example, were sown by the Stamp Act of 1765. Among the leading Philadelphia merchants who signed the "non-Importation Resolution," protesting this symbol of British imperialism, were Thomas Willing; Thomas, Charles, and John Wharton; Anthony, Israel, Isaac, Cadwalader, and Samuel Morris; Thomas, John, and Lambert Cadwalader; Owen and Clement Biddle; Israel and James Pemberton; Charles Coxe; John and Benjamin Chew; George Meade; Daniel and John Wister; William Rush; and Thomas and James Penrose.[10] All these men, of course, were members of families listed in Table 9. For convenience, in the discussion of the historic events of the Revolution and the founding of the new republic which follows in the next few pages, the names of Proper Philadelphians (listed in Table 9) will be italicized.

The "shot heard round the world," fired at Lexington on the 19th of April in 1775, brought a strong reaction in Philadelphia. The next morning, a crowd of some 8,000 people assembled in front of the State House. The Committee of Correspondence, which included *Thomas Wharton,* took charge; their authority was recognized and accepted. This small group of Philadelphia patriots had been formed the previous spring at a meeting at the City Tavern with Paul Revere who had come down from Boston seeking allies in the Quaker City. A single brief resolution was passed: "To associate together, to defend with arms their property, liberty, and lives against all attempts to deprive them of it."[11] The Committee immediately proceeded to organize a military establishment. Colonel *John Cadwalader,* the only gentleman in the city (besides the Governor) "who kept all sorts of carriages," trained and led the "Silk Stocking Company" which rendezvoused at his own house.* As Alexander Graydon wrote, "there were capacious demijohns of Madeira set out in the yard, where we formed for our refreshment before marching out to excercise. The ample fortune of Mr. *Cadwalader* had enabled him to fill his cellars with the choicest liquors; and it must be admitted that he dealt them out with the most gentlemanly liberality."[13] Among other patriotic volunteers, Captains *James Biddle* and *Lambert Cadwalader* organized local regiments; *Clement* and *Owen Biddle* were leaders in forming the "Quaker Blues"; and, finally, *Samuel Morris* who had helped to organize the most famous Philadelphia military organization, the First City Troop, in 1774, now assumed the Captaincy.[14]

On May 5th, 1775, Benjamin Franklin came back to Philadelphia from England and was immediately appointed to the Continental Congress. More important, he became head of the Committee of Safety, which replaced the Committee of Correspondence and governed the city during this early emergency with almost dictatorial powers.[15] The popular side no longer tolerated discussion.

---

* In Colonial Philadelphia, the term "Carriage Trade" had a rather precise meaning. A list of the 84 families with private equipages was published just before the Revolution (1772) and has been preserved to this day. Among the 84 families listed in this eighteenth-century *Social Register* were included Morrises, Norrises, Pembertons, Cadwaladers, Chews, and Willings. The eight "Coach" owners in the city (the loftiest "Carriage Trade" status) included Benjamin Chew, Thomas Willing, John Cadwalader and Joseph Pemberton.[12]

Along with Franklin, John Dickinson,* and other leading citizens, the Committee of Safety included *Edward Biddle, Thomas Willing, John Cadwalader, Owen Biddle* (Clement's brother), *Samuel Morris,* and *Thomas Wharton.*

The Declaration of Independence marked the final break with the British Empire. *Francis Hopkinson, Benjamin Rush,* and *Thomas McKean* were among the signers. Other Philadelphians, *Thomas Willing,* Robert Morris, *Edward Biddle,* and John Dickinson, were members of the Continental Congress on July 4th but did not sign the Declaration. Both *Willing* and Morris opposed it, *Edward Biddle* was on his death bed and unable to sign (he died in 1779), while Dickinson, who stood somewhat aloof from the revolutionary cause after this period, could not persuade himself to take this final step away from the mother country.[16]

After the Declaration, Penn's Proprietary Government was completely superseded by the Supreme Executive Council of Pennsylvania. Usually called the first Governor of the state, *Thomas Wharton* became *President of the Supreme Executive Council of Pennsylvania, Captain-General and Commander-in-chief in and over the same.*[17] Immediately a nine-man Board of War, with dictatorial powers, was set up with *Owen Biddle* and *Samuel* and *Cadwalader Morris* among its members.

In the meantime, the fortunes of war went against Washington all through the summer and fall of 1776. He retreated from New York, across New Jersey, and into Pennsylvania. Then on Christmas night, he recrossed the Delaware and captured about a thousand Hessians at Trenton. After this important psychological victory, his close friend, *Clement Biddle,* was delegated to receive the swords of the defeated Hessians.[18]

A week later Washington won another important battle at Princeton, often called "Philadelphia's Battle." We sometimes think of Washington as commanding a "ragtail and bobtail" army of farmers and mechanics. This was not always the case, especially at Princeton, where Proper Philadelphia's gentlemen-volunteers distinguished themselves in the field of battle. General *John Cadwalader,* who also fought at Trenton, Germantown, Brandywine, and Monmouth, played a major role in the victory, and the

---

* Dickinson was survived by two daughters only. While his brother founded a long Proper Philadelphia line, the family was not included in Table 9.

First City Troop, led by Captain *Samuel Morris,* captured double their number of British dragoons.[19] *Anthony Morris,* brother of Samuel, whose grandfather and great-grandfather had been colonial Mayors of Philadelphia, lost his life at Princeton.[20] When the First City Troop's term of volunteer service expired after the battle, Washington gave them a discharge over his own signature: "Though composed of gentlemen of fortune," it read, "they have shown a noble example of discipline and subordination, and in several actions have shown a spirit and bravery which will ever do honor to them and will be gratefully remembered by me."[21]

In the autumn of 1777, Lord Howe, instead of advancing up the Hudson, decided to attack Philadelphia. Washington's army offered little resistance. Howe defeated Washington (*Clement Biddle* was General Green's aide-de-camp in the battle) at Brandywine and occupied Philadelphia at the end of September.[22] A few days later, Washington attempted to surprise the British camp at Germantown, was defeated, and retired to Valley Forge, where he spent a disastrous winter. The Reverend *William White,* who later founded the Protestant Episcopal Church in America, was his army chaplain that winter, while Dr. *Benjamin Rush* was his Surgeon-General.[23]

While Washington was at Valley Forge, the Continental Congress met at York, and Pennsylvania's Supreme Executive Council met at Lancaster: here President *Thomas Wharton* died in May, 1778.[24] It was the most discouraging period of the war, and it was not surprising that an attempt was made to supplant Washington as Commander-in-Chief. But the movement, known as "Conway's Cabal," was defeated. General *John Cadwalader,* a close friend and admirer of Washington, strongly opposed the cabal and eventually fought a duel with General Conway in which the latter was severely wounded.[25]

Quakers, loyalists, and neutrals remained in Philadelphia throughout the occupation. Life was lonely for the neutrals and tragic for the Quakers who were stoned, molested, and suspected of treason because of their pacifist convictions.[26] But it was very pleasant for many of the fashionable loyalists whose lady-folk danced with the charming British officers who found their hospitable drawing-rooms "an agreeable substitute for their London clubs."[27]

Even though his daughters were belles of many a British

officer's ball, *Thomas Willing* managed to maintain a neutral position politically and remained in Philadelphia throughout the conflict.[28] This Anglican aristocrat had been the Quaker City's leading merchant and public servant for more than twenty years. He was Mayor in 1763, Justice of the Supreme Court in 1767-76, and a delegate to the Continental Congress in 1775-76. The family counting house, built up by *Thomas Willing's* father, became Willing and Morris when Robert Morris was taken into the firm as a junior partner, in 1757.[29] Morris was certainly the more colorful member of this most famous of Philadelphia counting houses. No kin of *Samuel* and *Anthony Morris,* he was a legendary self-made and-ruined man. But *Willing,* the aristocratic senior member of the firm, has been credited with the superior and sounder financial judgment and could even be called the "economic father of the Revolution."[30] At any rate, Willing and Morris were the leading financiers of the Revolution and *Thomas Willing* was rewarded after the war for his patriotic financial efforts by being placed in charge of the new nation's first financial system (president of the Bank of North America and later the Bank of the United States).

Unlike almost all other men of importance who remained in the city during the British occupation, *Thomas Willing* was unmolested by either the British occupying forces or the Americans after their return. The Americans appreciated his financial support, while the British hoped to make conciliatory use of such an important citizen. On the other hand, Chief Justice *Benjamin Chew* and the elder *Jared Ingersoll* (his son, *Jared,* was studying in London when war broke out), both of whom had held important colonial offices under the British crown, were arrested by the Supreme Executive Council before Lord Howe entered the city.[31] Along with John Penn, they were placed on parole and not allowed to go more than six miles from their houses. At the same time, *Thomas Wharton,* president of the Council, sent nineteen of the city's most prominent Quakers, including *Israel, James* and *John Pemberton, Henry Drinker,* and his cousin, *Thomas Wharton,* to be exiled as prisoners in Winchester, Virginia.[32]

The Pemberton family had had a long record of strict conformity to their Quaker pacifist convictions. The first *Israel Pemberton,* as we have seen, was an extremely wealthy Quaker merchant. His three sons, *Israel, James,* and *John,* were devout and philanthropic Friends. *Israel* was usually referred to as "King of the Quakers," because of his great wealth and power, and sometimes as "King Wampum," because of his sympathy for the Indians; most of his money and time went to support the *Friendly Association for Regaining and Preserving Peace with Indians by Pacific Measures.* He was arrested in 1739 for criticizing Thomas Penn; resigned from the Provincial Assembly because of his opposition to the Indian War, in 1756; and, after refusing to take an oath of allegiance to Pennsylvania, he was sent to Virginia, where he died in 1777.[33]

Lord Cornwallis surrendered at Yorktown on October 19, 1781, and the formal treaty of peace which ended the Revolutionary War was signed at Paris, in 1783. In the meantime, the Articles of Confederation had gone into effect in 1781, with *Thomas McKean,* now a Federalist and less liberal than when he signed the Declaration of Independence, as the first President of Congress. Meanwhile, *Thomas Willing* organized and became first president of the Bank of North America. This was the first corporate banking structure in America.[34]

Treated as a foreign country as far as trade was concerned by England and other European nations, and faced with a central government unable to raise revenue, America went through a depression in 1784-85. The Articles of Confederation were blamed, and held to be inadequate, especially by the merchant class. The weakness of the central government was dramatized by Shay's Rebellion in 1786. In that year Virginia invited all the states to send delegates to a convention at Annapolis in order to discuss the weaknesses of the government. Representatives of only five states, including the strong Federalist, *Tench Coxe,* attended, and another convention was called for May, 1787, in Philadelphia. After four months of secret deliberation, with representatives from all states save Rhode Island attending, the Constitution of the United States was signed by the delegates present. The younger *Jared Ingersoll,* who was now one of Philadelphia's rising young lawyers, was one of the signers from Pennsylvania.[35]

During the Constitutional period, and before the Capital of the new nation moved to Washington in 1800, Philadelphia was both the political and social center of the nation. Gracious Philadelphia hosts entertained the leaders of all the other states, as well as Washington and his cabinet, at their great Georgian mansions and their beloved dancing assemblies. While the Constitutional Convention was in progress, for example, Washington led an active social life after the hard days of deliberation: among other events, he dined with the forgiven loyalists, *Benjamin Chew* and John Penn, went to a dinner for the First City Troop, and partook of such relaxing diversions as going "up to Trenton on a fishing party with the *Morrises*."[36] *Thomas Willing*, who resembled Washington both in physique and temperament, was the grand old patriarch and fianancial leader of the period.[37] His daughter, *Anne*, wife of William Bingham, said to be the wealthiest man of his day, was the recognized leader of Federalist society in Philadelphia.

Economic growth and consolidation quite naturally followed the political founding of the nation. The First Bank of the United States was chartered by Congress in 1791, and *Thomas Willing*, who had been head of the Bank of North America during the trying period of the Articles of Confederation, was chosen president.[38] One of his first announcements was that the bank would do business in dollars and cents rather than in pounds, shillings, and pence. In 1792 America's oldest and most aristocratic joint-stock insurance company, the Insurance Company of North America, was founded.[39] It has written the cream of the fire and marine insurance business down to 1940, when *Benjamin Rush*, descendant of the great physician, was Chairman of the Board. Internal improvements were also stepped up during the 1790's. The Lancaster Turnpike, the earliest and for many years the best in the United States, received a charter in 1792, and another turnpike, from Philadelphia out to Germantown and Chestnut Hill, began construction in 1798.[40] Finally, as an expansive new nation felt the need for more relaxed and opulent leisure-time activities, the Puritan code of an earlier day was overthrown. Laws forbidding the theatre were repealed, in spite of the opposition of the church led by Bishop *White*. A new theatre, the Chestnut Street, was built in 1791.[41]

At the close of the eighteenth century, in 1798, *Robert Wharton* was elected Mayor of Philadelphia for the first of fifteen times.[42] A wealthy merchant and sportsman and the most popular member of the city's local aristocracy, he was president of the Gloucester Fox-Hunting Club, where the local gentry met to hunt the fox, sixteen times Governor of the Schuylkill Fishing Company, the oldest *gourmet* club in America today, and Captain of the First City Troop, in 1803-1810.[43]

At the same time that *Robert Wharton* was Mayor, *Thomas McKean,* after a bitter campaign, was elected Governor of Pennsylvania, in 1799.[44] Turning away from his Federalist convictions, he was elected by the Republicans and soon was known as the "father of the spoils system in Pennsylvania."[45] Among his other nepotistic appointments, he made his son, *Joseph Borden McKean,* Attorney-General.[46] Although *Thomas McKean* opposed the extreme Federalism of his Proper Philadelphia friends and family, his liberal political convictions were tempered with typical aristocratic restraint. Thus his main achievement during two turbulent terms as governor, according to a biographer, lay "in restraining the excesses of the Pennsylvania Jacobins."[47] When he died, in 1817, *McKean* left "a considerable fortune," including thousands of acres of land in Western Pennsylvania (much of it in what is now McKean County).

The year 1800 marked the beginning of the end of Federalist Philadelphia's golden age. Robert Morris, pillar of the nation's credit during the Revolution, master of stately town and country houses, and Washington's trusted friend and beloved host, had over-optimistically speculated in western lands and was now spending this fateful year of the century's turn in a debtor's prison.[48] Philadelphia was no longer to be the political capital of either the state or the nation. While Governor *Thomas McKean* rode west to the new capital on the Susquehanna, President Adams, his wife weeping at the thought of leaving her gay and charming Proper Philadelphia friends, drove south to the muddy banks of the Potomac. Perhaps John Adams was thinking how the change in the location of the nation's capital unhappily symbolized the final retreat of Federalism before the rising tide of Jeffersonian Republicans.

The Nineteenth Century: Prelude to the Victorian Age. Merchant capitalism produced the reluctant gentlemen-revolutionists and statesmen of the last quarter of the eighteenth century. History has few abrupt turning points. As one economic era dissolves gradually into another, wars and revolutions are but the blooming flowers of history with their roots dug deep in the nourishing soil of economic events. As far as the American upper class is concerned, just as the eighteenth century culminated in the great merchant aristocracy which founded the new republic in Philadelphia, so the industrial revolution of the nineteenth should be seen as a prelude to the creation of a business aristocracy which dominated America during the Victorian era. In the course of this century of industrial and technical progress, new mining, manufacturing, railroad, and banking families, and their fortunes, were alloyed with the descendants of the older merchant-capitalists to eventually create Proper Philadelphia's Victorian plutocracy on Rittenhouse Square.

Before entrance upon a more thorough analysis of the early stages of Philadelphia's industrial and transportation revolutions, a word should be said about the Proper Philadelphia bankers, the last of the merchant-shipper family founders, and the rise of urban real estate fortunes.

The Proper Philadelphia Bankers. Philadelphia has often been called the "cradle of American finance," and Thomas Willing was certainly the father of American banking.[49] As we have seen, he carried on the family counting house, which had been established by his father before him, throughout the revolutionary period. After the war, he was president of the Bank of North America during the ten years of its charter (1781-1791). When the First Bank of the United States came into being in 1791, Willing was again made president, a post which he held until the charter ran out in 1811.

At the same time, Stephen Girard, the largest stockholder in the First Bank, founded his own bank (Girard Bank) which carried the nation through the War of 1812. This patriotic Philadelphian, now forced to turn away from the sea he loved so well, even threw his own personal wealth behind the war. Of the $16,000,000 loan floated by the federal government, Stephen Girard and John Jacob Astor were the major subscribers.[50]

At the close of the war, in 1816, Congress chartered the Second Bank of the United States. For various reasons, the first five years of the Second Bank were filled with strife and disorder. Then President Monroe appointed his friend, Nicholas Biddle, to its presidency in 1823.[51]

Biddle became the central figure in American banking at the age of thirty-seven, but already he was one of Proper Philadelphia's most brilliant, accomplished, and polished gentlemen.[52] After graduating from the College of New Jersey (Princeton) as valedictorian of his class at the age of fifteen, he took the grand tour of Europe, where he delighted the Cambridge dons with his facility in Greek. Upon his return to Philadelphia, he studied law and was admitted to the bar in 1809. Before assuming the presidency of the bank, he had also gained some literary, diplomatic, and political experience. He was like a son to Ambassador James Monroe while acting as Secretary of Legation in London; and at a similar post in Paris, before he was twenty-one, he handled many of the details of the Louisiana Purchase. Thomas Jefferson was so impressed with Biddle at the time that he personally recommended his compiling and editing for publication, the journals of Lewis and Clark which became the definitive work on the subject for many years. Upon Biddle's return to Philadelphia after serving abroad, he edited the *Port Folio,* leading intellectual periodical of its day, before becoming a Pennsylvania State Senator.

As President of the Second Bank of the United States, Nicholas Biddle was czar of American finance for more than a decade. After his re-election in 1832, however, Andrew Jackson was determined to put an end to Proper Philadelphia's banking monopoly. Biddle was eventually defeated by the popular President, and the bank's charter automatically ran out in 1836.

Philadelphia's gradual decline from its Golden Age was now complete: it had lost the political leadership of the nation when the capital moved to Washington, in 1800; its commercial dominance passed to New York after the opening of the Erie Canal, in 1825; and Jackson's defeat of the Second Bank ended its financial monopoly. After his defeat, Biddle retired to "Andalusia," his stunning "Greek Revival" mansion on the banks of the Delaware, and the American people, drunk with the new democracy, entered upon an era of "wild-cat finance" which resulted in the panic of 1837.

Two of Philadelphia's most successful private banking houses were founded during the panic. In that year, Francis M. Drexel, charming Austrian portrait painter, who had dabbled in finance in many parts of the world, founded the famous family firm, first in Louisville, Kentucky, and then in Philadelphia.[53] Enoch W. Clark, a shrewd Yankee banker who had gone through difficult times in New England, came down to Philadelphia and opened up his own banking house in the same year.[54] Two years later, Jay Cooke, a young man from Ohio, began his fabulous banking career in the offices of Enoch W. Clark.[55] At the age of twenty-one, in

1842, Cooke became a partner in the Clark firm; he then founded
Jay Cooke & Company, in 1861, and eventually played the major
role in financing the Civil War. Cooke finally failed, however, when
the Northern Pacific carried him down in the railroad panic of
1873.[56]

Although all the profits of the Clark banking house between
1837 and 1844 were used to pay off debts acquired in Boston,
Enoch W. Clark left a considerable fortune when he died in 1856.
His two sons, Edward W. and Clarence H. Clark, and their descendants, have carried on the firm to the present day.

Anthony J. Drexel went to work for his father at the age of
thirteen and devoted the rest of his life to building up one of
America's greatest banking establishments.[57] While Drexel & Company soon had branch offices in London and Paris, their New
York connections were unsatisfactory. One day in the spring of
1871, Anthony J. Drexel wired young J. Pierpont Morgan asking
him down to Philadelphia for dinner.[58] After dinner the two men
went into the library: "Morgan, I want you to come into my firm
as a partner," said Drexel. Drexel, Morgan & Company opened for
business in 1871 and the two houses have been allied ever since.
After A. J. Drexel's death in 1893, Edward T. Stotesbury became
the senior Drexel-Morgan partner in Philadelphia, to be followed by
Thomas S. Gates, and Edward Hopkinson, Jr. (see later chapters).

The descendants of Alexander Brown run the oldest private
banking house in North America.[59] Although primarily a Baltimore
family, the Browns have been private bankers in Philadelphia for
over a century. The firm was still operating somewhat in the "Jack-
of-all-trades," merchant-banker tradition in 1940, and many Proper
Philadelphians retain their sense of history by banking at Brown
Brothers.

Alexander Brown, keeper of a linen store in Belfast, Ireland,
landed in Baltimore and founded Alexander Brown & Sons, in
1800. When he died in 1834, according to Frank R. Kent, "the only
fortunes that exceeded that of Alexander Brown were those of
Astor, Van Rensselaer, and Whitney. . . ."[60] Alexander Brown's
four sons supervised the firm's branch offices: one went to Liverpool, another to London, a third to New York, and a fourth, John
A. Brown, founded the Philadelphia office. That the original family
firm now goes under the style of Brown Brothers Harriman &
Company testifies to its vigor and judgment in choosing associates.

The End of the Merchant-Shipper Tradition. Although the main economic trend was westward with the advent of railroads and canals, many Philadelphians carried the eighteenth-century merchant-shipper tradition well into the nineteenth century, especially during the romantic clipper-ship era. Stephen Girard, a great deal of whose money had gone into western lands and internal improvements, nevertheless signed his will, "Stephen Girard, Merchant and Mariner," before he died in 1831.[61] Thomas Pym Cope, one of Girard's leading rivals and originator of the first packet line between Liverpool and America, and Thomas Ridgway, were two of Philadelphia's greatest merchants and philanthropists during this period. As Adolph Borie was listed in the *Dictionary of American Biography* and as the Borie family has been more consistently prolific down through the years (nine conjugal units listed in the 1940 *Social Register* and Charles Louis Borie listed in *Who's Who*), we have included this family in Table 9. Adolph Borie was the eldest of twelve children of John Joseph Borie, a Frenchman who had established himself as a Philadelphia merchant in the early nineteenth century.[62] After graduating from the University of Pennsylvania and obtaining additional education in France, Adolph Borie entered his father's firm in 1828. He and his brother, Charles Louis Borie, eventually married two of Thomas McKean's granddaughters and engaged in the clipper ship trade along with their brother-in-law, Henry Pratt McKean.[63] The firm "carried on trade with Mexico, the West Indies, and the Far East, engaging particularly in the silk and tea trade."[64] The magnitude of Adolph Borie's operations, which extended for almost thirty years during the sailing ship era, was indicated by his "property damage claims amounting to $100,000 in China during the disturbances of 1857-58."[65] During this period, he held several consular posts and, in 1869, was appointed Secretary of the Navy (due to health and business reasons he soon resigned) by his good friend U. S. Grant, with whom he toured the world a decade later. Although Adolph Borie had no children, his brothers founded an interesting Philadelphia clan which, in the French tradition of the arts, has produced several excellent architects and one of the city's distinguished artists, Adolph Borie (1877-1934).[66]

Landed Fortunes. Throughout history, landownership has been a staple bond between generations of aristocratic families. Although most family fortunes in commercial societies are originally built on some business enterprise, many of the greatest and most stable early American fortunes—Astor, Goelet, Rhinelander, or Schermerhorn in New York; Field in Chicago; Longworth in Cincinnati; and Girard in Philadelphia—were consolidated through landownership.[67] Nineteenth-century America's rapid population growth made investment in land, and especially urban property, as good as or better than gold.

The Pepper family created one of the largest early nineteenth-century, urban, real estate fortunes in Philadelphia. The family was founded in America by Henry Pepper (Johan Heinrich Pfeffer), of Strasburg, Germany, who came to Philadelphia in 1774 where he built up a prosperous brewing business.[68] Many prominent early Philadelphians, including Anthony Morris, were brewers. Although Madeira and claret were favored among "people of quality," the ubiquitous city taverns served locally brewed beer and imported rum to the lower orders: "The acquisition of a taste for Madeira in middle life is quite fatal to common people" was for many years a Proper Philadelphia comment on the *parvenu*.[69]

Henry Pepper left a considerable estate when he died in 1808. His son, George Pepper, took over the family brewery and proceeded to build up one of the city's largest fortunes. On January 8, 1846, the *Gazette of the United States* reported that "George Pepper, Esq., died on Tuesday night. . . . He was among the most respected and wealthy of our citizens, perhaps the wealthiest." The prominent Philadelphia lawyer Horace Binney, "received ten thousand dollars for drawing up his will."[70]

A large proportion of George Pepper's fortune consisted of urban real estate holdings, which were to be held in trust by his executors (George Seckel and William Pepper and his son-in-law, Isaac Norris) for his children and grandchildren, who carefully distributed several million dollars to the University of Pennsylvania, free public libraries, and many of the city's hospitals throughout the course of the nineteenth century.[71]

The American System: Manufacturing and Continental Imperialism. The versatile Irish publisher and publicist, Mathew Carey, and the Philadelphia patrician, Tench Coxe, were early and strong advocates of the development of American manufactures.[72] In many ways, Coxe was Proper Philadelphia's Alexander Hamilton, under whom he served as Assistant Secretary of the Treasury. Of secure, first-family position, Coxe's great-grandfather, Queen Anne's physician and member of the Royal Society, was a large landowner in West Jersey and a speculator in colonial proprietary rights.[73] His grandfather, Colonel Daniel Coxe, came to America in 1702 and was appointed commander of the armed forces of West Jersey. The Coxe family became part of Philadelphia history when, in 1707, Daniel Coxe, "a fine flaunting gentleman," eloped with Sarah Eckley, daughter of a devout Philadelphia Quaker.[74] In 1730, Daniel Coxe was deputized by the Duke of Norfolk, *Grand Master of the Grand Lodge of England*, as the *Provincial Grand Master of the Provinces of New York, New Jersey*, and *Pennsylvania*, and thus became the first Grand Master of Masons in America.[75]

Tench Coxe, both an intellectual and a man of affairs, had a somewhat vacillating and opportunistic political career.[76] In order to tend to his duties in his father's counting house, he remained in Philadelphia during Howe's occupation and was arrested and paroled after the British withdrew.[77] That he did not sacrifice his position among patriots, however, was attested to by his membership in both the Continental Congress and the Annapolis Convention. In every way a strong Federalist, his *An Examination of the Constitution for the United States* was one of the earliest and more well-known appeals for ratification.[78] Appointed Assistant Secretary of the Treasury by Washington and Commissioner of Revenue by Adams, Coxe eventually turned against the Federalists, and, in 1803, supported Jefferson, who appointed him Purveyor of Public Supplies, an office which he held until 1812.

Throughout his vacillating political career, however, Coxe maintained a consistent, strong nationalist position on economics. He worked closely with Hamilton in the Treasury Department and, according to Joseph Dorfman, his influence can be traced to Hamilton's famous *Report on Manufactures*.[79] In Philadelphia he devoted much of his time and energy to promoting *The United Company of Philadelphia for Promoting American Manufacturing*, and the *Pennsylvania Society for the Encouragement of Arts and Domestic Manufactures*, founded in 1775 and 1787, respectively.[80] He also encouraged the importation of Arkwright machinery for spinning cotton into the city in the last part of the eighteenth century, and consequently has often been called "the father of the American cotton industry."[81]

The War of 1812 was a more tangible, and perhaps more important, stimulus to both domestic manufactures and internal improvements (canals) in America than all the polemical writings of Hamilton, Coxe, or Carey. After 1807, when Jefferson imposed severe restraints on trade, the importation of European manufactures was brought to a halt and domestic goods could no longer be sent overseas. More important, due to inadequate means of transportation, domestic markets to the west were not yet available. (The poor communications existing at this time are indicated by the fact that, when Andrew Jackson, who had not yet been informed of the war's end, won the battle of New Orleans, on January 8, 1815, the news of his victory did not reach Philadelphia until a month later, on February 5.)[82]

Continental imperialism preoccupied the young nation throughout the rest of the century. The "Great Compromiser," Henry Clay, articulated America's rising nationalist spirit during and after the War of 1812. His ingenious "American System" combined the encouragement of domestic manufactures, the improvement of inland transportation, and the creation of home markets for southern agriculture, all of which persuaded his southern followers to accept a protective tariff, the first of which was passed in 1816.[83] Philadelphia's Henry C. Carey (Mathew's son) became the leading advocate of a high protective tariff, and canals, railroads, manufacturing, and mining absorbed the city's entrepreneurial ingenuity from 1816 to the Civil War. The remainder of this chapter will be devoted to the Philadelphia family founders who rose to power and wealth during this early period of industrial growth.

Manufacturing: Textiles and Chemicals. The *United Company of Philadelphia for Promoting American Manufactures,* the first joint-stock company engaged in the manufacture of cotton-goods in America (and believed by some authorities to be the first joint-stock company in this country), was formed, due to Tench Coxe's encouragement, in 1775, with Dr. Benjamin Rush as president.[84] From that day to the present, Philadelphia has been one of America's textile centers. In fact, textiles were so important in this early period in the northern part of Philadelphia around the Germantown area that for many years hosiery and knit-goods were known as "Germantown Goods."[85]

The first cotton mill in the city was established in 1810, by one Alfred Jenks, a pupil and collaborator of the famous Samuel Slater.[86] The more well-known textile manufacturers in nineteenth-century Philadelphia included William H. Horstmann & Sons (lace) established in 1815; John B. Ellison & Sons (cloth), established in 1823; Glen Riddle Mills, founded by Samuel Riddle, in 1842; John Bromley & Sons (carpets) founded in 1845; and J & J Dobson (woolens), established in 1855.[87] Although the family founders were not included in the *Dictionary of American Biography* (thus not in Table 9), descendants of all these early textile manufacturers were listed in the 1940 Philadelphia *Social Register* (not in *Who's Who*). Samuel Riddle, owner of the famous racehorse Man-of-War, and his wife (née Dobson) were living at the family homestead in Glen Riddle, just above the old mills, in 1940.

Thomas Dolan, one of Philadelphia's greatest nineteenth-century business tycoons, was listed in the "DAB."[88] He became one of the city's most prosperous textile manufacturers just before the Civil War. Born in rural Montgomery County of "obscure ancestry," and educated for a few years in the public schools, Dolan took a job in a dry-goods store at the age of fifteen. In 1861, he began the manufacture of "Germantown Goods" and speedily built up a prosperous trade, until, at the close of the Civil War, he was one of the wealthiest men in the city. At that time he founded the Keystone Knitting Mills which was doing $1,000,000 worth of business a year by 1871. Dolan eventually became one of the largest producers of men's wear in America, as well as a leader in the public utility field which will be discussed later in this chapter.

Many Proper Philadelphia fortunes can be traced to the chemical industry. "No doubt the chemical famine of the War of 1812," writes an historian of the American chemical industry, "encouraged apothecaries to become chemical manufacturers. Most of them must have been wiped out by the flood of postwar imports. At all events, the chronicle of the enterprises that eventually established the industry firmly in this country was written first in Philadelphia —then the unqualified chemical headquarters—and later in New York, Baltimore, and Boston."[89]

Samuel Wetherill, pious Quaker minister and leader of the "Fighting Quakers" who split off from the pacifist majority during the Revolution, eventually became America's pioneer paint and chemical manufacturer.[90] One of the original promoters of the *United Company of Pennsylvania for the Establishment of American Manufactures,* Wetherill set up his own textile establishment for making "jeans, fustians, everlastings, and coatings," in 1775.[91] As there were no dyers in the city at that time, he soon added this chemical process to his clothing venture. His interest in chemicals eventually led to the establishment of a white-lead manufacturing firm, Samuel Wetherill & Son, in 1804. The family firm, enlarged and consolidated with other ventures by his able and inventive descendants, was still prosperous in 1940.[92]

In this same year, 1804, John Harrison was listed in a city directory as a "druggist and *aqua fortis* manufacturer."[93] As a young man he had studied under the celebrated Dr. Priestly, a refugee from the French Revolution at the time; and as early as 1793 he was manufacturing sulphuric acid. Out of this drug store grew Harrison Brothers, eventually to be one of the city's larger chemical firms, with plants in New York, Maryland, and Philadelphia by the time of the Civil War.

Although founded in chemical manufactures, the great Harrison fortune was made primarily in sugar refining.[94] The Franklin Sugar Refining Company (Harrison, Newhall, & Welsh, and then Harrison, Havermeyer and Company until 1889) was founded in 1863 by John Harrison's son, George Leib Harrison. After graduating from Harvard, the younger Harrison read law under Joseph R. Ingersoll and was admitted to the bar just at the time of his father's death, in 1863.[95] He immediately abandoned his profession to help his brothers manage the family chemical works. He then became a partner in Powers & Weightman, a new chemical enterprise, and eventually bought an old sugar refinery in 1863. His great energy soon built up a firm which, under his son, Charles Custis Harrison, produced one of the city's greatest family fortunes. At the end of the century, the firm formed the basis of the famous "Sugar Trust" after its president, Charles Custis Harrison, had retired to become Provost of the University of Pennsylvania and one of its greatest benefactors (see Chapter XII). Harrison Brothers, the family chemical firm, was eventually purchased by Du Pont in 1917.[96]

Four prominent Philadelphia chemical fortunes were founded after the War of 1812: John T. Lewis & Brothers, in 1819, George D. Rosengarten & Sons, in 1823, Powers & Weightman, in 1825, and Nicholas Lennig & Company, in 1829.[97]

Mordecai Lewis actually founded the Lewis fortune when he grew from a small shopkeeper "into a great merchant, importer of foreign wares, exporter of colonial produce of all sorts, a ship owner and financier."[98] His sons carried on the family firm which eventually became so successful that they began to look for new lines. Their purchase of a white-lead factory, in 1819, marked the founding of John T. Lewis & Brothers and the beginning of a Proper Philadelphia chemical fortune.

John T. Lewis & Brothers Company eventually became a subsidiary of the Pennsylvania Salt Manufacturing Company, one of the largest and most successful chemical firms in the city. George T. Lewis, grandson of Mordecai, founded "Penn Salt" in 1850, although he himself remained a merchant all his life.[99] The family still retains control of both "Penn Salt" and its subsidiary, John T. Lewis & Brothers Company; Leonard T. Beale, a descendant of Mordecai Lewis, was president of both firms in 1940 (see Chapter XIV).

George D. Rosengarten founded a prolific and brilliant Proper Philadelphia family line. He was born in Cassell, Germany, in 1801, the son of a prominent banking family whose fortune was dissipated by the Napoleonic Wars. "Forced to seek his fortune abroad," according to William Haynes, "he went first to Amsterdam for a year's apprenticeship in banking in the great house of Hope, and in 1819 arrived in Philadelphia, armed with letters to bankers and merchants."[100] He was an excellent accountant and spoke both French and German as well as English. In the meantime, two recent immigrants, Seitler and Zeitler, one a Swiss speaking only French, and the other a German who spoke only his native tongue, were manufacturing fine chemicals. Excellent chemists, they were, nevertheless, poor businessmen, especially as they understood neither each other nor their clients. George D. Rosengarten, linguist, businessman, and banker, joined the firm in 1822 and became sole proprietor within a year.

George D. Rosengarten and William Weightman were two of the city's wealthiest men by the end of the nineteenth century. After Weightman's death in 1904 (he was said to be the largest real estate owner in Philadelphia and the wealthiest man in Pennsylvania at that time), the two family firms became Powers, Weightman, and Rosengarten.[101] The firm finally merged with Merck & Company, in 1927.[102] Since 1934, Merck has been the leader in the development and production of vitamins, and in 1940, first began the mass production of penicillin (Merck sales were $20,000,000 in 1939 and reached more than $68,000,000 by 1947). In 1940, Frederick Rosengarten, who had played a leading role in reorganizing the firm in 1927, was chairman of Merck's board of directors, which also included his two brothers, George D. and Adolph G. Rosengarten.[103]

Charles Lennig was Philadelphia's largest chemical manufacturer before the Civil War.[104] The family firm was carried on by his descendants until 1920 when it was purchased by Rohm & Haas, pioneers in the plastics field.[105] One of their products, Plextiglas, was used in every type of Army and Navy plane during World War II, and the Lennig family continues to prosper, although no longer in active management of the old family firm.

Many of the early chemists in Philadelphia, such as John Harrison, for instance, began as druggists. One of the ways for an enterprising young druggist to make his fortune was to enter the lucrative patent medicine field. Before the passage of the Pure Food and Drug Act in 1906, the gullible American public were victims of patent medicine peddlers whose claims for cure-alls and tonics far surpassed the modest claims of modern hucksters on Madison Avenue. These were the days of *Minard's Liniment,* "The Great Internal and External Remedy, for Man or Beast"; of *Herrick's Pills,* "For Dyspepsia, Colic, Sick Headache, Constipation, Diarrhoea, Worms, Fever and Ague, Indigestion"; or *Upham's* tonic, "Prepared according to the formula of Prof. Trousseau, of Paris, For the Prevention and Cure of Consumption, Lung Diseases, Bronchitis, Dyspepsia, Marasmus, Nervous Prostration, General Debility, and all morbid conditions of the system dependent on deficiency of Vital Force."[106] Experiments often found such cure-alls to have the alcoholic content of corn whiskey!

One of Proper Philadelphia's most fabulous nineteenth-century fortunes was built up by Dr. David Jayne with patent medicines: *Jayne's Expectorant,* "For Coughs, Croup Asthma, Bronchitis, and all Lung Diseases"; or *Jayne's Tonic Vermafuge,* "Strength for the Mother and Health for the Child: It Surely Expels Worms."[107] Their names became household words in America by mid-century: the rise of David Jayne was a typical nineteenth-century story.

Born in the village of Bushkill, in central Pennsylvania, the son of Ebenezer Jayne, a Baptist clergyman, young David had little opportunity of obtaining an education other than that afforded by the local schools, which was poor indeed. "Not satisfied therewith," according to a brief nineteenth-century eulogy of Dr. Jayne, "and nerved by the indomitable ambition within him, which manifested itself so forcibly throughout his after life, he entered upon a severe course of self-culture which fitted him for a higher sphere than that of a mechanic, which his father had intended for him, and enabled him, after pursuing a course of study in medicine under the guidance of a proper preceptor, and in the lecture courses of the University of Pennsylvania, to enter into the practice of medicine in the year 1825. Medicine promised little in pecuniary reward, but plenty of opportunity to acquire a practical knowledge of disease in its various forms, and the methods and remedies best adapted to its treatment and removal."[108]

Jayne first became a country doctor, but in 1831 he introduced the first of a long line of patent medicines. His product sold so rapidly that he soon had to give up the practice of medicine altogether. In 1849, in order to provide adequate quarters for David Jayne & Son, he built one of the first protoskyscrapers in America on Chestnut Street, in Philadelphia. The Jayne Building, as it is known today, was a landmark and a seminal influence in American architecture: Louis Sullivan, whose great work in Chicago set a pattern for skyscrapers all over the world, worked as a young architect in Philadelphia in an office across the street from the Jayne Building.[109]

In his later years, Dr. Jayne took in several of his family as partners, and then devoted more and more of his own time to real estate and the planning and building of other office buildings in the city. He was also active in the Baptist Church and the Native American, and Republican political parties. He married three times and had eight surviving children. Two of his sons, Horace Jayne, professor of biology and Dean of the College at the University of Pennsylvania under Charles Custis Harrison, and Henry Le Barre Jayne, member of the Biddle & Ward law firm, took no part in the family drug business.

Other fortunes in Philadelphia were made out of the American people's avid concern for health and physical appearance. Samuel Stockton White, born in Hulmeville, Bucks County, came down to Philadelphia in the 1840's at the age of fourteen "to learn the art and mystery of dentistry and the manufacture of incorruptible porcelain teeth."[110] In 1844, he set up his own business. The S. S. White Dental Manufacturing Company eventually became the largest false teeth firm in the world, a position it has held for over three-quarters of a century.[111]

Manufacturing: Iron Works and Machinery. Richard D. Wood

and Samuel Vaughan Merrick were two of the city's leading businessmen during the first part of the nineteenth century. Neither of them was a Philadelphian but both came from prominent families elsewhere. Richard D. Wood, whose father (Richard Wood) was the richest man in Salem County in southern New Jersey, came to the city in the 1820's and proceeded to build up one of the city's major pre-Civil War fortunes.[112] It derived from a rather diversified manufacturing base. In 1823, Richard D. Wood organized a wholesale dry-goods business in Philadelphia under the style of Wood, Abbott, and Wood, later Wood, Abbot & Company. The firm prospered and Richard D. Wood branched out into many other enterprises. He became a director and large owner in the Allentown Iron Works, the Cambria Iron Works, in Johnstown, Pennsylvania, and, in 1850, took over his half-brother's iron works outside of Camden, New Jersey. This last acquisition became R. D. Wood & Company and, in addition to manufacturing pipe and heavy machinery, included an extremely successful cotton mill and bleachery. Richard D. Wood also was a director of the Girard and Philadelphia (Philadelphia National) banks, the Insurance Company of North America, the Schuylkill Navigation Company, and a founder and director of the Pennsylvania Railroad. Both R. D. Wood & Company and Wood, Abbott & Company were run by various branches of the Wood family in 1940.

Samuel Vaughan Merrick came from a prosperous family in Hallowell, Maine. His father was a member of the Board of Overseers at Bowdoin College, 1805-1851.[113] But when he was fifteen he came down to Philadelphia under the sponsorship of his uncle, John Vaughan, who was not only a prosperous merchant but a leader of broad influence and remarkable character. After working for his uncle for several years, young Merrick found himself in charge of an insolvent plant which manufactured fire engines, a "gift" from his uncle, who had acquired the plant because of his generosity towards its incapable owners. In that day, to move from the counting house of a well-established merchant into a factory was something of a social degradation, but Samuel Vaughan Merrick was hardly bothered by any such petty considerations. He proceeded to build the insolvent company into one of the nation's finest in its field. Many years later an admirer of the firm, in an after-dinner address, recommended the superiority of Merrick's products because they were "used by professors in New

England colleges as illustrations in mechanics and specimens of American ingenuity and workmanship."[114]

Merrick would have liked this tribute. He placed a high value on mechanical skill and workmanship and the training of the younger generation therein. In fact, he has probably placed Philadelphians in debt to him more by his founding of The Franklin Institute "for the promotion of mechanical arts," in 1824, than for all his many other civic and industrial accomplishments.[115]

Among the original members of the Institute were such foremost figures in the city's affairs as Matthias Baldwin, Clement C. Biddle, Mathew Carey, James Rush, and Thomas Scattergood,* as well as other men from all walks of life including a "merchant, brewer, teacher, plasterer, saddler, plumber, marble mason, clothier, shot maker, counsellor-at-law, and blacksmith."[116] The Franklin Institute immediately began to take the lead in training Philadelphians in the pragmatic mechanical arts. In the first year, classes were begun in minerology and chemistry, natural philosophy and mechanics, architecture, drawing and design (machine design, naval architecture, and mathematics). In an early class in architecture, William Strictland taught a young bricklayer, Thomas U. Walter, who later went on to design Girard College, the United States Bank building (2nd bank), and the dome of the Capitol in Washington.[117]

Samuel Vaughan Merrick was actively absorbed in many other civic affairs, probably the most important of which was his exhaustive report to City Council on European lighting systems, which resulted in the erection of the first city gas works on the banks of the Schuylkill.[118] Soon after his report was released, in 1836, Philadelphia streets were lighted with gas for the first time.

That same year, the Pascall Iron-Works, a partnership composed of Stephen B. Morris, Henry S. Morris, and Thomas T. Tasker, began the manufacture of wrought-iron tubes and fittings, gas and water mains, and gas-heated hot water furnaces.[119] Philadelphia soon became the "chief seat of Gas-making Machinery in the United States," supplying all the principal cities of the South and West. The Pascall firm, which made 60,000 feet of wrought-iron tubes in 1838, was turning out nearly 5,000,000 feet annually

---

* One of the leading Quaker families in the city in 1940; see Chapter XI for a discussion of the Quaker Elite and upper class.

by the close of the Civil War (annually consuming 40,000 tons of anthracite).[120]

Charles Wheeler entered the employ of the Pascall Iron-Works in 1847, at the age of twenty.[121] Six years later, Stephen P. Morris, the original founder of the firm, retired and, "much to the surprise of everyone, sold out his interest to Mr. Wheeler."[122] Although young Wheeler, not yet thirty, had no capital of his own, he was able to pay Morris for his share in the firm within two years.

Charles Wheeler became one of the most versatile Philadelphia industrialists of his era. In 1864 he sold out his interest in the Pascall works ($800,000) and turned his entire attention to the Fairmount Iron Works, which he now owned. At the same time, he founded the Central National Bank. In 1876, having sold the Fairmount Iron Works to the Park Commission, he bought back a controlling interest in the Pascall Iron-Works. Two years later, he was made a senior partner of John Farnum & Company, one of the largest dry-goods houses in the city, at the request of his father-in-law, John Farnum, whose daughter he had married in 1867. At the time of his death, in addition to heading two of the largest business houses in the city, he was a director of the Insurance Company of North America, the Lehigh Coal and Navigation Company, the Pottstown and Cambria Iron companies, and the Seaboard Bank, in New York. Charles Wheeler was the leading layman in the Main Line's largest Episcopal church and his descendants were intimately connected with the founding of Proper Philadelphia's favorite boarding school, St. Paul's (see Chapter XII).

After successfully carrying through his efforts to persuade his fellow-Philadelphians to introduce gas lighting, Samuel Vaughan Merrick, in 1836, opened the Southwark Foundry with a young partner, John Henry Towne, who is remembered today through the Towne Scientific School which he founded and endowed at the University of Pennsylvania. (Towne later joined Isaac Pascall Morris, grandson of Captain Samuel Morris of the City Troop, in the management of the Port Richmond Iron Works.) The Southwark Foundry was the city's most impressive industrial establishment, comprising "a mechanics shop of three floors, a smith's shop with 18 forges, a foundry, and a boiler shop."[123] Merrick and Towne produced a wide variety of products including boilers, brass and iron castings, sugar mill machinery, ("every description of plantation machinery"), furnaces, steam hammers, high and low pressure steam engines for land and marine service, and iron lighthouses for the United States Lighthouse Service. The *U.S.S. Mississippi*, which took Perry to Japan, was one of the ships engineered by the Foundry.

While the Southwark Foundry prospered and its machinery was everywhere on the American continent, Samuel Vaughan Merrick continued to devote himself to outside civic duties. He was a prominent member of the Board of Trade and the Sanitary Commission, Warden of the Port, founder of the Western Savings Fund Society, and one of the delegated speakers at the celebration marking the consolidation of the City in 1854. A strong supporter of the Union during the Civil War, he afterwards devoted himself to the cause of educating the colored people in the South, making many generous gifts which he carefully concealed from the general public's knowledge. Not the least of his contributions to Philadelphia was the founding of the Pennsylvania Railroad.

Coal, Canals, and Railroads. Before the Pennsylvania Railroad opened up Philadelphia's western hinterland, the city had already lost commercial leadership of the nation to New York, especially after 1825 when the Erie Canal was completed. Unfortunately, while New Yorkers were busy exploiting the West, Philadelphians were building canals almost entirely for the purpose of hauling anthracite coal. This was understandable as the small area in northeastern Pennsylvania, along the valleys of the Wyoming, Lehigh, and Schuylkill Rivers, was the greatest anthracite producing region in the world (as of 1914, the source of 96 per cent of the nation's total output).[124]

The War of 1812 marked the beginning of the Pennsylvania anthracite industry. In that year, Colonel George Shoemaker brought nine wagonloads of anthracite down to Philadelphia from Pottsville, in the Schuylkill region of Pennsylvania.[125] Called an imposter for trying to pass off stone for coal, he was only able to sell two loads and was forced to give away the other seven. Fortunately, one of the loads was bought by Josiah White who used it in the furnace of his wire-mill on the Schuylkill near Manayunk, an early industrial suburb of Philadelphia.[126] Impressed with the qualities of this new fuel, White sold out his wire business and proceeded to spend the rest of his active business life in the upper Lehigh Valley.

Around the picturesque town of Mauch Chunk, where "bear, wolf, and panther roamed the river-slopes," White developed anthracite deposits, established the Lehigh Coal & Navigation Company (1820), and built a canal from Mauch Chunk, on the Lehigh River to the Delaware, which in turn flowed down to Philadelphia.[127] Anthracite shipments from the Mauch Chunk area increased from 365 tons in 1820 (the standard tables of hard coal shipments in Pennsylvania begin with this year) to 31,000 tons by 1826.[128] Erskine Hazard, White's partner, wrote in January, 1827: "Anthracite coal promises to become the largest and most profitable staple of Pennsylvania."[129] Hazard's prophesy came true, and countless Proper Philadelphia family fortunes were the result. But most of them awaited the development of the railroad. For example, while the Lehigh Valley and Reading railroads were already competing with the anthracite canals in the 1850's, these two leading coal-carrying railroads went through their period of most rapid growth after the Civil War.[130] This was also the period of family fortunes made in the coal industry.

What Philadelphia needed was a railroad across the Alleghenies to Pittsburgh and the West. A glance at a map of the United States will show why: rivers tend to flow in a northerly-southerly direction and America's problem has always been that of east-west transportation. The turnpikes, built at the close of the eighteenth century, were the first attempts to solve the problem. The completion of the Erie Canal was another: but while it helped New York, it was a defeat for Philadelphia.

A few far-sighted Philadelphians had been concerned with this defeat for some time, but the majority were still preoccupied with running factories, building canals, and opening up coal mines. Then, in the 1840's, the Baltimore & Ohio Railroad began the construction of a roadbed over the mountains into West Virginia.[131] Philadelphia would now be faced with competition from both New York and Baltimore.

Finally, in 1846, a group of prominent Philadelphia capitalists, including Samuel Vaughan Merrick and Richard D. Wood, organized what is now the Pennsylvania Railroad.[132] As he was the most respected and versatile businessman in the city, Merrick was per-

suaded to become the first president of the new railroad, a post
which he held for two years, in spite of his increasing responsi-
bilities at the Southwark Foundry and his pressing civic duties.
The road was completed to Pittsburgh in 1852, and Proper Philadelphia's proudest accomplishment—opening trade to the West with
the "Pennsy"—began to take shape as the Civil War approached.

CHAPTER VI

Post-Civil War Family Founders

> From Alaric to Napoleon the soldier had served
> as an independent vent to energy. Often, even when
> opposed to capital, he had been victorious, and the
> highest function of a leader of men had been, in
> theory at least, military command. The ideal states-
> man had been one who, like Cromwell, Frederick
> the Great, Henry IV, William III, and Washington,
> could lead his followers in battle, and . . . the
> aristocracy had professedly been a military caste.
> Only after 1871 came the new era, an era marked
> by many social changes. For the first time in history
> the ruler . . . of the people passed from the martial
> to the monied type, and everywhere the same phe-
> nomenon appeared: the whole administration of
> society fell into the hands of the economic man.
>
> BROOKS ADAMS

WITH the Civil War came the end of America's industrial youth
and the beginning of an accelerated growth which made this the
mightiest nation on earth by 1900—less than four decades after
Appomatox. Rarely pure tragedy, war was a financial blessing to
the Northern businessman. Chief Justice Oliver Wendell Holmes,
who was wounded in the breast at Ball's Bluff, in the neck at
Antietam, and in the foot at Fredericksburg, never forgot that his
contemporary, John Pierpont Morgan (they were born four years
apart), was simultaneously beginning a business career which
eventually was to lead beyond the dreams of avarice.[1]

With the inevitable war profiteering came the first but temporary Federal income tax, instituted by President Lincoln to help
defray the huge costs of war. A little pamphlet—*The Rich Men of
Philadelphia: Income Tax of the Residents of Philadelphia and
Bucks County for the Year Ending April 30, 1865*—provides considerable insight into the city's class structure at that time.[2] For
example, of the families listed in Table 9 in Chapter V, no less
than thirty-three—almost all those founded before the Civil War—
had one or more members who were among the wealthiest men in

(107)

the city as of 1865 (compare Table 10 with Table 9). Several things should be noted about these wealthy men.

First, the old family men—Morris, Norris, Cadwalader, Ingersoll, Biddle, etc. tend to cluster in the two groups with incomes below $50,000 and even more so at the $10,000 to $25,000 level. Thus the old colonial gentry, now physicians and lawyers and presumably possessed of inherited wealth (Dr. James Rush, for example, was the son-in-law of the late Jacob Ridgway, wealthy nineteenth-century merchant and philanthropist), were holding their own economically. But, *all* the wealthiest men (the twenty-three with incomes over $50,000) were either bankers or businessmen, and all save two, Stephen and Henry Morris (grandsons of Captain Samuel Morris of the First City Troop), were early nineteenth-

Table 10—*Proper Philadelphia Family Fortunes: Elite Incomes in 1864*

Incomes of Over $100,000		Incomes between $50,000 and $100,000	
Mathias Baldwin	$211,832	George D. Rosengarten	$98,526
Matthew Baird	208,049	E. W. Clark	97,362
Richard D. Wood	139,603	Charles Lennig	81,445
John A. Brown	137,536	William Weightman	83,255
Charles Wheeler	132,976	Samuel V. Merrick	82,704
A. J. Drexel	131,631	J. B. Lippincott	80,258
Francis A. Drexel	128,349	Stephen B. Morris	80,535
David Jayne	127,149	Henry S. Morris	79,693
Richard Norris	124,902	Clarence H. Clark	68,981
Joseph Harrison, Jr.	122,224	S. S. White	63,642
Thomas Dolan	109,207	Alan Wood	62,773
John H. Towne	109,204		

Incomes between $25,000 and $50,000		Incomes between $10,000 and $25,000	
C. Louis Borie	$48,285	Thomas A. Biddle	$24,918
Joseph W. Drexel	42,435	Isaac Norris	23,456
Isaac P. Morris	40,082	George Cadwalader	23,150
Henry Charles Lea	37,546	Henry H. Houston	22,065
Adolph Borie	33,820	Percival Roberts	21,883
Henry Pratt McKean	32,984	William C. Biddle	21,813
Israel P. Morris	32,341	Charles S. Coxe	18,854
Algernon S. Roberts	32,194	George S. Pepper	18,735
Horatio O. Wood	27,677	Morton McMichael	15,941
John Wanamaker	27,230	George Biddle	15,258
G. W. Wharton	26,608	Alexander Biddle	15,253
Harry Ingersoll	26,422	Joseph R. Ingersoll	14,690
Dr. James Rush	25,756		
George T. Lewis	25,627		
Henry P. Borie	25,414		
Clement Biddle	25,290		

* Incomes were taken from: *The Rich Men of Philadelphia, Income Tax of the Residents of Philadelphia and Bucks County* (Philadelphia, 1865).

century family founders. Although the two Morrises were exceptions as far as family origins were concerned, they fitted into this group economically in that they were extremely successful industrialists. Finally, these new and extremely wealthy members of the business and banking elite, were different from the men of older wealth in other ways. Most of them, for example, had *not* gone to college. As we have seen, Charles Wheeler, Samuel Vaughan Merrick, A. J. Drexel, Thomas Dolan, Matthew Baird, and others went to work in their teens. Of the twelve richest men ($100,000 or more), only Dr. Jayne possessed a college degree. These businessmen were different from the eighteenth-century merchants in another important respect: although they often were generous private benefactors and philanthropists—Samuel Vaughan Merrick, A. J. Drexel, and George D. Rosengarten, for example, were civic leaders of distinction on the whole, they avoided public office. This is an important pattern which business gentlemen in America have followed throughout the nineteenth and twentieth centuries.

It is important to note that all incomes listed in Table 10 were extremely high for that day. In that year, for example, Phillips Brooks, the rector of the city's most fashionable Episcopal Church, reported an income of only $3,600, while Dr. S. Weir Mitchell, a fashionable and successful physician, reported only $5,642. In fact, a perusal of the list of persons with incomes at that time between $5,000 and $10,000, reads like a list of families in the 1940 *Social Register*.

The Civil War finally opened upper-class doors to the successful members of the business, industrial, and banking elite. The genteel had always been comfortable; from now on they were definitely destined to be really rich. In the half century between the silence at Appomatox and the roar of howitzers on the Western Front, American society produced a flood of business Titans, "robber barons," and railroad, mining, and traction kings. Cast in the mold of the Renaissance Prince, most of these men were born in the 1830's, avoided service in the Civil War, and proceeded to pile up fabulous fortunes. It is no wonder that "tales of the conquests" made by hard cash constituted the staple conversation of ladies and gentlemen in the "Gilded Age."[3]

The Railroad Age. Frederick Townsend Martin, one of the more sophisticated participants in the "Gilded Age," said he once remarked to a railway king while basking in the Florida sunshine, "How lovely the earth is! I wonder if Heaven will be more beautiful than this scene?" To which his railroad friend replied, "Well, Fred, I guess I'll have no use for Heaven unless there are railways to be constructed there."[4]

The Civil War ushered in the railroad age in America. Four of the wealthiest men in Table 10, for example, Mathias Baldwin, Matthew Baird, Joseph Harrison, Jr., and Richard Norris, were builders of locomotives. (Joseph Harrison, Jr., and Richard Norris were not related to the sugar and chemical Harrisons or the Isaac Norris clan.) They were also adventurers and pioneers; even the farsighted businessmen of the day, however, were unaware of the importance of industrial strength in wartime. The unprecedented prosperity at the Baldwin Locomotive Works during the Civil War was not anticipated. As a brief history of the firm reports:

> The breaking out of the Civil War at first unsettled business, and by many it was thought that railroad traffic would be so largely reduced that the demand for locomotives must cease altogether. A large number of hands were discharged from the Works, and only forty locomotives were turned out during the year (1861). It was even seriously contemplated to turn the resources of the establishment to the manufacture of shot and shell, and other munitions of war, the belief being entertained that the building of locomotives would have to be altogether suspended. So far was this from being the case, however, that after the first excitement had subsided, it was found that the demand for transportation by the General Government, and by the branches of trade and production stimulated by the war, was likely to tax the carrying capacity of the principal Northern railroads to the fullest extent. The Government itself became a large purchaser of locomotives . . . [and] heavier machines than had ever before been built became the rule.[5]

Baldwin built 226 locomotives during the four years between 1858 and 1861 as against 416 between 1862 and 1865.

The Civil War, of course, was only the beginning. Baldwin proved to be a veritable Proper Philadelphia gold mine right up until the end of World War I. Production increased in each decade of the nineteenth century, until at the century's end, over 1,000 locomotives were turned out in one year. And, although not as fashionable or aristocratic in origin as their friends at the Pennsylvania Railroad, Baldwin partners and executives, in due course, founded several new Proper Philadelphia Lines, the most notable being the Bairds, Converses, and Vauclains.

The Baldwin Locomotive Works was founded in 1831, when Mathias Baldwin, a former jeweler, built *Old Ironsides,* one of the first locomotives to be used in rail transportation in America. Its first run was out to Philadelphia's oldest suburb of Germantown (see below, Chapter IX).[6] While Baldwin founded no family line, his partner, Matthew Baird, had many descendants—including Matthew III, a graduate of St. Paul's, Princeton, and Oxford—listed in the 1940 *Social Register.* Born in Londonderry, Ireland, Matthew Baird was brought to America in 1821 at the age of three.[7] At fifteen he went to work in a brickyard before taking a job in the new Baldwin shop where he became the foreman in 1838 at the age of twenty-one. He became a partner in the firm just before the Civil War and sole owner when Baldwin died in 1866. Despite the panic, when he sold out his interest in the firm in 1873, he was worth over two million dollars. Although hardly accepted by the Victorian gentry on Rittenhouse Square, Baird's descendants have been gradually assimilated into fashionable society along the Main Line (if not into the most exclusive clubs).

John H. Converse, a Presbyterian clergyman's son from Vermont, became the first president of the Baldwin Locomotive Works when it was incorporated in 1909, and remained as its head throughout World War I, the most profitable period in the firm's history.[8] In the three years between 1916 and 1918, for instance, 8306 locomotives, as against 867 in 1915, were produced. As early as 1915, through the close coöperation of Converse, J. P. Morgan, then representing His Majesty's Government, and Samuel M. Vauclain, first vice-president at Baldwin's, the firm began the manufacture of arms for the Allied cause.[9] The extent of the war activities of the Baldwin Locomotive Works and its war-created subsidiaries— the Standard Steel Works Company, the Eddystone Ammunition Company and the Eddystone Munitions Company—is shown by the following summary of materiel supplied "to the Allied Nations and the United States" (this in addition to a bulging private demand):[10]

Locomotives	5551
Gun Mounts (7 and 14 inch)	51
Foundations for 14 inch mounts	20
Trucks for gun and howitzer mounts	5
Total number of shells	6,565,355
Cartridge Cases	1,863,900
Miscellaneous ammunition items	1,905,213
Aggregate value of war contracts executed and delivered, approximately	$250,000,000

Baldwin's 50,000th locomotive was completed in September, 1918, a fitting symbol of the firm's accomplishment which spanned America's "Railroad Age." The following year, Samuel M. Vauclain, for many years a world recognized locomotive expert and now the holder of the D.S.M. for war service, moved up to the presidency.[11] A public school graduate from Altoona, Pennsylvania, he had joined the Baldwin Works after working ten years on the Pennsylvania Railroad. When he died in 1940, Vauclain was chairman of the board at Baldwin, according to *Who's Who,* and both he and his children and grandchildren were listed in the *Social Register.*

The main plant of the Baldwin Locomotive Works, which for many years sprawled over 19-1/10 mid-city acres in the shadow of "Billy Penn" atop City Hall, was a Philadelphia landmark for over half a century. It was torn down just before World War II and the plant remains in Eddystone, Pennsylvania. The railroad age had for some years been replaced by the age of the automobile and airplane.

Proper Philadelphia's Railroad. In the closing years of the nineteenth century, the Pennsylvania Railroad was America's largest, wealthiest, and proudest corporation, with a national prestige comparable to the present status of General Motors. Down through the years, although many of its presidents have been self-made men, they have usually been assimilated with ease into Proper Philadelphia's society of business gentlemen through the social standing of its fashionable board of directors.

The Pennsylvania went through its greatest period of geographical expansion between 1852 and 1874 when it changed from a local Philadelphia-to-Pittsburgh carrier into a sprawling 6,000 mile system.* Although its president, John Edgar Thomson (no family founder), was certainly the top executive during this period of expansion, many have given handsome and congenial Thomas A. Scott, the senior vice-president, most of the credit.[13]

At any rate, Thomas A. Scott, president between 1874 and 1880,

---

* As was the case with the Baldwin Locomotive Works, the Pennsylvania Railroad did very well during the Civil War, as the following figures for 1860-1865 indicate:[12]

Year	Total Revenue
1860	$ 5,933,000
1861	7,300,000
1862	10,730,000
1863	12,628,000
1864	15,890,000
1865	19,533,000

was one of the most colorful presidents of Proper Philadelphia's most conservative institution.[14] Born the son of a tavern-keeper in Franklin County, Pennsylvania, young Scott left school at the age of ten, worked as a handy man in a general supply store until he was seventeen, and, finally, after several private business ventures, went with the Railroad at the age of twenty-seven. He rose to become First Vice-President ten years later, in 1860.

In 1861, he handled President-elect Lincoln's secret inaugural trip down to Washington and was eventually made Assistant Secretary of War, in charge of all rail transportation.[15] After a year's service, during the course of which he and his personal assistant, Andrew Carnegie, then a young telegraphic operator, set up a completely new accounting system for the Army, Scott resigned, only to be called back a year later as an Army Colonel in General Joe Hooker's staff. He was immediately placed in charge of transporting some 13,000 troops, with their artillery, wagons, and horses, from Virginia, through Nashville, to Chattanooga, the greatest mass movement of troops by rail up to that time.[16]

After the war, Scott played a major role in expanding the Pennsylvania system. In contrast to the more conservative board of directors and leading executives of the Railroad, he was keenly interested in taking advantage of the western expansion of the nation. More in the tradition of a Hill or a Harriman, he was even something of a plunger. In 1871, for example, he took over the presidency of the Union Pacific after Oliver Ames got out, with the hope of consolidating it with the Pennsylvania system. A few years later, he almost ruined his career when he took over the presidency of the ailing Texas and Pacific for the same purpose. Finally, his ingenious development of the South Improvement Company, which was a pooling arrangement with the Standard Oil crowd in which the Pennsylvania was to handle 45 per cent of Rockefeller's eastbound oil shipments, was a tremendous financial success for a time, but eventually proved embarrassing for the Railroad.[17]

Handsome Tom Scott's expansive nature and winning ways won him endless friends both in business and in polite society. Unlike other self-made men, he was almost immediately accepted by Philadelphia's Victorian gentry. He joined the most fashionable clubs, and was something of a leader in Rittenhouse Square society.

He died at his country estate "Woodburne," in Darby, after a paralytic stroke and lingering illness, in 1881. Since then, his Harvard-educated descendants, through fashionable clubs and judicious marriage alliances, have carried on an impeccable Proper Philadelphia family tradition.

The fifth and seventh presidents of the Pennsylvania Railroad, George B. Roberts (1880-1897) and Alexander J. Cassatt (1899-1906), were the first of a presidential series drawn from wealthy upper-class backgrounds.

George B. Roberts was born at "Pencoyd Plantation," an estate in the old Welsh Barony along the Main Line which had been owned by his father's family for five generations.[18] Coal, iron and steel, and railroads were already in the Roberts tradition. His uncle, Algernon Sidney Roberts, had been active in the formation of the Pennsylvania Railroad and had been appointed State Commissioner at its original incorporation by the Legislature.[19] After retiring from a successful career in the drug business, Algernon Sidney Roberts developed important coal properties in Luzerne County and was a director of several railroads and coal companies as well as the Chesapeake and Delaware Canal. His two sons, Algernon Sidney and Percival (George B. Robert's first cousins) ran the Pencoyd Iron Works, a family firm situated on the banks of the Schuylkill near the family homestead (the firm was eventually absorbed by the United States Steel Company, with Percival Roberts, listed in *Who's Who* in 1940, as one of the original directors).

Adding to tradition and inheritance, young George Roberts entered Rensselaer Polytechnic Institute at the age of fifteen and completed its three-year course two years later.[20] After eleven years of experience in railroad location and construction as a private engineering consultant, he went with the Pennsylvania system as assistant to the president, a newly created office. "It was unusual then, as now, for the Pennsylvania to start so young a man, or, in fact, any man, in such an important position," writes the Railroad's official historian.[21] However, he rose rapidly, becoming a vice-president at the age of thirty-six, and president at the age of forty-one. "The rapid elevation of a young man with no previous experience in railroad operation or management," the company historian continues, "can only be explained by sheer hard-working ability."[22]

Perhaps the most dramatic event in Roberts' career as president of the Pennsylvania took place off Sandy Hook, aboard J. P. Morgan's yacht, the *Corsair*.[23] By the 1880's the New York Central and the Pennsylvania were the two mightiest railroads in the United States. The Pennsylvania was first, and the Central second. About this time the Central was in the process of building a road-bed for the South Pennsylvania Railroad which was to have run across the Alleghenies to Pittsburgh in order to compete with the Pennsylvania in this wealthy industrial region. Meanwhile, the Pennsylvania was quietly buying up the bankrupt West Shore Railroad in order to compete with the Central with a road up the west shore of the Hudson to Albany. Morgan, whose past three summers at "Cragston" (his country seat on the west shore of the Hudson) had been ruined by the infernal blastings of construction gangs working on the West Shore Road, quickly arranged a meeting aboard his *Corsair* between Chauncey Depew of the Central and George B. Roberts of the Pennsylvania.

This was Morgan's first attempt at playing the role of peace-maker in the competitive wars which were then spoiling the profits of the railroads and were soon to damage the steel industry. His plan was a simple trade: the Pennsylvania was to drop all interests in the West Shore and allow the Central to take it over, with the understanding that the Pennsylvania would be allowed to take over the South Pennsylvania. The *Corsair* steamed down the Hudson and out into New York Harbor as far as Sandy Hook. Morgan was mostly silent as the leaders of the Pennsylvania and the New York Central discussed his proposed trade from all possible angles. Roberts, trained as an engineer, and suspicious of New York money-men like Depew, held out until the last minute. As he was stepping ashore at the dock in Jersey City to catch the train back to Philadelphia, however, he shook hands with Morgan and said, "I will agree to your plan and do my part."[24] Quiet prevailed along the Hudson's west shore; weeds and bushes soon began to cover up the Southern Pennsylvania roadbed, now an un-noticed part of the Pennsylvania Turnpike for automobiles.

A. J. Cassatt became president of the Pennsylvania Railroad after the death of President Frank Thomson, in 1897. Severe competition had plagued the railroads despite such efforts as Morgan's settlement of the war between the Pennsylvania and the New York Central. The critical competitive situation at the time was summarized in the minutes of a meeting of the Pennsylvania's Board of Directors just after President Thomson's death. The minutes began as follows:

When Mr. Frank Thomson's untimely death occurred, the forces that had been steadily disrupting the fabric of railway prosperity had become so controlling that disaster was imminent. The recurrent waves of prosperity and adversity that marked almost every decade in our national life had strewn the path with the wrecks of railway enterprises, and the struggle for competitive traffic had forced down the actual rates paid by shippers to a point where none but the strongest and best equipped lines could earn a living profit. Agreements to maintain rates were not worth the paper upon which they were written, and the rebates extorted by large shippers under a threat to divert their traffic, had built up industries whose development often worked injustice to smaller combinations of capital.[25]

A. J. Cassatt's greatest achievement as president was the solution of the rebate problem. He believed that competition between smaller lines was responsible for the breakdown of published rates. Strong shippers such as the Carnegie Steel Company, for example, would play one small line off against another (and against the Pennsylvania) in order to secure rates, including rebates, almost on their own terms. In his typically bold and "free-enterprising" manner, Cassatt systematically proceeded to buy out weaker competitors soon after assuming the presidency.[26] In 1899 he bought heavily into the Chesapeake and Ohio and the Baltimore and Ohio railway companies and soon held a controlling interest in both. Large purchases of Reading, and, of Norfolk and Western stock were also made during the same period. By 1902 the Pennsylvania substantially controlled these competing lines and even elected one of its own vice-presidents as president of the Baltimore and Ohio. The assets of the Pennsylvania amounted to approximately $280,000,000 at the end of 1898 just before Cassatt became president. By the end of 1902 the expenditures in stock purchases were as follows:[27]

Chesapeake and Ohio stock	$ 5,569,000
Norfolk and Western stock	17,895,000
Baltimore and Ohio stock	65,042,000
Reading Company stock	21,563,000
	$110,069,000

A. J. Cassatt was an unusual president for the staid old Pennsy.[28] Born of wealthy parents in Pittsburgh, he spent much of his youth abroad where he attended continental schools and Darmstadt University. After returning from Europe, he graduated from Rensselaer Polytechnic Institute at the age of twenty. He first engaged in railroad location and construction in Georgia, but returned to the north because of the Civil War and joined the Pennsylvania in 1861. In 1880, at the age of forty, he became First Vice-President, only to retire two years later to devote his time to horse-breeding, eventually becoming one of the "two or three leading patrons of the American turf."[29] Seventeen years later he was called back from retirement to assume the presidency.

Less provincial, less conservative than many other Proper Philadelphians connected with the Railroad, A. J. Cassatt had long been convinced that New York would always outrank Philadelphia as the commercial center of the nation. When Cassatt assumed the office of president of the Pennsylvania, the New York Central was the only western line which reached Manhattan Island without a water transfer across the Hudson. This was only a slight advantage as far as freight was concerned, but it proved a definite advantage to the Central's passenger traffic. All passengers coming in from the West on the Pennsylvania, for example, had to leave the train with their baggage and complete the trip to New York by ferry. Under Cassatt's planning and leadership, the Pennsylvania began the construction of two tunnels under the Hudson and four under the East River, as well as the great Pennsylvania terminal in the heart of Manhattan.

A. J. Cassatt died in office (1906) before his bold plans for firmly establishing the Pennsylvania's position on Manhattan were completed. He did live to see the elimination of cutthroat rate competition, however. Before his death, the federal government finally assumed control over railroad rates through the passage of the Elkins Amendment (1903) and the Hepburn Act (1906), both of which he supported.[30] Thus in many ways A. J. Cassatt's presidency witnessed the beginning of the end of the great "free-enterprising" railroad age in America. The expansion of American railroad mileage reached its peak in 1916. Other forms of transportation seriously began to challenge the railroads after the war.[31] America's nineteenth-century preoccupation with creating its continental empire, in which the railroad played such a vital part, was diverted outward, and over the seas, in the twentieth century. Just as the War of 1812, the building of the Erie Canal, and Clay's

"American System" set the stage for America's nineteenth-century continental imperialism, so the Spanish War in 1898, the opening of the Panama Canal in 1914, World War I, and Wilson's dream of a League of Nations marked the nation's new internationalism and its world leadership in the twentieth.

Any discussion of Pennsylvania Railroad families would be incomplete without including Henry Howard Houston, one of Philadelphia's great family founders and public benefactors.[32] Born on his father's farm in Wrightsville, Pennsylvania, in 1820, he left school at fourteen and went to work for the local general store, where he remained until 1840 when he took a job at the Lucinda Furnace, owned by James Buchanan, Pennsylvania ironmaster and later President of the United States. After working at several other iron furnaces, Houston toured the Western and Southern states, in 1846, where he carefully observed the boundless business opportunities which were to be presented by the conquest of the American continent.

He then came to Philadelphia in 1847 where he worked for a canal company before going with the Pennsylvania Railroad in 1850. Although connected with the Pennsylvania for the rest of his life, first as General Freight Agent and eventually as a member of the Board of Directors, Houston was also involved in many outside business ventures. In addition to promoting and financing several other railroads, including the Texas and Pacific and Empire Lines, he was a successful speculator in California gold and Pennsylvania petroleum from which he accumulated a large fortune. Finally, Henry Howard Houston became one of the largest owners of Philadelphia suburban real estate. He is best remembered today as the developer of Chestnut Hill, the city's most fashionable suburb, and as a benefactor of the University of Pennsylvania.

Coal. If Proper Philadelphia can be said to be the capital of an empire, then its chief colony is the anthracite coal region of northeastern Pennsylvania. Profits from the "black gold" of Lehigh, Carbon, Wyoming, and Luzerne counties built many mansions around Rittenhouse Square and spacious estates along the Main Line. The Lehigh Coal and Navigation Company, often called the "Old Company," has been a veritable Proper Philadelphia institution down through the years. Edward W. Clark, son of Enoch, founder of the family banking house, was president of the "Old Company" for fifteen years after the Civil War. Another president, Edward B. Leisenring, whose father had supervised the building of the "Switchback Railroad" at Mauch Chunk in the 1840's, eventually moved down to Philadelphia.[33] Born in Mauch Chunk, where he was president of the First National Bank for many years, he moved down to Philadelphia after assuming the presidency of the Lehigh Coal and Navigation Company in the 1880's. His son, Edward B. Leisenring, Jr., was a very Proper Philadelphia member of the city's elite in 1940.[34] According to his *Who's Who* biography, he was a graduate of Hotchkiss School and Yale University; president of the Hazel Brook, Westmoreland, Wentz, and Virginia Coal & Iron coal companies; chairman of the board of the Stonega Coke and Coal Company; and a director of the Lehigh Coal & Navigation, Whitehall Cement, and Lehigh and New England Railroad companies. He belonged to the Philadelphia, Rittenhouse, Racquet, Gulph Mills Golf, and Merion Cricket Clubs, and lived with his family of four children in Ardmore along the Main Line.

But the story of all the Proper Philadelphia anthracite families cannot be related here; it is enough to show how the Coxe family mined one of the largest fortunes of them all, at Drifton, Pennsylvania, in the valley of the Lehigh not far from Mauch Chunk.

The origin of the Coxe family fortune goes back to Tench Coxe who, between 1790 and 1820, acquired large holdings of land in Luzerne, Carbon, Schuylkill, and Columbia counties, in what was eventually to become the heart of the Pennsylvania anthracite district. While the land at that time was open to homesteaders, Tench Coxe shrewdly took advantage of the situation by "grub-staking" a large number of settlers who were granted title to the land after fencing in 400 acres and building a home thereon. After supporting a homesteader for three years, Tench Coxe took two-thirds of the final title, and the valuable lands so acquired remain in the hands of his descendants to this day.[35]

Tench Coxe, whose first wife died without issue, had ten children by his second wife. His sixth child, Charles Sidney Coxe (see Table 10), judge of the District Court and President of the Board of Directors of the Eastern State Penitentiary at its founding, was a lawyer and civic leader of distinction in Philadelphia. But he made it the chief business of his life to hold intact the large body of coal lands inherited from his father. The estate, which was left entirely in his charge, was unproductive for many years. Annual taxes were large, squatters and timber-thieves abounded, and title disputes and conflicting surveys kept affairs in continual litigation. Judge Coxe, who knew every corner of the land which he succeeded in preserving for his descendants (he often sold or traded farming and timber producing land in order to retain the more valuable coal property), thoroughly trained his five sons to carry on after his death. His third son, Eckley Brinton Coxe, was carefully educated as a mining engineer.[36]

After graduating from the University of Pennsylvania at the age of nineteen, Eckley Brinton Coxe spent the summer of 1859 surveying the family land. In 1860 he went to Paris where he spent two years at the school of mines. After an additional year of study at the famous mining academy at Freiberg in Saxony, Coxe spent two more years in Europe observing the actual operation of mines in England and on the continent. He returned to America in 1864 and established Coxe Brothers and Company during the last year of the Civil War.

Thoroughly trained in both Europe and America, Coxe devoted the rest of his life to the coal industry. By 1886 the family firm controlled about 35,000 acres of coal property. Eckley Brinton Coxe held some seventy technical patents, built a technical school for coal miners' sons near his home in Drifton, Pennsylvania, founded the American Institute of Mining Engineers (president, 1878-1879), and became State Senator from Luzerne and Lackawanna counties in 1880, where he was instrumental in enacting beneficial legislation requiring the payment of wages to miners at a weekly rate.

From the early days, most of the railroads in Pennsylvania were closely associated with coal.[37] In 1872, even the Pennsylvania, primarily a national and diversified carrier, purchased some 28,000 acres of hard coal lands at a cost of about $5,000,000.[38] By 1907, over three-fourths (78.4 per cent) of the total anthracite coal output was being mined by railroad companies. The Coxe firm was one of the last large operators to sell out to the railroads.

Eckley Brinton Coxe and his wife Sophie, known as "the angel of the hard coal fields" because of her philanthropic devotion to the miners' welfare, spent their lives at Drifton, in the heart of the coal region.[40] But most of the Coxe family moved back to Philadelphia where they were leaders of fashionable society—captains of the City Troop, managers of the Assembly Balls, and presidents of the Philadelphia Club. This was especially true after the family firm sold out its mining rights (not the land) to the Lehigh Valley Railroad in 1906, for the sum of $19,000,000.[41]

Iron and Steel. The railroad age depended on iron and steel as well as coal. Before the development of the great Lake Superior and Chattanooga-Birmingham districts in the latter part of the nineteenth century (Masabi Range, 1890's), the mining of iron ore was widely dispersed in America.[42] In the eighteenth century, for example, the ubiquitous Pennsylvania ironmasters were famous throughout the colonies.[43] Captain Samuel Morris' grandfather, Anthony Morris, owned several large iron plantations, including the 400-acre Wells Ferry Forge and plantation, near New Hope (1724), the Durham Iron Works (1727), the Pool Forge, in Berks County (1731), and the Assumption Forge, near Trenton (1729).[44] The long rifle was the invention of Pennsylvania ironmasters, and General Washington was also thankful for the nearby forges (Valley Forge) which produced cannon balls, guns, and rims for the wheels of his army's caissons and wagons.[45]

Many Proper Philadelphia families carried on the tradition of the original ironmasters throughout the nineteenth century. The Roberts family ran the Pencoyd Iron Works, on the banks of the Schuylkill opposite Mannayunk, until they finally sold out to U. S. Steel after the turn of the century.[46] A few miles up the river, in Conshohocken, Alan and James Wood founded an iron works before the Civil War. Today, the Alan Wood Steel Company is one of the few large firms in this industry still owned and operated by the descendants of the original founders.[47] Finally, Henry Disston was not only the founder of one of the city's more prosperous steel companies but also produced a large and prolific family line.[48] Henry Disston & Sons, founded in 1840, became world famous through the "Disston saw" which followed the pioneers across the great American continent. The firm was run by the family for over a century (sold in 1955-1956).

In his day, Joseph Wharton was Philadelphia's greatest iron and steel capitalist.[49] The last of the Wharton line to attain national eminence, he founded the Bethlehem Iron Company just before the Civil War, and was the leading figure at Bethlehem until the company was finally bought by Charles M. Schwab, who had previously been one of the founders and the first president of U. S. Steel.[50]

Frederick W. Taylor, the father of scientific management and time-study engineering, performed many of his well-known experiments while employed by Joseph Wharton at Bethlehem.[51] In retrospect, this was one of the bleakest periods in the history of human engineering. When "that man Taylor" left Bethlehem after three years, he was undoubtedly one of the most hated individuals in the plant. Before going to Bethlehem, Frederick W. Taylor had been employed by the Midvale Steel Company, which had been founded by a group of Philadelphia capitalists headed by E. W. Clark shortly after the Civil War (1867).[52] The Clark and Taylor families had grown up together in Germantown, near the Midvale works in North Philadelphia (Taylor was E. W. Clark's brother-in-law).

Oil. Iron, coal, and petroleum are the three primary natural resources of the industrial state. After World War I, as the automobile began to challenge the railroad, petroleum gradually replaced coal as the dominant fuel in America. The rise of the petroleum industry began in 1859 when the Seneca Oil Company drilled the first commercial oil well in the United States at Titusville, Pennsylvania.[53] The discovery of oil at Titusville eventually led to the rise of the Pew family as one of the newer additions to Proper Philadelphia society.

Young Joseph Newton Pew, after selling real estate and teaching school in Mercer County where he was born on his family's farm, moved to Titusville and married Mary Anderson in 1874.[54] The Anderson family were pioneers in the early days of the oil industry in Titusville. In 1880, Pew founded the Sun Oil Company which has grown into one of the largest family-owned concerns in its field. At the same time, he and his wife moved down to Philadelphia where they built "Glenmede," the family estate in Bryn Mawr, on the Main Line.

Joseph Newton Pew, whose sons were carrying on the family business in 1940, died in 1912. His wife, Mary Anderson Pew, died at the age of eighty-five during the Depression. We are offered some insight into the stability of large family fortunes in our society, when we read of the final settlement of her estate. A year after her death, on September 3, 1936, her Sun Oil common and Sun Oil preferred were valued at $9,722,480 and $363,000, respectively. These same stocks had been valued at $7,777,984 and $354,750 as of her death in April, 1935.[56] Despite the Depression, her estate had appreciated in the amount of approximately $2,000,000 within one year.

Modern Merchant Princes. The department store—Macy's in New York, Harrod's in London, Maison Blanche in Paris, the G.U.M. (State Department Store) in Moscow, or Mitsukoshi in Japan—plays a vital role in modern metropolitan society.[57] With historical roots in the tradition of the itinerant peddler and the small-town general store, the modern department store was a result of the rapidly increasing standard of living and urbanization which characterized the second half of the nineteenth century. Most of the more fabulous American merchant princes—Jordan Marsh, Potter Palmer, Marshall Field, Rowland Hussey Macy, John Wanamaker, Adam Gimbel, and Alexander Turney Stewart—had already begun their merchant careers by the close of the Civil War.[58]

A. T. Stewart, America's leading mid-nineteenth-century merchant, opened the largest department store in the world, in New York in 1862. "I got it at Stewart's" became a national byword; even Mrs. Abraham Lincoln redecorated the White House with goods she charged at the store.[59]

John Wanamaker, the son of a bricklayer, became America's leading merchant prince when he bought A. T. Stewart's New York store in 1896, but it was in 1861 that he founded what is now Proper Philadelphia's favorite department store.[60] His first enterprise was called the Oak Hall Clothing Bazaar, which he founded with his brother-in-law in 1861; he soon became the leading clothing merchant in the city (see Table 10 where his income is shown as $27,230 as of 1865). Sometimes called "Pious John" by his more cynical rivals, Wanamaker was born into a vigorously pious, Baptist-Methodist family. All his life he was active in the Presbyterian Sunday School movement, the Young Men's Christian Association, and the Republican Party.[61] His religious convictions, which were continually publicized, so impressed the late Professor N. S. B. Gras, of the Harvard Business School, that he used Wanamaker as the classic American example of the affinity between the "Protestant ethic" and business success.[62]

Wanamaker was always a crusader for good government. Although he was defeated by Boies Penrose in an attempt to oust the notorious boss, Matthew Quay, from Republican rule in Pennsylvania, he did achieve national political recognition when President Harrison appointed him Postmaster General. He died in 1922, leaving a fortune of some twenty million dollars.[63]

Although Wanamaker's is *the* Proper Philadelphia store, Strawbridge and Clothier (Quaker) and Gimbel Brothers (Jewish) have old Philadelphia traditions. Isaac H. Clothier and Justus C. Strawbridge, who founded the Quakers' favorite store in 1862, and the Gimbel family will be discussed in a later chapter.

Utility Financiers. Rapid urban growth followed the industrialization of America during the last years of the nineteenth century. As the commercial and industrial masses were no longer able to walk from home to factory and office, Philadelphia became a "trolley-car city." The last of the great nineteenth-century business Titans in Philadelphia were masters at manipulating streetcar franchises, an art requiring both political and financial skill.

Theodore Dreiser immortalized in literature the stormy career of Charles T. Yerkes (1837-1905), a Philadelphia Quaker boy, who made and lost a great traction fortune.[64] Yerkes, who spent time in jail, went through an ugly divorce suit, and eventually left the city for Chicago, London, and New York, did not found a Proper Philadelphia family line, but his two friends and business associates, Peter A. B. Widener and William Lukens Elkins, both had descendants listed in *Who's Who* and the *Social Register* in 1940.

Peter A. B. Widener, whose father was a brickmaker of prerevolutionary stock, went to work in his older brother's butcher shop after two years at Philadelphia's famous Central High School.[65] He immediately became interested in politics and, when the Civil War broke out, secured a contract from the federal government to supply with mutton all troops located within ten miles of Philadelphia. With the $50,000 profits from this contract, a very large sum for that day, Widener bought several strategically located streetcar lines and a chain of meat stores throughout the city. Thereafter, his political influence grew rapidly. He was elected to several minor offices before being appointed City Treasurer in 1873. Two years later he and his partner, William L. Elkins, began buying up one streetcar line after another. By 1883, their Philadelphia Transportation Company, later the Philadelphia Rapid

Transit Company which carried Philadelphians to work in 1940, had control of all streetcar lines in the city. After obtaining a monopoly in Philadelphia, Widener turned to New York where he and his partners, William C. Whitney and Thomas Fortune Ryan, built up a notoriously profitable traction empire within a very few years. In addition to his traction interests in Philadelphia, New York, and several other cities, Peter A. B. Widener helped to organize both the United States Steel Company and the American Tobacco Company. He was also a large investor in the Pennsylvania Railroad, Standard Oil, and the United Gas Improvement Company.

William L. Elkins, a close friend and business partner of Peter A. B. Widener for many years, was born in Wheeling, West Virginia.[66] He left school at the age of fifteen and went to work in a grocery store. After ten years in his own produce business in New York City, Elkins spent the years 1861-1880 organizing oil companies in western Pennsylvania. He was one of the early partners in the Standard Oil Company, and about the same time he became interested in illuminating gas. According to the *Dictionary of American Biography*, William L. Elkins was a director of twenty-four companies and left an estate of approximately $25,000,000 when he died in 1903.[67]

One of Elkins' companies was the United Gas Improvement Company, organized in 1882 by a group of Philadelphia capitalists including Peter A. B. Widener, and Thomas Dolan. Ten years later, the "U.G.I." was America's largest public utility concern. Its management operated gas and electric companies "from Maine to Florida and from the Atlantic Seaboard to the Rockies. . . ."[68] Thomas Dolan, the company's president, became a national figure in the utility field, president of the National Association of Manufacturers, and advisor to the Republican National Committee.[69] Under his leadership, in 1897, the "U.G.I." obtained a thirty-year lease of Philadelphia's gas lighting system, and, needless to say, "U.G.I." stock became a staple item in many Proper Philadelphian's portfolio down through the years.

It is somehow fitting to close this discussion of Philadelphia's late-nineteenth-century money-makers with such men as Peter A. B. Widener and William Lukens Elkins. Moneyed men in many fields, they were typical of America's Renaissance Princes of the "Gilded Age." These two men, and their contemporaries, Thomas Dolan, Isaac H. Clothier, Justus C. Strawbridge, and John Wana·

maker, had several things in common. Born in the 1830's and
eligible for service in the Civil War, instead they all went to work
in their 'teens in retail establishments, and following the war proceeded to pile up considerable fortunes in commerce and industry in the next four decades. Perhaps more important, and in
contrast to many family founders of earlier wealth, none of these
men has produced, as of 1940, descendants who have established
themselves in the city as outstanding lawyers, physicians, statesmen,
or intellectuals. Plutocracy symbolizes the final triumph of the
commercial ethic: these men were of America's first plutocratic
generation.

Twentieth-Century Proper Philadelphia Fortunes. Edward T.
Stotesbury, John T. Dorrance, Clarence H. Geist, and A. Atwater
Kent added their fortunes to the Proper Philadelphia portfolios in
the twentieth century. Stotesbury went to work for the Drexels
right after the Civil War, at the age of seventeen. By 1900, according to the New York *Times,* he was one of a small group of Americans with international reputations in banking circles.[70] After A.
J. Drexel's death in 1893, Stotesebury was the firm's leading partner, a position which he held throughout the first quarter of the
century. In addition to his banking interests, Stotesbury was a
well-known patron of horse shows, painting, and the opera.

While he left no male heirs, Edward T. Stotesbury's fortune
flowed into various American first-family lines. His two daughters
married in the best Proper Philadelphia tradition. The Mitchell
family (as will be seen in Chapter VII, S. Weir Mitchell was Philadelphia's leading author and physician in the Victorian Age), for
instance, became really wealthy for the first time when S. Weir
Mitchell's grandson, John Kearsley III, married one of Stotesbury's
daughters.[71] Stotesbury's other daughter married Sydney Emlen
Hutchinson, a very Proper Philadelphian with a lifelong interest in
athletic affairs at the University of Pennsylvania. The Hutchinson
Gymnasium and Palestra, home of indoor athletics at the University
since 1927, were indirect beneficiaries of the Stotesbury fortune.[72]

After his second marriage, Edward T. Stotesbury became a
leading "socialite" in Philadelphia, but especially at Bar Harbor
and Palm Beach. Earlier, he "made" the coveted Assembly, no
mean accomplishment for A. J. Drexel's former office boy (Stotesbury often liked to relate how he went to work for the Drexels

at $6.00 a week, and began his fortune with the $200 Christmas bonus which he received during his first year there).[73]

When he remarried (his first wife died) in 1912, Stotesbury gave his new wife a $100,000 diamond and sapphire necklace and settled $4,000,000 in her name.[74] The second Mrs. Stotesbury and her children by a previous marriage seem to have had a flair for people of wealth and achievement. Her son, James Cromwell, was one of Doris Duke's husbands; her daughter was married to Douglas MacArthur, perhaps a more interesting alliance. Young Louise Cromwell met this brilliant young man of destiny, then a bachelor of forty-two in command of the Military Academy, at the nearby millionaire's country club in Tuxedo, a few miles from West Point.[75] They immediately fell in love and were married at a large and fashionable affair in Palm Beach. The newly-married couple were then ordered to the Philippines, hardly a resort for millionaires. The marriage did not last and is not even referred to by the General in his *Who's Who* biography.[76]

John T. Dorrance was the founder of the American canned soup industry.[77] After a private school education at the old Rugby Academy in Philadelphia, he obtained a degree from the Massachusetts Institute of Technology. He sailed for Europe where he obtained a Ph.D. in chemistry from Gottingen in 1897, and then spent some time in Paris exploring famous restaurants for soup recipes. Upon returning to Philadelphia, he turned down excellent academic appointments at Columbia, Cornell, and Bryn Mawr, in favor of a seven-dollar-a-week job in his uncle's firm, the Joseph Campbell Preserving Company. He rose to be vice-president and director of the family firm in 1900 and became President of the newly-formed Campbell Soup Company in 1914, a position which he held until his death in 1930. His daughters have added to several Proper Philadelphia family fortunes, while his only son now carries on the family tradition as a vice-president of Campbell Soup (Arthur C. Dorrance, the founder's younger brother, was president in 1940).[78]

Clarence H. Geist was one of Philadelphia's most colorful millionaires. Born on a farm in Indiana, Geist went west at eighteen and spent the next five years in the saddle, dealing in livestock and trading in horses. He then returned to Chicago because, as he once said, "No one in the West, at that time, had any money, and I discovered the fact that I could not make money where there wasn't any."[79] In Chicago, Geist, in partnership with Charles G. Dawes, later vice-president of the United States, entered the real estate business and began to buy up gas properties all over the Middle West. In 1900 he sold out all his real estate holdings and devoted his time to developing gas utilities. In 1907, Philadelphia's United Gas Improvement Company bought one of Geist's plants in South Bend, Indiana, for some two million dollars and the next year paid him nearly one and a half million for his Wyoming Valley Gas & Electric Company, in Pennsylvania.[80] Now pretty well integrated into the "U.G.I." crowd, he moved to Philadelphia and settled in Wynnefield (A. M. Greenfield, the city's wealthiest and most influential Russian Jew, lived in Geist's house in 1940). In 1933, Geist purchased the Clark estate on the Main Line (that year he contributed $50,000 to the United Campaign).[81] When he died in 1938, the local newspapers estimated his estate at $54,000,-000.[82] Although this later proved to be overly generous, his daughters (he had no sons) brought considerable wealth to two Proper Main Line families. *

A. Atwater Kent was Proper Philadelphia's last tycoon.[83] An inventive and mechanical genius, the first of whose ninety-seven patents was taken out in his teens, he was a pioneer in the automotive, telephone, and radio manufacturing industries. Born in Vermont and educated at the Worcester Polytechnic Institute, he came down to Philadelphia at the turn of the century and established the Atwater Kent Manufacturing Company in 1902, which first made telephones and volt-meters. Three years later he began to manufacture a revolutionary ignition system which was soon used by more than a dozen automobile manufacturers. During World War I, he made fuse-setters, panoramic sights, and cline-meters for the United States Government. After the war, the company reconverted to civilian production. It sold its first radio set in 1923 and at once became a leading producer in this new field. Three years later it sold its millionth set, and, at peak production,

---

* Geist's boundless energy and zest for conspicuous fun was hardly in the Proper Philadelphia tradition. He belonged to 26 clubs, including the Seaview Golf Club, in Atlantic City (where he entertained President Harding on the links) and the fabulous Boca Raton Club, in Palm Beach, both of which he built. His most famous party took place in 1910 when he entertained his entire home town including farmers from miles around, in La Porte County, Indiana. He rented the town's largest hall and hotel and imported a brass band from Chicago for the affair.

produced over 6,000 radios daily and employed 12,000 men and women.

Many laboring class families in and around North Philadelphia and Germantown will never forget the day when the Atwater Kent Company suddenly shut down in the Depression year of 1936. The owner's active mind had lost interest in the tedious problems of making money during a depression. Many times a millionaire, Atwater Kent proceeded to direct his boundless energy into two rather incongruous hobbies: the restoration of Old Philadelphia and extensive entertaining. In 1937 he restored the historic Betsy Ross house and the next year bought the old Franklin Institute Building, which he turned into the Atwater Kent Museum, now specializing in miscellaneous Old Philadelphiana. The same year, he was honored with the chairmanship of a committee to raise funds for the new Franklin Institute Building on Franklin Parkway (he contributed $225,000 to the drive).

All four of Philadelphia's twentieth-century multi-millionaires, and especially their energetic wives, were great party-givers and they were at the height of their powers during the twenties. The second Mrs. Stotesbury, for example, was for many years the arbiter of Palm Beach's fashionable whirl. Her husband, too, liked to entertain and danced at his eightieth birthday ball, an important event at this famous resort. Each summer, the Kents, Dorrances, and Stotesburys led the stiff and formal social life at Bar Harbor, on Proper Philadelphia's favorite island of Mount Desert. Although many eagerly accepted invitations to Kent's famous parties, both in Philadelphia and at Bar Harbor, the city's first families never accepted Atwater Kent himself as one of the family (or even as a distant cousin). Their sons, on the other hand, were not averse to marrying Kent's daughters, which was, of course, something different altogether.

It is fitting that Philadelphia's last tycoon should have died in 1949 at his Hollywood suburban estate. His $2,500,000, 750-acre show place on the Main Line (improved by $1,500,000 after its purchase in 1929) and his fabulous parties had failed to impress Philadelphia. After obtaining a divorce, he finally moved to Southern California, where he perhaps felt more at home with the publicity and party-loving tycoons of Hollywood.

CHAPTER VII

Proper Philadelphia Public Servants, Professionals, and Men of Letters

> I believe that ambitious men in democracies are less engrossed than any others with the interests and the judgment of posterity; the present moment alone engages and absorbs them . . . and they care much more for success than for fame. What appears to me most to be dreaded is that in the midst of the small, incessant occupations of private life, ambition should lose its vigor and its greatness . . . so that the march of society should every day become more tranquil and less aspiring.
>
> ALEXIS DE TOCQUEVILLE

WEALTH derived from business, industry, and trade, often consolidated through landownership, has always been the foundation for all commercial upper classes. Thus all upper classes have been based on inherited wealth. It is true, however, that the intellectual, professional and statesmanlike accomplishments of the moneymaker's descendants have always been recognized as the final flowering and ultimate justification of the existence of that wealth.

Moreover, it might be maintained that the Anglo-American heritage of freedom, both intellectual and political, has been in no small part a by-product of the existence in a democracy of a small class of men whose inherited wealth has freed them from the all-absorbing drive for economic independence. Theodore Roosevelt, for example, was aware of this function of inherited wealth: "I have known a few men of wealth who use their wealth to full advantage," he once wrote. "I have known plenty of men who are only able to do their work because they have inherited means. This is absolutely true of both Cabot [Lodge] and myself, for instance. Cabot is quite a rich man, but I am not; but each of us has been able to do what he has actually done because his father left him in such shape that he did not have to earn his own living."[1] Similarly in Philadelphia, when the wealthy reform Mayor, the great-grandson of Enoch W. Clark, recently told a local meeting of the Americans for Democratic Action that, of course, he was not in politics to make money, one had a right to note that there was some economic basis for his unquestionable integrity which did not in the least detract from his personal moral stature.

In other words, while any discussion of an upper-class family structure must of necessity concentrate on the money-making founders of family fortunes, their contemporaries and descendants in the law or medicine, in publishing and politics, or in pursuit of the arts may in fact be far more important to the enrichment of the life of the community as a whole. The more important professional men and public servants listed in Table 9, Chapter V, will be briefly discussed below. Although most of them did not found a Proper Philadelphia family, many attempted to justify their inherited position through valuable service to the larger community.

Public Servants: Soldiers and Statesmen. Proper Philadelphia has never produced great political families such as the Adamses and Lodges of Boston, the Tafts of Cincinnati, or the Roosevelts of New York. In discussing his appointment by the Governor of Pennsylvania to fill Boies Penrose's unexpired term in the Senate of the United States, George Wharton Pepper revealed an all-too-characteristic Proper Philadelphia trait: "The simple fact is," he wrote in his autobiography, "that never in my life have I felt the itch for public office, impossible as it may be to make people believe this."[2] It might indeed be hard to believe if it were not for the long Proper Philadelphia tradition behind Pepper. In fact, more than one Proper Philadelphian not only failed to possess the "itch for public office," but refused to serve when chosen. Anthony Morris, for example, was re-elected Mayor of the city in 1747, "but not desiring to serve, absented himself from home, and after a vain attempt to find him . . . William Atwood was selected in his stead."[3] Perhaps only a Proper Philadelphia patriot such as the great volunteer soldier, John Cadwalader, would have twice refused Washington's personal offer of a permanent general's commission in the Continental Army. Similarly, down through the nineteenth century, others were to refuse appointments to some of the highest offices in the land. John G. Johnson, the leading corporation lawyer of his day, turned down two appointments to the Supreme Court of the United States.[4] Perhaps this is only another instance of the constitutional Quaker passion for privacy, general distrust of the public show, and even governmental irresponsibility.*

Not that there were no exceptions to this prevailing upper-class tradition. Proper Philadelphians in the eighteenth century did in fact follow politics and the sword, in addition to their merchant or legal careers, and many of them took a prominent, if not always a leading part in the Revolution and the founding of the new republic. Later, too, there were important exceptions. Charles Jared Ingersoll and Richard Rush, lifelong friends from their days at Princeton together, were leading statesmen during the early nineteenth century. Both came from aristocratic families with an already established record of public service. In fact, Richard Rush was unique in his day, in that both his father, Dr. Benjamin Rush, and his grandfather, Richard Stockton, were signers of the Declaration of Independence.

It is traditional in America that the gentlemen of means and position support the rights of those less privileged than themselves, often in opposition to the privileged class that bred them. Rush and Ingersoll were in this tradition. Born and bred in the heart of Federalist Philadelphia, both became staunch Jeffersonians and eventual supporters of Andrew Jackson. As far as their fashionable families and friends were concerned, they were often branded as radical nonconformists. And while Proper Philadelphians love eccentrics and "characters," and assiduously cultivate them wherever possible, they mistrust, and produce surprisingly few nonconformists or radicals in politics.

Charles Jared Ingersoll grew up during the final flowering of Federalist Philadelphia, amidst the lively and brilliant pro-English and pro-French arguments resounding through America's most cosmopolitan and sophisticated drawing rooms.[5] After three years at Princeton, where his exuberant participation in extracurricular activities and political debates distracted him from his studies, he came down to Philadelphia to read law and become a member of the bar at the tender age of twenty. First turning to literature, he published a poem in the *Portfolio* and wrote a tragedy which was successfully produced at Philadelphia's leading theatre. He then

---

* The Quaker tradition in Philadelphia, which in a sense institutionalized governmental irresponsibility, will be discussed in more detail in Chapters X and XI.

proceeded to write two bold and fearless tracts against the fawning Anglophilia which was infecting the country, and especially Proper Philadelphia. His *View of the Rights and Wrongs, Power and Policy, of the United States of America* and his more famous *Inchiquin, The Jesuit Letters,* both of which took an anti-Federalist and anti-British view of foreign relations and pleaded for "a declaration of literary, social, and moral independence" from Great Britain, were widely read in Europe and America.

On the eve of the War of 1812, Ingersoll was elected to the United States Congress as a Republican, where he immediately attained an influential position as chairman of the judiciary committee and a member of the Foreign Relations Committee. As the Republicans were losing prestige in Philadelphia due to reverses in the War, Ingersoll was defeated for re-election, and returned to the practice of law. Politics and government, however, still absorbed much of his time. In 1815 he was appointed United States District Attorney, a post he held for fifteen years, and, during the Bank controversy, he took a strong Jacksonian position against his fellow-Philadelphian and Princetonian, Nicholas Biddle.

After serving his first term in Congress, Ingersoll, whose income was only about $6,000 a year at the time, had decided to devote himself to law for the rest of his life. He then proceeded to build up an extremely lucrative law practice during the next twenty-five years. After attaining an ample, independent income, he took advantage of the floodtide of Jacksonian political fortunes, ran again for Congress in 1840, and won. He remained in Congress until 1849, when he retired at the age of sixty-seven in order to devote himself once more to writing. Before his death in 1862, he published a four-volume history of the War of 1812, as well as two volumes of *Recollections.* A biographer sums up the life of this unusual nonconformist Proper Philadelphian as follows: "He was a man of vital personality, outstanding ability as a lawyer, and fascinating gifts as an orator. His career is mainly interesting because of his courage and vigor in championing causes and groups which were unpopular *in his own social environment.*"[6]

Pennsylvania got its first coonskin governor when Simon Snyder, of upstate German immigrant stock, led the left wing of the Republican party to victory in 1808.[7] The "best people" in Philadelphia, including the aging Dr. Rush, were horrified at this dangerously radical element now in control of the state. On the other

hand, John Binns, fiery editor of the *Aurora,* Charles Jared Ingersoll, and Richard Rush, became fast friends and ardent supporters
of this surge of frontier democracy.

Richard Rush, Jeffersonian Republican and Jacksonian Democrat of impeccable Proper Philadelphia position, was more rigidly
brahmin in bearing and temperament than his friend, Charles
Jared Ingersoll. While Ingersoll won congressional seats after some
of the roughest political campaigns in the city, Rush's career "depended rather upon the patronage and confidence of others of
superior political position."[8] Rush secured his first important political position, for example, when Governor Snyder, who needed
Philadelphia support in his campaign for re-election in 1811,
appointed him Attorney General of the State.

Richard Rush spent the next twenty-five years in important
appointive positions in the service of his state and nation. He
served President Madison both as Comptroller of the Treasury and
Attorney General, and was appointed Secretary of State immediately after the inauguration of Monroe. His negotiation of the
Rush-Bagot treaty, limiting naval armaments in the Great Lakes,
was one of the earliest United States treaties of its kind. He next
served his friend Monroe as minister to Great Britain (1817-1825).
To John Quincy Adams, of course, has gone the major credit for
the Monroe Doctrine, but Rush, according to Dexter Perkins,
played an important role in the extensive preliminary negotiations;
the British were more sympathetic with his polished, friendly ways,
so different from the colder, more moralistic approach characteristic of the Adamses.[9] In recognition of his capabilities, Rush was
appointed Secretary of the Treasury after John Quincy Adams
became President in 1825. Finally, in 1828, he ran for the vice
presidency under Adams; both were defeated.

Rush temporarily withdrew from public service and spent the
next two years abroad, negotiating important European loans for
the Chesapeake and Ohio Canal Company. In 1832 he was back
into politics again as an active supporter of Andrew Jackson.
Although he held no formal position in the government, Rush's
small estate, "Syndham" outside Philadelphia, soon became a familiar rendezvous for leading members of the Democratic Party in
the city. He had been against the renewal of the Bank while serving in the Treasury. Now his active support of Jackson led him to
oppose Nicholas Biddle in the Bank controversy. At about this

time, President Jackson appointed him as agent of the United States in London to secure the Smithsonian bequest. James Smithson, the bastard son of the Duke of Northumberland and an eminent British scientist, left a small fortune to the United States for the purpose of creating an "establishment for the increase and diffusion of knowledge among men."[10] Rush, who spent almost two years in London overcoming legalistic delays and various claims against the Smithson estate, returned to America with the bequest which eventually led to the founding of the valuable Smithsonian Institute.

Richard Rush spent his last, and perhaps most interesting, years in government service as minister to France. Late in 1846, President Polk had nominated Charles Jared Ingersoll, an ardent Francophile, as minister to France but the Senate refused to confirm the appointment. Rush had fought for Ingersoll, and when Polk offered him the post he was reluctant to take it. Ingersoll, however, urged him to accept, and Rush sailed for France at a time when that nation was seething with discontent; Louis Philippe, at seventy-five, was already in the seventeenth year of his reign. Soon after Rush's arrival in Paris, on Sunday evening, February 20, 1848, he attended a great ball at the Tuileries where he found "the King, Queen, and Royal family feeling secure in fancied strength."[11] On Wednesday morning he woke to find himself in the midst of civil war, and by Friday the King had fled.

Rush was immediately faced with the problem of recognizing the new French Republic. Instructions from Washington in those days would have taken a month's time. It was a difficult decision, but Rush acted, "not instantly, but promptly."[12] On Monday America became the first nation to recognize the new republic when Rush met the representatives of the Provisional Government at the Hotel de Ville, and offered the congratulations of the American people to the new regime, mentioning the ancient friendship of the two nations and their mutual adventure in republicanism. He repeated Washington's hope that the "friendship of the two Republics might be commensurate with their existence."[13]

After the election of Louis Napoleon to the presidency, Rush's real interest in the mission ceased. Napoleon was as adept at stalling reform as the old king. Rush had seen a whole cycle of history in the past year: boredom under the king, brave republicanism in February, chaos in the spring, dictatorship in the summer, and an elected president by the end of the year. While certain liberal illusions may have been shattered, he could be satisfied with a job well done in representing his country.

Perhaps Richard Rush's most pleasant hours in France were spent with his friend, Alexis de Tocqueville. Quite naturally, these two republican aristocrats felt at home with each other as they spent many long hours discussing America and France, and all the various aspects of the new world aborning in their native lands. At their last meeting, just before Rush departed for America, they talked long and sorrowfully of the cycle of political events. Zachary Taylor's Whiggery had triumphed in America, along with Bonapartism in France, and Rush returned to "Syndham" never to serve his country again. One of Proper Philadelphia's leading contributions to the national political scene, he somehow never lived up to his potential. "A certain fastidiousness," writes one authority on American diplomatic history, "may have had something to do with the limited character of his political success, as compared with other men decidedly his inferiors in capacity."[14]

Although the Ingersoll and Rush families have proved more prolific and prominent down through the years, the Dallas family produced Proper Philadelphia's leading public servant: George Mifflin Dallas (George Mifflin Dallas, IV was listed in the latest Philadelphia *Social Register*) was the only Proper Philadelphian to become Vice-President of the United States. His father, Alexander James Dallas, a Scotsman educated at Edinburgh, had come to Philadelphia from Jamaica, shortly after the founding of the nation, and soon took his place among the leading members of the bar in the city.[15] In 1791, already a power in local politics, he was appointed Secretary of the Commonwealth of Pennsylvania by Governor Thomas Mifflin and two years later founded the first Democratic Society in the nation. He was now the leader of a small group who founded the Democratic-Republican party in the State and, after Jefferson was elected President in 1801, he was appointed United States District Attorney for eastern Pennsylvania, a post he held for thirteen years.

An intimate friend of Albert Gallatin, Madison's Secretary of the Treasury, Alexander James Dallas played an important part in arranging the $16,000,000 war loan which kept the government solvent during the War of 1812. Later, in 1813, he was appointed Secretary of the Treasury by Madison and brought the nation through another financial crisis. While Secretary, he laid plans for the creation of the Second Bank and, just before his retirement in 1816, made detailed recommendations for a protective tariff which were largely adopted and became the basis for our tariff system for the next three decades. Energetic, brilliant, with an infinite capacity for legalistic detail in presenting his position, both at the bar and in government, Alexander James Dallas was one of Proper Philadelphia's most distinguished gentlemen. The Dallas family, with a fine mansion on Fourth Street and a country house "Devon," on the banks of the Schuylkill, was firmly established among the city's gentry when its founder, Alexander James Dallas died in 1817.

Born the son of a distinguished Philadelphia lawyer and statesman, George Mifflin Dallas, according to Roy F. Nichols, "bore the indelible stamp of his social environment [which] took its tone in the early days of the republic from a prosperous group, shrewd in business, conservative in politics, and manifesting a genteel interest in culture and the refinements of life."[16]

After graduating from Princeton and becoming a member of the Pennsylvania bar, George Mifflin Dallas became secretary to his father's old friend, Albert Gallatin, on a mission to Russia. When the treaty of peace was signed with Great Britain at Ghent in 1814, young Dallas was sent home with the peace terms in his possession. After a short term as a clerk in the Treasury Department under his father, he returned to Philadelphia to practice law.

While building up his private law practice, Dallas remained active in politics, first as a Republican and then as a Democrat. He was elected Mayor of Philadelphia in 1828 and then was appointed to fill an unexpired term in the Senate of the United States, in 1831. Although a strong supporter of Andrew Jackson, he was also a close friend of the Second Bank, which made his two years in Washington rather difficult ones. He retired at the end of his term because "he could not afford it." In 1837, Van Buren appointed him minister to Russia but "after two years of social gayety, he was recalled at his own request."

Although George Mifflin Dallas was now a decided enemy of James Buchanan, the leader of Democratic politics in Pennsylvania, he returned to the national political scene in 1844, when he was elected Vice-President of the United States along with James Polk who had outdistanced Van Buren, Cass, and Buchanan. He presided over the Senate during the difficult period of the Mexican War (the city of Dallas, Texas, was named in his honor).

George Mifflin Dallas's last official post was that of Minister to Great Britain. Appointed by President Franklin Pierce, he was kept in London by President Buchanan during his entire term. "The Civil War closed his career as it did those of so many Democrats," writes Roy F. Nichols, an authority on this critical period before the Civil War. "He had hated abolition and secession both, as he hated all extremes, and though he condemned the South for seceeding, he voted the Democratic ticket throughout the war, the end of which he failed to see. He was a striking figure with his shock of prematurely white hair, his strong face, and his distinguished manners. Conservative and cosmopolitan, precise and dignified, he may well be characterized as the gentleman in politics."[17]

Richard Vaux and Morton McMichael were two of Philadelphia's leading nineteenth-century political and civic reformers. Both became mayor of the city, and both had direct descendants by the same name listed in the 1940 *Social Register*.

Morton McMichael was born in Bordentown, New Jersey, where his father had been employed on the estate of the expatriate Frenchman, Joseph Bonaparte.[18] He came to Philadelphia as a young man and was admitted to the bar in 1827, after which he entered upon a long and successful career in journalism. After important positions as editor of the *Saturday Evening Post* and the extremely successful *Godey's Lady's Book*, McMichael became the sole owner of the Philadelphia *North American*, the leading Whig journal in America. A brilliant speaker as well as an editor of wide national influence, McMichael was active in politics and municipal reform all his life. As Sheriff of Philadelphia, he was commended for his part in ending the anti-Catholic riots of 1844. He lent editorial support to the movement to consolidate the city in 1854, and then served a term as Mayor between 1866-1869. He was the first president of Philadelphia's beloved Fairmount Park Commission, one of the founders of the Union League (4th President), and was recognized by President Grant with an appointment as minister to Great Britain, which he declined.

While Morton McMichael was a self-made family founder, Richard Vaux was born to the Quaker aristocracy.[19] His father, Roberts Vaux, was a very successful merchant before his retirement in favor of a life of public service and philanthropy. Although Roberts Vaux was connected "with almost every worthy public and private social welfare activity" in Philadelphia, he is best known for his role in penal reform. "From 1790 to 1829," writes Harry E. Barnes, "Pennsylvania was elaborating and perfecting one of the two great systems of prison administration which dominated the penology of the civilized world during the nineteenth century—the separate [and solitary] confinement of prisoners."[20] Roberts Vaux was on the commission which planned the Eastern State Penitentiary, which became "the pivotal point linking American and European penology for more than a generation after 1830."[21]

Richard Vaux carried on the family tradition. As president for forty years, he dominated the board of inspectors of the Eastern State Penitentiary. Like his father before him, he was a strong advocate of the Quaker concept of solitary confinement.

A gifted orator and possessed of a strikingly handsome and forceful appearance, Richard Vaux naturally gravitated towards politics. Often referred to as the "Bourbon war horse," this giant of a man "with noble face, tawney locks, and flowing mane of the king of the forest," was elected mayor and reorganized the city's government after consolidation.[22] Although a staunch Democrat all his life, he was president of the conservative Philadelphia Club between 1888 and 1894.[23]

The majority of Proper Philadelphians have been Republicans (especially the newly arrived and fashionable families) ever since the founding of the Union League during the war between the states. The Democratic Party, on the other hand, has always had a patrician elite down through the years. Charles Jared Ingersoll, Richard Rush, the two Dallases, and Richard Vaux, Jeffersonian Republicans and Jacksonian Democrats, were but outstanding examples of a long patrician tradition. Similarly, Judge John Cadwalader, eventually became a staunch admirer of that old soldier, Andrew Jackson, and a strong Democrat at a time when many of his contemporaries went over to the Whig and then the Republican parties.[24] The Democratic tradition among many of Philadelphia's oldest families, moreover, has carried down to 1940. A few contemporary members of the Norris, Ingersoll, Morris, Bullitt, and Biddle families, for instance, were Democrats even during the days of the New Deal when Franklin D. Roosevelt was so busy "betraying his class." Among the Proper Philadelphians listed in *Who's Who* in 1940, George Washington Norris, a lawyer and investment banker, was a Democrat; R. Sturgis Ingersoll, lawyer, was a Pennsylvania Chairman of the Democratic Victory Fund Campaign in 1932; Roland S. Morris, direct descendant of Captain Samuel Morris of the City Troop, was a delegate to the Democratic National Conventions of 1904, 1908, 1912, and 1928, although he mentions nothing about his party activities after 1930 in his *Who's Who* biography; finally, of course, William C. Bullitt and Francis Biddle were well-known New Dealers and served in various important appointive positions under Roosevelt, while A. J. Drexel Biddle, Jr., debonair expatriate, was Roosevelt's trusted ambassador to numerous exiled governments in London during World War II (his nephew, Angier Biddle Duke became America's youngest Ambassador when he was sent to El Salvador by President Truman).[25]

Boies Penrose, solidly in the Republican tradition, was unquestionably Proper Philadelphia's most interesting and gifted politician in the late nineteenth and early twentieth centuries.[26] Descendant of Bartholomew Penrose, a prominent colonial shipbuilder, Penrose came of a long line of highly cultivated, and not always conforming Proper Philadelphians. After private tutoring and attendance at the Episcopal Academy, he graduated from Harvard *magna cum laude*. As a young member of the Philadelphia bar, he became interested in municipal reform, publishing an extremely scholarly book on the subject.[27] He soon abandoned his youthful reforming ideas, however, and began to cultivate the practical Republican politicians of his own district, the Eighth, and became in 1884 its representative in the lower house of the State Legislature. The Eighth District included the fashionable Rittenhouse Square area as well as more rundown parts of the city. Penrose beat his Democratic opponent, William C. Bullitt (father of Roosevelt's Ambassador to France in 1940), because of his ability to cultivate the hardly fashionable voters and ward leaders east of Broad Street (see Map 1, Chapter IX).

This first victory led Penrose to further political conquests. After ten years in the State Senate, with the support of Pennsylvania's notorious boss, Matthew Quay, Penrose defeated John Wanamaker for the United States Senate in 1897, and served until his death in 1921. Upon Quay's death in 1904, Penrose became the undisputed boss of the Republican Party in Pennsylvania. In the Senate, although mainly interested in high tariff rates, he was an active opponent of prohibition, women's suffrage, and progressive policies in general.

Boies Penrose, who stood 6 feet, 4 inches in his stocking feet and loved all sorts of sports, especially big-game hunting and fishing, would have certainly measured up to Ernest Hemingway's ideal of the gentleman. He was aloof, dignified, and completely at ease with both his patrician peers and his less polished political cronies of the city machine. Although possessed of a devastatingly frank and sardonic manner and a keenly analytic mind, he was no orator and refused to speak in public if he could possibly avoid it. A man of inherited wealth and position, he kept his word absolutely, and "cared only for power, and nothing for pelf."[28]

Three Proper Philadelphia Soldiers. In the course of the nineteenth century, the ancient ideal of the chivalrous gentleman soldier, duty-bound and driven by the quest for glory, was gradually replaced by the more acquisitive ideals of bank and *bourse.* At the end of the century, Brooks Adams and T. R. Roosevelt saw the final doom of our civilization in the triumph of the commercial ethic. The young Roosevelt constantly flayed men of means who made the "till their fatherland."

At least three Proper Philadelphians, George Gordon Meade, John Clifford Pemberton, and Montgomery Cunningham Meigs, represented the older gentlemanly tradition. They graduated within three years of each other at West Point. Pemberton and Meade were friends and comrades-in-arms during the Mexican War, and eventually became generals in opposing armies in the tragic War between the States.

John Clifford Pemberton, a very Proper Philadelphian, whose great-great-grandfather, Israel II, had died while exiled in Virginia, came of a long line of strong-willed Quakers.[29] After graduating from West Point in 1833, young Pemberton served in the Florida Indian War (1837-1839), the Canadian Border War (1840-1842), and all through the Mexican War where he was brevetted Captain for bravery. Upon his return home, the citizens of Philadelphia presented him with a handsome sword as a token of their esteem. Just before the Civil War, he served under General Albert Sidney Johnson in the operations against the Mormons in Utah.

In 1861 Pemberton resigned his commission in the United States Army and went down to Richmond where he obtained a colonelcy in the Provisional Army of Virginia (General Winfield Scott had personally offered him a colonelcy in the Federal Army). Although many Southerners suspected his loyalty (petitions were made to the Confederate Secretary of War for his removal), Pemberton was promoted to Major-General in 1862, and placed in command of South Carolina, Georgia, and Florida. A year later, as Lieutenant-General in charge of the defense of Vicksburg, he attempted to "hold it at all costs," under personal orders from Jefferson Davis. Finally, on July 4, 1863, his garrison reduced to "eating rats, cane shoots, and bark," he was forced to accept the unconditional surrender terms imposed by U. S. Grant. After the war, Pemberton retired to a farm in Virginia before moving to Philadelphia where he spent the rest of his life with his sisters and brothers in Proper Philadelphia's most exclusive rural-suburb of Penllyn (see Chapter IX).

George Gordon Meade, commander of the Army of the Potomac during the Battle of Gettysburg, was a member of one of Philadelphia's oldest Catholic families. Because of this religious variation from the prevailing Proper Philadelphia norm, Meade's background will be treated in some detail. His grandfather, George Meade, had come to Philadelphia from the Barbados (where his Irish father had been a sea captain), and become one of the colonial city's more successful merchants. He was an ardent Catholic, a power in building St. Mary's, the city's oldest Catholic edifice, and an original founder of both the Friendly Sons of St. Patrick and the Hibernian Society, two of the oldest Catholic organizations in America. After the Revolution, this colorful Irish merchant and patriot (he signed the Non-Importation Resolution in 1765, and later contributed heavily to the revolutionary cause) invested heavily in western lands, and, like Robert Morris, failed in the panic of 1796. He died in bankruptcy.[30]

George Meade's son, Richard Worsam Meade, established a mercantile firm in the West Indies at about the time of his father's failure. At the turn of the century, he returned to Philadelphia with a considerable fortune. Several years later, after marrying in Philadelphia, he took his family to Spain. For seventeen years, he was a successful merchant in Cadiz where he lived in the lap of luxury, moved in the highest social circles, and bought pictures and statuary which later "formed one of the early, private collections in America."[31] The Meade family fortunes again took a turn for the worse. After the Peninsular War during which Meade helped the Spanish government financially (he never was able to collect a large debt owed him by the Spanish after the Treaty of 1819), he brought his family back to the United States, where he died in relative poverty in Washington, D. C.

George Gordon Meade was born in Cadiz, and was sent to West Point by his mother because of the family's impecunious circumstances during his youth.[32] Of a scholarly turn of mind, Meade looked down on a West Point education and resigned soon after graduation. He went to work as an engineer for several railroads, but returned to the regular army after his marriage in 1842 (he had to accept a lieutenancy, although most of his class were already captains). He fought all through the Mexican campaign and was brevetted at the Battle of Monterey "for performing a daring reconnaissance." His letters to his wife during the war, frequently mentioned his friend, John Clifford Pemberton.[33]

When the Civil War broke out, Governor Curtin of Pennsylvania had Meade appointed a Brigadier-General in the Pennsylvania volunteers in 1861. He was in charge of three brigades which saw action at Manassas, under General McDowell, and in the Peninsula campaign under General McClellan. In June of 1862, he was promoted to the rank of Major in the regular army and took part in the battles of Mechanicsville, Gaines's Mill, and Glendale, where he was wounded several times. A ball went above his hip, pierced his liver, and passed out near his spine. Another ball simultaneously went through his arm. Meade stuck to his horse, however, and directed his men until forced to quit the field because of loss of blood. He never was wounded in battle again, although his hat was riddled with balls while several mounts were shot out from under him.

After returning from the hospital, Meade took part in the second battle of Bull Run, the South Mountain campaign, and then was placed in command of the 1st Corps at Antietam, after General Hooker had been carried from the field. After the Fredericksburg disaster in November of 1862, he was placed in command of "V" Corps which he led through the battle of Chancellorsville. While leading the corps northward paralleling Lee, on June 28, 1863 Meade received a personal letter from President Lincoln, placing him in command of the Army of the Potomac just five days before the battle of Gettysburg. As he had been given this important command just a few days before this most decisive battle, it is no wonder Meade was roundly criticized by the somewhat hysterical Philadelphia press for his so-called faltering blunders in the early stages of the battle which finally turned back the high tide of the Confederacy.

Upon his retirement from the army at the conclusion of the war, Meade returned to Philadelphia where he devoted the rest of his life to the beautification of his native city. His energy and devotion as Commissioner of the Fairmount Park Art Association, have placed all Philadelphians in his debt. After his death, the Art Association, under the presidency of A. J. Drexel, erected a large equestrian statue in his memory.[34] Just before World War I, the State of Pennsylvania unveiled the Meade Memorial in Washington, located on the Mall in front of the Capitol, just south of the Grant Memorial.[35]

Although less spectacular than Meade and Pemberton, William Cunningham Meigs played an equally important role in the Civil War. Son of Dr. Charles DeLucena Meigs, the founder of the family in Philadelphia, he was born in Augusta, Georgia, where his father was living at the time (his grandfather had been President of the University of Georgia). After attending the University of Pennsylvania, he went on to West Point where he graduated fifth in his class in 1836 (Pemberton-1833; Meade-1835). An engineer of considerable brilliance, Meigs was placed in charge of the construction of the wings and dome of the Capitol Building and the project to enlarge the United States Post Office Building during the decade prior to the Civil War. In 1861 he was appointed a Brigadier-General and eventually became Quartermaster General of the Union Army. In addition to his important duties in Washington, he was in command of Grant's supplies at Fredericksburg and personally supervised the refitting and supplying of Sherman's army at Savannah. Meigs was brevetted Major-General in 1864. After the war, William H. Seward wrote that "without the services of this eminent soldier the national cause must have been lost or deeply imperiled," and James G. Blaine at the same time described General Meigs as "one of the ablest graduates of the Military Academy."[36]

Since the days of John Clifford Pemberton, George Gordon

Meade, and Montgomery Cunningham Meigs, few Proper Philadelphians have followed professional military careers. These few
careers have usually been in the Navy. General Meade's nephew,
Richard Worsam Meade, for example, was a dashingly handsome
naval officer. After graduating from Annapolis in his teens, Commander Meade had an eventful naval career, which included the
sporting command of the *America,* in the second America's Cup
Races, and a long Pacific cruise during which he concluded the first
American treaty with Samoa. It is of interest, finally, that the
latest John Cadwalader, who left the faculty of the University of
Pennsylvania to join the Navy in World War II, is now a regular
naval officer with the Admiral Byrd expedition to Antarctica.
Perhaps money-making just does not appeal to some families,
even in mid-twentieth-century America.

Proper Philadelphia Lawyers and Physicians. The charge of
subservience to middle-class money values has often been leveled
at Proper Philadelphians. Even Benjamin Franklin, the city's all-
time First Citizen, has often been dismissed, especially by Europeans such as D. H. Lawrence and Max Weber, as America's
"first bourgeois."[37] Nevertheless, since the days when the sons of
the city's colonial gentry were sent abroad to London's Inner
Temple, or to study medicine under the great physicians in
Edinburgh or Paris, Philadelphia has had a brilliant professional
elite.

Ever since Andrew Hamilton made the term "Philadelphia
lawyer" a national by-word because of his ability in defending
Peter Zenger in America's first, celebrated civil liberties trial, Philadelphia has been known for its gentlemen lawyers. Even a brief
discussion of each of the many Proper Philadelphian members of
the bar down through the years would be a tedious process and
would not add to our understanding of the city's upper-class
structure. It is enough to record that this gentlemanly legal tradition has been passed down since the nation's founding through
such men as Joseph Reed, Jared Ingersoll, Horace Binney, John
Cadwalader, William and Henry Rawle, Eli K. Price, George Shars-
wood, Richard Vaux, Theodore Cuyler, Thomas McKean, Craig
and George W. Biddle, and John G. Johnson, to such leading members of the contemporary bar as George Wharton Pepper, Thomas
S. Gates, R. Sturgis Ingersoll, Henry Drinker, Edward Hopkinson,
Jr., and United States Attorney General Francis Biddle, all of the

1940 elite. In short, it can be said that most of Philadelphia's First
Families (eighteenth and early nineteenth centuries), in striking
contrast to those founded in the late nineteenth and early twentieth
centuries, have produced leading members of the bar in each generation.

While many Proper Philadelphians have established prominent
reputations at the national as well as at the local bar, none has
risen to the United States Supreme Court, the highest honor in
judicial public service (Justice Owen Roberts, although listed in
both the *Social Register* and *Who's Who* and one of the city's most
distinguished citizens in 1940, was *not* one of the fashionable
Roberts clan). Undoubtedly, there are several reasons for this traditional failure to attain high public honor. The apparent absence
of any strong "itch for public office" is, of course, an important
factor. More basic, however, and perhaps a more important clue
to the Proper Philadelphian's values and traditions, may well be
the disinclination for sustained abstract reasoning. Learned in the
law and the practice thereof, the gentlemen lawyers of Philadelphia do not betray that love of abstract reasoning so characteristic,
for example, of men like Holmes or Brandeis of the Boston-Harvard
tradition. Abstract principles, rather than legal precedent alone,
guide the highest court of judicial review in a dynamic democracy.
In his highly perceptive criticism of the eighteenth century lawyers
in the middle colonies, Vernon Louis Parrington perhaps has provided a clue to a Proper Philadelphia cultural attitude which per-
sists to the present day: "The lawyers of the middle colonies,"
wrote Parrington, "were far better trained than those of New
England. Many were from the Inns of Court, where they had
steeped themselves in the Common Law and had imbibed profound respect for the orderly processes of English legal procedure.
They found intellectual satisfaction in tracing the evolution of constitutional practice and their methods of thought were too strictly
legal to suffer them to stray into the domain of extra-legal political
speculation. Their appeal was to law and the constitution; *never
to abstract principles.*"[38] George Wharton Pepper, dean of the
Philadelphia bar, learned in the law, and possessed of a prodigious
memory, remarks in his autobiography, *Philadelphia Lawyer*, that
he had to "struggle to˜develop a greater capacity for abstract
thought."[39]

The Proper Philadelphian's traditional avoidance of abstractions has been mentioned here at some length. Far from being characteristic of its lawyers alone, it must also be seen as a clue to values and attitudes of the upper class as a whole.

Although the Philadelphia Lawyer may justly deserve his national reputation, and while lawyers have been celebrated by historians as the most liberalizing influence in American culture, Philadelphia physicians have from colonial times made great cultural, humanitarian, and social contributions to their contemporary world in addition to their undoubted professional excellence. In the eighteenth century, Philadelphia was the medical center of the colonies. Educated in England, Scotland, and France, its doctors "constituted the most highly educated group in the city."[40] When John Morgan returned to Philadelphia after a European education to found in 1765 the Medical School at the University of Pennsylvania, he was, next to Franklin, the city's best educated gentleman. Moreover, the original staff at the Medical School was a remarkable group: all were born in the decade between 1735 and 1745; all were Bachelors of Arts; all were trained abroad with an M.D. from Edinburgh; all were men of wide culture, and all were successful in private practice.

John Kearsley, the founder of the medical profession in Philadelphia, came to the city in 1711 after a thoroughly liberal education in England. Ardent Anglican though he was, he soon matched the Quakers in the competition for patients, and became one of the town's civic, cultural, and artistic leaders. Carl and Jessica Bridenbaugh describe this man who set the tone for the future of Philadelphia medicine as follows:

With typical eighteenth-century virtuosity Kearsley was not only a doctor but scientist, artist, and politician as well. A vestryman of Christ Church, he was the principal architect of its lovely edifice, and years later shared with Robert Smith in drawing up the plans for St. Peter's, while his long service as Assemblyman naturally secured him a place on the committee to superintend the erection of the State House. During his leisure the Doctor made notes on his observations of comets and eclipses, which by the good offices of his friend Collinson of London were published in the *Philosophical Transactions* of the Royal Society.[41]

Over a century after Dr. Kearsley's time, Sir William Osler once described the Philadelphia medical tradition to the British Medical Association in the following glowing terms: "Morgan, Shippen, Redman, Rush, Coxe, the elder Wood, the elder Pepper, and the elder Mitchell [S. Weir Mitchell's father] of Philadelphia—Brahmins all, in the language of the greatest Brahmin among them, Oliver Wendell Holmes—these and men like them have been the leaven which has raised our profession above the dead level of a business."[42]

The first Benjamin Rush, Dr. Thomas Cadwalader, Dr. Charles Dc Lucena Meigs and, indeed, S. Weir Mitchell (see below), were first family founders. On the whole, however, most families have been founded by moneymakers, and it is the third and fourth generations which have distinguished themselves in medicine. Although their ancestors first made money as merchants and businessmen, the Norris, Wood, and Pepper families, for instance, have been leaders in Philadelphia medicine for over one hundred years. During that time the Pepper family has been a veritable dynasty at the Medical School of the University of Pennsylvania.

Publishing. Freedom of the press, sometimes an overworked slogan in modern America, is, of course, one of the most important guardians of political and intellectual freedom in any society. In Philadelphia, "nearly everybody" reads the *Bulletin.*[43] Today one of the five or ten best newspapers in the nation, and the largest and wealthiest of the afternoon papers, the *Bulletin* was founded in 1847 under the style of "Cummings Telegraphic Bulletin." William Lippard McLean came to Philadelphia from Pittsburgh and purchased the paper in 1895.[44] It was then one of twelve newspapers in the city. In his first year as publisher, circulation rose from 6,317 to 33,625, passed 100,000 in 1898, and reached 200,000 by 1905. William Lippard McLean died in 1931, and the paper has been managed by his sons ever since. Robert McLean ("The Major"), handsome Princetonian, member of the City Troop during World War I, and President of the Associated Press since 1938, carries on the family tradition as president of the *Bulletin;* his brother William held the office of Treasurer until his recent death.

Curtis Publishing Company and J. B. Lippincott Company are probably the best-known Philadelphia publishing houses today. Although Cyrus Hermann Kotzschmar Curtis (1850-1933) came to Philadelphia in 1876 and proceeded to build up one of America's most successful publishing enterprises—*Ladies' Home Journal, Saturday Evening Post,* and *The Country Gentleman*—he did not found a fashionable family line.[45] His only child, who married Edward Bok, however, was listed in the 1940 *Who's Who* as a philanthropist and civic leader, while his grandson, W. Curtis Bok, was one of the city's prominent jurists.

Joshua B. Lippincott founded the family publishing house in 1836.[46] Beginning with a staple line of Bibles, prayer books, and other religious works, the firm eventually introduced such nineteenth-century standbys as *Lippincott's Pronouncing Gazetteer* (1855); *Lippincott's Magazine* (1868); and the *Medical Times* (1870). J. B. Lippincott left four children and an estate of several million dollars when he died in 1886. His grandson, Joseph Wharton Lippincott, was president of the family firm in 1940.

The Leas, descendants of Mathew Carey, carried on the tradition of Philadelphia's great publisher, pamphleteer, and amateur political economist. Isaac Lea married Carey's daughter in 1823 and joined his father-in-law's firm which has remained in the Lea family down to the present day.[47] After his retirement in 1851, Lea's intellectual and scientific interests led him to the presidency of both the American Academy of Natural Sciences (1858-1863), and the American Association for the Advancement of Science (1860), and the vice-presidency of the American Philosophical Society.

Isaac Lea's son, Henry Charles Lea, was Proper Philadelphia's most profound scholar, ardent reformer, and an extremely successful publisher.[48] At the same time that he was building up the family publishing firm, he was actively engaged in various municipal reform movements. Henry Charles Lea first showed his sympathy for the underdog by actually shouldering a gun in defense of a Catholic church during the riots of 1844. One of the early members of the Union League, he eventually resigned when that bastion of conservatism refused to throw its weight on the side of municipal reform. He organized the Municipal Reform Association in 1870, the Committee of 100 (a leading reform group in the city today) in 1880, and was president of the Reform Club for many years.

Henry Charles Lea retired from business with a considerable fortune in 1880 and devoted the rest of his life to philanthropy and the writing of history. Sparing no expense, he sent agents exploring throughout the libraries of Europe in search of data. His *History of the Inquisition of the Middle Ages,* published in 1888, established his reputation as one of America's greatest historians, and it has remained the definitive work on the subject to this day. Recognized by such great historians as Lords Bryce and Acton, Lea worked steadily for the two years before his death in 1909, completing four volumes on the *History of the Inquisition of Spain.* Although the Lea family has gradually settled down into a solidly Proper Philadelphia pattern, Isaac and Henry Charles Lea, especially the latter, were in the intellectual and reforming tradition so characteristic of Proper Boston's best. Perhaps their Carey-Catholic background in a Quaker-turned-Episcopal Proper Philadelphia contributed to the Lea's intellectual vigor and social nonconformity.

Letters and Literature. Throughout most of the nineteenth and twentieth centuries, literary and intellectual Philadelphia remained in the shadow first of Boston, Salem, and Concord, and then of New York, which became the literary magnetic pole in America after William Dean Howells moved there from Boston in 1891.[49]

Philadelphia had been the cultural capital of the colonies during the eighteenth century. In his day, James Logan, a classicist schooled in Latin, Greek, and Hebrew, possessed perhaps the finest library in America. His young friend, and, in many ways his protegé, Benjamin Franklin, was, according to no less an authority than David Hume, "the first writer in America to obtain an international reputation and to be honored in France beyond Voltaire, Rousseau, and Turgot."[50] Franklin's *Autobiography* was the first book by an American to take its place among the classics in the English language.

As the second half of the eighteenth century began, William Smith surrounded himself with talented young scions of Philadelphia's best families: the net result was America's first consciously artistic circle.[51] After Franklin's death in 1790, the city became the center of polemical prose during the battle between the pro-British and aristocratic Federalists, and their Republican, pro-French, and more democratic opponents. Libel suits, even duels, were not unheard of as William Cobbett ("Peter Porcupine") aggressively argued the Federalist position against such Jeffersonian liberals as Mathew Carey, Phillip Freneau, and William Duane, whose *Aurora* became the leading Republican organ during the first two decades of the new century (Phillip Hamilton, like his famous father, who was a boyhood friend in Philadelphia of Charles Jared Ingersoll and part of the *Aurora* group, was killed in a duel).[52]

Mathew Carey founded the *American Museum,* the best of all the magazines during the 1790's. Born in Dublin, Carey eventually ran away to France where he worked in Benjamin Franklin's printing shop at Passy before entering the United States disguised as a woman. He soon became the leading American publisher and did more than anyone else to make Philadelphia the literary center of the new nation.

At the century's turn, Philadelphia produced America's first novelist, and first highbrow literary weekly. Charles Brockden Brown, whose hastily written Gothic tales were admired by Shelley, Scott, Keats, Cooper, and Poe, published his first successful novel *Weiland* in 1798.[53] Two years later, Joseph Dennie, a transplanted Bostonian and Harvard man, began publishing the *Portfolio,* devoted to "moral instruction and polite literature." Dennie ("Oliver Oldschool, Esq.") and a small group of his followers and contributors—including young Richard Rush, Charles Jared Ingersoll, Charles Brockden Brown, and Joseph Hopkinson—represented the literary after-glow of a dying federalism. Nicholas Biddle, aristocratic young Federalist, was the editor for a short period after Dennie's death in 1812.[54]

While most of the writers in Dennie's group were young dilettantes, Robert Walsh, son of the Irish peer Baron Shannon, founded America's first serious quarterly, the *American Review of History and Politics, and General Repository of Literature and State Papers,* in 1811 (four years before Dana founded the *North American Review*).[55] With the exception of the serious work done by this elegant and brilliant Irishman (he later edited the *American Quarterly Review*) Philadelphia's leadership in American letters began to wane after the War of 1812. As an author writing in the *American Quarterly* put it at the time: "the hiss of a locomotive is sweeter music than the happiest stanza. . . ."[56]

After the leadership of serious literature passed to New England, Philadelphia became a center of the new democratic journalism symbolized in the *Saturday Evening Post* and *Godey's Lady's Book.*[57] The modern *Post,* the survivor of Franklin's *Pennsylvania Gazette,* was put together in 1821 by Thomas Cottrell Clarke. Louis A. Godey, a self-educated New Yorker, came down to Philadelphia and founded the *Lady's Book* in the 1830's. It soon became an American institution, reaching its greatest popularity between 1840 and 1850, when this Barnum of American publishers had such men as Poe, Irving, Hawthorne, and the elder Holmes among his contributors.

At about this time, George Lippard, no genteel Philadelphian, became somewhat of a literary sensation. His tales of vice, horror, and political corruption, written in a flowing scarlet prose, reached their peak in his *Quaker City*, published in 1844.[58] The book was an immediate sensation, went through twenty-seven editions in five years, was published in London and translated into German, and was still being read twenty-five years later.

In striking contrast to the work of George Lippard, the city's literary tradition was taken over by genteel Anglophiles after the Civil War when S. Weir Mitchell—physician, psychiatrist, author, and conversationalist par excellence—became the First Citizen of Philadelphia as no one had been since Benjamin Franklin and Benjamin Rush.[59]

This brief outline of Philadelphia's literary history during its first two hundred years has been undertaken here for two reasons. First, it emphasizes the contrast between the money-making elite and the world of letters. Most of the business and banking leaders of this period discussed in earlier pages were family founders who quickly became assimilated into fashionable Proper Philadelphia society; this was not the case with the intellectuals. In social origin, however, the intellectual elite were also quite different. The first-rate men such as Mathew Carey and Robert Walsh, were Irish and Catholic. Perhaps even Agnes Repplier's Catholic background kept her somewhat apart from Proper Philadelphia's best. With the exception of the Bories who were French Catholics, the talented portrait painter and banker, Francis Drexel, who was Austrian Catholic, and the Irish Catholic Matthew Baird, (Baldwin's partner who was never really accepted by Proper Philadelphia anyway), all the Proper Philadelphia business leaders listed in Table 9 were Protestants. Second, one soon becomes aware of the fact that the few Proper Philadelphians who did contribute to this literary tradition invariably tended to be dilettantes and perhaps with the exception of Henry Charles Lea, whom James Bryce called "one of the three great scholars in the world," few produced work of lasting value.

Francis Hopkinson, S. Weir Mitchell, and Owen Wister were excellent representatives of the Proper Philadelphia literary tradition. All three were well-rounded and gifted men with a talent for friendship and worldly success; few, if any, of their literary accomplishments have proved to be of permanent importance. A brief discussion of their careers provides considerable insight into the Proper Philadelphia mind.

Francis Hopkinson—poet, portrait painter, essayist, musician, lawyer, patron of the arts, and patriot—came of aristocratic and wealthy stock.[60] His father, Thomas Hopkinson, an Englishman educated at Oxford, came to Philadelphia in the 1730's, became a prominent judge and provincial councillor, and was a founder and the first president of the American Philosophical Society. Francis Hopkinson was the first graduate of the College of Philadelphia, of which his father was a trustee. Often called Philadelphia's first dilettante, he was the most talented member of Provost William Smith's "Society of Gentlemen"—America's first literary circle.[61] "Witty and vastly popular not only among his own clique of wealthy Anglicans but with all groups in the city," Hopkinson produced some forty poems during his first decade out of college.[62] In 1765 he went abroad for an extended visit. As a kinsman of the Bishop of Worcester, he immediately began to move in the best English society and made the acquaintance of eminent men of all sorts, including the great Lord North. Upon returning to Philadelphia, he turned away from poetry in favor of the satirical essay, which proved to be a happy medium as the Revolution approached. In *A Pretty Story,* a political allegory which went through three editions in 1774, Hopkinson turned his cultivated and agile wit upon the pressing and serious problem of the day.[63] Alone among William Smith's circle of Anglican loyalists, he chose the side of Revolution and signed the Declaration of Independence. Thus this "genteel, well-bred, and very social" Philadelphian, as John Adams once remarked of Hopkinson, deliberately risked a life of ease and social position in favor of rebellion.[64] In addition to his witty political polemics in favor of the cause, he also designed the American flag. A biographer sums up his career as follows: "Though he was not prominent in any one field the bulk of his attainment is sufficient to make his place in American history secure."[65]

During the last decades of the nineteenth century, with men like Henry Charles Lea, S. Weir Mitchell, Horace Howard Furness, Owen Wister, and the artist Thomas Eakins, and women like Agnes Repplier, Mary Cassatt, and Agnes Irwin, Philadelphia went through its most recent renaissance. Especially after Henry Charles Lea's publication of the *History of the Inquisition* in 1888, Mitchell, Lea, and Furness brought a distinction to Philadelphia comparable to Lowell's and Holmes' in Boston. Certainly S. Weir Mitchell's autobiographical novels, *Characteristics* and its sequel *Dr. North and His Friends,* remind one of *The Autocrat of the Breakfast Table.*[66] Perhaps as a reaction to the crude industrial jungle which produced their wealth, the ladies and gentlemen in the Victorian drawing rooms oozed gentility. The earthy poetry of the unwashed Whitman or the fiercely realistic paintings of Thomas Eakins were strictly taboo.[67] Proper Philadelphia's two passions at the time were family history and the pleasures of the table. S. Weir Mitchell celebrated this latter passion in *A Madeira Party,* the tedious tale of a group of Proper Philadelphians eating terrapin and endlessly discussing the detailed history and merits of the wine they were drinking.[68]

Philadelphia's Victorian gentry on Rittenhouse Square were convinced that S. Weir Mitchell was the most versatile American since Franklin and probably a genius, too.[69] Certainly his accomplishments were many: his *Gunshot Wounds and Other Injuries to the Nerves,* published in 1864, was still used in France during the First World War I; his work on hysteria impressed Sigmund Freud as did his "rest cure" therapy which became famous in both Europe and America; and *Hugh Wynne* was favorably compared to *Henry Esmond.* In addition to publishing hundreds of medical papers, several volumes of verse, numerous short stories, two popular books on medicine, and a dozen novels, his medical practice brought him as much as $70,000 in one year. His wide circle of friends ranged from Oliver Wendell Holmes, Phillips Brooks, and William James, to Andrew Carnegie. He was constantly in demand as a speaker and sat on the boards of numerous trust companies, charitable institutions, and learned societies. His "Saturday evenings after nine" were famous for excellent food, wine, and conversation. Above all, S. Weir Mitchell was a very Proper Philadelphian: he lived on Walnut Street, belonged to the most exclusive clubs, went to Mount Desert every summer and after his first wife's death, married a Cadwalader.

Unfortunately, history has been less impressed with Mitchell's accomplishments than were his contemporaries. The following attempt of his most recent biographer to describe Mitchell's failure-in-success provides considerable insight into the Proper Philadelphia mind:

What then keeps Mitchell from being first rate? Certainly he was more adult than Winston Churchill, Owen Wister, Marion Crawford, or F. Hopkinson Smith. He has more grace than William Dean Howells, a deeper understanding of psychology. . . . In probing into the by-paths of psychology, the only contemporary who did as much was Henry James.

Part of the answer is Philadelphia. Mitchell never threw off its reticences, its social mores, its emphasis on class and family. He could help to support Walt Whitman, but he could never forget that Walt was not a gentleman. He was a friend of Carnegie's and he put Xerxes Crofter, the malefactor of great wealth, into his books, yet he has no conception of the America of *The Pit* and *The Octopus*. His people are the absentee owners of coal lands, the Philadelphia aristocracy of bankers and lawyers for inherited estates. In their unchallenged position they could afford generous charities, fine distinctions of business honor, and a discriminating taste in Madeira. They had not become the timid George Apleys and H. M. Pulhams of a later day.

His social order is paternalistic; it revolves around the dinner tables of the wealthy. Even the American Revolution becomes an affair of Philadelphia drawing rooms.

He was a regular churchgoer: St. Stephen's usually, but Christ Church on Easter. His friend Talcott Williams could say: "The winds of criticism and doubts of the day passed him by; he retained through all his life that simple and sincere faith he had early known and seen. . . ." It is one thing to win faith through doubt; it is often a sign of limitation to be untouched by doubt. Few intellectual leaders have achieved greatness without first seeing through the shams and stupidities of their times. Mitchell was a great man in his era; he did not transcend it.[70]

Owen Wister was Philadelphia's last distinguished gentleman of letters. Although a distant ancestor, Sally Wister, who is remembered because of her unique diaries full of chatty descriptions of Philadelphia at the end of the eighteenth century, is the only member of the family listed in the "DAB," the large Wister clan has populated Proper Philadelphia and its suburbs ever since the eighteenth century (Dr. Caspar Wistar [ar], of the famous "Wistar Parties," represented a different branch of the family). In addition to his fashionable Philadelphia ancestry, Owen Wister was, of course, proud of his grandmother, Fanny Kemble, an actress and herself an author, and of an artistic and creative family.[71]

After graduating from Harvard, where he had been an intimate friend and clubmate of Theodore Roosevelt, Wister spent several years abroad cultivating his first love, music. Forced to return to America because of poor health, he eventually settled down as a Philadelphia lawyer. One day in the 1880's, he went to his kinsman, S. Weir Mitchell, for a medical checkup. After carefully examining his patient, the eminent physician prescribed a rest cure in the West, and also suggested that his patient take a notebook along on the trip.

Perhaps the creative artist suffers from more than the ordinary amount of nostalgia. At any rate, many of the greatest characters in fiction have been created by authors who had witnessed the last stages of declining cultural epochs. Owen Wister and his friend Roosevelt (who bought two ranches in the Dakota badlands in 1883) both went West for their health at a time when America's romantic cowboy culture had largely lost out to the more stable family homestead.[72] Thus Wister's novel, *The Virginian,* was an attempt to portray a dying cultural type in the manner of Melville's whaling captains or Cooper's backwoodsmen.

Wister filled his notebooks with the local color of a dying West. Although his writing had been previously limited to essays on Beethoven for the *Atlantic Monthly,* he produced several novels upon his return to Philadelphia. His name will always be associated with *The Virginian*—"when you call me that, smile"—the tale of a gentleman-cowboy hero who went West from Virginia, bested the villain, and finally won the heart of a gentle schoolteacher from Vermont.[73] The book was a best-seller in 1902, sold over 1,500,000 copies, was widely produced on the stage, and resulted in two moving pictures. His other successful books included a popular biography of Theodore Roosevelt and *Lady Baltimore,* which made the best-seller lists in 1907.

Owen Wister was at the height of his creative powers at the time when S. Weir Mitchell was the patriarchal dean of Philadelphia letters. While Mitchell, who died in 1914, warmed his hands before fires burning in the many secure Victorian drawing rooms around Rittenhouse Square, Owen Wister unfortunately lived on into the crass and roaring twenties and the reforming New Deal thirties. A gentleman of the old school who abhorred the business civilization which surrounded him almost as much as he despised those who tried to reform it, he became an implacable enemy of both Wilson and the second Roosevelt. While his literary style was "tender and expressive," his polemical essays on current social and political issues became increasingly biting and bitter.

Of an ancient and talented pedigree, Wister was certainly appreciated by his Proper Philadelphia peers; they honored him with the presidency of their hallowed Philadelphia Club at its hundreth anniversary in 1934. This did not prevent him from making the following criticism of his home-town world when he wrote: "When in Boston any fellow-citizen paints a picture or writes a book, he is approached and fostered for Boston's sake and in Boston's name. We of Philadelphia steer quite wide of this amiable if hasty encouragement. We seem to distrust our own power to do anything out of the common; and when a young man tries to, our minds close against him with a civic instinct of disparagement. A Boston failure in art surprises Boston; it is success that surprises Philadelphia."[74]

Although she remained staunchly outside any Proper Philadelphia sociological catagories, Agnes Repplier, listed in both the *Social Register* and *Who's Who* in 1940, was certainly Philadelphia's most distinguished essayist. Discovered by Boston rather than her native city, she built up a secure reputation in the genteel tradition of letters. Anglophile, Catholic, strong-willed, and with an analytical mind superior to those of most males, she was, however, never impressed with feminism and other modern democratic dogmas. Her father had founded a modest family fortune (in 1865 he was one of the "Rich Men of Philadelphia" listed in the little pamphlet referred to in Table 9). Convent educated, Agnes Repplier remained a Roman Catholic, although for many years she was an intimate friend of the Irwin sisters who founded Proper Philadelphia's most fashionable girls' school. Always an individualist, she was living in an old Victorian house on a side street below Broad Street in 1940.[75]

CHAPTER VIII

The Old Family Core
of the 1940 Elite

> We all agree that he is a good member of society
> who works his way up from poverty to wealth, but
> as soon as he has worked his way up we begin to
> regard him with suspicion, as a dangerous member
> of society.
>
> WILLIAM GRAHAM SUMNER

SOCIAL MOBILITY, INDIVIDUALISM, and the attending decline in traditional family values are characteristic of modern metropolitan society where there are few fixed landmarks and where "every man is constantly spurred on by the desire to rise and the fear of falling."[1] But a traditional upper class composed of families with long established roots in the local community serves to balance the atomization of modern life, especially at the level of leadership. We have shown earlier, how the contemporary upper class in Philadelphia is composed of a group of families whose ancestors played a leading part in the economic, political, and social development of the city. The present chapter will show how those listed in the 1940 *Social Register* are less mobile and more familistic than the rest of those in *Who's Who*, before providing a more detailed analysis of the sociological characteristics of the "old family" core of the contemporary elite.

Some Demographic Characteristics of the Philadelphia Elite. *Who's Who* is an objective listing of the leading men and women in contemporary American life. The 770 listed members of the 1940 Philadelphia elite were drawn from a wide variety of cultural, class, ethnic, and even racial backgrounds. Although only two individuals were Negroes, no less than than 10 per cent were foreign born. No Negroes were listed in the *Social Register* and the few foreign-born members of the upper class were either born in Canada or in Europe where their families were traveling during the summer months. As one would expect, these prominent Philadelphians were older men and women; all were over thirty-six years of age and the majority were over sixty (Table 11).

Table 11—Philadelphians in Who's Who in 1940—Age as Related to Social Class

	SOCIAL		CLASS				
	Social Register		Non Social Register		Who's Who Total		Proportion in the Social Register by Age
Age by Decades	No.	%	No.	%	No.	%	
30-39	0	(—)	15	(3)*	15	(2)*	—
40-49	18	(8)	90	(17)	108	(14)	17
50-59	53	(22)	122	(22)	175	(23)	30
60-69	78	(35)	173	(32)	251	(33)	31
70-79	51	(23)	91	(17)	142	(18)	36
80 & over	14	(6)	14	(2)	28	(4)	50
No information	12	(5)	39	(7)	51	(6)	24
Total	226	(100)	544	(100)	770	(100)	29

* All Philadelphians in Who's Who were over 36 in 1940.

Successful Philadelphians are apparently more horizontally mobile than the rest of the city's population. Almost two-thirds of the elite were born outside the metropolitan area. One of the weakest aspects of many socio-anthropological studies of small American communities, particularly those done by the "Warner School," is the fact that they fail to make explicit that horizontal and vertical mobility are usually rather closely associated variables.[2] Especially in a small town, for example, one rarely crosses the tracks within the same community for the very reason that everyone knows "who" one is. On the contrary, one must move out, and usually to the large and anonymous city, in order to ascend successfully. Talented persons from small-town America have always found "bridges" across the tracks in the Greenwich Villages, the Broadways, and even the Wall Streets of our great cities.[3]

Philadelphia, of course, attracts ambitious men and women from small towns all over America, even though the members of the upper class are more likely to reflect the ties of place, family, and local tradition. Thus over half of the Philadelphians listed in both *Who's Who* and the *Social Register* were born in the city, as against less than one-third of the rest of the elite (Table 12).

The members of the Philadelphia upper class were not only less mobile than the rest of the elite; their movement was largely within an inter-city, predominantly eastern seaboard upper class; thus, geographical movement may very well not mean sociological mobility at all. A Proper Bostonian banker who moves to Philadelphia, has not been sociologically mobile in the same sense as an Iowa farmer's son who becomes one of Philadelphia's leading editors. Thus most of the members of the upper class were born in large cities and 64 per cent were born in one of the twelve *Social Register* cities. The rest of the elite, however, were more likely to have been born in small cities or rural areas.

The members of the upper class tend to have larger families than the rest of the Philadelphia elite. Of the 501 males listed in *Who's Who,* who reported the names of their children, for instance, those parents also listed in the *Social Register* report an average of 2.8 children, as against an average of 2.62 children reported by the rest. Finally, within each social class, the mobile parents have smaller families than the parents born in Philadelphia (Table 13). These differences are small but consistent.[4]

Due to a bias towards the sensational in the mass media of communications, the American public has come to identify "elite people," "personalities," and "socialites," with a high divorce rate. Even in Philadelphia, the conservative press is only too eager to spread a headline on the front page: "Socialite Sues for Divorce." "It just goes to show how times have changed," one Proper Philadelphian recently commented on a sensational socialite divorce headline: "Twenty-five years ago, it would have been routinely

Table 12—*Philadelphians in Who's Who in 1940—Size of Birthplace as Related to Social Class*

Size of Birthplace*	SOCIAL CLASS				Who's Who Total		Per Cent in Social Register
	Social Register		Non Social Register				
	No.	%	No.	%	No.	%	
Philadelphia†	118	(52)	160	(29)	278	(36)	42%
Over 100,000	37	(16)	61	(11)	98	(12)	38%
2,500-100,000	43	(19)	116	(22)	159	(21)	27%
Rural (under 2,500)	20	(9)	136	(25)	156	(21)	13%
Foreign born	8	(4)	63	(12)	71	(9)	11%
No information	—		8	(1)	8	(1)	—
Total	226	(100)	544	(100)	770	(100)	29%

* Size of birthplace was taken as of the 1900 census. This is the nearest census to 18-20 years after the median date of birth of the Philadelphia elite as a whole; presumably, the years from 18-20 are the most likely ages of first mobility away from place of birth.

† Philadelphia in this context is assumed to include the metropolitan area and not only the city proper.

reported in one of the back pages." As a matter of fact, within the upper class, where romantic love as a reason for marriage is deftly channeled within a relatively coherent subcultural circle, and the informal sanctions of relatives and friends are strong, one finds a relatively low divorce rate. Of the Philadelphians listed in *Who's Who* in 1940, only five—four men and one woman—reported divorce status; none of these was also listed in the *Social Register;* only one had been born in the city; and all were under sixty-five years of age—the younger generation among the elite.

The status of women in any society is an approximate index of family stability. On the whole, career women do not add to the stability of the home. In 1940, 7 per cent of the Philadelphians listed in *Who's Who* were women (5 per cent of the *Social Register* group as against 7 per cent of the rest). Women are somewhat less likely (26 per cent) than men (30 per cent) to be members of the upper class. In contrast to men, it is probably true that women are not rewarded socially, at least in the upper classes, by business or professional achievement.[5]

Even though she may have established herself in some career, the Proper Philadelphia woman is more or less bound by the patriarchal and familistic values of her class. A subtle difference between the women listed in the *Social Register* and the other elite females reflects these upper-class values. Upper-class women were almost twice as likely to be married (64 per cent) as the rest (37 per cent). The upper-class mothers also had larger families (upper class reported 2.66 children; the rest, 1.62). The only woman who reported a divorce was not listed in the *Social Register,* and she was not born in the city.

The occupational patterns of the upper-class women, as com-

Table 13—Philadelphians in Who's Who in 1940—Family Size as Related to Birthplace of Parent and Social Class*

	SOCIAL CLASS					
	SOCIAL REGISTER		NON SOCIAL REGISTER		WHO'S WHO TOTAL	
Birthplace of Parents	No. of Parents	Mean No. of Children	No. of Parents	Mean No. of Children	No. of Parents	Mean No. of Children
Philadelphia	73	2.90	97	2.72	170	2.80
All other areas	76	2.70	255	2.57	331	2.60
Total	149	2.80	352	2.62	501	2.67

* These are the 501 male parents who reported their place of birth and the names of their children.

pared to the rest of the women in *Who's Who,* suggest the paucity of real career women among the fashionable group. The upper-class women were almost all authors, artists, or civic leaders, achievements which can be combined with the role of mother and wife; the other women were engaged in a wide variety of professions (see Table 14). In the same vein, the women of the upper class had little formal education, while the less fashionable women contained among them five Medical Doctors, three Doctors of Philosophy, and one Phi Betta Kappa. The upper class boasted of only one Doctor of Philosophy, and she was not born in the city and had achieved upper-class status along with her husband (the only husband and wife listed in *Who's Who*).

Although not large, differences between the upper-class members and the rest of the 1940 elite consistently pointed to the greater stability of traditional values within the upper class, who were, on the whole, less mobile, more likely to be married and to have children, and less likely to be divorced and to produce the full-time career woman.

Table 14—Philadelphia Females in Who's Who in 1940—
Occupation as Related to Social Class

| | SOCIAL | | CLASS | | | |
| Occupation | Social Register | | Non Social Register | | Total | |
	No.	%	No.	%	No.	%
Artist	7	(50)	13	(33)	20	(37)
Author	3	(21)	10	(25)	13	(24)
Education	1	(8)	6*	(15)	7	(13)
Physician	0	(—)	4	(10)	4	(7)
Opinion	0	(—)	4	(10)	4	(7)
Librarian	0	(—)	2	(5)	2	(4)
Civic work	3	(21)	1	(2)	4	(7)
Total	14	(100)	40	(100)	54	(100)

* One M.D.

The Old Family Core of the 1940 Elite. Throughout this book, the terms upper class and Proper Philadelphia refer to a group of fashionable families listed in the contemporary *Social Register.* Thus the Proper Philadelphia world includes such patrician families of old wealth as the Morrises, Ingersolls, and Hopkinsons, as well as Wideners, Kents, and Dorrances of more recent money. This is a somewhat democratic use of these terms, at least as far as many "old families" in the city are concerned. Within the fashionable and sometimes snobbish world of Proper Philadelphia, for example, there are, of course, a few "old families" who consider themselves, and are reverently so considered by many others, to be "first families." In the local upper-class vernacular, these "first families" are known simply as "Philadelphians." One may have been born in Philadelphia, and one's ancestors may have been born there since colonial times, without ever presuming to call oneself a "Philadelphian," at least within the city's loftiest circles. This rather esoteric use of the term "Philadelphian" is altogether confusing to the outsider. It has been mentioned here only as a revealing comment on the subtle gradations within the city's upper class. The terms "old family" or "first family," however, will henceforth be used in the interest of clarity.

An annual invitation to the hallowed Assembly Balls, although recently tarnished by a few concessions to democratic progress and the power of wealth (E. T. Stotesbury eventually received a coveted invitation, for instance), is still the best index of first family status in the city. Every history of the city and almost every novel about Proper Philadelphia, including Christopher Morley's *Kitty Foyle*, has something to say about the Assembly. Attorney-General Francis Biddle, whose *The Llanfear Pattern* was his only venture as a novelist, devoted a whole chapter to "The Night of the Assembly."[6]

The oldest continuous series of fashionable balls in America, the Assemblies were established in 1748 by fifty-nine of Philadelphia's first citizens, including Thomas Willing, William Bingham, and Thomas Hopkinson, founder of the Hopkinson line and distinguished ancestor of Edward Hopkinson, Jr., a senior Morgan partner in the city in 1940.[7] George Washington danced at several Assemblies, including one held in his honor on February 23, 1793. To this day both the shabby genteel and presently prosperous "Philadelphians" are careful to make an annual appearance at this hallowed ball for the city's "best."

Unlike many such affairs held elsewhere in America, which are usually dominated by women (the men are too busy), the Philadelphia Assembly has always been run by men. Through the years, a small group of Assembly "Managers" have done their best to preserve the original tone of this ancient institution. These patriarchal arbiters of society still belong to families of pre-Civil War wealth and position. The remarkable continuity of first family

Philadelphia is reflected in the following "Managers" taken from three historical periods (compare with Table 9, Chapter V, above): Between 1800 and 1860, Thomas Willing, Charles Jared Ingersoll, Nicholas Biddle, J. P. Morris, Jr., James Rush, Thomas Cadwalader, George Meade, Richard Worsam Meade, and Richard Vaux were among the managers of the affair; between 1880 and 1900, S. Weir Mitchell, John Cadwalader, S. Warren Ingersoll, William Platt Pepper, Thomas McKean, Henry Brinton Coxe, Jr., W. Lyman Biddle, and Owen Wister decided who was to dance at the gala Victorian Assemblies; and between the two wars (1920-1940), Henry Brinton Coxe, Lambert Cadwalader, Caspar Wistar Morris, Beauveau Borie, Jr., Charles J. Biddle, John H. W. Ingersoll, Benjamin Chew, E. Shippen Willing, George L. Harrison, Arthur Ingersoll Meigs, George B. Roberts, Warwick Potter Scott, A. J. Drexel Paul, Anthony J. Cassatt, and R. Stockton Rush, helped to divide the old from the new within the swelling ranks of Proper Philadelphia society.

Patriarchal values still rule the Assembly, in spite of matriarchal dominance in modern suburbia. If a man marries outside the inner circle, his wife is usually asked to the Assembly. A cook once made the grade through the bonds of matrimony, but a woman rarely brings in a plebian husband. The Assembly helps to preserve the traditional family in other ways. Many "Philadelphians," including more than one "Manager" of the affair, for example, have been excluded because of divorce and remarriage, a hard and fast rule to this day. Many lengthy and faithful extra-marital romances have never led to divorce because of this traditional bulwark of family stability. In *The Llanfear Pattern*, Francis Biddle outlines the social structure of the Assembly as follows:

The Committee was self-perpetuating. It gave the ball, even if those fortunate ones whom it asked to subscribe paid for it. Certain rules, implicit in the bosom of succeeding secretaries, who made, like the popes, an unbroken succession, guided these careful gentlemen in their difficult task. Divorce barred a member, or rather an expectant member, for you had each year to be re-invited. And the ground of disbarment was not moral, because no distinction was made between the erring and the righteous. Again the husband's status, following the good analogy of the law, determined the wife's. Such cases were susceptible of firm treatment. But the exceptions were hard. Was the Governor entitled to belong if he were a gentleman though not a Philadelphian? Fortunately few governors were gentlemen. When old Dean Llanfear, the banker, insisted that his partner, Mr. Faircloud, should be admitted—sent out an ultimatum to that effect—Mr. Faircloud was admitted. Some rich men certainly could not get in, but other rich men certainly did.[8]

Peter A. B. Widener, baron of Lynnewood Hall and founder of his enormously wealthy family line, cared little for fashionable society and preferred a good game of shirt-sleeves poker with his cronies. His bridge-playing son, Joseph E. Widener, polished art connoisseur and turfman, however, apparently was hurt by the city's first families who, of course, excluded his wife from the Assembly list after she married across the tracks. In *Without Drums*, his son, P. A. B. Widener, betrays the feelings of a rich young man who felt that his family should belong to this fashionable group:

Back in the 'nineties Philadelphia society raised its eyebrows when Mother married Father. . . . She had married across the tracks!

As Ella Pancoast, daughter of one of the oldest families of Philadelphia, Mother had always attended the Assembly . . . she had always lived on the right side of the Market Street tracks. The Pancoast family address was 1911 Walnut Street [see Chapter XIII, Rittenhouse Club, 1811 Walnut Street].

But Father? Father was from North Broad Street. It made no difference that Grandfather had built one of the finest mansions in the city at Broad Street and Girard Avenue.

Market Street was the great divide in Philadelphia . . . North of Market was Nobody's Land—socially.

Grandfather was a self-made man; he had been in trade. It made no difference that he came from Revolutionary stock, that an ancestor had been a captain on General Washington's staff. Grandfather had been poor; he had been a butcher's boy. Now, he was rich, fabulously wealthy, and society called him and his sons *nouveau riche*.

Grandfather didn't care. But Father cared. It rankled for a long time, the slight to him and the Widener name. Later when Father had entertained and been entertained by princes and the nobility of Europe and by society leaders in other American cities, Philadelphia opened its doors.

It came about when my sister, Fifi, was invited to the Assembly Ball.

In 1919 Fifi made her debut at a tea attended by most of Philadelphia society. Later when invitations for the Assembly were out, Fifi was one of the many debutantes to be overlooked that season. About that time Father was asked to serve on one more of the many civic committees to which he had always contributed generously in time and money. The project was backed by some of the Assembly crowd.

Within a very short time an invitation arrived bidding Fifi to the Assembly. She was asked, of all things, as an "out-of-town" guest! Our home by then, as it is now, was just across the city line in Montgomery

County. The Assembly Committee was indulging in a bit of face-saving, but it didn't fool us. And I was not at all for Fifi's accepting. . . .

Father, however, was delighted. So was Fifi. And so Fifi went, and it was up to me to be her escort.

I went, but I was hot under the collar. I was mad clean through because it seemed to me the invitation to Fifi had contained a back-handed flip at Mother. It's the custom for a debutante to be chaperoned at the Assembly by her mother or some other woman member of the family. But Mother had not been asked; neither had any other of the Widener women. . . .

The ball is a very formal affair, and its etiquette is strict. All the women guests, old and young, must curtsy to the hostesses. I stood by as Fifi passed up the line.

As I watched sardonically, one of the hosts, who was also an old friend, came over to me. He made a very flattering speech of welcome to me. But I failed to assuage or cajole. I spoke out in hot-headed reply. "I know we're not wanted," I said to him, and I laughed shortly.

He looked thunderstruck. There was a titter from others who had overheard. But no titter could stop me now. "I'm only accompanying my sister," I rushed on, "or I wouldn't be here!" The whole business of Philadelphia's Assembly suddenly seemed idiotic. I enjoyed calling a slight a slight. You do when you're twenty-four.

I was tremendously pleased with myself as I took Fifi's arm. I waltzed her around the floor and then led her into supper. My face was flushed with triumph in spite of the head-nodding going on about me. People looked at me oddly, and I knew my remarks had already reached many pairs of ears.

After supper the dance floor was crowded. . . . I looked at Fifi. Her expression was not what you'd expect from a seventeen-year-old at her first big formal ball.

"Let's get out of here," I proposed, "and go someplace where we can have some fun."

"Great," she cried eagerly. . . .

And so we left the Assembly flat and went on to a livelier evening at the Ritz.[9]

One does not, of course, mention being on the Assembly list in one's *Who's Who* biography, or in the *Social Register*. As Struthers Burt has put it: "The Assembly excercises an altogether extraordinary power, both social and material, in the city, and to say you belong, which mustn't be said at all unless absolutely necessary, and then in the most casual manner, is exactly like announcing your rank in a country of Hereditary titles."[10]

Needless to say, a large majority of the 226 Philadelphians listed in both *Who's Who* and the *Social Register* in 1940 were not members of the inner circle of first families. In fact, of the

118 individuals born in the city, only 73 were listed in the *Social Register* as of 1900. Most of them had achieved this status within the past four decades (see Table 15).

Table 15—118 Philadelphians in Who's Who and the Social Register in 1940, Who Were Born in Philadelphia—Social Register Status by Decades, 1890-1940

	No. of Persons in Social Register	No. Increase by Decades	Per Cent Increase by Decades
1890	7	—	—
1900	73*	66	944
1910	90	17	23
1920	100	10	11
1930	109	9	9
1940	118	9	8

* Four females and sixty-nine males.

In the absence of public records of Assembly affiliation, we have used the sixty-nine males in the 1940 *Who's Who* who were listed in the 1900 *Social Register* (four of the total seventy-three were females) as examples of Philadelphia's first-family elite members in 1940. Presumably the patterns of behavior and institutional affiliations of these first family men set the style of life for the upper class as a whole. Their sociological characteristics have been summarized in Table 16, where they have been divided into two age groups in order to indicate trends which will be analyzed in more detail in the next five chapters. At this point, it is important to point out that the younger men are more likely to live in the most fashionable neighborhoods (Main Line-Chestnut Hill); to attend the Episcopal Church; to be privately educated; to attend fashionable universities; and to belong to the most exclusive club in the city (Philadelphia Club). They also reflect the historical trend towards an inter-community metropolitan upper class in that they were more likely to have attended one of the three fashionable New England boarding schools before going on to Harvard, Yale, or Princeton. On the whole, then, this difference between generations tends to substantiate our original hypothesis as to the changing American upper-class structure. That is to say, as the power of the family in relation to the total society declines, there is more pressure to conform to the prevailing pattern of neighborhood, religion, schools, college, and club affiliations.

The Peppers and Ingersolls have been leading Proper Philadelphia families for several generations. In 1940 there were nine
Pepper and ten Ingersoll conjugal family units listed in the *Social
Register;* three Peppers and two Ingersolls were also listed in
Who's Who. George Wharton Pepper and R. Sturgis Ingersoll
were leading members of the bar, C. Jared Ingersoll was a railroad
executive, and William Pepper and O. H. Perry Pepper were
physicians, Dean and Professor, respectively, of the University
of Pennsylvania Medical School. Brief biographical profiles of
George Wharton Pepper and R. Sturgis Ingersoll will indicate the
difference between the two generations of first-family Philadelphians. Pepper was of the older and Ingersoll of the younger
generation.

As we have seen, the Pepper fortune was founded by George
Pepper, a successful merchant and brewer, whose descendants
have been the city's first family of medicine for more than three
generations. George Pepper's great-grandson, George Wharton
Pepper, deviated slightly from family tradition when he entered
the legal profession. He was the dean of the Philadelphia bar
in 1940.

Born in 1867, George Wharton Pepper was the grandson of

Table 16—*Philadelphians in* Who's Who *in 1940 Who Were Also Listed in the
Social Register in 1900—Summary of Sociological Characteristics*

SOCIOLOGICAL CATEGORIES	AGE GROUPS			
	The 34 Males Who Were Over 65 in 1940		The 35 Males Who Were Under 65 in 1940	
Neighborhood				
Main Line-Chestnut Hill	61%		80%	
Religious Affiliation				
Episcopalian	56%		66%	
Type of Schooling				
Private Schools	50%		70%	
(Groton, St. Paul's, St. Mark's)		(3%)		(23%)
(Episcopal Academy)		(20%)		(9%)
College Attended				
University of Pennsylvania	53%		46%	
Harvard, Yale, Princeton	3%		40%	
Club Affiliation				
Philadelphia Club	39%		69%	
Rittenhouse Club	39%		26%	

Dr. William Pepper and William Mifflin Wharton, a Philadelphia lawyer.[11] His father, Dr. George Pepper, who fought in the Civil War where he was wounded at Fredericksburg, unfortunately died when young George was only six years of age. Although born in his grandmother Pepper's house on Walnut Street, "a mark of social respectability," George Wharton Pepper spent his boyhood on less fashionable Pine and South Sixteenth Streets, with pleasant summers at his grandmother's estate in Chestnut Hill. He was educated at home by his mother who believed in verbal memory of the Bible, the Book of Common Prayer, and a "considerable amount of poetry." The Peppers were devout Episcopalians, and young George was baptized and confirmed at St. Mark's Protestant Episcopal Church, at Sixteenth and Walnut Streets. He was a member of the parish in 1940.

In 1883, young Pepper entered the University of Pennsylvania as a rather "provincial but eager freshman." As he observes in his autobiography:

Those were the days when the son went to the father's college pretty much as a matter of course. In our case the ties that bound us to the University were unusually strong. My grandfather Wharton had been a trustee and my grandfather Pepper a professor in the Medical School. My father, my step-father and my uncle, Dr. William Pepper, had not only graduated from the college and its professional schools but had all been members of the same Greek letter fraternity. Moreover, my Uncle William had recently been elected provost of the University. Somebody, in speaking of the Pepper family in relation to the University, has remarked that it has not been a succession but a dynasty.[12]

After graduation from the University, Pepper went to the law school from which he graduated in 1889 with high honors. That summer he spent with his future father-in-law to be and his fiancée at Northeast Harbor, on Mt. Desert, which was destined to become his summer home for many years to come (this resort is probably the most fashonable and popular Proper Philadelphia resort to this day). The next fall, Pepper went to work for Biddle and Ward, a Philadelphia law firm and, in addition, held a teaching fellowship at the law school. For half a century, George Wharton Pepper has been one of the leading "Philadelphia lawyers."

Senator Boies Penrose died in office in 1921. The following January Governor Sproul came down to Philadelphia where he met George Wharton Pepper at the Philadelphia Club and offered him the Senate seat for Penrose's unexpired term. Pepper hesitated at first ("Never in my life have I felt the itch for public office. . . .") and asked for some time to think the matter over. Three days later, after talking the matter over with a few close friends, Pepper agreed to serve. On January 9, 1922, in the presence of Chief Justice Robert von Moschzisker and General W. W. Atterbury, President of the Pennsylvania Railroad, the Governor presented Pepper with his formal commission to serve.

Senator Pepper spent almost two terms in Washington, was re-elected in 1922, and finally defeated in 1927 due to the opposition of the powerful Vare machine which had consolidated itself in Philadelphia after the death of Boies Penrose. The years in the Senate had severely strained his financial resources and the return to Philadelphia, from this point of view, "was a welcome relief."

George Wharton Pepper has been a long-time and devoted trustee of the University of Pennsylvania, a member of the American Philosophical Society, a past president of the American Law Institute, a Fellow of the American Academy of Arts and Sciences, and a member of the Franklin Institute. He is the author of ten books, including, *The Borderland of Federal and State Decisions, Pleading at Common Law,* and *Digest of the Laws of Pennsylvania.* He is a member of the Rittenhouse, University, and Racquet clubs and his wife (deceased) was a member of the Acorn Club.

Senator Pepper, as he is even now called by his friends, married Charlotte Root Fisher, daughter of Professor George Park Fisher of New Haven and Yale, in 1890, and they had two children. Their son was an architect of some repute in the city, and their daughter is married to an investment banker and broker. The Pepper home is in Devon on the "Main Line."

This brief biography of Senator Pepper illuminates the nature of the gentleman of wide and worthwhile interests in the community. Characteristically, his earliest American ancestors were businessmen while their sons were physicians or lawyers. His early religious training was followed by a lifelong service to the Episcopal Church in many leading lay capacities. Although he knew little of practical politics, he served when called and was soon defeated, because, as he himself admits, he did not cater sufficiently to public opinion. His life has been both a happy and useful one with hard work sensibly blended with participation in athletics and life out of doors, a balance hardly attained by many leaders of the present "ulcer" generation. "Glancing astern" in his autobiography, Pepper observes that "after all, it is in the home that my greatest happiness has been found."

The Ingersolls have been prominent members of the Philadelphia bar since the eighteenth century. The first member of the family in America, John Ingersoll, came to Salem, Massachusetts, from Bedfordshire, England, in 1629.[13] His grandson, Jared Ingersoll, a distinguished lawyer and King's Attorney in Connecticut, was appointed Stamp-Master-General for New England, in 1765, and remained a Tory during the Revolution. At one point during the war, he was staying in the same Philadelphia boarding house with the fiery patriot, Samuel Adams. John Adams described his cousin's boarding house companions as "a curious group consisting of characters, as opposite as North and South. Ingersoll, the stamp man and Judge of Admiralty; Sherman, an old Puritan, as honest as an angel and as firm in the cause of American Independence as Mount Atlas; and Col. Thornton, as droll and funny as Tristram Shandy. Between the fun of Thornton, the gravity of Sherman, the formal Toryism of Ingersoll, Adams will have a curious time of it. The landlady, too, who has buried four husbands, one tailor, two shoemakers, and Gilbert Tenant, and still is ready for a fifth and still deserves him too, will add to the entertainment."[14]

Jared Ingersoll, son of Judge Ingersoll of Connecticut, was the founder of the Philadelphia Ingersoll clan. After graduating from Yale, in 1765, he came down to Philadelphia and read law under Joseph Reed. During the Revolution, he was in London completing his education at the Inner Temple. Upon his return to Philadelphia, he became the city's leading lawyer, including both Robert Morris and Stephen Girard among his clients. According to Charles A. Beard, his practice "was larger than any others . . . his opinions were taken on all important controversies, his services engaged in every litigation."[15]

Although primarily concerned with his private law practice, Ingersoll attained a certain prominence in public life: in addition to his membership in the Constitutional Convention, he was a delegate to the First Continental Congress, Attorney General of Pennsylvania for two brief periods, and a candidate for the Vice Presidency, on the Federalist ticket, in 1812.

Jared Ingersoll's great-great-grandson, R. Sturgis Ingersoll, carrying on the family legal tradition of five generations, was a distinguished member of the bar in 1940. He was educated at St. Paul's School, Princeton University, and received an LL.B. from the University of Pennsylvania in 1921. In addition to his law practice, Ingersoll was on the Board of Managers of the Philadelphia Savings Fund Society, and a director of several railroads. His wide civic and cultural activities include directorships in the Philadelphia Zoological Society, the Philadelphia Museum of Art, the Philadelphia Orchestra Association, the Fairmount Park Art Association, and the English Speaking Union. Carrying on a family tradition begun by Charles Jared Ingersoll, he was Pennsylvania Chairman of the Democratic Victory Fund Campaign in 1932. He belongs to the Philadelphia, Rittenhouse, Franklin Inn, Midday, and Print clubs, lives in Penllyn, a fashionable rural community beyond Chestnut Hill, attends the Episcopal Church, and has five children.

George Wharton Pepper and R. Sturgis Ingersoll are interesting examples of the generation differences within the old family members of the 1940 elite. Pepper was of the older generation and less likely to conform to fashionable trends than Ingersoll. Thus Pepper was educated locally and worked for the University of Pennsylvania all his life, whereas Ingersoll went away to boarding school and a fashionable university; Pepper preferred the Rittenhouse Club, while Ingersoll belonged to the more fashionable Philadelphia Club.

CHAPTER IX

Neighborhood and the Class Structure

> In every modern city it is possible to find local units which are self-contained for all ordinary social purposes. To their members, the city as a whole is simply a zone of exploitation, the region which the males go out to daily, returning to their band at night with their spoils.
>
> RALPH LINTON

THE NEIGHBORHOOD, like the tribe or band of an earlier era, is one of the basic social units of modern urban civilization. On the surface, the metropolitan environment is composed of a heterogeneous mass of isolated individuals, bound together by a complex web of impersonal social relations. In order to mitigate the loneliness and anonymity of metropolitan life men and their families have always banded together in relatively small and socially homogeneous neighborhoods within the city and its suburbs. The residential neighborhood, whether it be Park Avenue, Little Italy, Chinatown, Nob Hill, Hobohemia, or the Main Line, gradually develops a homogeneity and exclusiveness over the years, which, in turn, fosters a local loyalty and emotional security among its residents without which life in the large city would be unbearable. "In the course of time every sector and quarter of the city takes on something of the character and qualities of its inhabitants. The effect of this is to convert what was at first a mere geographical expression into a neighborhood, that is to say, a locality with sentiments, traditions, and a history of its own."[1]

The neighborhood is especially important where children are concerned. Such primary groups as the gang, the clique, the play group, and the school are essential aspects of neighborhood life. "From the child's point of view," writes Professor Bossard, "the neighborhood is the immediate area which he first explores outside the home. It is here that the first beyond-the-family sights, sounds, and words are encountered. . . . The neighborhood is for the child practically the whole world."[2]

Residential propinquity, by limiting social interaction, serves the function of creating and preserving the social heritage and style of life of the various subcultural units within the society as a whole. The higher the social class, the more social distance is reinforced by geographical isolation. The social life of the upper classes, both children and adults, tends to be *exclusive,* while that of the middle classes is *selective.* The exclusive neighborhood, then, with its distinctive architecture, fashionable churches, private schools, and sentimental traditions, is an indispensable factor in the development of an upper-class style of life, system of personal values, and distinct character structure.

The members of the Philadelphia elite in 1940 lived in many different parts of the city and its suburbs. The more important elite and upper-class neighborhoods, and the historical development of each, will be analyzed in this chapter. Both a description of the rise and fall of fashionable neighborhoods, and a tracing of the family migrations from one neighborhood to another in succeeding generations are indispensable means of understanding the contemporary class structure. The family founder Henry Disston, for example, lived in an undistinguished address on Front Street before the Civil War.[3] As his saw-works prospered along with the development of the American frontier, Mr. Disston was living in 1890 in the center of the "Disston Colony" on elite, if not fashionable, North Broad Street.[4] Finally, of course, his numerous descendants, very much a part of the contemporary upper class in the city, were spread out through Chestnut Hill and the Whitemarsh Valley in 1940.[5]

The Plan of Penn's City. Philadelphia was named, surveyed, plotted, and lots had begun to be occupied by settlers in July, 1682.[6] It was the first planned city in America. Thomas Holme, Penn's Surveyor-General, laid out a gridiron of streets running east and west between the broad Delaware and the muddy Schuylkill rivers, and north and south between Race and Pine Streets (Map 1). The two main streets were Broad Street, running north and south, and High (Market) Street between the two rivers. On this gridiron he placed five squares, arranged like the five spots on a die, with the center square (Penn Square) at the intersection of Broad and High Streets. What were eventually to be known as Logan and Franklin Squares were north of High (now Market) Street, while Washington and Rittenhouse Squares were in the southern and more fashionable part of the city. The founders of the city carefully preserved part of the virgin forest on these squares, which proved a blessing to many generations of Philadelphians.

Most Proper Philadelphians have always lived south of Market,

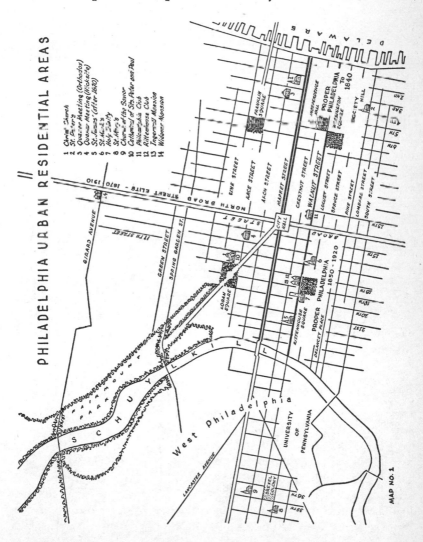

between Chestnut and Pine Streets. In colonial times and during the first part of the nineteenth century, however, although most fashionable families lived in the area below Washington Square, along Second, Third, and Fourth Streets, many Proper Philadelphians lived north of Market Street, especially along Arch Street. Rittenhouse Square became *the* address after the Civil War, while elite but unfashionable Philadelphians lived north of Market

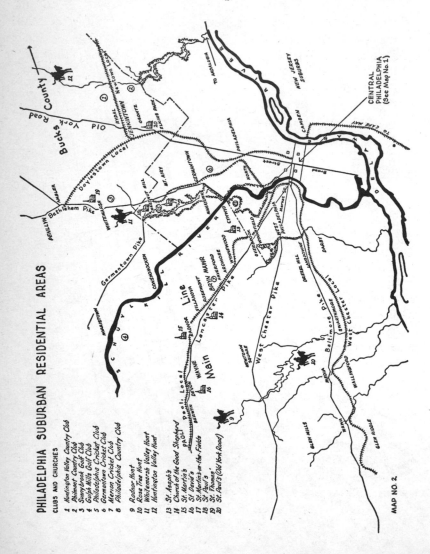

PHILADELPHIA SUBURBAN RESIDENTIAL AREAS

CLUBS AND CHURCHES

1 Huntington Valley Country Club
2 Philmont Country Club
3 Sunnybrook Golf Club
4 Gulph Mills Golf Club
5 Philadelphia Cricket Club
6 Germantown Cricket Club
7 Merion Cricket Club
8 Philadelphia Country Club
9 Radnor Hunt
10 Rose Tree Hunt
11 Whitemarsh Valley Hunt
12 Huntingdon Valley Hunt
13 St. Asaph's
14 Church of the Good Shepherd
15 St. Martin's
16 St. David's
17 St. Martins-in-the-Fields
18 St. Paul's
19 St. Thomas'
20 St. Paul's (Old York Road)

MAP NO. 2

Street, out along North Broad Street. In the last part of the nineteenth century "north of Market" was on the other side of the tracks as far as the Proper Philadelphians in the Rittenhouse Square area were concerned. Across the muddy Schuylkill, rural West Philadelphia became an elite neighborhood in the last part of the nineteenth century. Unlike Cambridge in Boston, however, West Philadelphia has never been a Proper Philadelphia address.

The beautiful Philadelphia suburbs (see Map 2) spread out from the center of the city along several ancient turnpikes: the northern suburbs, Jenkintown, Elkins Park, and Rydal, are contiguous to the Old York Road which is an extension of North Broad Street; Germantown, Chestnut Hill, and the Whitemarsh Valley developed along the Germantown and Bethlehem pikes leading out to the northwest of the city; the Main Line suburbs stretch out along the Lancaster Pike due west of the city; and finally, the Swarthmore, Wallingford, Rose Valley, and Wawa suburbs follow the Baltimore Pike to the southwest. The West Chester Pike, a continuation of Market Street, conveniently divides the Main Line suburbs from those along the Baltimore Pike.

Residential Distribution of the Elite in 1940. The 770 Philadelphians listed in *Who's Who* in 1940 lived in many parts of the city and its suburbs (Table 17). As one would expect, however, those persons also listed in the *Social Register* were more likely to reside in the few exclusive upper-class neighborhoods; the rest of the elite, or those of more diverse social origins, were found in all parts of the metropolitan area with considerably less concentration in any particular neighborhood.

The Main Line was the most popular elite suburb in Philadelphia; the Penllyn-Whitemarsh and Chestnut Hill areas were more exclusively upper class. Jenkintown and the Rittenhouse Square area, once fashionable, were primarily elite neighborhoods in 1940. Germantown, the oldest suburb in the city and once quite fashionable, was primarily an elite suburb, as were Swarthmore and West Philadelphia. North and South Philadelphia, although hardly homogeneous neighborhoods as of 1940, contained a few elite residents but no members of the upper class. The rest of the elite lived outside the suburban area in rural Bucks County or across the river in New Jersey.

The Rise and Fall of Upper-Class Neighborhoods. Every city has its well-known fashionable neighborhoods. As Americans are a restless people in a restless age, neighborhoods have a tendency to rise and fall in social prestige. Unlike the small town such as *Yankee City,* where upper-class families have been living in the same houses on the same street for many generations, in large cities such as New York or Philadelphia, the fashionable blocks rarely last for more than two or three generations. The growth of any large American city can usually be traced in the history of its residential architecture, especially in the history of houses built by the elite. The traditional practice of "building for the top" soon turns the wealthy merchant's family mansion into the tenement home of a dozen immigrant families. Thus the aristocratic ghosts of Washington Square in New York watch their descendants move north up on Park Avenue, out on Long Island, and up into Westchester County, while Beacon Street, after a long and losing struggle with "progress," is replaced by Brookline (Chestnut Hill), Milton, and Dedham as the address of proper Boston.

In Philadelphia, the rise and fall of upper-class neighborhoods

Table 17—Philadelphians in Who's Who in 1940—Neighborhood as Related to Social Class

Neighborhood	Social Register		Non Social Register		Who's Who Total		Percentage in Social Register in Each Neighborhood
	No.	%	No.	%	No.	%	
Upper Class							
Penllyn-Whitemarsh	12	(5)	2	(*)	14	(2)	86
Chestnut Hill	52	(23)	15	(3)	67	(9)	78
Main Line	75	(33)	80	(15)	155	(20)	48
Transition							
Rittenhouse Square	42	(19)	63	(12)	105	(14)	40
Jenkintown†	11	(5)	30	(5)	41	(5)	27
Elite							
Germantown	19	(8)	107	(20)	126	(17)	15
West Philadelphia	8	(4)	84	(16)	92	(12)	9
Swarthmore†	3	(1)	50	(9)	53	(7)	6
Other areas							
North Philadelphia	0	(—)	26	(5)	26	(3)	—
South Philadelphia	0	(—)	11	(2)	11	(1)	—
Outside Met. area	4	(2)	35	(6)	39	(5)	10
No information	0	(—)	41	(7)	41	(5)	—
Total	226	(100)	544	(100)	770	(100)	29

* Less than 1 per cent.

† For convenience, Jenkintown includes all the suburbs along the Old York Road, and Swarthmore all those along the Baltimore Pike.

can be divided, with some overlapping, of course, into three periods: (1) during the colonial period and through the first part of the nineteenth century, fashionable Philadelphians lived in what is now the downtown business district around Independence and Washington Squares (see Map 1); (2) after the Civil War, and until World War I, the upper-class center of gravity, as it were, became the Rittenhouse Square district; (3) after World War I, the center of society moved west once again out to the suburbs along the Main Line and in Chestnut Hill. At the same time, of course, many of the wealthier families had country places even as early as the eighteenth century.

The Pepper and Ingersoll families have followed the pattern of neighborhood change outlined above. In 1823, for example, Charles Jared Ingersoll lived on Walnut Street near Fourth, while George Pepper was living on Chestnut near Seventh [7] In 1890, the Ingersoll family mansion was on Walnut Street facing Rittenhouse Square, and George Wharton Pepper, born on Walnut Street several doors from the Ingersolls, lived on Spruce Street at Sixteenth.[8] Finally, in 1940, the Peppers lived in Devon on the Main Line while the Ingersoll clan spread out through the Whitemarsh Valley centering along the Penllyn Pike, the "Main Street" of this "Ingersoll-Cadwalader-Coxe" community.[9]

The Colonial Period. In the second half of the eighteenth century Philadelphia became the "Athens of America," the political capital and the wealthiest city in the colonies. The members of its thriving, mercantile aristocracy soon set themselves apart from the rest of the populace by "erecting country homes and city mansions, assembling libraries and art collections, attending concerts and the theatre, sitting for their portraits, and having their sons and daughters instructed in a variety of genteel accomplishments."[10] By the time of the Revolution, many fashionable Philadelphians were in the second and third generation of inherited wealth. William Bingham, often called the richest American of his day, for instance, was anything but a self-made man.[11] His great-grandfather, James Bingham, left a large estate when he died in 1714; his grandfather, James, married the daughter of one of New Jersey's largest landowners, William Budd, of Burlington; his father, William Bingham, Senior, added to the Budd and Bingham fortunes through a marriage to Mary, daughter of John Stamper, wealthy Mayor of Philadelphia; finally, William Bingham himself, after his return from the West Indies where he had augmented his fortune while acting as an agent for the colonies during the Revolution, married the daughter of Thomas Willing at Christ Church in 1780. In a poem called *The Times of 1788,* reflecting man's inevitable envy of the rich, a contemporary referred to wealthy William Bingham and life at the Bingham mansion in the following lines:

> Tho' to thy mansion wits and fops repair,
>   To game, to feast, to flatter and to stare.
> But say, from what bright deeds dost thou derive
>   That wealth which bids thee rival British Clive?
> Wrung from the hardy sons of toil and war,
>   By arts, which petty scoundrels would abhor.[12]

Philadelphia's colonial aristocracy lived near the Delaware River in the neighborhood below Washington Square (see Map 1). Several examples of America's finest colonial architecture are preserved to this day as a reminder that Second and Third Streets were once fashionable addresses in the city: Christ Church on Second Street just north of Market, and St. Peter's at Third and Pine, where the city's most elegant merchants once worshiped; the Powel House, 244 South Third Street, where Samuel Powel, inheritor of a large fortune from his father and grandfather, the last Colonial Mayor, and brother-in-law of both Thomas Willing and "The Third Byrd of Westover," once entertained all the great Americans of his day; and, finally, the Wharton House on Spruce Street above Third (Joseph Hopkinson wrote *Hail Columbia* in the house next door).

Although Christ Church, St. Peter's, and the Powel House are excellently preserved historical landmarks, the history of the succession of occupants of the Wharton House is a study in the sociology of neighborhood change in Philadelphia.[13] Between 1796 and 1799, the house was owned by Mordecai Lewis, a prominent merchant in the East India trade, director of the Bank of North America, the Philadelphia Contributionship for the Insurance of Houses from Loss by Fire, and the Library Company of Philadelphia, treasurer of the Pennsylvania Hospital, and founder of the Lewis family of Penn Salt (see Chapter V). In 1817, his son Samuel N. Lewis, also a prominent merchant, sold the house to another merchant, Samuel Fisher. Fisher bought the house as a wedding present for his daughter when she married William

Wharton. One of William Wharton's ten children, Joseph Wharton, financier, ironmaster (Bethlehem Steel Company), and founder of the Wharton School at the University of Pennsylvania, inherited the house when his mother died in 1888. In 1920, still owned by the Wharton estate, it was a cheap rooming house in a dilapidated slum area.

Even in the colonial period, affluent Philadelphians led a country life after the manner of the English gentleman. "The country estates around Philadelphia," write two historians of the period, "with their English and Scottish head gardeners and white servants, their groves, parks, stables, and kitchen gardens, bore greater likeness to an English country menage than did extended and isolated plantations manned by gangs of black slaves."[14]

Many of these beautiful country seats were built along the banks of the Delaware and Schuylkill Rivers. "Mount Pleasant," for example, remains today one of the finest examples of Georgian architecture in the city. Built in 1761 on the banks of the Schuylkill, in what is now Fairmount Park, it was purchased in 1779 by Benedict Arnold as a marriage gift for his bride Peggy Shippen, the belle of the colonial aristocracy.[15] In the nineteenth century, after the decline of the Georgian style of architecture, Nicholas Biddle, of the Bank of the United States, built his famous country seat on the banks of the Delaware. "Andalusia," a stunning Greek Revival mansion, still remains in the family, and in 1940 was owned by Charles J. Biddle, a prominent Philadelphia lawyer.

The Victorian Era and the Glory of Rittenhouse Square. During the course of the nineteenth century, the center of the growing city of Philadelphia moved westward. In response to the westward migration in the 1880's, City Hall (built between 1882 and 1907 at a cost of $25,000,000) moved from Fifth and Chestnut to its present location on Penn Square at Broad and Market Streets; the University of Pennsylvania moved out to West Philadelphia from Ninth and Chestnut in 1870; and, finally, in 1893, the Pennsylvania Railroad moved its terminal from Third Street to the Broad Street Station building, just west of City Hall.

The financial and business community, clinging to tradition and convenience, however, remained downtown throughout the nineteenth century. Third Streets, where Samuel Powel, William Bingham and Thomas Willing once lived, was the "Wall Street" of America until after the Civil War (Alexander Hamilton, the first Secretary of the Treasury, had an office at 79 South Third). In the days before the telephone, propinquity was especially important to the bankers and brokers. In 1858, for example, twenty-two (including E. W. Clark & Company, Drexel & Company, and Jay Cooke) of the twenty-four bankers and brokers listed in an early business directory of the city were located on Third Street.[16]

In recognition of the movement west, the financial community did make a two-block concession to progress in the eighties. In 1885, the Drexel firm moved into its beautiful new offices in the Drexel Building at Fifth and Chestnut Streets. Three years later, the Philadelphia Stock Exchange, which had been at Third and Walnut for many years, moved into the Drexel Building.[17]

After the Civil War, Philadelphia's banking and manufacturing aristocracy, which had been moving slowly westward along Walnut, Locust, and Spruce Streets for half a century, lived in an exclusive residential neighborhood between Broad Street and the Schuylkill River, bounded by Pine Street to the south and Market Street to the north (see Map 1). The center of this neighborhood was Rittenhouse Square.

The neighborhood migrations of fashionable society are conveniently traced by the churches they built. At one time, the "St. Peter's set" was as well known a stereotype of fashionable status in Philadelphia as the more secular term "Mainliner" is today. Just as Christ Church and St. Peter's marked the center of upper-class life in colonial Philadelphia, so St. Mark's and The Church of the Holy Trinity, built respectively in 1851 and 1859, were two of the city's most fashionable parishes during the Victorian era. Situated in the heart of the Rittenhouse Square neighborhood, these two Episcopal churches still remind one of the splendors and confidence of a departed age. As an architectural historian puts it: "The whole square was dominated by Holy Trinity and its seemly tower, the church of Quakers turned Episcopal. It was from the pulpit there that the *obiter dictum* was pronounced: 'I have always felt that Our Lord was a gentleman'—comfortable words for the dwellers nearby."[18]

During the second half of the nineteenth century, Rittenhouse Square was surrounded by the mansions of Philadelphia's Victorian aristocracy. At no other time in the city's history, before or since, have so many wealthy and fashionable families lived so near

one another. The more famous Philadelphians who resided on the
Square during this period are listed in Table 18. In addition to
families of older wealth, such as the Ingersolls and Peppers, the
residents of the Square included many of the city's wealthiest
mid-nineteenth-century family founders. The descendants of these
men of both old and new wealth, allied today through marriage
with each other and with other clans in the city, formed the backbone of the suburban upper class in 1940. Among other such
alliances, for example, an Ingersoll married a descendant of
William Weightman, the city's first chemical millionaire, in the
late 1930's. As he straightened his frock coat before the mirror on
the day of the wedding, the head of the older family was heard to
remark humorously: "We'll show these upstarts a thing or two."

In the early 1840's James Harper, an immigrant Irish contractor,
politician, and brick-maker, built the first house on Rittenhouse
Square at what is now 1811 Walnut Street.[19] (Today the Harper
house forms part of the *Rittenhouse* Club.) Curious Philadelphians
used to stroll out to the Square on Sundays in order to look at
Congressman Harper's handsome mansion. Most of the elegant
Victorian mansions on the Square, however, were built in the
fifties and sixties. In 1855, for example, Joseph Harrison, Jr.,
constructed the finest house ever built on the Square. While
accumulating a fortune in Russia (he built the St. Petersburg-
Moscow railroad), Mr. Harrison purchased almost a whole city
block to the east of the Square on 18th Street. The Harrison
house, copied from a St. Petersburg palace, contained the city's
finest private art collection, and its formal gardens extended over
a whole city block.

Joseph Harrison, Jr., had seven children and, like the Harrisons
of the sugar trust, he founded a Proper Philadelphia line and had
many descendants listed in the 1940 *Social Register*. His grandson,
Leland Harrison of New York, was listed in the 1940 *Who's Who*
as United States Ambassador to Switzerland. A brief outline of
Joseph Harrison, Jr.'s career suggests the mechanical and entrepreneurial genius of the Philadelphia Victorian elite.

Born of rather poor parents in the northern part of Philadelphia
in 1810, Joseph Harrison, Jr. was indentured to a steam-fitting
firm at the age of fifteen.[20] At twenty, before he was free of his
indenture, he was a foreman with forty men and boys under him.
In 1837, although he contributed no capital to the firm, he became

a partner in Garrett, Eastwick & Company, designers and builders of locomotives. In 1840 he designed an engine for the Reading Railroad which was considered to be "the most efficient locomotive for freight purposes that had been built anywhere." Russian engineers, who visited Philadelphia, made drawings of this remarkable locomotive, and in 1843, Emperor Nicholas invited Mr. Harrison to come to Russia. During most of the next two decades he was engaged in the construction and maintenance of the St. Petersburg-to-Moscow railroad. The need for rail transportation during the Crimean War, of course, increased the profits of the railroad beyond all expectations. Although twelve of the last twenty years of his life were spent abroad, Mr. Harrison built the famous mansion on the Square and was an imaginative civic leader in his native city where he died in 1874, a wealthy man, a world-famous engineer, and a recently-converted Episcopalian.

Table 18—Some Elite Philadelphians Residing in Rittenhouse Square
between 1850 and 1900

South Rittenhouse Square

W. W. Frazier—son-in-law of George L. Harrison, founder of the great sugar trust, Harrison, Havermeyer & Co.

J. William White—son of the first president and founder of S. S. White Dental Co., the world's largest dental manufacturers.

Thomas D. Smith—great-grandson of Rev. William Smith, first provost of the University of Pennsylvania.

Thomas A. Scott—president of the Pennsylvania Railroad.

Francis M. Drexel—founder of Drexel & Co. in 1838.

John D. Lankenau—son-in-law of Francis M. Drexel and the chief benefactor of the German Hospital, now the Lankenau Hospital, the most modern in Philadelphia today.

Thomas B. Wanamaker—son of the founder of John Wanamaker's, and the owner of *The North American*, leading newspaper of the day.

Solomon W. Roberts—civil engineer and builder of the Pennsylvania Railroad.

Theodore Cuyler—lawyer, founder and first president of the Social Art Club, later the *Rittenhouse* Club.

Frank Wyeth—president of John Wyeth & Brother, world renowned pharmaceutical manufacturers.

Nineteenth Street

Tench C. Coxe—descendant of Post-Revolutionary Period leader by the same name.

George D. Rosengarten—founder of Powers, Weightman, Rosengarten Co., pioneer chemical manufacturers (now Merck & Co.).

Samuel T. Bodine—president of the United Gas Improvement Co.

S. Weir Lewis—China merchant, banker.

Joshua B. Lippincott—founder of J. B. Lippincott, publishers.

A. J. Cassatt—president of Pennsylvania Railroad. The Cassatt house is now the diocesan headquarters of the Episcopal Church.

Walnut Street, between Broad Street and the Schuylkill River, was the most fashionable address in Victorian Philadelphia. "To mention Walnut Street to an old Philadelphian," writes George Wharton Pepper, "is to awaken memories of a departed glory. On bright Sundays, after church, there was always an informal parade of fashion on the south side of this thoroughfare. There the city's Four Hundred could be seen to great advantage. They were the blended congregation of half a dozen mid-city churches. They made upon the onlooker an impression of urbanity, of social experience and of entire self-satisfaction. If, during church-time, they had confessed themselves miserable sinners, by the time they appeared on parade their restoration to divine favor was seemingly complete."[21]

Walnut Street's popularity as an upper-class address reached its peak in the nineties. In 1890, for instance, there were more upper-class families living on Walnut Street (between Broad

Table 18 *(Continued)*

Walnut Street

John H. McFadden—cotton merchant, art connoisseur, philanthropist.

John A. Brown—Brown Brothers & Co., international bankers; one of four sons of the founder; was director of U. S. Bank when Nicholas Biddle was president.

Joseph Moore, Jr.—president of Pennsylvania Salt Manufacturing Co.

Charles Edward Ingersoll—lawyer and railroad executive.

Thomas Sparks—president of Pennsylvania Salt Manufacturing Co., one of the major chemical firms in the city.

George S. Pepper—lawyer, philanthropist, civic leader, and president of the *Rittenhouse Club.*

Alexander Van Rensselaer—clubman and son-in-law of A. J. Drexel.

Mrs. A. J. Drexel—lived on the Square after her husband's death.

William Weightman—founder of Powers, Weightman, & Rosengarten; pioneer American chemist and largest landowner in the city.

Thomas Dolan—founder of Thomas Dolan & Co. (1866) which became the Keystone Knitting Mills, one of the most successful textile firms in the city, doing $1,000,000 of business per year by 1871.

Algernon Sidney Roberts—born at "Pencoyd Plantation"; coal and railroad interests; one of the organizers of the Pennsylvania Railroad.

Eighteenth Street

Joseph Harrison, Jr.—railroad engineer and builder of the Moscow-St. Petersburg Railroad at the time of the Crimean War.

John Edgar Thomson—president of the Pennsylvania Railroad.

Charles Lennig—president of Nicholas Lennig & Co., founded 1831; philanthropist and benefactor of chemistry at the University of Pennsylvania.

George W. Childs Drexel—editor and owner of *Public Ledger,* most famous Philadelphia newspaper; son of A. J. Drexel.

Street and the Schuylkill River) than in all of Bryn Mawr on the Main Line.[22] Within half a century, however, commercial establishments had replaced the fashionable brownstones, and one old family after another moved out to the suburbs. The decline of Walnut Street as a Proper Philadelphia address is documented in Table 19. While there were 124 families living in the five blocks between Broad Street and Holy Trinity corner in 1890, there were fifty-five families listed there in 1914, and only three in 1940. Moreover, of the 124 original families, only seventeen remained in the same house until 1914; and only the Ingersoll family did not move for half a century. Since World War II, the old Ingersoll house has been torn down to make way for a municipal parking establishment.

In 1940 Walnut Street was the "Wall Street" of Philadelphia. As the banking gentlemen of Philadelphia moved their families

Table 19—Walnut Street, between Broad Street and Holy Trinity Church:
  Single Family Residences in 1890, 1914, and 1940

	Number of Single Family Residences			Number of Houses Owned by Same Family as in 1890	
	1890	1914	1940	In 1914	In 1940
Broad-15th	27	1	none	none	none
15th-16th	29	11	none	4	none
16th-17th	27	16	none	4	none
17th-18th	28	18	2	6	none
Square	13	9	1	3	1
Total	124	55	3	17	1

Number of Families
  Listed in Social Register   —   48*   3   17†   1‡

* All seven families not listed in the Social Register were M.D.'s. On the block between 16th and 17th, all families on one side of the street were listed in the Social Register; the five families that were not so listed were on the opposite side of the street.

† Of the 17 twenty-five year residents of Walnut Street in 1940, twelve of the families lived in either the Main line or Chestnut Hill, one family still lived in town on a side street in the Rittenhouse Square area, and four families have died out or moved elsewhere.

‡ The Ingersoll family lived at 1815 Walnut Street in 1890, 1914, and in 1940. After War II, the house was torn down to make way for a modern parking establishment run by the local municipal authority.

Source: Boyd's Blue Book, 1889-90; Social Register, 1914 and 1940.

out to the suburbs in the first part of the century, commuting to the downtown business section became less convenient. Just before World War I, the Philadelphia Stock Exchange moved to a new location on Walnut Street, west of Broad; soon afterwards, Drexel & Company built a six-story, granite banking establishment at the corner of Fifteenth and Walnut Streets.[23]

The era of the great houses on Walnut Street is passed if not forgotten and there are no longer any Proper Philadelphians living in private houses on the Square. Nevertheless, the members of many fashionable families, primarily those of the older generation with grown children, still prefer to live in town. In 1940, Delancey Place, near the Square, was the most fashionable center-city address, while many of the less affluent genteel lived in various alleys in the neighborhood which had been attractively rejuvenated during the Depression (the stables behind the large mansions usually faced on these alleys). In addition, there were several apartment houses surrounding the Square.

The most fashionable and expensive residential hotel on the Square, The Barclay, was completed in 1929. Here Philadelphia's wealthiest widows enjoy the best food in the city and congenial neighbors in the adjoining apartments. During the early years of the Depression an article in the local press brought back memories of the Victorian era on the Square. On February 11, 1933, the Philadelphia *Record*, the city's only Democratic newspaper at that time, reported that "the personal property holdings of some of the residents of 'millionaires row' in the Eighth Ward, which includes Rittenhouse Square, were opened to public gaze yesterday. . . . Edward T. Stotesbury, head of Drexel & Company, was revealed as one of several who will have to pay a 50 per cent penalty for failing to make returns."[24] Mr. Stotesbury, and several widows whose personal property holdings were listed in the *Record* article (all over $100,000) were all residents of The Barclay.

The Values of Philadelphia's Victorian Gentry. It is important to understand something of the values and attitudes of the residents of Rittenhouse Square in the Victorian era. As we have suggested above, the members of an upper class, in David Riesman's phrase, tend to be "tradition-directed." Most of the older members of the Philadelphia elite in 1940, men who had gone through World War I, the booming twenties, and the disillusionment of the thirties, spent their formative years in this Rittenhouse Square atmosphere. In so many ways, the cultural values of Philadelphia's, and America's, upper class on the eve of the Second War, especially the leaders among the older generation, were molded in the Victorian age.

The "Anglo-Saxon" ladies and gentlemen who developed the Rittenhouse Square neighborhood during and after the Civil War (even the new rich at that time were primarily of colonial stock) definitely felt themselves to be different, aloof and apart, from the rapidly developing heterogeneity of the rest of American society. While their ancestors in the days of the new republic came to the fore in public and military affairs, the Victorian gentlemen tended to withdraw from the world of public service into the counting house and factory. Their wives and children lived in a money-insulated world of the great houses, private schools, and fashionable churches surrounding the Square. There were many reasons for this "privatization" of the American upper classes after the Civil War. In Philadelphia, perhaps it goes back to the victory of Andrew Jackson over one of the city's most cultivated and aristocratic gentlemen, Nicholas Biddle. Certainly, on a national scale, President Jackson marked the end of aristocratic rule in America; the subsequent rise of modern political democracy has, in turn, been characterized by a plutocratic rather than an aristocratic upper class.

About this same period, the small and provincial Quaker City began to be invaded by a flood of immigrants from Ireland. The Native American party in Philadelphia was formed in Germantown in 1837, and the anti-Catholic riots soon frightened the city's more sober citizens.[25] In 1844, several Catholic churches in the city were burned to the ground or destroyed by mob violence; rape, arson, and murder were common in the streets of the Quaker City, and even the First City Troop was eventually called out to stem the tide of local unrest.* Then, in 1848, the government of France was overthrown and Louis Philippe escaped to England; the Italian government was attacked and the Bourbon King of Naples was forced to fly; and finally, there were the unsuccessful German revolutions.[26] At this same time, in Philadelphia, a grand meeting was held by the natives of these countries to celebrate the cause of freedom and revolution. The flags of France, Italy,

---

* The Borie and Drexel families, of French and Austrian descent respectively, were Roman Catholics (Episcopalian, with a few exceptions, after the Civil War) all through this trying period. As with other Catholic families who were educated and lived well, they almost entirely escaped this anti-Catholic feeling which was actually anti-Irish. A Roman Catholic prelate who was an Anglican convert did much to improve relations between the Anglican and Roman faiths: Bishop James Frederick Wood (1813-1883), who built the great Roman Catholic Cathedral on Logan Square (Logan Circle today), always remained unsympathetic towards the Irish, a feeling that was respected by his Protestant friends.

and Germany which were flown from the State House masts, along with the fiery speeches in alien tongues, symbolized the increasingly non-English character of the city's population. Although there was more noise than oratory, and more music than speeches, no doubt some of the city's gentry were set to thinking by the flamboyant demonstration at the State House.[27]

Finally, the great waves of immigrants from southern and eastern Europe which came to the city around the turn of the century reinforced the Rittenhouse Square gentry's sense of isolation and aloofness. A new anti-Semitism was added to an already prevalent anti-Catholicism. Such biblical given names as Levi, Isaac, Israel, and Jacob had a way of disappearing among the old-family members born after the turn of the century.

This sense of isolation from the ethnically diverse masses in America at the turn of the century quite naturally reinforced the need for conformity within the upper class itself. Moreover, the new-rich tone of the Victorian age increased this need. It must be remembered that even the old rich were newly wealthy at this time. Thus the "inner-directed" business and banking entrepeneurs of this buccaneering age were only too eager to conform to the strict Victorian code of manners when they entered the drawing-rooms of society. All this was quite in contrast to the present age where the rigid conformity of big business bureaucracy is balanced by a "bohemianization" of the private life of even the upper classes in America.

The Honorable William C. Bullitt, nonconformist Proper Philadelphian, brother-in-law of John Reed (who was buried in Lenin's Tomb), and Franklin D. Roosevelt's Ambassader to France in 1940, grew up on Rittenhouse Square, a few doors south of Holy Trinity Church (his father, William C. Bullitt, was a coal merchant and reform politician). Ambassador Bullitt once wrote a novel, *It's Not Done*, which was so popular that it went through more than seven printings the year it was published (1926).[28] *It's Not Done* was a saga of Rittenhouse Square family life in the early years of the century: "Is there any other city of a million in the world," asks one of the characters, "in which everyone who counts lives in an area three streets by eight surrounding a Sacred Square? I've been away twenty years and I'll wager I can tell you every person you've met at dinner in the interval and that there'll be no one I'll meet while I'm here who'll not call me by my first name. . . . I suppose the privilege of dancing at the Concourse [Assembly] is still the summum bonum."[29]

The following letter from the hero of *It's Not Done*, John Corsey, to his expatriate brother, Theodore, suggests something of the values and attitudes of Society on the Square, in the days of its decline after World War I, ("Chesterbridge" is of course, Philadelphia while the rest of the fictional disguises, highly transparent to the Proper Philadelphian, are unimportant to the outsider). "That night," William C. Bullitt writes, "John sat at the writing table of his room on the Square and addressed an envelope: The Right Honorable Lord Corsey, St. James's Square, London, England. Then he wrote:

Dear Ted:

I've been thinking of writing you this letter for some months. I haven't, I suppose, because I really don't like to write it. My roots in Chesterbridge are deeper than I know, and pulling up isn't easy. But I know now that I have to get out, so here goes: I want to resign the editorship of the Times. Please don't think I'm sore about anything or angry about anyone, except perhaps myself. I just want to get away to a new environment. I asked Wayne this morning to get me a job abroad, the embassy at home if he could manage it. . . .

Chesterbridge has changed, and I don't like the changes. Half the people I have respected and liked have moved into Hillcrest Cemetery, and I don't like the people who have taken their places. I suppose you know that John Collingwood died last week. (A funeral like the Concourse before 1900. Every one there. Eight tenants from his country place bearing the coffin and weeping as if their hearts were broken. 1776.) He's dead and the town is being run by Leather, Roediger, Yenks, Lowden et al. Wayne is Governor, but he is really Leather's office boy. Our beloved cousin Paul has just been interred in the State Supreme Court. Since Uncle Drayton has been President of the University he's had to spend his time going around hat in hand begging and, of course, his chief almoners are Leather, Roediger and Co., so that he's under their thumb, too. Dear old Fulke is slipping fast. He resigned from the Club last week after an incident of which you certainly haven't heard. A charwoman found him seated at six A.M. before a front window of the Club in one of the big leather armchairs reading the Sunday paper, naked except for a silk hat! Of course it was reported to the Governors and they spoke to him and he resigned. When I told him I regretted, etc., he merely said, "Doesn't it seem to you that Chesterbridge is becoming a bit stuffy, just a trifle stuffy!" . . .

Well, that's Chesterbridge 1921. . . . It's curious. There's an apparent success everywhere. Everybody in town is making and spending more money than ever before, but nobody seems to be getting any happiness out of it. And it's the same everywhere. The whole country is terribly successful, terribly in the Erehwon sense, devoured by the success of its own machines. The worst of it is that men who ought to be street cleaners and grocers and dry-goods clerks and butchers and mechanics, and would be in any other country, have millions and millions. They *are* the country to-day. We may have been here three hundred years and they may have been here twenty or fifty, but the whole taste of the country has become their taste and its standards have become their standards. What they want, they have. They're the market and the demand creates the supply. We don't count. The other day a German Jew banker had the nerve to write me that an editorial of mine was un-American. Un-American! The worst of it is I suspect he's right. . . .

Mildred left this morning for Palm Beach so that I'm all alone on the Square, and nowadays this house has a bad kind of sadness when you're alone in it—too full of ghosts—so you'll excuse me if I sound gloomy. . . . My regards to Pauline and my thanks to you for your long-suffering patience.

Yrs.
John.[30]

North and South Philadelphia: Decayed Elite Neighborhoods. There is an old saying among Proper Philadelphians that "Nobody lives north of Market." This meant, of course, that at one time, many prominent and prosperous, if not yet fashionable, families *did* live north of Market Street. After the Civil War, for example, North Broad Street was one of Philadelphia's leading elite addresses. A list of the families residing in the fifteen blocks north of City Hall on Broad Street in 1890 reads like a history of nineteenth-century business and manufacturing leadership in Philadelphia. Among other elite families whose descendants in 1940 were secure members of the contemporary upper class in Chestnut Hill or the Main Line, Disstons (Steel and Saws), Foerderers (Leather), Bromleys (Textiles), Hires (Root Beer), Dobsons (Textiles), Wideners (Traction and Utilities), Swains (Publishing), Cramps (Shipbuilding), Harrahs (Steel), and Elkinses (Traction and Oil), were all living along this elite thoroughfare in the 1890's.[31]

In the days when Rittenhouse Square was at the height of its glory, two of Philadelphia's most famous Victorian family founders, Peter A. B. Widener and William Lukens Elkins, built tremendous Victorian mansions at the corner of Broad Street and Girard Avenue (twelve blocks north of Market!). An excellent and realistic account of the life among the new-rich Philadelphians in the Girard Avenue neighborhood is found in *The Financier* by

Theodore Dreiser. When Dreiser's hero, Frank Algernon Cowperwood was thirty-four, he was worth well over two million dollars.
He built himself an outlandish Venetian-Victorian pile on Girard
Avenue in the early sixties. Cowperwood, as Dreiser meticulously
points out, was a long way socially from Rittenhouse Square
although he dealt in stocks and bonds with the Proper Philadelphia bankers along Third Street.[32]

In 1940, North Broad Street was almost entirely a commercial
thoroughfare. Only 3 per cent of those listed in *Who's Who* lived
in all of North Philadelphia. None of these families, of course,
were listed in the *Social Register*. A few members of the Jewish
elite in 1940 still lived on side streets in the North Broad Street
area. In the nineties, as the members of the gentile elite moved
away, this area became an elite Jewish residential area (see below,
Chapter XI). Today the Widener mansion, a Victorian landmark,
is a branch of the Philadelphia Public Library, and there are
small elite islands set in the seas of run-down neighborhoods
west of North Broad Street. The Pyramid Club, the Negro "Union
League," for example, is at 1517 West Girard Avenue, and Raymond
Pace Alexander, one of the city's wealthier and more powerful
Negroes, a lawyer, politician, and businessman, has a town residence at 1708 Jefferson Street (an elite North Broad address
in the 1890's) and a summer residence out along the Main Line,
beyond Paoli (see Map 2).

South Philadelphia has never been an upper-class neighborhood, and in 1940 only a few individuals listed in *Who's Who*
lived south of Pine Street. While elite mansions were being built
along North Broad Street after the Civil War, many Philadelphians
expected South Broad Street to develop in a similar manner. For
example, the Library Company ("Mr. Franklin's Library") completed the most imposing private library building in the city on
South Broad Street in 1878.[33] The Ridgway Library, an imposing
and impractical Doric temple, was endowed by Dr. James Rush,
son-in-law of Jacob Ridgway, merchant and chief rival of Stephen
Girard. This imposing library structure, which is hardly ever used by
Philadelphians today, although it houses one of the finest colonial
collections in America, was placed in South Philadelphia in anticipation of the development of the city down Broad Street, a
development which never materialized as far as the city's elite
were concerned. One of the few elite Broad Street mansions

south of Pine Street in the 1890's was owned by the famous Philadelphia lawyer and art collector, John G. Johnson.[34] The old mansion still stands but is surrounded by a commercial and Negro community. South Street, two blocks south of Pine Street, has been the chief Negro thoroughfare in the city for many years. Most of South Philadelphia, with its excellent Italian restaurants and picturesque Greek Orthodox mosques, has been populated by immigrants and their descendants from eastern and southern Europe. Marian Anderson, who was born in the city where she sang in the Union Baptist Choir as a child, was probably the most famous Philadelphian listed in *Who's Who* in 1940. Her home was in South Philadelphia.

West Philadelphia: Victorian Elite Neighborhood. Towards the end of the nineteenth century, members of the North Broad Street elite began to move out into the less congested areas of the city, the Disstons and Bromleys out to Chestnut Hill, Foerderers and Hires to the Main Line, and the Widener and Elkins families out along the Old York Road. Many families who were less fashionably inclined, however, moved over to West Philadelphia. Two of the finest examples of late Victorian architecture in West Philadelphia, for instance, were built by two Swain brothers who had grown up on elite North Broad Street. Their father, William M. Swain, was one of the greatest newspaper editors in nineteenth-century America. With his partner, Arunah S. Abell, he founded, owned, and edited both the Philadelphia *Public Ledger* and the Baltimore *Sun*.[35] One son, Charles M. Swain, bank president, built a large "Charles Addams-like" house at 45th and Spruce Streets, and his brother, William James Swain, founder of the Philadelphia *Record*, built himself a "Romanesque-Norman-Gothic" residence on Walnut Street opposite the "Drexel Colony."[36] The former house is now known as the deserted (some think haunted) "Bergdoll Mansion"; it had been owned by the wealthy, World War I draft-dodger. The latter mansion is now a stately funeral parlor. Willam Mosely Swain did not found a first-family in Philadelphia (his son William Mosely Swain, Jr., was listed in the Philadelphia *Social Register* in 1940 as living on "Belfair Plantation" in South Carolina), while his partner Arunah Abell with several descendants, including Arunah IV, listed in the Baltimore *Social Register*, apparently did. One is continually impressed with the fact that the sons of first-family founders usually moved to the more fashionable neighborhoods rather early in their careers.

The University moved out across the river to West Philadelphia in the seventies. Although many respectable upper-middle-class families, some of them extremely wealthy members of the elite, lived in West Philadelphia after the Civil War, it has never been a particularly fashionable neighborhood. It is said, for example, that some of the more exclusive fraternities at the University, in the 1870's and 1880's, when many sons of the best families still went to Pennsylvania, prided themselves on not having any members who lived west of the Schuylkill. Proper Philadelphians on Rittenhouse Square even credited their acquaintances across the river with "West Philadelphia accents." In contrast to the Georgian mansions along Brattle Street in Cambridge, across the Charles River from Boston, great houses built by new-rich Victorians are the most characteristic historical landmarks in the University neighborhood, across the Schuylkill in West Philadelphia.

Many wealthy and prominent Victorians, ancestors of some of today's most fashionable Philadelphians, built large mansions along Walnut, Locust, and Spruce Streets in West Philadelphia after the Civil War. In this period, for example, the "Drexel Colony" was the center of society across the river. A. J. Drexel, a firm believer in the lasting values of real estate investments, owned a great deal of land in West Philadelphia, including almost the entire block bounded by 38th and 39th and Walnut and Locust Streets where he built fine houses for himself and each of his children.[37] Totally absorbed in banking ever since joining his father's firm at the age of thirteen, Mr. Drexel was far less interested in fashionable Philadelphia than his children, all of whom eventually moved to more fashionable areas of the city after their father's death in 1893.

The house that Mr. Drexel built for his son, George W. Childs Drexel, at 39th and Locust Streets, for example, was sold to a wealthy coal merchant, E. B. Leisenring, whose son was listed in both *Who's Who* and the *Social Register* in 1940. The house then passed to Mr. Leisenring's brother-in-law, Dr. John S. Wentz, founder of John S. Wentz & Company (coal mining) and president of the Virginia Coal & Iron Company.[38] It is now a fraternity house at the University of Pennsylvania.

In 1940 West Philadelphia was second only to Germantown as the most frequent place of residence among those who were listed in *Who's Who*, but *not* in the *Social Register*. This was partly due to the large number of professors who lived in the University neighborhood. Many leading members of the contemporary business elite, however, still lived in West Philadelphia. Samuel S. Fels, soap manufacturer and one of the city's leading philanthropists, lived at 39th and Walnut Streets, on the same spot where A. J. Drexel had built his own fabulous mansion with forty-one rooms after the Civil War. The late Mr. Fels left his fine house to the *Institute of Local and State Government* which he endowed and founded at the University of Pennsylvania.

At the western boundary of the city, just inside the city line from the Main Line, lies the Wynnefield section of West Philadelphia. This neighborhood was built up before World War I by wealthy businessmen. Clarence H. Geist, one of the most fabulous, new-rich Philadelphians in the first part of the twentieth century, lived at 6399 Drexel Road, the elite street in Wynnefield at that time (Geist soon moved to the Main Line). In 1940, Wynnefield was primarily an elite Russian Jewish neighborhood. Many prominent businessmen and political leaders listed in *Who's Who* lived in this neighborhood, among them Albert M. Greenfield, perhaps the most powerful man in Philadelphia today, who lived in the former Geist residence on Drexel Road in 1940 (Greenfield has since moved to Chestnut Hill).

The Suburbs of Philadelphia. In Philadelphia, as in other eastern seaboard cities, the well-known suburban communities have passed through several more or less distinct sociological periods. Originally they were purely local communities situated along the old turnpikes leading out from the city. Germantown, for example, was an autonomous local community settled by Germans in the seventeenth century. Many of these local communities first became a part of upper-class Philadelphia during the eighteenth century. Two sociological processes were involved. First, many Philadelphia merchants and professional men built large country seats along these early turnpikes. Thus Chief Justice Benjamin Chew built "Cliveden," one of the few eighteenth-century country seats still in possession of the original owner's family, along the Germantown Pike in Germantown. Although he lived there in the summer months, he and his family returned to their winter house on Third Street where they were still a part of Philadelphia life both economically and socially.

At the same time that the wealthy city merchants were moving out into the surrounding countryside, many local ironmasters were building their own mansions outside various local communities. Then as they became more prosperous, and encountered Philadelphia merchants and bankers in business, these ironmasters began to differentiate themselves from the natives of the local community. In other words, these local first-families soon became part of Philadelphia's upper class both economically and socially; many moved to their city houses during the winter months, joining the city men's clubs, attending the Assembly Balls, and borrowing from the Philadelphia bankers. Many Proper Philadelphia families first made their money in small industrial communities, such as Conshohocken, Manayunk, or Norristown, along the Schuylkill River. George B. Roberts, president of the Pennsylvania Railroad from 1880 to 1897, for example, was born at "Pencoyd Farm" in Bala-Cynwyd along the Main Line where his family had lived for five generations.[39] His son, vice-president of the Philadelphia Savings Fund Society in 1940 and later president, still lives on the same property. The Roberts family had been ironmasters for several generations and the Pencoyd Iron Works were just below the family homestead on the Schuylkill River opposite Manayunk. Pencoyd specialized in making bridges, some of which were no doubt used by the Pennsylvania Railroad.[40] In 1900, the Roberts firm became part of the American Bridge Company and Percival Roberts, George B. Roberts's cousin, became a director of the newly-formed United States Steel Company. Just as the Roberts family of the old "Welsh Barony" eventually became part of Proper Philadelphia, so the family firm was absorbed by the large corporation.

This process of the absorption of the local ironmasters or manufacturers by the large city, at least socially, has continued down through the years. For example, the Alan Wood Iron & Steel Company, one of the few successful, family-owned steel companies in the Philadelphia area today, was founded by James Wood in 1832, in the small manufacturing community of Conshohocken, a few miles up the Schuylkill from the Pencoyd works.[41] James Wood's grandson, Alan Wood, Jr., built an impressive

"French Gothic chateau style" mansion, "Woodmont," on the bluffs above the Schuylkill across the river from Conshohocken.[42] In 1890, although they lived at "Woodmont," the Woods also spent the winter months in Philadelphia.[43] As early as the last part of the eighteenth, and continuing through the nineteenth century, then, urban imperialism at the upper-class level was working both ways: the wealthy Philadelphia merchant, banker, or businessman moved out to the country, while the prosperous local family on The Hill, outside of Conshohocken, Norristown, or Manayunk, moved into the city, economically, socially, or both.*

In the middle of the nineteenth century, a second period of migration to the suburbs began with the development of the suburban railroads which usually ran parallel to the old turnpike routes. The early suburbanites usually spent only the summer months in the country, the more wealthy in their country houses and their less affluent friends in various popular boarding houses. With the improvement in rail service in the last few decades of the nineteenth century, large suburban estates began to multiply, suburban developments were built, and many families remained the year round.

Finally, after World War I, the upper classes moved in large numbers to the suburbs. By the end of the twenties, most of the fashionable private schools had moved to the suburbs, the best indication that upper-class family life was now predominantly suburban. The neighborhood migrations of upper-class Philadelphia is summed up in Table 20 which shows where the directors of the Philadelphia National Bank lived in 1823, 1890, 1914, and 1940.

Germantown. The oldest real suburb in Philadelphia, and probably in America, Germantown was a leading elite suburb in 1940, though hardly as fashionable as the Main Line or Chestnut Hill. Of the Philadelphians listed in *Who's Who*, for example, 16 per cent lived in Germantown, as against 20 per cent along the Main Line, the most popular elite suburb (see Table 17). Moreover,

---

* As an ironic consequence of social change, it is interesting that today (1955) Father Divine and his Angels, leaders of a vigorous Negro sect, are the owners of "Woodmont." Residing in a former gatehouse on the estate, Francis Hopkinson (son of Edward Jr., and great-great-grandson of the signer of the Declaration of Independence) and his wife (great-granddaughter of Alan Wood) watch the Cadillacs going up to the former Wood castle on the hill with a certain amount of historical circumspection.

while almost half of the Main Line residents were also listed in the *Social Register,* only 15 per cent of the residents of Germantown were so listed. Although Germantown was primarily a middle-class suburb in 1940, more stately eighteenth-century mansions are found within a few miles of each other in this area than in all the rest of Philadelphia combined.

Germantown is almost as old as the city of Philadelphia. In 1683, Francis Daniel Pastorius, the son of a judge in Frankfürt, Germany, obtained a grant of some 6,000 acres of land from William Penn "in behalf of the German and Dutch purchasers."[44] Although primarily Lutherans and Methodists, the inhabitants of Germantown, from the beginning, have included members of the Society of Friends. Until the last decade of the eighteenth century, German was the official and spoken language in the community.

In 1793, Philadelphians invaded Germantown in large numbers. In that tragic year almost one-third of the city's residents fled the yellow-fever epidemic. According to the epidemic's historian, J. H. Powell, "Germantown, strangely uninfected, was the closest, and soon became the most crowded, resort of the fugitives."[45] Among the fugitives were many important members of the Federal Government. During November, for example, President Washington held several cabinet meetings in one of the present buildings of the Germantown Academy, where he was a guest of one of the school's masters.

Table 20—Directors of the Philadelphia National Bank— Residence in 1823, 1890, 1914, and 1940

Residence	Directors in 1823	Directors in 1890	Directors in 1914	Directors in 1940
Washington Square	74%	11%	6%	—
North of Market	26%	—	—	—
Rittenhouse Square	—	55%	41%	13%
West Philadelphia	—	6%	—	—
Germantown	—	11%	6%	4%
Chestnut Hill-Main Line	—	17%	41%	79%
Other areas	—	—	6%	4%
	100%	100%	100%	100%
	N-23	N-18	N-17	N-23

Source: the names of the directors were obtained in Nicholas B. Wainwright, *The Philadelphia National Bank, 1803-1953* (Philadelphia: Privately Printed, 1953), pp. 235-243. Addresses were checked in *The Philadelphia Index of Directory for 1823* (Philadelphia, 1823); *Boyd's Blue Book,* 1889-1890; *Boyd's Philadelphia Blue Book,* 1914; and the *Social Register* and Philadelphia Telephone Directory, 1940. Twenty of the twenty-three directors in 1940 were listed in the *Social Register.*

After their experience with the epidemic, many Philadelphia families bought land in Germantown and others spent the summer in various boarding houses. During this period, the residents of Germantown built the first church in which English was spoken from the pulpit. Encouraged by the Philadelphia invasion, in 1797, a local carpenter bought up a large tract of land in the southern part of Germantown in order to develop a new community. He subdivided the land into fifty building lots, laid out streets, and planned to call the new community "Manheim." "However, the site proved alluring to a number of wealthy Philadelphia families," writes an historian of Germantown, "who bought the entire tract and built country estates thereon. Ever since the locality has been known as Manheim, and in recent times most of the tract has been included in the grounds of the Germantown Cricket Club."[46]

In the 1830's, the first railroad to Germantown and another epidemic in Philadelphia contributed to the suburban trend. In 1832 Philadelphians were suffering from an epidemic of Asiatic cholera which swept the Atlantic coast that year. During the summer, it was estimated that between 500 and 600 people from elsewhere were boarding in Germantown.[47] In 1830 a group of Germantown civic leaders met to discuss the construction of a railroad from Philadelphia to Germantown. Reuben Haines, of "Wyck," one of Germantown's historic mansions today, presided over the meeting, while Benjamin Chew, Jr., of "Cliveden," the first Chief Justice's country seat, was secretary.[48] The next year, the Philadelphia, Germantown and Norristown Railroad Company was incorporated by an act of the State Legislature, and a five-mile track to Germantown was completed in 1832. Although many of the cars were still pulled by horses, "Old Ironsides," Matthias W. Baldwin's first locomotive, was used on the Germantown line. As late as the fifties, an early commuter car went in to Philadelphia propelled by the force of gravity. Each morning at six A.M. the car left Germantown after being started by workmen with crowbars.

In the nineties, the Germantown Cricket Club, often called "Manheim," was an important center of fashionable Philadelphia society. Cricket had been introduced into Germantown by English mill workers about 1844. In 1854 the first team composed wholly of Americans was organized and named the Germantown Cricket Club. William Wister taught the game to Philadelphia gentlemen at the Wister estate in Germantown. In 1855 the Young America

Cricket Club came into existence at the Newhall estate on Manheim Street (see Chapter XIV for a description of the modern Newhall family doings in banking circles).[49]

In 1891 the Germantown Cricket Club, now combined with the Young America, improved its grounds and completed a new clubhouse designed by McKim, Meade, and White, the famous New York architects. Excerpts from the club's annual report in November, 1892, suggest the flavor of fashionable life in Germantown in the nineties:

This, the thirty-eighth year of its existence, finds the club as a leading cricket organization of this country, its progress having far exceeded the greatest anticipation of its many well wishers.

The membership is now 1103, made up as follows: Honorary, 10; Life, 66; Family, 428; Senior, 228; Playing, 32; Active, 112; Junior, 181; Non-resident, 46. The number of tickets issued to ladies, through the privilege of family membership, brings the grand total of those interested in the welfare of the organization to nearly 2000.

The interest shown in the international cricket matches played on the grounds with Lord Hawke's team of English cricketers in September and October, has led the managers to believe that Manheim has been chosen as the international cricket grounds of America; and it may not be amiss to state that not only is the Germantown Cricket Club the only one in the United States that has ever attempted, singlehanded to bring a team of English cricketers to this country, but that it reflects honor upon the organization that an undertaking of such magnitude should have been so successful, not only financially, but from a cricketing point of view. During the six days of these matches nearly forty thousand people witnessed the play.

That the grounds are socially a success is now an undisputed fact, and too much credit cannot be given to the Ladies Committee for their untiring efforts to promote the welfare of the club in this direction. Ladies' teas have been served every Tuesday; Thursday has been made music day, and Saturday match day, so that the entire week has been made attractive, and the attendance consequently large. It is proposed that these attractions shall be continued and new ones added during the coming year.

The treasurer's report, which gave an excellent financial showing for the club, contained a statement that the total cost of the grounds and clubhouse at Manheim, was nearly $220,000.[50]

Not only was Manheim a center of fashionable life in the nineties, in addition, many Proper Philadelphians still lived in Germantown, especially along School Lane and Wissahickon Avenue. The Clark family, for instance, were leaders in the sporting and social life of the neighborhood: E. W. Clark, of Philadelphia's leading banking house, financiers of the Mexican War and first employers of Jay Cooke, was president of Manheim for over twenty years. He lived at the corner of School Lane and Wissahickon Avenue. Members of the Clark family were well known cricketers and tennis players; Clarence M. Clark and Frederick W. Taylor (as precise on the court as in his time-study work) were national doubles champions, and Joseph S. Clark, father of the present United States Senator from Pennsylvania, was national intercollegiate and Philadelphia champion.[51]

Although several Proper Philadelphians still lived in Germantown in 1940 (Attorney General Francis Biddle lived on School Lane), most of the families had moved away by the time of the first World War. In 1911, for example, the E. W. Clark estate was given to the citizens of Germantown as a public park (in the same year, "Cliveden Park" was given by the Chew family).[52] In 1912, the Clark family lived in a beautiful estate not far from the old Wissahickon Inn (Chestnut Hill Academy) and the Philadelphia Cricket Club in Chestnut Hill. At the same time, Oswald Chew, listed in *Who's Who* in 1940, and his brother Benjamin, were living on the large Chew estate in Radnor on the Main Line.

Although the Main Line and Chestnut Hill are fashionable and Episcopalian today, Germantown retains its original Quaker atmosphere. Something will be said of the Quaker elite in a later chapter.

The Main Line. The Main Line consists of a series of suburban communities—Overbrook, Merion, Wynnewood, Ardmore, Haverford, Bryn Mawr, Rosemont, Villa Nova, Radnor, Wayne, Devon, and Paoli—along the main line to the west of the Pennsylvania Railroad. The "Mainliner" commutes to the city on the "Paoli Local."

Exploited in literature and by the popular press, the famous Main Line is the most popular elite suburb in Philadelphia (see Table 17). Each Sunday, Philadelphians read all about upperclass social life in the Philadelphia *Inquirer's* popular society column, "The Mainliner" (the column has often been written by a resident of Chestnut Hill). As the column reports social minutiæ about fashionable Philadelphians throughout the city, the term "Mainliner" has become synonymous with "upper crust," "old family," or "socialite." This is especially true, of course, among outsiders and those below the upper-class level. It is no accident that Christopher Morley and Philip Barry exploited the "Main-liner" stereotype when writing about Philadelphia's "leisure classes enjoying their leisure."

As we noted earlier in these pages, the Pennsylvania Railroad has always been a very Proper Philadelphia business enterprise. The development of the Main Line has been intimately connected with the railroad. Many old Main Line families today are the descendants of leading executives of this venerable Philadelphia institution. All the presidents of the Pennsylvania Railroad since George B. Roberts, for example, have lived along the Main Line. In the nineties Frank Thomson, who became president when Mr. Roberts died in 1897, was a well-known host at his beautiful Merion estate; A. J. Cassatt, president from 1899 to 1906, lived at "Cheswold," one of the show places in Haverford. (As was the custom, Mr. Cassatt spent the winter months at 202 Rittenhouse Square.) James McCrea, who was president from 1907 to 1912, spent most of his railroad career in the lines west of Pittsburgh, but he was living at his Haverford estate, "Ballyweather," just before he died in 1913; Samuel Rea, president from 1913 to 1925, bought a modest house near the Bryn Mawr station while he was a vice-president and continued to live there for several years after he became president; when he died in 1929, however, he was living in a more pretentious estate, "Waverly Heights," in Bryn Mawr; W. W. Atterbury, president from 1925 to 1835, died a few months after his retirement at "Boudinot Farms" in Radnor.[53]

Martin W. Clement, listed in both the *Social Register* (M. Withington) and *Who's Who* (Martin W.) in 1940, became president of the Railroad in 1935. Born of colonial stock with a venerable military tradition in Sunbury, Pennsylvania, Mr. Clement achieved the Proper Philadelphia position befitting a president of the Pennsylvania Railroad. In his *Who's Who* biography, for instance, he listed membership in *The Sons of the Revolution, Society of the War of 1812, Baronial Order of Runnymede, Colonial Society of Pennsylvania,* and the Republican Party; his numerous directorships included the Girard Trust Company and the Philadelphia Savings Fund Society; he was a member of the *Philadelphia* and *Rittenhouse* clubs; finally, he lived at "Crefeld," his estate in Rosemont, and was a vestryman of the Church of the Redeemer, the Main Line's largest and most fashionable Episcopal church.[54]

The Pennsylvania Railroad built double tracks along the Main Line in the 1860's. With only six trains daily, lighted with oil lamps and heated with red-hot coal stoves, however, there was no commuter life as we know it today.[55] In this early period, Philadelphians came out for the summer months, and social life, even for the elite, centered around the many turnpike taverns and boarding houses. In 1874, in an advertisement extolling the advantages of the Main Line, the Pennsylvania Railroad listed some fifty boarding houses between Overbrook and Paoli. The "Wildgoss" boarding house, near Haverford College, was the most popular among fashionable Philadelphians; rooms could be rented only for the entire summer, and there was always a long waiting list (that refined and well-to-do families spent hot summers in boarding houses which were without bathtubs or running water is a reminder of social change since the sixties). In those more leisurely days, when young Victorian wives made a social event out of the arrival of their husbands from the city each evening, the suburban stations on the railroad were known as "kissing stops."[56]

The tempo of suburban development along the Main Line increased in the early seventies. The Pennsylvania Railroad, for example, bought up a large tract of land near the present Bryn Mawr station, marked off streets, planted the inevitable suburban saplings, and set up its own private zoning regulations which included minimum set-back and house value limits; no house on Montgomery Avenue, the principal street, was to cost less than $8,000.[57] In order to attract settlers in the new community, the Railroad also built the Bryn Mawr Hotel, an enormous Victorian structure now used by the Baldwin School for girls.

A. J. Cassatt, while a vice-president of the railroad, was one of the first guests (along with his now-famous artist sister, Mary) at the old Bryn Mawr Hotel. Cassatt was one of the more colorful Main Line personalities in this early era; in the seventies—a free-enterprising decade—he and a group of his friends bought up some fifteen miles of the Lancaster Pike between Bryn Mawr and Paoli, made it into a first-class macadamized road, and charged a toll to keep it in order for carriage driving, one of Cassatt's favorite sports.[58]

Among the first Philadelphians to build a large country estate in Bryn Mawr was George W. Childs, editor of one of the city's leading newspapers, the *Public Ledger*. At "Wootton," Mr. Childs, a generous host, entertained many prominent Americans of his day: "General Grant planted a memorial tree on the Wootton lawn, as did also General Sherman, President Hayes, Mrs. Grover Cleveland, A. J. Drexel and many other noted people."[59] In 1881, George W. Childs and his close friend, A. J. Drexel, anticipating George Babbitt by more than a generation, built America's first suburban development in Wayne, several miles beyond Bryn Mawr on the Main Line. South of the railroad tracks, they erected fifty modern homes which included spacious lawns, ample shade trees, and such conveniences of the city as water, sewer, and gas mains. When asked why he built this new development so far out in the country, Childs quickly replied that it would give the residents more time to read the *Ledger*.

George W. Childs Drexel, named for his father's close friend, was one of the three "retired capitalists" listed in both *Who's Who* and the *Social Register* in 1940. In 1903 he sold the *Ledger*, which he had inherited, and retired from his post as publisher. (Few people knew that for thirty years during George W. Childs' lifetime A. J. Drexel and his brothers held three-fourths of the ownership in the paper to Child's one-fourth.)[61] In 1940, George W. Childs Drexel lived in retirement at "Wootton" (his widow lived there until 1949, after which the property was cut up by a modern developer into more modest "estates" for junior executives).

The era between 1890 and 1929 produced many big men and a fabulously prosperous American upper class (in 1890, for example, foreign stockholders owned 47.46 per cent of the total outstanding shares of the Pennsylvania Railroad Company, as against 1.54 per cent in 1920).[62] These big men built large estates along the Main Line, with "formal gardens," "sunken gardens," "Italian gardens," or "Japanese gardens," all as unlike nature as possible. Certainly men who had built cities of concrete and spanned a continent with steel rails were hardly likely to be satisfied with natural surroundings, which, after all, would not cost enough. Not to be outdone by the railroad, at least seven executives of the Baldwin Locomotive Works also built show places along the Main Line. On Bryn Mawr Avenue, opposite Mr. Child's "Wootton," one imaginative Baldwin executive built a large mansion whose outlines resembled a locomotive.[63] Fortunately for the preservation of neighborhood standards, the less affluent members of the upper class, often more discriminating in their taste, built smaller sub-urban houses along the Main Line during this period.

Chestnut Hill: Suburban Upper-Class Neighborhood. Although the better-known Main Line is the most popular upper-class neighborhood in Philadelphia, Chestnut Hill is more homogeneous and exclusively upper class (see Table 17). Quantitatively, there are more families listed in the *Social Register* per square mile in Chestnut Hill than anywhere else in the metropolitan area. While it is, of course, absurd to say that the residents of Chestnut Hill are socially superior to those on the Main Line, it is true, never-theless, that the relatively small area of Chestnut Hill is more provincially upper class in atmosphere than the more cosmopolitan Main Line. At the upper-class level, for instance, Chestnut Hill has all the qualities of the small village: the social life is inbred, as it were; everyone knows everyone else; gossip travels very fast. Above all, there is the quaint ethnocentrism of the village, with more than the normal amount of pride of place. One local resident of Chestnut Hill betrays this attitude in the following remark: "We went slumming for the first time in years last night," he reported to John Gunther. "We dined with people on the Main Line."[64] More than one wife in Chestnut Hill has refused to move to the Main Line, even though the latter suburb was far more convenient to her husband's job in a suburban industrial concern located in the southern part of the city. Perhaps the most important contrast between these two suburbs is the fact that an outsider— a psychiatrist or lawyer from another city, for instance—would certainly find the cosmopolitan Main Line friendlier and more congenial than Chestnut Hill; especially if he were from the Middle West and entertained "peculiar" ideas about the demo-cratic value of public, as against private, school education. "No-body" sends his children to public school in Chestnut Hill; but the Main Line boasts of, and supports, several of the finest public schools in the nation.

Chestnut Hill, in contrast to the sprawling Main Line suburbs, is a relatively small, built-up community within the city limits about twelve miles northwest of the downtown business and shop-ping district (see Map 2). When the Reading Railroad came out to Chestnut Hill in 1854, this small village on the outskirts of Germantown began its early development as a Philadelphia suburb. The parish of St. Paul's Episcopal Church, today's most fashionable church in Chestnut Hill, for example, was organized by several prominent residents in 1855, and the original church building dates from 1856.[65] It is interesting that Chestnut Hill, Boston's most exclusive suburb, was developed in this same period by a group of merchants who planned the community in the counting room of Lee, Higginson & Company.[66]

In the eighties, Chestnut Hill went through a period of rapid development. Henry Howard Houston, whose son and son-in-law were both listed in *Who's Who* and the *Socal Register* in 1940, was one of the early, and largest, landowners in the southern part of Chestnut Hill. A successful financier, steamship executive, and speculator in both California gold and Pennsylvania oil, Mr. Houston was also a director of the Pennsylvania Railroad between 1881 and 1895. Due to his vision and encouragement, the Pennsylvania built a commuter line out to Chestnut Hill in 1884.[67]

At this same time Mr. Houston made many other contributions to the development of the neighborhood: in 1884 he built the Wissahickon Inn in order to encourage summer residents to come out from the city; this period piece, like the old Bryn Mawr Hotel it resembles, is today a private school for boys, Chestnut Hill Academy; in the same year, Mr. Houston built the St. Martin's Episcopal Church; and finally, the Philadelphia Cricket Club, founded in 1854, moved to its present location next to St. Martin's Church in 1884 (the grounds were given to the club by Mr. Houston).

In 1892 the Philadelphia Horse Show was held on the Houston land near the Cricket Club and the Wissahickon Inn. The Horse Show has always been an important event in the city's sporting and fashionable life; for many years Edward T. Stotesbury, local Morgan partner and director of the Philadelphia, New York, and London horse shows, carried off the blue ribbon in the trotter or "Gentlemen's Roadster" class.

The Philadelphia Horse Show remained in Chestnut Hill until 1908, when it moved to its present location at Devon on the Main Line: "As the neighborhood grew in handsome residences, attracted by the Cricket Club, Horse Show and Church," writes Horace Mather Lippincott, an historian (and resident) of Chestnut Hill, "the residents objected to the many inflammable frame buildings of the Horse Show grounds . . ."[68]

While the Main Line was a popular suburb among executives

of the Pennsylvania Railroad, many leading Philadelphians came
out to Chestnut Hill because it was convenient to the industrial
northern part of the city and because it was within the city limits,
a factor appealing to those men who were interested in the city's
government. The Disston family, for instance, have been residents
of Chestnut Hill for three generations. In the 1890's while Henry
Disston still lived at 1505 North Broad Street, which was convenient to his saw-works in the northern part of the city on the
Delaware River, his sons moved out to Chestnut Hill. "Norwood
Hall," Jacob S. Disston's castle-like mansion, was one of Chestunt
Hill's landmarks for many years, especially for those boys in the
neighborhood who had read the romances of Walter Scott. Another
well-known estate in Chestnut Hill was built by the father of
"Scientific Management," Frederick W. Taylor. "Boxly," named
for its famous and scientifically developed boxwood gardens, was
convenient to "Speedy" Taylor's work at the Midvale Steel Works
in North Philadelphia.

One of the unfortunate consequences of the modern suburban
trend has been the fact that many responsible members of the
urban business community cannot vote in city elections. Many of
the city's more civic-minded leaders, therefore, prefer to live in
Chestnut Hill rather than on the Main Line which is outside the
city limits.

Richard Vaux, Secretary of the American Legation in London
in 1838, Mayor of Philadelphia in 1856, and a Congressman in
1890, was one of the most picturesque residents of Chestnut Hill.
He was a Quaker and an ardent Democrat who, it is said, would
never walk past the Union League. When the local papers reported
that her son had danced with Queen Victoria, Richard Vaux's
mother, a good Quaker, is reported to have said: "I do hope
Richard will not marry out of meeting."[69]

Today's residents of Chestnut Hill are not Quakers, and do
not belong to the Democratic party. After Richard Vaux, the
next Proper Philadelphia resident of Chestnut Hill to be elected
Mayor of Philadelphia, however, was Joseph S. Clark, Jr. In 1951,
Mayor Clark not only ran on the Democratic ticket but carried
Chestnut Hill (the 22nd Ward) which went Democratic in a
mayoralty election for the first time in the twentieth century.*

---

* Mrs. George M. Dallas III, still followed the Dallas family's Democratic
traditions. An ardent Democratic committeewoman, she did a great deal to
bring about Clark's local victory (see George M. Dallas, Chapter VII).

Unlike most of the fashionable residents of Chestnut Hill, who are Republican and Episcopalian, Mayor Clark is both a Democrat and a Unitarian.

Chestnut Hill has remained a surprisingly stable suburb over the years. In comparison to other American suburbs, the neighborhood has changed very little in over half a century. Many of the local merchants have been serving the same families for several generations: Whittem's pharmacy, which has not bowed to the drug store trend even to this day, has been run by the same family since 1874. Frank Streeper, trained by the elder Whittem, opened his own drug store in 1892, and today Streeper's is the gathering place for Chestnut Hill's young, soda-drinking set, as it has been for several generations. The Streepers, at one time the largest landowners in Chestnut Hill and residents since the eighteenth century, are the oldest, if not the most fashionable, family in Chestnut Hill.[70]

Several things have contributed to the stability of Chestnut Hill as an upper-class suburb. First, even in the early part of the century, although the houses were large and comfortable, they were built fairly close together and protected by judicious planting rather than numerous acres. Thus these original estates have remained intact through the years, even when the lack of gardeners and servants caused the break-up of larger estates elsewhere. Schools are both good, and within walking distance; commuting to town is easy. Finally, one of the most stabilizing factors in Chestnut Hill is the fact that, to this day, many smaller houses are owned by the Houston estate. Rented at reasonable rates, usually to the impecunious genteel, the houses in this somewhat feudalistic real estate venture have served to conserve the neighborhood to an unusual degree. It is the profit motive, after all, which drives the usual suburb in America from shirt-sleeves to shirt-sleeves in two or three generations. Although the Houston estate has undoubtedly done well in its venture into medium-priced housing for the genteel, it has always placed neighborhood stability above immediate and maximum profits.

The Andorra Nurseries have been responsible for much of the fine planting around Chestnut Hill. They occupy a thousand acres purchased by Henry H. Houston in 1886.[71] The offices of the Andorra Nurseries are in an old farmhouse on the outskirts of Chestnut Hill, once owned by John Yerkes who supplied grain for Washington's army at Valley Forge and whose descendant, Charles T. Yerkes, built the London and Chicago subways and supplied the model for Theodore Dreiser's hero, Frank Algernon Cowperwood in *The Financier.*

Penllyn-Whitemarsh's Rural Gentlemen's Retreat. In many ways the Penllyn-Whitemarsh area is a sociological extension of Chestnut Hill as far as upper-class neighborhoods are concerned. As the original Philadelphia Cadwalader came to America in 1697 from the Comot of Penllyn, County Meredith, Wales, the most exclusive village in this area has an appropriate name.[72] This charming rural area, with its many turnpike taverns, old Pennsylvania stone farmhouses, and stately colonial mansions such as "Hope Lodge" built by Samuel Morris in 1723, is Philadelphia's most genteel residential neighborhood. Of all the residents of this area listed in *Who's Who* in 1940, for instance, over 80 per cent were also listed in the *Social Register* (Table 17). Moreover, three of the six managers of the Assembly Ball in 1940 lived in or near Penllyn.

Most of the familes in this area—Ingersolls, Cadwaladers, Coxes, Vauxes, Bullitts, Beales of older wealth, and Wideners, Klines, Cookes, and McLeans of more recent wealth—have had money for several generations. In this almost studied atmosphere of old money, one finds few of the formal estates with manicured lawns, baroque formal gardens, and high, wrought-iron fences so characteristic of many of the larger estates along the Main Line. Privacy and hard-riding simplicity suits these gentlemen-farmers, who have a tendency to feel somewhat different, if not aloof from the fashionable families in the more typically suburban areas of the city. It is not that they are snobbish. On the contrary, they are usually rather shy with strangers, and if anything, the few large clans in and around Penllyn and Fort Washington, relatives or friends of many years, simply do not feel the need for enlarging their circle of acquaintances. What little organized club life there was in the area centered around the Whitemarsh Valley Hunt, recently defunct, and the small Penllyn Club where polo was played until it died a natural death after 1929.

On the whole, the clannishness, combined with extreme individuality, which marks the families in this area, is a reminder of an earlier America. In recent years, one or two extra-marital romances have precipitated extremely individualistic behavior. Early one morning, for instance, a very Proper Philadelphian turned up at a hunt meeting, gun in hand, prepared to go after a close friend who had been a bit too intimate with his wife. One could not help thinking of the days when gentlemen were more ready to protect their honor at pistol point.

The Jenkintown Suburbs: The Rise and Fall of a Fashionable Suburb. A continuation of North Broad Street, geographically and in many ways socially, the Old York Road, built in 1711, leads to the north of Philadelphia, up through Bucks County to New Hope on the Delaware River (see Map 2). The Jenkintown suburbs—Elkins Park, Ogontz, Jenkintown, Abington, Rydal, Meadowbrook, and Huntington Valley—are all in the neighborhood of this famous old turnpike.

Before World War I, many old Philadelphia families, and many famous Americans—the publishers, Cyrus Curtiss, George Horace Lorrimer, and J. Bertram Lippincott, and the well-known traction magnates, P. A. B. Widener and William Lukens Elkins—lived along the Old York Road. According to Horace Mather Lippincott, who grew up in the area but was listed as a resident of Chestnut hill in the 1940 *Who's Who* and *Social Register,* the following famous Americans were neighbors in the late nineteenth century: "Owen Wister, the novelist; Joseph Wharton, ironmaster and philanthropist; Lucretia Mott, Quaker Minister, abolitionist and women's suffrage leader; John B. Stetson, hat manufacturer; John Wanamaker, merchant and Postmaster General; and Edward T. Stotesbury and Jay Cooke, financiers of national distinction."[73] Representing two important, if not always compatible social forces in the "Gilded Age," the fast friendship between the financial buccaneer, Jay Cooke, and Lucretia Mott, reforming suffragette, was all the more interesting.

In the eighteen-eighties, the traction magnates, William L. Elkins and P. A. B. Widener bought up large tracts of land in what is now Elkins Park (so named in 1899). A genealogist of the Elkins family describes here how they built the first housing development in the area:

Following the examples, it may be said, of the Astors and Rhinelanders in New York, Mr. Elkins, in company with his friend and esteemed business associate, Mr. P. A. B. Widener, of Philadelphia, has recently turned his attention to real estate investments in the Quaker city, and together they have purchased large tracts of land in the northern section, upon which they have erected upwards of three thousand houses. This magnificent effort in the line of urban development has been of great practical advantage to the city and its people, as well as profitable to the enterprising projectors.[74]

The Jenkintown neighborhood, once quite fashionable and in many ways more colorful than the Main Line or Chestnut Hill, has not maintained its upper-class status over the years. Of all the Philadelphians listed in *Who's Who* in 1940, for example, 78 per cent of the Chestnut Hill, and 48 per cent of the Main Line residents, as against only 27 per cent of the residents of Jenkintown, were also listed in the *Social Register* (see Table 17). Although many old families continue to remain loyal to the Old York Road, the younger generation has been moving away for several decades. In 1940, for example, Joseph Wharton Lippincott, listed in both *Who's Who* and the *Social Register*, and president of the family publishing house, J. B. Lippincott Company, still lived at "Oak Hill" in the Old York Road neighborhood, while his two sons and married daughter now live on the Main Line.

The story of the rise and fall of the Old York Road neighborhood is reflected in the history of the families of Jay Cooke and P. A. B. Widener. Jay Cooke, who had privately financed the Civil War for the United States Government, started to build one of the first great mansions in Pennsylvania, "Ogontz," in 1865.[75] Cooke himself planned and supervised the building of this curiously baroque Victorian mansion. The house included the inevitable Italian garden, the imported ruins of a European castle, music and entertainment rooms complete with stage and scenery, and numerous statues and fountains placed along the many "vistas" which were cut through some two hundred acres of forest. Its fifty-two rooms, maintained by over seventy servants, were used to entertain such intimate friends as President Grant, who attended the five-hundred-guest house-warming ceremonies in 1867. The cost of "Ogontz," over one million dollars, was unusual for that day. Just ten years after he had completed "Ogontz," Jay Cooke, like a former Philadelphian, Robert Morris, financier of the Revolution, went through bankruptcy in the panic of 1873. "Ogontz" became a young ladies' finishing school.

In 1900, Peter Arrell Brown Widener moved from his city residence at Broad and Girard Avenue out to the Old York Road neighborhood where he and his partner William L. Elkins had been buying land for some time. In that year, this former butcher's boy who now owned over 500 miles of car tracks in Philadelphia, New York, Chicago, Baltimore, and Pittsburgh, completed a 110-room mansion, "Lynnewood Hall," on a 300-acre tract of land in Elkins Park.[76] This American Versailles, a mansion in the then popular Georgian style, was designed by the architect, Horace Trumbauer; the formal French gardens were laid out by Jacques Greber, who redesigned the outskirts of Paris. At "Lynnewood Hall," Mr. Widener and his son, Joseph E. Widener, built up one of the finest private art collections in the world.

When P. A. B. Widener died in 1914, he left one of the city's greatest fortunes. The estate included the famous art collection, left under the care of his son, Joseph E. Widener, with instructions that it eventually be given to a public museum in either Philadelphia, New York, or Washington.[77]

Today there are no Cookes and Wideners living along the Old York Road. A year before his death in 1943, Joseph E. Widener gave the family art collection, some 300 paintings, including sixteen Rembrandts, and Titians, Raphaels, Gainsboroughs, Van Dycks, Holbeins, and Millets, to the National Gallery (for tax purposes, the collection was valued at $7,141,060). As the local newspapers reported at the time, Mr. Widener had "cut off the Philadelphia Museum without a single painting."[78]

In 1944, 220 acres of the Widener estate, including a private race track, were sold to a developer; "Lynnewood Gardens," a twenty-million-dollar housing development, helped to alleviate the postwar housing shortage in Philadelphia by providing attractive apartments for upper-middle-class families. "Lynnewood Hall" is now in the possession of a theological seminary.

Perhaps the fabulous ghosts of "Ogontz" and "Lynnewood Hall" are now watching their descendants huddling with their kind in Chestnut Hill and Whitemarsh Valley or scattering with the wind. In the 1955 *Social Register*, for example, one of P. A. B. Widener's grandsons, George D. Widener, was listed as a resident of New York, although he still maintains a beautiful estate in the Whitemarsh Valley just beyond Chestnut Hill. His sister, Mrs. Widener Dixon, was living in Chestnut Hill. In 1916, after her divorce, she bought Jay Cooke's "Ogontz," tore down the original mansion and built a new one "in the English style." After living at "Ogontz" for many years, she finally moved to Chestnut Hill when World War II made convenience of location a vital necessity. Two other Wide-

ners were listed in the 1955 *Social Register:* Mrs. (Peter A. B.)
was listed as living in Northeast Harbor, Maine, and Peter A. B.
III, in Lexington, Kentucky. Jay Cooke, the great-grandson of the
builder of "Ogontz," lived in the Whitemarsh Valley.

Among the various reasons for the decline of the Old York Road
neighborhood during the past few decades two appear to be more
important than the rest: First, the "big men" who first moved out
to this area were of a subtly different breed than their peers along
the Main Line or in Chestnut Hill. The wealthy men in the latter
suburbs, for instance, tended to be successful *executives,* while
the tone of the Jenkintown neighborhood was set by typical Victorian *entrepreneurs.* The presidents and vice-presidents of the Pennsylvania Railroad, whose style of life dominated the Main Line,
were employees, and, equally important, they were engineers by
profession and experience. Men like John Wanamaker, William
L. Elkins, P. A. B. Widener, and, above all, Jay Cooke were
entrepreneurs (never employees)—promoters by temperament if
not by profession. And if they were more colorful in their day,
the families of the less exciting executives have proved, at least
more stable in succeeding generations. The estates along the Main
Line may not stand comparison with "Ogontz" or "Lynnewood
Hall," but they have remained intact longer. The rise and fall of
the Jenkintown neighborhood bears out the thesis, stressed by
Pitirim A. Sorokin in his *Social Mobility,* that communities distinguished by rapid success and accumulation of great wealth
have less staying power than communities with more moderate
rates of social mobility.[79] Business giants settled the Old York
Road, but most of Philadelphia's upper-class family clans are now
spread out along the Main Line, Chestnut Hill, and the Whitemarsh
Valley.

The location of the fashionable private school is, of course,
always a vital factor in upper-class neighborhood development.
Before the first War, when many families still lived in the city
during the winter, the fashionable schools were also in town (see
Chapter XII). If a family chose to spend the winter in Ogontz
or Rydal, the sons could still commute by train to the traditional
family school, the Episcopal Academy or Penn Charter, for instance,
both of which were then located in the city. Train service from
the center of the city to all suburbs was excellent. However, there
was no means of public transportation between the suburbs (see

Map 2): the only way to get from Bryn Mawr to Chestnut Hill, or from Chestnut Hill to Jenkintown, was to use an automobile (or to take the train all the way into town and out again). Consequently, after World War I, when both families and schools moved to the suburbs, the Jenkintown families either had to send their sons to local schools (the Meadowbrook School grew up in this period) or drive them to the nearest schools in Germantown (Penn Charter) or Chestnut Hill. This was a plausible solution as long as chauffeurs were available. During the thirties, it was not unusual to find boys from the various Old York Road communities at Penn Charter in Germantown or even at Episcopal Academy on the Main Line.

After the Depression, however, and especially because of the scarcity of servants following the second War, the younger generation of parents prefer to live near the traditionally fashionable schools rather than turn their wives into school-bus drivers (which many of them are anyway, as they drive their children to school, parties, dancing-class, and to the dentist, up and down the Main Line).

The Jenkintown neighborhood, then, is an interesting example of a community which has changed its character in the first half of the twentieth century. As the family has become weaker, the sons and grandsons of the big men along the Old York Road have moved increasingly to the Main Line or Chestnut Hill where they can be nearer their friends and the fashionable schools.

No longer an upper-class neighborhood, the Old York Road area is, nevertheless, an important elite suburb of Philadelphia. Today, for example, many successful executives from the industrial northern part of the city, men from such plants as the Philco Radio and Television Corporation and SKF Industries Inc., have settled in the Huntington Valley area. The Huntington Valley Country Club was one of the most fashionable clubs in Philadelphia at one time (see Map 2). While all officers of the club (John W. Pepper, president; E. T. Stotesbury and George W. Elkins, vice-presidents) were listed in the *Social Register* in 1914, forty years later, in 1954, none of the officers was so listed.

An important characteristic of the modern managerial elite suggests itself at this point. Leading business executives at the turn of the century were absorbed into, if not drawn from, the existing upper class, but the new executive elite in Huntington

Valley, presumably having few contacts socially with the older upper class in the city, do not aspire to upper-class status as symbolized by *Social Register* listing.

This new type of executive, wealthy in salary and expense account, if not in bank account, has been interestingly described by William H. Whyte, Jr., in *Fortune* magazine. These men and their families are company, rather than community or "clan," oriented (some of the younger generation, for example, now refer to the Huntington Valley Country Club as "The Philco Country Club"). Several things follow from this new situation. In this corporate feudalism, for instance, where one's primary status referent is the corporation, top executives—supposedly mature men—compete for all kinds of simple status symbols in their place of work: who gets the corner office, the new rug on the floor, the fancy ashtrays, the new air-conditioner, or the mahogany desk. This type of competition appears somewhat pointless and immature to the Proper Philadelphian who does not require these status props to emotional security. *Time* magazine, for example, in a recent article describing the modern executive scramble, used a Philadelphia firm as a conspicuous exception to this widespread practice in America: "The chairman of the board, department heads and general employees," so *Time* describes this firm, "all look at the same green-painted walls, rugless floors and utilitarian furniture."[80] *Time* failed to point out, however, that the president of this Proper Philadelphia firm was a graduate of Groton and Harvard, and that both the junior and senior executive levels of management were heavily staffed with members of the Philadelphia upper class who are deeply rooted in the local community.* A powerful, wealthy, yet declassed elite may be one of the greatest threats to freedom in modern American society. At the higher levels of corporate control, perhaps the existence of an upper class is a protection against the dangers of corporate feudalism.[81]

Along with the decline of upper-class status, the Old York Road neighborhood has become an increasingly popular elite German-Jewish suburb (see below). The Philmont Country Club, the oldest Jewish country club in the city, for example, is located in this area (see Map 2). Founded by the great Philadelphia merchant and philanthropist, Ellis Gimbel, in 1906, the charter mem-

---

* Both the president and chairman of the board (and major owner) of this old family firm live in the Penllyn-Whitemarsh area.

bers of Philmont included such well-known families as the Fleishers, Lits, Loebs, Newbergers, Snellenbergs, Sterns, Wassermans, and Wolfs.[82]

This movement to the Old York Road suburbs was started by members of Philadelphia's older German-Jewish elite. In 1915, Howard A. Loeb succeeded his father, August B. Loeb, as president of the Tradesmen's National Bank to become one of the youngest bank presidents in the city. At that time Mr. Loeb was a resident of Elkins Park and a charter member of the Philmont Country Club. In 1940, he was chairman of the board of the Tradesmen's and listed in *Who's Who* as a resident of Rydal in the Old York Road area.

Another distinguished resident of the Old York Road Jewish community was Dr. David Riesman, physician, author, intellectual, historian of the Italian Renaissance, and a favorite lecturer in the city. Born the son of a merchant in Saxe-Weimar, Germany, he came to Philadelphia where he married the daughter of Penrose Fleisher and graduated from the medical school at the University of Pennsylvania. His son, David, the author of *The Lonely Crowd,* one of the most perceptive psycho-sociological analyses of American society since Tocqueville's *Democracy in America,* commuted to Penn Charter School before going on to Harvard.[83]

Swarthmore: More Intellectual than Fashionable. The Swarthmore suburbs—Lansdowne, Drexel Hill, Swarthmore, Media, Wallingford, Rose Valley, and Wawa—lie to the southwest of Philadelphia, along the Baltimore Pike and the West Chester branch of the Pennsylvania Railroad (see Map 2). This beautiful Quaker suburban area is sharply divided from the Main Line, at least sociologically, by the West Chester Pike (an extension of Market Street). Of the Philadelphians listed in *Who's Who* in 1940, for example, only three persons also listed in the *Social Register* lived south of this convenient dividing line. (This sociological "Chinese Wall" placed fashionable Philadelphians to the south within the city, and to the North in the suburbs.)

In contrast to Germantown or the Old York Road suburbs, this part of Philadelphia has never been particularly fashionable. Lansdowne, for example, is a very old community, now *petit bourgeois* in tone. Once inhabited by wealthy Philadelphians from John Penn to A. J. Drexel who built country places there, Lansdowne and

Drexel Hill have in more modern times, always been a suburban extension of West Philadelphia rather than Rittenhouse Square. Even though several prominent ancestors of fashionable Philadelphians of today, such as the banker A. J. Drexel, Ellis Yarnall, prominent Quaker merchant, and Thomas Scott, president of the Pennsylvania Railroad, had fine estates in the Lansdowne area during the eighties, their descendants lived along the Main Line in 1940.[84]

The communities further out along the Baltimore Pike, even during the first part of the present century, have never had the same suburban atmosphere as, for example, the Main Line. Media, in contrast to Bryn Mawr or Ardmore, has always had the air of a country town (at least until the rapid suburbanization after World War II). The few upper-class families who chose to live in this area presumably preferred a simple rural atmosphere rather than the conventional suburb. The Shakespearean scholar, Henry Howard Furness, for example, was one of the older generation of Philadelphians to settle in Wallingford, near Media. To this day, the tone of the neighborhood has been more intellectual than fashionable. In contrast to the suburban cricket club atmosphere along the Main Line, such institutions as Swarthmore College and the Hedgerow Theatre in Rose Valley are more characteristic of this neighborhood. In short, this area might be described as the rural Greenwich Village of Philadelphia.

The differences between Swarthmore and Haverford Colleges provide some insight into the atmosphere of the communities in which each is located. These differences may be traced back into the early nineteenth century; historical origins are persistent in Philadelphia. In 1827, Philadelphia's Quaker community was divided into two sects—the Orthodox and the Hicksite.[85] This unfortunate "separation," so-called by the famous Quaker Philosopher, the late Rufus Jones, lasted for over one hundred years (only in 1955, did the two sects of Friends reunite). In most schisms within Protestantism social status bears some correlation to conviction, and the division within the Society of Friends was apparently no exception. The essayist and expatriate, Logan Pearsall Smith, for instance, grew up in one of Germantown's old Quaker families of the Orthodox persuasion. Writing of his youth in Germantown, he recalls his horror when a boyhood friend, a member of a prominent Orthodox family, "played with Hicksite boys in the street," and goes on to say that "this sense of social superiority among Orthodox Friends is the main religious feeling which I still retain."[86]

In 1833, soon after the "separation," Haverford College was founded by Orthodox Friends. Swarthmore was not founded until 1873, and, from the beginning, it has been Hicksite.[87] While Haverford, following a more conventional path, limits its student body to men (Orthodox Bryn Mawr educates the women on the Main Line), Swarthmore has always been a coeducational institution (eighty-eight boys and eighty-two girls were in the first graduating class).[88] Just as Haverford has been more conventional, more conservative, than Swarthmore, so the families along the Main Line tend to fit more closely the upper-class stereotype than do their friends south of the West Chester Pike.

For many years two interesting Proper Philadelphia families have lived south of the West Chester Pike—the Furnesses in Wallingford and the Willcoxes in Ivy Mills, near Wawa. Geographical exceptions to the Main Line-Chestnut Hill pattern, these two families differ from the usual upper-class Philadelphians in other respects as well.

The Willcox family settled in Ivy Mills in the early part of the eighteenth century.[89] The first member of the family in America, Thomas Willcox, came to the area in 1827 and two years later established the family paper mill at Ivy Mills (this was the second paper mill in Pennsylvania; the first was established by the Rittenhouse family on the Wissahickon Creek, near Chestnut Hill). Until late in the nineteenth century the Willcox family, at Ivy Mills and later at Glen Mills, were one of the leading paper manufacturers in America. Thomas Willcox supplied the paper for Benjamin Franklin's Pennsylvania *Gazette* but the Willcox mills were best known as the primary manufacturers of paper currency for the national government (from its founding until 1878), as well as for Germany, Japan, Greece, Venezuela and other South American countries. Unlike most of their Episcopalian friends along the Main Line, members of the Willcox family to this day have always been leaders and generous benefactors of the Catholic Church in Philadelphia. Said to be the second Catholic family to settle in the city of Philadelphia, the Willcoxes celebrated mass in a room set aside for the purpose in their old family homestead at Ivy Mills even before the first Catholic church in the city, St. Joseph's, was built in 1732. The family now worships in the local Catholic church in Ivy Mills which was built and supported by Willcoxes for many years.

The Furness family were originally New England Unitarians. Perhaps this accounts for the individualistic and scholarly family tradition distinguishing it from the more extroverted congenial Proper Philadelphians as a whole. William Henry Furness, after graduating from Harvard in 1820, came down to Philadelphia at the suggestion of his friend, Ralph Waldo Emerson, and became the first regular minister of the Unitarian church in the city.[90] He was the church's minister for over fifty years. A rather unpopular reformer in the early years of his ministry, he gradually withdrew from worldly controversy into his study, where he produced many scholarly works on religious subjects. At his retirement, he was one of the most respected clergymen in the city. His son, Horace Howard Furness, intimate friend of S. Weir Mitchell, lawyer, trustee of the University, and Philadelphia's most famous Shakespearean scholar, carried on the family's intellectual traditions.[91] His brother, Frank Furness, was a well-known architect. At the same time that H. H. Richardson and Richard Morris Hunt were doing their best work in Boston and New York, Frank Furness, although perhaps less well-known nationally, was doing more original work in Philadelphia.[92] Neglected for many years, he is now gaining critical recognition for such major works as the old Broad Street Station Building of the Pennsylvania Railroad (recently torn down), the Academy of Fine Arts, and the Library of the University of Pennsylvania. Frank Furness was one of the important influences on Louis Sullivan, who was, in turn, Frank Lloyd Wright's master. This has, perhaps, helped stimulate the contemporary interest in his work.

Just as the beloved Shakespearean scholar, Henry Howard Furness, remained downtown on Washington Square many years after most of Proper Philadelphia had long since moved up to Rittenhouse Square, so he eventually moved to his lovely country estate, "Lindenshade," in Wallingford, while other people of fashion chose Chestnut Hill or the Main Line. "Lindenshade" has remained in the family to the present, and Horace Howard Furness Jayne, archaeologist and curator of the University of Pennsylvania Museum (listed in *Who's Who* and the *Social Register*), was its master in 1940.

Benjamin Disraeli, in an age less addicted to environmental determinism than our own, once said that man is not the creature of circumstances but circumstances are the creatures of men. Thus, as the "promoters"—Jay Cooke, Peter A. B. Widener, and John Wanamaker—set the tone of the Old York Road neighborhood, or Baldwin and Pennsylvania Railroad executives put their stamp on the Main Line, the less conforming, more intellectual families like the Furnesses and Willcoxes symbolized the atmosphere of Media, Wawa, or Wallingford which has persisted to the present day.

The Summer Resort: an Inter-city Upper-Class Neighborhood. For many generations, the American upper classes have gathered during the summer months at various fashionable summer resorts. Newport and Saratoga Springs were popular as early as the eighteenth century: "Over a hundred Philadelphians, for instance, voyaged to Newport for summer sojourns between 1767 and 1775, there to mingle not only with native New Englanders but also with wealthy South Carolinians, Georgians, and West Indians who were likewise investing the profits from commercial enterprise in a few months of expensive recreation in the refreshing northern climate."[93]

From the beginning, these fashionable resorts have been inter-city upper-class neighborhoods. As recently as 1930, Newport was the birthplace of James W. Gerard's famous list of the "Sixty-Four Men Who Run America." Of these sixty-four men, according to Cleveland Amory, "no less than fifty were recognized men-about-resorts."[94] J. P. Morgan, a well-known man-about-resorts, once described the beauty of escaping from the world of affairs to a homogeneous summer neighborhood such as Bar Harbor: "You can do business with anyone," he said, "but you can only sail a boat with a gentleman."[95]

Mount Desert, a beautiful island "down east" on the coast of Maine, has been the most popular Proper Philadelphia summer resort for over half a century. On the island formal and fashionable Bar Harbor, and more informal and wholesome Northeast Harbor, are summer versions of Boston and Philadelphia. Mount Desert is a national upper-class summer resort where the winter residents of Chestnut Hill (in Boston or Philadelphia), meet their more opulent friends from Park Avenue, Lake Forest, or Grosse Point. Several generations of Pulitzers, Fords, Rockefellers, Palmers, and McCormicks have grown up on this fashionable island.

The earliest summer visitors to Mount Desert were artists. They were soon followed by intellectuals and clergymen who enjoyed the beauty and simplicity of life on the island. President Eliot of Harvard, Bishop Lawrence of Massachusetts, and Bishop William Duane of New York ("William of Albany" who wore gaiters after the Anglican tradition) were leaders, sometimes autocratic, of the early island community. The intellectual tradition has been carried on by such permanent summer residents as Walter Lippman, Arthur Train, F. Marion Crawford, Mary Roberts Rinehart, and Philadelphia's S. Weir Mitchell and Horace Howard Furness.

S. Weir Mitchell, who had returned to Newport each year since he first visited relatives there at the age of twelve in 1844, came to Bar Harbor for the first time in 1891 in order to avoid the new-rich then taking over Newport.[96] For many years Mitchell was the recognized leader of the walking and talking set which was the backbone of Bar Harbor society in the days before the cocktail turned conversation into chatter and the automobile abolished walking. In those days George Wharton Pepper was one of the leaders of the vigorous life on the island. In September, 1900, he was the first "to walk in one day from Bar Harbor to Northeast over nine intervening mountains."[97]

The early city visitors to the island stayed at farmhouses; later, boarding houses were opened; and, finally, hotels and cottages were built. The most famous early hotel in Bar Harbor, "Rodick's," was built in 1882. Between 1890 and World War I, Bar Harbor became one of America's most stylish resorts. By 1894, the year Joseph Pulitzer built the resort's first hundred-thousand-dollar "cottage," Morgan and Standard Oil partners were the bastions of Bar Harbor's wealthy community. After the turn of the century, Philadelphia's A. J. Cassatt and E. T. Stotesbury were energetic leaders of summer society; they were followed by the Dorrances and Atwater Kents after the first war.

The Proper Philadelphia tradition is symbolized at Bar Harbor by the Pot and Kettle Club which was founded in 1899 by six members of Philadelphia's Rabbit Club.[98] The membership is limited to fifty men, who, at one time, were said to control 85 per cent of the nation's wealth. Although this is certainly an exaggeration, there were often as many as thirty-five yachts anchored off the club's float during a regular dinner meeting. Like the Rabbit and the Fish House in Philadelphia, the Pot and Kettle is a gentlemen's eating club where numerous toasts, including one to the President of the United States, are an important part of every formal occasion. One summer tradition was slightly altered. Dur-

ing the height of the New Deal, in spite of the fact that Franklin
D. Roosevelt was one of five Presidents ever to have been enter-
tained at the club, the traditional toast to the President of the
United States was replaced by a toast to the Constitution of the
United States.

One of the very few Proper Philadelphia women listed in *Who's
Who* in 1940, Mrs. J. Madison Taylor, a distinguished miniature
painter, was a leader in Bar Harbor's intellectual, artistic, and fashionable worlds for many years. When she died in 1952, Mrs. Taylor
was preparing for her seventy-fifth consecutive summer on the
island.

The fashionable (Episcopalian) churches have always played
an important part in the Island's social life. During the summer,
when life during the week is less hectic, many Easter-Christmas-
funeral-wedding families attend church every Sunday. While morning prayer is usually held in the church, evensong is often held on
the lawn of some estate overlooking the sea. The headmasters of
Groton and St. Paul's—Endicott Peabody and S. S. Drury—were
summer residents of Northeast Harbor for many years. Each summer on a Sunday in August, Dr. Drury held communion service for
boys and alumni of his school.

The fashionable summer neighborhood fosters the development
of upper-class solidarity on a national scale in America, and summer romances on the enchanting island of Mount Desert have not
infrequently resulted in inter-city family alliances. Among other
such alliances, the grandson of Joseph Pulitzer (St. Louis) is now
married to a granddaughter of Samuel M. Vauclain, a former president of the Baldwin Locomotive Works who built one of the Main
Line's show places; the wife of Nelson Rockefeller (New York)
is the granddaughter of George Roberts of the Pennsylvania Railroad; and the former Louise De Koven Bowen, descendant of an
old Bar Harborite from Chicago who lent her social prestige to the
service of Jane Addams' Hull House, now lives in Chestnut Hill
as the wife of young John Wanamaker, vice-president of his great-
grandfather's department store.

Romance has brought great loyalty to this romantic island. In
1889, for example, George Wharton Pepper, who spent that summer with his fiancée and father-in-law-to-be, saw Mount Desert
for the first time. "Thereafter," he writes in his autobiography,
"there have been only three summers in fifty-four years when we
have failed to visit our beloved Mt. Desert."[99]

CHAPTER X

Religion and the Class Structure

> Hardly a generation ago when business men were
> establishing themselves and making new social con-
> tacts, they encountered the question: "To what
> church do you belong?" . . . Evidently it was never
> asked accidentally.
>
> MAX WEBER

COMMENTING on the mores of the carriage trade, Ralph Waldo
Emerson once remarked that "no dissenter rides in his coach for
three generations; he invariably falls onto the Establishment." This
chapter will attempt to show how the members of the American
metropolitan upper class, deeply rooted though their ancestors
were in the Calvinism of New England or the Quaker faith of Philadelphia, gradually returned to the Anglican communion of the
Protestant Episcopal Church. Before discussing this Episcopalian
upper class, especially Philadelphia's Quaker-turned-Episcopal
gentry, a word should be said about religion and the class structure as a whole in America.

Religion and the American Class Structure. "However much
details may differ," writes Liston Pope of the Yale Divinity School,
"stratification is found in all American communities, and religion
is always one of its salient features."[1] The middle classes in America
have been traditionally Protestant, while labor, especially the unskilled, has tended to be Catholic. Historical circumstance, rather
than the "Protestant ethic" alone, has been the most important
factor in the American situation. On the whole, throughout our
history, the earliest arrivals have constantly been thrust upward
in the social and economic structure as each new wave of immigrants has taken its place at the bottom of the occupational hierarchy. Colonial stock in this country was primarily Protestant; even
as late as the first census in 1790, for example, Catholics made up
less than 1 per cent of the population. But the Irish who came in
the eighteen-forties and fifties, and the millions of immigrants from
southern and eastern Europe who flooded these shores at the turn

of the century were more likely to belong to the Catholic and Jewish faiths.

During a famous and bitter coal strike in 1902, when George F. Baer, then president of the Philadelphia and Reading Railroad, spoke out in defense of the "men and women to whom God in His infinite wisdom has entrusted the property interests of this country," he was referring, no doubt, to a Protestant elite. Certainly the more than 150,000 men and boys striking for better working conditions in the anthracite mines of Pennsylvania at the time, many of whom had been brought to America as contract laborers after the Civil War, were predominantly good Catholics from Poland, Lithuania, Czechoslovakia, or Italy. The fabulous railroad baron, James Hill, took a realistic view of the Catholic church in American society. Hill, himself a Protestant, when asked why he had suddenly donated a million dollars for the establishment of a Roman Catholic theological seminary in St. Paul, Minnesota, quickly replied: "Look at the millions of foreigners pouring into this country to whom the Roman Catholic Church represents the only authority they fear or respect."[2]

One of the important consequences of the Reformation has been the fact that whereas the Catholic Church traditionally ministered to all social strata, the numerous Protestant sects and denominations have been divided along class lines virtually from the beginning. Today, while each individual Protestant congregation tends towards class homogeneity, the Catholic parish, larger in size and geographically organized, ministers to the whole community. The differential segregation of races as between Protestantism and Catholicism serves as a dramatic clue to the one-class-church policy within Protestantism. It has recently been reported, for instance, that over *one-third* of the Catholic Negroes in America, as against almost *none* (less than one-tenth of 1 per cent) of the Negro Protestants, attend mixed churches.[3] Liston Pope, in *Millhands and Preachers*, found that the Catholic Church was not popular in the mill-towns of North Carolina because, as the millhands say with a chuckle, "Catholics use the same church for both white people and niggers."[4]

Although the Catholic Church appeals to the whole community, due to historical circumstance in America, it has been predominantly the church of the urban industrial masses. The business and professional community, on the other hand, has been dominated by Protestantism which, in turn, is subtly stratified along denominational lines. On the whole, while the educated elite tend to worship in Presbyterian or Episcopalian churches, the Lutheran, Methodist, and Baptist congregations appeal to the urban middle classes and rural farmers. At the same time, of course, certain smaller denominations—Congregationalists, Unitarians, Christian Scientists, and Quakers—tend toward elite or middle-class status, depending on local conditions. Finally, the Protestants within the laboring classes, disenchanted with the middle-class smugness which characterizes the major denominations, often prefer the more radical sects—the Jehovah's Witnesses, for example, or the Four Square Gospel Churches, or the Adventists. The relationship between religion and the class situation in America has been amusingly summed up by a Jesuit friend of the author's: "The average American is born the son of a Baptist or Methodist farmer; after obtaining an education, he becomes a businessman in a large city where he joins a suburban, Presbyterian church; finally, upon achieving the acme of economic success, he joins a fashionable Episcopal church in order to satisfy his wife's social ambitions; in a materially secure old age, of course, this unusually successful American is converted to the Catholic Church as a hedge against failure in the after life."

The Episcopalian Upper Class in America. John Calvin was the spiritual father of the union of *Bourse* and Bible which has long been recognized as an important characteristic of Western civilization. Thus the opening paragraph in Max Weber's classic essay, *The Protestant Ethic and the Spirit of Capitalism,* reads as follows: "A glance at the occupational statistics of any country of mixed religious composition brings to light with remarkable frequency a situation which has several times provoked discussion in the Catholic press and literature, namely, the fact that business leaders and owners of capital . . . are overwhelmingly Protestant."[5]

The "Protestant ethic" of hard work and worldly asceticism paid dividends in a business civilization. In both Europe and America, most of the great Victorian capitalists were faithful Protestants, while many of them, including Cecil Rhodes and E. H. Harriman, grew up in the pious homes of Protestant clergymen. John D. Rockefeller, who always led the simple life and taught Sunday school for many years, quite naturally felt that "God gave me money." Even the notorious Daniel Drew was founding a Methodist theological seminary and faithfully attending prayer meetings when he was not printing bogus shares and devising techniques for watering stock. It was no wonder that a leading Protestant spokesman could declare in an American religious periodical in the 1870's, "that there is no sleeping partner in any business who can compare with the Almighty."[6]

Following its reverence for British traditions of all sorts, members of the American upper class of second- and third-generation wealth quite naturally prefer the Episcopal Church to the more aggressively Protestant denominations. In the "good taste of its architecture, the dignity and breeding of its clergy, and the richness of its ritual," the Episcopal Church reflects the values of the cultivated classes in this country.

Clarence Day, a graduate of fashionable St. Paul's School and Harvard University, once began an analysis of his father's religious convictions as follows:

My father's ideas of religion seemed straightforward and simple. He had noticed when he was a boy that there were buildings called churches; he had accepted them as a natural part of the surroundings in which he had been born. He would never have invented such things himself. Nevertheless they were here. As he grew up he regarded them as unquestionably as he did banks. They were substantial old structures, they were respectable, decent, and venerable. They were frequented by the right sort of people. Well, that was enough.

As to creeds, he knew nothing about them, and cared nothing either; yet he seemed to know which sect he belonged with. It had to be a sect with a minimum of nonsense about it; no total immersion, no exhorters, no holy confession. Since he was a respectable New Yorker, he belonged to the Episcopal Church.[7]

In 1907 the General Convention of the Protestant Episcopal Church met in Richmond, Virginia. One of the most eloquent speakers there, George Wharton Pepper, recalls in his autobiography that this was the 300th anniversary of the establishment of "English Christianity" in the New World.[8] Thus the Anglican Church first achieved its aristocratic position in America among the tidewater squires of Virginia where it was the established church until late in the eighteenth century. As with the abolition of entail and primogeniture, Thomas Jefferson, deist and democrat, played a leading role in disestablishing the Anglican Church in 1786. Although the separation of church and state in America has been official doctrine ever since the founding of the Republic, "the affiliation of George Washington and other Virginia patricians with the Episcopal Church, and the fact that after the Inauguration he, the Vice-President, cabinet officers, and many senators and representatives repaired to, St. Paul's Chapel in Broadway where Doctor Provost invoked the blessings of God upon the Administration, lent a new semi-official character to the Church."[9] Today, the National Cathedral on beautiful Mount St. Albans, towering above both the Capitol and the Washington Monument, symbolizes the semi-official character of the Episcopal Church. For many years, Philadelphia's George Wharton Pepper was the leading fundraiser and supporter of the Cathedral, which was appropriately designed by a British architect in the Gothic tradition.

In contrast to the Virginia cavaliers, most of the oldest first-families in the other colonies along the eastern seaboard were, of course, not originally Anglicans. In the course of the second half of the eighteenth century, however, many fashionable descendants of Puritan, Dutch Reformed, Quaker, and Huguenot families in Boston, New York, Philadelphia, and Charles Town, gradually returned to the Anglican communion. In *Cities in Revolt,* a study of American urban life during the second half of the eighteenth century, Carl Bridenbaugh writes that "the spread of Anglicanism in the Northern colonies was one of the most significant religious and social developments of the period."[10] The opening of King's Chapel in Boston for worship in 1754 symbolized the social triumph of Anglicanism there, and similarly, St. George's Chapel in New York was opened in 1752 to relieve the pressure on Trinity Church. At the same time, "the most fashionable religion" gained control of King's College (Columbia University) in 1754, and the ardent Anglican, William Smith, was made Provost of the College of Philadelphia (University of Pennsylvania) in the same year. Even in Charles Town many Huguenots "changed over to the modish liturgy," and a new Anglican Church was completed in 1751.

After the turn of the nineteenth century, the Protestant Episcopal Church soon absorbed many members of the newer planter aristocracy which grew up in the Deep South during the five decades preceding the Civil War. These romantic cotton aristocrats, primarily of Scotch-Irish Presbyterian descent, lost no time in absorbing the manners and values of the Virginia gentry.[11]

Of all the northern colonists, the original Quaker families in

Philadelphia were the first to return to the church of their Anglican ancestors. By the time the Protestant Episcopal Church in
America was founded in 1789 at Christ Church, in Philadelphia,
most of the city's wealthier citizens had gone over to the Anglican
Church.[12] President Washington had his own pew in Christ Church
as well as in St. Peter's, which was erected in 1758 to take care of
the swelling congregation at Christ Church (for many years both
churches were under the same rectorship). The elite, or semi-
official, status of the Episcopal Church in the "Quaker City" during
the early years of the new republic is indicated by the fact that
Robert Morris, James Wilson, John Penn, Payton Randolph, Francis
Hopkinson, Benjamin Rush, Generals Charles and Jacob Morgan
of the Continental Army, Commodores Truxton, Bainbridge and
James Biddle of the Navy, and even the famous deist, Benjamin
Franklin, are all buried in the churchyard of Christ Church.[13]

There were, of course, important exceptions to this trend towards upper-class Episcopalian uniformity in America. In Boston,
for instance, a hard core of top-drawer families have retained
their Unitarian or Congregationalist convictions to this day; many
Proper Baltimorians, in the Calvert and Carroll tradition, have
remained loyal to Catholicism, and even the hardest riders out
in "The Valley" are seen at early Mass on Sunday after a Hunt
Ball; and, finally, the Creole aristocrat in New Orleans has never
seen any reason why he should forsake the Catholicism of his
ancestors. Even in Philadelphia there are a few fashionable weddings held in the quaint suburban Friends' meeting houses. The
fashionable Friends, however, do not as a rule attend meeting
regularly, nor do they participate in the intricate web of Quaker
institutions, such as the American Friends Service Committee, which
do good works throughout the world.

On the eve of the Civil War, then, with certain exceptions—
Baltimore and New Orleans, for instance—the Episcopal Church
was firmly established among the planter aristocracy throughout
the South. Although perhaps to a lesser extent, this same pattern
prevailed among the upper classes in the northern commercial
cities.

After the Civil War the Episcopal Church experienced another
period of rapid growth when fashionable Episcopalian congregations in the northern cities were flooded with converts from the

ranks of the new plutocracy. Jay Cooke, the financier of the Civil War, eventually gave up his Methodist affiliations and became a devout Episcopalian. Philadelphia's greatest financial genius, Cooke, in addition to teaching Sunday school, supporting struggling young ministers, and organizing adult Bible classes, also built beautiful St. Paul's Protestant Episcopal Church near his celebrated mansion, "Ogontz," in the Old York Road area.[14] The affinity between the gentleman-businessman of the "Gilded Age" and the Episcopal Church is illustrated in the career of Henry Clay Frick, the "Coke King" from Pittsburgh. Mr. Frick who was "the child of Pennsylvania Dutch ancestors, ended by departing from the plain Lutheran faith of his fathers and 'later in life' attended the Protestant Episcopal Church whose form of service appealed more strongly to his sense of dignity, harmony and beauty."[15] Perhaps the conversion of other new-rich gentlemen like Henry Clay Frick and Jay Cooke helped to swell the Episcopal Church from 160,000 communicants in 1866 to 720,000 in 1900.[16]

Apparently, the members of America's new industrial elite were only too eager to conform to the customs of the class to which they aspired. The fashionable New England boarding schools, many of them first established in the "Gilded Age," were educating the sons of the new elite in an Episcopalian atmosphere. Young Endicott Peabody, for example, returned from an English education at Winchester and Cambridge to establish the Groton School in 1884.[17] In response to an increasing demand, St. Paul's School went through its period of most rapid growth during the last two decades of the nineteenth century. "Never forget," the first Rector, Henry Coit, once said to a St. Paul's parent, "that in the life to come the Presbyterians will not be on the same plane as the Episcopalians."[18]

Proper Boston also changed. After the Tories' exodus during the Revolution, fashionable King's Chapel (Anglican), in Boston, became the first Unitarian church in America. Under the leadership of such "priestly men of letters" as Emerson and Channing, Proper Boston became staunchly Unitarian, as did Harvard College. In 1836, for example, of the fifty-one churches in Boston, thirteen were Unitarian, eleven were Congregationalist, and only six were Episcopalian.[19] As Lyman Beecher put it: "All the literary men were Unitarians; all the trustees of Harvard College were Unitarians; and all the elite of fashion and wealth crowded the Unitarian Churches."[20] But after the Civil War Proper Boston also underwent an Episcopalian renaissance.

Henry Adams, whose *Education* was a pessimistic analysis of post-Civil War America, drifted away from his family's Unitarian faith into an urbane scepticism with leanings towards the Roman Catholicism of *Mont Saint-Michel and Chartres*. At the same time, many of his contemporaries reverted to an Anglo-Catholicism which reflected an aesthetic revival in America and a Europeanization of the leisured classes. While men of enterprise unleashed their acquisitive instincts on the western frontier, those of a more sensitive and critical mind turned to Europe for spiritual and aesthetic enrichment. After the Civil War, the artists flocked abroad as usual. More important, however, was the birth of the modern American tourist in the seventies. A wave of art treasures, bric-a-brac, and a new respect for European culture soon rolled westward across the Atlantic.

Proper Boston, rooted in Anglophilia, responded to this aesthetic revival with its first Museum of Fine Arts, founded in 1870; young men of decided ability, such as Ralph Adams Cram, developed rigid High Church views, founded a "Medieval Academy of America," and dreamed of a new scholasticism in stone, the American cathedral; Mrs. Jack Gardiner, who combined an interest in art with High Church Anglicanism, ostentatiously scrubbed the steps of the Church of the Advent before the Good Friday services; and, finally, Trinity Church, rebuilt in 1877 by Richardson with the aid of John La Farge, Sanford White, and the sculptor, Saint-Gaudens, became the decisive symbol of this aesthetic and Episcopalian revival. Boston had buried its Puritan past.[21]

Phillips Brooks was the clerical leader of Boston's Episcopalian renaissance. A very Proper Bostonian, who had already made a name for himself in the Church as the Rector of Holy Trinity on Philadelphia's Rittenhouse Square, young Phillips Brooks was called to fashionable Trinity Church in Boston in 1869. Born a Unitarian and a direct descendant of John Cotton, the founder of Calvinism in New England, Phillips Brooks became a Boston institution in the course of the seventies and eighties. A handsome man whose preaching rivalled the great Henry Ward Beecher's, he was especially successful with Proper Boston's females: "With ringing rhetoric from his Trinity Church pulpit, Brooks soon had even such staunch Unitarian feminists as the daughters of James Russell Lowell, and Dr. Oliver Wendell Holmes proudly referring to him as 'our bishop.' "[21] Aristocratic Bostonians had travelled a long way from the Puritan convictions of Cotton and Increase Mather when they turned to the teachings of the Right Reverend Phillips Brooks, Bishop of Massachusetts, who was once referred to by a Philadelphian as "an Episcopalian—with leaning towards Christianity."[23] When he died in 1892, Phillips Brooks' funeral attracted the largest crowd in Boston's history.[24]

Throughout the nineteenth century, the leading bishops of the Protestant Episcopal Church were intimately allied by birth and breeding with the eastern seaboard aristocracy: "The social as well as apostolic succession was unbroken through such bishops of blue blood as William Ongreham Kip, Mark Anthony De Wolfe Howe, and William Heathcote De Lancey."[25] Many of the Church's greatest leaders were, like Phillips Brooks, recent converts to the Episcopal Church. Of the twenty Presiding Bishops of the Church, from the first Bishop, William White of Philadelphia, through Henry Knox Sherrill, who took office in 1947, only eight were of Episcopalian lineage.[26]

Frederick Dan Huntington, for instance, a graduate of Harvard and a Unitarian, was appointed Plummer Professor of Christian Morals and preacher in the Harvard College Chapel in 1855.[27] A contemporary Congregationalist review stated that "Professor Huntington occupies a public position of incalculable power over the religious convictions of the American people."[28] Although his father was a Unitarian clergyman, and his grandfather had been a staunch Calvinist, in 1860, he resigned from his position at Harvard, joined the Episcopal Church, and eventually became Bishop of the newly created diocese of central New York in 1869.

Similarly, the Right Reverend Alonso Potter, the third Episcopal bishop of Pennsylvania, was the first of a great family of the cloth.[29] Although himself the son of a Quaker farmer, in Duchess County, New York, he was confirmed an Episcopalian by Bishop White in Philadelphia, and elected Bishop of Pennsylvania in 1845. His brother, Horatio Potter, also became an Episcopalian clergyman and eventually Bishop of New York. His wife was the daughter of Dr. Eliphalet Nott, the great Presbyterian preacher and president of Union College. Of their six sons, two entered the Church. One son, Eliphalet Nott Potter, became president of Episcopalian Hobart College, and the other, Henry Codman Potter, succeeded his uncle, Horatio Potter, as Bishop of New York. Bishop Henry Codman Potter, generally considered to be New York's first citizen at the turn of the century, was very proud that "English visitors often pronounced him to be 'a typical mid-Victorian Bishop,' and was never happier than when officiating at the titled marriage of a Vanderbilt or a Goelet, or travelling to a church convention in the private car of J. P. Morgan."[30]

The great Episcopalian bishops, of course, usually officiated at the more important marriages which allied America's new-rich heiresses with many an impecunious European nobleman, thus helping to create an international Victorian aristocracy. The era of international marriages began when Jennie Jerome, the daughter of a New York broker and sportsman, married Winston Churchill's father, the Duke of Marlborough, in 1874. Between that date and 1909, more than 500 American women married titled foreigners; an estimated $220,000,000 followed them to Europe.[31] Bishop Henry Codman Potter cemented the most celebrated international alliance of the era when he blessed the marriage of Consuelo Vanderbilt and the ninth Duke of Marlborough in 1895 at St. Thomas's Church on Fifth Avenue. St. Thomas's, one of Ralph Adams Cram's more well-known Gothic creations, "contains two significant details inserted by a waggish young architect in Mr. Cram's employ—a dollar-sign worked into the tracery over the Bride's Door, and three money-bags initialed 'J. P. M.' carved above the choir-stalls."[32]

In many ways the elder Morgan, who collected the autographs of Episcopal bishops in his youth, was a symbol of the close relationship between the Episcopal Church and America's business aristocracy.[33] In addition to being a constant contributor to various church causes, he was on the original board of Groton School (along with his close friend, Bishop Lawrence), the senior warden of fashionable St. George's Church on Stuyvesant Square, and the leading lay figure at every General Convention of the Protestant Episcopal Church. In 1907, for example, "two special cars took him and his guests—who included three American Bishops and the gaitored Bishop of London—to Richmond, where they took up residence in the Rutherford House on Grace Street, which Morgan had engaged for the occasion, with Louis Sherry once more serving as Major-domo."[34]

While attending the Richmond convention J. P. Morgan first

heard of the approaching panic of 1907. The ominous messages and telegrams received by Mr. Morgan during the last days of this auspicious gathering of bishops and prosperous laymen of the Episcopal Church seem somehow symbolic of the shallow confidence and optimism of wealthy Americans in the "Gilded Age." Outside the calm Victorian drawing-room, the two decades prior to 1907 were marked by unrest and revolt: the tragic Haymarket Riot, for example, shook the nation in the spring of 1886 and the American Federation of Labor was formed the following December; the "Gay" nineties, ushered in by the Sherman Act, witnessed the Homestead and Pullman strikes, the populist revolt, and the march of "Coxey's Army" on Washington; and, finally, at the end of this gay decade, Andrew Carnegie, a former immigrant boy, was enjoying an *income*, according to Frederic Lewis Allen, of something like fifteen million dollars a year (the income tax had been declared unconstitutional in a test case in 1895), while the mass of unskilled workers in the North received less than $460 a year in wages—in the South the figure was less than $300.[35]

If their congregations were saturated with upper-class complacency and conformity, it is true, nevertheless, that many Episcopalian clergymen were vitally concerned both with the corruption at the top of society and the cruel living and working conditions of the urban masses. In one of the most popular novels of its day, *Inside of the Cup*, novelist Winston Churchill dramatized the struggle of a young Episcopalian minister with corrupt "pillars of the church" within his congregation. The elder Morgan's rector, Dr. Rainsford, was surely morally concerned about the role of the Episcopal Church among the poor of New York City. Although he never carried out his threat, J. P. Morgan almost resigned as the senior warden of his beloved St. George's when Dr. Rainsford placed a member of the working class on the parish board (Admiral Mahan did resign as a result of the rector's democratic ways). Mr. Morgan summed up his position as follows: ". . . The rector wants to democratize the church, and we agree with him and will help him as far as we can. But I do not want the vestry democratized. I want it to remain a body of gentlemen whom I can ask to meet me in my study."[36] Dr. Rainsford, who came to this country in 1880, was an enthusiastic supporter of Kingsley's "muscular Christianity" and admired the work of the English church among the poor. As the once-fashionable mansions on

Stuyvesant Square gradually became tenements, he eventually built up St. George's from 200 to 4,000 communicants. Although Morgan certainly never understood Dr. Rainsford's brand of Christianity, he continued to admire him and took care of him for life in the form of a legacy.

Allied with the reforming clergymen were many laymen of second- and third-generation wealth who were overly sensitive to the crude materialism so characteristic of the new-rich in the "Gilded Age." In *A Hazard of New Fortunes,* for example, William Dean Howells shows how Conrad Dryfoos, the son of a crude, new-rich millionaire, and his old-family friend, Margaret Vance, both High Church members, become interested in the rights of labor through the Episcopal Church. In the end, Miss Vance enters an Episcopal religious order and Dryfoos, symbolically enough, is accidentally killed in the course of a streetcar strike.

The Episcopal Church was the first Protestant denomination to recognize the right of labor to organize for its own protection. In an age when the Protestant churches, especially the Calvinist pulpits, regarded poverty as a sin, Bishop Henry Codman Potter of New York repeatedly stated in public: "It is because they have helped to teach the lesson of fellow service that modern civilization may well thank God—however impatient capitalists or the public may from time to time have been of them—for trade unions."[37]

The two leading reform organizations within the Protestant Church in America—The Church Association for the Advancement of the Interests of Labor (CAIL) and the Christian Social Union (CSU)—were founded and led by Episcopalians in the last part of the nineteenth century.[38] Father James Otis Sargent Huntington, founder of the Order of the Holy Cross and a member of the old Knights of Labor, was the first Protestant clergyman to devote his life to the labor question. After the Haymarket tragedy, Father Huntington and other church leaders founded the CAIL in 1887. Bishop Huntington, Father Huntington's father, was the first president of the CAIL, and Bishop Henry Codman Potter, a seasoned and respected arbitrator of strikes and lockouts, became the second president in 1904 upon the death of Bishop Huntington. The Christian Social Union, an American branch of the British organization of the same name, was founded in 1891, with Bishop Huntington as president, and the economist and lay Episcopalian, Richard T. Ely, as secretary. All through the nineties and until World War I, these two organizations took the lead in the American social gospel movement.

It was often difficult for contemporary church leaders to understand why "the Church of wealth, culture, and aristocratic lineage" was leading the way. The fashionable clergymen in America, however, were strongly influenced by the Christian socialism of their British cousins. In his *Protestant Churches and Industrial America,* Henry F. May explains the leadership of the Episcopalians in the American Social Gospel movement:

The most obvious explanation of Episcopalian social emphasis is the influence of English Christian Socialism, which all Episcopalian progressives and radicals heartily acknowledged. Perhaps a more fundamental explanation is the persistence of authoritative, disciplined, "church" tendencies in the American as well as in the English Episcopal tradition. Episcopalianism had never lost touch completely with the medieval dream of society guided and led by the church.

Significantly, many of the most outspoken Episcopalian Social Gospel leaders belonged to the High Church wing of the denomination, and thus had an especially lofty conception of their own status as priests. The fact that Bishops Huntington and Potter consistently backed the C.A.I.L. made it difficult for even the most conservative Episcopal laymen to believe it altogether bad. Similarly, Morgan yielded not to Rainsford's arguments but to his priestly authority.[39]

In an age when the great capitalist entrepreneurs were unifying the nation and even the world with trusts and giant corporation structures, leading bishops of the Protestant Episcopal Church became the moral spokesmen of this new national upper class in America. Bishop Henry Codman Potter, the "first citizen of New York," was not only a national but an international leader of his age. As his biographer put it: "He was called, indeed, to be the pastor of the rich. In Boston and New York he was brought into intimate relations with the most privileged people. Wherever he went, he entered naturally, as by right, into the best society. It was as a matter of course that at Baden-Baden he walked with the Prince of Wales, and that in London, even while he was a parish minister, content with 'humble lodgings,' he was sought out by the Archbishop of Canterbury."[40] Steeped as they were in the ideas of British Christian socialism, on the other hand, these great men of the cloth took the concept of *noblesse oblige* much more seriously than the business gentlemen who conscientiously filled the pews of the more fashionable churches on Sunday mornings. When Bishop

Potter died in 1908, for example, Samuel Gompers, on behalf of the American Federation of Labor, wrote: "A movement for the social betterment of all the people had no stauncher advocate nor more earnest worker than Bishop Potter. His every work, his every act, was an effort and an appeal for a higher and better life for all."[41]

In the course of the twentieth century, the Episcopalianization of the American business aristocracy has been a continuous process. One was reminded of this never-ending process by the recent marriage of the first John D. Rockefeller's great-granddaughter at St. Paul's Episcopal Church in Tarrytown, New York.[42] The Suffragen Bishop of New York performed the ceremony. The bride, a great-granddaughter of the wealthiest Baptist of his day, was also a great-granddaughter of both E. W. Clark, Philadelphia banker and founder of the first Unitarian Church in Germantown, and George B. Roberts, fifth president of the Pennsylvania Railroad, whose good Quaker ancestors had owned land in the "Welsh Barony" since the seventeenth century.

Proper Philadelphia: Quaker-Turned-Episcopal Gentry. In accord with most studies reporting on the relationship between religion and educational and economic position in America, the Philadelphia elite in 1940 was predominantly Protestant (Table 21).

While the Presbyterians and Episcopalians in Philadelphia were about equally represented in *Who's Who,* the Episcopalians were definitely more likely to be listed in the *Social Register.* Before

Table 21—Philadelphians in Who's Who in 1940—Religious Affiliations as Related to Social Class

Religious Affiliation	SOCIAL CLASS				Who's Who Total		Per Cent in Social Register
	Social Register		Non Social Register				
	No.	%	No.	%	No.	%	
Episcopalian	95	(42)	75	(14)	170	(22)	56
Presbyterian	30	(13)	107	(20)	137	(18)	22
Quaker	7	(3)	15	(3)	22	(3)	32
Baptist	2	(1)	22	(4)	24	(3)	8
Methodist	0	(—)	26	(5)	26	(10)	—
Other Protestant	10	(5)	70	(12)	80	(10)	13
Catholic	2	(1)	25	(5)	27	(4)	7
Jewish	1	(—)	26	(5)	27	(4)	3
No information	79	(35)	178	(32)	257	(33)	31
Total	226	(100)	544	(100)	770	(100)	29

proceeding to a detailed discussion of Philadelphia's Episcopalian upper class, something should be said about the Presbyterians. In 1940 there were vigorous Presbyterian congregations in all the fashionable suburbs of the city as well as the downtown residential areas around Rittenhouse Square. On the whole, however, the parishioners of these churches were less inclined to participate in the city's fashionable social life than were their neighbors in the Episcopal churches. There were a few exceptions: for example, Henry S. Drinker (the brother of Catherine Drinker Bowen, biographer and historian), descendant of the Quaker merchant, Henry Drinker (Table 9), who was exiled to Virginia along with Pembertons and Norrises in 1777, was both a Calvinist and a very Proper Philadelphian. He was senior partner of Drinker, Biddle, and Reath, one of the city's leading law firms, a member of the Philadelphia Club, a trustee of the University of Pennsylvania, and on the board of the Philadelphia Savings Fund Society (see Chapter XIV).

More representative of the Presbyterians, however, was J. Howard Pew, also listed in both *Who's Who* and the *Social Register*, and head of one of the newer Proper Philadelphia families. President of the family-owned Sun Oil Company since 1912 and one of the most influential Republicans in Pennsylvania and in the nation, J. Howard Pew was not interested in conforming to the mores of Proper Philadelphia's inner circles (he belonged to the Union League rather than the Philadelphia Club). His wide civic interests included the chairmanship of the board and principal benefactor of Grove City College, a Presbyterian college in the western part of the state, presidency of the board of the Presbyterian Church, and chief benefactor of his local Main Line Presbyterian church. The Calvinist ethic was still strong, at least in this generation of the Pew family.

Perhaps the career of Henry Pitney Van Dusen, president of Union Theological Seminary, best reflects the difference between the Episcopalian and Calvinist traditions in America. Van Dusen grew up in Chestnut Hill before World War I, where he attended St. Paul's Episcopal Church (he is still a nominal member in good standing). After attending Penn Charter School, he went on to Princeton. As an undergraduate he captained the debating team, headed the undergraduate council, was class valedictorian, Ivy Orator, Phi Beta Kappa, and an active member of the Student

Christian Association. During his summers he served as a counselor in a Princeton-run camp for underprivileged boys. Maintaining that the system of exclusion was "undemocratic and un-Christian," he joined a boycott of the Princeton eating clubs.

After Princeton, although there was a strong family tradition in the law (his father was a Philadelphia lawyer and his uncle a Supreme Court Justice—1912-1922), Henry Pitney Van Dusen finally chose the ministry as his career. Although a communicant at St. Paul's—his mother was a devout Presbyterian—he chose the Presbyterian Church. "I wasn't keen about the liturgical emphasis in the Episcopal Church," he once said. "I also thought it contained more charming Christians than any other. I missed its lack of moral drive. My religious motivation is primarily moral, and always will be. I didn't have to read Reinhold Niebuhr to know about original sin. The forces of evil are always gaining ground, and must be stopped again and again. This is a continuous battle."[43]

While members of most of the Protestant denominations were represented in the *Social Register* in 1940, a detailed analysis of the historical development of Philadelphia's Anglo-Catholic gentry is necessary for an understanding of the city's upper-class traditions and values.

The Colonial Period. The spirit of tolerance which prevailed in Penn's City from the very beginning, and the absence of an established church, drew settlers of diverse religious beliefs, or of no faith at all, to the Quaker colony. Although one of the last colonies to be established in the New World, Philadelphia grew rapidly and prospered.

During the first three decades of the eighteenth century, the Society of Friends gradually lost its numerical superiority in Philadelphia. The steady stream of Englishmen to Pennsylvania, for example, was stepped up by a wave of Scotch-Irish Presbyterians in the 1720's. A flood of Germans arrived during the 1730's. The Society's failure to proselytize, and its frequent expulsion of members for "marrying out of meeting" or for "disunity," contributed to its failure to keep pace with the city's growth. By 1750, Philadelphia was the Quaker City in name only; less than one-fourth of its inhabitants were members of the Society of Friends.[44]

In spite of their loss of numerical superiority, however, "wealthy God-fearing Quakers" formed the backbone of the city's merchant elite throughout the first half of the eighteenth century. Friends who had come to the New World "to do *good* ended up by doing extremely *well*." When the Philadelphia Contributionship for the Insurance of Houses from Loss by Fire, America's oldest fire insurance company, was founded in 1752, all the twelve original directors save three—one of them Benjamin Franklin—were members of the Society of Friends (of the three non-Friends on the board, one Amos Strettell had only recently been read out of meeting for "disunity").[45]

After accumulating fortunes in trade and finance, the vigorous Quaker aristocrats built large country houses, collected books for their libraries (paintings were discouraged), laid out fine formal gardens, and founded such civic and intellectual institutions as the Pennsylvania Hospital and the American Philosophical Society. Of the nine founders of the American Philosophical Society, five were Quakers.[46] The Pennsylvania Hospital, the first in the New World, was financed and run by the Quaker elite in its early years. Of the twelve original managers, nine were Quakers. At the time the hospital was founded, the Quaker majority in the Assembly had blocked all appropriations for the military defense of the frontier. It was said that the generosity of the wealthy Quaker merchants towards the hospital was calculated to show that "when they are not restrained by principle they can be as liberal as others."[47]

The Quaker merchant oligarchy was no closed aristocratic circle. There were great opportunities for advancement in the world of trade for diligent Quakers like the first Samuel Powel, carpenter, who accumulated enough capital to launch his own mercantile ventures, buy up quantities of valuable real estate, and, finally, to leave a sizeable fortune to his children. The ethic of the meeting house was congenial to success in the counting house. Long before Poor Richard made Benjamin Franklin famous as the "first Bourgeois," William Penn was advising his children to "think only of present Business . . . First, it is the way to Wealth: *The diligent Hand makes Rich . . . Seest thou a Man diligent in his Business he shall stand before Kings.*"[48] The way to wealth in early colonial Philadelphia is nicely documented in the following passage by a Quaker historian:

The history of John Bringhurst (1691-1750) may be taken as a representative Philadelphia Quaker success story. Son of a London printer, he was apprenticed at the age of ten to a cooper in Philadelphia, whither his mother had brought him. After serving out his time and working for a few years as journeyman cooper, he concluded, in hopes of faster advancement, to go to sea. Shipping first as a cooper, he learned navigation, and made several voyages to Barbados, Curacua, and Surinam as mate. Having accumulated about forty pounds, he decided to remain ashore and resume the cooperage business. "Under Providence," he recorded, "I got beforehand and Carried on a Trade of Merchandise with a small Stock which helped me forward into a good way of getting." Beginning to be recognized as a Friend of some weight in the affairs of the meeting, he was made an Overseer of the Poor in 1728 and two years later an Overseer of the Friends School. By 1736 he was able to purchase a one-third share in the brigantine *Joseph* which made numerous voyages to Barbados, Lisbon, and Madeira, freighted with provisions. Within a few years he was also half owner of the sloop *James,* which carried pipestaves and beeswax to the Wine Islands. Two years before he died, he was named an Elder of the meeting. His three sons engaged in mercantile undertakings and amassed considerable wealth; James, the second son, was to be styled "gentleman" in the city Directory.[49]

The "Protestant ethic" may be especially congenial to the *parvenu.* Quaker convictions, however, have never endorsed the more conspicuous forms of worldly display so dear to the hearts of the aristocratic classes. Small wonder that many of the more elegant and urbane members of the Quaker elite, especially those of second- and third-generation wealth, preferred the ritual and drama of the Anglican Church and the more worldly social life of its members to the plain living and high thinking of the meeting house. After William Penn died in 1718, the province passed to his sons who hardly shared their father's strong Quaker convictions: John attended meeting only infrequently; Richard joined the Anglican Church at an early age; and Thomas openly avowed his lack of sympathy with the Society of Friends, although he delayed in joining the Church until the 1750's.[50] John Penn, grandson of William, was a pew-holder at both Christ Church (1778-81) and St. Peter's (1782-92).[51]

Towards the middle of the century, it was said in Philadelphia that one could be a Christian in "any church, but not a gentleman outside the Church of England." After 1750, "Quakerism had to share wealth and influence with the Church of England. Though never so numerous as the Friends, Presbyterians, or even the Lutherans, the Anglicans became definitely the congregation of wealth, fashion and position."[52] Samuel Powel III—last colonial mayor of Philadelphia, patron of artists such as Benjamin West, trustee of the College of Philadelphia, and the city's most elegant host—provides an excellent example of the city's Quaker-turned-Anglican gentry. After inheriting the largest Quaker fortune in Pennsylvania and graduating from the College in 1760, young Samuel Powel "found ready welcome among a group, made up principally of young Quakers, who called themselves the Society Meeting Weekly in the City of Philadephia for Their Mutual Improvement in Useful Knowledge."[53] Perhaps the earnest ethics of the Friends, so useful to the *parvenu,* bored the young Quaker aristocrat? At any rate, he soon sailed for England "to begin a quest for European culture and experience that was to last for seven years."

After several years spent in the best of London Society, and the usual Grand Tour of the continent which included a reception with Voltaire at Verney and a familiar conversation with the Pope, the sophisticated young Quaker returned to Philadelphia in 1767. How far he had traveled was soon demonstrated "when shortly he was baptized by the city's most fashionable prelate and became a communicant of St. Peter's Church."[54] Undoubtedly the Church of England provided this cultivated young Philadelphian with a comfortable compromise between the provincial Protestantism of the New World and the pagan and Catholic world view opened up to him by the great Renaissance art of Italy.

In the 1750's Christ Church, the only Anglican church in the city, began to feel the pressure caused by the rising tide of wealthy and fashionable converts: "The long tramp through filthy muddy streets to the very overcrowded Christ Church was becoming more and more distasteful to these fine gentlemen and beautiful belles, in damasks and brocades, velvet breeches and silk stockings, powdered hair and periwigs."[55] To take care of the overflowing congregation at Christ Church, Robert Smith, the designer of Carpenter's Hall, the famous Walnut Street prison, and Nassau Hall at the College of New Jersey, produced his masterpiece in St. Peter's, the second Anglican church in the city. Situated on Pine Street, around the corner from the Powel and Bingham mansions on Third Street, St. Peter's was conveniently located in the midst of the Society Hill district, where many prominent merchants then lived.[56] The new church was opened in 1761, with Provost Smith of the College preaching the first sermon to the city's most distinguished congregation.

It was significant that St. Peter's should have been founded at the close of the 1750's. During this decade, the Quaker oligarchy finally lost control of Philadelphia and the Colony of Pennsylvania. In 1755, the Pennsylvania Assembly, deadlocked in a contest for power with the Governor, failed to appropriate adequate funds for Braddock's expedition to Fort Duquesne. With Braddock's defeat, conditions deteriorated on the frontier, and, after three-quarters of a century of peace with the Indians, Pennsylvania found itself at war in 1755. The Quaker leadership in the Assembly ("The Norris Party") had held up appropriations partly because of pacifist convictions and partly because of opposition to placing money at the disposal of the Governor. At any rate, after war was declared, six of the leading Quakers in the Assembly resigned. As they put it, "the present Situation of Public Affairs calls upon us for Services in a Military Way, which, from a Conviction of Judgement, after mature Deliberation, we cannot comply with."[57]

Pacifist convictions plagued the Quakers right through the Revolutionary period. Gallantry on the battlefield, of course, has been the mark of the aristocrat in all ages. During the Revolution, the "Fighting Quakers" included many young men such as Owen and Clement Biddle, and Samuel and Anthony Morris, whose descendants became the core of the city's Episcopalian upper class. The Philadelphia Troop of Light Horse, now the First City Troop, was organized by aristocratic young Philadelphians in 1774. As we have seen, Quaker Sam Morris, "Christian Sam," was Captain of the Troop and served at Princeton, Brandywine, and Germantown, while his brother, Anthony Morris, gave his life at Princeton. Other Quaker blades formed their own company of light infantry: "Notwithstanding their endeavors to keep aloof from the contest," writes Alexander Graydon in his memoirs, "a good many Quakers swerved from their tenets, and, affecting cockades and uniforms, openly avowed themselves fighting men. They went so far as to form a company of light infantry . . . which was called the *Quaker Blues,* and instituted a spirit of competition with the *Greens,* as they were sneeringly styled, the *silk stocking company,* commanded by Mr. John Cadwalader, and which, having associated early, had already acquired celebrity."[58] Finally, the Board of War, instituted in 1777, included such prominent Friends as Owen Biddle, Samuel Morris, Sr. (Captain Sam's uncle), and Samuel Cadwalader Morris.

Anglican communicants in America also went through a soul-searching period during the Revolution. Unlike King's Chapel in Boston which became a Unitarian Church after its Tory communicants fled from the city during the war, most of the parishioners of Christ Church and St. Peter's remained Whigs and loyal supporters of the Revolution.[59] Several Anglicans who had held important posts in the King's colonial government, however, were temporarily arrested as Tories during the scare which preceded Howe's march on Philadelphia (John Penn and Benjamin Chew were among those arrested and · placed on parole, forbidden to go more than six miles from their houses).[60] The patriotic position taken by most Philadelphia Anglicans can partly be explained by their opposition to the Quakers' record of pacifism.

Although most of the prominent Anglican laymen supported the war, Jacob Duché, the Rector of the United Churches (Christ Church and St. Peter's) finally chose the Tory position after some vacillation. In 1774 and 1775 Duché had served as the official chaplain to the first and second Continental Congresses (Sam Adams, the crafty patriot from Boston, nominated him for the job because he thought it "prudent" to have the rector of such a prominent congregation on the side of rebellion).[61] After the Declaration of Independence was signed in 1776, Duché again showed his patriotism by omitting the prayers for the King at both Christ Church and St. Peter's on Sunday, July 7th (these were the first Anglican churches in America to make this omission). Three months later, however, Duché reversed his position and resigned as Chaplain to Congress because of the "State of his health." Although now no longer in charge of the United Churches, he remained in Philadelphia during Howe's occupation and finally fled to England.

After the Revolution, William White, who had served as a chaplain with Washington's army at Valley Forge, became the leading Anglican clergyman in the New World. In 1787 he was consecrated a bishop of the Anglican Church by the Archbishop of Canterbury, assisted by the Archbishops of York, Bath, and Peterborough. After returning to Philadelphia, he took the lead in founding the Protestant Episcopal Church in America at Christ Church in 1789. William White was the ideal leader of the Episcopal Church which has been closely associated with Philadelphia's gentry from its inception. He was a leader of both inherited and acquired position. His father, who had practiced law at the Maryland bar representing the Lord Proprietary, was a great landowner, who left 7,772 acres of taxable land in Baltimore County alone when he died in 1779.[62] William White, brother-in-law of Robert Morris, took an active part in all aspects of Philadelphia life. He was one of the founders of the Protestant Episcopal Academy and at the age of twenty-six became a trustee of the College of Philadelphia, a post which he held for sixty-two years.

By the end of the eighteenth century, then, the Episcopal Church was clearly the church of the aristocratic elite in the Quaker City. The Philadelphia Contributionship, which was founded only a half century earlier by a dominant Quaker elite, was, by 1782, virtually an Anglican gentleman's club which it has continued to be to the present day.[63] Even the sceptical deist, Benjamin Franklin, who was amused to find that most Europeans considered him a good Philadelphia Quaker, was a pew-holder at Christ Church (No. 59) between 1778 and 1790.[64] We have already listed the distinguished Americans of this period who are buried at Christ Church.

In the early years of the new republic, St. Peter's was probably the most fashionable church in the city. Among its pew-holders were Samuel Powel and William Bingham, two of the wealthiest men in the city, Robert Morris and Thomas Willing, financiers of the Revolutionary period, the artist, Charles Wilson Peale, Chief Justices of the Supreme Court of Pennsylvania, Benjamin Chew and Edward Shippen, Doctors Benjamin Rush, John Morgan (founder of the medical school at the college) and Thomas Bond, and General John Cadwalader, colonel of the "Silk Stocking" Battalion (Cadwalader, Shippen, Morgan, Bond, and Powel all had fathers who were birthright Friends). George Washington, who usually attended Christ Church, used the Powel-Willing pew (No. 41) at St. Peter's during the entire winter of 1781-82, after renting a house nearby.[65]

There were probably several reasons why so many leading citizens of the Quaker City returned to the Anglican Church at the end of the colonial period and during the founding of the new republic. The drabness of Quakerism hardly suited a mercantile aristocracy bent on modeling itself after the Georgian gentlemen of England. Even the descendants of such staunch Quakers as the two Israel Pembertons were not immune to the fashionable trend. Joseph Pemberton, for example, was the son of

Israel, Jr., who had been exiled to Virginia during the Revolution because of his moral convictions: "Though both Joseph Pemberton and his wife came of strict Quaker families," writes John W. Jordan, in his *Colonial Families of Philadelphia*, "they appear to have renounced the plain dress of their ancestors, as attested by two handsome oil paintings of them now in the possession of their grandson, Henry Pemberton, which showed them attired in the height of the mode of their day. It was in their time, too, that the name of Pemberton first appeared on the list of the Philadelphia Dancing Assemblies." (One can usually gauge the dates of old Quaker family conversions to Anglicanism by noting when they first appear on the Assembly lists.)[66]

As this is primarily a sociological analysis of stratification, we have naturally stressed the congeniality of the Anglican ritual to the aristocratic mind. But sociological causation should not be over-emphasized. The moral conflict surrounding the extreme pacifist position, which even James Logan, the leading Quaker in Penn's young city, could not abide, was unquestionably an important factor in causing the decline of the influence of the Society of Friends in Philadelphia after 1750. This position on war, of course, was but one aspect of a consistent and extreme form of Protestantism which, perhaps inadvertently, tended to institutionalize an irresponsibility towards the state which, in modern society, must always include military power. Philadelphia Quakers took no part in the Revolution or the founding of the republic. To have refrained from participating in the series of stirring events which took place in Philadelphia between 1776 and 1787 was to have missed one of the greatest opportunities for statesmanship in world history. In fact, it may be argued that the attitudes of Proper Philadelphians toward governmental service down through the years, and the fact of their relatively small number of distinguished public servants, are deeply rooted in their Quaker heritage. Traditions die hard, and the extreme withdrawal from the world so characteristic of eighteenth- and early-nineteenth-century Quakerism has left a definite mark on even the contemporary Proper Philadelphia mind.

This is not the place to discuss theological matters. A brief mention of the "Keith Controversy," however, will provide a theological balance to our more worldly analysis. The fact that Rufus Jones, distinguished Quaker philosopher and member of the Philadelphia elite in 1940, could sum up the controversial career of

George Keith in the following words testifies to the existence of legitimate doubts about the tenets of Quakerism among sincere Friends in the seventeenth and eighteenth centuries. "The writings of George Keith," Rufus Jones wrote, "both before and after his repudiation of Quakerism, are marked by an excellent style, an earnest spirit, much clearness in thought, and moderation of temper. . . . Had he died in 1690, they would have ranked high as Quaker classics. . . . He was intellectually a great man. His changes from Presbyterianism to Quakerism, from this, after nearly thirty years' advocacy, to Independency, and from this again to Episcopalianism, necessarily made many enemies and required many explanations. His biographies have been mainly written by his opponents who emphasize his faults and his apostacy."[67]

The Victorian Age: The Church on Rittenhouse Square. The Protestant Episcopal Church in Philadelphia continued to grow throughout the nineteenth century. The most fashionable churches in the city and its suburbs are shown in Table 22. Soon after the turn of the century, St. James' on Seventh Street just north of Market Street, became part of the United Churches under the rectorship of Bishop White. The building of the church was "projected in the year 1806 to supply the want of church accommodation in what was then the western part of the city."[68] St. James', St. Peter's, and Christ Church, under the leadership of Bishop White until his death in 1836, took care of the spiritual needs of fashionable Philadelphians during the first four decades of the nineteenth century. During this period, St. Mary's Church (1827) was built west of the Schuylkill River in Hamilton Village, a small rural community near the "Woodlands," the famous mansion built by the family of Andrew Hamilton, the Philadelphia lawyer in the Peter Zenger case.[69]

As the population of Philadelphia expanded, the upper classes moved westward, and St. Mark's (1848) and the Church of the Holy Trinity (1857) were built in the newly fashionable "West End," in the neighborhood of Rittenhouse Square. At this same time, across the river in the elite neighborhood of West Philadelphia, some parishioners of St. Mary's, Hamilton Village, established the Church of the Savior (1852), at 38th and Chestnut, just down the street from the Drexel colony. A. J. Drexel and his family were members of the parish from the beginning; he was a vestryman between 1856 and 1889 and Accounting Warden from 1889 until his death in 1893.[70]

After the Civil War, as the figures in Table 22 illustrate, the Victorian gentry filled the three churches in the Rittenhouse Square neighborhood. In addition to St. Mark's and Holy Trinity, St. James' finally followed the fashionable westward trend and moved to 22nd and Walnut Streets in 1870.[71] The fact that these three churches had an increase in communicants of over 300 per cent (see Table 22) between 1860 and 1900, is indicative of the growing influence of the Episcopal Church upon the Victorian upper class. Christ Church and St. Peter's also held their own during this period as many old families remained loyal to their family traditions. "The present John Cadwalader, Senior, has been a vestryman for forty years," wrote a St. Peter's historian in 1923. "In his pew three generations of John Cadwaladers are represented each Sunday."[72] Even as late as 1940, Cadwaladers were still associated with St. Peter's.

The Rittenhouse Square parishes not only increased in size but also in wealth during the prosperous Victorian period. The Parochial Reports of St. James' Church between 1833 and 1899 are revealing:[73] Whereas the total annual offerings of the parish never exceeded $3,000 during the 1830's, $4,000 during the 1840's, and only twice exceeded $5,000 in any one year during the 1850's, things were quite different after the Civil War. During the 1860's, for instance, even though most of the parishioners had already moved away and "had to depend on their carriages and ultimately on street cars for reaching their place of worship," the annual offerings only once fell below $5,000 and were usually between $8,000 and $10,000 per year. Finally, after removal of the church to the fashionable "West End" in 1870, the annual offerings at St. James' remained between $20,000 and $60,000, most often nearer the higher figure, for the remainder of the century.

The list of vestrymen at St. James' during the nineteenth century included many ex-Quaker family names. Dr. Edward Shippen (vestryman 1879-1895), for example, recalls the Quaker merchant of the same name who owned the "biggest house and the biggest coach in Philadelphia" at the end of the seventeenth century; Senator Pepper's grandfather, George Mifflin Wharton, himself a birthright Friend and the son of the wealthy Quaker merchant, William

Table 22—Fashionable Episcopal Churches in Philadelphia—Number of Communicants 1860-1940

		1860	1880	1900	1920	1940	1860-1900	1900-1940
URBAN CHURCHES								
Old Philadelphia								
Christ Church	(1695)	353	392	566	492	509		
St. Peter's	(1761)	502	754	931	825	637		
		855	1146	1497	1317	1146	+75%	−24%
Rittenhouse Square								
St. James'	(1810)	250	400	944	1118	546		
St. Mark's	(1848)	294	850	1627	1520	720		
Holy Trinity	(1857)	268	900	988	1789	1091		
		812	2150	3559	4427	2357	+338%	−34%
West Philadelphia								
St. Mary's	(1827)	104	311	544	479	261		
The Savior	(1852)	110	452	1221	1807	914		
		214	763	1765	2286	1175	+725%	−33%
SUBURBAN CHURCHES								
Chestnut Hill-Whitemarsh								
St. Paul's	(1856)	54	122	306	625	1198		
St. Martin's	(1884)	–	–	368	473	605		
St. Thomas'	(1710)	98	110	220	375	846		
		152	232	894	1473	2649		+197%
Main Line								
Redeemer	(1852)	29	150	318	601	831		
Good Shepherd	(1871)	–	121	200	471	699		
St. Asaph's	(1888)	–	–	261	480	644		
St. Martin's	(1887)	–	–	77	152	290		
St. David's	(1715)	80	52	130	116	390		
		109	323	986	1820	2854		+189%
Old York Road								
St. Paul's	(1861)	–	155	257	418	836		+225%
SUMMARY:								
Urban Communicants		1881	4059	6821	8030	4678	+263%	−31%
Suburban Communicants		261	710	2137	3711	6339	+719%	+196%
Total Communicants		2142	4769	8958	11741	11017	+318%	+23%
Population: Philadelphia County:		565,529	847,170	1,293,697	1,823,779	1,931,334	+130%	+49%

Source: Journals of the Annual Conventions of the Protestant Episcopal Church in the Diocese of Pennsylvania—1861, 1881, 1901, 1921, 1941.

Fishbourne Wharton, served as a vestryman between 1837 and 1870; finally, James C. Biddle, grandson of Owen Biddle, a leader of the "Free" or "Fighting" Quakers during the Revolution, served St. James' between 1834 and 1839. The old Episcopalian Cadwaladers and the newer Episcopalian Biddles were nicely blended in the person of Mr. Cadwalader Biddle, vestryman and accounting warden at St. James' in the 1880's. It is said that the Biddles and Cadwaladers are to Philadelphia what the Cabots and Lowells are to Proper Boston: While the "Cabots speak only to Lowells and the Lowells speak only to God," as the saying goes, "when a Biddle gets drunk, he thinks he's a Cadwalader."

St. Mark's Church, on Locust Street just east of Rittenhouse Square, is the finest example of Gothic church architecture in the city. Founded by men who were vitally concerned with the Oxford movement in England (the Oxford movement was founded to combat the various attempts to disestablish the Church after the Reform Bill of 1832), the High Church services at St. Mark's closely resemble the form of the Anglican communion.[74] The building and furnishing of St. Mark's over the years suggest the nostalgia for Europe, the Anglophilia of the American Victorian gentry. The plans of the church, "suggested by an old abby, were drawn up by the Ecclesiological Society of London," and executed by John Notman, leading Society architect, who also designed the Church of the Holy Trinity, and the first brownstone-front house in the Square area.[75] St. Mark's was decorated "in the style which prevailed in the last quarter of the Fourteenth Century, a period when Gothic architecture attained its highest point of perfection and beauty."[76]

Like Henry Adams, the parishioners of St. Mark's dreamed of the days of Mont St. Michel and Chartres. "Love for the church in the Middle Ages," a new rector told his parishioners in the nineties, "led people not only to build and adorn beautiful churches but to store them with costly vessels and vestments. The churches were possessed of great treasures of gold, silver, and precious stones, the work of the most celebrated artists of the time. In our time churches too often suggest cheapness rather than simplicity."[77]

Rodman Wanamaker, the son of Philadelphia's most famous department store merchant and devout Presbyterian, John Wanamaker, was St. Mark's greatest single benefactor. A man of exquisite taste, Rodman Wanamaker had represented the family interests in Europe for many years. When his wife died in 1900, he donated the Lady Chapel at St. Mark's, including many priceless furnishings gathered from all over Europe. His gift of a silver altar was the chief treasure of St. Mark's: "This altar is without doubt the greatest work of English ecclesiastical art in twentieth century America," writes the Church's historian, "and the first such example since the Fifteenth Century, when one was made in Florence by Pallajuolo (1429-98) and his associates."[78] The altar was, of course, designed in London "by Messrs. Barkentin and Krall of Regent Street." The American merchant prince, the spiritual cousin of the Medici of Renaissance Italy rather than the knight of the Middle Ages, certainly would have been extremely cramped by the style of the Quaker meeting house.

The installation of the bells at St. Mark's, cast in 1875 by the Whitechapel Bell Foundry in London, the same firm which had cast the bells of Christ Church and St. Peter's, was responsible for one of the most curious cases in the history of American jurisprudence. According to the best historical opinion, the steeple at St. Mark's was so low that the sound of the new bells was a definite nuisance in the community. Although the following account by the church's historian of the bell controversy at St. Mark's in the seventies may be overdrawn, it does illustrate the typical tenacity of Proper Philadelphians in defending their creature comforts:

In January, 1875, while the bells were being cast, nineteen over-imaginative neighbors remonstrated to the vestry concerning the proposed installation of the bells. They said their nervous systems could not be shocked by sharp, sudden, or loud noises, such as chimes being rung. They estimated their properties would decrease in value to the extent of $5,000 apiece, if St. Mark's installed the bells. . . .

On Whitsunday, 1876, the four bells arrived from London. . . . Protests began anew. Philadelphia society was rent in twain. Matrons had to select their dinner guests, all of whom either favored or opposed the bells of St. Mark's. The Centennial Exposition and the Pennsylvania-Princeton football game were nearly eclipsed.

A bill for injunction was finally filed against St. Mark's. The case came up for hearing in February, 1877, in Court of Common Pleas No. 2, Judge Hare, presiding. Philadelphia lawyer was arrayed against Philadelphia lawyer—P. Pemberton Morris and George W. Biddle for St. Mark's and William Henry Rawls and R. C. McMurtrie for the plaintiffs. The latter averred that the environs of the 16th and Locust Streets were replete with handsome and expensive residences which were enhanced by their supposed immunity from nuisances. However, the present bell ringing was harsh, loud, high, sharp, clanging, discordant, and the noise was an intolerable nuisance. The bells shook the very walls of the houses, made conversation impossible in the immediate vicinity of the tower, disturbed the sleep of infants and children, distracted the mind from serious employment, and destroyed social and domestic intercourse and much of all that goes to make up the peace and happiness of home life. All this was so increased in summer that departure from the city was necessary. (It is hard to imagine any of these gentle folk staying in town during the summer. To do so would have been very unfashionable.) The nuisance became much intensified for those who were ill. Property values were depreciating in the neighborhood because of bell ringing. This action of the defendants was not a secular work carried on for private profit nor was it part of the necessary apparatus or machinery by which a great city had its wants supplied. It certainly was not a work of benevolence, charity, or education. The fact that for the last quarter century the prosperity of the defendants had increased, during all of which time they had not a single bell, showed that bell ringing was neither essential to their worship nor their wordly welfare. Dr. S. Weir Mitchell, probably influenced by his more affluent patients, testified that "medical treatment of the neighbourhood had to be regulated by the hours of the defendants' bell ringing." Thus ran the curious reasoning of the complainants, many of whom were Episcopalians. Apparently their belief in the Holy Catholic Church was on the condition of personal convenience.[79]

The plaintiffs won their case, and the bells of St. Mark's rang no more. The day following the court's decision, a ballad appeared in the Philadelphia *Sunday Dispatch:*

IN STATU QUO ANTE BELLUM

No more the clanging sound of bells shall fright the quiet air;
No more the tolling 'country chimes' will agitate the fair;
And drowsy Cit may sweetly doze upon his easy chair.
No chiming now for brownstone folks
Who live in St. Mark's square.

At midnight now the soldier 'swell' from club may safely reel,
And, pausing at his lofty door, for friendly latch-key feel;
His morning nap is all secure—his dream's his own affair.
No matin-bell for brownstone folks
Who live in St. Mark's square.

To Justice—sweet and noble maid, with balances so true,
Who blindly weighs the good and bad—our thanks are warmly due;
But loftier, greater, grander, still is Equity so rare,
Who guards the nerves of brownstone folks,
Who live in St. Mark's square.[80]

General George Gordon Meade was one of St. Mark's most famous parishioners. After his sudden death from pneumonia in

1872, his funeral was held in the church and was attended by federal, state, and city officials, a host of relatives and friends, and the President of the United States, Ulysses S. Grant. Born to one of the city's most distinguished Catholic families, Meade had been baptized in the parish of "Nuestra Senora del Rosario," at Cadiz, Spain. According to parish records, he had been confirmed at St. Mark's in 1855 at the age of forty.[81]

Across the Square from St. Mark's, on Walnut Street, the Church of the Holy Trinity ministered to Low Church fashionable Philadelphians. Simple in ritual and decor, Holy Trinity became the leading Philadelphia congregation under the great Phillips Brooks.[82] After graduating from the Virginia Theological Seminary, the most fashionable in the Episcopal Church, Phillips Brooks began his ministry in 1859 at a rather poor parish, the Church of the Advent, in North Philadelphia. He attracted city-wide fame in a very short time and was called to Holy Trinity in 1860. Phillips Brooks' influence on Philadelphia is described here by a contemporary observer:

The costly, spacious Church of the Holy Trinity, in Rittenhouse Square, was always filled, crowded in all weathers, whenever it was known that he was going to preach. And yet to the breathless multitudes who came and went under the spell of his unique eloquence as certainly as the tides, he stood an insoluble puzzle and wonder. Perhaps there never was developed in any pulpit a parallel experience. Here were thousands crowding the pews and standing room of the Holy Trinity Church, Sunday after Sunday, and year after year. . . .[83]

In 1869 Phillips Brooks left Philadelphia to become the famous rector of Trinity Church in Boston. In a memorial service for Dr. Alexander Hamilton Vinton, a Proper Bostonian and his predecessor at Holy Trinity in Philadelphia, Phillips Brooks summed up his impressions of the Philadelphia upper class:

Philadelphia is a city where the Episcopal Church is thoroughly at home. Side by side with the gentler Puritanism of that sunnier clime, the Quakerism which quarrelled and protested, but always quarrelled and protested peacefully, the Church of England had lived and flourished in colonial days, and handed down a well-established life to the new Church which sprang out of her veins at the Revolution. It was the temperate zone of religious life with all its quiet richness. Free from antagonism, among a genial and social people, with just enough internal debate and difference to insure her life, enlisting the enthusiastic activity of her laity to a degree which we in Boston know nothing of, with a more demonstrative if not a deeper piety, with a confidence in herself which goes forth in a sense of responsibility for the community and a ready missionary zeal, the Church in Philadelphia was to the Church in Boston much like what a broad Pennsylvania valley is to a rough New England hillside.[84]

The fashionable Philadelphians on Rittenhouse Square were unquestionably a devout and charming people whose well-regulated social world included firm religious habits. Cordelia Drexel Biddle, who grew up on Rittenhouse Square and attended Holy Trinity, recalls in her chatty biography of her father that grace was always said at the Biddle table and that "all the Philadelphia families we knew were strict about daily prayers, regular church attendance, and spiritual duties."[85] George Wharton Pepper, a vestryman and warden at St. Mark's for over half a century, attended the 7:45 A.M. service daily when he lived in the neighborhood of Rittenhouse Square. Always an advocate of action and the cultivation of worth-while habits as a defense against doubt-producing introspection, Senator Pepper records in his autobiography that "it is not in analysis but in actual experience that the power of the Sacrament is to be found."[86]

Anthony J. Drexel Biddle, Cordelia Biddle's father, was perhaps Holy Trinity's most colorful parishioner. An intimate friend of pugilists, from Jack Lawless to Gene Tunney, and of revivalists such as Billy Sunday, Tony Biddle built the men's Bible class at Holy Trinity from a feeble three participants into a thriving enterprise.[87] His "Athletic Christianity" movement, started at Holy Trinity, eventually spread all over the world. With only a minimum of formal education, Tony Biddle published several books and hundreds of articles during his active and busy life. He was an officer in the United States Marine Corps during both wars and a special consultant to the Federal Bureau of Investigation (as specialist in the art of self-defense) until his death in 1948. Needless to say, he was one of the most interesting Proper Philadelphians listed in *Who's Who* in 1940.

Despite the popular notion that high prestige accrues to the businessman in America, men such as the Biddles and Cadwaladers—military and professional men, not businessmen—have always out-ranked, in the minds of the public, men more adept in the affairs of money. Charming, romantic, cerebral rather than acquisitive, and always with an eye on a chance for glory and adventure, the Biddle family have never been conspicuous money-makers. Nevertheless, they seem to have had the happy faculty, in the tradition of the British gentleman, of marrying well. Anthony J. Drexel Biddle, Senior, as his name suggests, was the great Philadelphia banker's grandson. Even more spectacular wealth was absorbed by the family, however, when Anthony J. Drexel Biddle, Jr., Franklin Roosevelt's ambassador to most of the exiled governments of Europe during World War II, married into the Duke fortune. His charming sister, Cordelia, married her brother's new brother-in-law, Angier Duke, six months later. Both marriages eventually ended in divorce.[88]

Divorce was not acceptable to Rittenhouse Square society at the height of its glory. Both the Protestant Episcopal Church, which stands nearer to Rome on the matter of divorce than the other Protestant denominations, and the rules of the dancing Assembly, foster and defend the sanctity of the Proper Philadelphia family. Thus the Episcopal Church does not sanction the marriage of a divorced person, and invitations to the annual Assembly Balls are never sent to divorced persons who have taken a second spouse. The power of the Assembly in regulating upper-class mores is suggested by the ex-Philadelphian, Cordelia Biddle, who recalls that "any family not getting a bid might as well jump from the City Hall dome."[89]

While the upper-class mores included a rigid code of personal morality, no one on Victorian Rittenhouse Square would ever have thought of questioning the essential rightness of the social structure. The conscientious parishioners of Holy Trinity, St. Mark's, and St. James' certainly felt it their duty to help those less fortunate than themselves and responded generously to the founding of slum parishes and city missions as well as a multitude of other charitable causes. Any suggestion, however, that the basic institutional pattern needed reforming, generally found the Proper Philadelphian either indifferent or adamantly in opposition. Even the great Phillips Brooks, who had vigorously preached the cause of anti-slavery from the Holy Trinity pulpit, felt that the Church should deal with private spiritual problems rather than the social question. He did not approve of the "fact that the English Episcopalians were turning some of their attention from spiritual to social questions."[90] The Proper Philadelphian's attitude towards social inequality, for instance, is probably stated as well as anywhere else in the following remarks of Phillips Brooks, taken from a sermon he preached in Boston many years after he had left the Quaker City:

> There can be no doubt, I think, whatever puzzling questions it may bring with it, that it is the fact of privilege and inequalities among men for which they do not seem to be responsible, which makes a large part of the interest and richness of human experience. . . . I believe that the more we think, the more we become convinced that the instinct which asks for equality is a low one, and that equality, if it were completely brought about, would furnish play only for the low instincts and impulses of man.[91]

Despite Christian doctrine to the effect that poverty is a virtue and great wealth conducive to sin, complete material equality—the basis of pernicious ideologies in every age—has not always been stressed by the Church. It is hard to understand, however, how good Christian men and women with advantages of "wealth, influence, Catholic traditions, and ceremonial," as one rector once described his parishioners at St. Mark's, could have remained unconcerned with the underlying causes of corruption and cruel inequalities such as the sweat-shop and child labor, which festered beneath the calm surface of the Victorian drawing rooms on Rittenhouse Square. At any rate, aristocrats such as the Harvard-educated "Socialist Priest," Father J. O. S. Huntington, founder of the Order of the Holy Cross, were never bred on Rittenhouse Square. Perhaps George Wharton Pepper's honest and frank confession of his own inability "to appreciate the anxieties of the so-called 'underprivileged' " may be indicative of the state of mind of his class. In 1944, over half a century after the days of his youth on the Square, he wrote in his autobiography:

> In the past I have repeatedly tried to imagine what it is like to be hungry and cold and harassed by debts but I have always ended by admitting the inadequacy of mere imagination. Rolling along in a comfortable car, spending my days in congenial work, going back at nightfall to a happy home without fear of landlord or sheriff, I simply could not imagine what it is like to be an elevator boy or a taxi driver or a share cropper or a coal miner or a veteran too old to be employed or a man with a sick wife or child and unable to afford medical care or nursing comforts or a white-collar worker conscious of inherent capacity but up against a dead end with no chance of promotion.[92]

The mores of Proper Philadelphia society allow and even foster individuality and eccentricity but never nonconformity. At the turn of the century, Lincoln Steffens found Philadelphia "corrupt and contented." He might also have added "unimaginative."

The glory of Rittenhouse Square, and the fashionable Episcopal churches in the neighborhood, reached its height in the 1890's. On Saturday afternoon, January 20, 1894, the pomp and power of Philadelphia's and America's business upper class were symbolized at a service held in memory of the city's greatest Victorian banker, Anthony J. Drexel, who had recently passed away at the height of the panic of 1893.[93] The memorial service, attended by fashionable, official, and business gentlemen from Philadelphia, New York, and other cities along the eastern seaboard was held at Drexel Institute of Technology in West Philadelphia. Bishops of the Protestant Episcopal Church led the ceremonies. The opening prayer was given by William B. Bodine, Rector of the Church of the Savior, the memorial address by the Right Reverend Henry Codman Potter, Bishop of New York, and the final benediction by the Right Reverend Ozi William Whitaker, Bishop of the Diocese of Pennsylvania.*

The Twentieth Century: Decline of the Urban Family Church. After the First World War, the fashionable churches around the Square gradually ceased to be family parishes and increasingly ministered to a mobile population of apartment-dwellers and a few members of the older generation whose children had moved to the suburbs. This trend, of course, started much earlier. The historian of St. Mark's, for example, writes that in 1909, "the Sunday School numbered about 50 pupils as compared with 100 pupils in 1894."[95]

Although St. Mark's and Holy Trinity survived the suburban exodus, St. James' eventually became a casualty when it was sold to the Atlantic Refining Company (a convenient spot to refuel before taking the Parkway to the suburbs) during World War II.[96] St. James' struggle for survival in its last years provides an inter-

---

* Although A. J. Drexel was baptized a Roman Catholic in infancy, he and his brother, Joseph W. Drexel, who married a Wharton, eventually went over to the Episcopal Church. Their older brother, Francis A. Drexel, however, remained a Catholic and one of the Church's leading benefactors. For years, on specified occasions, Holy Mass was celebrated at "St. Michel" the estate of this branch of the family in Torresdale, on the Delaware, and at 1503 Walnut Street, their winter residence. Francis A. Drexel's daughter, Katherine, eventually became a nun and founded the Sisters of the Blessed Sacrament, which used the Drexel country place, "St. Michel," as a novitiate.[94]

esting case history of the atomization of urban life in the twentieth century. The exodus of old families to the suburbs accelerated in the twenties. Finally, in 1925, it was decided to do away with the "family pew" at St. James'. At that time, the Philadelphia *Evening Bulletin* reported the decision as follows: "St. James' is finally open to the masses. Pew rents have finally been dropped. It is reported that some of the pews here rent for as high as $2,000 a year. Often the same family rents the same pew for several generations."[97]

The final step in attempting to reach the urban masses at St. James' was taken when the vestry called the Reverend Joseph Fort Newton to be co-rector along with Dr. John C. H. Mockridge, rector of the parish since 1915. John C. H. Mockridge had been one of the most respected high churchmen in the city for many years. He was a strict Anglo-Catholic, born in Canada, and educated at Trinity College, Toronto. He was often mentioned as the High Church candidate for Bishop of the Diocese of Pennsylvania and was well known in church circles and throughout the city as a vigorous opponent of divorce. For many years he was president of the board of the Episcopal Academy and an overseer of the Philadelphia Divinity School. For the sake of his beloved St. James', he finally consented to the appointment of Dr. Newton in 1930.[98]

During World War I, Joseph Fort Newton had gained a world-wide reputation as the rector of the City Temple, often referred to as "The Cathedral of Nonconformity," in the heart of London.[99] A few years before coming to St. James', Dr. Newton had been confirmed before a small group of Episcopal clergymen and later ordained at an "imposing ceremony in Old Christ Church." Together with other plans for popularizing the work of St. James'— concerts, recitals, lectures, and sermons—the appointment of a "man of vigorous and vital utterance, eloquent, and with a voice which charms" should have revived the staid, old, first-family church.[100] If not exactly a typical Anglo-Catholic rector, Joseph Fort Newton was certainly in the tradition of the best American pastors.

He was born in a small town in Texas, graduated from the Southern Baptist Seminary, and ordained in the Baptist ministry in 1893.[101] During his vigorous career, he had written some thirty books and numerous pamphlets on patriotic, religious, and Masonic subjects. Dr. Newton's career was a personification of the secular twentieth century's attempt to compromise with Christianity. His pastorships included the First Baptist Church, Paris, Texas, the

Non-Sectarian Church, St. Louis, Missouri, the People's Church, Dixon, Illinois, the Liberal Christian Church, Cedar Rapids, Iowa, the City Temple, London, and the Church of the Divine Paternity, New York City.

Both Joseph Fort Newton and John C. H. Mockridge were listed in *Who's Who* in 1940, but only the latter was listed also in the *Social Register*. Dr. Newton left St. James' in 1938, and Dr. Mockridge retired in 1940. The church did not survive the pressures of urban democracy.

The Twentieth Century: Rise of the Suburban Church. During the second half of the nineteenth century, urban centers went through a period of rapid growth. As we have seen, the wealthier classes in Philadelphia moved away from the older parts of the city, west to Rittenhouse Square and West Philadelphia, and north on Broad Street. At the same time, the development of the railroad made it possible for more and more families to escape from urban congestion altogether by moving out to the suburbs. All the suburban churches listed in Table 22 had been built by 1900.

The two oldest Episcopal Churches in the Philadelphia suburbs are Old St. David's in Wayne, on the Main Line, and St. Thomas' Church in the Whitemarsh Valley. In the eighteenth century these rural churches were served by circuit missionaries sent from London by the "Society for Propagating the Gospel in Foreign Parts."[102] The first congregation at St. David's, interestingly enough, was composed of Welsh Quakers who had gone over to the Church of England as a result of the Keithian schism mentioned above.[103] These two churches served the local people primarily and did not become fashionable suburban churches until the last two decades of the nineteenth century. In 1880, for example, one finds that Mr. W. H. Drayton and Mr. J. W. Sharp, two fashionable Philadelphians, were the senior wardens of St. Thomas' and St. David's, respectively.[104] Since the total annual offerings of these two parishes in that year were $92.42 and $60.76, however, they were hardly thriving suburban churches. Their eventual growth into full-fledged suburban (rather than rural) churches between 1920 and 1940 is indicated by the fact that each church recorded total annual offerings of over $10,000 (St. David's) and over $40,000 (St. Thomas') in 1940.

In the 1850's, new Episcopal churches came to Chestnut Hill and the Main Line. In 1852, the Church of the Redeemer was built on a hill overlooking the old Bryn Mawr Hotel in Lower Merion Township.[105] St. Paul's became the first Episcopal church in Chestnut Hill when it was completed in 1856.[106] Both churches were founded by fashionable Philadelphians, many of whom were still parishioners in St. James', St. Mark's, or Holy Trinity during the winter months. Continuity, always dear to the hearts of Proper Philadelphians, was maintained in the person of the first rector of St. Paul's, William Hobart Hare, who was the son of one of the great headmasters of Episcopal Academy and a grandson of Bishop Hobart of New York.[107]

The construction of these two Episcopal churches marked the beginning of the suburban trend. Both Chestnut Hill and Lower Merion Township, of course, were old communities in 1850. In Chestnut Hill, for instance, the Baptist, Methodist, Presbyterian, and Roman Catholic churches, all still standing on their original sites in 1940, were all built before St. Paul's.[108] There was no Quaker meeting house in the early days of Chestnut Hill because, although the original settlers were German Friends, they were members of the Germantown meeting.[109] Lower Merion Township was settled by Welsh Quakers in 1681 and the old Meeting House was built in 1695. The Lutheran and Baptist churches were built well before the advent of the Church of the Redeemer, in 1765 and 1808, respectively.[110]

Both the Redeemer and St. Paul's were relatively small parishes before 1900 and went through their period of most rapid growth during the first four decades of the present century. Due to the pressures of an expanding congregation, a large and impressive Gothic church, built on the same site as the original St. Paul's, was completed in 1929, under the leadership of Reverend Malcolm Peabody, son of Endicott Peabody of Groton.[111] St. Paul's Church in Chestnut Hill has always maintained a close relationship with St. Paul's School, in Concord, New Hampshire (see below). The rector of St. Paul's Church in 1940, listed in both *Who's Who* and the *Social Register*, had been a master at the School for a short period, while the rector of St. Paul's School at its 100th anniversary in 1956, had once been a young curate in Chestnut Hill under Dr. Peabody.[112]

The other St. Paul's Church, along the Old York Road in Elkins Park, was built in 1861, largely due to the generosity of the master of "Ogontz," Jay Cooke.[113] For many years, Jay Cooke was a vestryman at St. Paul's where he took an active part in the Sunday School and other church activities. In 1940, Charles D. Barney, Jay Cooke's son-in-law, kept up the family traditions at St. Paul's where he was the senior warden.[114]

The four remaining fashionable churches listed in Table 22—St. Martin's-in-the-Fields in Chestnut Hill, and the Church of the Good Shepherd, St. Asaph's, and St. Martin's on the Main Line—were all built in the eighteen-eighties. The first was named as a private chapel for the "Druim Moir" estate of Henry Howard Houston. The Church of the Good Shepherd, with its fine Gothic architecture and Anglican form of service, is the St. Mark's of the Main Line. St. Martin's-in-the-Fields, St. Martin's in Radnor, and St. Asaph's in Cynwyd, have been intimately allied with the Houston, Chew, and Roberts families, respectively, from their very beginning. In 1940, moreover, the same families were all active in these three churches: Samuel F. Houston, for example, was a warden at St. Martin's in Chestnut Hill, Benjamin Chew was a warden at St. Martin's in Radnor, and I. W. Roberts and T. W. Roberts, sons of George Roberts, late president of the Pennsylvania Railroad, were wardens at St. Asaph's.[115]

The Episcopal Church probably played a lesser role in the social life of the Proper Philadelphians in 1940 than it did in the Victorian period. No clergyman had the same influence on either the upper class or the rest of the city's population as did Phillips Brooks in Boston and Philadelphia, or Henry Codman Potter in New York. The Church was, nevertheless, still intimately connected with Philadelphia's contemporary, suburban upper class. Five of the eight Episcopalian clergymen listed in *Who's Who* in 1940, including the Bishop of the Diocese of Pennsylvania, were also listed in the *Social Register*. Of the five members of the Standing Committee of the Diocese of Pennsylvania and the four Delegates to the General Assembly—the nine most important lay positions in the Church hierarchy—seven were listed in the 1940 *Social Register*.[116] At the same time, the presidents of the Pennsylvania Railroad, the Philadelphia Savings Fund Society, the Fidelity Philadelphia Trust Company, the Real Estate Land Title and Trust Company, and the president of the University of Pennsylvania, all were active church leaders, as wardens of their respective suburban parishes or lay officials in the Diocese. Finally, in 1940, *all* the wardens of the churches listed in Table 22 (with the exception of the two West Philadelphia churches which were no longer fashionable) were listed in the *Social Register*. It is no wonder that in the diocesan headquarters and in the parish offices the little orange and black book is always available for convenient reference.

By 1920 the urban churches in Philadelphia reached their peak in number of communicants. By 1940, however, the fashionable suburban churches became the center of upper-class Episcopalianism. As a fitting symbol of this change, in 1940, the First City Troop, always, and still, closely connected with St. Peter's, marched to the Church of the Redeemer where a service was held to mark its departure for active service.[117]

CHAPTER XI

Parallel Upper-Class Structures

> To the extent that ethnic factors in combination with social class factors tend to delimit the area of intimate social contact in the adult world, and concomitantly provide the particular setting for the socialization of the child, it is clear that American society consists of a series of "invisibly" delineated smaller societal units with varying degrees of interrelationship, and each with its own variation and version of the American culture pattern.
>
> MILTON M. GORDON

AMERICAN society is a symphony of many and diverse racial, ethnic, religious, and subcultural traditions. Sociologists have long been aware of the fact that, in addition to the various *horizontal* class levels in American society, within each horizontal class there are *vertical* differentiations based on religion, race, and ethnic origins. To put it another way, within each racial, religious, or ethnic community, there are distinct horizontal social classes. In summing up a great deal of painstaking research on the social structure of New Haven, the Yale sociologist, August B. Hollingshead, has recently described these horizontal and vertical cleavages as follows:

The New Haven community's current social structure is differentiated *vertically* along racial, ethnic, and religious lines, and each of these vertical cleavages, in turn, is differentiated horizontally by a series of strata or classes that are encompassed within it. Around the socio-biological axis of race two social worlds have evolved—a Negro world and a white world. The white world is divided by ethnic origin and religion into Catholic, Protestant, and Jewish contingents. Within these divisions there are numerous ethnic schisms. The Irish hold aloof from the Italians, and the Italians move in different circles from the Poles. The Jews maintain a religious and social life separate from the Gentiles.

In short, a major trend in the social structure of the New Haven community during the last half-century has been the development of *parallel class structures* within the limits of race, ethnic origin, and religion. This development may be illustrated by the fact that there are seven different Junior Leagues in the white segment of the community for appropriately affiliated upper class young women. The top ranking organization is the New Haven Junior League which draws its membership from "Old Yankee" Protestant families whose daughters have been educated in private schools. The Catholic Charity League is next in rank and age—its membership is drawn from Irish-American families. In addition to this organization there are Italian and Polish Junior Leagues within the Catholic division of the society. The Swedish and Danish Junior Leagues are for properly connected young women in these ethnic groups, but they are Protestant. Then too, the upper-class Jewish families have their Junior League. The Negroes have a Junior League for their top-drawer young women. This principle of parallel structures for a given class level, by religious, ethnic, and racial groups, proliferates throughout the community.[1]

Professor Hollingshead, of course, is referring to the existence of many different subcultural worlds within the social structure of New Haven as a whole. Each subculture, in turn, has its own class structure, associational complex, charitable institutions, and its own distinctive customs and value systems. Throughout this book we have been primarily concerned with the development and structure of the fashionable, Episcopalian, upper-class subculture. In this chapter, however, we will deal with the upper-class structures within two other subcultural worlds—the Quaker and the Jewish.

In Philadelphia in 1940, there were many subcultural worlds with parallel class structures roughly similar to those Hollingshead found in New Haven. These diverse and more or less isolated, racial, religious, or ethnic worlds were, in turn, represented in the elite. The 770 Philadelphians listed in *Who's Who*, for example, included two leading members of the Negro community; at least twenty-seven Catholics, most of whom were leaders in the Irish-Catholic community; twenty-two members of the somewhat isolated Quaker community; two wealthy and influential brothers, Harold Frederick and Raymond Pitcairn, officers and owners of the Pitcairn Autogiro and Pittsburgh Plate Glass companies, who were the patriarchal leaders of the unique Swedenborgian community (a highly integrated theocracy, complete with Gothic cathedral and private academy), in the suburb of Bryn Athyn; and, finally, there were twenty-seven members of the Jewish community.

A brief discussion of the Quaker and Jewish upper classes in Philadelphia should shed some light on this extremely important aspect of American urban society. While the Quaker world was isolated from the rest of the community because of its religious traditions and autonomous social institutions, the Jewish community, on the other hand, was both ethnically and religiously differentiated from the Gentile world. As a great deal has already been said, at least indirectly, about the Philadelphia Quakers in our previous discussion of the Quaker-turned-Episcopal gentry, the structure and traditions of the Jewish upper class will be analyzed in somewhat more detail. Furthermore, the social isolation of the Jewish community is of wider sociological interest because of its existence in all urban social structures.

Quaker Philadelphia: A Parallel Elite and Upper Class. As we have seen, the members of the Society of Friends lost political control of Pennsylvania in the 1750's as a result of their refusal to support the wars against the Indians. The Revolutionary War period divided the Friends into a minority of "Fighting" or "Free" Quakers and a pacifist majority. Those who believed, following the position taken by James Logan in the early eighteenth century, that a defensive war was morally justifiable, broke off from the main body and formed the Society of Free Quakers—which eventually died out in 1836. Betsy Ross, the flag-maker, was the last of the original members. The majority, who stood by their pacifist principles, went through a very unpleasant period. They were suspected of treason, fined, thrown into jail, and many of their houses were burned. Despite their wish to remain neutral, they were never left alone.

The seclusiveness, simplicity, moral fervor, and clannishness of the Philadelphia Quakers began with their final withdrawal as a group from the world of affairs during the Revolutionary period. Rufus M. Jones, Quaker historian, philosopher, religious leader, and beloved Haverford College professor, was a leading member of the Philadelphia intellectual elite in 1940. He attempted to explain the Philadelphia Quaker community as follows:

> The Revolutionary War left the Philadelphia Yearly Meeting more moral internally, more devoted to moral reforms, more conservative of ancient tradition, custom, and doctrine, more separate from the world, more introversive in spirit, than it found it. . . . Had the active public-spirited Friends, who went off with the revolutionary movement, remained to mould their generation, a type more outward, more progressive, more intellectual would have resulted. . . . As a result of the narrowing and uniting processes combined Friends are what they are.

What they would have been with a wider outlook upon life and a looser standard of conduct, we can only conjecture. But he who understands Philadelphia Quakerism of a century past must read it in the light of the Revolution—a revolution not less in Quaker development than in American history.[2]

At the upper-class level, Philadelphia's Quaker aristocracy remained apart from the fashionable Episcopalian world down to the period when most of the men in the 1940 elite were growing up; they lived isolated lives on Rittenhouse Square, north of Market Street, or in Germantown. For example, after graduating from the University of Pennsylvania in 1887, George Wharton Pepper and two college friends spent the summer abroad. Among the passengers on the ship on which they sailed were "some interesting Philadelphia Quakers; Robert Pearsall Smith, his young and attractive unmarried daughter and several friends of hers," records Senator Pepper, a half century later in his autobiography. "That I had never heard of these fellow-townsmen of mine," he continues, "was due to the fact that within the limits of Philadelphia we had lived in different worlds. The Quaker community, with its center in Germantown, was effectually set off from the social group into which I was born as if between us there had been a Chinese wall." Young George Pepper soon found out that the Smiths were a prosperous and aristocratic family as well as important religious leaders in the Society of Friends. He also observed, in the Smiths, the usual circumspection and the habit of probing into the social credentials of strangers so characteristic of his own world: "When we struck up an acquaintance with the young people of his party," writes Senator Pepper, "Mr. Smith was careful to interview us and to subject us to a rather severe examination respecting our social qualifications. I was somewhat puzzled, in Mr. Smith's case, by the combination of evangelistic ardor and an attitude not far removed from snobbishness. I was to find confirmation fifty years later for my boyish suspicion that worldliness may penetrate even a Chinese wall, when I read the reminiscences of Mr. Smith's son Logan Pearsall Smith, entitled *Unforgotten Years*. In this most interesting, if rather cynical, volume one reads of the social contacts between Philadelphia Quakers and prominent English members of their Society."[3]

Logan Pearsall Smith, expatriate intellectual, friend of Henry James and George Santayana, and brother-in-law of Bernard Berenson, was born in 1865, just two years before the birth of his fellow-Philadelphian, George Wharton Pepper. While the latter grew up in the fashionable world of Rittenhouse Square and St. Mark's Church, his contemporary spent his youth in the "Quaker suburb" of Germantown, which he describes in *Unforgotten Years* as follows:

The life of the Quakers in Philadelphia, where we lived as children, was that of a secluded community, carefully entrenched and guarded from all contact with what we called the "World"—that dangerous world of wickedness which, we vaguely knew, lay all about us. With that world and its guilty splendors we had no contact; of the fashionable American aristocracy (and every population has its aristocracy and fashion) we were not members; and I can make no claim, as Americans abroad are apt to claim, that I belong to one of what are called America's first families. With members of this greater world, like Edith Wharton and Mrs. Winthrop Chandler, I became acquainted only after I had come to live in Europe.[4]

In striking contrast to George Wharton Pepper's open and frank autobiography, Logan Pearsall Smith's urbane comments on his world remind one of Boston's Henry Adams. But then the Quaker side of Philadelphia's Victorian Chinese wall was far more intellectual and introspective, on the whole, than the Episcopalian side. Both sides, however, had a strong sense of family tradition, caste, and an admiration for their spiritual British cousins whether Anglican or Quaker.

Logan Pearsall Smith, a direct descendant of James Logan, was literally a member of one of the city's First Families. His somewhat snobbish comments on the social class superiority of the Orthodox over the Hicksite Friends were noted in an earlier chapter. His insight into the basic ideals of Philadelphia's business aristocracy applies both to the Quaker and Episcopalian sides of the Chinese wall. A man of inherited wealth, as was his father before him, Logan Pearsall Smith had no desire to take over the family business. He soon saw the difficulties of justifying the life of scholarship to the American upper classes: "That every American should make money, that even those who already possessed it should devote their lives to making more, that all of them without exception should betake themselves every morning to their offices and spend all the hours of sunlight in these great business buildings—this was the universally accepted and grotesque ideal of life in the world we lived in."[5] His friend Benjamin Jowett, master of Balliol and famous Oxford classicist, once summed up the curious blend of middle-class striving and aristocratic ideal of aloofness which makes up the modern gentleman's social code. In giving advice to a young gentleman at Balliol, Jowett said: "It is most important in this world to be pushing; it is fatal to seem so."[6]

After the Society of Friends lost control of the city, partly due to its failure to support the Indian Wars, its primary strength lay in the rural meetings surrounding Philadelphia. Isaac Sharpless, president of Haverford College between 1887 and 1917, for example, was born on the same farm owned by his great-grandfather along the West Chester Pike in Chester County. The first member of his family in America, John Sharpless, came over with William Penn in 1682. Isaac Sharpless, friend of both Lowell and Eliot of Harvard, and respected by presidents of the United States, was Haverford's greatest president and built it into one of the best small colleges in America.[7]

In 1940 Philadelphia's Quaker gentry were spread throughout the city's suburbs, with centers in Germantown and in the college communities of Haverford, Bryn Mawr, and Swarthmore. Even in the Victorian era, the most prominent Friends did not live in the Rittenhouse Square area. Within the city, in fact, both of the Friends meeting houses and urban headquarters were situated north of Market Street from the very beginning. In 1940, the original Philadelphia Yearly Meeting (Orthodox) was in the older part of the city at 4th and Arch Streets; the newer (Hicksite) Meeting House and Headquarters was uptown at 15th and Race Streets. While the fashionable Episcopal churches moved west, south of Market, during the nineteenth century, the Friends moved west, on the *northern* side of the Chinese wall.

By 1940, a sharp but subtle line divided the fashionable world in Philadelphia from their more earnest peers in the Society of Friends. In an increasingly secular and mobile world, however, the Chinese wall which characterized the boyhood days of George Wharton Pepper and Logan Pearsall Smith (also listed in the 1940 *Who's Who*) was slowly crumbling. An analysis of the brief *Who's Who* biographies of several leading members of the Philadelphia elite will outline the spectrum of Quaker separation from the "world" of fashionable Philadelphia.

At the turn of the century, Morris E. Leeds founded one of the city's leading manufacturing companies, Leeds and Northrup. He was president of the company from 1903 until 1939, when he became Chairman of the Board. Born in Philadelphia, Mr. Leeds was educated at the Westtown Boarding School, Haverford College, and the University of Berlin. He was a member of Phi Beta Kappa and the recipient of several honorary degrees. He was president of the Haverford College Corporation, president of the Philadelphia Board of Public Education, chairman of the Pennsylvania State Unemployment Commission, and served under President Roosevelt on the Committee on Economic Security and the Business Advisory Council to the Department of Commerce. Morris Leeds lived in Germantown, where he attended the Quaker Meeting (Orthodox) with his wife and two daughters. His clubs included the *Engineers, University,* and the *Cosmos* in Washington, D.C.[8]

The Scattergoods have been leaders within the Society of Friends, and in the Philadelphia business community, since the eighteenth century. Thomas Scattergood, born in Burlington, New Jersey in 1748, was an active Quaker minister in Philadelphia and vicinity.[9] In the 1860's the firm of Carter and Scattergood were "probably the largest manufacturers in this country of Yellow and Red Prussiates of Potash."[10] At the same time, good Quaker Henry Sharpless was engaged in the manufacture of dye stuffs and chemicals. His father, Townsend Sharpless had founded the family firm in 1835.[11] In 1895 the Sharpless Dyewood Extracts Company was incorporated; Thomas Scattergood was president.[12] His two sons J. Henry Scattergood and Alfred Garrett Scattergood were listed in *Who's Who* in 1940.

J. Henry Scattergood was with the American Pulley Company (1897-1900), the Sharpless Dyewood Extracts Company (1900-1904), and secretary of the newly formed American Dyewood Company between 1904 and 1906, when he became a "trustee of estates." Since 1916 he has been treasurer of Haverford College and, since 1927, treasurer of Bryn Mawr College. He was born in Philadelphia and educated at Haverford and Harvard. His directorships in the business world included the American Dyewood Company, the United Dyewood Corporation, First National Bank, Provident Mutual Life Insurance Company, American Pulley Company, Philadelphia Transportation Company, Lehigh Coal and Navigation Company, and the Vicksburg Bridge Company. Among his many good works, Mr. Scattergood was chairman of the board of trustees of the Hampton Institute, an original member of both the

Committee of 70 (Philadelphia's prestige committee fostering good government in a variety of ways) and the American Friends Service Committee, and a member of the original Red Cross commission sent to France in World War I. He belonged to the Historical Society of Pennsylvania, Academy of Natural Sciences, Pennsylvania Geneological Society, American Philosophical Society, Numismatic and Antiquarian Society, American Alpine Club, and the Republican Party. His five grown children were all married and he lived with his second wife (first wife, *nee* Morris, deceased) on the large Morris tract of land in Villanova, on the Main Line. His club memberships included the *Union League, University,* and *Merion Cricket,* in Philadelphia, and the *Cosmos,* in Washington.[13]

Alfred Garrett Scattergood, vice-president of the Provident Trust Company, was educated at Haverford and Harvard. He was director of the Mine Hill and Schuylkill Haven Railroad Company, the Saving Fund Society of Germantown, Friends Hospital, Pennsylvania Hospital, and chairman of the board of directors of Penn Charter School. Alfred Scattergood belonged to the University Club and lived with his wife (Emlen) at "Awbury" in Germantown. "Awbury," a kind of Quaker plantation in the heart of Germantown, is the home of the many descendants of George Emlen, brewer, merchant, and leading Friend in eighteenth-century Philadelphia. In many ways, the Emlens are in the Quaker world what the Biddles or Cadwaladers are to Proper Philadelphia.

The Quakers are most well known and respected in Philadelphia for their educational institutions and the world-wide charitable work of the American Friends Service Committee. We have seen how these three leading Friends were connected with Haverford and Bryn Mawr Colleges (both Orthodox), and Penn Charter School—the oldest day school in the city (1689)—and run by a self-perpetuating board of Friends. The American Friends Service Committee was founded during the first war. Its original chairman was Rufus Jones and its chairman in 1940 was Clarence Pickett, a member of the Quaker elite, living in Wallingford, Pennsylvania (Swarthmore area). Soon after the Committee's founding, J. Henry Scattergood and Morris E. Leeds were sent abroad to make arrangements for the future work of its first relief unit in Europe. When, at the invitation of Herbert Hoover, the American Friends Service Committee took charge of the feeding of German children after the first war, Alfred G. Scattergood was chief of that unit.[14]

These three Quaker (Orthodox) businessmen differed from their more fashionable peers in a number of subtle ways. First, their family and educational background was Quaker. They attended Quaker educational institutions and served them in later life as trustees and managers. All three were leaders in the Quaker world of good works, especially in their connections with the American Friends Service Committee. While the Scattergood brothers listed many important directorships in the business world, it is important to note that they did not list such fashionable directorships as the Philadelphia National Bank, the Girard Trust Company, or the Quaker-founded Philadelphia Contributionship. Finally, all these three men limited their downtown club memberships to the hardly fashionable University and Union League Clubs. In other words, although the two Scattergood brothers were old family Philadelphians and listed in the *Social Register* in 1940, they participated in the Quaker upper class, and not in the world of Proper Philadelphia. Morris Leeds, of an old Quaker family, was not listed in the *Social Register*. From his point of view, of course, this was of no importance. It was, however, of sociological interest because it illustrated that many wealthy and influential Friends lived in a world where this kind of social position or recognition was of no consequence. Most successful industrialists of Mr. Leeds' stature in the city, had they been Episcopalians, would undoubtedly have been listed in the *Social Register* in 1940. The difference has nothing to do with snobbery or social exclusiveness, but refers rather to differences in subcultural values or religious convictions.

Strawbridge & Clothier is one of Philadelphia's three leading department stores. It was founded in 1862 by two members of the Society of Friends, Justus C. Strawbridge (Orthodox) and Isaac Hollowell Clothier (Hicksite).[15] Three descendants of these two family founders were listed in both the *Social Register* and *Who's Who* in 1940. While the members of the Strawbridge family have remained in the Quaker tradition, the Clothiers have gradually gone over to the more fashionable world of Proper Philadelphians.

Isaac Hollowell Clothier was a devout member of the Society of Friends and generous benefactor of many Quaker institutions in the city. Two of his four sons, Morris and William J. Clothier, were members of the 1940 Philadelphia elite. Morris Clothier, a graduate of Swarthmore College and one of its principal benefactors, was the senior partner of the family department store for many years and in 1940 was chairman of the board of directors. Although he was a member of the Society of Friends and a benefactor of such Quaker institutions as Swarthmore College, Morris Clothier participated primarily in the world of fashionable Philadelphia. Among his many directorships in 1940, for example, Mr. Clothier listed the Philadelphia National Bank, the Girard Trust Company, and the University of Pennsylvania (he did not list a Swarthmore College directorship); moreover, his memberships in the Rittenhouse and Racquet clubs, in addition to the inevitable Union League, were also indicative. (The other more strictly Quaker members of this elite limit themselves to one downtown club—the University.)

William J. Clothier, although a birth-right Friend (no religious affiliation listed in *Who's Who*), was even less involved in the Philadelphia Quaker community than his brother. A great Harvard athlete and former lawn tennis champion of the United States, he was one of Philadelphia's leading gentlemen-sportsmen. His social life quite naturally centered in the fashionable word of the Newport Casino, the Pickering Hunt (where he was M.F.H. for many years), and the Merion Cricket Club, as well as the downtown world of exclusive clubs (Philadelphia, Rittenhouse, and Racquet), brokerage offices, investment houses, and absentee coal operations. He was married to a beautiful and talented Proper Philadelphian, and his children and grandchildren were brought up in the world of St. Paul's School, Harvard and Princeton, and the Main Line.

Justus C. Strawbridge, son of Dr. George F. Strawbridge, a graduate of the University of Pennsylvania, was born near Reading, Pennsylvania. After his father's death at an early age, young Strawbridge came down to Philadelphia and eventually went into business with Isaac Hollowell Clothier in 1862. Their store soon became the largest dry-goods store in the world. While his partner was one of the managers of Swarthmore College for many years, Strawbridge was on the board of Haverford College.

Frederick Heap Strawbridge, son of the family founder, was listed in both *Who's Who* and the *Social Register* in 1940. He became a member of the family firm in 1900, and in 1940 was a director of Strawbridge & Clothier. His educational interests included membership in the board of directors of both Bryn Mawr and Haverford colleges. Like Morris Leeds and the two Scattergoods, he limited his downtown club memberships to the University Club. He lived in Chestnut Hill and attended the German-town (Orthodox) Meeting of the Society of Friends. His sons and grandsons, unlike the Clothiers who went away to Harvard and Princeton, attended Haverford College in the good Quaker tradition.

These brief profiles of the Strawbridge and the Clothier families not only delineate the subtle differences between the Quaker and Proper Philadelphia communities in 1940; they also mirror the historical movement of successful Philadelphia families away from the Quaker and into the more worldly community during a period of almost two hundred years. While there was a coherent and autonomous Quaker community in Philadelphia even in 1940; at the peak of wealth and influence in each generation, the lure of fashionable (that is, powerful) society was too great a temptation for all but a few to resist.

This analysis of the Quaker community and its leaders would be incomplete without a brief outline of the biography of Charles James Rhoads, the most influential Quaker in the city in 1940. The Rhoads family have been rural Philadelphia Quakers since the seventeenth century. Charles J. Rhoads' father, James E. Rhoads, retired physician, Quaker philanthropist and the first president of Bryn Mawr College, grew up along with six brothers and sisters, on a farm in Delaware County (south of the West Chester Pike) which had been owned by his family since 1690.[16] Charles J. Rhoads was educated at Penn Charter School and Haverford College (Phi Beta Kappa). Along with J. Henry Scattergood and Morris Leeds, he was attached to the Quaker unit of the American Red Cross in Paris during the First World War. Charles J. Rhoads was one of the leading bankers in Philadelphia. He was a vice-president of the Girard Trust Company from 1904 to 1914 when he resigned to become governor of the Federal Reserve Bank of Philadelphia. He was a partner of Brown Brothers and Company, investment bankers, from 1921 to 1929.

Charles J. Rhoads adroitly bridged the gap between the Quaker and *Social Register* worlds: in the city he was very much the powerful Proper Philadelphian; in his private and civic interests he was a leader within the Quaker community. In the city, for example, he was a director of the Philadelphia Savings Fund Society, the Philadelphia Contributionship, and the Girard Trust Company, and a member of the exclusive Philadelphia Club. In the country, as it were, he was a member of the board of managers of Haverford College and president of the board of trustees of Bryn Mawr College. He listed himself as an Orthodox Friend in *Who's Who* and lived in Bryn Mawr on the Main Line.

The Jewish Elite and Upper Class. The Jewish community in Philadelphia is one of the oldest and most influential in America. Socially isolated from the Gentile world in an infinite variety of ways, this ethnic and religious community perpetuates an ancient and rich cultural tradition. Its highly developed institutional structure, which parallels that of the Gentiles, is supported by a highly articulated associational and class structure.

A small but important part of the Philadelphia elite in 1940 was drawn from the Jewish community. Only one member of the Jewish elite, Dr. David Riesman, Sr., was also listed in the *Social Register.* As we have pointed out, Dr. Riesman grew up in Saxe Weimar, Germany, where members of the Jewish elite traditionally participated in the Gentile world. Although he married the daughter of Penrose Fleisher, a member of one of the most prominent and aristocratic Jewish families in the city, Dr. Riesman's background probably explained his participation in Proper Philadelphia's society. The fact that he was a fashionable physician was also of importance.

The twenty-seven members of the Philadelphia Jewish community listed in *Who's Who* in 1940 held important positions in a wide variety of occupations and professions: There were seven businessmen, five lawyers—two of whom were distinguished judges —two physicians, three journalists, three Rabbis, and a Congressman, a college president, an author, artist, historian, psychologist, and a world-famous bibliophile. Fourteen of these twenty-seven members of the elite were also members of the Jewish upper class. Within the Jewish community, upper-class membership was based on German ethnic origins and family position, which, as in the Gentile world, meant "old wealth." While all the upper-class members of the elite were born in the United States, seven of the thirteen other members of the elite were born in Russia or Poland. The members of the Jewish upper class were even less horizontally mobile than the upper-class members of the Gentile elite. Of those listed in both *Who's Who* and the *Social Register,* for instance, 54 per cent were born in Philadelphia; but 57 per cent of the upperclass members of the small Jewish elite were born in the city.

Just about the same proportion of the Jewish elite were college graduates (74 per cent) as was the case for the whole Philadelphia elite (75 per cent, see Table 29). While eleven of the fourteen members of the Jewish upper class were college graduates, nine of the thirteen other members of the Jewish elite reported college degrees. Unlike the Quakers, and the Gentile upper-class communities as a whole, the Jewish community in Philadelphia did not have its own private schools. All save two upper-class members (both attended Quaker schools) were educated in the public school system.

The following members of the Jewish upper class were also prominent members of the Philadelphia elite in 1940: Abraham Simon Wolfe Rosenbach, the famous bibliophile; Justice Horace Stern of the State Supreme Court; Julius David Stern, publisher of the Philadelphia *Record,* the only Democratic newspaper in the city; Lessing J. Rosenwald, of the Sears Roebuck family; Dr. Solomon Solis-Cohen; Morris Wolf, senior partner of the city's leading Jewish law firm; Howard A. Loeb, who followed his father as president of one of the city's principal banks; Samuel Fels and S. S. Fleisher, two of the city's leading philanthropists; Cyrus Adler, president of Dropsie College and a force in American Jewry as a whole; and Ellis Gimbel, distinguished department store executive, philanthropist, and civic leader.[17]

Howard Loeb, chairman of the board of the Tradesmen's National Bank, was the only member of this group to be employed by a Gentile institution. He and his father before him, in fact, were the only members of the Jewish community ever to attain the presidency of a large Proper Philadelphia banking institution. All the other members of this Jewish upper class were either heads of their own, or family businesses, or they were independent professionals such as lawyers or physicians. In other words, with certain important exceptions, the members of the Jewish elite in Philadelphia were isolated, both socially and economically, from the elite members of the Gentile community.

Historical Development of the Jewish Community. The Jews of Europe are composed of two basically different cultural traditions: the Sephardic Jews of Iberian extraction; and the Ashkenazic Jews of central European (east of the Rhine) origins. The basic difference between them is cultural, rather than ethnic or racial. The Sephardim have both a different form of worship (the ritual is more similar to that followed in the Orient), and a different pronunciation of the Hebrew language from the Ashkenazim who, at least in Europe, spoke Yiddish which is predominantly German, blended with various local idioms.[18]

After the medieval period in Europe, the majority of European Jews were settled in the Iberian peninsula or in central Europe, east of the Rhine. In 1492 the Jews were expelled from Spain by Ferdinand and Isabella. At this time the Jewish community in Venice, about which Shakespeare wrote, came into being. Other Sephardic Jews settled in the free port of Hamburg and in the Netherlands where they were given "burger rights" after 1648. After 1664 Jews were unofficially admitted into England, and the old Sephardic communities formed at this time. During the late seventeenth and eighteenth centuries the Sephardim prospered and became well integrated into the commercial and trading elites of London, Hamburg, and Amsterdam.

In the meantime, the Ashkenazic, or central European Jews, persecuted west of the Rhine, were welcomed by the Dukes of Poland during the sixteenth century. According to one authority, between 1500 and 1648, the Jewish communities in the Polish principalities increased from some 50,000 to over 500,000 souls.[19] Civil War came to Poland in 1648, however, and both sides massacred the Jews. A westward migration was set in motion. All wanted to get to Hamburg or Amsterdam, but many settled down elsewhere, especially in Germany, where the Age of Reason and Enlightenment was slowly creating a tolerant atmosphere. As the Sephardic Jews were already established, and more or less integrated into such commercial communities as Hamburg, Amsterdam, and London, the new immigrants, the Ashkenazim, were relegated to a lower caste position within the Jewish community.

The first Jewish colonists in America arrived at New Amsterdam in 1654. They were Sephardim who had originally gone out to Brazil as crypto-Jews in the sixteenth century or later, along with the early Dutch colonists. When the Portuguese conquered Brazil, the Jews spread north into the West Indies and into the British and Dutch colonies of North America. Eventually, in all other colonial cities, in Newport, Charleston, Savannah, and Philadelphia, there were a small number of Sephardic Jews.

In the early eighteenth century, the Ashkenazim came to America. They came originally from Poland, thence through Germany to Amsterdam or London, and, finally, if they had not settled in these centers, they came to the New World. The eight-eenth-century migrants to America were largely Ashkenazim, be-cause the well-established Sephardim in Amsterdam or London stayed at home. By mid-eighteenth century, the majority of Jews in America were Ashkenazim.

The earliest synagogues in America, on the other hand, were Sephardic, that is, in ritual and language.[20] The early Jewish im-migrants from middle Europe, Ashkenazic or German in origin, were only too glad to join the established synagogues and thus become acculturated Sephardim. Many of the Sephardic aristo-crats of eighteenth-century American Jewry, then, were actually Yiddish-speaking Ashkenazim in background. The sharply-drawn European caste line between Sephardim and Ashkenazim was blurred in America, almost from the beginning.

The Jewish Upper Class and Elite in Philadelphia. In Philadel-phia, the development of a Jewish elite and upper class can con-veniently be divided into five historical periods: (1) elite Jews in Philadelphia but too few to form a distinct Jewish community (1747-1782); (2) formation of an elite Jewish community, but Jews still participated in both the social and business life of the Gentile upper class (1782-1840); (3) formation of the modern Jewish upper class, composed of German (or Ashkenazic) Jews (1840-1882); (4) mass Russian immigration resulting in German-Russian caste division (1882-1920); (5) Russian Jews attain elite status, followed by faint beginnings of acceptance into the Jewish upper class which was, in 1940, still almost entirely German in ethnic origins (1920-1940).

The Colonial Period up to 1782. For all practical purposes there was no coherent Jewish community in Philadelphia during most of the eighteenth century. During the early years of the century, however, there were probably a few leading Jews among the merchant elite. Early records are inadequate. In the 1740's, however, it is believed that a small group of Jews began holding divine services in a house in Sterling Alley.[21] On the other hand, with no synagogue or formal Jewish community, and consequently little prejudice, if any, these early Philadelphia Jews participated in the social and economic life of the community as individuals. When the exclusive Dancing Assembly, the oldest organization of its kind in America, was formed in 1748 by fifty-nine of the city's most prominent families, for example, two Jews, David Franks and Samson Levy, were among the original subscribers.[22]

As the sex ratio was unbalanced during this early period, many Jews were absorbed by the Gentile community. David Franks and Samson Levy were both married to Christians and their children were baptized. Although her father remained a Jew all his life, Rebecca Franks was baptized at aristocratic Christ Church. Once referred to by General Charles Lee as a lady of "every human and divine advantage," Rebecca Franks was one of the most popular belles of Revolutionary society in Philadelphia. According to Dixon Wecter, she "visited and corresponded charmingly with Chews, Allens, and Penns, married Lieutenant-General Sir Henry Johnston, and finished her days as the grande dame of Bath, most aristocratic of English watering places."[23]

The First Jewish Community (1782-1840). The formal Jewish community in Philadelphia began with the construction of the first synagogue, Mikveh Israel. Mikveh Israel was Sephardic in ritual and language. There was a small nucleus of Sephardim in the original congregation, and the first Rabbi, Gershom Mendes Israel Seixas, was a Sephardic Jew from New York. But many of the original founders, including such leading Philadelphians as Bernard Gratz, Manuel Josephson, Methias Bush, and Jonas Phillips, were of German origins. Haym Solomon, a Polish Jew who worked closely with Robert Morris during the Revolution, was one of the original members of the Mikveh Israel synagogue, as were several men whose descendants were leading members of Proper Philadelphia society in 1940.

There was no anti-Semitism as we know it today in colonial Philadelphia. The construction of Mikveh Israel, and hence the formation of a visible Jewish community, however, resulted in the first overt expression of anti-Semitism in Philadelphia. The Jewish congregation had purchased a lot in Sterling Alley where they planned to build a synagogue. The lot, however, was "contiguous" to a German Reformed congregation. Such vigorous protests were raised by this Protestant group that the Jewish leaders finally purchased a new lot, north of High (Market) Street in Cherry Alley, between 3rd and 4th Streets, where the first Mikveh Israel synagogue was erected in 1782 (see Map 3).[24]

During the second half of the eighteenth century, Jewish im-

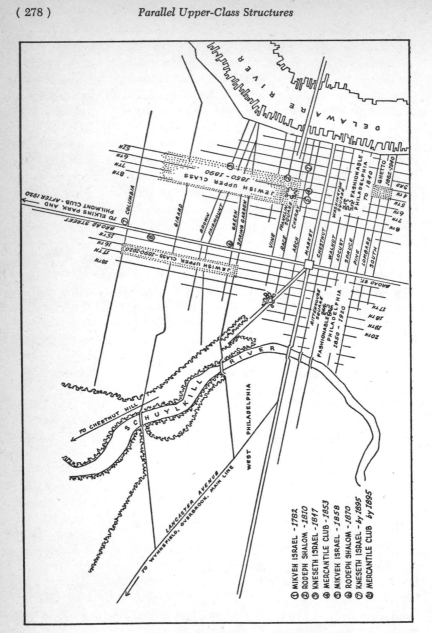

MAP 3

migrants continued to come to Philadelphia. They were almost over-whelmingly Ashkenazim. Those who were accepted were only too glad to join Mikveh Israel and thus "become" Sephardim. By 1795 the German Jews in the city had formed the first Ashkenazic con-gregation, Rodeph Sholom.[25] Within a few years, interestingly enough, many of the founders of Rodeph Sholom went back and joined Mikveh Israel. At this time Ashkenazi-Sephardic caste lines were not sharply drawn. In other words, the upper-class Jews in early Philadelphia were almost entirely Ashkenazim, but brought up in the Sephardic tradition. Bernard Gratz, for example, although an acculturated Sephardi, was from the upper-Silesian part of the Polish kingdoms. Perhaps the appeal of the Sephardic ritual to the successful Ashkenazi merchants in colonial Philadelphia was not unlike the appeal of the Anglican ritual to his Gentile peers of Quaker or Presbyterian origins.

The 1830's were a kind of watershed in upper-class Jewish history in Philadelphia. Although there was by then a definite Jewish community in the city, the families that had made their money and consolidated their position by the 1830's—the Gratz family, for instance—took their place in the social, cultural, and business life of the city along side of, and participating in the Gentile world. Five members of the Gratz family, for example, were taken into the oldest and most exclusive men's club in the city, the Philadelphia Club, before the Civil War.[26] Hyman Gratz, wealthy merchant, respected civic leader, and member of Mikveh Israel, was so popular in Gentile circles that he was elected tempo-rary president of the Philadelphia Club while its first president, Commodore James Biddle, was serving in the Mexican War.[27] In addition to the Gratzes, other leading Sephardic and German Jews married outside the Jewish faith and became assimilated into Proper Philadelphia society during this same period.

The 1830's were also somewhat of a watershed in the relation-ships between the upper-class Jewish and Gentile communities in other American cities. According to Dixon Wecter, for instance, "the last Jew to enter the arcana of smart New York Society before the bars went up was August Belmont."[28] Born in Germany, August Belmont came to America as an agent of the Rothschilds, and "after the panic of 1837—still with the approval of the greatest banking house in the world—he set up his own firm of August Belmont and Company." He became a United States citizen, served as Consul-General to Austria and Minister to the Netherlands, and rendered valuable financial aid to the Union during the Civil War. The Belmonts have been leaders in New York society for over three generations. August Belmont married a Miss Perry, of the family of naval heroes, and his grandson—his namesake—married a Boston Saltonstall.

Formation of the Jewish Upper Class (1840-1892). After the defeat of Napoleon, immigrants from Europe came to America in increasing numbers. The Congress of Vienna, of course, marked a reaction to the more liberal Enlightenment. Due to unrest and, finally to revolution, the immigration of Jews along with other Germans was accelerated during the three decades prior to the Civil War. For example, while 7,583 Germans entered America during the 1820's, 148,204 came during the 1830's.[29] Even more came in the forties and fifties. As the Jews played active roles in the revolutions of 1848, failure sent many to America. (Many of the Jewish forty-eighters were assimilated into the various German-American communities during this period.)[30]

It is estimated that, while there were some 4,000 Jews in America in 1820, by 1860 there were close to 150,000.[31] Along with the increasing size of the Jewish community in Philadelphia, the modern upper class began to take shape in this pre-Civil War period. The three leading members of this new upper class were Isadore Binswanger, Abraham Simon Wolf, and Morris Rosenbach. All three married sisters, the daughters of Hyman Polock, and sisters, too, of one of the city's leading booksellers and bibliophiles, Moses Polock. Hyman Polock, born in Amsterdam in 1786, was married by the most fashionable German-Jewish Rabbi in London, in 1811, and came to America in 1813. He joined the Mikveh Israel congregation and was a moderately successful jeweler and civic leader in the Jewish community for many years. He was an original member of the Hebrew Society for Visitation of Sick and Mutual Assistance, founded in 1813, and one of the founders and directors of the Hebrew Education Society in 1847.[32]

Before the Civil War, the Jewish upper class lived along 5th, 6th, 7th, and 8th Streets, north of Franklin Square (see Table 23 and Map 3). In 1858, the Mikveh Israel congregation built a new synagogue at 7th and Arch Streets (Abraham S. Wolf was on the building committee).[33] At the same time, upper-class social life centered around the Mercantile Club, founded in 1853 (Abraham

S. Wolf, Morris Rosenbach, and Isadore Binswanger were among
the eighteen charter members).[34] Just down the street from Mikveh
Israel, at 6th and Arch, this exclusive club was limited to 400
families as late as the year 1894.[35]

Table 23—Leading Jewish Upper-Class Families in Philadelphia—
Residence in 1859, 1890, 1914, and 1940

Residential Areas[e]	1859 (N—14)[a] %	1890 (N—41)[b] %	1914 (N—37)[c] %	1940 (N—58)[d] %
Franklin Square	100	80	8	—
North Broad	—	20	54	3
Old York Road	—	—	24	81[g]
Rittenhouse Square	—	—	6	13
Other Areas	—	—	8[f]	3[h]
All Areas	100	100	100	100

a. There were 18 founders of the Mercantile Club in 1854. There are the 14 family heads which
could be traced in McElroy's *Philadelphia City Directory*, 1859. The names of the founders of the
Mercantile Club were taken from Henry Samuel Morais, *op. cit.*, p. 193.

b. These are the 41 traceable residences of the families of the men who founded the Philmont
Country Club in 1906. For example, the residential address of Adam Gimbel, father of Ellis A.
Gimbel, founder and president of the Philmont Club 1906-1946, is included here as Ellis Gimbel
was presumably living at home at that time. Similarly, N. Snellenburg, founder of N. Snellenburg and Company, the city's leading middle-class department store, is included here, although
his descendants were Philmont founders. The addresses were obtained from Boyd's *Blue Book*,
1889-90.

c. This list includes 37 charter members of the Philmont Country Club. The charter members
and their addresses were both taken from Boyd's *Philadelphia Blue Book, Elite Directory and
Club List*, 1914.

d. There were 19 charter members of the Locust Club, founded in 1920. As many of these
charter members were deceased in 1940, this list includes the residences of 58 members of their
families. The addresses were obtained from the Philadelphia and Suburban telephone directories
for the year 1940.

e. See Maps 1 and 2 (Chapter IX); and Map 3, above.

f. All lived in West Philadelphia.

g. 31 of the 47 families living in this area lived in Elkins Park.

h. These families lived in the Whitemarsh Valley area.

One's social position within the Jewish community is perhaps
more dependent upon his charitable contributions than is the case
with the Gentile community. Consequently, the members of the
Jewish upper class in Philadelphia took the lead in founding various charitable organizations. The first Hebrew Charity Ball was
organized in 1843 and soon became the most fashionable event
of the year.[36] It was held annually until 1901 when the Federation
of Jewish Charities was organized to replace this informal method
of raising money. After the Civil War, the Jewish Hospital Association (1865) and the United Hebrew Charities (1869) were
formed with Messers. Binswanger, Wolf, and Rosenbach again
among the founders of each institution.[37]

By 1882, then, there was a tightly structured German-Jewish upper class in Philadelphia. It centered around the Franklin Square neighborhood, north of Market Street, and its social life included the synagogue, the Mercantile Club, and charitable work. It has been shown how every upper-class institution was originally guided by members of the Wolf, Binswanger, and Rosenbach families. These first-family founders were, at the same time, the wealthiest members of the early Jewish community. In 1865, for example, the four richest Jews in Philadelphia were R. H. Gratz, Isadore Binswanger, Morris Rosenbach, and Abraham S. Wolf. The incomes of Philadelphians were published in a pamphlet entitled "Rich Men of Philadelphia": R. H. Gratz's income was reported as $102,042, Isadore Binswanger's as $65,143, Morris Rosenbach's as $25,452, and Abraham S. Wolf's as $12,507.[38] All were sizeable incomes for that day. The Gratz family were not only wealthier than the other three, but, as descendants of the pre-1830's generation, they were less a part of the formal Jewish upper class as it took shape at the time of the Civil War. According to a Philadelphia City Directory of 1859, the Binswanger, Wolf, and Rosenbach families all lived in the Franklin Square area, but three Gratz family heads (an attorney, a merchant, and a gentleman) were living west of Broad Street and north of Market Strteet (at that time, the elite new-rich, but not upper-class, Gentile neighborhood) and a fourth Gratz listed his address as 1309 Locust Street in the fashionable Gentile neighborhood.[39]

In other words, the members of the Gratz family were no longer to be considered part of the Jewish community. Many of them had married Christians by this time and had even been baptized themselves. At the upper-class level, the forces of assimilation were such that, by the end of the Civil War, most of the descendants of the eighteenth-century Jewish upper class—the original founders of Mikveh Israel, for example—had become Christians and were completely accepted in fashionable Gentile society. Prominent early-nineteenth-century families—the Binswangers, Wolfs, and Rosenbachs—not families who had founded Mikveh Israel such as the Gratzes, were leaders in the first coherent Jewish upper class in the city.

Russian Immigration (1882-1920). In the year 1881, after Alexander II was assassinated and his son Alexander III became Czar, the pogrom became part of the policy of the Russian regime. The formula was simple: "a third of the Jews in Russia would be forced to emigrate, a third would accept baptism and the remaining third would be starved to death."[40] On Christmas night in that same year the streets of Warsaw were bathed in Jewish blood, in Europe's most terrible massacre since St. Bartholomew's Day in 1572 when the Huguenots were shot down without warning in the streets of Paris. Between 1881 and 1914 some two millions were added to the American Jewish community from the lands that lay under the scepter of the Czars.

Russia's regression to barbarism shocked the western world. A mass meeting of protest took place in Paris under the chairmanship of Victor Hugo and a similar meeting was held in London with the Lord Mayor presiding. In New York the Mayor led a meeting of protest in February, 1882, and on March 4th, Philadelphia's civic, religious, and governmental leaders, both Gentile and Jew, gathered in the staid Academy of Music to discuss the Russian atrocities.[41]

The central problem confronting the Philadelphia Jewish community during the next four decades was the assimilation of the mass of immigrants from Russia, Poland, Hungary, and Rumania. Many were penniless when they arrived in Philadelphia, and, of course, most of them were ignorant of American language and customs. Fortunately, there was an established and prosperous Jewish community in the city with habits of charity based on an ancient tradition of *noblesse oblige*. After 1882 most of the charitable resources of the German-Jewish upper class went toward the aid of the less fortunate Russian immigrants. The United Hebrew Charities in Philadelphia, for example, obtained subscriptions from 682 individuals for $14,773.32 in the year 1870; in 1894, 7,968 individuals gave $52,916.04.[42]

A great deal of financial aid also came from the more fortunate members of the Russian-Jewish community in the city. For example, the Association of Jewish Immigrants, all the officers of which were Russian Jews, was formed in 1884 at 931 South 4th Street.[43] During the year 1885, the Association afforded shelter to 848 newly-arrived immigrants, processed 900 applications for employment, and provided many other services, including protection from sharpers bent on taking advantage of ignorant immigrants.

From the point of view of Philadelphia's Victorian gentry on Rittenhouse Square "nobody" lived north of Market Street. Within the Jewish upper class, on the other hand, "everybody" lived north of Market Street, especially after the phenomenal growth of the Russian-Jewish "ghetto" in South Philadelphia. Between 1882 and 1914, thousands of Jewish immigrants settled within a small area along 4th and 5th Streets, south of Pine Street, which became known as Philadelphia's "East Side." The east European Jews who poured into South Philadelphia during this period were a pious people with their own religious ritual, language, and traditions. They soon built their own synagogues. Of the eight synagogues in Philadelphia in 1882, for example, only one (417 Pine) was south of Market.[44] By 1900 the number of synagogues in the city had doubled, and five of the eight new synagogues were located within an area of two city blocks in the Russian-Jewish ghetto. (In addition to the existing synagogue at 417 Pine, five new ones were located at 4th and Lombard, 420 Lombard, 5th and Lombard, 518 South Street, and on 5th Street, between South and Lombard Streets.)[45]

At the same time that the "East Side" was developing in South Philadelphia, significant changes were taking place within the upper-class community, including several indications of increasing affluence. In the nineties, for example, the Jewish upper class began to move uptown to the elite area of the city, north of Market Street. At about the same time, as members of the Gentile North Broad Street elite were beginning to move to the Old York Road, the Main Line, and Chestnut Hill, a new Jewish upper-class neighborhood was developing from North 17th to Broad Street, between Spring Garden and Columbia Avenue (see Map 3). Members of the Wolf, Fleisher, and Binswanger families moved into this area in the nineties. In 1890, for example, Barnett Binswanger lived at 1414 North 16th Street, a few houses north of Meyer Guggenheim (1400 North 16th), founder of the Guggenheim dynasty and benefactor of the first Jewish hospital in Philadelphia.[46] Spring Garden Street, where the Gratz family lived in 1860 (see above) was one of the elite Gentile streets during and immediately after the Civil War. Charles T. Yerkes, the traction magnate who made the classic remark, "It's the straphanger who pays the dividends," lived on Spring Garden during this period (Theodore Dreiser, who fictionalized Yerkes' career in the *Financier* had Copperwood living on Girard Avenue; both streets were elite addresses so that Dreiser's fiction rang true to the initiated).[47] In 1890, prominent Jews such as Penrose Fleisher and August and Edward Loeb had mansions on elite Spring Garden Street.[48]

By 1895, both the Rodeph Sholom and Keneseth Israel congregations had built large and impressive new synagogues on North Broad Street (see Table 24). The new Rodeph Sholom synagogue was situated at a point where Green Street, one of the most fashionable Jewish addresses at the turn of the century, ran into Broad Street. At the same time, the first summer resort synagogues along the New Jersey coast were built at Long Branch (1890), Atlantic City (1893), and Asbury Park (1896).[49]

The development of the Jewish summer resort was not solely due to the increasing affluence of the Jewish upper class. It was partly a reflection of the increasing anti-Semitism which charac-

Table 24—Upper-Class Synagogues in Philadelphia—location in 1860, 1895, and 1940

	First Synagogue	1860	1895	1940
Sephardic				
Mikveh Israel	(1782)	7th & Arch	7th & Arch	Broad & York
Ashkenazic				
Rodeph Sholom	(1810)	5th & Vine	Broad & Green	Broad & Green
Keneseth Israel	(1847)	5th & Brown	Broad & Columbia	Broad & Columbia

a. Rodeph Sholom, originally Orthodox, changed to the Reform service in 1870, when the new synagogue was built on North Broad Street.

b. Keneseth Israel was founded as a reform congregation. This congregation led the "Radical Reform" movement in Philadelphia.

c. Since the 1920's, the members of Rodeph Sholom and Keneseth Israel have largely moved to the Old York Road suburbs. During the 1920's and 1930's the suburban members of the synagogues commuted to town for divine worship. Since World War II, these two congregations have run a co-operative Sunday School for the children of their suburban members, in Elkins Park. Keneseth Israel is planning to build in the Old York Road area as this is being written. In addition, land has been purchased and plans made for another synagogue, by Frank Lloyd Wright, in the Old York Road area.

terized even the educated classes in America after the turn of the century. In the 1880's and early 1890's, for instance, many prominent Jewish Philadelphians spent their summers in such popular Proper Philadelphia resorts as Cape May.[50] The exclusion of members of the Jewish community from hotels, resorts, clubs, and neighborhoods, however, was more rigidly and overtly enforced after this period. (It was in the 1890's that the sign, "No Jews and Dogs Admitted Here," was supposed to have been displayed at fashionable Saratoga.)[51]

According to most observers, anti-Semitism was much more prevalent among the fashionable classes in America than was the case in France or England where many ancient Gentile lines had absorbed members of the Jewish community. This has been explained in part by the timidity and conventionality so characteristic of the American open-class system. More important, however, was the fact that the masses of Jewish immigrants who came to these shores between 1882 and 1914 were primarily members of the uneducated classes and possessed of quite alien cultural and religious traditions.[52] The tremendous growth of the lower-class Jewish community, moreover, coincided with the mass immigration of southern Europeans who also differed in language, religion, and temperament from the dominant Angló-Saxon majority in America. Thus anti-Semitism was but one aspect of a growing antagonism towards all non-Anglo-Saxon Americans. According to H. L. Mencken, for instance, the prevalent use of such terms as "kike," "bohunk," and "wop," originated in the last part of the nineteenth century.[53] In the twentieth century, old-stock Americans replaced the anti-Irish-Catholicism of their ancestors with a new and sometimes more open anti-Semitism.

Unfortunately, as with all forms of group prejudice, the dominant majority failed to differentiate between the various social, economic, or cultural levels which exist within all minority groups. Thus the cultivated Jewish aristocrat was often discriminated against because of a prejudicial stereotype derived from the behavior of lower-class immigrants. Quite naturally, this produced an all-too-human resentment and anti-Semitism within the Jewish community itself. The derogatory term, "kike," for example, was first used in America by German Jews when referring to the less polished and often aggressive members of the east European Jewish community.[54] One need not go back too far in history to find similar ethnic origins in German and eastern European Jews. Many of the ancestors of the "German" Jews in Philadelphia—Hyman Polock, for example, or Hyman Gratz—were originally Polish. It was, then, primarily a different historical, and consequently cultural, experience which differentiated the Jews from Germany, Russia, or Poland. The Germans had the first and longest contacts with both western European and American culture. In other words, the members of the German-Jewish community, who came to America largely before 1870, were Americanized earlier than the Jews from eastern Europe. These historical and cultural differences were also reinforced by religious differences. In Philadelphia and elsewhere, for example, most of the upper-class German Jews belonged to Reform synagogues, while Russian and Polish Jews were members of the Orthodox faith. Within the Jewish community in the twentieth century, membership in a fashionable Reform congregation became a symbol of social and economic achievement and acculturation. It was much the same as the Quaker-turned-Episcopal or the Ashkenazim-turned-Sephardim process of an earlier Philadelphia. Today, several of the newest Reform synagogues in the city are made up primarily of east European Jews, which is, of course, an index of their continuing acculturation.

By 1900, most of Philadelphia's upper-class Jewish families had moved uptown to the new neighborhood, west of Broad Street. In 1895 the Mercantile Club built an impressive new clubhouse on North Broad Street (1422 North Broad), about halfway between Rodeph Sholom and Keneseth Israel.[55] Several of the wealthier families, such as the Gimbels, had purchased mansions along Broad Street itself after the members of the Gentile elite had migrated out to the suburbs. At the same time, a few Jewish families began to move out to the suburbs along the Old York Road. The first symptom of this Old York Road trend was the founding of the Philmont Country Club in 1906.[56] Founded by Gimbels, Snellenburgs, Loebs, and Wolfs this was the original and is still the most exclusive upper-class Jewish country club in the city. By 1914, as the figures in Table 23 suggest, the movement to the suburbs was well under way.

East European Jews Attain Elite Status (1920-1940). American ideals and aspirations are closely bound to the success saga. Most Americans strongly identify with the stories of Horatio Alger and with the lives of such men as Abraham Lincoln and Andrew Carnegie or the fabulous cinema Cinderellas of Hollywood. The rise of the east European Jewish community, within approximately half a century, from the American ghetto to middle-class comfort and even affluence is probably the most fabulous ethnic group success story of all. At the turn of the century, most of the east European Jews were concentrated in the garment or handicraft industries, if they were not earning a precarious living as small shopkeepers, drummers, or peddlers. By the 1920's many had risen into the middle-class white-collar world, and some had even attained elite status.[57]

Albert Monroe Greenfield, Philadelphia's most recent example of the Horatio Alger tradition, was listed in the 1940 *Who's Who*. In that year he was the most powerful member of the Jewish community and one of the wealthiest and most influential men in the whole city. Born in the Ukraine in 1887, he was brought to America at the age of six. His father eventually became the proprietor of a small furniture store in North Philadelphia where he probably never made more than $4,000 a year.[58] Young Albert graduated from Central High School, attended the University of Pennsylvania for two years, and entered the real estate business in 1903. In 1914 Mr. Greenfield married a Miss Kraus, who had studied at Bryn Mawr College and whose father was a successful building and loan magnate (Mr. Kraus was one of the original officers of the Association of Jewish Immigrants at its founding in 1884). By 1920, at the time of his father-in-law's death, Albert M. Greenfield had accumulated twenty-seven building and loan associations with total assets of approximately $35,000,000. He was also the owner (at the age of thirty-five) of the largest real estate business in the city, and one of the largest in the nation (Albert M. Greenfield and Company was doing about $127,000,000 worth of business a year at that time).[59]

The phenomenal achievements of the members of the Jewish community had some unfortunate consequences. The 1920's was one of the most anti-Semitic decades in American history. Throughout, there was a rising tide of resentment against the alien, the foreigner, the Jew, the Negro, and the "Yellow Peril." Madison Grant's *The Passing of the Great Race* (1916) and Lothrop Stoddard's *The Rising Tide of Color* (1920) were passionate defenses of Anglo-Saxon superiority after the style of Houston Stewart Chamberlain. Both books were fabulously successful; the latter went through fourteen editions and became somewhat of an "international sensation."[60] At a graduation address at Harvard in 1922, President Lowell advocated quotas against Jews, Henry Ford's Dearborn *Independent* carried on a relentless anti-Semitic campaign between 1920 and 1927, and, finally, the Immigration Act of 1924 considerably reduced further immigration into the United States, especially from southern and eastern Europe and from the Orient.[61]

Perhaps partly as a reaction to outside pressures and partly due to developments within the Jewish community itself, the 1920's marked the beginning of a gradual breakdown of the caste-like barriers between the German and Russian Jewish communities in Philadelphia, at least at the elite level. The first signs of change came in 1919. Three days after the end of World War I, for example, the Board of Directors of the Federation of Jewish Charities, following the leadership of their president, Louis Wolf, voted for "a 100 per cent federation." In other words, for the first time in Philadelphia, leading German and Russian charitable institutions were combined within one large organization.[62] Founded by upper-class German Jews such as Jacob Gimbel in 1901, the Federation, with eighteen supporting agencies, had been raising about $200,000 per year in the decade before 1918. On the other hand, the first "100 per cent campaign" in 1919, under the chairmanship of Colonel Samuel D. Lit, set a goal of $750,000 and raised $800,000 (in 1920 there were fifty-three German- and Russian-run charities included in the Federation).[63]

Philanthropy, as we have said, has always played an important role in the determination of social status within the Jewish community. As successful Russian Jews, symbolized by Mr. Greenfield, rose to influential positions within the city's business community, it was quite natural that they should assume their share of the charitable burden. It was also quite in accord with the mores and values of the Jewish community (much more so than in the Gentile community) to accept these new benefactors, or "big givers" as they were often called, within the higher associational levels of the social structure. In 1923, Albert M. Greenfield, who was now on the board of directors of the Federation, led the annual fund-raising drive.[64] Moreover, in 1925, while the most prominent upper-class members of the Jewish elite in 1940, A. S. W. Rosenbach, Ellis Gimbel, Morris Wolf, Howard Loeb, Dr. Solis-Cohen, Judge Stern, Lessing J. Rosenwald, Samuel Fels, S. S. Fleisher, and Cyrus Adler contributed a combined total of $52,775 to the annual drive in that year, Mr. and Mrs. Greenfield alone gave $31,000.[65] At about this same time, the ethnic line was broken at the upper-class Mercantile Club when Albert M. Greenfield became one of the first two members of the club who were not of German origins.[66] By 1940, Mr. Greenfield and other east European members of the Philadelphia elite listed membership in both the Philmont Country Club, along the Old York Road, and the most exclusive Jewish urban men's club, the Locust, often known as the Jewish Union League.

The Locust Club was founded in 1920 by leading members of the Jewish business community.[67] In addition to Clarence Wolf, then president of the Mercantile Club, the charter members of the Locust included Gimbels, Fleishers, Lits, and Snellenburgs. This new urban men's club was somewhat different from the older Mercantile Club which was located in the heart of the Jewish community and was the center of family social life. With the suburbanization of the Jewish upper class, however, there was a need for a downtown club for businessmen. Of course, the leading members of the Jewish business community, unlike the Gratz family of an earlier day, were not accepted within the halls of the Union League or the Philadelphia Club. And while the Mercantile Club was voluntarily Jewish in membership, culture, and character, the Locust Club, from the start, was open to both Jews and Gentiles. As a gesture towards anti-exclusiveness, Francis Shunk Brown, one of the leading members of the Philadelphia bar and the grandson of two former governers of the state of Pennsylvania, was chosen to be the club's first president, while a promising young Irish-Catholic politician, a law partner of Morris Wolf, was one of the original directors. Although only one non-Jewish member of the 1940 elite in Philadelphia reported membership in the Locust Club, the ideals of the club still exist.

By 1929 most of the members of the Jewish upper class had moved to the Old York Road suburbs, centering in Elkins Park. At the same time, but especially during the 1930's, many of the old Jewish families had moved into apartments in the Rittenhouse Square neighborhood (see Table 23), and the more successful members of the east European community moved out of South Philadelphia, especially into West Philadelphia and Germantown. In 1940 the elite Russian-Jewish neighborhood in the city was Wynnefield-Overbrook, a West Philadelphia residential area just inside the city line from the Main Line. Albert M. Greenfield moved into this area and in 1940 occupied a large mansion previously owned by Clarence Geist, one of Philadelphia's more colorful utility tycoons.

The residential distribution of the small Jewish elite in 1940 indicated that the caste-like divisions between the Russian and German communities were slowly dissolving by this time (Table 25). It must be borne in mind however that these were older men with grown families, and, therefore, less likely to reflect actual neighborhood patterns. After all, it is largely for the children's sake that people move to the "right" neighborhoods.

Table 25—Philadelphia Jews in Who's Who in 1940—
Residential Distribution as Related to Social Class

Residence	Upper Class	Rest of the Elite
Rittenhouse Square	6	1
Old York Road	3	2
North Philadelphia	2*	2
Germantown	2	2
West Philadelphia	1†	3‡
South Philadelphia	0	2
Swarthmore	0	1

* S. S. Fleisher lived in the same house, on once-fashionable Green Street, as his family did in 1890.

† Samuel Fels lived at 39th and Walnut in a beautiful house which has since become the home of the Institute of Local and State Government, of the University of Pennsylvania. The Institute was endowed and founded by Mr. Fels. This address was, of course, the center of the "Drexel Colony" in the 1880's and 1890's when the great A. M. Drexel lived there.

‡ These three men lived in the Wynnefield-Overbrook section, mentioned above as the elite east European neighborhood in West Philadelphia.

CHAPTER XII

Education and Status Ascription

Today the certificate of education becomes what
the test for ancestors has been in the past.

MAX WEBER

ALONG with the decreasing importance of the hereditary principle in Western civilization, especially since the Enlightenment and
the rise to power of the urban middle classes, men have been placed
increasingly in the social hierarchy by their educational attain-
ments. The American people, following the lead of such men of the
Enlightenment as Thomas Jefferson and Benjamin Franklin, have
traditionally placed more faith in universal education than in
any particular political system. After all, democratic political institutions ultimately depend upon an educated and informed
citizenry. More important perhaps, is the fact that education in
America, from the very beginning, has been an important factor
in assimilating the immigrant from foreign lands as well as a means
of social mobility and the improvement of one's social status. In
other words, in a highly utilitarian civilization such as ours, education has always been bound to pragmatic ends.

Benjamin Franklin, for example, advanced highly practical reasons for the founding of the *Academy* (later the University of
Pennsylvania) in Philadelphia. His original prospectus, printed in
the *Pennsylvania Gazette*, 24 August 1749, opened as follows:

In the settling of new countries, the first care of the planters must
be to provide and to secure the necessaries of life; this engrosses their
attention, and affords them little time to think of anything further. We
may therefore excuse our ancestors, that they established no ACADEMY
or college in this province, wherein their youth might receive a polite
and learned education. *Agriculture* and *mechanic arts,* were of the most
immediate importance; the *culture* of *minds* by the *finer arts* and *sciences,* was necessarily postpon'd to times of more wealth and leisure.

Since those times are come, and numbers of our inhabitants are both
able and willing to give their sons a good education, if it might be had

at home, free from the extraordinary expense and hazard in sending them abroad for that purpose; and since a proportion of men of learning is useful in every country, and those who of late years come to settle among us, are chiefly foreigners, unacquainted with our language, laws and customs; it is thought a proposal for establishing an ACADEMY in this province, will not now be deemed unseasonable.[1]

At the same time that Franklin was making his proposal for founding an Academy, Edward Shippen, young Philadelphia aristocrat, illustrated this pragmatic American point of view towards education in the following letter written while traveling in Europe to his younger brother who was struggling through a private Latin school in Philadelphia: "If you ever travel," he writes in 1749, "you'll find men of letters are everywhere respected; you'll see the ascendency the knowing man has over the blockhead; you'll have a friend which will stand by you when all others fail. Be a man of learning and you'll be a man of consequence wherever you go."[2] For generations Americans have followed this wise advice.

On the whole, in America social class position and educational attainment are positively correlated. On the other hand, the level of educational attainment does not differentiate the members of the American upper class from the rest of the elite. Of those Philadelphians listed in *Who's Who* in 1940, for example, approximately three-fourths were college graduates regardless of their social class origins. It was the type of educational institution attended, however, which differentiated the members of the upper class from the other members of the elite. It is the purpose of this chapter to show how the private secondary school—both the local day school and the boarding school—and certain fashionable eastern universities serve the sociological function of differentiating the upper classes in America from the rest of the population. In other words, in addition to their manifest and most important function, that of providing an education, these private educational institutions serve the latent function of acculturating the members of the younger generation, especially those not quite to the manor born, into an upper-class style of life. As the educative role of the family declines, as it must in a democratic as against an aristocratic age, the private school and college increasingly become a kind of surrogate family.

In social if not in educational terms the graduate of Groton and Harvard is subculturally as different from the graduate of the local high school and city college as the latter is from the laborer who left school in the eighth grade. Moreover, the Harvard of the clubs and the private school graduates is, in turn, very far removed from the Harvard world of the earnest scholars who have graduated from public high schools all over America. Charles McArthur of the Office of Tests at Harvard University, for example, has found some interesting differences between private and publicly educated Harvard students. Using Dr. Florence Kluckhohn's theoretical structure (see above, Chapter IV), he found that the public school boy's dominant values emphasized "the *Future* as the important time, the *Indvidual* as the important person, and *Doing* as the important aspect of personality."[3] In contrast, he found that among the private school boys from "the Eastern upper class . . . the time most valued was the *Past,* the persons who matter bore a *Lineal relation* to oneself, and *Being* was the most valued aspect of the person."[4] For example, the doing-oriented boys from the public schools make A's in Chemistry while the being boys are satisfied with a "gentleman's C"; the doing and future-oriented boys come to Harvard with a definite, usually pre-technical major in mind; the being and past-oriented boys usually drift into the Humanities. The public school boys worry about marks; but the deans find the private school boys more likely to be concerned about their personalities, whether they are going to make the right friends and the proper clubs. Interestingly enough, Dr. McArthur also found significant differences between these two types of Harvard boys when comparing the results of Thematic Apperception Tests in terms of Dr. Kluckhohn's theory. There were other extremely suggestive findings in this work at the Office of Tests at Harvard. The point to be made here, however, is that there are real differences between the privately and publicly educated subcultures in America.

Private school attendance clearly differentiated the members of the upper class from the rest of the Philadelphia elite in 1940.[5] Of the Philadelphians listed in *Who's Who,* 41 per cent of those also listed in the *Social Register,* as against only 15 per cent of those who were not, reported attendance at some private school (see Table 26). If the private school is such an important part of the upper-class way of life, one is inclined to ask why more upper-class members did not report a private school education. There are several reasons for this. First, there is the inevitable factor of inadequate reporting; many individuals list only their college or university in their *Who's Who* biographies. More important, however, is the fact that private school attendance is the best index of ascribed upper-class position, even more indicative than neighborhood, religion, or *Social Register* affiliation. One attends private school only if one's family can afford it. In other words, many of the members of the upper class in 1940 who did not go to private school presumably had achieved upper-class membership. The president of one of the city's leading banks, for example, was listed in the *Social Register* in 1940, lived in Chestnut Hill, went to the Episcopal Church, and belonged to the Rittenhouse Club (never a member of the Philadelphia Club, he was not taken into the Rittenhouse Club until after he became a bank president); he attended the city's public schools and did not go to college, however, and he was not listed in the *Social Register* until after his marriage into one of the wealthier Philadelphia families.

Finally, of course, it is important to realize that the importance of a private school education varies directly with the decline of the strength of the family. Thus the older generation (over sixty-five in 1940) were less likely to report a private school education than the younger members of the upper class (see above Table 27). This difference was partly due to the fact that many of the older men were educated at home. George Wharton Pepper, for example, was educated by his mother until he went to the University; George W. Childs Drexel was educated by private tutors.

It is interesting that while the private school was of increasing

Table 26—*Philadelphians in Who's Who in 1940—Secondary Education as Related to Social Class*

	SOCIAL	CLASS					Per Cent of Each Educ. Type in the Social Register
Type of Schooling	Social Register		Non Social Register		Who's Who Total		
	No.	%	No.	%	No.	%	
Episcopalian Church boarding schools†	14	(6)	1	(*)	15	(2)	94%
Other private schools	78	(35)	79	(15)	157	(20)	50%
No private schooling reported‡	134	(59)	464	(85)	598	(78)	22%
Total	226	(100)	544	(100)	770	(100)	29%

* Less than 1 per cent.
† Three schools are included here—Groton School, St. Paul's School, and St. Mark's School.
‡ In this book, parochial schools are not considered as private.

importance within the upper class (*Social Register*—over 65, 32 per cent; under 65, 46 per cent), among the rest of the elite the younger generation were less likely to have attended private school than the older men (over 65, 16 per cent; under 65, 13 per cent). This is, of course, a reflection of the growth of the public secondary school in America during the last part of the nineteenth century. Of the older college graduates in this elite, for example, the private school may well have been the only available means of obtaining a secondary education at the time when they were of school age. In other words, as the public school has become available to all Americans, the private school then becomes the differentiating factor in a social class sense. At one time, however, education itself was the sole differentiating factor.

The Private Day School in Philadelphia: Provincial Family-Surrogate. Like Boston and other eastern seaboard cities, Philadelphia has an excellent system of private day schools. There are the well-known Quaker schools—Germantown Friends, Friends Select, in the center of the city, Friends Central on the Main Line (all of which are co-educational), and the William Penn Charter School in Germantown which is for boys only. While many members of the upper class attend these Quaker schools, they are more likely to go to such boys' schools as the Protestant Episcopal Academy and the Haverford School, on the Main Line, or the Chestnut Hill Academy.

The William Penn Charter School is considered to be the oldest private boys school in Philadelphia, having been granted a charter by William Penn in 1689.[6] It had been the custom among English Quakers to establish day schools "to which Friends were advised

Table 27—*Philadelphia Males in* Who's Who *in 1940—Secondary School Education as Related to Age and Social Class*

| | SOCIAL CLASS | | | | | |
| | SOCIAL REGISTER | | NON SOCIAL REGISTER | | WHO'S WHO TOTAL | |
Secondary Schooling	65 & Over	Under 65	65 & Over	Under 65	65 & Over	Under 65
Private schooling	32%	46%*	16%	13%	22%	22%
No private schooling	68%	54%	84%	87%	78%	78%
Total	100%	100%	100%	100%	100%	100%
(Number of cases)	(94)	(112)	(185)	(304)	(279)	(416)

* 14 out of 15 of those who reported attendance at the three Episcopalian Church boarding schools were of the younger age group.

by the Yearly Meeting to send their children." Actually, Penn
Charter was originally a part of the public school system in Philadelphia for most of its history. It was not until 1875 that the
William Penn Charter School was opened as a private Quaker
school for boys at Eight South Twelfth Street in the center of the
city.

Germantown Academy is the oldest suburban day school in
Philadelphia and possibly in America.[7] Founded in 1760, it has
been nonsectarian from the beginning. The main school building
today is the oldest building in the United States which has been
continuously devoted to secondary education. (In the 1830's,
A. Bronson Alcott was a teacher at the school and his famous daughter, Louisa May Alcott, was born in Germantown in 1832. Although
Alcott later became famous as the friend of Emerson and the
leader of the Concord School of Philosophy, his teaching at Germantown was a failure. Somewhat of an idealist, in many ways a
forerunner of the progressive school—he was interested in meaning
rather than memory—he could not keep discipline.) As Germantown was a suburb by the end of the eighteenth century, there
were several boarding schools for girls there as early as the 1830's.

Along with the suburban trend in the last part of the nineteenth
century, Haverford School, on the Main Line, was opened as a
part of Haverford College in 1884.[8] It is now an independent
and nonsectarian school. Although its charter goes back to 1861,
Chestnut Hill Academy began its life in the fall of 1895 with
thirty-five boys enrolled.[9] In 1898, through the generosity of
the Houston family, it moved into the old Wissahickon Inn, where
it remains to this day (the building belonged to the Houston
Estate until 1941).

*The Protestant Episcopal Academy: Proper Philadelphia Family-
Surrogate.* The Protestant Episcopal Academy has been intimately
associated with Philadelphia's Anglo-Catholic gentry since the
eighteenth century. According to Porter Sargent, who has published *A Handbook of Private Schools* for more than thirty years,
"over sixty-five hundred boys of old Philadelphia families have
attended the academy since 1850, and it is today the largest of the
Episcopal schools."[10]

On the first of January, 1785, a group of subscribers met at
Christ Church to found the Protestant Episcopal Academy: they
elected sixteen trustees, including Thomas Willing, Edward Ship-

pen, Robert Morris, Francis Hopkinson, and, of course, the Reverend William White. School opened in April "on ye back part of a lot on ye east side of Fourth Street, a few feet south of Market Street."[11] Benjamin Franklin lived next door. In 1788, the school moved to a newly constructed building between Sixth and Seventh on Chestnut Street. Noah Webster, of dictionary fame, taught mathematics and English, and Commodore Stephen Decatur and Bishop John Henry Hobart were among the first pupils.

Although the records are rather obscure, it is believed that the academy was run as a charity school between 1805 and 1846.[12] Some support came from the government as it became necessary to get boys and girls off the street. The parents of the pupils at this time were required to take the pauper's oath.

The modern era at Episcopal Academy began in 1846.[13] Under the leadership of Bishop Alonzo Potter, a boys' day school was opened and the Reverend George Emlen Hare (father of Bishop William Hobart Hare—see above) was headmaster. In 1850, the Academy moved into a newly constructed school building on Locust Street several blocks below St. Mark's Church and convenient to the Rittenhouse Square neighborhood.

During Rittenhouse Square's "Golden Day," the sons of Proper Philadelphians were educated at the Episcopal Academy and the Delancey School. Founded by Henry Hobart Brown in 1877, Delancey School was at the corner of Seventeenth and Delancey Streets during the 1880's, a convenient location for the Rittenhouse Square gentry.[14] The tone of the school is suggested by the names of the trustees in 1898 when the school was incorporated after the death of its founder. Among the eleven trustees were Thomas DeWitt Cuyler, president of the Rittenhouse Club, John H. Converse, later president of the Baldwin Locomotive Works, Effingham B. Morris, president of the Girard Trust Company between 1887 and 1928, J. Rodman Paul, Senator Pepper's former law partner, and Alexander Van Rensselaer, A. J. Drexel's son-in-law.[15]

In 1915 the Delancey School merged with the Episcopal Academy. The first class to graduate after the merger included the sons of many Philadelphia families mentioned in previous chapters. According to the class yearbook for that year, Horace Howard Furness Jayne was the class poet, John Frederick Lewis, "one of the strangest," Bertram Lippincott, "most original fellow in the class," Henry Rawle Pemberton, "most musical," Benjamin Rush,

Jr., "leader in the class in regard to clothes," and Elias Wolf, who "was always riding around in his automobile."[16]

The sixteen members of the board of trustees of the Academy in 1915 were representative Proper Philadelphians of the period.[17] All of them were listed in the *Social Register:* ten were graduates of the University of Pennsylvania; three did not graduate from college; one, the youngest, was a graduate of Princeton, one of Trinity College, and Bishop Rhinelander was a Harvard man; all save two were members of either the Philadelphia (six members) or Rittenhouse (seven members) Clubs; eleven lived in the Rittenhouse Square neighborhood, two on the Main Line, three in Chestnut Hill, and one in Germantown. It is safe to assume that all were members of the Episcopal Church.

In response to the upper-class suburban trend, the Episcopal Academy moved out to the Main Line in 1921.[18] In that same year, Greville Haslam, a graduate and former master at St. Paul's School, became the first nonclerical headmaster. Upper-class suburbanization during this postwar period was a national phenomenon which can be accurately measured by the location of the fashionable private schools in the larger cities throughout America. Noble and Greenough, Proper Boston's most exclusive day school, for example, moved from Beacon Street to Dedham in 1922.[19]

In 1940 the twenty trustees of the Academy were primarily Proper Philadelphians. The fact that three of the trustees were not listed in the *Social Register,* however, reflected the changes in the city's elite structure since the days before the first World War when all the trustees were quite naturally listed in the little black and orange book. As in 1915, of the seventeen Proper Philadelphia trustees, twelve were members of the Rittenhouse and Philadelphia Clubs. On the other hand, while a majority of the trustees in 1915 were alumni of the University of Pennsylvania, seven sons of Pennsylvania now shared the leadership of the school with three Princetonians, four Harvard men, a Yale man, and the headmaster and the Reverend John Mockridge, who were graduates of the Massachusetts Institute of Technology and Trinity College in Canada respectively. Finally, of course, the trustees now lived primarily in the suburbs—nine on the Main Line, two in Chestnut Hill, two in Germantown, and only four in the Rittenhouse Square area.[20]

The move to the suburbs proved successful and the Academy grew in size all during the two postwar decades. By 1940 there were almost six hundred boys in the school who commuted each day from all parts of the city and its suburbs, from the Old York Road area, from Chestnut Hill and Germantown, and from Wallingford and Wawa.[21] In contrast to the provincial Rittenhouse Square atmosphere of the pre-war years, the school enlarged its scope both geographically and socially. Like all the more fashionable country day schools, the Academy increasingly drew boys from more diverse social backgrounds, especially at the high school level. As many of the sons of Proper Philadelphians, for example, began to go away to New England boarding schools for their last four or five years of secondary education, vacancies were created in the higher forms at Episcopal and other fashionable day schools. To fill this gap many boys came in from the public school system and spent their last few years at the Episcopal Academy. There is always a tendency to stress the exclusive aspects of all fashionable institutions. Actually, such institutions are always assimilating new material, as it were; in each generation capable boys with ambition and an eye to the main chance have gotten a start towards success through schoolboy "contacts" made at such schools as Episcopal. This is especially true of the sons of the new-rich. The private day schools, especially during the Depression, needed pupils who could pay full tuition. Newly rich fathers and mothers were, in turn, eager for their sons to meet "nice people." Moreover, the private school, with its personal supervision and consequently higher academic standards, often made it possible for these boys from the local high schools to get into the better colleges.

Proper Philadelphia Daughters: Pre-debutante Education. While most Proper Philadelphia gentlemen are products of Episcopal, Haverford, Penn Charter, or Chestnut Hill Academy, their wives are invariably alumnae of Springside School in Chestnut Hill, or the Shipley and Agnes Irwin schools along the Main Line. Springside and Shipley, founded in 1879 and 1894 respectively, were suburban schools from the very beginning.[22] It is interesting that they were founded in the last part of the nineteenth century when Proper Philadelphians were moving out to these two suburbs in increasing numbers.

The Agnes Irwin School, the traditional Proper Philadelphia school for girls, was founded in the Rittenhouse Square neighborhood in 1869.[23] Agnes Irwin, friend of S. Weir Mitchell, Horace Howard Furness, and Agnes Repplier, and a witty member of the "walking and talking" set in the early days of Mount Desert, was a nationally known educator of young ladies. As Porter Sargent puts it: "The more conservative of Philadelphia's elite still send their daughters to Miss Irwin's School as in the days before 1894 when her work here won her so great a reputation that she was called to be the first dean of Radcliffe College."[24] Young ladies from both Chestnut Hill and the Main Line, as well as those from Rittenhouse Square, attended Miss Irwin's school until 1933 when the school moved from DeLancey Place out to Isaac H. Clothier's former estate in Wynnewood on the Main Line.

Although Philadelphia's most fashionable girls' school was founded and dominated for many years by Agnes Irwin, a strong-willed feminist and pioneer in women's education, most of the Irwin girls, even as of the nineteen-thirties, terminated their education at the secondary level and entered into the debutante world on graduation. All this has been changed since World War II. Daughters of even the most traditional and fashionable families now go on to college.

The Boarding School: Cosmopolitan Family-Surrogate. Before the turn of the nineteenth century, a majority of Philadelphia's Rittenhouse Square gentry were either educated at home or at local private academies. In the last years of the nineteenth century, and especially in the twentieth, however, the sons of Proper Bostonians, New Yorkers, Chicagoans, and Philadelphians began to go away to school in New England in ever-increasing numbers. In a previous chapter, for example, it was shown how only sixty-nine men who were listed in *Who's Who* in 1940 were also listed in the Philadelphia *Social Register* in 1900. Within this small group of old Philadelphians, of those who reported a private school education, 40 per cent of the older generation (over twenty-five in 1900) were graduates of the Episcopal Academy, while 34 per cent of the younger men (under twenty-five in 1900) had gone to either St. Paul's, Groton, or St. Mark's Schools.

While a few old-family members of the Philadelphia elite, such as the Ingersolls, began the movement to the fashionable New England boarding schools between the Civil War and the First World War, it was their sons and grandsons who filled these New England schools during the 1920's and 1930's. Two old Philadelphians listed in *Who's Who* in 1940—Benjamin Rush, chairman of the board of the Insurance Company of North America, and

Joseph Wharton Lippincott, president of J. B. Lippincott Company
—were both graduates of the Episcopal Academy. Between 1920
and 1940, however, four members of the Rush family as well as
Joseph Wharton Lippincott, Jr., were students at St. Paul's School
(one member of the Rush family was a master in the school in
1940).[25] During the same period, Senator Pepper, educated at
home by his mother, had three grandsons at the Kent School.

The growth in popularity of the New England boarding school
coincided with, and reinforced, the development of a national
upper class in America. Both the growth of these inter-city, educational institutions and the national upper class which supported
them, however, were a product of tremendous technological and
economic changes in American society during the half century
preceding 1940. In other words, the demand for these schools was
the result of the same social forces which produced the national
corporation, the nationally advertised brand, the national market,
and an increasingly centralized government. The following well-
known schools, for example, were founded within a decade, before
or after, of the formation of the United States Steel Company in
1901:[26] The Taft School in Watertown, Connecticut, was founded
by Horace Dutton Taft, a brother of President Taft, in 1890; the
Hotchkiss School, Lakeville, Connecticut, was founded and endowed by Maria Hotchkiss, widow of the inventor of the famous
machine-gun, in 1892; St. George's School, Newport, Rhode Island,
which has a million-dollar Gothic chapel built by John Nicholas
Brown, was founded in 1896; in the same year, Choate School,
whose benefactors and friends include such prominent businessmen as Andrew Mellon and Owen D. Young, was founded by
Judge William G. Choate, at Wallingford, Connecticut; while the
elder Morgan was forming his steel company in New York and
Pittsburgh in 1901, seven Proper Bostonians, including Francis
Lowell, W. Cameron Forbes, and Henry Lee Higginson, were
founding Middlesex School, near Concord, Massachusetts; Deerfield, which had been a local academy since 1797, was reorganized
as a modern boarding school by its great headmaster, Frank L.
Boydon, in 1902; and, finally, Father Sill of the Order of the Holy
Cross, founded Kent School in 1906.*

---

* Boarding schools for girls are also increasingly popular. Such schools as
Farmington (1843), Foxcroft (1914), Westover (1909), and St. Timothy's
(1882) have educated many Proper Philadelphia females.

More than any other single individual, J. Pierpont Morgan was responsible for the beginning of the trend towards the centralization of industry in the large corporation which began in the final years of the nineteenth century. Just as Morgan symbolized the gentleman banker, so Peabody of Groton was the prototypical upper-class schoolmaster of his age. The Morgans and Peabodys were allies in more ways than one. Thus young Endicott Peabody, whose father was a partner in the Morgan firm in London, spent five years at Cheltenham, an English public school, before going up to Cambridge.[27] Upon his return to America after his British education, Peabody first went to work in Wall Street. After deciding that life on the Street was not entirely satisfactory, however, he went to divinity school in Cambridge, spent some time as a missionary after his ordination, and finally founded Groton School on the premise that the traditions of the Episcopal Church, combined with the values of the English public school, would be most likely to produce the ideal "Christian Gentleman" in America. The first trustees of Groton School, Phillips Brooks and William Lawrence (Bishops of Massachusetts in that order), William C. Endicott, James Lawrence, J. Pierpont Morgan, S. E. Peabody, and Endicott Peabody, were a judicious blend of clerical, financial, and family prestige in America. The announcement of the new school included, among other items, the following statement:

In the early part of 1883, Endicott Peabody . . . wished to make an attempt to found a boys' school in this country somewhat after the manner of the Public Schools in England.

As these schools, under the influence of the Church of England, have developed a type of manly Christian character, he believed that a school, under the influence of the Protestant Episcopal Church would do a similar work in this country.[28]

The vital role which schools such as Groton have played in creating an upper-class subculture on almost a national scale in America is best understood if they are seen as *surrogate families* whose latent function is that of status ascription in an increasingly individualistic and centralized society. As a biographer of Endicott Peabody has said: "In the first place, to understand Groton one must understand the importance of the family idea . . . it was the most natural thing in the world for him [Peabody] to think of his school as being simply a large family. At the center of the big school family his own family grew and the beautiful home and

family life was presided over by Mrs. Peabody, the most gracious
and beautiful of wives and mothers. . . . He and she said good-
night to every boy in the school every night when they were
there."[29]

Over the years, Groton has become somewhat of an incestuous
family-surrogate. The first son of a Groton alumnus graduated from
the school in 1915. By the nineteen-thirties, however, approximately two-thirds of the boys at the school were from old Groton
families.[30] Of the thirty-six members of the class of 1934, for example, no less than twenty-five, including Theodore Roosevelt's grandson and Franklin Roosevelt's son, such scions of old eastern seaboard families as Alsop, Coolidge, Gerard, Saltonstall, Welles, and
Whitney, and a Deering McCormick and a McCormick Blair, of
the harvester families in Chicago, were the sons of old Grotties.

The social equality within the bosom of the school family is an
important feature of its role as both a socializing and status-
ascribing institution. "Despite great differences in physical equipment, life in most boarding schools is on the whole simple," writes
Allan V. Heely in *Why the Private School.* "More important," he
continues, "it is the same for everyone. . . . The regime provides
no opportunities for ostentation by the well-to-do. . . . Such considerations as money, dress, automobiles, social standing, financial
position, which plague the day school, whether it is public or
private, have little if any influence in the boarding school community."[31]

At the same time that these new schools were being founded,
older schools were going through a period of rapid growth. St.
Paul's School, founded in 1856, for example, graduated an average
of 16.3 boys per year during the 1860's, 45 during the 1870's, 84.8
in the 1880's, 104.2 in the 1890's, and has leveled out at about 100
boys per year during the first four decades of the twentieth century.[32] The Phillips Exeter Academy, which went through its most
rapid period of growth somewhat later than St. Paul's, more than
doubled its enrollment between 1900 and 1920 (290 to 660 students).[33]

In so many ways, as Helen Merrell Lynd observed in her pene-
trating study of *England in the 1880's,* the American social and
economic structure has experienced important changes approximately half a century behind the English.[34] Thus, while many new
boarding schools were founded at the turn of the century in order

to take care of the sons of America's new industrial aristocracy,
the British public school system had expanded about a half-century
earlier, in a period when England went through its great industrial
and imperial expansion after the Napoleonic Wars.[35] This was, of
course, the era when Thomas Arnold was the great headmaster of
Rugby (1828-1842). In order to accommodate England's increasingly prosperous middle classes, moreover, many new public
schools, such as Cheltenham (1841), Marlborough (1843), Rossall
(1844), Radley (1847), Bradford (1850), Wellington (1852), and
Epsom (1835), were founded during this period. (It is interesting
that Cheltenham was founded almost a half century before its
most famous American alumnus, Endicott Peabody, founded Groton
School.)

It was the sociological function of these public schools, especially the older and more aristocratic schools such as Eton, Harrow, and Winchester, to fuse the landed aristocracy with the
second-generation industrialists.[36] Thus the sons of the wealthiest
industrial families, such as the Gladstones, were assimilated into
that exclusive circle of public school men who ran the British
Empire throughout the nineteenth century. As a report of the
Public School Commission put it in 1864: "These schools have been
the chief nurseries of our statesmen: in them, and in the schools
modeled after them, men of all the various classes which make up
English society, destined for every profession and career, have
been brought up on a footing of social equality, and have contracted the most enduring friendships, and some of the ruling
habits, of their lives; and they have had perhaps the largest share
in moulding the character of an English gentleman."[37] Of course,
the inclusion of sons of wealthy manufacturers within these "nurseries of statesmen" may have seemed democratic in 1864, but the
fact is that "the various classes" at these public schools were pretty
well limited to the sons of the nobility and the mercantile classes
who could afford to pay.

The leading Protestant boarding schools in America in 1940
included twelve in New England, two in the Middle Atlantic
States, and two in Virginia (see Table 28).[38] While there are many
other private boarding schools in all parts of the country, and
especially in New England, these sixteen schools set the pace and
bore the brunt of the criticism received by private schools for
their so-called "snobbish," "un-democratic," and even "un-Ameri-

Table 28—Leading New England-Type Boarding Schools in the United States in 1940

Type of School	Location	Date Founded	No. of Students in 1940	Estimated Endowment in 1936*	Tuition in 1940
Old New England Undenominational					
Andover	Mass.	1778	650	$6,000,000	$1,100
Exeter	N.H.	1783	700	$8,000,000	$700-1,050
New England Episcopalian					
St. Paul's	N.H.	1856	400	$1,500,000	$1,400
St. Mark's	Mass.	1865	160	$900,000	$1,400
Groton	Mass.	1884	175	$1,500,000	$1,400
St. George's	R.I.	1896	175	†	$1,600
Kent	Conn.	1906	295	$13,500	none to $1,500
New England Undenominational					
Taft	Conn.	1890	300	†	$1,550
Hotchkiss	Conn.	1892	300	$400,000	$1,500
Choate	Conn.	1896	450	†	$1,825
Middlesex	Mass.	1901	150	†	$1,650
Deerfield	Mass.	1902	400	$330,000	$1,800
New England Catholic					
Portsmouth Priory	R.I.	1926	130	†	$1,700
Canterbury	Conn.	1915	130	†	$1,700
Middle States Undenominational					
Lawrenceville	N.J.	1810	450	$290,000	$1,500
Hill	Pa.	1851	400	$971,798	$1,550
Southern Episcopalian					
Episcopal High School	Va.	1839	250	†	$1,200
Southern Undenominational					
Woodbury Forest	Va.	1889	250	†	$1,400

* Estimates taken from *Fortune*, January, 1936.
† No information.

can" values. There were also two New England boarding schools run by and for Catholics. Although many fashionable Catholics attended the older Protestant schools, the fact that Portsmouth Priory and Canterbury School were founded in 1926 and 1915 respectively attested to the growing number of upper-class Catholics in America.

None of these schools was secular in the public school sense; divine worship was part of the daily schedule at all of them. All save St. Paul's, Groton, St. Mark's, St. George's, Kent, and the Episcopal High School were undenominational. Hill and Lawrenceville, however, were founded by Presbyterians, and Phillips Exeter and Phillips Andover had ancient Unitarian and Calvinist traditions. For generations, for example, Exeter, "one of the most precious institutions in the country," according to President Eliot, has sent most of its graduates to Harvard, while most of the graduates of Andover have gone to Yale because of the early Calvinist traditions at both institutions.[39]

Needless to say, the Episcopalian schools (including Middlesex) are the most fashionable while the two richest and oldest schools, Exeter and Andover, are the least exclusive socially. The other schools vary between these two extremes. Unlike the Episcopalian schools, which have five or six forms (grades) and prefer to take boys for at least five years, Exeter and Andover take boys only during the high school years (Junior, Lower Middle, Upper Middle, and Senior). Moreover, they often encourage exceptional students from the public high school system to take their last two years there. In contrast to the paternalistic and highly supervised life at the church schools, Exeter and Andover are more like small colleges and encourage self-reliance in a more permissive atmosphere. On the whole, while the upper-class church schools are in the tradition of Lord Chesterfield, Andover and Exeter would have appealed to Ralph Waldo Emerson with his emphasis on self-reliance as the highest American virtue.[40]

St. Paul's School: Proper Philadelphia Ideal. St. Paul's is the oldest, largest, and wealthiest of the Episcopal Church boarding schools. While Groton tends to be the American version of Tory and aristocratic Eton, St. Paul's is more in the tradition of Harrow, which drew its boys from the wealthy Whig families of nineteenth-century England. Although St. Paul's was founded by Dr. George Shattuck, a Proper Boston physician and philanthropist, Proper

Philadelphia families have been closely connected with the school from the very beginning. Less direct than the relationship between Groton and Boston, the original ties between Philadelphia and St. Paul's are all the more interesting.

William Augustus Muhlenberg, whose great-grandfather was the first Speaker of the House of Representatives in Washington's administration, was born in Philadelphia in 1796.[41] Although brought up in the church of his Lutheran ancestors, he became an Episcopalian and was baptized by Bishop White at the age of seventeen. After graduating from the University of Pennsylvania, Muhlenberg was ordained in 1817. His first three years in the ministry were spent in Philadelphia as an assistant to Bishop White in the united parishes of Christ Church, St. Peter's, and St. James. Always a restless and pioneering churchman, he finally decided to devote his life to the Christianizing of education. In 1828 he became the first headmaster of a church boarding school on Long Island, called at first the "Flushing Institute" and later St. Paul's College. "Here for the next eighteen years," according to James Thayer Addison, "he became the pioneer and the inspiration of Church schools in America."[42] Henry Codman Potter, later Bishop of New York and a friend of Muhlenberg's for many years, described the atmosphere at this pioneering Church school as follows:

The whole system of teaching was brought into healthful subordination to sound principles of Christian nurture. The college chapel, that bugbear of most youths in our ordinary American institutions, was made at once the center of the whole school life and a place of genuine attractiveness. The Church Year, which has so much in its beautiful order to appeal to the young mind, was made practically the school year; and today, among hundreds of men in all ranks of life who have gone forth from College Point [St. Paul's College], there is scarce one who does not date his first appreciation of the Church's feasts and fasts from the solemn and glowing services in its chapel. . . . The secret of this success was not any system, however excellent, nor any skill, however thorough. It was in the rare and happy qualities of the presiding mind. That mind possessed the magnetism of [Thomas] Arnold without his impatience; the religious earnestness of Arnold without his tendency to speculation. And the boys caught and reflected the master's spirit. . . .[43]

Henry Augustus Coit, a shy and sensitive young man whose personality was to dominate St. Paul's School in Concord, New Hampshire, for half a century, was one of Dr. Muhlenberg's pupils at College Point and one of his most devoted admirers.[44]

In predominantly Congregationalist and Unitarian New England, Dr. George Shattuck founded staunchly Episcopalian St. Paul's School in 1856.[45] With the usual zeal of a convert, however, he was rather proud of bringing such a Church institution into "enemy territory." Although brought up a Unitarian, Dr. Shattuck was one of the founders and for many years a warden of the Church of the Advent in Boston (it is recorded that he once put a check for $20,000 in the collection plate on a Sunday morning). As he probably numbered more Episcopal clergymen among his friends than did any other layman in America, Dr. Shattuck knew what he was about when he chose young Henry Augustus Coit to head his new school.

In the spring of 1856, Henry Coit and three pupils set up a school two miles from President Franklin Pierce's home town, Concord, New Hampshire. That spring even New Englanders were horrified by the news telling how John Brown and his sons "had dragged three members of one family from their beds and slain them with sabres."[46] The school had been incorporated the previous year, and some fifty acres of land, including a large house which had been the Shattuck family's country place since 1807, were deeded as a gift to the school on condition that the property should never be mortgaged, that the trustees of the school corporation should always be communicants of the Episcopal Church, and that the religious education at the school be in conformity with the doctrines and ritual of that church.[47]

Henry Augustus Coit's religious zeal almost matched the abolitionist fanaticism of John Brown. An austere and rigidly devout Episcopalian, he sternly guided his graduates away from Harvard for many years because of its Godless Unitarian atmosphere.

Young Henry Coit was ordained by Bishop Alonzo Potter at St. James' Church in Philadelphia.[48] His first ministry was under Reverend Samuel Bowman, later Bishop of Pennsylvania, whose niece, Mary Bowman Wheeler, he married in 1856 and brought to the school that first spring. Had Henry Coit been a bachelor, his austere manner would doubtless have frightened away most parents. But his wife, who came from a large and genial Philadelphia family (see family-founder, Charles Wheeler, Table 9), was an ideal mother substitute for the younger boys at the school. She cared for them when they were sick and consoled them in their periods of depression and homesickness. Many Philadelphia boys went to St. Paul's because of Mrs. Coit's wide circle of friends and relatives in the city.[49]

The link between St. Paul's and Philadelphia was interestingly maintained through the Wheeler family and their friends in the twentieth centuy.[50] Of the many Wheeler alumni of St. Paul's, for example, Samuel Bowman Wheeler graduated from the school in 1897 and from Harvard in 1901. Two of his classmates and friends at Harvard were Gibson Bell and Samuel S. Drury. The Reverend Samuel S. Drury, Rector of St. Paul's from 1911 until his death in 1938, became one of the great American headmasters of his era (as was Dr. Drury of Harrow in the nineteenth century). Upon his graduation from Harvard, Gibson Bell went up to Concord where he was a master at the School for almost a decade. In 1915, after his marriage to a Wheeler widow, he established the Montgomery County Day School at Wynnewood on Philadelphia's Main Line.[51] For almost twenty-five years until his retirement and the school's reorganization in 1938, the Reverend Gibson Bell ("The King"), whose strong sense of humor often broke through his stern façade, ran a very personal school which specialized in preparing the sons of Proper Philadelphians for boarding school, especially, of course, for St. Paul's. After 1928, when J. Vaughan Merrick, III—a graduate and master at St. Paul's, whose father and grandfather were trustees of Episcopal Academy and whose great-grandfather founded the Pennsylvania Railroad—became the headmaster of St. George's School, many Montgomery boys went there.

St. Paul's has always been closely tied to the Protestant Episcopal Church. Among the eighty-one trustees of the school between its founding and 1940, for example, fourteen were clergymen (the influence of the clergy may be dying; all save three of these clergymen-trustees took office before 1900) and nine of these were Bishops of the Episcopal Church (including Frederick D. Huntington). All of the rectors during this period were Episcopalian clergymen. Although the Right Reverend Alexander Mackey-Smith, Bishop of Pennsylvania and a graduate of the class of 1868, was the first Philadelphia clergyman to become a trustee, the school was closely allied to Philadelphia through Bishop Alonzo Potter and his family. He sent his sons to St. Paul's (the first one graduating in 1871) while a member of the fourth generation of the Potter family graduated from the school in 1929.[52]

The Ingersoll family, as we have said, usually initiates the fashionable thing to do in Philadelphia. Charles Edward Ingersoll, who graduated from St. Paul's in 1878, was a trustee of the school from 1909 to 1929. His son, C. Jared Ingersoll,, was a trustee in 1940. R. Sturgis Ingersoll, of course, graduated from the school, as did his oldest son. A perusal of the list of his son's classmates (class of 1934) at St. Paul's is a useful way of demonstrating the function of the school as a Philadelphia, and national, upper-class family surrogate. In the class of 1934 at St. Paul's, in addition to an Ingersoll, there were direct descendants (sons, grandsons, great grandsons, etc.) of Bishop William White, Anthony J. Drexel, Enoch W. Clark, George B. Roberts, George D. Rosengarten, William Weightmen, John B. Ellison, and Isaac H. Clothier, all past members of the Philadelphia elite (see Table 9, Chapter V); in addition, these young men from Philadelphia were classmates of the descendants of George F. Baker, James B. Duke, Marshall Field, Bradley Martin (of the famous party), and President Theodore Roosevelt. Although the composition of this one class clearly demonstrates the nature of the school, it is interesting that these boys of the class of 1934 also sat in chapel with (in the classes of 1933 and 1935) Chews, Cadwaladers, Morrises and Wheelers from Philadelphia, as well as Pillsburys (flour). Widdicombes (furniture), Vanderbilts, Rockefellers, Schleys (railroads and Chase National Bank), McLeans (Hope Diamond), Dillinghams (Hawaiian Oligarchy), and a host of other famous American family names too numerous to mention.

Phillips Brooks was impressed by the famous American families whose sons were nurtured on the playing fields of St. Paul's School. Having come up to preach a Founders' Day sermon at the school in the 1870's, he was pleased to run into his old Philadelphia friend, S. Weir Mitchell, who was visiting his son at the school. While watching various sporting events, Phillips Brooks remarked to his old friend: "How interesting it is to hear these fellows shouting to one another names that are historically familiar."[53]

Although Franklin D. Roosevelt was the first graduate of an exclusive American boarding school to become President of the United States, since the Civil War seven presidents have sent their sons to these schools: the sons of presidents Lincoln, Grant, and Cleveland went to Phillips Exeter; Theodore and Franklin Roosevelt sent their boys to Groton; Robert A. Taft, of course, graduated from his uncle's school; and St. Paul's educated the sons of James A. Garfield.

Historical and family continuity at St. Paul's continues down through the years. Of the 101 "new boys" entering the school in the fall of 1953, for example, 56 were descendants of alumni (42 were sons, 16 grandsons, and five were great-grandsons). One of the boys (both a son and grandson of alumni) was a great-grandson of President Cleveland, while a classmate was a great-grandson of J. P. Morgan.[54] Although the elder Morgan was an original trustee of Groton School at its founding in 1884, his son graduated from St. Paul's in that same year [55]

The Boarding School Graduate and the American Elite. After the prayer and the anthem at the Founders' Day service, Phillips Brooks stood up in the pulpit of St. Paul's School Chapel in his habitual hesitating way. After taking off his glasses, wiping them, and putting them on once again, he announced his text: "Render unto Caesar the things. . . ." He closed his Bible, and, after another long pause, began his sermon: "As I watched your sports today," he said, "I heard many of the names great in American history. It is only worthwhile to have had ancestors who have served their country well, if out of the pride of birth you win high-minded reasons and desires to follow nobly where they led so well."[56]

Where has "pride of birth" and an expensive education led the graduates of the leading New England boarding schools later in life? Perhaps participation in public service is the most obvious way to pay the debt of special privilege. On this score, Groton and Exeter were probably the leading schools as of 1940. However, of all the graduates of these schools since the founding of Andover in 1778, according to the editors of *Fortune* magazine, only Daniel Webster (Exeter) and Franklin D. Roosevelt (Groton) could be classed as statesmen of the first rank.[57] During this same period, while thousands of highly successful lawyers have been graduates of America's leading boarding schools, only one (Exeter) has ever been a Justice of the Supreme Court. Out of approximately 20,000 Exeter graduates between 1783 and 1940, in addition to one member of the Supreme Court, ten graduates have been cabinet members, nine have been United States senators, twenty-five have sat in the House of Representatives, and fourteen have been state governors.[58]

Groton, a much younger school than Exeter, achieved national recognition, of course, when Franklin D. Roosevelt became President of the United States. Of the members of Roosevelt's cabinet during the New Deal days however, only one, Henry Morgenthau, Jr. (Exeter) was a graduate of a leading boarding school. As *Fortune* wrote at the time: "It is true that Morgenthau is not the only private school boy in the Roosevelt Administration. There have also been Acheson and Coolidge of Groton and St. Mark's, Lloyd Garrison and John G. Winant of St. Paul's, and James Moffett of Lawrenceville. But only Morgenthau can accurately be described as a New Dealer."[59]

Thoughtful Americans, including many who have graduated from exclusive New England schools, have often compared the records of graduates of Exeter, Andover, Groton, or St. Paul's, with records of their English counterparts from schools such as Eton and Harrow. Seventeen old Etonians, for example, have been Prime Ministers of England, while no less than five Prime Ministers between 1800 and 1860 were graduates of Harrow. Peel and Palmerston were Harrow men; Wellington, Gladstone, Charles James Fox, and the first Earl of Chatham went to Eton.

In the face of this record, the American schools are certainly open to criticism. While the statesman from the private school in America is conspicuously the exception, the graduates of New England boarding schools have been leaders in the business and financial community. It has always been true that "you can hardly throw a stone in Wall Street without hitting a Groton or St. Mark's or Hotchkiss or St. Paul's banker or broker or corporation lawyer."[60] George Biddle, Grotonian of Proper Philadelphia stock, describes his impression of his old school as follows:

Ninety-five per cent of these boys came from what they considered the aristocracy of America. Their fathers belonged to the Somerset, the Knickerbocker, the Philadelphia or the Baltimore Clubs. Among them was a goodly slice of the wealth of the nation, little Morgans, Harrimans, Whitneys, Webbs, McCormicks, Crockers, Stillmans. On the whole the equipment and the teaching were more admirable than at any other school in America.

Generally speaking, this aristocracy, this wealth, this admirable educational training was destined to flow into one channel: Wall Street or its equivalent. There were, of course, exceptions. Of the fifty-six of my two Groton forms the names of seven have even been listed in *Who's Who in America*. The greater number, however, could, in terms purely of manhood, be listed as absolute failures: parasites on the community, cheats, drunkards, lechers, panhandlers, suicides. This is not entirely—considering the investment in money, in zeal, in single-mindedness, in purity—a successful experiment. Is it the educational system or the material—the social and financial aristocracy of America—that is responsible?[61]

George Biddle may have been a little harsh in his evaluation of his old school. Yet there is some evidence to support the thesis that the second ·and third generation of America's plutocracy produce more than their share of failures. Perhaps this is understandable in a society which, ideologically and morally, places such an emphasis on material success. The drive to make money comes naturally to those born to poverty; it may make little sense to those born to wealth. And there is a danger that the exclusive American schools have imitated only the superficialities of the British public school system. Both produce polished gentlemen who are accepted into the best clubs, banks, and law firms, but, in addition, the British system has produced great public servants. Perhaps it is unfair to criticize the schools themselves. It has been argued justifiably that the American people do not want leaders from this sort of background. But, the conspicuous exceptions often belie this excuse. Franklin D. Roosevelt's Groton and Harvard accent did not stand in the way of his popularity, and some think it helped. Moreover, if more members of the American upper class had the strength of their convictions, and took pride in their background, perhaps the situation would be different. In the 1938 senatorial elections, for example, Mrs. Robert A. Taft made a statement to the mine-workers of Ohio which the political pundits branded as political suicide. "My husband is not a simple man," she said during the campaign. "He did not start from humble beginnings. My husband is a very brilliant man. He had a fine education at Yale. He has been well trained for his job. Isn't that what you prefer when you pick leaders to work for you?" Robert A. Taft won this election. In contrast to Mrs. Taft's convictions, it is indicative of our conforming age that Adlai Stevenson, a product of Choate and Princeton, was told to "humanize" his Ivy League diction by his expert and "other-directed" advisors.[62]

The exclusive schools also have to face the fact that the family environment of their students does not always foster the ideals of political leadership. During the last years of his life,[63] Endicott Peabody, for example, was in constant correspondence with his most famous graduate. Although a great admirer, though not uncritically so, of President Rooscvelt, Peabody knew the sentiments of most Groton alumni. In 1934, when Groton celebrated its fiftieth anniversary, Dr. Peabody let it be known that alumni who were unprepared to be polite to Mr. and Mrs. Roosevelt need not return to Groton for the celebrations. Again, George Biddle has made some interesting comments on the American upper class value system:

Not so long ago I attended at the Union Club on Park Avenue and 69th Street a dinner given by the graduates to commemorate the happy and complete recovery of Mr. Peabody from a long and serious illness. He was approaching his eighty-first birthday. I had not seen him for twenty-seven years. He had changed singularly little. His hair grayer; his face less pink and white. But he had the same vitality, the same clear eye, the same indestructible dominance and untiring energy. He looked more than ever like some splendid eleventh- or twelfth-century Crusader; the militant Christian, half warrior, half priest. He spoke for an hour, with the occasional use of a note, and during that hour held all of us in the hollow of his hand. He was the father; we, his boys. There was much easy wise-cracking—as of old—and much reassuring statistical proof of the high standing of recent classes at Harvard, at Yale and at Princeton. He spoke about purity in the home and said that home life and purity were at the basis of our civilization. The audience responded with laughter or applause. Then the Rector spoke to this effect:

"Something has troubled me a good deal lately. Personally I don't pretend to know much about politics or economics. [A little ripple of gaiety spread among us.] But in a national crisis like the present one, we get pretty excited and perhaps we give vent to expressions that later on we are sorry for. I believe Franklin Roosevelt to be a gallant and courageous gentleman. I am happy to count him as my friend."

There was complete silence.

Now the dramatic meaning of this incident was *not* that the school was completely hostile to Mr. Peabody in his loyalty to perhaps the most popular president since Washington, to one of the half-dozen admittedly most important people in the world today, to the only preeminent living Grotonian. It was rather—if I analyzed the Groton mind correctly—that they were silenced for a moment in admiration at his courage in thus daring, at a completely friendly, family meeting, to step into the breach and alone undertake to defend the President. I take it that what ran through their minds was something like this: "Good old Rector! By jove he has nerve. And perhaps—after all—he may be partly right. Perhaps we should not *talk* the way we do. Not in public. Not of a fellow Grotonian."[64]

It is interesting that such a large number of the distinguished political and governmental leaders drawn from the American upper class (and Groton), in recent years, have been members of the Democratic party. But they were exceptions to the rule in their chosen vocations ("politicians" rather than respectable bankers or brokers), and given the correlations between social facts it is quite natural. The vast majority of their families were conservative and tied to the money interests of the country. The consistently conservative attitudes of St. Paul's boys have a long tradition. Arthur Stanwood Pier, for example, writes of the presidential election of 1860 as follows: "The result of the boys' ballot for President indicates how conservative in their political views were the families from which many of them came. Nineteen votes were cast for Bell and Everett, of the National Constitutional Union, the party which in the crisis confronting the country had—to quote Professor Morrison [a graduate and trustee of S.P.S.]—'no political principle other than the Constitution and the Country, the Union of the States, and the enforcement of the Laws,' and which Lincoln said was composed of 'the nice exclusive sort' of people. Fifteen voted for Lincoln and Hamlin, five for Douglas and Johnson, and two for Breckenbridge and Lane, the secession candidates."[65] Four years later, the boys of St. Paul's defeated Lincoln when McClellan received thirty-three out of the fifty-three votes cast that year at the school. The straw votes of the St. Paul's community down through the years, of certain quantitative sociological interest, were cast as follows:[66]

1888:   Harrison, 188; Cleveland, 101.
1892:   Harrison, 186; Cleveland, 108.
1896:   McKinley, 200; Palmer, 35; Bryan, 12.
1900:   McKinley by a very large majority; no figures.
1904:   Roosevelt, 239; Parker, 51; Swallow, 7.
1908:   Taft, 286; Debs, 40; Bryan, 26.
1912:   Wilson, 133; Taft, 130; Roosevelt, 90.
1916:   Hughes, 251; Wilson, 73.
1920:   Harding, 329; Cox, 46; Debs, 3.
1924:   Coolidge, 335; Davis, 62; LaFollette, 10.
1928:   Hoover, 216; Smith, 88; Thomas, 47; Will Rogers, 10.
1932:   Hoover, 276; Roosevelt, 76; Thomas, 60.

On the whole, then, both the political and social attitudes of St. Paul's boys and their families have been conservative and conformist. It is ironic, but perhaps all too true, that Henry Codman Potter's judgment of his friend, William Augustus Muhlenberg, caught the spirit of the leadership of St. Paul's School down through

the years. It will be recalled that Bishop Potter once contrasted
Muhlenberg of College Point with Thomas Arnold of Rugby as
follows: "Muhlenberg," he wrote, "possessed the magnetism of
Arnold *without his impatience; the* religious *earnestness* of Arnold
without his *tendency to speculation*."[67] It may be true that a certain
amount of *impatience* combined with a tendency to *speculation* are
indispensable prerequisites of the reforming zeal so characteristic
of the gentleman in American politics, such, for example, as the
two Roosevelts. In the closing paragraphs of his sympathetically
critical history of St. Paul's School, Arthur Stanwood Pier, in emphasizing the patient, unspeculative, and earnest qualities of St.
Paul's boys, echoes Bishop Potter's estimate of William Augustus
Muhlenberg. His *St. Paul's School 1855-1934* ended on the following note:

What is the spirit of St. Paul's? In the accepted meaning, the boy
who has school spirit, the right "attitude," is one who conforms cheer-
fully to regulations and customs, . . . is energetic and enthusiastic in
club athletics, is pleasant and friendly with masters and never "two-
faced" with boys, and is quite uncritical in his outlook. The boys who
are thoroughly imbued with it go on into a larger world with an appealing enthusiasm, a radiant ingenuousness, an eagerness to join in some
common effort for the good of all—if only one will direct them where
that common effort is being made![68]

Ours is an age when the terms "good" and "democratic" have
tended to become synonymous. Even democratic societies, however,
cannot get along without aristocratic as well as democratic virtues.
Thus it seems important that institutions such as Groton, Exeter,
and St. Paul's live up to genuine aristocratic standards. All human
institutions, like the men who run them, fall far short of perfection,
but the New England boarding school has not even begun to produce the type of leadership in America which has characterized
the British public school. In effect, the schools have failed in their
aristocratic function primarily because of the values and attitudes
of the upper-class parents who have patronized them, and, partly,
though less than those who fall back on this excuse like to think,
because the American people have not whole-heartedly supported,
if they have even known about, this kind of exclusive educational
system. To call the New England boarding school un-American,
however, is absurd and short-sighted, though understandable if its
graduates do not prove themselves valuable to society as a whole.

The British public school, on the other hand, has gained national respect; even under a Socialist regime, with its extreme emphasis on equality, it is still valued. (A recent Royal Commission report on Population was extremely concerned about the fact that middle- and upper-middle-class parents were severely limiting family size in order to afford public school education for their sons.)[69] Although the public school has been criticized on every side, especially by gifted and literate alumni, the British people have begun to recognize the value of these schools now that they have been threatend with extinction.

Many great aristocratic institutions, as well as a great many aristocrats, have been highly democratic. The New England boarding school, then, has an important democratic as well as aristocratic function in modern American society. It would be unrealistic to hope that all Americans should or could be automatically provided with such an expensive and exclusive education as that obtained at Exeter or Groton. More could have such an education, however, if educational excellence were valued in America above such material comforts as the Cadillac automobile and other expensive gadgets so dear to the hearts of so many members of the nation's wealthier classes. All would agree, on the other hand, that these exclusive schools should not limit their enrollment to the sons of the wealthy. The New England boarding schools have always been aware of this. Through scholarship endowments and other means, they have attempted to provide tuition reductions for a large proportion of their students each year. It is probably true, however, that most of these scholarship boys, especially at such familistic schools as St. Paul's and Groton, come from impecunious upper-class families. This is quite natural and not wholly undesirable. It should not be used as the principal argument in defense of the democratic nature of the schools' admission policies, however. On the contrary, in America in the middle of the twentieth century, a school which charged high tuition rates and had no scholarships could conceivably be more socially democratic than one with many scholarships awarded only to the sons of the impecunious genteel. One wonders if the New England boarding schools are truly encouraging unfashionable, and, particularly, ethnic or racially different families (who may well be able to afford full tuition) to send their sons there.

If the boarding schools are to be truly democratic, true "public schools" for the sons of the successful, they must appeal to a broad cross-section of the American elite. To justify their importance in an ethnically mixed democracy, these schools must resist the danger of becoming purely Anglo-Saxon, colonial-stock, upper-class preserves. The democratic function of Groton School, for example, was recently (1955) brought to the author's attention when a Groton parent (and alumnus) faced the problem of asking his son's Negro classmate to visit in an exclusive suburb of Washington, D.C. Surrounded with many Southern neighbors, the parent faced the incident with some trepidation but could hardly deny his son's convictions of racial equality gained at exclusive and "snobbish" Groton school. As happens more often than not, the whole family was pleased with the pleasant results of their invitation.

Perhaps it is somewhat naïve, and bad sociology as well, to expect a democratic society to provide the opportunity for members of minority groups to climb the ladder of success and social acceptance if the ladder does not have any rungs. Just as Groton, in the days of Peabody, assimilated the sons of newly-rich Yankees, so today its democratic function is to provide a rung in the ladder of assimilation for the sons of the newly successful ethnic and racial minority group members. It is entirely possible that among the sons of the successful in America the *segregated democracy* of the boarding school may produce more democratic citizens than the *selective snobbery* so characteristic of the modern suburban high school.

College Education and Social Class. Within the upper class, and especially along the eastern seaboard, colleges are socially stratified. *Where* one goes is far more important than going. It is more advantageous, socially, and economically, to have graduated from Harvard, Yale, or Princeton with a low academic standing than to have been a Phi Beta Kappa at some less fashionable institution. Thus the sixty-nine Philadelphians who were listed both in *Who's Who* in 1940 and the *Social Register* in 1900—the old-family core of the contemporary elite (see Table 16, Chapter VIII)—limited themselves to attendance at the University of Pennsylvania, Haverford, Swarthmore, Harvard, Yale, and Princeton. The increasing importance attached to Harvard, Yale, and Princeton, moreover, is indicated by the fact that, while 53 per cent of the older men (over sixty-five) went to the University of Pennsylvania as against

3 per cent to the "big three," the younger men (under sixty-five) preferred the three fashionable universities (46 per cent) to the local University (40 per cent).

The pattern set by these old-family elite members was followed by the rest of the upper-class members of the Philadelphia elite. Of the Philadelphians listed in *Who's Who* in 1940, for example, over half of those also listed in the *Social Register* were graduates of the University of Pennsylvania, Harvard, Yale, or Princeton, while at least three-fourths of those not in the upper class were graduates of other institutions (Table 29). The figures in the last column of Table 29 provide a fairly accurate index of the prestige

**Table 29—Philadelphians in Who's Who in 1940—College Attended
as Related to Social Class**

	SOCIAL		CLASS				
	Social Register		Non Social Register		Who's Who Total		Per Cent in Social
College Attended	No.	%	No.	%	No.	%	Register
Univ. of Penna.	63	(28)	108	(20)	171	(22)	37%
Haverford-Swarthmore	8	(7)	12	(8)	20	(8)	40%
Other Phila. colleges	7		33		40		17%
Harvard	22		8		30		73%
Yale	11	(23)	8	(5)	19	(10)	58%
Princeton	18		10		28		64%
Other Ivy colleges†	12	(5)	15	(3)	27	(4)	44%
All other colleges	36	(16)	204	(38)	240	(31)	15%
Noncollege graduates	49	(22)	140	(26)	189	(25)	26%
No information	—		6	(1)	6	(*)	—
Total	226	(100)	544	(100)	770	(100)	29%

* Less than 1 per cent.
† This category includes—M.I.T., Columbia, Cornell, Dartmouth, Amherst, Trinity, Williams, and the University of Virginia. By and large they are second choices for those of the upper class who for one reason or another do not go to one of the "big three."

rankings of the various types of colleges and universities in America, at least as far as the Philadelphia upper class is concerned.

The University of Pennsylvania and the Philadelphia Upper Class. Since the eighteenth century, prominent Philadelphians have been intimately associated with the University of Pennsylvania. More Philadelphians listed in *Who's Who* in 1940 were graduates of the University than of any other institution of higher learning. This was true of both the members of the upper class and the rest of the elite.

The eighteenth century, the "Age of Benevolence," witnessed

the opening of hundreds of privately supported schools for the poor. In 1739, the Reverend George Whitefield, a young Anglican clergyman and among the greatest revivalists of all time, arrived in Philadelphia. In spite of his cool reason and sceptical attitude toward religion, even Benjamin Franklin was impressed by the eloquence and sincerity of this young divine.[70] The religious revival which followed Whitefield's arrival in the Quaker City resulted in the founding of a charity school in 1740. This charity school eventually became the University of Pennsylvania.

The American people, who purportedly love nothing more than change and the newest model, have, nevertheless, a great respect for the antique and the early date. The official date of the founding of the University of Pennsylvania is 1740, although the Board of Trustees date their origin from the founding of Franklin's Academy in 1749; instruction actually began in 1751, the Board of Trustees was not incorporated until 1753, and official power to grant degrees was not obtained until 1755.[71] At any rate, the founding date, 1740, allows Pennsylvania men to boast of a greater antiquity than their rivals in Princeton Town (1746).

In 1749, a group of twenty-four trustees, with Benjamin Franklin as their president, signed the "Constitutions for a Public Academy in the City of Philadelphia."[72] These original trustees of the Academy, "the principal Gentlemen in the Province" according to Franklin, were the most prominent Philadelphians of their day. Aristocratic Philadelphians have run the University, except for the decade immediately after the Revolution, down to the first part of the twentieth century. As one historian of the University puts it:

> Eight of [the original trustees] were notably wealthy merchants, four were prominent physicians, several were or had been judges, and most of them were also members of the Provincial Assembly or City Council. The only two who were in any sense artisans were Franklin who, with the pride of the self-made man, signed himself "Printer," and Philip Syng, "Silversmith." Syng was an artist in his craft, a scientific observer, member of the Junto, a director of the Library, a man of good social standing, and a vestryman of Christ Church. . . .
> The requirement of frequent meetings and detailed oversight made it necessary, as indeed was recognized in the Constitution, that the Trustees should be chosen from Philadelphia; and the provision for filling their own vacancies made it practically certain that they would, as in fact they did, continue to draw their members from among the prominent men of the city and of their own class, often their own families, foregoing such vivifying influence and support as might come

from drawing on other regions and other classes in the community. Except for a short period after the Revolution, until very recent times through all its history the Academy and its successors have had the advantages and disadvantages of control by a Board of Trustees of individual ability, eminence, and social position, but drawn from a narrow geographical radius and a closed social circle.[73]

Unlike most of the other early colleges and universities in America from its beginning the College of Philadelphia was non-sectarian. Although never under the supervision of any Protestant sect, the University has always been dominated by Episcopalians. As the trustees were selected on the basis of wealth, influence, and social position, however, Episcopalian dominance was primarily social rather than religious. The first Provost (the Provost was the head of the University until Thomas S. Gates became President in 1930; the term is derived from the traditional title of the heads of certain Colleges at Oxford), the Reverend William Smith, a Scotchman chosen by Franklin, turned out to be a devoted and ardent Episcopalian. Two of the greatest Provosts, William Pepper (1881-1894), and Charles C. Harrison (1894-1911), in the Proper Philadelphia tradition, were communicants of St. Mark's Church, while the president in 1940, Thomas S. Gates, was a vestryman at St. Paul's in Chestnut Hill, and a devoted lay official of the Diocese of Pennsylvania.

It is interesting that the Quakers, who founded such excellent colleges as Swarthmore, Haverford, and Bryn Mawr, did not play an important role in the early history of higher education in the Quaker City. This was so for two reasons: one, according to Rufus Jones, was that the early Friends did not necessarily believe in the value of higher education;[74] and, two, they had no need to educate a clergy—a factor responsible for the early founding of Harvard, Yale, and Princeton.

Although Proper Philadelphians sat on the Board of Trustees and sent their sons there, the University remained a small local institution, with no national reputation, throughout the major part of the nineteenth century. For eighty years before 1866, for example, Philadelphians expressed their generosity and loyalty towards the University with only one gift of $5,000 "to provide instruction in drawing."[75]

During the 1870's the University moved out to its present site in West Philadelphia. With gifts amounting to less than $500,000 during the decade of the seventies, the debt continued to increase. Many alumni and friends of the University, including Provost Stillé, felt that nothing would ever be accomplished as long as the trustees ran the University by committee without any central authority. The Provost never had any real powers, and S. Weir Mitchell even went so far as to say that what the University needed was a real autocrat at its head.[76]

The expansion of the University into a nationally recognized institution began with the election of Dr. William Pepper as Provost in 1881. Although the formal powers of the Provostship remained unchanged, Dr. Pepper, through the force of his personality and dedication to his job, dominated the University for the next thirteen years. "He found the University a respectable school," writes his biographer, "he transformed it into a real University—created thirteen departments, erected twenty costly and appropriate buildings for its use, increased the Faculty from a corps of ninety to one of nearly three hundred, and the attendance from eight hundred to above twenty-eight hundred. For the endowment and use of the institution he raised over four million dollars, and added more than forty acres in the heart of the city to its campus."[77]

A wealthy and well-connected Philadelphian, Dr. Pepper virtually gave his life to the University and other civic projects in the city. Even his summers at Northeast Harbor, "a tiresome place and too far away," were devoted to raising funds and talking up the University.[78] Dr. Pepper sought the support of all groups in the city: "Wealthy members might provide funds, scholars might bring celebrity, society leaders might make the work popular and through the glamor of fashion promote the undertaking. Men of affairs might contribute practical suggestions, and politicians real power."[79]

Perhaps Dr. Pepper was most successful in making support of the University fashionable, a tribute to his understanding of the psychology of the Proper Philadelphia mind. Many fashionable families rallied to his support.[80] On the day he assumed the position of Provost in 1881, he was able to announce the contribution of $100,000 for the founding of the Wharton School by Joseph Wharton; in 1881 J. B. Lippincott gave $10,000 towards the founding of a veterinary school; in 1884 Dr. Horace Jayne, heir to the patent medicine fortune and Dean of the College at the time, contributed $100,000 toward the building of Biological Hall; in 1888 the Library was built by Frank Furness and some $200,000 was contributed by a host of Dr. Pepper's friends including $25,000 by Joseph Wharton; in 1892, the Hygiene Laboratory was completed through the generous donations of Henry C. Lea, wealthy Philadelphian and famous historian of the Counter-Reformation; and finally, during Dr. Pepper's last year in office, the Harrison Laboratory of Chemistry, a gift of Charles Custis Harrison, was completed in 1893.

This great expansion was carried on by Charles Custis Harrison, who took office in 1894. Interestingly enough, William Pepper, Charles Custis Harrison, and John Cadwalader, a devoted trustee at the time, were all members of the class of 1862 at the University. Provost Harrison was the greatest builder in the history of the University.[81] Among the major additions to the physical plant at the University were the University Museum; Houston Hall, a students' recreation and eating hall given by the Houston family; the Physics Laboratory, built by Randall Morgan, philanthropist, lawyer, and financier; and the Law School, which was begun by a gift of $100,000 from Thomas McKean, descendant of the signer of the Declaration of Independence of the same name. The Harrison family itself made the most important contribution of all. Soon after taking office, Charles Custis Harrison announced a gift of $500,000 to establish a graduate school in 1895.*

The University of Pennsylvania reached the zenith of its prestige as a Proper Philadelphia institution at the turn of the century. The trustees and principal benefactors of the University were primarily composed of wealthy and fashionable citizens. Among the twenty-four trustees in 1903, for example, were such eminent Proper Philadelphians as John Vaughan Merrick, Richard D. Wood, S. Weir Mitchell, Charles Custis Harrison, Horace Howard Furness, Bishop Ozi William Whitaker, Joseph George Rosengarten, Randal Morgan, Samuel Frederic Houston, and Joshua Bertram Lippincott.[82]

While William Pepper and Charles Custis Harrison were certainly successful in interesting the prominent members of old-Philadelphia families in the University, they were less successul in drawing upon many of the most prominent new fortunes of their day. The largest single donation to the University up until 1913 was a bequest of over $900,000, left by Dr. Louis A. Duhring, a

---

* Confirmed repeaters in donations under Harrison's regime included Joseph G. Rosengarten, Dr. and Mrs. Pepper, as well as the Harrison and Houston families.

bachelor who had been a professor in the Medical School most of his life.[83] Four of the city's wealthiest families, however—Widener, Elkins, Stotesbury, and Drexel—made no major contributions to the University, a fact Dr. Pepper realized only too well when A. J. Drexel suddenly died in 1893: "It is very disturbing," he wrote at the time, "a few years ago what great hopes all would have had; now, of course, whatever is done must and should be altogether for the Drexel Institute."[84] Perhaps the vein of snobbery which runs beneath the surface of fashionable Philadelphia—for example, their attitude toward eligibility for Assembly invitations (see the Widener case above)—may have had something to do with this failure to obtain really large contributions.

In 1940, although the Board of Trustees at the University had been enlarged since 1927 to include ten Life Trustees, twenty Term Trustees, and ten Alumni Trustees, it was still dominated by old Philadelphians.[85] Of the nineteen trustees from Philadelphia who were listed in *Who's Who,* for example, fourteen were also listed in the *Social Register.* The first President of the University of Pennsylvania, Thomas S. Gates, who had been in office since 1930 was the most respected and influential Philadelphian at the time. After the stock market collapse of 1929, he gave up his partnership in the Drexel firm and devoted himself to carrying the University through the Depression years. Also on the board were George Wharton Pepper, Samuel F. Houston, Morris L. Clothier, and Edward Hopkinson, Jr., all Life Trustees; among the Term Trustees were Adolph George Rosengarten and Joseph Wharton Lippincott; and, finally, Thomas Francis Cadwalader and J. Vaughan Merrick III, were among the Alumni Trustees.[86] In other words, although its leadership had been given officially a broader base since the first war (partly arising out of the controversy over the Scott Nearing case), the University was still dominated by the Philadelphia upper class in 1940.

The social life at the University of Pennsylvania revolves around the fraternities. In 1940 there were forty undergraduate male fraternities (twenty-eight "A," or Gentile, and twelve "B," or Jewish). The four oldest, Delta Psi (St. Anthony), Delta Phi (St. Elmo), Phi Kappa Sigma, and Zeta Psi, all founded in the years 1849-1850, have remained through the years the most exclusive upper-class fraternities on the campus.[87] Although they have nothing like the national upper-class reputation of Porcellian at Harvard,

Fence at Yale, or Ivy at Princeton, they do draw members from the best Philadelphia families. Most of the benefactors and trustees of the University discussed above belonged to one or another of these four original fraternities: countless members of the Pepper, Hopkinson, and Lippincott families have been members of Zeta Psi; Cadwaladers prefer Delta Phi; Phi Kappa Sigma is the home of Merricks, DuPonts, and President Gates; and the Houston family, as well as many Pembertons, Woods, Fraziers, Biddles, Clarks, and Harrisons have been brothers at St. Anthony Hall.

Harvard, Yale, and Princeton: National Upper-Class Institutions. As far as the Board of Trustees was concerned, the University of Pennsylvania was still a very Proper Philadelphia institution in 1940. But graduates of other "Ivy League" universities were more likely to be listed in the Philadelphia *Social Register*. Of the Philadelphians listed in *Who's Who*, for instance, only 37 per cent of the University of Pennsylvania graduates, as against 73 per cent of the Harvard men, 64 per cent of the Princetonians, and 58 per cent of the graduates of Yale, were also listed in the *Social Register* (see Table 29, above). Not only is the University considered to be socially inferior to Harvard, Yale, or Princeton; more important, upper-class loyalty to such local institutions as the University of Pennsylvania, Haverford, and even Swarthmore has been weakened throughout the twentieth century as fashionable Philadelphians have gone away increasingly to one of the three, nationally recognized, upper-class universities. While only 22 per cent of the older generation of the upper-class members of the Philadelphia elite (see Table 30) were graduates of Harvard, Yale, Princeton, and other "Ivy League" institutions, this proportion was increased to 36 per cent among the younger men. At the same time, of course, the younger members of the upper class were less likely to have graduated from the three local institutions (31 per cent as against 42 per cent). For the rest of the Philadelphia elite, local loyalty had remained the same over the generations. The trend to Harvard, Yale, and Princeton, then, was an upper class rather than an elite trend. In effect, these prestige institutions were not educating a larger proportion of Philadelphia's leaders, but more of its fashionable leaders.

In order to provide additional quantitative evidence of this centralizing trend, a 25 per cent sample of all the college graduates listed in the 1940 Philadelphia *Social Register* was obtained (see

Table 31). This larger sample of upper-class Philadelphians illustrates this same trend in somewhat more detail. First, of the 990 college graduates in this sample taken from the *Social Register,* no less than 78 per cent were graduates of either the University of Pennsylvania or Harvard, Yale, and Princeton. More important, however, is the fact that the trend towards the "big three" continued throughout the whole period from 1870 to 1940, and was accelerated during the two decades following the First World War. While 48 per cent of the men who had graduated from college before the turn of the century went to the University of Pennsylvania, as against only 24 per cent to Harvard, Yale, and Princeton, the reverse was true of the graduates during the 1920's and 1930's; 22 per cent graduated from the local university compared to the 57 per cent who went away to one of the "big three."

The fashionable trend to Princeton was most pronounced. Princeton has, of course, educated the sons of the American upper classes since colonial times. Of the 230 men graduating from Princeton between 1766 and 1776 (then the College of New Jersey), James Madison became President of the United States, twelve sat in the Continental Congress, six sat in the Constitutional Convention, twelve were members of Congress, three were Judges of the Supreme Court of the United States, three Attorney-Generals, two foreign ministers, one Secretary of State, and one became Vice-President.[88] But the point to be made here is that only in F. Scott Fitzgerald's era of gin, jazz and the suburban country club, well-stocked with bond salesmen, did the Princetonian become an upper-

Table 30—Philadelphia Males in Who's Who in 1940—College Attended as Related to Age and Social Class

College Attended	SOCIAL CLASS					
	Social Register		Non Social Register		Who's Who Total	
	65 & Over	Under 65	65 & Over	Under 65	65 & Over	Under 65
Local institutions (U. of P., Hav., Swarth., other Phila.)	42%	31%	27%	32%	32%	32%
Harvard-Yale-Princeton	18%	29%	5%	5%	10%	12%
Other Ivy colleges	4%	7%	2%	3%	3%	4%
All other colleges	15%	17%	37%	39%	29%	33%
Noncollege graduates	21%	16%	28%	21%	26%	19%
Total	100%	100%	100%	100%	100%	100%
(Number of cases)	(94)	(112)	(185)	(304)	(279)	(416)

class stereotype in America. Apparently Proper Philadelphians followed fashion. During the 1920's—and even through the Depres- sion years when sending a son out of town to college was a con- siderable strain on the family budget—for the first time, more upper-class Philadelphians went to Princeton than to the University of Pennsylvania (see Table 31). Even old, and previously loyal, Pennsylvanians surrendered to the trend. Although most of the old trustee families in 1940, including Hopkinsons, Peppers, and Cad- waladers, still sent their sons to the University, both Adolph G. Rosengarten (Pennsylvania 1892) and Joseph Wharton Lippincott (Pennsylvania 1908), whose fathers had preceded them as trustees, sent their sons away to St. Paul's and Princeton in the postwar decades (their sons were Princeton 1927 and 1937 respectively). The trend is unabated and local pride continues to wane: President Gates' son remained a loyal Pennsylvanian, became a campus leader as an undergraduate, and later a trustee; Thomas Sovereign Gates, III, however, went to St. Paul's and Harvard.

The New England boarding schools are closely connected by tradition with the fashionable universities. Approximately three- fourths of the Exeter boys have gone to Harvard for generations, just as their rivals at Andover have gone to Yale (in spite of this

**Table 31—Philadelphians in the 1940 Social Register—College Attended,
by Decade, 1870-1940**

Decade Graduated	COLLEGE ATTENDED					
	Harvard	Yale	Princeton	Pennsylvania	All Other	Total
1870's	1	1	0	7	2	11
1880's	2	3	0	28	8	41
1890's	6	15	16	50	40	127
1900's	18	13	29	63	39	162
1910's	24	23	28	90	42	207
1920's	21	32	76	55	48	232
1930's	25	27	72	43	43	210
Total	97	114	221	336	222	990
Percentage Summary						
1870-1900	5%	10%	9%	48%	28%	179-100%
1900-1920	11%	10%	15%	42%	22%	369-100%
1920-1940	10%	13%	34%	22%	21%	442-100%
Total						
1870-1940	10%	12%	22%	34%	22%	990-100%

Source: In the *Social Register*, after the name of every male college graduate, his college and year of graduation are listed (i.e., P'36, H'08, PA'00, etc.). This sample was obtained by taking all the graduates listed on each fourth page of the 1940 Philadelphia *Social Register*.

tradition, the class of 1929 at Princeton included fifty-seven Exeter and Andover alumni). Quite naturally, a vast majority of the Groton and St. Paul's boys go on to Harvard, Yale, or Princeton each year. In 1934 (see above, the discussion of the class of 1934 at St. Paul's) over 95 per cent of the 106 graduates of St. Paul's went to one of the "big three"; of the thirty-two Grotonians entering college that year, twenty-one went to Harvard, nine to Yale, and one each to Princeton and Cambridge, England.[89]

The interrelationships among the family, the private school, and the university are illustrated by the following characteristics of three entering classes at Princeton:[90]

Year of Entrance	Number in the Class	Per Cent Sons of Princeton Graduates	Per Cent Graduating Private School
1922	607	10.8	81.4
1930	631	15.8	84.9
1940	645	20.4	77.7

In spite of an admissions policy in these years which attempted to take boys on their merits, regardless of social background, over three-fourths of each class were products of private schools, and the amount of family in-breeding (sons of alumni) almost doubled in the course of two decades. The changing religious composition of the student body during the early decades of the twentieth century may be an additional clue to the changing class structure at Princeton. Of the 203 members of the class of 1900, for instance, 111 were Presbyterians and 36 were Episcopalians; of the 607 members of the class of 1926, on the other hand, 227 were Episcopalians as against 190 Presbyterians.[91] Finally, the number of exclusive eating clubs at Princeton, the bane of such liberal reformers as Woodrow Wilson, multiplied during this same period. Of the eighteen eating clubs at Princeton in 1929, for instance, only two, Ivy (1879) and Cottage (1887) were in existence before 1890. Five came into being during the 1890's, and the rest were founded in the twentieth century.

An intricate system of exclusive clubs, like the fraternities on less rarified American campuses, serves to insulate the members of the upper class from the rest of the students at Harvard, Yale, and Princeton. There are virtually "two nations" at Harvard. The private-school boys, with their accents, final clubs, and Boston debutante parties—about one-fifth of the student body—stand aloof and apart from the ambitious, talented, and less polished boys who come to Cambridge each year from public high schools over the nation. The Apley family, of J. P. Marquand's Boston, were members of the same club at Harvard for generations. George Apley explains the importance of the Harvard club to his son, John, in the following letter: "I am still quite well-known around the Club, you know, and your first object must be to 'make' the Club. I believe that everything else, including your studies, should be secondary to this. You may call this a piece of worldly counsel but it is worth while. I don't know what I should have done in life without the Club. When I leave Boston it is my shield. When I am in Boston it is one of my greatest diversions. The best people are always in it, the sort that you will understand and like. I once tried to understand a number of other people, but I am not so sure now that it was not a waste of time. Your own sort are the best friends and you will do well not to forget it."[92]

While the Exeter and Andover graduates are likely to participate in the life of the whole college community, as members of the student council, editors, managers, debaters, and prom chairmen, the Groton and St. Paul's boys, on the whole, limit their social life to the club world. Porcellian and A.D., the top clubs at Harvard, are followed by Fly, Spee, Delphic, and Owl.[93] Porcellian, founded in 1791 and including the loftiest names in Proper Boston history among its members, was the first college club in America. Owen Wister and his friend T. R. Roosevelt were both members of Porcellian. When asked about Porcellian, Owen Wister is said to have remarked: "Nothing has ever meant so much to me. It is a bond which can be felt but not analyzed."[94] Although a few have belonged to Porcellian and A. D., most Proper Philadelphians are members of the Fly Club (F. D. Roosevelt's).

New Haven is marked by a somewhat more democratic atmosphere than Cambridge. The exclusive top drawer at Yale includes the Fence Club (Groton and St. Paul's), Delta Kappa Epsilon (Exeter and Andover), and Zeta Psi, as well as St. Anthony Hall, the leading fraternity at the Sheffield Scientific School. Perhaps the senior societies are even more important than the social clubs. The two most important are Skull and Bones, founded in 1832, and Scroll and Key, which opened ten years later. Each year Skull and Bones "taps" about fifteen or twenty of the campus leaders, football captains, editors of the *News,* and so forth, while Scroll and Key prefers the more polished members of the senior class. As

Dixon Wecter puts it: "Skull and Bones has even been known to smile upon graduates of high schools; to Scroll and Key this anarchy would be unthinkable"[95] (since World War II, a Negro was elected captain of the football team and tapped by Skull and Bones).

More homogeneous, more suburban than New Haven or Cambridge, the Princeton campus is both more democratic and more snobbish. Traditionally, almost two-thirds of the students have been members of one or another of the eighteen eating clubs (since World War II the policy calls for including the whole student body within clubland). The Ivy Club is the oldest (1879), wealthiest, and most exclusive of the Princeton eating clubs.[96] For many Princetonians, to say "I am an Ivy man" is like the proud declaration of the ancient Roman, "I am a Roman citizen." Proper Philadelphia is tied to the Ivy Club in much the same way as Proper Boston is linked to Porcellian. Of the sixteen Board of Governors of the club in 1929 (all listed in the *Social Register* for various cities), six, including Edgar Allen Poe, Isaac W. Roberts, L. Caspar Wister, Fitz Eugene Dixon (P. A. B. Widener's grandson-in-law), and P. Blair Lee, president of the board, were residents of Philadelphia (Senator Blair Lee was one of the club's founders).[97] Philadelphia alumni of the Ivy Club include descendants of William Disston, William Weightman, P. A. B. Widener, William L. Elkins, George D. Rosengarten, Isaac H. Clothier, and many Ingersolls and Robertses. It is worth noting that of all the graduates of Princeton listed in *Who's Who* from Philadelphia in 1940, only those who were members of the Ivy Club saw fit to list their undergraduate club affiliations in their *Who's Who* biographies.

Election to membership in an appropriate club has usually been the main concern of upper-class boys at Harvard, Yale, and Princeton. "Thirty years ago," writes George Biddle in his autobiography, "the standard at Harvard was established by the socially well born; and those who were not socially well born sensed this standard . . . by the measure of undergraduate and graduate prestige—college activities far outweighed scholarship; athletics outweighed undergraduate activities; social standing—the importance of club life—outweighed them all. At Harvard, then, the New England boarding-school boy went in for clubs—social success."[98] In a similar vein, Arthur Stanwood Pier writes that, "of the boys who come to St. Paul's there are always some who have no serious interest in acquiring an education, and whose families do not encourage them to have such an intetrest. They go to college frankly to have a good time, to . . . make certain clubs; and having made their clubs they have acquired what they and their families regard as the hallmark of a college education—something more prized than the college diploma. College students may be classified into three groups: those who regard college as mainly an intellectual experience, those who regard it as both a social and an intellectual experience, and those who regard it as merely a social experience. By far the greater number of St. Paul's boys are found in the second of these categories, very few in the first, too many in the third."[99]

Alarmed at the power of the clubs, and convinced that "the side shows" were swallowing up the circus at Princeton, Woodrow Wilson included the following statement in his annual report to the Trustees, in 1906: "It would be difficult to exaggerate the importance in the life of the undergraduate of the question whether at the end of his Sophomore year he is going to be taken in to one of the upper-class clubs. His thought is constantly fixed upon that object throughout the first two years of his university course with a great intensity and uneasiness whenever he thinks either of his social standing, his comradeship, or his general social considerations among his fellows. The clubs do not take in all the members of the Junior and Senior classes. About one-third are left out in the elections; and their lot is little less than deplorable. . . . It often happens that men who fail of election into one of the clubs at the end of the Sophomore year leave the University and go to some other college or abandon altogether the idea of completing their university course."[100] Moses Taylor Pyne, an Ivy man and financial power among the Trustees, was one of Wilson's strongest opponents in the famous club controversy.

The ultimate in social success at college is not always an unmixed blessing, and even exclusion may have its compensations. No doubt John P. Marquand's keen insight into, and life-long interest in the American upper-class mind is related to the fact that he could not afford the world of undergraduate clubland when he went to Harvard. And perhaps the contrasting literary statures of Booth Tarkington and F. Scott Fitzgerald—both small town boys from the Middle West who lived through the Princeton social system—are partially the result of the latter's failure to achieve the ultimate in social success in his youth. Tarkington, a graduate of Exeter, was a member of the Ivy Club, while Fitzgerald belonged to a club of somewhat less upper-class prestige (his daughter married a St. Paul's and Ivy man).[101]

The injured oyster produces the pearl. Thus George Biddle sensed a correlation between failure to attain the ultimate in social success at Harvard and success in later life. Among the men who eventually became pre-eminent in his class at Harvard were Van Wyck Brooks, Samuel Eliot Morison, George Richards Minot, George Howe, Edward Brewster Sheldon, John Hall Wheelock, Alfred Vincent Kidder, Joseph Pulitzer, Charles Louis Seeger, and Warren Delano Robbins. "I happened to know all of these men fairly intimately as undergraduates," writes Biddle. "They then showed every promise of brilliance. Two or three of them told me during those years that they felt their college life a failure because they had not been elected into certain of the purely social final clubs. They felt that their fathers or uncles were ashamed of them. Some doubted whether in after-life they could ever live down the fact that they had made fairly good—but not the best—social clubs in college. Remember, I am not speaking of average undergraduates. I am speaking of the men who as undergraduates excelled in their chosen fields of scholarship, writing, drama or music."[102]

The American upper-class mind, a product of the playing fields of Groton or St. Paul's and the rarefied air of Porcellian or Ivy, has never been more deftly described than in the opening lines of Fitzgerald's short story, *The Rich Boy*. Perhaps he was using his Princeton classmates, graduates of St. Paul's and members of the Ivy Club, as his inspiration when he wrote: "They are different from you and me. They possess and enjoy early, and it does something to them, makes them soft where we are hard, and cynical where we are trustful, in a way that unless you are born rich, it is very difficult to understand. They think, deep in their hearts, that they are better than we are because we had to discover the compensations and refuges from life for ourselves. Even when they enter deep into our world or sink below us, they still think they are better than we are. They are different."[103] And the difference was not only, or primarily, "money," as Ernest Hemingway once remarked, in a superficially cynical way.

This chapter has been concerned with the sociological role of the New England boarding school and the "Ivy" university in fostering the growth of a national upper class in America at the expense of a declining local loyalty and pride. Before the turn of the nineteenth century, the sons of Philadelphia's moneyed aristocracy grew up in the center of the city where they went to school and college. Presumably they knew their "home town" pretty well, and were proud of it. Their sons and grandsons, however, led a more sheltered existence in spite of the "democratization" of American society. The residential suburb protected them from the ugliness of the heterogeneous urban melting pot; the local country day school prepared them for four or five years in some utopian New England boarding school community; and finally, they spent four more years amid the Gothic seclusion of an "Ivy League" university. One wonders if these class-insulated years of their youth prepared them as well for the various tasks of civic improvement so satisfying to the citizens of great local loyalty. Over 200 years ago, Benjamin Franklin referred his fellow Philadelphians to the *Letters of Pliny the Consul* when he proposed the founding of an academy in his adopted Quaker City. In the letter Franklin refers to, the younger Pliny addressed Cornelius Tacitus on the advantages of being educated in one's native city: "Your sons should receive their education here, rather than anywhere else," he wrote. "They will, by this means, receive their education where they receive their birth, and be accustomed, from their infancy, to inhabit and affect their native soil."[104]

CHAPTER XIII

Social Clubs and the Class Structure

> In the past and up to the very present, it has been
> a characteristic precisely of the specifically American
> democracy that it did *not* constitute a formless sand
> heap of individuals, but rather a buzzing complex of
> strictly exclusive, yet voluntary associations.
>
> MAX WEBER

IN MODERN metropolitan America, the club serves to place the
adult members of society and their families within the social hierarchy.[1] These voluntary associations to which members are elected
by ballot provide an intricate web of primary group milieux which
give form and structure to an otherwise impersonal urban society
composed of secondary groups. The social club, according to Crane
Brinton, "may perhaps be regarded as taking the place of those
extensions of the family, such as the clan and the brotherhood,
which have disappeared from advanced societies."[2]

Of the 770 Philadelphians listed in *Who's Who* in 1940, 490 or
64 per cent report membership in at least one club in the city or
its suburbs. The sense of clan and brotherhood is apparently
stronger within the upper class (90 per cent report club membership) than among the rest of the elite members (53 per cent belong
to clubs).[3] Moreover, the members of the business elite, where
organizing and personal influence are important, are more likely to
join clubs than the technical and intellectual elites. Of the businessmen listed in *Who's Who*, 97 per cent of those also listed in
the *Social Register*, and 76 per cent of the rest, report membership
in at least one club.

Two Types of Clubs. Within the metropolitan upper class
in America, there exist two types of social clubs: the metropolitan
clubs containing adult members, usually, but not always, of one
sex, and whose primary function is to provide a convenient place
to meet one's friends for meals and other social activities within
the city; and the suburban clubs, often called "country clubs," to

which the whole family usually belongs and where members spend much of their leisure time in various sporting activities and social events.

Contrary to the stereotype which equates the upper class with the "country club set" (and all its "leisure class" implications), the structure of the social class hierarchy, especially the upper classes, in Philadelphia is best understood in terms of the web of metropolitan club membership. Unlike the American middle classes, and resembling the lower classes, in fact, the Philadelphia upper class is largely male dominated and patriarchal. The social standing of the male family head, the best index of which is his metropolitan club affiliations, usually determines the social position of the family as a whole.[4] Even in familistic and conservative Proper Boston, according to Cleveland Amory, the leading men's clubs rather than the family are the core of the social system: "So severe are Boston's leading clubs," he writes, "that even the blue bloods have had to watch their step to gain admission."[5]

The Metropolitan Men's Club: National Elite and Upper-Class Brotherhood. In most major American cities there are one or two distinguished metropolitan men's clubs whose members dominate the social and economic life of the community. Max Weber, on a visit to America more than half a century ago, observed that "affiliation with a distinguished club is essential above all else. He who did not succeed in joining was no gentleman."[6]

The metropolitan men's club, traditionally an Anglo-Saxon rather than a Latin institution, began with the introduction of coffee-drinking into seventeenth-century England. Coffee houses sprang up all over London during the Commonwealth and continued to flourish after the Restoration. In an age not yet blessed with the daily press, the radio, or the telephone, the coffee house provided a convenient means of communicating the latest news. Gradually, the various London coffee houses attracted men with common or similar interests.

The original Lloyd set up his coffee house in Tower Street and later in Abchurch Lane and found his patrons among marine insurers. For city men there was likewise Garraway's. . . . Soldiers frequented Young Man's and stockjobbers Old Man's; lawyers the Grecian near the Temple and clergymen Child's in St. Paul's Churchyard. There were the men of fashion who wanted to talk their own particular talk, so interesting to themselves, so tiresome to those who have not the clue. White's Chocolate House in St. James's Street was from 1693 their place of resort. Finally there were the literary gentlemen who wanted to talk of books and talked for glory. . . . The most famous coffee house in the days of its zenith was Will's in Convent Gardens, where Dryden held undisputed sway. . . .⁷

In the course of the eighteenth century these informal coffee house gatherings evolved into permanent and private clubs, often retaining the name of the original tavern-keeper. White's, Brooke's, Arthur's, and Boodle's, for example, are among the leading London clubs to this day. During the nineteenth century, the number of London clubs multiplied. Among the more famous ones founded in this period were the Carlton (Wellington and the Tories) and the Reform, where political leaders gathered, and the Athenium, where one met the scientific and literary giants of London. The district of St. James' in London is known as "clubland" and this typically British institution has gradually spread all over the English-speaking world.

Following the British pattern, the Philadelphia Club, which began as an informal coffee house gathering of congenial friends, is the oldest of the well-known metropolitan men's clubs in America. "As early as 1830 a few gentlemen met at Mrs. Rubicam's Coffee-House at Fifth and Minor Streets to play cards. Joined by friends they organized the Adelphia Club in 1834; it soon came to be called the Philadelphia Club. Henry Bohlen, George Cadwalader, James Markoe, and Henry Pratt McKean were among the guiding lights. In 1835 the club rented the old house where Joseph Bonaparte, King of Naples, had lived in exile, and became officially the Philadelphia Club."⁸ The Philadelphia Club moved into a stately brick dwelling at Thirteenth and Walnut Streets in 1850, where it has remained for over a hundred years. Between the club's founding and 1940, ladies had been admitted on only three occasions, for balls in 1851 and 1869 and at the 100th anniversary celebration, in 1934, when Mrs. John Markoe, a belle of the ball in 1869, poured tea.⁹

The second oldest club in America is the Union in New York (1836); it was followed by the Century in New York (1847); the Somerset in Boston (1851); the Pacific Union in San Francisco (1852); and the Maryland in Baltimore (1857). Early metropolitan clubs were not founded in such old cities as Richmond and Charleston because of the habits of plantation living, and, of course, this peculiarly Anglo-American tradition did not appeal to the

Creole aristocracy in New Orleans. Since the Civil War, exclusive upper-class men's clubs have been founded in most major cities. Today the more distinguished clubs in America include the Somerset and Union in Boston; the Union and Knickerbocker in New York; the Duquesne and Pittsburgh in Pittsburgh; the Pacific Union in San Francisco; the Queen City and Cincinnati in Cincinnati; the Chicago in Chicago; the Maryland in Baltimore; the Buffalo Club in Buffalo; the Detroit Club in Detroit; and the Philadelphia and Rittenhouse in Philadelphia. Only St. Louis of the larger cities in the country did not have such a club in 1940, the St. Louis Club having been discontinued. This may be related to the fact that upper-class life in that city seems to be unusually closely allied to the country club. Even the Pulitzers have an estate contiguous to *the* country club, and on Thursday nights, when the servants are out (as in all cities), fashionable families have dinner and attend movies there.

The metropolitan club subculture, with its distinctive mores, values, and rituals, is perceptively outlined in the following passage:

The social club in America has done a great deal to keep alive the gentleman in the courtly sense. Here is his peculiar asylum from the pandemonium of commerce, the bumptiousness of democracy, and the feminism of his own household. Here he is technically invisible from the critical female eye—a state of bliss reflected in the convention that a gentleman never bows to a lady from a club window, nor according to the best form discusses ladies there. The club is his Great Good Place, with its comfortable and slightly shabby leather chairs, the pleasantly malt-like effluvium of its bar, the newspaper room with a club servant to repair quickly the symptoms of disarray, the catholicity of magazines from highbrows to *La Vie Parisienne* which in less stately company would seem a trifle sophomoric, the abundant newspaper, the good cigars and hearty carnivorous menus, and the waiters who are not to be tipped from New Year to Christmas. And perhaps most important of all, the friends with whom one sits down to a rubber of bridge after five o'clock, on the way home. They are the men with whom one grew up, saw through prep school and college, attended at their weddings— and whom the survivors will accompany decently in gloves to their long home in Mount Auburn or Sleepy Hollow [or Laurel Hill, on the bluffs of the Schuylkill]. They are the good fellows in whose essential infallibility one is bound to believe. Here we have no poor losers, bounders, muckers, or cads—and if one should take a cocktail too many and speak with loosened tongue, nobody outside is the wiser. And if by inconceivable chance one finds himself unable immediately to go home, there is always a pleasant bed upstairs in a room of bachelor's asceticism still redolent of pipe tobacco and toilet water.

One is likely to meet doctors here and most certainly surgeons, but never a dentist. There will be many lawyers—barristers, as they style them in Pall Mall, but not solicitors. Bankers and brokers, of course, who come from the best Nordic families, and wholesale merchants rather than retail. Retired military officers, with their excellent horsemanship, their erect carriage, white hair, and fine apoplectic flush, are also in the best Piccadilly tradition. Two or three Episcopal clergymen, preferably deans, lie lightly upon the consciences and budget of the club. Artists, musicians, and authors are regarded with suspicion unless their family names and background are quite trustworthy, and set them clear of raffish bohemia. The Union, the Knickerbocker, the Racquet, and the Metropolitan condescend to the Century, where achievement outweighs blood and wealth. A stage player is very seldom seen, though the fashionable architect—as the tradition of Richard Hunt and Stanford White, or even Addison Mizner in Palm Beach, demonstrates—may be quite a swell and amusing fellow. With what Henry James called "a certain light of the fine old gentlemanly prejudice to guide it," the preeminently social club welcomes the serious frivolity of horses, hounds, foxes, and boats, but not the effeminate frivolity of aestheticism. Pedantry is also frowned upon; except for the *Social Register,* the *World Almanac,* and Lloyd's *Register of American Yachts* not a volume in the club library has been taken down since the cross-word puzzle craze. It is comforting to think that one's sons and grandsons will sit in these same chairs, and firelight will flicker on the same steel engravings and oil portraits of past presidents—and though the stars may wheel in their courses and crowned heads totter to the guillotine, this little world will remain, so long as first mortgages and government bonds endure.[10]

Below the level of such patrician strongholds as the Somerset, Knickerbocker, or Philadelphia Clubs, a hierarchy of lesser clubs follows a fairly uniform pattern from city to city. First, there are the Union Leagues in Philadelphia (the oldest), New York, and Chicago. These strongholds of Republican respectability are more indicative of elite than upper-class status. At approximately the same social level as the Union Leagues, although perhaps attracting a professional rather than business membership, there are University clubs in most large cities. Finally, there are the athletic clubs. These are of two sorts and must not be confused. In each city the Racquet Club is favored by the more fashionable young bloods with an athletic turn of mind who pride themselves on "keeping in shape." The various "Athletic Clubs" such as the New York A. C., the Chicago A. C., or the Penn A. C. in Philadelphia, mark the lower fringes of clubdom in most cities. Quite different in atmosphere and criteria for membership (Jews are usually not taboo) are the gentlemen-intellectual clubs such as the Tavern in Boston, the Franklin Inn in Philadelphia, or the Century in New York. In the Athletic Club lounge a loyal member of the Century once overheard his club referred to as follows: "Did you know there was a club down on Forty-third Street that chose its members for intellectual eminence? Isn't that a hell of a way to run a club?"[11]

The circulation of elites in America and the assimilation of new men of power and influence into the upper class takes place primarily through the medium of urban clubdom. Aristocracy of birth is replaced by an aristocracy of ballot. Frederick Lewis Allen showed how this process operated in the case of the nine "Lords of Creation" who were listed in the New York *Social Register* as of 1905 (see Chapter III above): "The nine men who were listed [in the *Social Register*] were recorded as belonging to 9.4 clubs apiece," wrote Allen. "Though only two of them, Morgan and Vanderbilt, belonged to the Knickerbocker Club (the citadel of Patrician families), Stillman and Harriman joined these two in the membership of the almost equally fashionable Union Club; Baker joined these four in the membership of the Metropolitan Club (Magnificent, but easier of access to new wealth); John D. Rockefeller, William Rockefeller, and Rogers, along with Morgan and Baker were listed as members of the Union League Club (the stronghold of Republican respectability); seven of the group belonged to the New York Yacht Club. Morgan belonged to nineteen clubs in all; Vanderbilt, to fifteen; Harriman, to fourteen." Allen then goes on to show how the descendants of these financial giants were assimilated into the upper class: "By way of footnote it may be added that although in that year [1905] only two of our ten financiers belonged to the Knickerbocker Club, in 1933 the sons and grandsons of six of them did. The following progress is characteristic: John D. Rockefeller, Union League Club; John D. Rockefeller, Jr., University Club; John D. Rockefeller, 3rd, Knickerbocker Club. Thus is the American aristocracy recruited."[12]

In these days of the national corporation and the national market, most gentlemen-businessmen of any stature belong to distinguished clubs in more than one city. The younger J. P. Morgan, for instance, listed thirteen club memberships in his 1940 *Who's Who* biography. The catholicity of his interests was shown by the fact that, in addition to the Union and Knickerbocker in New York, he belonged to the Somerset in Boston, the Metropolitan in Washington, and to the Athenaeum, Garrick, and White's in London. Of the Philadelphians listed in *Who's Who* in 1940, 27 per cent— and over half (51 per cent) of the businessmen also listed in the *Social Register*—reported club membership in other cities. Upper-class Philadelphia businessmen were most likely to report membership in the Harvard, Yale, or Princeton Clubs in New York. These graduate clubs, which list out-of-town memberships from all over the country, do not automatically accept all alumni of their respective universities for membership. As with any other top-drawer club, one must be proposed, seconded, and approved by the membership committee. (At least one Proper New Yorker recently went through a trying experience when a Harvard classmate and professional associate, who happened also to be Jewish, asked to be proposed for membership in the Harvard Club. Although the Semitic dividing line is not absolutely impassable, as it is at the Union or Racquet, the situation is always difficult.) At any rate, these three prestige university clubs conveniently contribute to the solidarity of a national upper class: out-of-town businessmen stop in with old friends and often make business engagements there when they are in New York; in addition, countless small-town boys at Princeton, Harvard, or Yale live at their respective graduate clubs during their first years out of college if they happen to be among that large group of Ivy alumni who seek their fortunes each year among the caverns of Wall Street, or, in more recent years, along Madison Avenue. Many of these young men buy their clothes at America's most well-known "Gentleman's Tailor," Brooks Brothers, which is conveniently located on Madison Avenue, only a few blocks away from all three clubs. The cut of one's coat is a manifestly superficial, but perhaps not unimportant, mark of social standing. Not only is Brooks Brothers conveniently located in New York; it also contributes to the creation of a national upper-class uniform for men, as it were, through its branch stores in Boston, Chicago, San Francisco, and Los Angeles, as well as its traveling representatives who visit America's major cities several times each year. Neither "nationally advertised" nor quantitatively produced, this venerable old clothing firm has set a pattern for the gentleman's suit and shirt in America.

The metropolitan club system is simulated in smaller American communities. One meets ex-governors and senators as well as wealthy coal barons at the Westmoreland Club in Wilkes-Barre, Pennsylvania. Of the fourteen residents of Wilkes-Barre listed in the 1940 *Who's Who*, for example, ten—a congressman, a public utility executive, capitalist, lawyer, two publishers, the two leading bankers, and two coal operators—were members of the Westmoreland Club (characteristically, a composer, a clergyman, psychiatrist, and a journalist were not members). Sinclair Lewis describes the club system in smalltown America with characteristic insight. George Babbitt and his fellow-members of the Zenith Athletic Club, according to Lewis, "envy the conservative Union Club, which all sound members of the Athletic call 'a rotten, snobbish, dull, expensive old hole—not one Good Mixer in the place—you couldn't hire me to join!' Statistics show that no member of the Athletic has ever refused election to the Union, and of those who are elected, sixty-seven per cent resign from the Athletic and are thereafter heard to say, in the drowsy sanctity of the Union lounge, 'The Athletic would be a pretty good hotel, if it were more exclusive.' "[13]

Finally, the metropolitan club serves as a social bond between small-town leaders and their metropolitan peers. Of the eight residents of Muncie (*Middletown*), Indiana, listed in the 1940 *Who's Who*, six, including two members of the Ball family, the presidents of the Merchants National Bank and Ball State Teachers College, and the president of Glascock Brothers, a local manufacturing establishment, were members of the Columbia Club in Indianapolis. The national club membership of Charles S. Davis, president of Glascock Brothers, aptly illustrates the nature of the national elite in America. His ten club memberships listed in *Who's Who* included, in addition to the Columbia in Indianapolis, the Chicago and Union League in Chicago, the Northport Yacht in Michigan, and the Bath and Tennis and Everglades Clubs in Palm Beach, Florida. A graduate of Harvard in 1899, his residences included an apartment in Chicago, a house in Muncie, and resort residences in Michigan and Palm Beach. It is interesting that the two Ball brothers, the original family founders, limited their out-of-town clubs to the Columbia Club, and also belonged to the Athletic and Rotary Clubs in Muncie; both were educated in the public schools and did not graduate from college. As a footnote, however, to increasing centralization of the upper class in America, Edmund F.

Ball, president of the family firm today, was a graduate of Ashville School, a boarding school of which he is now a trustee, and Yale College in 1928; his clubs include the Columbia in Indianapolis, and the Yale Club in New York City.

The Philadelphia Metropolitan Club Hierarchy. Like other large cities in the English-speaking world, Philadelphia has a well-structured club hierarchy. Fifteen metropolitan clubs were mentioned most frequently by Philadelphians in their *Who's Who* biographies (see Table 32). Most of the city's prominent business, professional, and civic leaders were members of either the Philadelphia, Rittenhouse, Union League, or Locust Clubs. The Philadelphia and Rittenhouse Clubs, most of whose members were listed in the *Social Register,* were the most important upper-class clubs; the less fashionable Union League was the most popular elite club; while the Locust, often referred to as the "Jewish Union League," was the leading Jewish club in the city. As membership in any of these clubs was a symbol of power and influence in the city, as might be expected, 59 per cent of the Union League, 67 per cent of the Philadelphia, 68 per cent of the Rittenhouse, and 86 per cent of the Locust Club membership within the elite were businessmen, lawyers, or engineers (the business elite, as defined in Chapter III).

The Franklin Inn, Art Alliance, and University clubs were far less important factors in the distribution of power and prestige in the city (only 20, 16, and 39 per cent, respectively, of the members of these three clubs were drawn from the business elite). Membership in any one of these clubs was almost entirely a matter of intellectual, artistic, or literary interest and accomplishment. The Franklin Inn, a male club in the tradition of London's Athenaeum, was composed of those who had either published something themselves, were in the publishing field, or had an interest in literature (S. Weir Mitchell was a founder and first president of the club). The University Club was made up of a congenial group of university men. Finally, the Art Alliance, whose membership included both men and women, was devoted to the promotion of the arts and crafts. In contrast to the other metropolitan clubs, both the Art Alliance and the Franklin Inn draw members from both the Gentile and Jewish communities.

The Racquet and Penn Athletic Clubs were, as their names imply, male clubs with athletic facilities. The former was an upper-class club while the latter had a predominantly middle-class membership. The rest of the clubs in Table 32 were common-interest and functionally oriented. Their titles explain their purpose and criteria for membership (the Lenape Club is a private eating club run by members of the faculty at the University of Pennsylvania).

The Union League, in the considered judgment of the city's major historians and a vast majority of its citizens, is "the leading club in the Quaker City."[14] Situated south of City Hall on Broad Street, in the heart of commercial Philadelphia, the Union League club-house, a massive and impressive Victorian structure, is a familiar Philadelphia landmark. Founded in 1862 by such prominent members of the Philadelphia elite as Morton McMichael, editor (*Saturday Evening Post*), mayor, and first president of the city's beloved Park Commission, and George H. Boker, poet, diplomat (Minister to Turkey and Russia), and the handsomest Philadelphian of his day, the League rapidly assumed a commanding position in national politics. Leagues were founded in other northern cities, of which the New York and Chicago Union League still remain. During the Civil War the Union League, whose mem-

Table 32—*Philadelphians in Who's Who in 1940—Reported Memberships in Metropolitan Clubs as Related to Social Class*

| | SOCIAL | | CLASS | |
| | Social Register | | Non Social Register | |
	No.	%	No.	%
Male Social Clubs				
*Philadelphia Club	56	(98)	1	(2)
*Rittenhouse Club	58	(88)	8	(12)
*Union League	57	(42)	80	(58)
Locust Club	0	(—)	7	(100)
Common Interest Clubs				
*Franklin Inn Club	22	(61)	14	(39)
*University Club	47	(54)	40	(46)
*Art Alliance	43	(59)	30	(41)
Athletic Clubs				
*Racquet Club	41	(80)	10	(20)
Penn Athletic Club	11	(29)	27	(71)
Functional Clubs				
Lawyers Club	1	(9)	10	(91)
Engineers Club	11	(39)	17	(61)
Mfg. & Bankers Club	9	(20)	37	(80)
Lenape Club†	3	(21)	11	(79)
Rotary	1	(6)	17	(94)

* These clubs are listed in the *Social Register*; the rest are not so listed.
† This club is the faculty club at the University of Pennsylvania. All members of the faculty do not neecessarily belong as it is a private club run by the members.

bers included one thousand of Philadelphia's wealthiest citizens, "sent into the field nine regiments, two battalions, and a troop of cavalry, all armed and equipped at the expense of the club."[15] The present club-house, "one of the finest in the world," was built in 1865 at the high cost for that day of $200,000. A bastion of business and Republican respectability down through the years, "the Union League has been noted for the beauty and elegance of its receptions, which have invariably been attended by the highest society in Philadelphia."[16] The first grand reception at the Union League was tendered to Lieutenant-General U. S. Grant after the Union victory in 1865. President McKinley, whose term in office marked the high watermark of Republican and business power in America, was a frequent visitor at the Union League (this author's ancient barber had the honor of cutting President McKinley's hair at the Union League just two days before his assassination in 1901 in Buffalo, New York).

In 1940 more Philadelphians listed in *Who's Who* were members of the Union League than any other club in the city, and it is safe to say that most Philadelphians have stereotyped this Republican stronghold as the center of "upper crust" dominance in the city's affairs—"Union Leaguers run the city whichever party is in power."

Social perspective varies, however, with one's position in the social structure. Thus the Proper Philadelphian regards membership in the Philadelphia Club, and not the Union League, as the hallmark of gentlemanly antecedents and business accomplishment (see Table 32, where 98 per cent of the Philadelphia Club members, as against 42 per cent of the members of the Union League, were also listed in the *Social Register*). Moreover, contrary to the popular stereotype, the Philadelphia Club, and the somewhat less exclusive Rittenhouse Club, were more powerful and influential forces in the business and cultural life of the city in 1940 than the Union League (see below, Chapter XIV).

The Philadelphia and Rittenhouse Clubs: Upper-Class Status-Ascribing Associations. The primary function of the Philadelphia and Rittenhouse clubs is the ascription of upper-class status. The continuing strength of the British aristocracy has been partly due to the fact that an hereditary nobility was always balanced by an ample supply of new titled men of merit. While titles are taboo in

Table 33—Philadelphians in Who's Who in 1940—High Prestige Social Characteristics as Related to Philadelphia and Rittenhouse Club Membership, and Social Register and Non-Social Register Affiliation

High Prestige Social Characteristics	Philadelphia Club Members		Rittenhouse Club Members		Social Register		Non Social Register	
	No.	%	No.	%	No.	%	No.	%
Born in Philadelphia	43	(75)	34	(52)	118	(52)	160	(29)
Listed in Social Register as of 1900	35	(61)	19	(30)	69	(30)	—	
Reside in Chestnut Hill or the Main Line	44	(77)	44	(67)	139	(61)	97	(18)
Episcopalians	33	(58)	27	(41)	95	(42)	74	(14)
Attend St. Paul's, Groton or St. Mark's	10	(18)	2	(3)	14	(6)	1	(—)
Attended University of Pennsylvania	16	(28)	20	(30)	63	(28)	108	(20)
Attended Harvard, Yale, or Princeton	21	(37)	14	(21)	51	(22)	26	(5)
Engaged in Finance	14	(25)	12	(18)	24	(11)	8	(1)
Total Number in Each Category	57	(100)	66	(100)	226	(100)	544	(100)
Mean Number of Children Reported Per Parent	3.30		2.89		2.80		2.61	

our democratic society, business gentlemen of distinguished antecedents are continuously blended with men of distinguished achievement within the halls of the aristocratic Philadelphia and
Rittenhouse clubs. On the whole, pedigree and fashionable background is more highly valued at the Philadelphia Club: thus
the members of the Philadelphia Club are more likely than their
peers in the Rittenhouse Club to have been born in Philadelphia;
to have been listed in the *Social Register* in 1900; to have attended
fashionable schools and colleges; and to be Episcopalians and
financiers. Finally, as family size may vary directly with high
ascribed status and inherited wealth, the large families reported
by its members is further evidence of the aristocratic standing of
the Philadelphia Club (see Table 33).

The Philadelphia Club has been a Proper Philadelphia stronghold since its founding in 1834. The first Chairman of the club was
George Cadwalader (1834), the first president was Commodore
James Biddle (1845-1848), and the president at its 100th anniversary was Owen Wister.[17] Through the years members of the
Philadelphia Club have, of course, dominated the management of
the annual Assembly Balls.* Of the eighteen directors of the Assembly between 1820 and 1840, eight were founding members of the
club; in 1940, five of the six Assembly Managers were club
members.[18] An inspection of the names of the 2,101 members of
the club between 1834 and 1940 reads like an economic and social
history of Philadelphia. Among the old-family members of the
club there have been thirty-five Biddles, seventeen Morrises, sixteen Coxes, fourteen Peppers, thirteen Cadwaladers (three presidents), twelve Whartons, eleven Ingersolls, ten Bories, ten Willings,
ten Woods, seven Merricks, seven Rushes, and six Drexels, as well
as several Pembertons, Pemroses, Chews, Hopkinsons, Walns,
Ridgeways, Dallases, Meades, Lippincotts, Harrisons, Rosengartens, and Cassatts. Such members as Anthony Drexel Cassatt,
A. J. Drexel Paul, and the two A. J. Drexel Biddles suggest the
consanguinity of the membership as well as the prestige of the
great banker's name.[19]

The circulation of elites in Philadelphia is stabilized in each
generation by the assimilation of the descendants of newer family
founders within this inner circle of Proper Philadelphians. Thus

---

* Since 1940, all the Assembly Managers have also been members of the
Philadelphia Club.

a Biddle, Borie, Pepper, Cadwalader, Norris, Wharton, Ingersoll, Willing, Chew, Waln, Dallas, and a Ridgeway were among the original members of the club at its founding in 1834, while Morrises, Coxes, Rosengartens, and Hopkinsons joined soon afterwards; Drexels, Lippincotts, and Cassatts were assimilated between the Civil War and 1900; finally, between 1920 and 1940, the club absorbed one member from each of the Elkins, Widener, Disston, Clothier, and Wanamaker families.[20]

There are, by and large, two ways to enter the Philadelphia Club. First, every year a small group of younger men in their twenties and thirties, invariably relatives of present members, are taken into the club. This group of younger men forms the nucleus of ascribed members in their generation. Second, certain capable men who have achieved a high and respected position in the business and cultural life of the city are taken into the club each year. As they meet, and are liked by Philadelphia Club members —on school and hospital boards, in the neighborhood, through civic and charitable activities of all kinds, and through common membership in other clubs and associations—these new men are asked to join. They are rarely proposed for membership, however, until they have proved themselves occupationally. A room-mate at Princeton, for instance, would not be asked to join the club by his old Philadelphia friends when he was still in his twenties. They would wait until he had made his mark in business. In other words, as each generation of ascribed members of the Philadelphia Club take their places in the business and cultural life of the city, they bring into the club those of their contemporaries whom they (and their fathers) consider "worth-while" and, above all, congenial. These "new men," in turn, have sons who will become ascribed members of the club at a young age. The self-made man finds that club membership is one of the best entrées into the upper class, and one of the best ways of passing on his achieved position to his family.

One might meet among the old-family members of the Philadelphia Club, some charming and congenial wastrels and even nonconformist intellectuals. The new men, however, are invariably worth-while men of power and influence, with more than the ordinary desire to conform to upper-class values and rituals. These new men are most likely to be men of executive ability and leadership rather than men of purely professional accomplishment. In short, they are prominent members of the goal-integrating elite, as defined in Chapter III. Needless to say, few, if any, professors have ever been among the achieved generation of club members.

Of the Philadelphia Club members listed in *Who's Who* in 1940, no less than two-thirds were engaged in finance, law, or business. Partly, this results from the fact that the old-family ascribed members who are making a career in business, finance, or law are most likely to find the Philadelphia Club of use to them in their careers. Membership may be a luxury to those in other lines of work, although they may be of similar social background. And, as we have said, the new men are predominantly businessmen. This is aptly illustrated, for example, in the backgrounds of the fifty-seven members of the club who were listed in the 1940 *Who's Who*. Twenty-five, or less than one-half, had been members of the club since World War I. Of these twenty-five men, ten were physicians, professors (in the medical and law schools of the University), architects, or authors; all ten were listed in the *Social Register* as of 1900—the ascribed generation. But, of the eleven men taken into the club since 1930—the achived generation—*all* were either bankers, lawyers, or businessmen.

The assimilation of powerful outsiders within the halls of the Philadelphia Club does not always please all members, especially those who revere tradition or, for one reason or another, are no longer active in business. That classic Proper Bostonian, "The Late George Apley," the protagonist in J. P. Marquand's novel, illustrates a point of view which might easily apply at the Philadelphia Club. When two of his more opportunistic peers at the Province Club, "the best club in Boston," proposed a prominent businessman for membership, George Apley, holding steadfast to principle, wrote the following letter to the Admissions Committee:

My dear Sirs:—

I noticed today on the bulletin board that the name of Marcus Ransome has been proposed by Mr. Storrel Moore and Mr. Franklin Fields for resident membership in the Province Club. I wish to express myself as unalterably opposed to his admission.

I do not object to Ransome personally and I have sat with him about the directors' tables of several small companies in which we are both associated. Although he has only been in Boston for ten years, he has good manners and is superficially a gentleman. He may not possess the same background and antecedents which characterize most members of the Province Club but I do not believe that his appearance here would be objectionable. I wish to make it clear that it is not because of Ransome personally that I move to oppose him.

Rather, I move to oppose the motive which actuates Messrs. Moore and Fields in putting this man up for membership. They are not doing so because of family connections, nor because of disinterested friendship, but rather because of business reasons. It is, perhaps, too well known for me to mention it that Mr. Ransome has been instrumental in bringing a very large amount of New York business to the banking house of Moore and Fields. This I do not think is reason enough to admit Mr. Ransome to the Province Club, a club which exists for social and not for business purposes. I, for one, shall feel that the Club has lost much of what is good in it if the Committee acts favorably on Mr. Ransome. I am sending a copy of this letter to Mr. Moore and another to Mr. Fields. . . .[21]

Business mores and the profit motive, despite the stereotypes held by the liberal reformer, have a way of destroying caste. At any rate, sociological continuity is inevitably a balance between the aristocratic and democratic aspects of social organization. The exclusive Philadelphia Club functions to provide a congenial, primary-group setting where Proper Philadelphians may spend their leisure time among their friends; there is also the latent, and perhaps more important, function of blending men of ascribed and achieved upper-class status, in order to maintain a continuity of control over important positions in the business world (see Chapter XIV). While Philadelphia Club membership is the final criterion of Proper Philadelphia's acceptance of new men of power, the Rittenhouse Club has an important role to play in the process of assimilation.

The Rittenhouse Club is younger than the Philadelphia Club and easier of access. Although members of distinguished old Philadelphia families belong to both clubs—some Peppers belong to the Philadelphia and some to the Rittenhouse—on the whole, the younger club is the first to accept worth-while self-made men. That is to say, while the Philadelphia Club passes the final word on acceptance within the inner circles of Proper Philadelphia, membership in the Rittenhouse Club is often the first step toward attaining this exalted status. Of the eleven businessmen taken into the Philadelphia Club since 1930, for example, seven had previously been members of the Rittenhouse Club (from between two to eighteen years). The new and ambitious men of power in the city move from the Union League, to the Rittenhouse, and, eventually, to the Philadelphia Club. Many men of older pedigree happen to prefer the Rittenhouse, and some of these, with more than the usual sense of humor, rather cynically regard their more aggressive peers as using the Rittenhouse as a "waiting-club" before the final conquest.

Founded in 1875 by such leading Philadelphians as S. Weir Mitchell and William Pepper (both Philadelphia Club members), the Rittenhouse Club is located on Walnut Street in one of the few remaining Victorian mansions on the Square.[22] It is appropriate that this younger club, founded as it was in the days of Rittenhouse Square's greatest glory, should be located uptown on Walnut Street, while the older club remains downtown in the older part of the city (see Map 1). Originally founded as the "Social Art Club" (changed to the "Rittenhouse Club" in 1888), the members of the Rittenhouse Club are somewhat more intellectually and artistically inclined than their more sporting peers in the older club. This difference is, of course, a subtle one; the fact that the Diocesan Headquarters of the Episcopal Church is across the street, and that the club is nearer the University of Pennsylvania out in West Philadelphia may contribute to this atmosphere. At lunchtime, at the Rittenhouse, one is more likely to meet men of the cloth, and even professors. While presidents of the Pennsylvania Railroad and the city's leading bankers eventually gravitate towards the Philadelphia Club, the Provosts and Presidents of the University often find the Rittenhouse Club quite satisfactory.

The Rittenhouse Club is not only more closely associated with the University, but in almost every way its members tend to have been less rigidly brought up in the orthodox fashionable tradition (see Table 33). Consistently, the members of the younger club who were listed in *Who's Who* were less likely to have been born in the city, listed in the 1900 *Social Register,* to have been educated at the prestige schools and colleges, and to reside in the fashionable neighborhoods. Finally, of course, of the nine members of the Rittenhouse and Philadelphia clubs who were not listed in the *Social Register,* all save one belonged to the Rittenhouse Club only. The one member of the Philadelphia Club who was not listed in the *Social Register,* the exception which proves (illustrates) the rule, was a member of both clubs in 1940. A brief outline of his career will illustrate the roles played by these two clubs in the structuring of the upper class.

This deviant Philadelphia Club member was born in Philadelphia in 1867, and was educated in the public schools and at Lafayette College. He was a Justice of the Supreme Court of Pennsylvania from 1921 to 1940 when he became Chief Justice. A leading member of the bench and bar, he was taken into the Rittenhouse Club in 1926, at the age of fifty-nine, and the Philadelphia Club in 1935, at the age of sixty-eight. He is married and reports no children in his *Who's Who* biography. A man with no children to place in "society," perhaps the Chief Justice has no need for *Social Register* listing. He probably enjoys the company of Philadelphia gentlemen, who, in turn, welcome (the older club more belatedly) a man of such prestige and power in the community. That he has no son eligible for ascribed Philadelphia Club membership may conceivably have been a factor in the situation.

Following the pattern outlined by Frederick Lewis Allen (with reference to the leading financiers in New York at the turn of the century), the aristocratic mold in Philadelphia is fired in the halls of these two leading upper-class clubs. Each has its subtle role to play in the process: on the whole, the younger club is a testing ground for final inclusion in the older club. First of all, younger men in each generation who are sons and relatives of present members are taken into the Rittenhouse Club in much the same way as was shown to be the case with the older club. In addition, however, the younger club is more likely to admit promising young men who are friends of the younger members. One could, for example, bring one's college roommate from out-of-town into the Rittenhouse Club. This rarely happens at the older club. Of course, the crucial difference between the two clubs comes at the older ages. Pedigree and power are less important as far as the Rittenhouse Club is concerned. Moreover, as we have seen, the new men of power are usually accepted by the Rittenhouse Club first. Concretely, the pattern is somewhat as follows: A member of the Philadelphia elite in 1940 was not listed in the *Social Register* until just before the First World War; he was a member of the Rittenhouse Club and listed in the *Social Register* as of 1930; and, finally, in 1940, he was a member of both the Rittenhouse and Philadelphia clubs; his sons prefer the Philadelphia Club only. Thus is the Philadelphia aristocracy recruited. And it is a surprisingly democratic process, and, in a sense, open to talent—provided one wants to play the game.

While the upper class is differentiated from the rest of the elite by the Philadelphia and Rittenhouse Clubs, other clubs in the city are more or less important links in the chain of social prestige. Members of both these two leading clubs belong to other clubs in the city. The overlapping of memberships in the Philadelphia, Rittenhouse and Union League Clubs takes on an interesting pattern. A higher proportion of Philadelphia Club members belong to the Rittenhouse Club than vice versa (39 per cent versus 33 per cent). Thus, at least for one generation, those who have achieved Philadelphia Club membership, still retain membership in their older club. More important, except for their retention of membership in the Rittenhouse, the members of the more exclusive club are less likely to belong to any of the other metropolitan clubs. This is especially marked in the case of the Union League. Thus only 14 per cent of the Philadelphia Club members belong to the Union League as against almost half or 38 per cent of the Rittenhouse Club members who retain membership in this elite club. The pattern is clear. As new men succeed in business, they join the Union League as a matter of course. If they eventually join the Rittenhouse, often at advanced ages, they retain membership in the Union League. If they then go on to the Philadelphia Club, however, they may drop out of the League. One gentleman in the 1940 elite, for example, was quite a clubman back before the First World War. His club listings in a pre-war *Social Register* amounted to ten clubs in all, including the Union League, University, and Rittenhouse Clubs. With his entrance into the Philadelphia Club in the late thirties, however, his club listings in *Who's Who* in 1940, included the Philadelphia and Rittenhouse only.

The Racquet Club, different in kind from the Philadelphia, Rittenhouse, and Union League, is only in a limited sense a "waiting-club" for inclusion in one of the two exclusive men's club. More sporting and democratic in atmosphere, it is, nevertheless, typed among Philadelphia citizenry as definitely upper-class. Although not limited by any means to members of the upper class, the Racquet serves as the one city club for a large number of fashionable Philadelphians. Especially is this the case in these days of suburban living. Many very Proper Philadelphians are perfectly content with this club as their only in-town affiliation. In fact, many Racquet Club members only reluctantly join the Philadelphia Club in their later years because of its usefulness in business, especially at the higher echelons. As a matter of subtle fact, it is probably true that, at the younger ages, more Philadelphia Club talent, as it were, limits its membership to the Racquet Club than men of the same age in the Rittenhouse Club.

In order to complete the picture of the metropolitan club structure in Philadelphia and its relationship to upper-class formation, additional data on upper-class wives should be provided. In every large city there are one or two upper-class clubs for women (called "hen clubs" in London). "Seemingly patterned on an English men's club rather than the usual American informal type of women's club," writes Cleveland Amory, "the Chilton is in reality Boston's female Somerset . . . in the Proper Boston woman's parlance 'everybody in Boston' belongs to it, everybody being understood to mean a select five hundred, or about one-tenth of one per cent of the city's female population."[23]

In Philadelphia, the Acorn Club is the female Philadelphia Club. Like the Chilton in Boston, "everybody" belongs. Of the fifty-four females listed in *Who's Who*, only six report membership in the Acorn Club; all six were also listed in the *Social Register*. On the other hand, seventy-seven of the males listed in *Who's Who* had wives who were members of this exclusive female version of the Philadelphia Club. Of these seventy-seven wives of the elite members of the upper class, 56, or 73 per cent, had husbands who belonged to either the Philadelphia or Rittenhouse Clubs. Moreover, the members of the older men's club were more likely to have wives in the Acorn Club; 68 per cent of the elite members of the Philadelphia Club, as against 47 per cent of the Rittenhouse Club members, had wives who lunched at the Acorn Club. Whether the wives of patriarchal Proper Philadelphians lunch at the Acorn Club before going to the Orchestra on Friday afternoons, is related presumably to whether their husbands walk down, or up, Walnut Street for lunch. Attendance at the Friday afternoon concerts of the Philadelphia Orchestra is an upper-class ritual among Proper Philadelphia females as well as males with a free afternoon. On winter Friday afternoons, Locust Street, from just off the Square where the Acorn Club is located, to the old Academy of Music at Broad Street, is a parade of fashionably-dressed women and chauffeur-driven black automobiles.

The Suburban Clubs: Family Centers of Sporting Activities. Membership in the correct country club, often the decisive index of social position in the small American community, is not necessarily an accurate indicator of social prestige within Philadelphia's upper class. The gentry in John O'Hara's coal towns of Pennsylvania are known as the "country club set." And perhaps the term even applies in such cities as Minneapolis, Cincinnati, or St. Louis. In Philadelphia, however, the higher one goes in the social class hierarchy, the less important the role of the country club is in leisure-time activities. There are numerous first families along the Main Line and in Chestnut Hill who are never seen at country clubs even if they belong, and many do not. A Proper Chicagoan, who visits in Chestnut Hill, would meet his host's friends in their own houses; in Lake Forest, the Philadelphian would be more likely to meet his Proper Chicagoan's friends at various elaborate country clubs. In contrast to the seriousness surrounding one's metropolitan club standing, the Proper Philadelphian does not think of the suburban club in terms of social exclusiveness, but in terms of the congeniality of sporting interests. The inevitable restriction on membership is made largely to avoid overcrowding the athletic facilities. All this is not to say that certain suburban clubs are not exclusive and extremely homogeneous in membership. They are, and to achieve membership is considered quite an accomplishment by many people, especially those who are excluded, for one reason or another.

The nine suburban clubs listed most frequently in the *Who's Who* biographies of the Philadelphia elite were the Radnor Hunt, Gulph Mills, Merion Cricket, and Philadelphia Country Club, on the Main Line; the Philadelphia Cricket and Sunnybrook in Chestnut Hill; the Germantown Cricket in Germantown; and the Huntington Valley Country and Philmont Country in the Jenkintown or Old York Road area (see Table 34 and Map 2). All these clubs are listed in the *Social Register* except the Philmont Country Club which is the leading upper-class Jewish suburban club in the city. The fact that so few (less than 50 in each case) members of the Philadelphia elite, even upper-class members, bother to list these clubs in their *Who's Who* biographies indicates the low value, in terms of social status, placed on membership. A Proper Philadelphian would be sure to list the fact that he belonged to the Philadelphia Club as a mark of his superior standing in the community; he would feel his membership in the Merion Cricket Club to be quite incidental. The somewhat insecure new man may feel compelled to list a multitude of club memberships in his *Who's Who* biographies, including his suburban clubs and such resort clubs as the Bar Harbor, or Mount Desert, or the Bath and Tennis in Palm Beach. To the uninitiated, the Proper Philadelphian who lists only the Philadelphia Club in his *Who's Who* biography may be socially inferior to his fellow-elite member with a dozen lesser clubs after his name. This lack of appreciation of the former gentleman's superior position by the masses, of course, pleases the Proper Philadelphian who prefers to impress his peers but is rather uninterested in, and almost prefers not to be recognized by, the rest of the population. It is no accident that a new-rich, parvenu culture such as ours values quantity rather than quality. A clubman is a clubman, and the more clubs the better.

The country club is a peculiarly American institution. In many ways it is America's associational answer to the British country-house weekend. The exclusive American country club is, in a sense, a highly democratic institution: here, for the first time, is a club that does not discriminate on the basis of age or sex; whole families belong to these private weekend suburban resorts with their all-

Table 34—*Philadelphians in Who's Who in 1940—Selected Suburban Clubs in the Philadelphia Area as Related to Neighborhood and Social Class**

	SOCIAL		CLASS	
	Social Register		Non Social Register	
Neighborhood				
Suburban Club	No.	%	No.	%
Main Line				
Radnor Hunt Club	9	(100)	—	
Gulph Mills Golf Club	13	(100)	—	
Merion Cricket Club	33	(72)	13	(28)
Philadelphia Country Club†	13	(38)	21	(62)
Chestnut Hill				
Sunnybrook Golf Club	21	(96)	1	(4)
Philadelphia Cricket Club	25	(86)	4	(14)
Germantown				
Germantown Cricket Club	7	(70)	3	(30)
Jenkintown				
Huntington Valley Country Club	12	(75)	4	(25)
Philmont Country Club	—		10	(100)

* These suburban clubs were the ones most frequently listed by those in *Who's Who*. All but the Philmont Country Club are also listed in the *Social Register*.
† The Philadelphia Country Club is actually located both in the West Philadelphia area as shown in Map 1, and on the Main Line. The main club-house is situated within the city limits but the golf course is further out on the Main Line. Sociologically, we shall consider it a Main Line, although hardly an upper-class, club.

inclusive athletic facilities from golf and tennis to drinking and dancing. Along with the suburban trend which characterized the 1920's, the great American middle class turned "cowpastures into rich tourney fields," as Sinclair Lewis has it, and the golf course, locker-room, and Saturday night dance at the country club became indispensable partners in every bond or real estate salesman's family success story. A thoroughly middle-class institution today, the country club idea took hold among the wealthy elite in America in the last part of the nineteenth century. Henry James, whose whole world was limited to "society," found in the country club after the turn of the century, a "deeply significant American symbol."

The "millionaire's colony" at Tuxedo Park, New York, is often considered to be the first American country club. This honor belongs, however, to The Country Club, founded in Brookline (Chestnut Hill), Massachusetts in 1882.[24] According to Dixon Wecter, Tuxedo, although hardly a typical country club, has remained the "prince of the type" down through the years.[25] It was founded in 1886 by Pierre Lorillard II, of the snuff and tobacco family, on some 600,000 acres of his own land, and built at the cost of two million dollars. Situated west of the vast Harriman holdings, near Bear Mountain, Tuxedo is a kind of country club *cum* family resort where some two or three hundred of New York's "Best People who were growing tired of resort-hotels at Saratoga or Richfield Springs might come to hunt, fish, and skate."[26] From 1886 to the present day, the New York social season unofficially opens each autumn with the launching of a selected group of fashionable debutantes at the Tuxedo Ball.

There is no "millionaire's colony" like Tuxedo in suburban Philadelphia. True to form, the Proper Philadelphian is more likely to model his suburban clubs along the Main Line and Chestnut Hill in the British tradition. American and British club mores are nicely contrasted by an Englishman, George Birmingham, in the following passage:

There are also all over England clubs especially devoted to particular objects, golf clubs, yacht clubs, and so forth. In these the members are drawn together by their interest in a common pursuit, and are forced into some kind of acquaintanceship. But these are very different in spirit and intention from the American country club. It exists as a kind of center of the social life of the neighborhood. Sport is encouraged by these clubs for the sake of general sociability. In England sociability is a by-product of an interest in sport.

The country club at Tuxedo is not perhaps the oldest, but it is one of the oldest institutions of its kind in America. At the proper time of year there are dances, and a debutante acquires, I believe, a certain prestige by "coming out" at one of them. But the club exists primarily as the social center of Tuxedo. It is in one way the ideal, the perfect country club. It not only fosters, it regulates and governs the social life of the place.[27]

Cricket clubs, rather than the typical American country clubs, have been centers of Proper Philadelphia sporting activities since before the Civil War. Although the leisurely game of cricket died out in Philadelphia due to the increasingly rapid pace of life required by the getting and spending of the booming twenties, three of the oldest cricket clubs, the Philadelphia (1854), Germantown (1855), and Merion (1865), are today among the leading tennis and squash racquet clubs in the city. The Philadelphia and Merion Cricket Clubs also have excellent golf facilities.

Cricket was probably introduced into the American colonies during the eighteenth century.[28] Benjamin Franklin brought back a copy of the laws of cricket after one of his trips to England, and John Adams, in a discussion of an appropriate name for the chief executive, referred to the fact that there were "presidents of fire companies and of a cricket club." The history of the rise and fall of Philadelphia cricket provides interesting insight into the nature of the social structure of the city as a whole and the upper class in particular.

The British gentleman, "whose cricket is his chivalry," supposedly absorbed his code of manners and morals on the playing fields of Eton and other public schools. This gentlemen's game, however, reached maturity in England during the half-century preceding the Reform Bill, a rough-and-tumble age when cricket-players smelled of the pub and the betting ring, matches were bought and sold, players bribed, and bookmakers "shouted the odds in front of the pavilion at Lord's."[29] Modern American baseball is milk-toast mild compared to this "gentlemen's" game in its early days.

In Philadelphia, cricket probably first became popular among the lower classes. Originally played on the southern downs, cricket spread to the great industrial centers of northern England in the early nineteenth century. A rapidly expanding textile industry drew many skilled hands from the dark satanic mills of Nottingham and Lancaster to Philadelphia. In the 1840's, wrote an early historian of the game, "most of the players in Germantown were Nottingham men."[30] As the first cricket in Philadelphia was closely bound up with "stakes and ale," cricket clubs were formed by anxious parents in the 1850's to protect their sons from contaminating associations. The cricket clubs gave the game an air of respectability.

Proper Philadelphia sporting life centered around the cricket clubs during the period between the Civil War and World War I. Haverford College is traditionally credited with having the first cricket club composed of all native-born American youth, and during the last part of the nineteenth century many local schools and some two hundred private clubs participated in the game.[31] The first international matches in Philadelphia were played in 1868 and 1872; an Australian eleven visited the city in 1878, and Philadelphia teams visited England in 1889 and 1897. The two best-known Philadelphia cricket families were the Newhalls and the Clarks who played for Germantown in the days of that suburb's greatest glory. Two members of the Newhall family were listed in *Who's Who* in 1940, as were J. Henry Scattergood and George Wharton Pepper, leading cricketeers of this earlier era. In 1895, a visiting British eleven was surprised to find four top cricket clubs (Germantown, Philadelphia, Merion, and Belmont) in Philadelphia, while London boasted only two of comparable stature.[32]

Cricket was an important connecting link between St. Paul's School and Proper Philadelphia for many years.[33] More than at any other school, cricket was a major sport at St. Paul's for almost fifty years. Through the arrangements of Thomas McKean, president of the Germantown club, the school eleven played a week's cricket in Philadelphia three times between 1884 and 1891, and Haverford College went up to Concord for a match in 1893. Germantown Academy was the most important day school in the history of Philadelphia cricket, while the University of Pennsylvania had excellent teams in the days when a majority of Proper Philadelphians still went there (Horace Mather Lippincott, an author listed in *Who's Who* in 1940, was a member of the University's eleven when it visited England in 1902).[34]

This gentlemen's game in Philadelphia began to decline just

before the first war. Writing in 1951, in *A Century of Philadelphia Cricket,* John A. Lester described the causes of this decline as follows:

> It is easy to overemphasize the change that has taken place since George Wharton Pepper defined sport as "the gentleman at play" in his great address at the Merion Cricket Club fifty years ago. It was that change that caused Paul Gallico to bid good-by to amateur sport in America in 1938.
>
> In Philadelphia, cricket was affected by both the impact of the industrial age, and by the recoil from that impact. Its impact built factories on cricket patches, and caused the genuine sportsman to seek relaxation in briefer and stronger doses; it created the money-seekers to supply them; it kept driving the vicarious sportsman to more hectic spectacles.[35]

The sociology of sport, a neglected aspect of the scientific literature, often provides fruitful insights into the nature of society at any given time. Changing sporting mores, and the changing social origins of the sportsmen, are often sensitive seismographs of social upheaval. During the 1920's the "gentleman at play" was replaced by the expert, and sport evolved from an avocation into a profession. The last qualified eleven of Philadelphia cricketeers visited England, for example, in 1921.[36] The English tour of the "Philadelphia Pilgrims"—the eleven included Morrises, Newhalls, Clothiers, and Edward Hopkinson, Jr., the senior Morgan partner in the city in 1940—symbolized the end of an era. Although the gentleman's game of cricket was soon replaced by more vigorous forms of sport which, like the martini, produces the desired results in a briefer period of time, the Merion, Germantown, and Philadelphia Cricket Clubs continued to prosper as centers of sporting activities, especially lawn tennis.

The 1920's witnessed the decline of lawn tennis as an upper-class sporting activity. Previous upper-class dominance of the game was symbolized by two Proper Philadelphia members of the Merion Cricket Club in 1940, William Jackson Clothier and Richard Norris Williams, who were champions of the United States in 1906, 1914, and 1916 respectively. Perhaps William Tatum Tilden, world lawn tennis champion in the age of ballyhoo, symbolized better than anyone the transition of American sport from an upper-class leisure-time pursuit to a full-time profession. Tilden was born in Philadelphia where he attended the Germantown Academy and the University of Pennsylvania and learned his tennis on the lawns of the Germantown Cricket Club. In 1929, after winning the United

States Championship for the seventh time, he became the most celebrated and notorious professional tennis player in the world. And it was a very different world from the cricket-playing Germantown of his youth.

The famous old Philadelphia cricket clubs continued to be active centers of tennis in 1940, even though Proper Philadelphians no longer played tennis of championship grade. In fact, the Australians took the Davis Cup back home after defeating the Americans in an historic match at the Merion Cricket Club just before World War II broke out in 1939 (the Australian victory over the United States in 1914 marked the beginning of the First World War).

At the time of World War I, when cricket was dying on the vine and golf was still an exclusively upper-class ritual, Proper Philadelphia golfing enthusiasts founded two golf clubs, Sunnybrook, on the Chestnut Hill side of the Schuylkill, and Gulph Mills on the Main Line. These were the most exclusive upper-class suburban clubs in 1940 (see Table 34). The Proper Philadelphia gentleman lunches at the Philadelphia and Rittenhouse Clubs during the week and plays golf at Sunnybrook or Gulph Mills over the weekend. Of the thirteen Gulph Mills and twenty-two Sunnybrook members listed in *Who's Who* in 1940, twelve and twenty one, respectively, also belonged to the Philadelphia or Rittenhouse Clubs in town. Although the members of these two clubs are, of course, primarily interested in using the athletic facilities, many are in the habit of bringing-out their daughters at dinner dances which are usually held each June and September in the modest ballrooms of these two clubs. By 1940, the cricket clubs were too democratic in atmosphere to suit the more socially circumspect Proper Philadelphia parents.

On the whole, the social prestige of the suburban clubs in Philadelphia tends to follow neighborhood. As the more exclusive neighborhoods are usually farther out from the center of the city, it is of interest to see that, on both the Main Line and in Chestnut Hill, the more exclusively upper-class clubs are farther out in the country than those of lesser status. On the Main Line, the Philadelphia Country, the Merion Cricket, the Gulph Mills Golf, and, finally, the Radnor Hunt are progressively farther from town, and, at the same time, have a progressively higher proportion of their members listed in the *Social Register*. Similarly, on the other side of the river, in Germantown and Chestnut Hill, the Germantown Cricket, Philadelphia Cricket, and, finally, the Sunnybrook Golf are increasingly upper-class clubs. As the facilities of the clubs nearer town become crowded and the neighborhood deteriorates, upper-class families move further out into the country and eventually build clubs for themselves. Before the first war, and even during the 1920's, for example, the Philadelphia Country Club was a stronghold of upper-class families; today it is no longer fashionable.

Most upper-class members of the elite belong to clubs on the Main Line or in Chestnut Hill. Just as persons also listed in the *Social Register* are unlikely to live south of the West Chester Pike, so none of the clubs listed in Table 3 are located in the Swarthmore-Wallingford-Media area. The Old York Road club pattern, moreover, reflects its changing social status. As we have seen, the Huntington Valley Country Club, although built by fashionable members of the upper class, is now primarily an elite club patronized by members of the North Philadelphia industrial elite. Appropriately enough, the first ranking country club in the Philadelphia Jewish community, Philmont, is located along the Old York Road.

For many parts of the English-speaking world, pink-coated gentlemen have traditionally hunted the fox, over hill and dale, on the back of a horse. Riding to the hounds has been the Philadelphia gentleman's favorite pastime ever since the eighteenth century. The first hunt club in Philadelphia was founded by a congenial group of gentlemen who had been in the habit of riding to the hounds in beautiful Gloucester County, New Jersey, across the Delaware River from Philadelphia. At a meeting in the Philadelphia Coffee House, at the southwest corner of Front and Market Streets, in 1766, the Gloucester Fox Hunting Club was founded by twenty-seven Proper Philadelphians with Benjamin Chew and Thomas Willing presiding and including John Cadwalader, Samuel, Anthony and Israel Morris, James Wharton, and Levi Hollingsworth, Robert Morris, John Dickinson, and Andrew Hamilton.[37] The city's first hunt club had a brief although vigorous history. The Revolution dispersed most of its members as "the intrepid hunter's spirit became the soldier's, and with very few exceptions, the club entered with an ardor and alacrity worthy of patriot souls into the service of the noble cause of an oppressed country."[38] No less than twenty-two members of the club were original members of the "First Troop of Philadelphia City Cavalry." After the Revolution the club was revived. Samuel Morris, Captain of the First City Troop during the conflict and Governor of the Schuylkill Fishing Company, was elected first president of the club, a post which he held until his death in 1812. The Gloucester Fox Hunting Club disbanded a few years later in 1818.

In 1940 there were various hunt clubs in all the Philadelphia suburbs. The Huntington Valley hounds chased the fox over the rolling Bucks County countryside; the gentlemen farmers of Penllyn and Fort Washington met their suburban friends from Chestnut Hill several times each week for an early morning hunt, at the Whitemarsh Valley Hunt Club, before going into town for a hard day of work; Mainliners follow the hounds at Radnor, Pickering, or out beyond Paoli, at Unionville; and those who live south of the West Chester Pike ride to the hounds at the Rose Tree Fox Hunting Club. Only the members of Radnor and Rose Tree see fit to list their hunt club affiliations in the *Social Register;* the others apparently do not bother. Of the Philadelphians in *Who's Who,* nine upper-class members listed membership in the Radnor Hunt Club (Table 34). It is interesting that, although most of the members of Radnor are quite naturally "to the saddle born," the fashionable hunt probably has more than the usual number of new horsemen who are just acquiring a taste for this aristocratic ritual. Many years ago, a caustic British Colonel remarked that one Radnor enthusiast, who has since devoted his life to the sport, was "the horsiest man on foot, and the footiest man on a horse" he had ever met.

The familistic simplicity of a great deal of upper-class life along the Main Line and Chestnut Hill sides of the river is reflected in small tennis and swimming clubs with unpretentious old Pennsylvania farm houses serving as club houses. No one would think of listing their membership in these clubs either in the *Social Register* or in *Who's Who,* yet the members are almost exclusively congenial, "nice" people from upper-class backgrounds. There are no cocktail bars, dining-rooms, or other conveniences so vital to the average country club. Social activities are centered around the family, especially young children. Far removed from the conspicuous leisure of the Veblen era, many Proper Philadelphians place a high value on these clubs. The dues are purposely nominal which is in accord with these days of declining upper-class opulence.

CHAPTER XIV

A Primary Group
of Prestige and Power

> The small group of individuals who control big-
> business and banking in this country are probably
> more conscious of their common interests than the
> members of any other so-called classes.
> RALPH LINTON

POMP without power paves the way for revolution. In the final
analysis, social stratification is an outgrowth of, and ultimately dependent on, the differential distribution of social power within any
community, and, of course, economic and political power are in-
divisible aspects of social power. In analyzing the growth of an
upper-class way of life in metropolitan America, and especially in
describing the social patina of Proper Philadelphia, there is a
danger that we lose sight of the main function of an upper class:
the perpetuation of its power in the world of affairs, whether in
the bank, the factory, or in the halls of the legislature. Whenever
an upper-class way of life becomes an end in itself, rather than a
means for consolidating its power and influence, that upper class
has outlived its function.

Although it may well be true that the ultimate social power in
America passed from Wall Street to Washington under the New
Deal, considerable financial and business power in Philadelphia remained in upper-class hands down to the eve of the Second World
War. Unlike his British prototype, as a matter of fact, the Proper
Philadelphian has always been, and still remains, a moneyed, rather
than a political, aristocrat. This chapter will be devoted to re-
emphasizing the nature of upper-class leadership in the economic
life of Philadelphia before 1940.

Where power is concerned, modern America often tends to be
hypocritical. Its leaders, especially the leaders of American busi-

ness, tend deliberately to perpetuate this hypocrisy. Perhaps this is to their own advantage, or perhaps they themselves really believe the myth of their own impotence. At any rate the facts of power, ideologically taboo in a democracy, are often hidden from the ordinary American citizen. In *The Irony of American History*, Reinhold Niebuhr finds this to be true to an alarming degree: "The knight of old knew about power," he writes. "He sat on a horse, the symbol of military power. But the power of the modern commercial community is contained in the 'counters' of stocks and bonds which are stored in the vaults of the bank. Such a community creates a culture in which nothing is known about power, however desperate the power struggles within it."[1]

Although it is manifestly difficult, for the reasons suggested by Niebuhr, to understand and articulate the power structure in Philadelphia, it is possible to state that in the 1930's the economic and cultural life of the city was still dominated by a small nucleus of Philadelphia and Rittenhouse Club members.

The close relationship which exists between a fashionable institution, e.g., the metropolitan men's club, and important executive decisions within the business community is of great importance. A surgeon makes a decision to operate after consultation at the hospital; the mergers of banks or industrial concerns are often planned by gentlemen of power within the halls of their exclusive clubs. Thus on the evening of December 12, 1900, two New Yorkers gave a dinner to Charles M. Schwab at the University Club; J. Pierpont Morgan accepted the invitation to attend.[2] The seed which was to eventually grow into the United States Steel Company was sown that night at the University Club. It is of sociological interest to record that the golf club also played a part in this historic business merger. After carefully consulting Mrs. Carnegie as to the best way of approaching her husband, Schwab persuaded the canny Scotch steelmaster to sell the Carnegie works to the Morgan group during a friendly round of golf on the St. Andrew's links in Westchester County.[3]

High-level executive decisions are often made by Proper Philadelphia bankers and businessmen within the halls of the Philadelphia and Rittenhouse Clubs. Out of the 770 Philadelphians listed in *Who's Who* in 1940, a small group—forty-two members of these two clubs—can be said to constitute a primary group of power and influence at the top of the social structure. We have placed these

Table 35—Philadelphians in Who's Who in 1940—Sociological Profiles of 42 Upper-Class Directors of High Prestige Economic and Cultural Institutions

Career Profiles

24 Males Born in Philadelphia and in Social Register in 1900

	A	B	C	D	E	F	G	H	I	J	K	L	M	N	O	P	Q	R	S	T	U	V	W	X
Directorships (Economic)																								
Phila. Saving Fund Soc.				x										P	x				x		x	x	x	
Western Saving Fund Soc.					x				x	x	P					C	x		x		x	x	x	
Penna. Co.*	x														x							x		x
Phila. Nat'l. Bank			x		x				x	x				x		P		x						
Fidelity Phila. Trust Co.				x																				
Girard Trust Co.								x	x	x			P					x	x					
Insurance Co. of N. Am.			x						x	x			x					C						
Penn Mutual Life Ins. Co.			x						x	x			x					x	x					
Penna. Railroad			x					x			x		x				x							
Directorships (Cultural)																								
Univ. of Penna.				x	x								x					x			x		x	
Franklin Institute				x	x				x	x												x		
Phila. Museum of Art									x	x		x												
Fairmont Park Art Assoc.																P								
Penna. Academy of Fine Arts						x				x					x									
Phila. Free Library							x						x											
Phila. Orchestra Assoc.										x													x	
Occupation																								
Finance	x	x	x		x	x		x	x	x	x	x	x	x	x		x	x	x	x	x	x	x	x
Law			x	x																				
Business	x	x	x		x	x		x	x		x	x	x		x		x	x	x	x	x	x	x	
Opinion													x											
Education																								

Neighborhood
  Main Line
  Chestnut Hill
  Other

Religion
  Episcopal
  Other Protestant
  No answer

Schooling
  Fashionable church schools
  Other private
  No private

College
  Univ. of Penna.
  Harvard-Yale-Princeton
  Other college
  No college

Family Size
  No. children

City Clubs
  Philadelphia Club
  Rittenhouse Club

P These men are Presidents of these institutions.
C These men were chairman of the Board of Directors.
* The Pennsylvania Company for Insurance on Lives and Granting of Annuities.

Table 35 (Continued)

Career Profiles	Born Philadelphia but not in S.R. 1900							Not Born Philadelphia in S.R. 1900					Not Born Philadelphia not in S.R. 1900					
	1	2	3	4	5	6	7	10	11	12	13	14	20	21	22	23	24	25
Directorships (Economic)																		
Phila. Saving Fund Soc.	x	x						x	x									
Western Saving Fund Soc.		x	x	x	x		x	x	x	x				x		x	x	
Penna. Co.*										x						x	x	
Phila. Nat'l Bank				x			P	x										
Fidelity Phila. Trust Co.						x												
Girard Trust Co.	x	C								x			x		x			x
Insurance Co. of N. Am.			x	x	x		x	x	x			x	x		x		x	
Penn Mutual Life Ins. Co.		x	x	x	x				P				x		P	x	x	
Penna. Railroad			x	x			x	x			x	x	x			x		
Directorships (Cultural)																		
University of Penna.	x			x	x							x	x	x	x	P		
Franklin Institute															x			
Phila. Museum of Art				x						x								
Fairmont Park Art Assoc.																		
Penna. Acad. of the Fine Arts				x							x							
Phila. Free Library																		
Phila. Orchestra Assoc.						x												
Occupation																		
Finance	x	x	x	x			x	x	x	x		x	x		x	x	x	
Law			x	x	x						x							
Business		x	x	x	x			x	x	x		x	x		x	x	x	x
Opinion						x												
Education				x										x			x	x

Neighborhood																	
Main Line	x	x	x		x	x	x	x	x	x	x	x		x	x	x	x
Chestnut Hill		x	x										x			x	
Other									x								
Religion																	
Episcopal	x	x	x		x	x	x	x	x	x	x	x		x	x	x	x
Other Protestant					x								x			x	
No answer			x														
Schooling																	
Fashionable church school	x	x	x	x	x	x	x	x			x	x		x	x	x	x
Other private		x	x		x								x			x	
No private	x																
College																	
Univ. of Penna.	x							x	x	x	x	x		x		x	x
Harvard-Yale-Princeton		x			x	x	x						x		x	x	
Other college			x														
No college		x			P								x				
Family Size																	
No. children	5	M	3	2	1	5	2	5	3	5	M	5	2	M	1	2	4	3
City Clubs																	
Philadelphia Club	x	x	x	x	x	x	x	x	x	x		x	x	x	x	x	x
Rittenhouse Club	x	x	x	x	x	x	x	x	x	x	x	x	x	x	x	x	x

P Presidents.

* The Pennsylvania Company for Insurance on Lives and Granting of Annuities.

influential gentlemen in this group for a number of reasons. First, they were all listed in the *Social Register*. All were directors in one or more of the sixteen leading cultural and economic institutions in the city (see Table 35). In fact, of the 131 directorships in these sixteen institutions listed by *all* 770 Philadelphians in the 1940 *Who's Who,* 116, or 80 per cent, were listed by these 42 gentlemen. Finally, within this group of leading Philadelphians were included the presidents of the city's six largest banks, two largest insurance

Table 36—*Philadelphians in Who's Who in 1940—Profile Summaries of 42 Upper-Class Directors of High Prestige Institutions*

	"Old Family" Directors	Other Directors	Total
Occupation			
Bankers	42%	22%	33%
Law	21	17	20
Business	33	44	37
Opinion	4	6	5
Education		11	5
	100%	100%	100%
Neighborhood			
Main Line	46%	44%	45%
Chestnut Hill	42	33	38
Other Neighborhoods	12	23	17
	100%	100%	100%
Religion			
Episcopal	70%	50%	60%
Other Protestant	5	17	11
No information	25	33	29
	100%	100%	100%
Secondary Schooling			
Private Schooling	70%	28%	52%
No private school	30	72	48
	100%	100%	100%
College Attended			
University of Penna.	38%	28%	33%
Harvard-Yale-Princeton	33	33	33
Other colleges	4	22	12
No college	25	17	22
	100%	100%	100%
Family Size			
Mean no. Children per parent	3.50	3.20	3.36
Proportion married	92%	100%	95%
Metropolitan Clubs			
Philadelphia Club	46%	22%	36%
Rittenhouse Club	21	50	33
Both Phila. & Rittenhouse Clubs	33	28	31
	100%	100%	100%
Number of cases	(24)	(18)	(42)

companies, the Pennsylvania Railroad, the University of Pennsylvania, and the Franklin Institute. The presidents of the five other cultural institutions—the Art Museum, the Fairmount Park Art Association, the Academy of the Fine Arts, the Free Library, and the Philadelphia Orchestra—were listed in the *Social Register* as members of the Philadelphia or Rittenhouse Clubs. They were not included in this group because they were not listed in *Who's Who*.

This small, common-interest group, which included members of the Ingersoll, Hopkinson, Lippincott, Pepper, Drinker, Rush, Houston, Newhall, Houston, Elkins, Clothier, and Dorrance families, as well as a number of men of newer wealth and position, judiciously blended historical tradition with current achievement. The profile summaries in Table 36, show how the old-family men differ from the rest. Brief sociological biographies of several members of the group will serve to illustrate the pattern of power in the city more concretely. Each biography more or less typifies one of the four background categories shown in Table 35. Edward Hopkinson, Jr., Leonard T. Beale, Benjamin Rush, and C. Stevenson Newhall were old Philadelphians; Thomas Gates and Joseph Wayne, Jr., were highly respected Philadelphians of newer position; Nathan Hayward was a transplanted Proper Bostonian; and, finally, John A. Stevenson and Samuel Dexter Warriner were typical of newer men of power from outside Philadelphia.

Educator, Financier, and the Most Influential Member of the Upper Class in Philadelphia. Thomas Sovereign Gates was the most influential and respected member of the upper class in Philadelphia in 1940.[4] In 1930, already many times a millionaire, he resigned his senior partnerships in both J. P. Morgan and Drexel and Company to become President of the University of Pennsylvania.

Dr. Gates was wont to repudiate the statement that he had been born with a silver spoon in his mouth. However, although not of fashionable society, his parents were in better than average circumstances as his father, Jabez Gates, was President of the Mutual Life Insurance Company, of Germantown.

Gates was born in Germantown in 1873. He grew up in this suburb of Philadelphia where he was educated at Germantown Academy before going on to Haverford College for two years and then graduating from the University of Pennsylvania in 1893 and its law school in 1896. On being admitted to the bar in 1896, Gates entered the office of the famous lawyer and art collecter, John G. Johnson. In 1906, he left the formal practice of law to become a trust officer of the Pennsylvania Company for Insurance on Lives and Granting of Annuities. In 1912, he became President of the Philadelphia Trust Company, a post which he held until 1918 when he became a partner in Drexel and Company. He became a Morgan partner in 1921.

Dr. Gates married three times. His first wife had two children. The sister-in-law of Owen J. Roberts, former Justice of the Supreme Court, she died in 1910. In 1925, Dr. Gates' second wife died, and he married again in 1929.

All his life, Dr. Gates was active in civic, financial, and industrial affairs. His civic work won him the *Bok Philadelphia* award in 1939. He served on the boards of the Chestnut Hill Hospital, the Southeastern Pennsylvania Chapter of the American Red Cross, the Bethesda Children's Christian Home in Chestnut Hill, the Board of City Trusts, the Leamy Home, the Museum of Natural History in New York, the Philadelphia Orchestra Association, the Pennsylvania Academy of Fine Arts and was a director of the National Community Fund. At the time of his death in 1948, Dr. Gates was serving his third term as President of the American Philosophical Society.

Dr. Gates held many directorships in industry and finance. During the war, while he was guiding the University through one of the most critical periods in its history, he accepted service on the boards of several large corporations engaged in war production. He was a director of the Pennsylvania Railroad, the Penn Mutual Life Insurance Company, the Fidelity-Philadelphia Trust Company, the Philadelphia Saving Fund Society, the Public Service Corporation of New Jersey, the Standard Steel Works, the Midvale Company, the Baldwin Locomotive Company, the John B. Stetson Company, and the Pittsburgh Equitable Motor Company.

Quite naturally, a man of Dr. Gates' stature in the city would have been a member of numerous clubs. He was, of course, a member of both the Rittenhouse and Philadelphia Clubs, having joined the younger club in 1912 at the age of thirty-nine and the older club in 1927 at the age of fifty-four. He also belonged to the Downtown, Church, Racquet, University, Mask and Wig, Huntington Valley Country, Philadelphia Cricket, Sunnybrook Golf, Art, Lenape, and Manufacturers Clubs in Philadelphia as well as the Banks in London, Rolling Rock in Pittsburgh, and the Broad Street in New York.

As President of the University of Pennsylvania, Dr. Gates served without pay. He was Treasurer of the Pennsylvania Diocese of the Protestant Episcopal Church as well as a member of the Committee of 100, a local good-government organization (founded by Henry Charles Lea). He lived in Chestnut Hill until his death in 1948.

Old Family Financier and Civic Leader. Edward Hopkinson, Jr., Philadelphia lawyer and financier, after the death of Thomas Gates in 1948 became the most influential member of the upper class in the city.[5] He is the senior partner of Drexel and Company, the leading investment bankers in the city.

A fine example of family continuity in community leadership, Edward Hopkinson is the great-great-great-grandson of Thomas Hopkinson, a founder of the American Philosophical Society, and a great-great-grandson of Francis Hopkinson, signer of the Declaration of Independence.

Hopkinson was born in Philadelphia in 1885 and grew up in the city. He was graduated from the University of Pennsylvania, where he received an A.B. in 1907 and an LL.B. in 1910. In 1911, at the age of twenty-six, he married. He has six children, three boys and three girls by this marriage. His first wife died, and in 1928 he married again. There is one son by this marriage.

After practicing law for many years as a member of the firm of Dickson, Beitler and McCouch which became the firm of Drinker, Biddle, and Reath in 1932, Hopkinson became a senior partner in Drexel and Company. His financial, industrial, and cultural interests include directorships in the Keystone Watch Case Corporation, Pennsylvania Fire Insurance Company, the Riverside Metal Company, the Insurance Company of North America, the Alliance Insurance Company, the Indemnity Insurance Company of North America, the Philadelphia Fire and Marine Insurance Company, the Parkway Company, the Baldwin Locomotive Works, and the Reading Company, and membership in the board of managers of the Philadelphia Saving Fund Society; he was also on the boards of the University of Pennsylvania, the Wister Institute, the Free Library of Philadelphia, and the Pennsylvania Institute for the Instruction of the Blind.

Edward Hopkinson joined the Philadelphia Club in 1920 at the age of thirty-five, and the Rittenhouse Club in 1924 at the age of thirty-nine. He also belonged to the Penn Athletic, Philadelphia Cricket, and Sunnybrook Golf clubs, in Philadelphia, as well as the Incogniti in London. He lived in Chestnut Hill and attended St. Paul's Episcopal Church.

Old Family Insurance Executive. The Insurance Company of North America, founded in 1792, is one of the oldest property insurance companies in America and has been closely associated with the upper class in the city for generations. Benjamin Rush was president of the company from 1916 until 1939 when he resigned to become chairman of the board of directors.[6]

Benjamin Rush belongs to an old Philadelphia family with a long and illustrious tradition. His great-grandfather was Dr. Benjamin Rush, signer of the Declaration of Independence, Surgeon-General of the Revolutionary Army under George Washington, and a member of the convention which adopted and drafted the United States Constitution. His grandfather was Richard Rush, Attorney General of Pennsylvania, United States Secretary of the Treasury, Acting Secretary of State, and United States Minister to the Court of St. James and to France. Benjamin Rush's father, Colonel Richard Henry Rush, raised and commanded the Sixth Pennsylvania Cavalry in the Civil War.

Born in Chestnut Hill in 1869, Benjamin Rush grew up in Philadelphia where he went to the Protestant Episcopal Academy which was then located in the center of the city. He did not go to college.

In 1895, at the age of 26, he married a Miss Lockwood of Stamford, Connecticut. He had three sons and two daughters. He lives in the country near West Chester, Pennsylvania.

Benjamin Rush was a director of the Fidelity-Philadelphia Trust Company and a trustee of the Penn Mutual Life Insurance Company. He was a member of the Pennsylvania Academy of Fine Arts and the Historical Society of Pennsylvania and was for many years a trustee of the Episcopal Academy, a director of the Children's Hospital, and manager of the Preston Maternity Hospital. Benjamin Rush went to the Episcopal Church, voted as a Republican, and was a member of the Philadelphia Club (joined in 1904 at the age of thirty-five).

Proper Philadelphia Industrialist. While the Philadelphia gentleman usually prefers to exercise his talents as a lawyer or financier, several leading industrialists were included in this group of civic and business leaders in 1940. Leonard T. Beale, President of the Pennsylvania Salt Manufacturing Company, ideally combined the roles of business, civic, and social leadership in Philadelphia in 1940.[7] In addition to his wide business interests, he was one of the five managers of the Assembly, the most coveted mark of social position in the city.

Leonard T. Beale was born in Philadelphia, attended the Haverford School, Princeton University, and the University of Pennsylvania, where he obtained an advanced degree in engineering. He was a director of the Pennsylvania Company for Insurance on Lives and Granting Annuities, the Penn Mutual Life Insurance Company, the Philadelphia Contributionship, National Lead Company, Titanium Pigment Company, Bell Telephone Company of Pennsylvania, Fire Association of Philadelphia, Titan Company, and the John T. Lewis & Brothers, Company.

Mr. Beale's directorship in the John T. Lewis & Brothers, Company is a reminder of his family's long tradition as manufacturing chemists. In the second half of the eighteenth century, Mordecai Lewis (see Chapter VI) was a prominent East India merchant, director of the Bank of North America, the Philadelphia Contributionship, and treasurer of the Pennsylvania Hospital. His two sons, Mordecai and Samuel N. Lewis, carried on the family mercantile business. In 1819, the firm of M & SN Lewis purchased a small white lead manufactory which grew into the largest firm of its kind in the United States by mid-century. Samuel N. Lewis had nine chilldren. John Thompson Lewis, his eldest son, took over the business and the firm became John T. Lewis & Brothers. John Thompson Lewis, the family patriarch, had five daughters who, in turn, married five capable Philadelphia gentlemen, including Theodore De-Witt Cuyler, leading member of the bar and first president of the Rittenhouse Club, and Edward Fitzgerald Beale, who eventually became president of John T. Lewis & Brothers, Company. Leonard T. Beale followed his father (Edward Fitzgerald) into the chemical business and eventually became president of the Pennsylvania Salt Manufacturing Company when the family firm became part of this larger concern.

Leonard T. Beale married Anna Lewis and they had three children (Edward Fitzgerald Beale III is now a vice-president of Penn Salt).

His clubs included the Philadelphia, Midday, and Chemists (New York), The family lived on DeLancey Place in town, and in Penllyn, where they attended the Episcopal Church and voted the Republican ticket.

Pennsylvania Hard Coal Executive. Samuel Dexter Warriner, born in Lancaster, Pennsylvania, in 1867, was the son of Reverend Edward and Louisa Voorhis Warriner.[8] After graduating from Amherst College and Lehigh University in 1890, he went to work for the Liberty Iron Company in Virginia. Five years later, he became general superintendent of the Lehigh Valley Coal Company, and in 1912, he was elected President of the Lehigh Coal and Navigation Company, a position which he held until 1937 when he became Chairman of the Board.

The history of the Lehigh Coal and Navigation Company, established in 1817-1820, spans the rise and decline of the anthracite industry in Pennsylvania (see Chapter VI). Mr. Warriner was manager of the company during the crucial years when hard coal was gradually forced out of the market by other fuels. During the 1920's, as Chairman of the Anthracite Operators Conference Committee, he led the fight with John L. Lewis which culminated in a disastrous strike in 1925. As a result of this strike by the mine-workers, other fuels necessarily were used in place of the nation's dwindling supply of anthracite, and hard coal has been a sick industry ever since.

In addition to being the symbol of leadership in the hard coal industry for many years, Samuel Dexter Warriner was also prominent in the business community of Philadelphia and Pennsylvania as a whole. His thirty-three directorships in a wide variety of business concerns included the Lehigh and New England R.R. Company, Allentown Iron Company, Allentown Terminal R.R. Company, Pennsylvania Salt Manufacturing Company, Westmoreland Coal Company, Insurance Company of North America, Philadelphia National Bank, and the Penn Mutual Life Insurance Company. In addition to his business interests, he was a trustee and president of the alumni society of Lehigh University, where he had been a football and baseball star in his undergraduate days.

Mr. Warriner's broad interests included memberships in numerous clubs: he belonged to the Rittenhouse, Union League, Engineers, Philadelphia Country, and Merion Cricket in Philadelphia; the Railroad-Machinery Club in New York; and the Westmoreland Club in Wilkes-Barre, in addition to eight other sporting, golfing, and resort clubs in various parts of the country. He was married and had three children who were married and living along the Main Line. Mr. Warriner's country seat, "Fernheim," was in Montrose, Pennsylvania, while his Philadelphia residence was on 18th Street in the neighborhood of Rittenhouse Square.

Executive of Achieved Upper-Class Status. John A. Stevenson, President of the Penn Mutual Life Insurance Company, had the longest *Who's Who* biography in this study of the Philadelphia elite. It has been said that he was one of Philadelphia's best-known citizens in local and national business, education, and civic councils.[9]

John A. Stevenson was born in 1886 at Cobden, Illinois. He graduated from the Cobden High School and the Southern Illinois Normal University in 1905. After graduating from college, he was assistant principal of the Nashville, Illinois, High School, and at the age of twenty-three, he was superintendent of schools in Olney, Illinois. He then returned to the University of Wisconsin where he received an A.M. in 1912. The following year he became manager of the Department of Music, Drawing, and Manual Arts for the Scott, Foresman & Company, Chicago publishers. Four years later he became a lecturer in the Department of Education at the University of Illinois where he received a Ph.D. in 1918. Due to some of his progressive ideas on education, he became a professor in Education and Director of the School of Life Insurance Salesmanship at the Carnegie Institute of Technology, in Pittsburgh, where he remained from 1919 to 1920. In 1920, he became third vice-president of the Equitable Life Assurance Society of the United States, in New York, where he was in charge of the company's training program. In 1928, he was called to Philadelphia where he became manager of the John A. Stevenson agency of the Penn Mutual Life Insurance Company. He became a vice-president of the company in 1931 and president in 1939.

John A. Stevenson was active in many business, cultural, and educational organizations. He was a trustee of Temple University, the University of Pennsylvania, the University of Chicago, the George Peabody College for Teachers, and a director of the Southern Illinois University Foundation. He was a director and a member of the executive committee of the Institute of Life Insurance; a director of the Insurance Federation of Pennsylvania; a member of the board and secretary of the American College of Life Underwriters; a member of the executive committee and president of the marketing executives society; a director and member of the executive committee of the American Management Association; a member of the Pennsylvania State Board of Public Assistance; a director of the Young Men's Christian Association, in Philadelphia; a director of the Community Fund and the Salvation Army, in Philadelphia; president of the Friends of the University of Pennsylvania Library; chairman of the executive committee and member of the board of directors of the Ministers and Missionaries Benefit Board of the Northern Baptist Convention; a charter member of the American Association of University Teachers of Insurance; and a director of the Better Business Bureau of Philadelphia. He was a member of the National Society for the Study of Education, the American Academy of Political and Social Science, the National Institute of Social Science, the St. Andrews Society, Sigma Nu, Kappa Delta Pi, Phi Delta Kappa, Phi Eta, and Pi Gamma Mu.

John A. Stevenson held the following directorships in the business world: Girard Trust Company, Home Insurance Company of New York, Bell Telephone Company of Pennsylvania, Pullman Company, Avco Manufacturing Company, Fire Association of Philadelphia, Reliance Insurance Company, Lumberman's Insurance Company, Philadelphia

National Insurance Company, and the Penn Mutual Life Insurance Company.

Stevenson was the author of several books on teaching, salesmanship, and philanthropy, and a co-editor of the Harper's Life Insurance Library.

As an important and influential executive, Stevenson's club memberships were extensive. He was a member of the Union League, Rittenhouse, Franklin Inn, and Merion Cricket clubs in Philadelphia; the Metropolitan, Canadian, and Grolier clubs in New York; the Chicago Club in Chicago; the Bath Club in Miami Beach; and the Bar Harbor Club in Bar Harbor, Maine. He joined the Rittenhouse Club, after becoming a Vice-President of the Penn Mutual Life in 1932 at the age of forty-six.

Stevenson married Josephine Reese, of Chicago, and they had one son (educated at Exeter and Princeton, where he was a member of the Ivy Club). He was a Baptist and lived at his suburban estate, "The Chimneys," at Bryn Mawr on the Main Line.

Transplanted Proper Bostonian. Nathan Hayward was born in Boston in 1872. He was a student at the Roxbury Latin School and graduated from Harvard College in 1895.[10] In 1897 he received an S.B. degree from the Massachusetts Institute of Technology where he was an instructor for two years before going to work for the Bell Telephone Company of Pennsylvania. Nathan Hayward was a construction engineer for the Telephone Company from 1898 until 1922. He has been President of the American Dredging Company since 1917 and the American Shipyard Company since 1919.

Nathan Hayward had many and varied interests in both economic and cultural affairs. He was President of the Franklin Institute from 1925 to 1937, a member of the American Philosophical Society, the Newcomen Society, the American Institute of Electrical Engineers, the Historical Society of Pennsylvania, the Academy of Natural Sciences of Philadelphia, and the Fairmount Park Art Association, and, finally, he was a member of the Board of Overseers of Harvard University.

His directorships in industry and finance included the following: Bell Telephone Company of Pennsylvania, Philadelphia and Reading Coal and Iron Corporation, Philadelphia Saving Fund Society (his brother-in-law is listed in Table 35 as President of the P.S.F.S.), Philadelphia Belt Line Railroad Company, and the Fidelity-Philadelphia Trust Company.

Nathan Hayward was a member of the Rittenhouse Club, the Engineers Club, and the Harvard Club in Philadelphia.[16] He also belonged to the Harvard Clubs in Boston and in New York, as well as the Manchester Yacht Club in Manchester, Massachusetts. He married at the age of thirty-five and had five children. He belonged to the Unitarian church, was a Republican, and lived in Wayne on the Main Line.

Two Proper Philadelphia Bankers. It has been estimated that the Proper Philadelphia lady and gentleman have between three and four billion dollars invested in various forms of trusts. Just as power in a commercial community is stored in the vaults of banks, so the continuity and life blood of an upper class depend on inherited trust funds. At least until the rapid increase in the size of government, the ultimate source of capital, the arbitrator of business expansion, lay in the hands of gentlemen bankers all over America but especially in the larger metropolitan areas. C. Stevenson Newhall and Joseph Wayne, Jr. were two of the leading commercial bankers in Philadelphia in 1940.

C. Stevenson Newhall was born on the Newhall family estate at Midvale Avenue and Stockley Street in Germantown in 1877.[11] In 1940, he and his sister were still living on the estate, which by that time had become something of a landmark; passersby could see cows grazing in this rural oasis in the heart of Germantown. The Newhalls were the most famous Philadelphia cricket family and C. Stevenson Newhall, an ardent player in his youth, had been a member of the "Newhall Eleven" a team made up entirely of members of the family.

After graduating from the Germantown Academy, young Newhall went to work for the Pennsylvania Company for Insurance on Lives and Granting Annuities where he remained all his life. In 1940 he was Chairman of the Board of Directors. He was a director of eighteen business and financial concerns including the Westmoreland Coal Company, Home Insurance Company of New York, Philadelphia Suburban Water Company, Philadelphia Transportation Company, North Penn Railroad, Reading Company, and John B. Stetson, Limited.

C. Stevenson Newhall was unmarried, belonged to the Racquet and Rittenhouse Clubs, and was the Rector's warden of Germantown's most charming Episcopal church, St. James the Less, situated on the fringes of the city's booming industrial northern part of the city.

Joseph Wayne, Jr. was born in Philadelphia where he was educated in the public schools.[12] At the age of seventeen he went to work for the old Girard National Bank where "he didn't watch the clock and liked his work." In 1914, at the age of forty-one, he became the youngest bank president in the city. When the Girard National Bank was consolidated with the Franklin-Fourth Street National Bank, under the title of the Philadelphia National Bank, Joseph Wayne, Jr. became president of the city's largest bank. In 1940 he was the highest paid banker in the city with a salary reported as $108,342. He was president of the Philadelphia Clearing House, and a director of the Federal Reserve Bank of Philadelphia, the Philadelphia Savings Fund Society, Provident Mutual Life Insurance Company, Insurance Company of North America, Pennsylvania Railroad, Reading Coal and Iron Corporation, Midvale Company, Baldwin-Southwark Company, and the Provident Trust Company.

An excellent cricketer in his youth, Joseph Wayne, Jr. was one of the founders of the Philadelphia Cricket Club in Chestnut Hill. In addition to the Cricket Club, he also belonged to the Union League, Rittenhouse (joined at forty-six), Racquet, Sunnybrook Golf, and the Germantown Cricket Clubs. He married Laura B. Jayne, of the patent medicine family in 1902, and had three children, now wives of P. Blair Lee, banker, Ivy Club director and descendant of Senator Blair Lee, founder of Ivy; James S. Hatfield, Princetonian and architect; and G. Willing Pepper, vice-president of the Scott Paper Company. He lived in Chestnut Hill where the family attended the Episcopal church.

The great utility, railroad, and coal fortunes in America were made before World War I. During the twenties and thirties, consumer goods began to replace heavy industry as the dominant money-makers in America (the New Deal, for instance, favored the former). With the coming of the automobile, oil became the leading fuel, and the age of chemistry took hold. But the directorships listed by Messers. Gates, Hopkinson, Rush, Newhall, and Wayne indicated that Proper Philadelphia power was primarily limited to coal, utilities, and railroads, in addition to banks and insurance companies. Thus, with such important exceptions as Arthur Dorrance, President of Campbell Soup, and Leonard T. Beale, President of Penn Salt, this small group of Philadelphia and Rittenhouse Club members tended to be leaders in areas of waning power in 1940.

The Philadelphia elite, of course, included other men of wealth and power who were not members of these two exclusive clubs. J. Howard Pew, a staunch Presbyterian and leading member of the Union League, was not only head of the family firm (Sun Oil and Sun Ship); he was also one of the leaders in the Republican party in the city and in the state as a whole.

Perhaps Albert M. Greenfield, often referred to as "Mr. Philadelphia" in the popular press, was the most interesting member of the Philadelphia elite to rise to power in the period after the First World War. In many ways, he was the most powerful single individual in the city in 1940. Albert M. Greenfield & Company was the largest real estate firm in the state of Pennsylvania. Every resident of Philadelphia knows Mr. Greenfield through his firm's ubiquitous green and white "For Sale" signs on factories, apartment houses, and skyscrapers throughout the city and its suburbs. In addition to his real estate interests, Albert M. Greenfield was a banker, department-store and newspaper-owner, utility executive, and a powerful behind-the-scenes politician.

He was chairman of the board of the Bankers Securities Corporation and the Bankers Bond and Mortgage Guaranty Company of America, and president of the U. S. Mortgage & Title Guaranty Company of New Jersey.[13] Among his many department-store

interests he was chairman of the board of Lit Brothers Department Store and Bonwit Teller Company in Philadelphia, and the
City Stores Company in New York, a multi-million dollar corporation which owned such department stores as the Maison Blanche
Company in New Orleans, B. Lowenstein & Brother, Memphis,
Kaufman, Straus Company, Louisville, and Loveman, Joseph &
Loeb, in Birmingham, Alabama. He was a director and part owner
of the Philadelphia *Record*, the city's only Democratic newspaper
(now defunct), as well as a director of the Camden *Courier Post*,
and the New York *Post*. His interest in public utilities included a
strategic and influential directorship in the Philadelphia Rapid
Transit Company which handled all of Philadelphia's streetcar
and subway services.

Albert M. Greenfield started out as a member of the Republican party. He was a member of the City Council under the
Republicans, in 1918-1920, and a delegate to the Republican
National Convention in 1928. But in 1936, he became chairman of
the All-Philadelphia Citizens Committee on Arrangements for the
Democratic National Convention and a member of the finance
committee of the Democratic party. In an unostentatious and old-
fashioned office in his own Bankers Securities Building on Juniper
Street, one of Philadelphia's numerous alleys in the center of the
city, Mr. Greenfield has hung signed portraits of both Herbert
Hoover and Franklin D. Roosevelt, a tribute to his broad political
views.

Thus while the banker and business gentlemen in the Rittenhouse and Philadelphia clubs tended to dominate economic life
in Philadelphia before the Second World War, there were certainly other centers of influence, such as, for example, the powerful
and independent Pew family or Albert M. Greenfield.

It would be sociologically fruitful to ascertain how day-to-day
decisions are related to the power structure in a metropolitan community. This is an extremely difficult, if not impossible, task. Day-
to-day decisions, unimportant in isolation, are so often made, by
default or tradition, in informal personal relationships or in loosely
structured committees. Moreover, a traditional society such as
Philadelphia is probably much more difficult to understand, fortunately, than a coercive and revolutionary centralized society. However, the invisible workings of the power structure, and the nature
of decision-making, sometimes come to light in crisis situations,

e.g., the disastrous bank failures in the early years of the great Depression. When the Bankers Trust Company, owned by Albert M. Greenfield, was obliged to close its doors just before Christmas in 1930, the sociologically inclined observer was provided with some insight into the nature of power and influence in the city.[14]

The details surrounding the failure of the Bankers Trust, and even its ownership and control, were, of course, obscure and hidden from the view of the ordinary citizen. Albert M. Greenfield was supposed to have owned and controlled the Bankers Trust, and was generally blamed for the failure. In the spring of 1931, however, during the period when the State Banking Commission was still trying to revive the bank, a special committee of the bank's board of directors reported that "Mr. Greenfield was an important factor in the building up of Bankers Trust Company but was at no time in control either of the board of directors or the management, either by stock ownership or otherwise."[15] That the general public and the bank's depositors thought that Mr. Greenfield was more than an important director in Bankers Trust is suggested by the following announcement, made some time after the bank's failure: "Neither Albert M. Greenfield nor any of his representatives," declared the bank's president, "will be on the board of directors of the new bank, which it is proposed to reorganize from the old, nor will they have any voice in its management or direction."[16]

Although the circumstances surrounding the ownership of the Bankers Trust Company and the responsibility for its collapse are controversial, and the "facts" have not been agreed upon, the story of the bank's failure was told in some detail by Russell W. Davenport in *Fortune* magazine in June, 1936. In addition to his prestige as an editor of *Fortune*, Russell Davenport had other qualifications which provided an entrée into Proper Philadelphia.[17] His father, one of the first young men to graduate from the Sheffield Scientific School at Yale University, came down to Philadelphia before the first war and became the general manager of the Midvale Steel Company and then the Bethlehem Iron Company (he worked at both plants with the famous management engineer, Frederick W. Taylor). Russell Davenport's mother, a Philadelphia beauty, née Cornelia Farnum, was headmistress of a fashionable girls' school in the city. In other words, Davenport had had intimate first-hand knowledge of the city where he had spent part of his youth.

In his *Fortune* article, "Philadelphia," Russell Davenport described the failure of the Bankers Trust Company in 1930 as follows:

In 1925 Mr. Greenfield bought a small bank in West Philadelphia, moved it to Walnut Street, and dubbed it Bankers' Trust Co. There were 128 banks in Philadelphia at that time, and having tasted the blood of high finance, Mr. Greenfield, or rather Bankers' Trust Co., proceeded to buy up nine of them during the next five years. Its action forestalled several failures but into the bargain it helped to cloak the dangerous situation that the mortgage extravaganza had created. By 1930 Bankers' Trust, with eleven offices throughout the city, had 115,000 depositors and a total of $35,000,000 in deposits.

In July of that year a bank out in North Philadelphia called the Bank of Philadelphia & Trust Co., which had $15,000,000 in deposits and did a big business in builders' construction mortgages, showed signs of going under. And in line with his policy during the past several years, Mr. Greenfield pricked up his ears. Unfortunately the careful historian is faced at this point with a contradiction in his sources, and it is impossible to say precisely what happened. On the one hand, Mr. Greenfield says that the leading bankers came to him and urged him with very cogent arguments to buy up the Bank of Philadelphia. On the other hand the bankers, and specifically Mr. C. Stevenson Newhall, whom we shall identify presently, assert they did not urge Mr. Greenfield at all; that the idea of buying up the Bank of Philadelphia was his and his alone; and that they were not a little surprised when he decided to take it. But whichever way it was, on July 22, following a hectic weekend, the Bank of Philadelphia & Trust Co. and all its nine branches opened for business under the name of the Bankers' Trust Co., bringing the deposits of the latter institution up to $50,000,000; not, however, before Mr. Greenfield had sounded out Mr. Newhall, and Mr. Joseph Wayne, Jr. of the Philadelphia National Bank, and had received from them the assurance that they would extend loans to Bankers' Trust upon good and sufficient collateral. . . .

The Philadelphia bankers themselves are a conservative lot. Joseph Wayne, Jr., President of the Philadelphia National Bank with $400,000,-000 in deposits, has the biggest institution (it is often colloquially referred to as "the Philadelphia bank") and is that institution's biggest intangible asset. A large, ruddy man of sixty-three, his head crowned by a shock of square-cut snow-white hair, former baseball player, former cricketer (a sport that used to be extremely popular in Philadelphia until about the time of the World War), he is hailed by almost everyone passing in or out of the bank with a "Hello Joe," and he always answers "Hello there," even when he doesn't know who it is or hasn't got time to look. Just a block up Chestnut Street, in a walnut-paneled office in the Packard Building, sits soft-spoken, beaverlike C. Stevenson Newhall, President of the bank with the most absurd name in the world—the Pennsylvania Company for Insurance on Lives and Granting Annuities, with deposits of $231,000,000. A bachelor with a dry grin and sometimes a petulant frown, whose single and absorbing passion is the Pennsylvania Co., Mr. Newhall is in many ways the opposite of the aggressive, outdoorsy Wayne; but the two of them are a kind of team and they acted as spokesmen for all the commercial banks in the crisis that was approaching. . . .

Not long after its purchase of the Philadelphia Bank & Trust Co., the Bankers' Trust Co. began to feel the effects of that acquisition (which, however, was not strictly a merger), or at any rate people thought that it ought to be feeling them, for a run on the bank started in September, 1930. True to their promise, Messrs. Wayne and Newhall backed Bankers' Trust all during November, but by December 18, when they had loaned $7,000,000, it was obvious that the dike would not hold with any such patching as this. In a series of strained conferences it became apparent that, while everyone dreaded the effects of the forthcoming collapse, no one was willing to step forward to the rescue. The banking interests, however, went so far as to make certain demands, which in the aggregate required the replacement of $10,000,-000 of Bankers' Trust assets with cash, and supposing that this indicated a willingness on the part of some of the members of the Clearing House to save Bankers' Trust, Mr. Greenfield (together with William Fox, Hollywood's ex-tycoon, who was a Bankers' Trust stockholder and was then solvent) asserted that he was prepared to meet their conditions. But in a final conference during the night of December 21 at Mr. Gest's house on the Main Line (to which Mr. Greenfield was not invited) the leaders unexpectedly decided to let the bank go. On December 22 some 135,000 Philadelphians awoke to their first real taste of the great depression.[18]

CHAPTER XV

Summary and Conclusion

> The wealthier, or, as they would prefer to style themselves the "upper" classes, tend distinctly towards the bourgeois type, and an individual in the bourgeois stage of development, while honest, industrious, and virtuous, is also not unapt to be a miracle of timid and short-sighted selfishness. The commercial classes are only too likely to regard everything merely from the standpoint of "Does it pay?" and many a merchant does not take any part in politics because he is short-sighted enough to think that it will pay him better to attend purely to making money, and too selfish to be willing to undergo any trouble for the sake of abstract duty; while the younger men of this type are too much engrossed in their various social pleasures to be willing to give up their time to anything else.
>
> THEODORE ROOSEVELT

CONCEIVED in a new world which was free of the traditional authority of an established church and a feudal nobility, and born in a revolt from the tyranny of a centralized government symbolized in the British monarchy and mercantilism, American institutions have, virtually from the beginning, been shaped in a laissez-faire capitalist climate. The merchant, mining, manufacturing, railroad, and finance capitalists, each in their day, were the most powerful members of the elite in nineteenth- and early twentieth-century America. As "old family" is usually found to be synonymous with "old money," the leading capitalists in the pre-Civil War period were the "old-family" founders in America. In the 1870's, the families of these men and their descendants formed local business aristocracies in the older cities such as Boston, New York, and Philadelphia. Living near one another, on the gentle slope of Murray Hill in New York, on Beacon Street in Boston, or around Rittenhouse Square in Philadelphia, the members of these families knew "who" belonged within this formal and well-structured world of polite society.

In the last two decades of the nineteenth century, these provincial aristocracies of birth and breeding (old money) merged with a new and more conspicuously colorful world known as "Society." It was in the 1880's that New York Society with a capital "S," then moving uptown to the newly fashionable Fifth Avenue district, came under the tutelage of Mrs. Astor and her right-hand man, Ward McAlister. It was Mr. McAlister who coined the snobbish term "Four Hundred" and finally gave his official list to the New York *Times* on the occasion of Mrs. Astor's famous ball on February 1, 1892. During this same period, as millionaires multiplied and had to be accepted, as one lost track of "who" people were and had to recognize "what" they were worth, the *Social Register* became an index of a new upper class in America.

But this new upper class was soon to be organized on a national rather than a local scale. In an age which marked the centralization of economic power under the control of the finance capitalists, the gentlemen bankers and lawyers on Wall Street, Walnut Street, State Street, and La Salle Street began to send their sons to Groton, St. Mark's, or St. Paul's and afterwards to Harvard, Yale, or Princeton where they joined such exclusive clubs as Porcellian, Fence, or Ivy. These polished young men from many cities were educated together, and introduced to one another's sisters at debutante parties and fashionable weddings in Old Westbury, Mount Kisco, or Far Hills, on the Main Line or in Chestnut Hill, in Dedham, Brookline, or Milton, or in Lake Forest. After marriage at some fashionable Episcopal church, almost invariably within this select, endogamous circle, they lived in these same socially circumspect suburbs and commuted to the city where they lunched with their fathers and grandfathers at the Union, Philadelphia, Somerset, or Chicago clubs. Several generations repeat this cycle, and a centralized business aristocracy thus becomes a reality in America. The *Social Register,* first published in 1888, lists the families of this business aristocracy and their relatives and friends, in New York, Chicago, Boston, Philadelphia, Baltimore, San Francisco, St. Louis, Buffalo, Pittsburgh, Cleveland, Cincinnati-Dayton, and Washington, D.C. In 1940, approximately one-fourth of the residents of these twelve metropolitan areas who were listed in *Who's Who* in that year were also listed in the *Social Register.* Thus the members of this contemporary American upper class, descendants of leaders in American life from colonial times to the present, had considerable influence on the elite in 1940.

The Philadelphia Business Aristocracy. In 1940 the Proper
Philadelphian tended "distinctly towards the bourgeois type" as
Theodore Roosevelt would have put it. While 29 per cent of the
Philadelphians listed in *Who's Who* were also listed in the *Social
Register,* the upper class contributed considerably more than its
share of leaders within the business community: 75 per cent of the
bankers, 51 per cent of the lawyers, 45 per cent of the engineers,
and 42 per cent of the businessmen listed in *Who's Who* were also
members of the upper class. In addition, of the 532 directorships
in industrial and financial institutions reported by *all* the members
of the elite, 60 per cent were reported by members of the upper
class. Finally, the leading bankers and lawyers in the city were
members of the upper class. The presidents, and over 80 per cent
of the directors in the six largest banks were Proper Philadelphians,
as were the senior partners in the largest law firms. And Dr. Thomas
S. Gates, lawyer, former senior Morgan partner, and President of
the University of Pennsylvania in 1940, was not only the most influential and respected member of the upper class but also the most
powerful man in the city.

Within the upper class as a whole, moreover, business power
tended to be correlated with the various attributes of high social
class position. Thus, the members of the business elite, both those
in the upper class and the rest, were more likely to live in the
more fashionable neighborhoods, to attend the Episcopal churches,
to have graduated from the right educational institutions, and to
have grown up in the city (see Table 37).

In 1940 the ideal-typical Proper Philadelphian at the apex of
the pyramid of social prestige and economic power in the city,
may be said to have had the following attributes:

(1) Of English or Welsh descent, his great-great-great-grandfather
would have been a prominent Philadelphian in the great age of the
new republic. Somewhere along the line an ancestor would have made
money, or married wisely. And along with money and social position,
some good Quaker ancestor would have preferred the Episcopal Church,
or have been banished from the Society of Friends for marrying "out of
meeting."

(2) His family would have been listed in the *Social Register* at the
turn of the nineteenth century.

(3) He would have been born on Walnut Street, facing Rittenhouse Square.

(4) After an early education at the Episcopal Academy or some

other private school in the city, he would have gone away to one of the fashionable Episcopalian boarding schools in New England.

(5) Unless his parents felt an unusual loyalty and pride in local institutions, he would have gone to either Harvard, Yale, or Princeton where he would have belonged to one of the more exclusive clubs.

(6) After attending the law school at the University of Pennsylvania, this young Proper Philadelphian would enter one of the fashionable and powerful law firms in the city and eventually become a partner; or enter the field of banking or finance. He would be on the board of directors of several cultural and economic institutions (Pennsylvania Railroad, a bank such as the Girard Trust Company, and perhaps the Fairmount Park Art Association).

(7) Finally, the Proper Philadelphian would live either in Chestnut Hill or the Main Line in 1940, attend the Episcopal Church, be married with three or four children, and walk either up or down Walnut Street to lunch with his peers at the Rittenhouse, or preferably the Philadelphia Club.

As Proper Philadelphia has been democratically assimilating new men or power and wealth into its ranks, most of the upper-class members of the elite in 1940, of course, do not measure up to this exalted ideal-typical status. By way of a quantitative summary of the various attributes of social class position discussed throughout this book, the Philadelphia elite as a whole in 1940 has been broken down (in Table 38) into various levels which more or less approach this ideal-typical status. Columns 1 and 3 are made up of upper-class directors in certain prestige institutions

Table 37—Philadelphians in Who's Who in 1940—Attributes of High Social Class Position as Related to Functional Elites

| | SOCIAL CLASS | | | |
| | SOCIAL REGISTER | | NON SOCIAL REGISTER | |
Attributes of High Social Class Position	Business Elite Members	All Other Elite Members	Business Elite Members	All Other Elite Members
Neighborhood:				
Main Line & Chestnut Hill	80%	44%	32%	14%
Religion:				
Episcopalian	48	37	21	12
Education:				
Private School	44	37	25	12
Harvard-Yale-Princeton	28	18	4	5*
Birthplace:				
Philadelphia	55	49	37	27
(Number of cases)	(107)	(119)	(111)	(433)

* Upper-class graduates of Harvard, Yale, or Princeton go into business, while the other graduates are more likely to go into church or education. This may explain this deviant case.

Table 38—Philadelphians in Who's Who in 1940—Attributes of High Social Class Position as Related to Specified Levels of Prestige and Power

Attributes of High Class Social Position	1 "Old Family" Prestige Directors	2 Philadelphia Club Members	3 Prestige Directors, Not "Old Family"	4 Rittenhouse Club Members	5 Social Register	6 Non Social Register
Neighborhood:						
Main Line & Chestnut Hill	88%	77%	77%	67%	61%	18%
Religion:						
Episcopalian	70%	58%	50%	41%	42%	14%
Education:						
Private School	70%	52%	28%	35%	41%	15%
Harvard-Yale-Princeton	33%	37%	33%	21%	22%	5%
Birthplace:						
Philadelphia	100%	75%	28%	52%	52%	29%
Occupation:						
Banker	42%	25%	22%	18%	11%	1%
Lawyer	21%	12%	17%	17%	9%	4%
(Number of cases)	(24)	(57)	(18)	(66)	(226)	(544)
Family Size:						
Mean number of children per Male Parent	3.50	3.30	3.20	2.89	2.80	2.61

discussed in the previous chapter; the men in column 1 were born in Philadelphia and were listed in the 1900 *Social Register,* while those in column 3 were not. Column 1, then, includes old-family men of power while column 3 includes men of newer power and position. The rest of the columns in Table 38 are self-explanatory. As we have said, the Philadelphia Club is both more socially circumspect and more influential than the younger Rittenhouse. In fact, the younger club is best understood as the first rung in the ladder of ascent into the upper class (except for columns 5 and 6, of course, the various subgroups in Table 38 have overlapping and not mutually exclusive memberships).

In a very real sense, Table 38 summarizes this book. Thus Proper Philadelphia was a business aristocracy in 1940 wherein social class position and commercial and financial power in the community were positively correlated variables in the total class situation. Throughout its history, and especially since the Civil War, the Philadelphia upper class closely approximated R. H. Tawney's description of the British aristocracy which most American patricians, of course, both emulate and respect: "It is a subtle combination of both—a blend of a crude plutocratic reality with the sentimental aroma of an aristocratic legend—which gives the English class system its peculiar toughness and cohesion. It is at once as businesslike as Manchester and as gentlemanly as Eton. . . ."[1]

After this brief summary of the characteristics of the Philadelphia upper class in 1940, several things pertaining to the American metropolitan upper class as a whole should be emphasized in closing.

It is important to stress once again the fact that, while there are many middle and lower classes in America, and in Philadelphia, there exists one metropolitan upper class with a common cultural tradition, consciousness of kind, and "we" feeling of solidarity which tends to be national in scope. The origin and development of this inter-city moneyed aristocracy in America quite naturally paralleled the rise of rapid communications and the national corporate enterprise. Moreover, just as economic control of the various local firms in the "Yankee Cities" and "Middletowns" of America have gradually gravitated to such metropolitan centers as Boston, New York, or Chicago, so upper-class prestige has, over the years, become increasingly centralized in the fashionable metropolitan suburbs.

The growth and structure of this national upper class has, in turn, been supported by various institutions. First and most important, of course, are the New England boarding schools and the fashionable Eastern universities. Whereas the older generation of Proper Philadelphians were educated at home or in local schools and colleges, at the turn of the century, and especially after the First World War, these national upper-class family-surrogates began to educate the children of the rich and well-born from all cities in ever-increasing numbers. At the same time, the Episcopal Church also developed into a national upper-class institution. By the end of the nineteenth century, the process of upper-class conversion, which had actually begun in the previous century, was virtually complete. In the twentieth century, the fashionable descendants of staunch New England Calvinists or pious Philadelphia Quakers almost invariably worshipped in the Episcopal churches in the metropolitan suburbs of America. And the Episcopal Church is also an important part of the summer social life at such fashionable resorts as Mount Desert which do so much to foster inter-city family alliances.

Several things follow from the development of this national upper class and its supporting institutions. On the whole, of course, the family is weakened and increasingly replaced by an associational aristocracy. The family firm gives way to the large and anonymously owned corporation with the attending consequences of declining family pride and responsibility. The entrepreneur who founded the family firm and fortune is replaced by the hired executive, and the corporation soon becomes an impersonal source of dividends which conveniently supports a suitable style of life. At the same time, the fashionable school, college, and club replace the family as the chief status-ascribing institutions: often isolated geographically as well as socially from the rest of the community, these fashionable associations tend to make for less social contact between classes than was the case in an earlier day when the members of polite society, although undoubtedly protected by a formal social distance recognized by all classes, may well have interacted more frequently in the local community with the members of the middle and lower classes. George Wharton Pepper, for instance, met and befriended a Negro boy while he was growing up in the neighborhood of stiff and fashionable Rittenhouse Square; his grandsons, reared in the social homogeneity of the Main Line and a New England boarding school, were more geographically isolated even though born in a more egalitarian age. Finally, the Episcopalianization of the whole American upper class also tends to foster uniformity and class isolation. This is, of course, part of a general trend throughout Protestantism. The Catholic Church has traditionally been an altar before which men of all walks of life bow down together, but the various Protestant denominations have, almost from the beginning, been organized along class lines. Certainly most Protestant churches today are social centers where families of similar backgrounds assemble together for worship. One often wonders if fashionable Episcopalians, in their aversion to the middle-class drabness of the "Protestant ethic," have not thereby substituted a convenient conventionality for their ancestors' more rigid convictions. At any rate, these developments in upper-class institutions tend to make for an increasing conformity and uniformity, a decline in local color and originality, and perhaps, at the same time, a new snobbishness which inevitably follows the increasing importance now attached to proper associational affiliation.

Arnold Toynbee has written that whereas Western civilization has been preoccupied for several generations with the building of roads, the challenge before us today is one of regulating the traffic thereon. American civilization, led by businessmen of daring enterprise and ingenuity ("know how"), has produced the highest standard of living the world has ever known. And these business leaders and producers of wealth have been the backbone of its upper class. "New occasions teach new duties," however, and today, in the atomic age of abundant consumption, the continuing, or perhaps, new greatness of America will presumably depend on the nation's ability to shoulder the burden of world leadership in creating and defending, to use Toynbee's analogy, some sort of world traffic rules. At the same time, domestic government, at the local, state, and national level, is playing a larger and larger role in the lives of American citizens, both as the defender of law and order and the redistributor of wealth in a host of welfare activities. In short, while entrepreneurial and financial genius may have built up America, statesmen and political leaders are rapidly becoming the most powerful and important members of the contemporary elite.

On the whole, the American upper class, with such outstanding exceptions as the Roosevelts, Adamses, Lodges, and Tafts, has produced few great statesmen in modern times. As we have seen, this has been especially true of Proper Philadelphia. As young Theodore Roosevelt once wrote: "There are not a few men of means who have always made the till their fatherland, and are always ready to balance a temporary interruption of money-making, or a temporary financial and commercial disaster, against the self-sacrifice necessary in upholding the honor of the nation and the glory of the flag."[2] The vigor and continuity of an upper class depends, not on its social prestige and style of life, but rather on its continuing contribution of men who are both willing and able to assume positions of power and leadership in the world of affairs. As the seat of power moves from State Street to the State House, from Wall Street to Washington, one wonders if the American business aristocracy discussed in this volume will be capable of supplying its share of leaders in local, national, and international governmental affairs. There are several reasons for believing that it will.

First, Philadelphia has been going through a cultural, civic, and political renaissance since the close of the Second World War. The political renaissance has been led by two members of the upper class, Richardson Dilworth, a transplanted member of an old Pittsburgh family, and Joseph Sill Clark, descendant of Enoch W. Clark, founder of one of the city's leading banking families. Both men had distinguished war records; Dilworth with the Marine Corps at Guadalcanal and Clark with the United States Air Force in the Far East. Both were distinguished lawyers and former Republicans who became Democrats rather than attempt to reform the corrupt Republican party from within. Their fight for reform began when Dilworth ran for mayor in 1947 and was defeated by the entrenched Republican machine. Four years later, however, Clark and Dilworth waged a vigorous campaign and won; Clark became the city's first Democratic mayor in the twentieth century, and Dilworth was elected district attorney. Two years later the local Democratic revival was tested again when in Philadelphia Adlai Stevenson ran 162,000 votes ahead of Dwight D. Eisenhower in a conspicuous reversal of the national Republican landslide. Finally, in 1955, Dilworth was elected to succeed Clark as mayor.*

Ever since the reluctant gentlemen-revolutionists founded the Republic in the late eighteenth century, Philadelphians have preferred to have their radical reform movements guided by people of substance and position. While Clark and Dilworth were rejuvenating the Democratic party, other reform groups were forming in the city. Walter Phillips, a Proper Philadelphian and birthright Republican who as a student at Harvard during the Depression came all the way down from Cambridge (much against his father's will) in order to cast his vote for Franklin D. Roosevelt, organized and led the "Republicans for Clark and Dilworth."† At the same time, John Frederick Lewis, Jr. and his wife were instrumental in organizing the local chapter of the Americans for Democratic Action, a so-called radical group with a very responsible and politically concerned membership in Philadelphia.

John Frederick Lewis, Jr. was a wealthy Proper Philadelphia lawyer and philanthropist whose intellectual and nonconformist propensities (see Class of 1915, Episcopal Academy, Chapter XII) were more in the tradition of Proper Boston's greatest days when "everybody talked of reform." His grandfather, S. Weir Lewis, founded the family fortune in the China trade before the Civil War (see Table 9, Chapter V) and lived a few doors south of Holy Trinity Church on Rittenhouse Square. His father, John Frederick Lewis, Senior, a Philadelphia lawyer, augmented the family fortune by shrewd investments in urban real estate.

The Lewises have been leaders in the cultural life of Philadelphia for two generations. John Frederick Lewis, Senior, was president of the Academy of the Fine Arts, Academy of Music, Mercantile Library, and the Historical Society of Pennsylvania. His

---

* In this most recent mayoralty contest it is interesting and perhaps a sign of the times, that Richardson Dilworth, one-time end on the Yale football team, and W. Thacher Longstreth, of Princeton gridiron fame, led their respective political parties.

† Phillips was also responsible for the founding of Philadelphia's first City Planning Commission (one of the nation's finest today). Appropriately enough, its first Chairman was Edward Hopkinson, Jr. He remained at the helm throughout Mayor Clark's Democratic administration but was replaced by Albert M. Greenfield after Richardson Dilworth became Mayor. Jared Ingersoll announced his resignation from the Commission after Greenfield's appointment as Chairman; such are the ways of social change.

son followed in his footsteps as president of the Academy of the
Fine Arts and the Academy of Music. In accordance with his civic
and cultural interests, John Frederick Lewis, Jr. limited his club
memberships to the Franklin Inn and Art Alliance, in both of
which he has held the office of president in recent years. The
Philadelphia chapter of the Americans for Democratic Action was
founded at an informal meeting in the Lewis mansion at 1916
Spruce Street, where the family has lived continuously since 1856.

On the national scene, men of means and background are
following the example set by Franklin D. Roosevelt in the 1930's.
In fact the Democratic party, in the tradition of Jefferson and that
colorful frontier aristocrat, Andrew Jackson (who of course, appealed to such patrician Philadelphians as Richard Rush and
Charles Jared Ingersoll), has probably taken on more of an
aristocratic pattern of leadership than at any other time in its
long history. Such men as Adlai Stevenson of Choate School and
Princeton, G. Mennon Williams of Salisbury School and Princeton,
John F. Kennedy of Choate and Harvard, and both Dean Acheson
and Averell Harriman of Groton and Yale are all representative
of the trend.* Descendants of "robber barons" would hardly be
satisfied with the confining life of the corporation executive or a
partnership in a large metropolitan law firm.

Even Proper Philadelphians are participating in this trend on
the national scene. Apparently the voters of Pennsylvania, who
re-elected President Eisenhower by an overwhelming majority,
also had enough confidence in Proper Philadelphia's millionaire
socialite, Joseph Sill Clark, to send him to Washington as their
junior Senator. And he was the descendant of a long line of investment bankers who had never had the "itch for public office"
in over one hundred years. Finally, of course, America's most
important ambassadorial post was held recently by a Proper Philadelphian. The former American Ambassador to Moscow, ex-Philadelphian Charles E. Bohlen, a product of St. Paul's and Harvard

---

* A comparison of the biographies of Adlai Stevenson, Averell Harriman,
and Dean Acheson as reported in *Who's Who* (British) and *Who's Who in
America* reveals some interesting cultural contrasts. Hobbies are, of course,
reported in the British version only. More interesting, however, is the fact that
while all three report their boarding school in their British biographies, none
does so in the American volume. One often observes this sort of reverse snob-
bism in this country where egalitarianism often is preferred to the truth.

(Porcellian), and his brother-in-law, Charles Wheeler Thayer,* one of the few Proper Philadelphia graduates of West Point in modern times, are both thorough students of the Russian language and culture, having long since anticipated the present contest between this country and the Soviet Union. Perhaps gentlemen of means and secure leisure have often been leaders in new movements and ideas. After all, Thomas Jefferson, Oliver Cromwell, Franklin Roosevelt, and George Washington were country squires. Isaiah Berlin may well have a point when he writes: "There is something singularly attractive about men who retained, throughout life, the manners, the texture of being, the habits and style of a civilized and refined *milieu*. Such men exercise a peculiar kind of personal freedom which combines spontaneity with distinction. Their minds see large and generous horizons, and, above all, reveal a unique intellectual gaiety of a kind that aristocratic education tends to produce. At the same time, they are intellectually on the side of everything that is new, progressive, rebellious, young, untried, of that which is about to come into being, of the open sea whether or not there is land that lies beyond. To this type belong those intermediate figures, like Mirabeau, Charles James Fox, Franklin Roosevelt, who live near the frontier that divides old from new, between the *douceur de la vie* which is about to pass and the tantalising future, the dangerous new age that they themselves do much to bring into being."[3] Perhaps America as a whole will benefit from the patrician's modern emancipation from the counting house.

One more question remains to be raised even if it cannot be answered: What is the future function of a predominantly Anglo-Saxon and Protestant upper class in an ethnically and religiously heterogeneous democracy? In many ways, this is the most important question of all. As Joseph Patrick Kennedy, Boston millionaire and American Ambassador to the Court of St. James under Roosevelt, once put it: "How long does our family have to be here before we are called Americans rather than Irish-Americans?" As has been shown throughout this volume, the American upper class has been from the beginning open to new men of talent and power and their families. By the middle of the twentieth century,

---

* Descendant of Charles Wheeler, family founder, discussed in Chapter V.

however, upper-class status appears to be limited primarily to families of colonial and northern European stock and Protestant affiliations. Glancing back to the turn of the century, when a flood-tide of immigrants came to these shores from southern and eastern Europe, to say nothing of the Irish Catholics who came earlier, one wonders if this American democracy has not produced some-what of a caste situation at the upper-class level. Or are the talented and powerful descendants of these newer immigrants going to be assimilated into some future upper-class way of life and social organization?

It has been shown how parallel upper classes existed in Philadelphia in 1940. On a national scale, "café society" as well as the business executive society of rank, although perhaps not as permanent or community-rooted as the upper class, have been firmly institutionalized in recent decades as parallel social organizations. Whether this contemporary situation is a sign of a healthy social structure of leadership is a problem which needs a great deal of careful research. At any rate, the description of the wealthy and talented expense-account elite in A. C. Spectorsky's *The Exurbanites* or William H. Whyte, Jr.'s *The Organization Man* appears to suggest that large numbers of this new American elite are living in a nightmare of insecurity and conformity.[4] Nor does C. Wright Mills offer much hope; his *The Power Elite* adds up to a "higher im-morality."[5]

In closing it should be said that, although a "classless society" is manifestly a contradiction in terms, this democracy surely cannot survive so long as upper-class status is still denied to those families with minority ethnic and religious affiliations. In this young nation, an ancient mansion of democracy, the stairway of social prestige has been "forever echoing with the wooden shoe going up, and the polished boot descending." When the echoes die, however, the ancient mansion will have been deserted.

The American Aristocrat
and Other-Direction

THE ideal-typical constructs of tradition-, inner-, and other-direction are now firmly fixed both in the jargon of social science and in the minds of most modern social critics. They not only provided a useful theoretical point of departure for Riesman's brilliant analysis of American social character; they have also been extremely useful in stimulating other studies of contemporary trends toward conformity in America, such, for instance, as the *Organization Man,* by William H. Whyte, Jr. While Riesman rightly focused his attention, in *The Lonely Crowd,* on middle-class social character, this paper will attempt to apply his theoretical constructs in an analysis of American upper-class social character, especially as it has been changing in central tendency since the Second World War.

According to Riesman, it is "the upper socioeconomic levels in the western democracies today, *except for the aristocracy,* which are most strongly permeated by other-direction."[1] In a recently published monograph (this book), I tried to show how America had produced a business aristocracy that maintained a continuous tradition of leadership and power, especially in the older cities along the eastern seaboard, from colonial times to the Second World War.[2] As Riesman suggests above, it was apparent that the social character of this prewar aristocracy, especially in Philadelphia, was a blend of tradition- and *inner*-direction.[3] Here it will be our purpose to show, on the other hand, that the postwar generation of Proper Philadelphians, along with their peers in Boston, New York, or San Francisco, may be increasingly tending toward a *new* social character marked by tradition-

This essay first appeared in *Culture and Social Character: The Work of David Riesman Reviewed,* edited by Seymour Martin Lipset and Leo Lowenthal (Glencoe: The Free Press, 1961), copyright © 1961 by The Free Press of Glencoe, Inc., and reprinted here by permission of The Macmillan Company.

and *other*-direction. But while the pressures for a new type of conformity are very definitely a part of their postwar social situation, the members of the established upper class are still far more resistant to other-direction than the more mobile members of the new American leadership.

Whereas the members of an hereditary upper class—most of whom have parents, or ancestors, of greater stature than themselves —stand for stability and tradition, middle class membership means mobility and change. Thus tradition-direction is always the basis of upper-class social character. Moreover in a stable, preindustrial society, both the hereditary aristocracy *and* the people are characterized by tradition-direction. But with the rise of an urban-industrial civilization, middle-class values will eventually permeate the whole social structure. While the style of life of the "old" middle class produced an inner-directed social character, other-direction is a product of the rise of the "new" middle class to a dominant position in modern society. When the entrepreneur and the "old" middle class produced the typical mobile men, the members of the upper class, in self-defense as it were, took on many of the characteristics of inner-direction. The Protestant, business aristocrat in America, and even in England, was always quite different from his counterpart in preindustrial and Catholic Spain. In our era, when the "new" middle class of white collar employees, led by managers and bureaucrats rather than entrepreneurs, becomes the predominant mobile type, other-direction not only becomes the middle-class mode; it also permeates both the upper and lower classes. The gentlemen of inherited means and traditions who dealt with such new men as Dreiser's Frank Cowperwood were of a very different breed from their descendants who are now dealing with new men of the style of Marquand's Willis Wade. While buccaneering Frank Cowperwood was ostensibly ostracized by Proper Philadelphians because of his irregular private life, sincere Willis Wade had no time for a private life as he fought his way up in a large corporation world. Thus in a country such as America where middle-class values dominate the whole society, one would expect the social character of the upper class to change along with the changing modes of mobility. Of equal importance, however, is the fact that, beginning in the 1930's and accelerated since the Second World War, there has been a gradual but fundamental change in the ethnic composition of America's mobile middle class.

The Rise and Fall
of Anglo-Saxon–Protestant Rule in America

Contrary to the melting-pot ideologies, American leadership has been dominated by an Anglo-Saxon–Protestant minority for most of its history. Between the close of the Civil War and the onset of the great depression, business gentlemen of Anglo-Saxon descent and Protestant affiliations became the most powerful members of the American community; and they and their children were rapidly assimilated into an already established upper class, composed of the descendants of colonial and pre–Civil War merchants, statesmen, and soldiers. In the course of the twentieth century the new upper-class suburbs with their fashionable Episcopalian churches, exclusive country clubs and country day schools, as well as New England boarding schools and Ivy League universities, all served the purpose of assimilating the sons of the newly rich and powerful into this traditional upper-class way of life. The polished graduates of Groton and Harvard went easily into the best law firms and banks, and eventually on to the Supreme Court, the Senate, the Cabinet, or to some choice ambassadorial post abroad; the best medical schools were almost hereditary preserves for these sons of the fortunate; and for those with a less professional turn of mind, there was always the securely held family firm, waiting for heirs to move into top management. And above all, these exclusive institutions were run and supported by families with a nationally recognized monopoly of power and caste-like security of social position.

In many ways of course this caste-like situation in America depended on, and was fostered by, the flood of immigrants, first from Ireland and then later from southern and eastern Europe, who came to these shores each year, primarily to fill the lower socioeconomic positions in our steadily expanding economy. At first these immigrants, who after all were used to an inferior and fixed status in Europe, were only too glad to defer to their "betters" here in democratic America. Even though the more ambitious members of these various hyphenated-American groups eventually obtained power and wealth as leaders of our urban political machines, more often than not these machines were subservient locally to the respectable business interests and represented on the national scene by such men of older stock as Mark Hanna, Nelson Aldrich, or Boies Penrose. "Ed Flynn might boss the Bronx," writes Andrew Hacker, "but he would defer to Franklin D. Roosevelt (of Harvard); Carmine De Sapio rides behind Averell Harriman (of Yale); and Jake Arvey cleared the way for Adlai Stevenson (of Princeton)."[4]

Protected by this nationally recognized caste position and assuming a monopoly of ultimate power through a kind of natural rights tradition, it is no wonder that America's business aristocrats of the old regime manifested a strong tradition- and inner-directed social character. In the first quarter of the twentieth century, anti-Semitism and anti-Irish Catholicism were taken for granted among American aristocrats, while any form of ethnic "tolerance"—so characteristic, at least on the surface and in public, of our more other-directed age—was unheard of.[5] After all it was America's "best people" who strongly supported the tragic decision in the Sacco-Vanzetti trial; upper-class anti-Semitism was perhaps more blatantly displayed in the five decades after 1880 than at any other time in our history; and even more indicative of these last days of Anglo-Saxon–Protestant assumed superiority were the tracts of Madison Grant, himself a product of one of old New York's most patrician families and of the most exclusive clubs in the city.[6] But perhaps the very success of Grant's books during the twenties was a warning of an era's end and the shape of things to come.

The assumed superiority of this older business aristocracy in America has been seriously challenged, if not defeated, by the revolutionary changes in our society brought on by the depression, the war, and especially the postwar boom. In this connection, the two most important developments have been (1) the unprecedented expansion of our economy since the war and (2) the consequent need for rapidly assimilating new groups, including large numbers of hyphenated-Americans, into the central stream of our national life and *leadership*. We are now witnessing, as never before, the ethnic democratization of plutocracy in America. As a sign of the times, Grace Kelly, of Philadelphia's most eminent Irish-Catholic clan, was not only Hollywood's leading postwar patrician heroine but also went on to marry royalty in the traditional American pattern, set by the Vanderbilts and Astors, of the old-stock plutocracy.

This new democratization of plutocracy has created a social situation where the old deference to caste leadership is being replaced by competing ethnic and functional veto groups, to borrow from Riesman's vocabulary. This is so because the new men of power, due to their great number, their interests and values, or their ethnicity, are *not* being assimilated into any traditional upper-class way of life and social organization. With no established tradition of their own, and no traditional group to break into, their social position is probably more slippery than that of any previous group of leaders in our history. In place of the family traditions and the assumptions of Anglo-Saxon superiority which legitimized the power of the old regime, these new men and women (one hesitates to call them families) have had to resort to public relations, manipulation of mass media, and all sorts of social engineering to sell the American public on their new right to rule. The press agent has replaced the genealogist, and the white-collar millions who dream of a place in the sun now prefer the racy style of the gossip columnist to the dreary and dwindling reports of the society editors.

But it is one of the tragic ironies of modern life and leadership that these skillful manipulators of others may themselves have become the most manipulated segment of the population. It is no accident that the hidden persuaders, who have so little respect for the privacy or dignity of the average citizen, are living in an exurban nightmare of insecurity and sophisticated conformity. While Riesman has a charming way (perhaps an other-directed way?) of qualifying and minimizing the unpleasant implications of many of his insights, surely anyone who takes seriously such blunter books as the *Hidden Persuaders,* the *Organization Man,* or *The Exurbanites* must be impressed and depressed by the other-directed conformity that characterizes the lives of the most talented and ambitious members of America's postwar generation.

Finally, of course, this atomization of American leadership has affected the security of the old upper class, which is now being forced to share its power with others. Both the late Senator McCarthy's rise to power and Madison Avenue's skillful handling of a Republican campaign that focused its attack on the supposed treason of prominent members of the opposition were symptoms of this new power struggle. The tragic tale of Alger Hiss and the well-publicized dismissal of a number of Ivy League diplomats on the grounds of degeneracy were sold as solemn warnings to the American people that proper, Anglo-Saxon Protestants no longer had an exclusive claim on 100 per cent

Americanism. In the course of this power struggle, Dean Acheson was politically crucified, among other reasons, for his rather inner-directed and hardly public-relations-minded definition of what friendship means; and Secretary Stevens, a fellow Yaleman of patrician New England stock, was humiliated before the American public on our most publicized postwar television investigation. But the panic politics of the McCarthy era were only symptoms of much more basic social trends.

The Decline of Family Capitalism

Family power in America has been traditionally based on family capitalism. Yet one of the most important consequences of the postwar economic boom has been the rapid absorption of the family firm by the large corporation. And the decline of family power in America has been an important factor in the growth of other-direction in our managerial society.

The old business aristocracy in America was of course based on families of inherited wealth. And this wealth was produced and preserved by a succession of entrepreneurial founders of family firms. While the modern manager tends to be but a shadow of the established corporation's prestige and power, the old family firm and the upper class upon which it was based to a great extent were the lengthened shadows of these family founders. These family firms were not only a source of wealth and income; they were also the basis of family pride and tradition as well as an important source of parental discipline. Family capitalism fostered paternalism in the home as well as in the factory. Sons and grandsons grew up on the legends of their ancestors' accomplishments; at an early age they were taken to the plant or office, where they often knew many of the employees and sometimes their families; and they were disciplined and inspired by their responsibility as sons and heirs. As an ideal at least, continuity of family ownership created a sense of *noblesse oblige* among the rich and powerful that was not unlike that which went with landed wealth in an earlier era. In vivid contrast to this ideal, which was of course not always lived up to, absentee corporate ownership demands no sense of personal involvement or continuity of responsibility; the dividend playboys who can be found gambling in oil wells around the "brunch" table at El Morocco or the Stork every afternoon are heirs to the modern atomization of ownership.

The current tax structure is of course an important factor in the accelerated postwar decline in family capitalism. The family firm is often sold, not because of inefficiency or lack of competitive success, but rather because inheritance taxes have reached a point where an owner cannot afford to pass on his partnership or firm to his heirs intact; it is far more expedient to sell out to the large corporation in return for stock, which can be divided among the heirs. Although often overlooked, the effect of inheritance taxes in inhibiting the passing on of family enterprises is far more damaging to the heirs psychologically, and to the family sociologically, than is its intended function of limiting large inheritances of more liquid corporate wealth. Whereas, for example, the patriarchal continuity of the Du Pont clan has flourished along with their control of the family enterprise, the publicity-seeking, café society crowd draws many of its most prominent members—such as the divorcing John Jacob Astor III (three wives), Cornelius Vanderbilt, Jr. (five wives), Tommy Manville (nine wives), or the Topping brothers (ten wives between them)—from the ranks of the dividend heirs with no locus of responsibility. In this connection it was interesting to watch the individual members' reactions to the recent sale of one of Philadelphia's oldest and well-known family firms to a Cash McCall type of modern buccaneer. The family patriarch was dead, while the members of the present generation were clamoring for more dividends. Since the sale of the firm, the heirs, now scattered around this country and Europe with little sense of community roots, are far better off financially, but the family's influence on the business and cultural life of the city is now reduced to a minimum. At any rate, just as the tradition- and inner-direction and family conformity so characteristic of the old upper class in America were fostered by family capitalism, so the new peer, and publicity-dependent, conformity thrives in a social structure that undermines the power of parents and encourages other-directed social situations.

If the inheritance tax atomizes established family power, the income tax makes it far more difficult for the new men of power and ambition to establish new families. While the bank account and community roots create family strength and continuity, corporate loyalty and the expense account life may have quite the opposite effect. The new manager virtually marries the corporation, which, in return, provides him with a generous expense account life, especially when away from home; retirement benefits replace private savings, make it increasingly hard for him to resign, and encourage an other-directed conformity in his slow struggle to the top. In response to the persistent corporate cooption of the private sectors of modern life, it is not surprising that, since the war, countless numbers of Proper Philadelphians have resigned from promising positions in nationally famous firms. At least one member of an old Proper Philadelphia clan was able to resist, for a time, this modern trend. Possessed of ambition, ability, and drive, this young man was doing very well in the local office of a national corporation. Several years ago, he was moved to New York. Rather than move his family from his beloved Main Line, he arose each morning at five-thirty, took the Paoli Local to the city, where he caught the New York express and arrived promptly at his desk before nine o'clock. But this was not enough for his boss, who felt that he should be available in New York after business hours in order to entertain customers. He refused to move, however, even after several threats from the front office. About a year later, he was not only still with the firm but had been transferred back to Philadelphia with a raise in salary and a far more responsible position. In relating the story of his corporate life to the writer, he was careful to stress that his peers in the New York office were horrified at what they called his arrogant behavior; he had not of course let it be known that he would never have been able to do what he did (he had three children) had he not had ample private means. It is indicative that, since his recent divorce, this ambitious Proper Philadelphian has been working for the same firm out in the West. He is now willing and anxious to travel anywhere they so desire, which of course makes him a far more valuable member of the corporate team.

Corporate Contacts, Family Friends, and Other-Direction

One of the important developments making for an increase in other-direction is of course the fact that modern managers of large corporations, as well as men of affairs in general, have less and less private social life because they spend so many of their leisure hours with contacts within the bureaucratic hierarchy, if not with customers. Inevitably one begins to treat everyone as a customer who is always right and wants to be a friend. This new type of social life, which so often confuses contacts with friends, is reflected in the living language. In the recent past, for example, the inner-directed business gentleman, at least in Philadelphia, carefully structured his human relations in graded levels of intimacy. Thus he addressed his many business contacts in a formal way (Mr. Smith); at a more intimate level of association, business contacts of long standing as well as most of his office colleagues were addressed by their surnames only (Smith); finally given names (Joe) were reserved for his closest associates in the firm and friends he had known for years if not since childhood. At the same time, he reserved such terms as "dear" and "darling" for a rather intimate circle of relatives and friends of the opposite sex. Today, when public relations have made private relations old hat, everyone is "Joe" and almost anyone may be "darling." As the *gemeinschaft* barriers of class, community, and family have largely broken down, even the most patrician businessman or politician must conform to this new pattern of pseudo-gemeinschaft. Although he realizes that resistance to the trend is both ridiculous and reactionary, one can understand his sardonic smile when a new business contact immediately addresses him by his first name when his friends and family have always used his middle name (often an abbreviation of a famous ancestor's surname).

But this new pseudo-gemeinschaft lends warmth to the human relations of a lonely crowd of leaders whose social position is no longer anchored in family, class, or community but is solely due to their status in the corporate hierarchy. Philadelphia, however, sometimes provides a colder climate for new men, especially in those firms where the top executive positions are in the hands of members of the established upper class, who still maintain family and class traditions in their private social life if not in the office downtown. An extremely talented executive from a more progressive city in the Middle West, for example, was brought into Philadelphia recently as president of one of these established firms. He was immediately elected to membership in an elite country club where his new associates entertained customers. But he was surprised that, after about two years as president of this national corporation, he had not yet been asked to join the upper-class golf club to which most of his closest associates in the firm belonged. He had of course assumed that, as was the case with the western branch of the firm, he would automatically take his place in the social group that his high position in the firm warranted.

This unfortunate conflict between upper-class traditions and the new corporate mores illustrates several important things about the new leadership structure in America, and even in Philadelphia. In the first place, this old Philadelphia firm, like many others of its kind in the city since the war, desperately needed new talent at the top. And it is significant that the more progressive Proper Philadelphia members of the firm (the younger rather than the older generation) were extremely upset by the incident and did all in their power to pressure their club's admission committee into accepting their new president.[7] A generation ago, so argued the more traditional and inner-directed older men of the present management, this situation would not have arisen (even if an outsider had been given the presidency, which would have been unlikely).

In our rapidly expanding economy, where new men are needed more than ever before, this incident also serves to emphasize the important function of the new corporate cooption of the social life of its executives. Expense accounts, company-owned country clubs, hunting lodges, and dude ranches are excellent and rapid devices for assimilating new men of talent into the leisure-time aspects of their new station in life. At least at first, most of these new men do not feel that their private life has been infringed upon by the corporation because they probably have had very little, at least of the kind they are being introduced to. A Proper Philadelphian, for example, recently dined at the home of a talented new executive of the "X" Company, one of the more progressive firms in the city (most of its top executives belong to the same country club, all the officers in which are also officers of the "X" Company). After dinner, he strolled into his host's den and pulled out a blue, leather-bound volume from the small bookshelf. Entitled *Ranching It: 1952*, the little volume contained a snapshot record of a brief vacation his hosts, along with five other executives and their wives from the "X" Company, had spent at a company-sponsored hideaway in the West. Characteristically enough, our Proper Philadelphian, whose family had gone to the same summer resort in Maine for two generations, was surprised that his host not only enjoyed spending his vacation with business contacts but was very proud of this little volume.

Caveat

The postwar economic boom in America has accelerated the decline of the old family-capitalism and increased the importance of the large corporation as well as the other-directed conformity of the new managerial society. At the same time, we have tried to show how the traditional upper-class social organization has been somewhat of a defense against this other-directed trend. It would be entirely misleading, however, to create the impression that the members of the old upper class have in the recent past, or will in the future, remain aloof from these trends. As a matter of fact, they are increasingly taking part and only feel more frustrated because they know what they have to lose in the way of their traditional freedoms.

Moreover, while many of the old established family firms have now been absorbed by large corporations, a host of new and exceedingly prosperous enterprises have grown up during and since the war; these are almost invariably run by rugged new men of the old entrepreneurial mold. But whereas the man of patrician background is most welcome to a modern management that lays such stress on polished human relations in both office and plant, it is the somewhat rougher diamond, often of minority ethnic origins, who is forced to build his own enterprise as the only available way to wealth and power. After a decade of teaching at the Wharton School of Finance and Commerce, for example, one has the definite impression that the *undergraduate* student body has an unusually high proportion of sons of individual entrepreneurs. These boys are not wasting time on "culture" but are preparing to take over from dad (many of the more intellectual among them bemoan the fact that their fathers simply will not pay for the trappings of "culture"). At the Wharton graduate level, on the other hand, polished alumni of the best liberal arts colleges are preparing themselves, by and large, for careers in well-established corporations. Many informal polls in the classroom also reveal that the *undergraduates* at Wharton include a large proportion of second and third generation Americans.

Although impossible to document in a brief paper such as this, there is good reason to believe that the individual enterprisers who have produced real wealth in Philadelphia since the war—appliance and automobile dealers, contractors and construction engineers, food-fair magnates, restaurateurs, and so forth, all of whom have benefited from the rising standard of living in our consumer economy—have come predominantly from second and third generation American backgrounds. A wartime friend of the newer immigrant stock, for instance, made a small fortune right after the war in secondhand automobiles, sold out at the peak of the boom, and is now on the way to real wealth as a successful manufacturer of storm sash and metal windows, with a lucrative sideline investment in a string of "motels" along a prominent highway leading out of the city.[8] And he has a crowd of affluent friends among the Italian- and Irish-American nabobs of South Philadelphia. In describing the elaborate Catholic wedding-party of one of them, to which, as he put it, "no one worth less than a million got an invite," this former bombardier for democracy opened up to the writer a prosperous world that we sociologists have not begun to explore systematically. And these inner-directed buccaneers are very different from the other-directed, corporate managers, public relations experts, and Madison Avenue manipulators who are, after all, rapidly rising in somewhat more Brooks-Brothers-suited channels to power.

At the same time, few if any members of the upper class in Philadelphia have started and succeeded in building up their own firms since the war. It is socially acceptable to become a junior executive at General Motors but hardly proper to run the local Buick agency. Even in the law, traditionally the way to power in America, the well-connected young men are usually found in the old established firms. Again it is rather the new ethnic groups who are contributing the legal entrepreneurs of ability and independent imagination. In 1957, for instance, one of the writer's keenest former students founded his own law partnership. Irish Catholic in background, he remarked while talking over his plans and dreams with his old teacher: "You know that not a single white-Protestant friend [deep in local Democratic politics, this language is second nature] has started a new law firm in the city since the war."

One final point should be made concerning the other-directed leadership that has emerged since the war. The progressive large corporation, with its elaborate devices for acculturating its new executives into the kind of social life proper to their achieved positions in the corporate hierarchy, may *seem* to be far more "democratic" than the community- and family-rooted criteria of social position that characterized the way of life of the old upper class. But this new democratic camaraderie cuts two ways: if every new president or vice-president is to be automatically accepted in the company-owned or -sponsored country club life, this very warm and democratic way may have the unanticipated consequence of narrowing the background qualifications for working in the firm in the first place. In other words, in the days when one was not expected to play golf with business contacts, or bring them home to dinner, it made little difference what their backgrounds were so long as they did a good job in the office.[9] But when friends and business contacts are fused, the ground is laid for an even more selective recruitment of management material, on the basis of ethnicity or religion. One often wonders if, in the long run, the new corporate feudalism in America will not eventually prove to be far more socially stultifying than the traditional community, family, and class hierarchies of the past.

The Younger Generation and Other-Direction

The members of the younger generation are always a mystery to their elders, and we shall not attempt to assess the values and attitudes of upper-class youths who are coming to maturity in this postwar era. Nevertheless there are ascertainable trends in upper-class social organization, especially in the fashionable suburbs, private schools, and colleges, that may be sowing the seeds of other-direction.

In our democracy, ecological stratification has replaced the older and aristocratic barriers of class and family. The fashionable suburb plays such a vital role in modern society primarily because *where* one lives, rather than *who* one is, is a *visible* status referent in an increasingly amorphous social structure. The Main Line, Philadelphia's most publicized elite address today, first became fashionable when the city's leading coal barons, railroad kings, merchant princes, and utility tycoons built houses there around the turn of the century.[10] The tycoons' wives were executive directors of large households staffed with housemaids, chambermaids, parlormaids, waitresses, butlers, cooks, governesses, gardeners, and coachmen. As a result, they were often only indirectly involved with their children and hardly concerned with their social life, which, at the younger ages, usually revolved around the fascinating and congenial life backstairs—in the nursery, in the kitchen, and out in the stable. In this extended-family kind of world, the children's characters were molded largely by the servants who, if anything, overemphasized the patriarchal and class values of their employers. As most of these servants had themselves been reared in the "old country" patriarchal ways, this was inevitable.

This way of life was maintained by many proper Main Line families until the war. As labor was cheap during the depression, even the impecunious genteel usually had a servant or two. With the modern exodus of servants from all but the wealthiest households, however, this world has gone forever. Since the war, most of the old estates have been sold to the Catholic Church, been remodeled into modern country clubs, or been subdivided into smaller "estates," more in keeping with a servantless, do-it-yourself age. And even along the prosperous Main Line, these changes have produced a mother-organized and child-centered world, where the smaller household is now served by a host of outside associations, from the diaper service and play school to the country club and summer camp. Before the war, for instance, very few if any upper-class children went to school before the age of six; today all of them go to play school for two or three years (and of course are now far better adjusted to the group). Moreover, as the children grow older their lives are highly organized in activities outside the home: their personalities are developed by an endless round of dancing, skating, ballet, music, tennis, and golf lessons, and devoted mothers are having nervous breakdowns as they transport Johnny and Joan from one activity to another in the course of each over-steered week.

Modern life along the Main Line has become increasingly organized and competitive because, although it is still an extremely exclusive suburb from the point of view of society as a whole, from the standpoint of old families, it has been democratized to an alarming degree since the war. The members of the new plutocracy, only too glad to pay for this prominent and patrician address, are often avid participants in the social game: there are now five "exclusive" dancing class groups where there used to be one; numerous mutually excluding country club sets are now spread throughout the countryside, and one former Proper Philadelphia mansion has recently been remodeled into the first Jewish country club in the area; and the local social columns report the leisure-time activities of these new families, many of whose names suggest their Irish background.[11] Whereas the Proper Philadelphia clans who built up the old Main Line were servant- and property-protected and could afford to stand aloof from the crowd, today even long-established families are forced by circumstance to be snobbishly selective, especially where their children are concerned. And this new heterogeneous atmosphere, along with the selective and highly organized associational life it fosters, is bound, in the long run, to produce a more other-directed younger generation.

The private schools, always extremely sensitive to social change at the higher levels of society, have of course been flooded with students from both old and newly prosperous homes since the war. Not only have they had to take care of an ever increasing number of students in Latin, mathematics, and English; they have also had to handle all sorts of extra-educational functions that used to be done in the home by parents or servants. Discipline alone has been vastly complicated by the commingling of students from different backgrounds. Several years ago, for example, the school authorities were extremely concerned about the steadily increasing amount of serious juvenile delinquency among teenage children from wealthy and prominent Main Line homes. At an evening class at the University of Pennsylvania that same winter, one of the author's students, a Main Line matron of an inner-directed and intellectual turn-of-mind, brought the Agnes Irwin School "news" up to the desk after class. Founded by Agnes Irwin, the first dean of Radcliffe College and a well-known Victorian educator, this is Philadelphia's most patrician school for young ladies. At any rate, the school newspaper reported the formation of an association of the leading schools, both public and private, along the Main Line. The purpose of this association was to set up and attempt to enforce a series of rules for parents to follow with their teen-age children: when and where they should be allowed to date, when they should be home at night, and the type of chaperonage required at parties. In exercising this kind of authority over modern parents, the private schools have come a long way from the days when, as Riesman put it, the upper-class mother could say to the headmaster: "I don't see why the masters can't get along with Johnny; all the servants do."[12] But in an other-directed age when "Joan's mother allows it, why don't you?" is so often given in to by overworked and distracted mothers, even the most traditional Main Line matron (whose fifteen-year-old daughter can't possibly be prevented from driving forty miles to hear a "name-band" with some new-rich contractor's son in his red Jaguar) must welcome this kind of regimentation by the school authorities. After all, when class lines and values are breaking down, her daughter can ill afford to lose caste with her popular peers.

The New England boarding schools have played an important role in educating the sons of the Eastern seaboard aristocracy for several generations. Just as they succeeded in acculturating the sons of the new rich of Anglo-Saxon Protestant stock at the turn of the century, so many of them are now aware of the problems of assimilating the sons of the modern, and often ethnic, plutocracy. Thus since the war these schools have been changing rapidly. And perhaps St. Paul's School, in Concord, New Hampshire, the favorite Proper Philadelphia school, has changed even more than the rest. Its extremely inner-directed and puritanical traditions, however, remained intact throughout the thirties.[13] The curriculum was routine and classical, with only the few students who hated Latin majoring in science; there was little if any emphasis on the arts. The masters were often gentlemen of inherited means who found teaching highly rewarding as a way of life rather than as a profession. Their duty was to build character. Intellectual excellence and the rounded personality were secondary and boys were rarely expelled for scholastic failure. And most of them followed their fathers on to Harvard, Yale, and Princeton.

But it was for its extracurricular programs that St. Paul's was most criticized before the war; they were said to be puritanical, in-breeding, and snobbish. There were, for example, very few athletic contests with other schools. The student body was divided into three clubs, Isthmian, Delphian, and Old Hundred, and all took part in intramural contests. In the fall, *everyone,* including the more gentle and bookish seniors, was expected to represent his club in football; in the winter everyone played ice hockey; and in the spring, which eventually came after endless, bleak days of New England thaw when the boys had to *amuse themselves* (see below), everyone played baseball, rowed, or ran around the track. While other minor sports were available, they were not encouraged as a major activity. On the whole, four or five years in this rather rigid atmosphere were likely to produce a moralistic, inner-directed, and often unimaginatively snobbish young man. But of course the boys were drawn to begin with from fashionable and conservative homes where the old Republican-Protestant values were the norm.

The changes at the school since the war have been far-reaching and progressive. A less puritanical and more permissive atmosphere has been consciously created in order to set a more democratic, tolerant, and possibly other-directed tone to school life. First of all, the curriculum has been broadened and intellectual excellence has been emphasized. Both the sciences and the arts have come into their own. In accord with the times, in fact, science, with excellent new equipment and instruction, has become one of the most popular majors. Music, dramatics, and the plastic arts have assumed a much more prominent place in the whole school community. Honors programs and wide elective choices for the keener students have produced a far more varied intellectual diet. And above all, the postwar faculty appears to be far better trained if not better educated. In place of the traditional gentlemen of inherited means whose primary purpose was to mold character, the new masters are more likely to be specialists in their respective fields, with an increasing number holding advanced degrees. Their social backgrounds are far more diverse, many having graduated from public rather than private schools. As a democratic example to the boys, one of the latest appointments to the faculty happens to be a Negro.[14]

Extracurricular activities are now far more diverse and attractive. To combat the old provincialism and isolation of life at the school, competition with other schools, both public and private, is now being encouraged. Within the school, the boys may now choose between a wide variety of minor sports rather than being forced into playing football or some other major sport each term. There is also a much closer coordination with both private and public schools in the intellectual sphere through increased membership in outside educational associations and participation in inter-school programs and contests.[15]

But probably two developments at the school have been most disconcerting to the more traditionally minded parents and alumni. First of all, due to our expanding economy and the consequent increase in the number of newly wealthy and talented families coming to the fore in the postwar America, there has been a tremendous pressure both for admission to the school and admission from the school into college. At the same time both schools like St. Paul's and the prestige universities like Harvard, Yale, and Princeton are definitely attempting to broaden the social base and improve the intellectual standards of their student bodies. One no longer goes to Groton or St. Paul's and then on to Harvard or Yale just because one's father or grandfather did so.

Moreover, to broaden the geographic and social representativeness of the student body, the administrative staff of the school has been enlarged so as to improve its admissions and public relations policies. Among other things, the school sends representatives annually to our major cities, where they meet with specially arranged parent groups. Talks and informal discussions serve to acquaint new families with the advantages of the school and to encourage them to send their sons there. Planned public relations of this sort would have been unheard of during the old regime. Not only are those admitted to the school chosen from a more democratic base; its graduates are also having a much more diverse and democratic college experience. Whereas, for instance, in 1935 all save two or three of the graduating class went on to either Harvard, Yale, or Princeton, approximately the same number of graduates in 1955 went on to some twenty different institutions of higher learning.

As we have stressed before, many of these changes have been forced on a progressive and realistic administration at the school by the profound changes in America's postwar elite structure. Certainly the best forms of tolerance and other-direction must result from this new social situation. But vices lay hidden in all virtues. The overbusy and overorganized life at the school, and the emphasis on personality development and intellectual excellence at the possible expense of character, may not all be to the good. In contrast to Europe, for example, where formal extracurricular activities among students—regular drill and rigid schedules, paid coaches and officials, elaborate and uniform uniforms and equipment, and so forth—are rare, the overorganizing of both school and college life in America is certainly a factor in fostering other-directed conformity. The recently completed indoor athletic building at St. Paul's, costing in the neighborhood of a million dollars, is an example of this modern propensity for organized activities. This expensive building now provides efficiently directed activities for boys who previously were forced to spend rainy days and almost the whole New England "thaw" season between February and early April in *amusing themselves*. But perhaps the following anecdote is appropriate here: while talking with an official of the school who was visiting the University of Pennsylvania last spring, the author suggested that the new athletic building was not necessarily a mark of progress. The official replied somewhat as follows: "Many of us at the school might agree with you but let me tell you a story: two years ago we had two very fine sons of a prosperous, Midwestern industrialist visit the school. We had met the boys the year before and they had excellent records at their local high school. They were just the type we wanted. In the course of looking around the school grounds, however, one of them remarked that we had no indoor athletic facilities. Well, we never got those two boys, as it turned out, because they liked the gym, swimming pool, and baseball cage down at 'X' school. As we had thought we had sold the parents on St. Paul's, we were obviously disappointed. So you can see why those of us who were in favor of the new facilities had a good argument. . . . Anyway the thing is simply built and not too conspicuous, as it is hidden in the woods just above the old baseball field."

Like the boarding schools, the prestige institutions of higher learning are also responding to the postwar democratization of plutocracy. The pressure for admission rises along with the rapid rise in tuition fees. Although the sons and grandsons of alumni are given special consideration, many are being turned down because of increasingly democratic admissions policies, which want intelligent boys from a broad cross-section of American life. The story of the representative from Yale or Princeton who addressed a local alumni group in a large Eastern city and ended his talk on the modern pressures for admission by reminding his distinguished audience that two out of three of them would not qualify for admission by today's standards is well known. The sons of disappointed loyal alumni of Harvard, Yale, and Princeton are now getting to know about colleges all over the nation, and even fashionable Foxcroft mothers are having to face the fact that they may lose their dear daughters forever if they can't get into Vassar or Radcliffe and end up instead in the fraternity, courting life at Stanford or California.

This new pattern of college attendance being forced on the Eastern seaboard aristocracy will inevitably break down parental power and family continuity, which depends on the maintenance of long-established community roots. Whereas in the nineteen thirties nine out of ten Proper Philadelphia daughters did *not* go to college, and spent their entire post-school year as debutantes in their local community and under parental supervision, today a vast majority of them go to college in various parts of the country where they are on their own in a more or less peer-supervised world. And as Proper Philadelphia sons, before the war, were invariably enrolled at the traditional Eastern universities, which were convenient to the debutante functions, class endogamy and family continuity were fostered by a world that has now been modified considerably.

This modern breakdown of class endogamy and parental authority has considerably modified upper-class courting mores. There is reason to believe that the "steady dating" mores in America are partly due to the insecurity fostered by social mobility. Thus the mobile youth substitutes stable emotional ties with his *peers* for the traditional ties with *parents*. Before the war, upper-class youth, by and large, snobbishly looked down on "steady dating" and dismissed it as "middle-class." In a parent-supervised and class-protected world, young gentlemen "played the field." On the other hand, it is indicative of the changes in the postwar upper-class world that the present generation invariably follows these same "steady dating" mores that their fathers once looked down upon.

Upper-Class Social Character and
Political Leadership

The need for governmental interference in our large corporation economy was first brought home to the American people by the Great Depression and the New Deal; the locus of ultimate power in America moved from Wall Street to Washington, and the days of the indirect control of the reins of government by the all-powerful money-power came to an end. At the same time, Franklin D. Roosevelt and his patrician friends in the Democratic party symbolized the return once more of American aristocrats to positions of direct governmental leadership.

It is perhaps ironic that, just when the assumed superiority of, and traditional deference to, the old-stock aristocracy is being challenged by the postwar democratization of plutocracy, this same aristocracy of overwhelmingly Republican businessmen is now producing great political leaders who, with certain outstanding exceptions, are Democrats, the party in the North of the urban ethnic masses. But America has a long tradition of this kind of leadership: "In a very real sense," writes S. M. Lipset, "the abolitionists and Progressives were American Tory radicals, men of upper-class backgrounds and values, who as Conservatives also helped to democratize the society as part of their struggle against the vulgar *nouveaux riches* businessmen."[16] From Thomas Jefferson, through the two Roosevelts, to Adlai Stevenson, Averell Harriman or Mennon Williams, the Tory radical in American politics has led the people in their fight for social equality.

But according to Riesman's thesis today and Tocqueville's before him, it is the very triumph of egalitarian values in modern America that has fostered the trend to other-direction. As Riesman writes in *The Lonely Crowd:*

My general thesis is that the inner-directed character tended and still tends in politics to express himself in the style of the "moralizer," while the other-directed character tends to express himself politically in the style of an "inside-dopester." These styles are also linked with a shift in political mood from "indignation" to "tolerance," and a shift in political decision from dominance by a ruling class to power dispersal among many marginally competing pressure groups.[17]

As everything we have said so far in this paper would suggest, we are in complete agreement with Riesman's thesis relating the rise of other-direction to the decline of class rule in America. On the other hand, it is also our thesis that the modern patrician politician in the Democratic party, to a far greater extent than most members of the class from which they came and now depart in political persuasion, are, by and large, *inner-directed moralizers* with, at the same time, a great respect and sympathy for the so-called *tolerance* that Riesman finds characteristic of the political public in our other-directed age. It is no accident that the specialists in "inside-dope" along Madison Avenue handled two political campaigns—probably the most other-directed and cynically moralistic in our history—against Adlai Stevenson, who was drawn into politics after the war for deeply moral reasons before leading the Democrats to their first defeat in one of the most inner-directed campaigns since the puritanical Woodrow Wilson ran for office. But, it will be said, these inner-directed moralizers are psychological deviants from their own social backgrounds and from the other-directed political climate that is a vital part of their postwar world.

Psychological deviants only become sociologically relevant when they also form part of a class of persons with a similarly deviant social character. Classes of patrician deviants are usually thrust upon the political scene during periods of rapid social change and class realignment. Such a class of deviants, for instance, grew up in Philadelphia during the early nineteenth century, when talented and wealthy scions of the city's most prominent Federalist families became Republicans, then Democrats, and eventually supported Andrew Jackson. Just as Tocqueville's America witnessed the decline of the once dominant Colonial aristocracy before the surge of frontier egalitarianism, so Riesman's America is now witnessing a similar egalitarian trend as minority ethnic groups are being absorbed into the main stream of American life and leadership.

Ever since New Deal days, minority aspirations in this country have by and large been voiced through the Democratic party. And such men as Stevenson and other patrician leaders who have turned away from their families' traditional Republicanism may be but outstanding examples of a social character characteristic of a whole class of upper-class members who have been workers and supporters as well as leaders in the Democratic party since the war. Of the members of the upper-class generation that came to maturity in America during the nineteen twenties and thirties, for example, most of those who have had active governmental careers have also been Democrats. And like most of the "do-good" members of the Americans for Democratic Action regardless of background, they have taken a moral rather than opportunistic approach to politics. It is no accident that former Attorney General Francis Biddle, scion of one of Philadelphia's most patrician clans, was very active in founding ADA, besides acting as its long-time leader in Washington. At the same time, the Philadelphia chapter of ADA was founded in the home of a wealthy philanthropist whose family had continuously occupied that home since 1856, and its president for many years was the overly conscientious heir-through-marriage of one of the city's greatest nineteenth-century family fortunes. On the whole then, this class of deviant patricians is the product of several generations of inherited wealth and social position. The wealthiest among them often feel guilty about their inherited fortunes and are compulsively driven by overly egalitarian convictions. The social character of this whole generation of Tory radicals, however, includes a common conviction in the rightness of accepting persons on their merits and accomplishments rather than their racial, ethnic, or religious backgrounds. Brought up in homes where Jews were rarely seen and never accepted, they are often avidly anti-anti-Semitic.[18]

But what one generation often remembers the next generation never knew. Thus social change is not only extremely complex; it is also *generationally discontinuous*. It must be remembered that today's patrician Democratic leaders grew up in a traditionally inner-directed and class-protected world. While they are predominantly liberal conservatives with strong egalitarian convictions, the members of the upper class who are now coming to maturity in a more other-directed and far less class-protected world may produce quite different leadership material. Whereas the bright and talented undergraduates in even the best Ivy League colleges tended to be liberal egalitarians during the prewar period, this very well may not be so today. The keenest undergraduate at the University of Pennsylvania since the war, for example, came of a very good family, was senior editor of the newspaper, a campus leader in general, and possessed of a brilliantly conservative turn of mind. And it may be significant that, of the younger generation of gentlemen from old Eastern seaboard families who are beginning their political careers today, several are now sitting on the Republican rather than the Democratic side of the House of Representatives. Whatever the character and convictions of this postwar generation, in the long run, they will have to deal with an ethnically mixed society that is no longer dominated by a traditionally inner-directed and property-protected minority of Anglo-Saxon-Protestant patricians.

Both the aristocratic and the egalitarian dreams are inspiring as a hope but hopeless as a reality. Like Tocqueville before him, Riesman fears the egalitarian trends of his own generation. As egalitarian caesarism marches across our modern world, perhaps the class of deviant patricians in modern American politics will serve a truly conservative function by preserving the best from the past in an other-directed age in which masses of rootless men and their rootless leaders are desperately seeking a brave new world.

Postscript

Philadelphia Gentlemen, researched and originally published in the 1950's, is an analysis of the structure, function, and historical formation of an American upper class during the *inner-directed* and Protestant era of our history which came to an end in 1940, on the eve of our entry into World War II.

This Afterword, published in 1961, attempts to show how our postwar upper-class institutions are producing a new social character which tends to be more and more *other-directed.*

In the same year (1961), I began working on a book which was essentially an elaboration of the ideas contained in this essay. The book, *The Protestant Establishment,* was finished on July 4, 1963, a

few months before the assassination of John F. Kennedy. Its con-
cluding chapter opened as follows: "Essentially this book has been
an attempt to analyze the decline of authority in America in the
course of the twentieth century."

It is my contention that this *decline of authority* is intimately
bound up with the movement from tradition- and inner-direction,
from parental and principled modes of conformity (and guilt), to
other-direction or peer conformity (and anxiety). Moreover, peer-
fear and other-directed conformity tend to be antithetical to all forms
of hierarchical authority. It is no wonder, then, that, in the decade
since the publication of the above essay, both class and parental
authority in America have declined at a steadily accelerating rate.

I doubt if anyone will ever be able to explain why the present
drug problem came to plague America, like a bolt from the blue, as it
were, in the decade of the 1960's. But I do think, on the other hand,
that the rapid rise of the drug problem into the middle and upper
classes was partly due to the other-directed social character of even
our most privileged youth. Deprived of the protection of class and
parental authority, it is no wonder they succumbed to a peer-fear of
panic proportions.

In the meantime, what has happened to the American upper
class? The class remains, but its authority, like that of parents, has
rapidly declined. It is increasingly a shadow without substance. In
Philadelphia today, for example, new heads of local institutions imported from other cities are often given a copy of *Philadelphia Gentlemen* to help them understand the local power structure. It may
help—the class is still around; where the locus of authority resides,
however, is anybody's guess.

But of course this is a national and world-wide problem. Thus I
am afraid that the structure of American leadership increasingly approximates the lonely crowd of other-directed and traditionless
strangers which the brilliant West German sociologist Ralf Dahren-
dorf found to be characteristic of his own nation's leadership: "When
we look at the present West German elite," he wrote in his *Society
and Democracy in Germany* (1967), "we encounter a set of people
united at best by their common membership in the German Elite.
Presumably, this tie would be their only subject of conversation; they
might find some common ground in a fairly amused discussion of the
absurdity of sociological analysis. But leaving irony aside, apart from
politics, in which every one of these men is involved in one way or

another, there would probably not be a common subject of conversation for all or indeed, any three of them; the restriction of their conversations to shop-talk, on the other hand, betrays the absence of any kind of social coherence. There is no school they might all have attended; not even law faculties unite this elite; it is hard to imagine a club in which they might all be members; it is unlikely that they would all meet sailing or watching football; in so far as they are married, a ladies' tea of their wives would be likely to produce rather strained conversation; even their children live in different worlds. Those at the top of German society are essentially strangers to each other."

Perhaps, let us hope, we have not gone quite as far as the West Germans, though our direction is the same. In our anxious era of lonely leaders, then, I should like to think that a reading of *Philadelphia Gentlemen* may be even more instructive than it was when first published in the 1950's. For, as Abraham Lincoln once said, "If we could first know where we are, and whither we are tending, we could better judge what to do, and how to do it." Or, as W. H. Auden has recently put it:

> The class whose vices
> he pilloried was his own,
> now extinct, except
> for lone survivors like him
> who remember its virtues.

Notes

Chapter I

INTRODUCTION

1. Robert Michels, *Political Parties*, translated by Eden and Cedar Paul, (New York: Hearst's International Library Company, 1915).

2. For an excellent discussion of the problem of the recruitment and accountability of oligarchic elites see James Burnham, *The Machiavellians, Defenders of Freedom* (New York: The John Day Company, Inc., 1943), pp. 205-220.

Also see Vilfredo Pareto, *The Mind and Society*, edited by Arthur Livingston with the advice and active coöperation of James Harvey Rogers (New York: Harcourt, Brace and Company, 1935), 4 volumes; Gaetano Mosca, *The Ruling Class*, edited and revised, with an Introduction, by Arthur Livingston. Translated by Hannah D. Kahn (New York: McGraw-Hill Book Company, 1939); Jose Ortega Y Gasset, *The Revolt of the Masses* (New York: W. W. Norton and Company, 1932); and Arnold J. Toynbee, *A Study of History*, Abridgment of Volumes I-VI by D. C. Somervell (New York and London: Oxford University Press, 1947).

3. Milton M. Gordon, "Social Class in American Sociology," *The American Journal of Sociology*, Vol. LV, No. 3, (Nov. 1949), pp. 262-68.

The steadily increasing literature on stratification in the small American community reminds one of Toynbee's comments on the Western excavator in Egypt. He observes that, after Alexander the Great had broken up the Achaemenian Empire, there arose the two great dynasties of the Ptolemies and the Seleucids. Although the history of the Seleucid monarchy was infinitely more *important*, the raw materials pertaining to the Ptolemies were more *accessible* to the scholar: "The significant point is that the Ptolemaic papyri have attracted al-most all the spare energies of Western scholarship in the field of Ancient History, and . . . scholars . . . have tended to measure the historical importance of the Ptolemaic Monarchy by the amount of raw material accessible. . . . The scholar has seldom asked himself the prior question: 'Is Ptolemaic Egypt the most interesting and important phenomenon to study in the particular age of the particular society to which it belonged.'" Arnold J. Toynbee, *A Study of History* (London: Oxford University Press, 1934), Volume I, pp. 6-7.

4. W. Lloyd Warner and Paul S. Lunt, *The Social Life of a Modern Community*, (New Haven: Yale University Press, 1941), Chapter V.

Perhaps Marx once said, "je ne suis pas un marxiste," precisely because he saw the reification of his abstractions as inevitable. It may be observed that "by their abstractions ye shall know them" and the reification of the *social climbing man* found in contemporary social science thought is not unrelated to the modern preference for *Vogue* and *Esquire* rather than *Horatio Alger*.

For an interesting discussion of the whole problem of reification—"the taking as real that which is only conceptual"—see James Wroten Woodard, *Reification and Supernaturalism as Factors in Social Rigidity and Social Change*, (Philadelphia: University of Pennsylvania, 1935).

5. Robert S. Lynd and Helen Merrill Lynd, *Middletown in Transition*, (New York: Harcourt, Brace and Company, 1937), p. 96.

6. Barrington Moore, Jr., *Soviet Politics—The Dilemma of Power* (Cambridge: Harvard University Press, 1950), pp. 245-46.

7. Edward Hallett Carr, *The New Society* (London: Macmillan & Co., Ltd., 1951), p. 23.

8. Dixon Wecter, *The Saga of American Society* (New York: Charles Scribner's Sons, 1937), p. 6.

9. See C. Wright Mills' excellent

review of *The Social Life of a Modern Community* in the *American Sociological Review,* Vol. VII, No. 2 (April, 1942), pp. 263-71.

10. *Who's Who in America* (Chicago: The A. N. Marquis Company, 1940), Vol. 21. *Social Register* (New York: The Social Register Association, 1940). Twelve volumes are issued early in November.

11. Proper Philadelphia has, however, been more receptive to new wealth than Proper Boston. See Cleveland Amory, *The Proper Bostonians* (New York: E. P. Dutton and Co., Inc., 1947), esp. pp. 39-40.

12. Most books about Philadelphia tend to stress the charming and eccentric ways of upper-class members. See, for example, Cordelia Drexel Biddle, *My Philadelphia Father* (Garden City, New York: Doubleday and Company, Inc., 1955).

13. This is, of course, true primarily of his most well-known book, *The Theory of the Leisure Class.*

14. It is no accident that the introductory textbooks in Sociology today abound with discussions of taste, including the clothing advertisements of Brooks Brothers or the wine-drinking habits of upper-and middle-brows. Needless to say, the student rarely is confronted with a discussion of the writings of Karl Marx or any other studies of the historical development of social classes.

15. Harvey Warren Zorbaugh, *The Gold Coast and the Slum* (Chicago: University of Chicago Press, 1929).

16. *Ibid.,* p. 49.

Chapter II

THE AMERICAN METROPOLITAN UPPER CLASS AND THE ELITE

1. W. Lloyd Warner and J. O. Low, *The Social System of the Modern Factory,* (New Haven: Yale University Press, 1947), p. 153.

2. *Ibid.,* p. 156.

3. Brooks Adams, *The Law of Civilization and Decay,* (New York: The Macmillan Company, 1896), pp. 186ff.

4. Cleveland Amory, *The Proper Bostonians,* (New York: E. P. Dutton and Co., Inc., 1947), pp. 39-40.

5. Charles A. Beard and Mary R. Beard, *The Rise of American Civilization,* (New York: The Macmillan Company, 1937), Vol. II, pp. 383-84.

6. See Van Wyck Brooks, *The Ordeal of Mark Twain,* (New York: E. P. Dutton and Co., Inc., 1920), Chapter V.

7. Charles A. Beard and Mary R. Beard, *op. cit.,* Vol. II, p. 388.

8. *Social Register,* (New York: The Social Register Association, 1888).

9. *Ibid.,* preface.

10. Dixon Wecter, *The Saga of American Society,* (New York: Charles Scribner's Sons, 1937), p. 233.

11. This information was obtained by checking the volumes of the *Social Register* in the stacks of the Library of Congress.

In 1937, according to Dixon Wecter, about 10 per cent of the total copies of the *Social Register* sold in that year went to commercial firms, *ibid.,* p. 235.

12. *Ibid.,* pp. 232-36.

Herbert Spencer saw "progress" in terms of the movement of society from the militant to the industrial type of social structure. In the modern state where social and functional classes merge in one all-inclusive bureaucratic hierarchy, Spencer's ideal-typical militant social structure may well be a cogent description of the "Brave New World." See Herbert Spencer, *The Principles of Sociology,* (New York: D. Appleton and Company, 1896), Vol. II, Chapter XVII.

13. Frederick Lewis Allen, *The Lords of Creation,* (New York: Harper and Brothers, 1935), pp. 98-99.

14. Ferdinand Lundberg, *America's 60 Families,* (New York: Vanguard Press, 1937).

15. Gustavus Myers, *History of the Great American Fortunes,* (New York: The Modern Library, 1937).

16. Frank D. Ashburn, *Peabody of Groton,* (New York: Coward McCann, Inc., 1944), p. 5.

17. *Independent Schools,* Meridan, Conn., 1943.

18. W. Lloyd Warner and Paul S. Lunt, *The Social Life of a Modern*

Community, (New Haven: Yale University Press, 1941), p. 136.

19. *Ibid.*, p. 135.

20. This is an interesting example of how functional achievement was more important in *Middletown* than in *Yankee City.*

21. *Who's Who in America*, (Chicago: The A. N. Marquis Company), by permission of the publisher.

22. *Ibid.*, pp. 1-2.

23. *Statistical Abstract of the United States*, (Washington: U. S. Government Printing Office, 1947), p. 47.

Chapter III

THE PHILADELPHIA
UPPER CLASS AND
THE ELITE IN 1940

1. Robert Douglas Bowden, *Boies Penrose*, (New York: Greenberg, 1937), pp. 7-8.

2. Talcott Parsons, *Essays in Sociological Theory Pure and Applied*, (Glencoe: The Free Press, 1949), p. 193.

3. W. Lloyd Warner and Paul S. Lunt, *The Social Life of a Modern Community*, (New Haven: Yale University Press, 1941), p. 135.

4. James Burnham, *The Managerial Revolution*, (New York: The John Day Company, 1941).

5. *Fortune*, vol. XIII, no. 6, (June 1936), p. 208.

6. Frederick Lewis Allen, *The Lords of Creation*, (New York: Harper and Brothers, 1935), p. 104.

7. Studies of small American communities have consistently shown that the upper classes are closely allied with the business, and especially the financial elites. In post-1929 Middletown, the upper class, centering in the X family, was extremely influential in local business affairs and especially in the control of credit. After the bank holiday of 1933, "on the board of directors of the one remaining bank are three members of the X family, with one of them as chairman; while on the board of the trust company are the X member who is chairman

of the bank's board, one of the sons and a son-in-law." Robert S. and Helen M. Lynd, *Middletown in Transition*, (New York: Harcourt, Brace, and Co., 1937), p. 78.

August Hollingshead has also shown how the members of the upper class in Elmtown owned the two banks, the larger business concerns, and most of the commercial buildings in town. August Hollingshead, *Elmtown's Youth*, (New York: John Wiley, 1949), pp. 85-86.

8. Brooks Adams, *The Law of Civilization and Decay*, (New York: The Macmillan Company, 1896) p. vii.

For an interesting discussion of "The Rise and Fall of Families" see Joseph A. Schumpeter, *Imperialism and Social Classes*, translated by Heinz Norden, edited and with an Introduction by Paul M. Sweezy, (New York: August M. Kelley, Inc., 1951), pp. 148-162.

9. Peter Drucker, *The Future of Industrial Man*, (New York: The John Day Company, 1942), pp. 242-43.

For a sophisticated discussion of the compatibility of freedom and pluralistic elite structure, see Raymond Aron, "Social Structure and the Ruling Class," *The British Journal of Sociology*, Vol. I, No. 1, (March 1950), pp. 1-16.

10. Alexis de Tocqueville, *L'Ancien Regime*, translated by M. W. Patterson, (Oxford: Basil Blackwell, 1952), p. 151.

Chapter IV

THE STRUCTURE AND
FUNCTION OF AN UPPER CLASS

1. The word usage of the British and American upper classes overlap in many cases: see, for example, Alan C. Ross, Nancy Mitford, Evelyn Waugh, 'Strix,' Christopher Sykes, and John Betjeman, *Noblesse Oblige: An Inquiry into the Identifiable Characteristics of the English Aristocracy*, (London: Hamish Hamilton, 1956).

2. Florence Rockwood Kluckhohn, "Dominant and Substitute Profiles of Cultural Orientations: Their Signifi-

cance for the Analysis of Social Stratification," *Social Forces*, Vol. 28, No. 4, (May 1950), pp. 376-93.

3. *A History of the Schuylkill Fishing Company of the State in Schuylkill, 1732-1888*, (Philadelphia, Privately Printed, 1889).

4. *History of the First Troop Philadelphia City Cavalry, 1914-1948*: Together with an introductory chapter summarizing its early history and The Rolls complete from 1774, (Philadelphia, Privately Printed, 1948), p. 74.

5. Nicholas B. Wainwright, *A Philadelphia Story: The Philadelphia Contributionship for the Insurance of Houses from Loss by Fire*, (Philadelphia, 1952).

6. *Ibid.*, pp. 179-180.

7. *Ibid.*, pp. 180-181.

8. *Ibid.*, pp. 185-186.

9. David Riesman, in collaboration with Reuel Denney and Nathan Glazer, *The Lonely Crowd: A Study of the Changing American Character*, (New Haven: Yale University Press, 1950).

10. George Wharton Pepper, *Philadelphia Lawyer: An Autobiography*, (Philadelphia: J. B. Lippincott Company, 1944), pp. 53-54.

11. A. Davis, B. B. Gardner, and M. R. Gardner, *Deep South: Social Anthropological Study of Caste and Class*, (Chicago: University of Chicago Press, 1941), p. 59.

12. W. L. Warner and others, *Democracy in Jonesville*, (New York: Harper and Brothers, 1949), p. xv.

13. Seymour M. Lipset and Reinhard Bendix, "Social Status and Social Structure: A Re-examination of Data and Interpretations: I," *The British Journal of Sociology*, Vol. II, No. 2, (June 1951), p. 168.

14. Richard Hofstadter, *The American Political Tradition*, (New York: Alfred A. Knopf, 1948), p. 204.

15. Alexis de Tocqueville, *Democracy in America*, The Henry Reeve Text as revised by Francis Bowen. Now further corrected and edited with introduction, editorial notes, and bibliographies by Phillips Bradley, (New York: Alfred A. Knopf, 1945), Volume II, p. 242.

16. Ralph Linton, *The Study of Man*, (New York: D. Appleton-Century Company, 1936), p. 111.

17. Stanley Baldwin, *On England*,

(New York: Frederick Stokes and Company, 1927), p. 266.

18. Quoted in Robert A. Nisbet, *The Quest for Community*, (New York: Oxford University Press, 1953), p. 292.

19. Louis M. Hacker and Benjamin B. Kendrick, *The United States Since 1865*, (New York: Appleton-Century-Crofts, Inc., 1949), p. 128.

20. Quoted in George C. Homans, *The Human Group*, (New York: Harcourt, Brace and Company, 1950), p. 463.

21. Robert A. Nisbet, *op. cit.*, p. 109.

22. *Ibid.*, p. 278.

23. William Graham Sumner, *Folkways*, (Boston: Ginn and Company, 1906), p. 107.

24. Ralph Linton, *op. cit.*, p. 216.

25. *Ibid.*, p. 131.

26. Cleveland Amory, *The Proper Bostonians*, (New York: E. P. Dutton and Company, Inc., 1947), p. 289.

27. *Ibid.*, p. 299.

28. Florence Rockwood Kluckhohn, *op. cit.*, p. 384.

29. William Miller, "American Historians and the Business Elite," *The Journal of Economic History*, Vol. IX, No. 2 (November 1949), pp. 184-208.

Chapter V

PRE-CIVIL WAR
FIRST FAMILY FOUNDERS

1. *Dictionary of American Biography*, (New York: Charles Scribner's Sons, 1929-1946).

2. See Frederick B. Tolles, *Meeting House and Counting House: The Quaker Merchants of Colonial Philadelphia 1682-1763*, (Chapel Hill: University of North Carolina Press, 1948).

3. See John W. Jordan, *Colonial Families of Philadelphia*, (New York: The Lewis Publishing Company, 1911), 2 Volumes.

4. *Who Was Who in America*, (Chicago: The A. N. Marquis Company, 1942), Vol. 1, 1897-1942.

5. See Isaac Norris, "DAB" biography.

6. See Isaac Norris, "DAB" biography.

7. Tolles, *op. cit.*, pp. 120-21.

8. See Anthony Morris (1654-1721), "DAB" biography.

9. "DAB", Vol. XIII, p. 200.

10. See list of signers in J. Thomas Scharf and Thompson Westcott, *History of Philadelphia 1609-1884*, (Philadelphia: L. H. Everts & Co., 1884), Vol. I, pp. 272-273.

11. *Ibid.*, p. 295.

12. *Ibid.*, p. 295.

13. *Ibid.*, p. 883.

14. *Ibid.*, pp. 296-297.

15. *Ibid.*, p. 300.

16. *Ibid.*, pp. 317-318. For the role of Edward Biddle, see also the *Autobiography of Charles Biddle; Vice President of the Supreme Executive Council of Pennsylvania*, (Philadelphia: Privately Printed, 1883), p. 390.

17. William C. Armor, *Lives of the Governors of Pennsylvania 1609-1872*, (Philadelphia: James K. Simon, 1872), p. 194.

18. See Clement Biddle (1740-1814), "DAB," Vol. II, p. 239.

19. Scharf and Westcott, *op. cit.*, p. 337.

20. *Ibid.*, p. 337.

21. *Ibid.*, p. 337.

22. "DAB," Vol. II, p. 239.

23. See William White (1748-1836), "DAB" biog.; and Benjamin Rush (1745-1813), "DAB" biog.; also see *The Autobiography of Benjamin Rush*, Edited with Introduction and Notes by George W. Corner, (Princeton: Princeton University Press, 1948), pp. 131-138.

24. William C. Armor, *op. cit.*, p. 208.

25. See John Cadwalader (1742-1786), "DAB," Vol. III, p. 398.

26. See Rufus M. Jones, *The Quakers in the American Colonies*, (London: Macmillan and Co., Limited, 1911).

27. For a detailed study of the Loyalists in the Revolution, see Lorenzo Sabine, *Biographical Sketches of Loyalists of the American Revolution with an Historical Essay*, (Boston: Little, Brown and Company, 1864), 2 vols.

28. Thomas Willing (1731-1821), "DAB," biog., also Burton A. Konkle, *Thomas Willing and the First American Financial System*, (Philadelphia: Univeristy of Pennsylvania Press, 1937), p. 80.

29. *Ibid.*, p. 28.

30. *Ibid.*, p. 2.

31. See Sabine, *op. cit.*, (Chew), Vol. I, p. 310; (Ingersoll) Vol. I, pp. 561-562; also see Lawrence Henry Gipson, *Jared Ingersoll: A Study of American Loyalism in Relation to British Colonial Government*, (New Haven: Yale University Press, 1920); also see Scharf and Westcott, *op. cit.*, Vol. I, p. 343.

32. See Thomas Wharton, "DAB" biog. For a fascinating fictional account of the lives of the Quaker exiles to Virginia, see Elizabeth Gray Vining, *The Virginia Exiles*, (Philadelphia and New York: J. B. Lippincott Company, 1955).

33. See Israel Pemberton, "DAB" biography.

34. Konkle, *op. cit.*, p. 2.

35. See Jared Ingersoll, "DAB" biography.

36. Washington spent the winter of 1781-82 in a house rented from Benjamin Chew, with whom he was on friendly terms, Konkle, *op. cit.*, p. 102.

37. Konkle, *op. cit.*, pp. 214-221.

38. *Ibid.*, pp. 146-161.

39. See Marquis James, *Biography of a Business 1792-1942: Insurance Company of North America*, (New York: The Bobbs-Merrill Company, 1942).

40. John Russell Young, *Memorial History of Philadelphia*, (New York: New York History Company, 1895), pp. 405-406.

41. *Ibid.*, p. 407.

42. See Robert Wharton, "DAB" biography.

43. *Ibid.*

44. See Thomas McKean, "DAB" biography and Armor, *op. cit.*, pp. 289-307.

45. "DAB" biography.

46. Joseph Borden McKean, "DAB" biography.

47. Thomas McKean, "DAB" biography.

48. Robert Morris, "DAB" biography.

49. Konkle, *op. cit.*

50. John Bach McMaster, *The Life and Times of Stephen Girard, Mariner and Merchant*, (Philadelphia and London: J. B. Lippincott Company, 1918), Vol. II, pp. 246-50.

51. Nicholas Biddle, "DAB" biography.
52. *Ibid.*
53. Francis M. Drexel, "DAB" biography; also Scharf and Westcott, *op. cit.*, Vol. III, p. 2101.
54. Scharf and Westcott, *op. cit.*, Vol. III, p. 2100.
55. *Ibid.*, Vol. III, p. 2101; also see Ellis Paxson Oberholtzer, *Jay Cooke, Financier of the Civil War*, (Philadelphia: George W. Jacobs & Co., 1907), 2 volumes.
56. Oberholtzer, *op. cit.*, Vol. II, pp. 378-439.
57. Anthony J. Drexel, "DAB" biography; also see Scharf and Westcott, *op. cit.*, Vol. III, pp. 2101-2102.
58. Frederick Lewis Allen, *The Great Pierpont Morgan*, (New York: Harper & Brothers, 1949), pp. 37-38.
59. Alexander Brown, "DAB" biography; also see Frank R. Kent, *The Story of Alexander Brown & Sons*, (Baltimore: Privately Printed, 1925).
60. Frank R. Kent, *op. cit.*, p. 20.
61. McMaster, *op. cit.*, Vol. II, pp. 441-460.
62. Adolph Borie, "DAB" biography.
63. See McKean Family, in Jordan, *op. cit.*, Vol. I, pp. 916-917.
64. Adolph Borie, "DAB" biography.
65. *Ibid.*
66. *Who Was Who in America 1897-1942.*
67. See Gustavus Myers, *History of the Great American Fortunes*, (New York: The Modern Library, 1936), Part II, The Great Land Fortunes.
68. Francis Newton Thorpe, *William Pepper*, (Philadelphia and London, J. B. Lippincott Company, 1904), pp. 21-22.
69. Ernest Earnest, S. *Weir Mitchell, Novelist and Physician*, (Philadelphia: University of Pennsylvania Press, 1950), p. 133.
70. Francis Newton Thorpe, *op. cit.*, p. 22.
71. *Ibid.*, p. 22.
72. See Joseph Dorfman, *The Economic Mind in American Civilization 1606-1865*, (New York: The Viking Press, 1946), Volume I.
73. See Daniel Coxe, "DAB" biography.
74. *Ibid.*

75. Scharf and Westcott, *op. cit.*, Vol. I, p. 233.
76. Tench Coxe, "DAB" biography.
77. *Ibid.*
78. Dorfman, *op. cit.*, pp. 280-295.
79. *Ibid.*, p. 290.
80. Tench Coxe, "DAB" biography. Also see Dorfman, *op. cit.*, pp. 253-256.
81. *Ibid.*
82. John Russell Young, *op. cit.*, p. 439.
83. Samuel Eliot Morrison and Henry Steele Commager, *The Growth of the American Republic*, (New York: Oxford University Press, 1953), Fourth Edition, Vol. I, pp. 438-49.
84. Scharf and Westcott, *op. cit.*, Vol. III, p. 2228.
85. *Ibid.*, p. 2305.
86. Edwin T. Freedley, *Philadelphia and its Manufacturers*, (Philadelphia: Edward Young & Co., 1867), p. 587 ff.
87. Scharf and Westcott, *op. cit.*, Vol. III, pp. 2303-2310.
88. Thomas Dolan, "DAB" biography.
89. Williams Haynes, *American Chemical Industry, A History*, (New York: D. Van Nostrand Co., Inc., 1954), Vol. I, p. 180.
90. Samuel Wetherill, "DAB" biography.
91. Mrs. S. P. Wetherill, *Samuel Wetherill and The Early Paint Industry of Philadelphia*, (Philadelphia: City History Society, 1916), p. 6. Fustian is a cloth, the warp of which is linen and the woof thick cotton. It derived its name from Fusht, a town on the Nile where it was first made.
92. See Miriam Hussey, *From Merchants to "Colour Men," Five Generations of Samuel Wetherill's White Lead Business*, (Philadelphia: University of Pennsylvania Press, 1956).
93. Freedley, *op. cit.*, p. 196.
94. *Philadelphia and Popular Philadelphians*, (Philadelphia: The North American, 1891), pp. 186-188. Also see Gustavus Myers, *op. cit.*, pp. 697 ff.
95. *Ibid.*, p. 188.
96. Williams Haynes, *op. cit.*, Vol. I, p. 179.
97. *Ibid.*, p. 180.
98. Williams Haynes, *Chemical Pioneers, The Founders of the Ameri-*

can *Chemical Industry,* (New York: D. Van Nostrand Company, Inc., 1939), p. 111.

99. *Ibid.,* pp. 107-123.

100. Williams Haynes, *American Chemical Industry, A History,* Vol. I, p. 214n; also *Chemical Pioneers,* pp. 26-41.

101. *Chemical Pioneers,* p. 39.

102. *American Chemical Industry,* Vol. VI, pp. 274-275.

103. *Ibid.,* Vol. VI, p. 275.

104. *Ibid.,* Vol. I, pp. 180-181.

105. *Ibid.,* pp. 358-359.

106. Slogans taken from labels photographed in "Who put the borax in Dr. Wiley's butter," *American Heritage,* Vol. VII, No. 5, (Aug. 1950), pp. 59-63.

107. *Ibid.,* p. 63.

108. *Philadelphia and Popular Philadelphians,* p. 174.

109. See Theo. B. White, Editor, *Philadelphia Architecture in the Nineteenth Century,* (Philadelphia: University of Pennsylvania Press, 1953), Plate 45; also see Louis H. Sullivan, *Kindergarten Chats,* (New York: Wittenborn, Schultz, Inc., 1947), p. 7.

110. Samuel Stockton White, "DAB" biography.

111. *Ibid.*

112. Scharf and Westcott, *op. cit.,* Vol. III, p. 2237.

113. Samuel Vaughan Merrick, "DAB" biography.

114. Thomas Coulson, "Some Prominent Members of the Franklin Institute: 1. Samuel Vaughan Merrick, 1801-1870," *Journal of The Franklin Institute,* Vol. 258, No. 5, (November 1954), p. 338.

115. Thomas Coulson, *The Franklin Institute 1824 to 1949.*

116. *Ibid.,* p. 4.

117. *Ibid.,* p. 4.

118. Thomas Coulson, *Samuel Vaughan Merrick,* p. 339.

119. Edwin T. Freedley, *op. cit.,* p. 343.

120. *Ibid.,* pp. 597-598.

121. Scharf and Westcott, *op. cit.,* Vol. III, p. 2252.

122. *Ibid.*

123. Thomas Coulson, *Samuel Vaughan Merrick.*

124. Eliot Jones, *The Anthracite Coal Combination in the United States,* (Cambridge: Harvard University Press, 1914), p. 5.

125. *Ibid.,* p. 17; also see Eleanor Morton, *Josiah White,* (New York: Stephen Daye Press, 1946), p. 86.

126. Eleanor Morton, *op. cit.,* pp. 92-93.

127. *Ibid.,* pp. 108-109.

128. Eliot Jones, *op. cit.,* p. 223.

129. Eleanor Morton, *op. cit.,* p. 260.

130. Eliot Jones, *op. cit.,* pp. 30-35.

131. Thomas Coulson, *Samuel Vaughan Merrick,* pp. 342-343.

132. *Ibid.,* p. 343.

Chapter VI

POST-CIVIL WAR
FAMILY FOUNDERS

1. See Justice Oliver Wendell Holmes, *Who Was Who in America, 1897-1942,* (Chicago: The A. N. Marquis Company, 1942), p. 582.

2. *The Rich Men of Philadelphia: Income Tax of the Residents of Philadelphia and Bucks County for the Year Ending April 30, 1865,* (Philadelphia: For Sale By All Booksellers, 1865).

3. Charles A. Beard and Mary R. Beard, *The Rise of American Civilization,* (New York: The Macmillan Company, 1937), p. 389.

4. *Ibid.*

5. *History of the Baldwin Locomotive Works, 1831-1920,* (Privately Printed), p. 57.

6. *Ibid.,* p. 9.

7. See Matthew Baird, "DAB" biography.

8. *History of the Baldwin Locomotive Works,* pp. 104-105.

9. *Ibid.,* p. 126.

10. *Ibid.,* p. 130.

11. *Ibid.,* p. 135.

12. George H. Burgess and Miles C. Kennedy, *Centennial History of the Pennsylvania Railroad Company,* (Philadelphia: The Pennsylvania Railroad Company, 1949), pp. 61-340.

13. *Ibid.,* pp. 346-347.

14. *Ibid.*, p. 343.

15. *Ibid.*, p. 345.

16. *Ibid.*

17. See "Pennsylvania Railroad: I," *Fortune*, Vol. XIII, No. 5 (May 1936), pp. 67-68.

18. George B. Roberts, "DAB" biography.

19. John W. Jordan, *Colonial Families of Philadelphia*, (New York: The Lewis Publishing Company, 1911), Volume 1, pp. 456-457.

20. George B. Roberts, "DAB" biography.

21. George H. Burgess and Miles C. Kennedy, *op. cit.*, p. 385.

22. *Ibid.*, p. 387.

23. Frederick Lewis Allen, *The Great Pierpont Morgan*, (New York: Harper & Brothers, 1949), pp. 47-53.

24. *Ibid.*, p. 53.

25. Quoted in George H. Burgess and Miles C. Kennedy, *op. cit.*, p. 455.

26. *Ibid.*, p. 458.

27. *Ibid.*, p. 460.

28. A. J. Cassatt, "DAB" biography.

29. *Ibid.*

30. *Ibid.*

31. See Edward C. Kirkland, *A History of American Economic Life*, (New York: F. S. Crofts & Co., 1941), Chapter X, "The Railroad Age," (1850-1915).

32. Henry Howard Houston, "DAB" biography.

33. See biography of E. B. Leisenring (1845-1894), in Frederic A. Godcharles, Editor, *Encyclopedia of Pennsylvania Biography*, (New York: Lewis Historical Publishing Company, 1931), volume 17.

34. See Edward B. Leisenring, *Who's Who*, 1940.

35. For background of Coxe family and acquisition of coal lands, see Alexander DuBin, *Coxe Family*, (Philadelphia: The Historical Publications Society, 1936).

36. See Eckley B. Coxe, "DAB" biography.

37. Eliot Jones, *The Anthracite Coal Combination in the United States*, (Cambridge: Harvard University Press, 1914), p. 23.

38. George H. Burgess and Miles C. Kennedy, *op. cit.*, pp. 283-284.

39. Eliot Jones, *op. cit.*, p. 105.

40. Carl Corlsen, *Buried Black Treasure, The Story of Pennsylvania Anthracite*, (Danville, New York: F. A. Owen Publishing Company, 1954), p. 45.

41. The sale was rather complicated. Professor Eliot Jones describes the transaction as follows: "Coxe Brothers was, at this time, the largest independent firm in the field, possessing over 5000 acres of coal lands, and mining in 1905 over 1,300,000 tons. It owned, also, the Delaware, Susquehanna and Schuylkill Railroad (a gathering line with 50 miles of track in the Lehigh region), which had been built in 1890-1892 in order to connect the collieries of Coxe Brothers with a number of railroads to tidewater. In 1905, however, Coxe Brothers was shipping its output and that of the other collieries on its line over the tracks of the Lehigh Valley, the cars and crews being supplied and manned by the Delaware, Susquehanna and Schuylkill Railroad, the Lehigh Valley supplying merely the track. The entire capital stock of Coxe Brothers ($2,910,150), and the stock of its controlled railroad ($1,500,000) and $60,000 of the stock of four subsidiary companies were purchased by the Lehigh Valley Railroad, on November 1, 1905, for the sum of $19,000,000." Eliot Jones, *op. cit.*, p. 86.

42. Edward C. Kirkland, *op. cit.*, p. 415.

43. See Arthur Cecil Bining, *Pennsylvania Iron Manufacture in the Eighteenth Century*, (Harrisburg: Pennsylvania Historical Commission, 1938).

44. John W. Jordan, *op. cit.*, Vol. 1, p. 51.

45. Arthur Cecil Bining, *op. cit.*, p. 136.

46. E. Gordon Alderfer, *The Montgomery County Story*, (Norristown, Pennsylvania: Commissioners of Montgomery County, 1951), p. 259.

47. *Ibid.* As of this writing (1957) the Wood firm has offered stock on the public exchange for the first time.

48. Henry Disston, "DAB" biography.

49. Joseph Wharton, "DAB" biography.

50. Charles M. Schwab, "DAB" biography.

51. Frank Barkley Copley, *Fred-*

erick W. Taylor, *Father of Scientific Management,* (New York: Harper & Brothers, 1923), 2 Vols.

52. *Ibid.,* Vol. I, pp. 106-107.

53. Edward C. Kirkland, *op. cit.,* p. 412.

54. See biography of Joseph Newton Pew in Frederick A. Godcharles, Editor, *op. cit.,* Volume 19, pp. 334-337.

55. Philadelphia *Inquirer,* August 11, 1935.

56. *Ibid.,* September 3, 1936.

57. Tom Mahoney, *The Great Merchants,* (New York: Harper & Brothers, 1955).

58. *Ibid.,* pp. 5-9.

59. *Ibid.,* p. 8.

60. *Ibid.,* p. 9.

61. John Wanamaker, "DAB" biography.

62. Professor Gras devoted a week to the study of Wanamaker and used him as the prototypical example of the "Protestant ethic." Often called "Pious John," Wanamaker firmly believed, in his own words, that "The Golden Rule of the New Testament has become the Golden Rule of business": See Joseph H. Appel, *The Business Biography of John Wanamaker,* (New York: The Macmillan Company, 1930), pp. XIV-XV.

63. "DAB" biography.

64. Compare Dreiser's *Financier* with Charles T. Yerkes, "DAB" biography.

65. Peter A. B. Widener, "DAB" biography.

66. William L. Elkins, "DAB" biography.

67. *Ibid.*

68. "The United Gas Improvement Company," *Philadelphia and Popular Philadelphians,* (Philadelphia: The North American, 1891), p. 130.

69. Thomas Dolan, "DAB" biography.

70. See obituary of Edward T. Stotesbury, New York *Times,* May 17, 1938. The obituary appeared on the front page of the paper that day.

71. *Ibid.*

72. Edward Potts Cheyney, *History of the University of Pennsylvania,* (Philadelphia: University of Pennsylvania Press, 1940), p. 424.

73. Horace Mather Lippincott, *A Narrative of Springfield, Whitemarsh and Cheltenham Townships in Mont-*gomery *County, Pennsylvania,* (Jenkintown, Pennsylvania: Old York Road Publishing Company, 1948), pp. 146-162. Horace Mather Lippincott comments on how Stotesbury, although he "never read a book," rose by "sheer ability" from office boy to partnership in the world's greatest banking house, accumulated a fortune of a hundred million dollars, and "went to the Assembly Ball."

74. New York *Times* obituary, *op. cit.*

75. John Gunther, *The Riddle of MacArthur,* (New York: Harper & Brothers, 1950), pp. 44-46.

76. See current *Who's Who in America.*

77. Obituary of John T. Dorrance, New York *Times,* September 22, 1930.

78. Arthur C. Dorrance, *Who's Who* biography, 1940.

79. See brief biography of Clarence H. Geist in U.G.I. *Circle,* Vol. XI, No. 2, (August 1930).

80. Obituary, Philadelphia Evening *Bulletin,* June 13, 1938.

81. Philadelphia Evening *Bulletin,* July 19, 1933.

82. *Ibid.,* June 13, 1938.

83. See obituary of A. Atwater Kent, New York *Times,* March 5, 1949.

Chapter VII

PROPER PHILADELPHIA PUBLIC SERVANTS, PROFESSIONALS, AND MEN OF LETTERS

1. *The Letters of Theodore Roosevelt,* Selected and Edited by Elting Morison, (Cambridge: Harvard University Press, 1951), p. 108.

2. George Wharton Pepper, *Philadelphia Lawyer,* (Philadelphia: J. B. Lippincott Company, 1944), p. 137.

3. John W. Jordan, *Colonial Families of Philadelphia,* (New York: The Lewis Publishing Company, 1911), Vol. 1, p. 51.

4. John G. Johnson, Philadelphia lawyer and art patron, turned down appointments to U. S. Supreme Court tendered by Presidents Garfield and

Cleveland, and the Attorney General-ship of the U. S., under President Mc-Kinley. See his biography in *Who Was Who in America,* Vol. 1, 1897-1942.

5. See Charles Jared Ingersoll, "DAB" biography.

6. *Ibid.*

7. William C. Armor, *Lives of the Governors of Pennsylvania,* 1609-1872, (Philadelphia: James K. Simon, 1872), pp. 308 ff.

8. See William M. Meigs, *The Life of Charles Jared Ingersoll,* (Philadel-phia: J. B. Lippincott Company, 1897), and J. H. Powell, *Richard Rush,* (Philadelphia: University of Pennsylvania Press, 1942).

9. See Richard Rush, "DAB" biog-raphy.

10. J. H. Powell, *op. cit.,* p. 237.

11. *Ibid.,* p. 259.

12. *Ibid.,* p. 261.

13. *Ibid.,* p. 262.

14. See Richard Rush, "DAB" biography.

15. See Alexander James Dallas, "DAB" biography, and Raymond Walters, Jr., *Alexander James Dallas,* (Philadelphia: University of Pennsyl-vania Press, 1943).

16. See George Mifflin Dallas, "DAB" biography.

17. *Ibid.*

18. See Morton McMichael, "DAB" biography.

19. See Richard Vaux, "DAB" biog-raphy.

20. See Harry Elmer Barnes, *The Evolution of Penology in Pennsyl-vania,* (Indianapolis: The Bobbs-Mer-rill Company, 1927).

21. *Ibid.,* p. 141.

22. J. Thomas Scharf and Thomp-son Westcott, *History of Philadelphia,* (Philadelphia: L. H. Everts & Co., 1884), Vol. II, p. 1544.

23. See *The Philadelphia Club, 1834-1934,* (Privately Printed, 1934).

24. Judge John Cadwalader was elected to the U. S. Congress on the Democratic ticket in 1855, represent-ing Philadelphia and Montgomery Counties, see Scharf and Westcott, *op. cit.,* Vol. II, p. 1538.

25. See latest *Who's Who* biog-raphies of A. J. Drexel Biddle, Jr., and Angier Biddle Duke.

26. See Boies Penrose, "DAB" biog-raphy, and Robert Douglas Bowden,

Boies Penrose, (New York: Green-berg, 1937).

27. See Edward P. Allinson and Boies Penrose, *Philadelphia 1681-1887, A History of Municipal Devel-opment,* (Philadelphia: Allen, Lane & Scott, 1887).

28. Boies Penrose, "DAB" biog-raphy.

29. John W. Jordan, *op. cit.,* Vol 1, pp. 276-315; and John Clifford Pem-berton, "DAB" biography.

30. See George Meade, "DAB" biography.

31. See Richard Worsam Meade, "DAB" biography.

32. See George Gordon Meade, "DAB" biography.

33. George Meade, *The Life and Letters of George Gordon Meade,* (New York: Charles Scribner's Sons, 1913), Vol. 1, pp. 140-141.

34. See *Fairmount Park Art Asso-ciation,* Unveiling of the Equestrian Statue of Major-General George Gor-don Meade, (Philadelphia, 1887).

35. See *The Memorial to Major-General George Gordon Meade* in Washington, D.C. (Meade Memorial Commission of Pennsylvania, 1927).

36. See William Cunningham Meigs, "DAB" biography.

37. See D. H. Lawrence, *Studies in Classic American Literature,* (Garden City, New York: Doubleday & Com-pany, Inc., Anchor Books, 1953), pp. 19-31. Also see criticism of such for-eign observers as Max Weber and D. H. Lawrence in Robert E. Spiller, "Franklin on the Art of Being Human," *Proceedings of the American Philosophical Society,* Vol. 100, No. 4, (August, 1956), pp. 304-15.

38. Vernon Louis Parrington, *Main Currents in American Thought,* (New York: Harcourt, Brace and Company, 1930), Volume One, p. 222. Italics mine.

39. George Wharton Pepper, *op. cit.,* p. 20.

40. Carl and Jessica Bridenbaugh, *Rebels and Gentlemen,* (New York: Reynal and Hitchcock, 1942), pp. 263-303.

41. *Ibid.,* p. 264.

42. Ernest Earnest, *S. Weir Mitch-ell, Novelist and Physician,* (Philadel-phia: University of Pennsylvania Press, 1950), pp. 175-176.

43. For a detailed review of the

history of Philadelphia's leading evening newspaper, see The Evening *Bulletin*, June 1, 1955.

44. William Lippard McLean, "DAB" biography.

45. See Cyrus Hermann Kotzschmar Curtis, *Who Was Who in America*, Vol. 1, 1897-1942.

46. Joshua B. Lippincott, "DAB" biography.

47. Isaac Lea, "DAB" biography.

48. See Henry Charles Lea, "DAB" biography, and Edward Sculley Bradley, *Henry Charles Lea*, (Philadelphia: University of Pennsylvania Press, 1931).

49. See Everett Carter, *Howells and the Age of Realism*, (Philadelphia: J. B. Lippincott Company, 1954).

50. Ellis Paxson Oberholtzer, *The Literary History of Philadelphia*, (Philadelphia: George W. Jacobs & Co., 1906), p. 48.

51. Carl and Jessica Bridenbaugh, *op. cit.*, p. 103.

52. Ellis Paxson Oberholtzer, *op. cit.*, p. 177.

53. *Ibid.*, p. 159.

54. Nicholas Biddle, "DAB" biography.

55. Ellis Paxson Oberholtzer, *op. cit.*, pp. 190-192.

56. *Ibid.*, p. 226.

57. *Ibid.*, pp. 228-229.

58. *Ibid.*, p. 254.

59. Van Wyck Brooks, *The Confident Years: 1885-1915*, (New York: E. P. Dutton & Co., Inc., 1952), p. 28.

60. Francis Hopkinson, "DAB" biography.

61. Carl and Jessica Bridenbaugh, *op. cit.*, p. 103.

62. *Ibid.*, p. 105.

63. Vernon Louis Parrington, *op. cit.*, Vol. 1, pp. 253-54; and Carl and Jessica Bridenbaugh, *op. cit.*, p. 106.

64. Parrington, *ibid.*, p. 255.

65. Francis Hopkinson, "DAB" biography.

66. *Characteristics* was published in 1891, and *Dr. North and His Friends*, in 1900.

67. Ernest Earnest, *op. cit.*, pp. 114-115.

68. *A Madeira Party*, published in 1895, was characteristic of Victorian Proper Philadelphia. Van Wyck Brooks quotes one writer as saying that the art of giving successful dinners was a fetish at that time, and another, Charles Godfrey Leland, as saying that "what was on the table was more carefully considered than what was placed around it." Van Wyck Brooks, *op. cit.*, p. 23.

69. Ernest Earnest, *op. cit.*, pp. V-VI.

70. *Ibid.*, pp. 233-236.

71. See the Preface to Owen Wister, *Safe in the Arms of Croesus*, (New York: The Macmillan Company, 1928).

72. Van Wyck Brooks, *The Confident Years*, pp. 85-87.

73. See obituary of Owen Wister, New York *Times*, July 22, 1938.

74. Introduction to Thomas Wharton, *Bobo and Other Fancies*, (New York: Harper & Brothers, 1897), p. xiv.

75. See George Stewart Stokes, *Agnes Repplier, Lady of Letters*, (Philadelphia: University of Pennsylvania Press, 1949).

Chapter VIII

THE OLD FAMILY CORE OF THE 1940 PHILADELPHIA ELITE

1. Alexis de Tocqueville, *The Old Regime and the Revolution*, translated by John Bonner, (New York: Harper & Brothers, 1856), p. ix.

2. Florence Kluckhohn makes a similar criticism of the small community study when she says, "Only in indirect statements or in the quoted interview material can one find evidence of the importance of outward migration for the problem of vertical mobility." Florence Rockwood Kluckhohn, "Dominant and Substitute Profiles of Cultural Orientations: Their Significance for the Analysis of Social Stratification," Social Forces, Vol. 28, No. 4, (May 1950), p. 387.

"Passing," among Negroes, is the extreme example of vertical mobility. In *Deep South*, it is noted that the Negro must move to another community, usually the Northern cities, in order to permit "sociological death" and a "rebirth" within the white community. See A. Davis, B. B. Gardner, and M. R. Gardner, *Deep South: A*

Social Anthropological Study of Caste and Class, (Chicago: University of Chicago Press, 1941), p. 42.

3. Again the novelist contributes insight when J. P. Marquand shows how Charles Grey, blocked by the status system in "Yankee City," goes to Boston and New York in order to *achieve* success. J. P. Marquand, *Point of No Return,* (Boston: Little Brown & Company, 1949).

4. For a more detailed treatment of this relationship, see E. Digby Baltzell, "Social Mobility and Fertility within an Elite Group," *The Milbank Memorial Fund Quarterly,* (October 1953), Vol. XXXI, No. 4, pp. 412-420.

5. A similar "double standard" was observed in a study of eminent English women. See Joseph Schneider, "Class Origin and Fame: Eminent English Women," *American Sociological Review,* Vol. 5, No. 5, (October 1940), pp. 700-712.

6. Francis Biddle, *The Llanfear Pattern,* (New York: Charles Scribner's Sons, 1927).

7. *The Philadelphia Assemblies, 1748-1948,* Edited by Joseph P. Sims, (Privately Printed).

8. Francis Biddle, *op. cit.,* p. 96.

9. See P. A. B. Widener, *Without Drums,* (New York: G. P. Putnam's Sons, 1940), pp. 9-12.

10. Struthers Burt, *Philadelphia Holy Experiment,* (Garden City, New York: Doubleday, Doran & Company, Inc., 1945), p. 363.

11. George Wharton Pepper, *Philadelphia Lawyer,* (Philadelphia: J. B. Lippincott Company).

12. *Ibid.,* p. 31.

13. For the background material on the Ingersoll family I have used the following: William M. Meigs, *The Life of Charles Jared Ingersoll,* (Philadelphia: J. B. Lippincott Company, 1897); Lawrence Henry Gipson, *Jared Ingersoll, A Study of American Loyalism in Relation to British Colonial Government,* (New Haven: Yale University Press, 1920); the "DAB" biographies of Jared and Charles Jared Ingersoll; *Who Was Who in America,* 1897-1942; and *Who's Who in America,* Vol. 21, 1940-41.

14. Quoted in Lawrence Henry Gipson, *op. cit.,* p. 356.

15. Charles A. Beard, *An Economic*

Interpretation of the Constitution of the United States, (New York: The Macmillan Company, 1913), p. 116.

Chapter IX

NEIGHBORHOOD AND
THE CLASS STRUCTURE

1. Robert E. Park, Ernest W. Burgess, and Roderick D. McKenzie, *The City,* (Chicago: The University of Chicago Press, 1925), p. 3.

2. James H. S. Bossard, *The Sociology of Child Development,* (New York: Harper & Bros., 1948), p. 525.

3. His residence, 944 North Front Street, was listed in *McElroy's Philadelphia City Directory for 1859,* (Philadelphia: Edward C. & John Biddle, 1859), p. 174.

4. See *Boyd's Blue Book, The Ladies' Visiting and Shopping Guide,* for the year ending April, 1890, (Philadelphia, C. E. Howe Co., 1890).

5. See six conjugal Disston family units listed in the 1940 *Social Register.*

6. J. Thomas Scharf and Thompson Westcott, *History of Philadelphia,* (Philadelphia: L. H. Everts & Co., 1884), Vol. 1, pp. 72-76.

7. Robert Desilver, *The Philadelphia Index or Directory for 1823, containing the Names, Professions, and Residence, of all the Heads of Families and Persons in Business of the City and Suburbs, with other useful information,* (Philadelphia, 1823).

8. See *Boyd's Blue Book* for 1890.

9. See 1940 *Social Register.*

10. Carl and Jessica Bridenbaugh, *Rebels and Gentlemen, Philadelphia in the Age of Franklin,* (New York: Reynal & Hitchcock, 1942), p. 222.

11. Scharf and Westcott, *op. cit.,* Vol. II, p. 1180.

12. John Frederick Lewis, *The History of an Old Philadelphia Land Title, 208 South Fourth Street,* (Philadelphia: Privately Printed, 1934), pp. 202-203.

13. Frank Cousins and Phil M. Riley, *The Colonial Architecture of Philadelphia,* (Boston: Little, Brown, and Company, 1920), pp. 44-46.

14. Carl and Jessica Bridenbaugh, *op. cit.*, p. 222.

15. Frank Cousins and Phil M. Riley, *op. cit.*, pp. 75-76.

16. The Drexel firm was then located at 34 South 3rd Street while E. W. Clark & Co., and young Jay Cooke were across the street at 35 South 3rd; see *McElroy's Philadelphia Directory, A Business Directory,* (Philadelphia: Edward C. and John Biddle, 1859).

17. See *A New Home for an Old House,* (Philadelphia: Drexel & Co., privately printed, 1927). An attractively illustrated brief history of this famous old Philadelphia banking house.

18. Theo. B. White, Editor, *Philadelphia Architecture in the Nineteenth Century,* (Philadelphia: University of Pennsylvania Press, 1953), p. 9.

19. See Charles J. Cohen, *Rittenhouse Square,* (Privately Printed, 1922).

20. The fascinating career of Joseph Harrison, Jr. was pieced together from: Scharf and Westcott, *op. cit.,* Vol. III, pp. 2258-2259; Charles J. Cohen, *op. cit.,* pp. 259-266; and Joseph Harrison, Jr., *The Iron Worker and King Solomon,* with a Memoir and an Appendix, (Philadelphia: J. B. Lippincott & Co., 1868).

21. George Wharton Pepper, *Philadelphia Lawyer,* (Philadelphia: J. B. Lippincott Company, 1944), p. 17.

22. Two hundred and twenty-three families were listed in *Boyd's Blue Book* (1890) as living on Walnut Street between Broad Street and the Schuylkill River (The Rittenhouse Square blocks). At the same time, only 126 families were listed in *Boyd's* as living in Bryn Mawr.

23. See *A New Home for an Old House, op. cit.*

24. Philadelphia *Record,* February 11, 1933.

25. See Ray Allen Billington, *The Protestant Crusade 1800-1860,* (New York: The Macmillan Company, 1938), and Scharf and Westcott, *op. cit.,* Vol I, pp. 663-664.

26. Scharf and Westcott, *op. cit.,* Vol. I, pp. 666-667.

27. *Ibid.*

28. William C. Bullitt, *It's Not Done,* (New York: Harcourt, Brace and Company, 1926).

29. *Ibid.,* p. 7.

30. *Ibid.,* pp. 305-308.

31. *Boyd's Blue Book, op. cit.,* pp. 181-183.

32. See Theodore Dreiser, *The Financier,* (New York: John Day Company, 1912).

33. Theo. B. White, Editor, *op. cit.,* p. 63.

34. *Ibid.,* p. 100.

35. Scharf and Westcott, *op. cit.,* Vol. III, pp. 2004-2005.

36. Moses King, *Philadelphia and Notable Philadelphians,* (New York: Moses King, 1901), p. 69.

37. Cordelia Drexel Biddle, as told to Kyle Crichton, *My Philadelphia Father,* (Garden City, New York: Doubleday & Company, Inc., 1955), p. 30.

38. Moses King, *op. cit.,* p. 68.

39. George H. Burgess and Miles C. Kennedy, *Centennial History of the Pennsylvania Railroad Company, 1846-1946,* (Philadelphia: The Pennsylvania Railroad Company, 1949), p. 386.

40. E. Gordon Alderfer, *The Montgomery County Story,* (Norristown, Pennsylvania: County Commissioners, 1951), p. 259.

41. *Ibid.,* p. 202-203.

42. Moses King, *op. cit.,* p. 92.

43. *Boyd's Blue Book* (1890).

44. Edward W. Hocker, *Germantown, 1683-1933,* (Germantown, Philadelphia: Published by the Author, 1933), pp. 13-14.

45. J. H. Powell, *Bring Out Your Dead,* The Great Plague of Yellow Fever in Philadelphia in 1793, (Philadelphia: University of Pennsylvania Press, 1949), p. 230.

46. Edward W. Hocker, *op. cit.,* pp. 133-134.

47. *Ibid.,* p. 162.

48. *Ibid.,* p. 164.

49. *Ibid.,* pp. 241-242.

50. John A. Lester, Editor, *A Century of Philadelphia Cricket,* (Philadelphia: University of Pennsylvania Press, 1951), pp. 312-313.

51. The Clark brothers were also friends of the founder of Scientific Management, Frederick W. Taylor. For a description of life on the Clark Estate, see Frank Barkley Copley, *Frederick W. Taylor,* Father of Scientific Management, (New York: Harper and Brothers, 1923), pp. 61-62.

52. Edward W. Hocker, *op. cit.,* p. 274.

53. George H. Burgess and Miles C. Kennedy, *op. cit.,* p. 645.

54. See *Who's Who* biography.

55. J. W. Townsend, *The Old "Main Line,"* (Philadelphia: Privately Printed, 1922), p. 21.

56. *Ibid.,* p. 28.

57. *Ibid.,* pp. 51-52.

58. *Ibid.,* pp. 60-61.

59. *Ibid.,* p. 83.

60. *Ibid.,* p. 84.

61. *Ibid.,* pp. 83-84.

62. George H. Burgess and Miles C. Kennedy, *op. cit.,* Appendix E.

63. J. W. Townsend, *op. cit.,* p. 86.

64. John Gunther, *Inside U.S.A.,* (New York: Harper & Brothers, 1947), p. 604.

65. John J. Macfarlane, *History of Early Chestnut Hill,* (Philadelphia: City History Society, 1927), p. 68.

66. Cleveland Amory, *The Proper Bostonians,* (New York: E. P. Dutton & Co., Inc., 1947), p. 196.

67. Horace Mather Lippincott, *A Narrative of Chestnut Hill, Philadelphia with some account of Springfield, Whitemarsh, and Cheltenham Townships in Montgomery County, Pennsylvania,* (Jenkintown, Pennsylvania, Old York Road Publishing Company, 1948), p. 18.

68. *Ibid.,* p. 78.

69. *Ibid.,* p. 86.

70. *Ibid.,* p. 87.

71. *Ibid.,* pp. 115-116.

72. Frank Willing Leach, "Old Philadelphia Families XLIV," *The North American,* Philadelphia, June 16, 1907.

73. Horace Mather Lippincott, *op. cit.,* p. 133.

74. Josiah Granville Leach, *Genealogical and Biographical Memorials of the Reading, Howell, Yerkes, Watts, Latham, and Elkins Families,* (Philadelphia: J. B. Lippincott Company, 1898), p. 257.

75. Ellis Paxson Oberholtzer, *Jay Cooke, Financier of the Civil War,* (Philadelphia: George W. Jacobs & Co., 1907), Vol. II, p. 33.

76. P. A. B. Widener, *Without Drums,* (New York: G. P. Putnam's Sons, 1940), Chapter III.

77. *Ibid.,* pp. 52-53.

78. Philadelphia Evening *Bulletin,* October 26, 1943.

79. Pitirim Sorokin, *Social Mobility,* (New York: Harper & Brothers, 1927).

80. See "Executive Trappings," *Time,* Jan. 24, 1955.

81. See Robert Strausz-Hupe, *Power and Community,* (New York: Frederick A. Praeger, 1956). This excellent collection of essays points out the dangers of a society of *rank* and the consequent weakening of "the private sectors of society."

82. Compare *Boyd's Blue Book, Elite Directory with Philadelphia Club List* (1914).

83. See obituary of Dr. David Riesman, Sr., Philadelphia *Evening Bulletin,* June 4, 1940.

84. See 1940 *Social Register.*

85. Rufus M. Jones, *Haverford College, A History and an Interpretation,* (New York: The Macmillan Company, 1933), p. 1.

86. Logan Pearsall Smith, *Unforgotten Years,* (Boston: Little, Brown and Company, 1949), p. 31.

87. John W. Jordan, *A History of Delaware County Pennsylvania and its People,* (New York: Lewis Historical Publishing Company, 1914), Volume II, pp. 460-461.

88. *Ibid.*

89. Scharf and Westcott, *op. cit.,* Vol. III, pp. 2321-2322.

90. *Ibid.,* Vol. II, p. 1406.

91. Joshua L. Chamberlain, *University of Pennsylvania, Its History, Influence, Equipment, and Characteristics, with Biographical Sketches,* (Boston: R. Herndon Company, 1901), p. 384. Also see Horace Howard Furness, "DAB" biography.

92. See *Philadelphia Architecture in the Nineteenth Century* for examples of Frank Furness's work.

93. Carl and Jessica Bridenbaugh, *op. cit.,* p. 7.

94. Cleveland Amory, *The Last Resorts,* (New York: Harper & Brothers, 1952), p. 8.

95. *Ibid.,* p. 4.

96. Ernest Earnest, S. *Weir Mitchell,* (Philadelphia: University of Pennsylvania Press, 1950), p. 15.

97. George Wharton Pepper, *op. cit.,* p. 318.

98. Cleveland Amory, *op. cit.,* p. 308.

99. George Wharton Pepper, *op. cit.,* p. 318.

Chapter X

RELIGION AND
THE CLASS STRUCTURE

1. Liston Pope, "Religion and the Class Structure," *The Annals of the American Academy of Political and Social Science*, Vol. 256, (March 1948), p. 89. See also the classic work on this subject, H. Richard Niebuhr, *The Social Sources of Denominationalism*, (New York: Henry Holt and Co., Inc., 1929).

2. Matthew Josephson, *The Robber Barons: The Great American Capitalists, 1861-1901*, (New York: Harcourt, Brace and Company, 1934), pp. 320-321.

3. George Eaton Simpson and J. Milton Yinger, *Racial and Cultural Minorities: An Analysis of Prejudice and Discrimination*, (New York: Harper and Brothers, 1953), p. 515.

4. Liston Pope, *Millhands and Preachers*, (New Haven: Yale University Press, 1942), p. 124.

5. Max Weber, *The Protestant Ethic and the Spirit of Capitalism*, translated by Talcott Parsons, (London: Allen and Unwin, 1930), p. 1.

6. *Congregationalist*, June 21, 1876, p. 196. Quoted in Henry F. May, *Protestant Churches and Industrial America*, (New York: Harper and Brothers, 1949), p. 51.

7. Clarence Day, *God and My Father*, from *The Best of Clarence Day*, (New York: Alfred A. Knopf, 1948), p. 5.

8. George Wharton Pepper, *Philadelphia Lawyer*, (Philadelphia: J. B. Lippincott Company, 1944), p. 98.

9. Dixon Wecter, *The Saga of American Society*, (New York: Charles Scribner's Sons, 1937), p. 478.

10. Carl Bridenbaugh, *Cities in Revolt*, (New York: Alfred A. Knopf, 1955), p. 152.

11. See W. J. Cash, *The Mind of the South*, (New York: Doubleday Anchor Books, 1954).

12. See James Thayer Addison, *The Episcopal Church in the United States, 1789-1931*, (New York: Charles Scribner's Sons, 1951), pp. 65-73. An ex-cellent description of the founding of the Episcopal Church.

13. Frank Cousins and Phil M. Riley, *The Colonial Architecture of Philadelphia*, (Boston: Little, Brown and Company, 1920), p. 221.

14. Ellis Paxson Oberholtzer, *Jay Cooke, Financier of the Civil War*, (Philadelphia: George W. Jacobs and Company, 1907), Vol. II, pp. 483-485.

15. Matthew Josephson, *op. cit.*, p. 319.

16. James Thayer Addison, *op cit.*, p. 205.

17. Frank D. Ashburn, *Peabody of Groton*, (New York: Coward McCann, Inc., 1944), p. 30.

18. Cleveland Amory, *The Proper Bostonians*, (New York: E. P. Dutton and Company, Inc., 1947), p. 107.

19. Boston *Daily Herald*, May 15, 1836. Taken from a student's dissertation in progress.

20. Andrew Landale Drummond, *Story of American Protestantism*, (Boston: The Beacon Press, 1951), p. 187.

21. Van Wyck Brooks, *New England: Indian Summer, 1865-1915*, (New York: E. P. Dutton and Company, Inc., 1940), pp. 184-203.

22. Cleveland Amory, *op. cit.*, p. 105.

23. Charles J. Cohen, *Rittenhouse Square*, (Philadelphia: Privately Printed, 1922).

24. Alexander V. G. Allen, *Life and Letters of Phillips Brooks*, (New York: E. P. Dutton and Company, 1901).

25. Dixon Wecter, *op. cit.*, p. 478.

26. Robert K. Bosch, *Ecclesiastical Background of the American Episcopate*, (Unpublished manuscript in the author's possession).

27. See Vida Dutton Scudder, *Father Huntington, Founder of the Order of the Holy Cross*, (New York: E. P. Dutton and Company, Inc., 1940).

28. *Ibid.*, p. 35.

29. See George Hodges, *Henry Codman Potter, Seventh Bishop of New York*, (New York: The Macmillan Company, 1915).

30. Dixon Wecter, *op. cit.*, p. 479.

31. Gustavus Myers, *History of the Great American Fortunes*, (New York: The Modern Library, 1937), p. 378.

32. Dixon Wecter, *op. cit.*, p. 480.

33. See Frederick Lewis Allen, *The*

Great Pierpont Morgan, (New York: Harper and Brothers, 1949).

34. *Ibid.,* p. 240.

35. *Ibid.,* p. 153.

36. *Ibid.,* p. 133.

37. Spencer Miller, Jr., and Joseph F. Fletcher, *The Church and Industry,* (New York: Longmans, Green and Company, 1930), p. 219.

38. *Ibid.,* pp. 52-111.

39. Henry F. May, *Protestant Churches and Industrial America,* (New York: Harper and Brothers, 1949), p. 186.

40. George Hodges, *op. cit.,* pp. 343-344.

41. Spencer Miller, Jr., and Joseph F. Fletcher, *op. cit.,* p. 71.

42. New York *Times,* June 25, 1955.

43. *Time,* April 19, 1945, p. 62.

44. Carl and Jessica Bridenbaugh, *Rebels and Gentlemen, Philadelphia in the Age of Franklin,* (New York: Reynal & Hitchcock, 1942), p. 16.

45. Nicholas B. Wainwright, *A Philadelphia Story, The Philadelphia Contributionship for the Insurance of Houses from Loss by Fire,* (Philadelphia: Privately Printed, 1952), p. 30. Amos Strettell was married at Christ Church in 1752, and was one of the petitioners for land on which to build St. Peter's in 1754.

46. Frederick B. Tolles, *Meeting House and Counting House, The Quaker Merchants of Colonial Philadelphia, 1682-1763,* (Chapel Hill, The University of North Carolina Press, 1948), p. 221.

47. *Ibid.,* p. 229n.

48. *Ibid.,* p. 45.

49. *Ibid.,* pp. 115-116.

50. *Ibid.,* p. 19.

51. William W. Montgomery, *Pew Renters of Christ Church, St. Peter's and St. James's, From 1776 to 1815,* (unpublished manuscript, Philadelphia, 1948).

52. Carl and Jessica Bridenbaugh, *op. cit.,* p. 17.

53. *Ibid.,* p. 208.

54. *Ibid.,* p. 211.

55. C. P. B. Jefferys, *The Provincial and Revolutionary History of St. Peter's Church, Philadelphia, 1753-1783,* (Philadelphia: Privately Printed, 1923), p. 14.

56. "Society Hill" was so called long before St. Peter's and the mansions of wealthy Philadelphians were built there. According to Christopher Tunnard, Society Hill may have been the first suburban development in America. See Christopher Tunnard, *The City of Man,* (New York: Charles Scribner's Sons, 1953), p. 113.

57. Frederick B. Tolles, *op. cit.,* p. 27.

58. Quoted in J. Thomas Scharf and Thomas Westcott, *History of Philadelphia, 1609-1884,* (Philadelphia: G. Everts & Co., 1884), Vol. I, p. 296n.

59. C. P. B. Jefferys, *op. cit.,* pp. 66-76.

60. J. Thomas Scharf and Thomas Westcott, *op. cit.,* Vol. I, p. 393.

61. C. P. B. Jefferys, *op. cit.,* p. 63.

62. John W. Jordan, Editor, *Colonial Families of Philadelphia,* (New York: The Lewis Publishing Company, 1911), Vol. II, p. 1746.

63. Nicholas B. Wainwright, *op. cit.,* p. 132.

64. William W. Montgomery, *op. cit.* Even the great sociologist of religion, Ernest Troeltsch, called Franklin a Quaker. *Le bon Quaker,* of course, was part of the *philosophes'* heavenly city in the eighteenth century.

65. C. P. B. Jeffery's, *op. cit.,* p. 88.

66. John W. Jordan, *op. cit.,* Vol. I, p. 293.

67. Rufus M. Jones, *The Quakers in the American Colonies,* (London: Macmillan and Co., Limited, 1911), pp. 457-458.

68. A. E. Browne, *A Sketch of St. James's Parish,* (Philadelphia, 1899), p. 7.

69. J. Thomas Scharf and Thomas Westcott, *op. cit.,* Vol. II, p. 1352.

70. *The Church of the Savior,* 100th Anniversary, November, 1950. (pamphlet)

71. A. E. Browne, *op. cit.,* pp. 23-27.

72. C. P. B. Jeffery's, *op. cit.,* p. 89.

73. See summary of these reports in A. E. Browne, *op. cit.*

74. Claude Gilkyson, *St. Mark's, One Hundred Years on Locust Street,* (Philadelphia, 1948).

75. *Ibid.,* p. 9.

76. *Ibid.,* p. 9.

77. *Ibid.,* p. 45.

78. *Ibid.,* p. 60.

79. *Ibid.,* pp. 26-33.

80. *Ibid.,* p. 33.

81. *Ibid.*, pp. 16-25.

82. Alexander V. G. Allen, *op. cit.*, Vol. I, p. 293.

83. *Ibid.*, Vol. II, pp. 113-114.

84. *Ibid.*, Vol. II, p. 113.

85. Cordelia Drexel Biddle (as told to Kyle Crichton), *My Philadelphia Father*, (Garden City, N. Y.: Doubleday & Company, Inc., 1955), p. 71.

86. George Wharton Pepper, *op. cit.*, p. 313.

87. Cordelia Drexel Biddle, *op. cit.*, p. 71.

88. *Ibid.*, p. 135.

89. *Ibid.*, p. 91.

90. Henry F. May, *op. cit.*, p. 64.

91. *Ibid.*, p. 65.

92. George Wharton Pepper, *op. cit.*, p. 278.

93. *Service in Memory of Anthony J. Drexel, Founder of the Drexel Institute of Art, Science and Industry*, (Philadelphia; privately printed, 1896).

94. Sister M. Dolores, *The Francis A. Drexel Family*, (Cornwells Heights, Pa.: The Sisters of the Blessed Sacrament).

95. Claude Gilkyson, *op. cit.*, p. 63. Even in the 1880's parishioners were moving out to the country. In 1883, for example, while twenty-six children entered the parish school, twenty-seven left because their parents had moved from the neighborhood. *Ibid.*, p. 39.

96. St. James was sold to the Atlantic Refining Company "due to financial difficulties caused by changing neighborhood conditions." Philadelphia *Evening Bulletin*, September 8, 1945.

97. Philadelphia *Evening Bulletin*, December 21, 1925.

98. *Ibid.*, November 7, 1930.

99. *Ibid.*

100. *Ibid.*

101. *Ibid.*

102. John T. Faris, *Old Churches and Meeting Houses in and around Philadelphia*, (Philadelphia: J. B. Lippincott Company, 1926), p. 203.

103. *Ibid.*, p. 206.

104. Journal of the *Annual Convention of the Protestant Episcopal Church in the Diocese of Pennsylvania*, (Philadelphia, 1881).

105. Ernest C. Earp, *The Church of the Redeemer, Bryn Mawr, Lower Merion, Montgomery County, Pennsylvania*.

106. *Centennial History of St. Paul's Church, Chestnut Hill, 1856-1956*.

107. James Thayer Addison, *op. cit.*, pp. 254-62. William Hobart Hare became one of the pioneering missionary bishops of the Episcopal Church. He devoted the prime of his life to the Indians of the Dakotas.

108. *Centennial History of St. Paul's Church*.

109. Horace Mather Lippincott, *A Narrative of Chestnut Hill, Philadelphia, with some account of Springfield, Whitemarsh, and Cheltenham Townships in Montgomery County, Pennsylvania*, (Jenkintown, Pennsylvania: Old York Road Publishing Company, 1948), p. 29.

110. Ernest C. Earp, *op. cit.* (no pages are numbered).

111. *Centennial History of St. Paul's Church*.

112. *Ibid.*

113. Ellis Paxson Oberholtzer, *op. cit.*, Vol. II, pp. 483-485.

114. Journal of the *Annual Convention*, 1941.

115. *Ibid.*

116. *Ibid.*

117. Ernest C. Earp, *op. cit.*

Chapter XI

PARALLEL UPPER-CLASS STRUCTURES

1. August B. Hollingshead, "Trends in Social Stratification: A Case Study," *American Sociological Review*, Vol. 17, No. 6, (December 1952), pp. 685-86.

2. Rufus M. Jones, *The Quakers in the American Colonies*, (London: Macmillan and Co., Limited, 1911), pp. 579-580.

3. George Wharton Pepper, *Philadelphia Lawyer*, (Philadelphia: J. B. Lippincott Company, 1944), p. 44.

4. Logan Pearsall Smith, *Unforgotten Years*, (Boston: Little, Brown and Company, 1949), p. 17.

5. *Ibid.*, p. 80.

6. *Ibid.*, p. 139.

7. Rufus M. Jones, *Haverford College, A History and an Interpretation,* (New York: The Macmillan Company, 1933), pp. 82-93.

8. *Who's Who in America,* (Chicago: The A. N. Marquis Company, 1940).

9. J. Thomas Scharf and Thomas Westcott, *History of Philadelphia, 1609-1884,* (Philadelphia: L. H. Everts & Co., 1884), Vol. I, p. 535.

10. Edwin T. Freedley, *Philadelphia and its Manufactures,* (Philadelphia: Edward Young & Co., 1867), p. 203.

11. *Ibid.,* p. 215. See also J. Thomas Scharf and Thomas Westcott, *op. cit.,* Vol. I, pp. 810-811.

12. Moses King, *Philadelphia and Notable Philadelphians,* (New York: Moses King, Publisher, 1901), pp. 40a and 60.

13. *Who's Who in America.*

14. Rufus M. Jones, *op. cit.* (Haverford College), pp. 176-77.

15. *Philadelphia and Popular Philadelphians,* (Philadelphia: The North American, 1891), pp. 198-199.

16. See James E. Rhoads, "DAB" biography.

17. No index used in the social sciences, of course, is completely accurate. All the gentlemen named here were listed in *Who's Who,* except Morris Wolf. As he was the senior partner in the top Jewish law firm in the city, a firm which includes Sterns and Solis-Cohens as well as Wolfe, this is certainly a weakness in our index. As the Wolfs are such an important upper-class Jewish family, I have included Morris Wolf within the elite as if he were listed in *Who's Who.* Let us never be bound, and blinded, by our too-often mechanistic methods in the social sciences!

18. Background material on the Jews of Europe was obtained in: Jacob Radar Marcus, *Early American Jewry, the Jews of New York, New England, and Canada, 1649-1794,* (Philadelphia: The Jewish Publications Society of America, 1951), Vol. I, pp. 3-24; Oscar Handlin, *Adventure in Freedom, Three Hundrd Years of Jewish Life in America,* (New York: McGraw-Hill Book Company, Inc., 1954), pp. 3-22; and Rufus Learsi, *The Jews in America,* (New York: The World Publishing Company, 1954), pp. 3-26.

19. S. M. Dubnow, translated from the Russian by I. Friedlaender, *History of the Jews in Russia and Poland,* (Philadelphia: The Jewish Publication Society of America, 1920), 3 Volumes.

20. Early Sephardic Synagogues were erected in New Amsterdam (Shearith Israel 1730), Newport (Jeshuat Israel 1768), Charleston (Beth Elohim 1750), Savannah (Mikveh Israel 1735), and Philadelphia (Mikveh Israel, 1782).

According to Rufus Learsi, by 1754 "most of the first-grade members of Shearith Israel were Ashkenazim, although worship followed the Sephardic ritual." Rufus Learsi, *op. cit.,* p. 30.

21. Henry Samuel Morias, *The Jews of Philadelphia,* (Philadelphia: The Levytype Company, 1894), p. 11.

22. See list of original subscribers to the Dancing Assemblies in: Joseph P. Sims, Editor, *The Philadelphia Assemblies, 1748-1948,* p. 10; and J. Thomas Scharf and Thomas Westcott, *op. cit.,* Vol. II, p. 864.

According to Morias, *op. cit.,* p. 34, David Franks was a member of Mikveh Israel but was "lax in his adherence to Judaism, and married outside the pale of his religion."

23. Dixon Wecter, *The Saga of American Society,* (New York: Charles Scribner's Sons, 1937), p. 153.

24. For a more detailed discussion of the building of Mikveh Israel on Cherry Alley, see Jacob Radar Marcus, *op. cit.,* Vol. II, pp. 125-131.

25. Henry Samuel Morias, *op. cit.,* pp. 70-71.

26. *The Philadelphia Club, 1834-1934,* (Philadelphia: Privately Printed, 1934).

27. *Ibid.*

28. Dixon Wecter, *op. cit.,* pp. 153-154.

29. Francis J. Brown and Joseph S. Roucek, *One America, The History, Contributions, and Present Problems of our Racial and National Minorities,* (New York: Prentice-Hall, Inc., 1953), p. 663. Between 1841 and 1850, 434,626 Germans came to America and between 1851 and 1860 the figure had increased to 951,667.

30. See Carl Wittke, *Refugees of Revolution, The German Forty-Eighters in America*, (Philadelphia: University of Pennsylvania Press, 1952), pp. 78-91.

31. Rufus Learsi, *op. cit.*, p. 64.

32. Henry Samuel Morias, *op. cit.*, pp. 294-295.

33. *Ibid.*, p. 64.

34. *Ibid.*, p. 193.

35. *Ibid.*, p. 194.

36. *Ibid.*, pp. 135-138.

37. *Ibid.*, pp. 112-120.

38. *The Rich Men of Philadelphia, Income Tax of the Residents of Philadelphia and Bucks County for the Year Ending April 30, 1865.* (Philadelphia, 1865), pp. 5-9.

39. *McElroy's Philadelphia City Directory for 1859*, (Philadelphia: Edward C. and John Biddle, 1859).

40. Rufus Learsi, *op. cit.*, p. 124.

41. Henry Samuel Morias, *op. cit.*, pp. 207-208; and Rufus Learsi, *op. cit.*, p. 125.

42. *Ibid.*, p. 114.

43. *Ibid.*, pp. 131-135.

44. *Gopsill's Philadelphia City Directory, 1882*, (Philadelphia: James Gopsill, 1882).

45. *Ibid.*, 1900.

46. *Boyd's Blue Book*, (Philadelphia: C. E. Howe Co., 1890.)

47. This information as to Charles T. Yerkes's Philadelphia address at this time was obtained from the curator of the Dreiser Collection at the University of Pennsylvania Library.

48. *Boyd's Blue Book*, 1890.

49. Henry Samuel Morias, *op. cit.*, pp. 109-110.

50. See *Boyd's Blue Book*, Editions during 1880's and in 1890. Prominent families often named their summer residences along with their city addresses.

51. Dixon Wecter, *op. cit.*, p. 438n. Most writers on the subject date the beginning of the modern American practice of exclusion of Jews from summer resorts, hotels, and clubs in 1877. In that year Joseph Seligman was openly excluded from the Grand Union Hotel in Saratoga. When Joseph Seligman, a distinguished financier, friend of both presidents Lincoln and Grant (who offered him the post of Secretary of the Treasury), and one of the major financiers of the North in the Civil War, was told by the Grand Union manager that "no Israelite shall be permitted in the future to stop in the hotel," the "news" made headlines all over the country. See Rufus Learsi, *op. cit.*, pp. 172-173.

52. Between 1882 and 1914, some two million east European Jews came to America. Almost twenty million other immigrants arrived in America during this period.

53. See H. L. Mencken, *The American Language, Supplement I*, (New York: Alfred A. Knopf, 1945), pp. 601-14.

54. According to H. L. Mencken, the most commonly accepted etymology for *kike* was thus stated in *American Speech* in 1926 by J. H. A. Lacher:

"In Russia there began some forty years ago a fierce persecution of the Jews. . . . Many found their way to the United States. . . . Here they offered keen competition to their brethren of German origin, who soon insisted that the business ethics and standards of living and culture of these Russians were far lower than theirs. Since the names of so many of these Eastern Jews ended in *-ki* or *-ky*, German-American Jewish traveling men designated them contemptuously as *kikis*, a term which, naturally, was soon contracted to *kikes.*"

For the above and other claims and counter-claims as to origins, see *ibid.*, pp. 614-617.

55. Henry Samuel Morias, *op. cit.*, p. 193.

56. See obituary notices of Ellis A. Gimbel, Philadelphia Evening *Bulletin*, March 17, 1950.

57. See Oscar Handlin, *op. cit.*, pp. 143-174; and Carey McWilliams, *A Mask for Privilege*, (Boston: Little, Brown and Company, 1948), pp. 36-37. According to McWilliams, "after 1924 the Jewish population tended to become predominantly middle class."

58. *Fortune*, Volume XIII, No. 6, (June, 1936), p. 186.

59. *Ibid.*, p. 186.

60. Carey McWilliams, *op. cit.*, pp. 58-63.

61. *Ibid.*, pp. 34-40.

62. The history of the Federation was obtained in an interview with Mr. Roman Slobodin, director.

63. *Report of the Federation of*

Jewish Charities of Philadelphia and its Affiliated Organizations, for the Year Ending April 30, 1920, Vol. XIX.

Upper-class families still held the dominant positions in the Federation: Louis Wolf was President, Jacob Gimbel, Honorary President, Samuel S. Fels, Honorary First Vice-President, and the Directors included Cyrus Adler, Fleishers, Gimbels, Lits, Snellenburgs, and Wolfs.

64. *Report of the Federation,* April 30, 1923.

65. *Ibid.,* A list of the Annual Subscribers to the Federation as of July 15, 1925.

66. *Polk's Philadelphia Blue Book, Elite Directory and Club List,* (Philadelphia: R. L. Polk & Co., 1924), p. 624.

67. Information on the founding of the Locust Club was obtained from the club's president in 1955, Raymond A. Speiser.

Chapter XII

EDUCATION AND STATUS ASCRIPTION

1. Quoted in Thomas Harrison Montgomery, *A History of the University of Pennsylvania from its Foundation to A.D. 1770,* (Philadelphia: George W. Jacobs & Co., A.D. 1900), p. 11.

2. Quoted in Carl and Jessica Bridenbaugh, *Rebels and Gentlemen,* (New York: Reynal & Hitchcock, 1942), p. 47.

3. Charles McArthur, "Personalities of Public and Private School Boys," *The Harvard Educational Review,* Vol. XXIV, No. 4, (Fall, 1954), pp. 256-62.

4. *Ibid.,* p. 257.

5. This is a general pattern in the older eastern seaboard cities in America. In *Yankee City,* for instance, "The members of the upper-upper and the lower-upper classes give their children a different formal and informal education. No children of the former attended the local high school . . . only four lower-upper class children

were enrolled in the high school. Most of the children of the two upper classes are sent to private preparatory schools, where they . . . acquire the etiquette and attributes of their group." W. Lloyd Warner and Paul S. Lunt, *The Social Life of a Modern Community,* (New Haven: Yale University Press, 1941), p. 426.

6. *Catalog of the William Penn Charter School Alumni,* (Philadelphia: The Overseers, 1948), pp. v-x.

7. Porter Sargent, *A Handbook of Private Schools,* (Boston: Porter Sargent, 1950), pp. 404-405.

8. *Ibid.,* pp. 394-395.

9. *The Quarter Century Review of the Chestnut Hill Academy,* (Chestnut Hill, Philadelphia: The Chestnut Hill Academy, 1920).

10. Porter Sargent, *op. cit.,* p. 403.

11. *Register of the Academy of the Protestant Episcopal Church,* (Philadelphia, 1915), p. 17.

12. *Ibid.,* p. 10.

13. *Ibid.,* p. 18.

14. *Ibid.,* p. 10.

15. *Ibid.*

16. The *Tabula* of the Class of 1916 (Class Yearbook at the Episcopal Academy).

17. This data was obtained by checking the Class Yearbook list of trustees with the *Social Register,* for the same year.

18. Porter Sargent, *op. cit.,* p. 404.

19. *Ibid.,* p. 244.

20. Yearbook, *Tabula,* 1940 checked with the contemporary *Social Register.*

21. Yearbook, *Tabula,* 1940.

22. Porter Sargent, *op. cit.,* p. 409.

23. Agnes Repplier, *Agnes Irwin,* (New York: Doubleday, Doran & Company, Inc., 1934).

24. Porter Sargent, *op. cit.,* p. 416.

25. Alumni Directory of St. Paul's School, (Concord, New Hampshire, 1956).

26. See Porter Sargent, *op. cit.,* and

27. Frank D. Ashburn, *Peabody of Groton,* (New York: Coward McCann, Inc., 1944), p. 30.

28. *Ibid.,* pp. 67-68.

29. *Ibid.,* p. 71. The school family is also closely related to the families of its pupils and its alumni. For example, "For ten years (1933-43), Hotchkiss School in Lakeville, Conn.,

watched the young Fords go by—Henry II, Benson, and William, sons of Automagnate Edsel Ford . . . This week, in memory of their father, the Fords and their mother gave Hotchkiss $350,000 to build a new library, something Hotchkiss has wanted for more than 20 years." *Time,* November 20, 1950.

30. *The Groton School Address Book,* 1953.

31. Allan V. Heely, *Why the Private School,* (New York: Harper & Brothers, 1951), pp. 94-95.

The *selective* snobbery in the local high schools is far different from the *segregated* democracy of the boarding school. As a business-class daughter in "Middletown" reported to the Lynds: "There are special cliques in high school according to what Sunday school you go to. . . . The social emphasis of the most prominent of these Sunday-school classes, that in the Presbyterian Church, is enhanced by such class affairs as stylishly appointed luncheons at the Country Club." Robert S. Lynd and Helen Merrell Lynd, *Middletown in Transition,* (New York: Harcourt, Brace and Company, 1937), p. 306.

32. *Alumni Directory of St. Paul's School,* 1956.

33. *Phillips Exeter Bulletin,* Special Issue, Volume XLIV, Number 4, (March, 1948).

34. Helen Merrell Lynd, *England in the Eighteen-Eighties,* (London and New York: Oxford University Press, 1945).

35. Rex Warner, *English Public Schools,* (London: Collins, 1945), pp. 8-9.

36. *The Public Schools and the General Educational System,* (London: His Majesty's Stationery Office, 1944), p. 19.

37. Quoted in Rex Warner, *op. cit.,* p. 32.

38. "Boys Schools," *Fortune,* Vol. XIII, No. 1, (January, 1936), pp. 48-55.

39. *Phillips Exeter Bulletin, op. cit.*

40. See *Fortune* article.

41. Paul A. W. Wallace, *The Muhlenbergs of Pennsylvania,* (Philadelphia: University of Pennsylvania Press, 1950).

42. James Thayer Addison, *The Episcopal Church in the United*

States, 1789-1931, (New York: Charles Scribner's Sons, 1951), p. 165.

It is interesting that James Thayer Addison, himself a graduate of Groton School, does not discuss such schools as Groton or St. Paul's in his history of the Episcopal Church.

43. *Ibid.,* pp. 165-66.

44. Arthur Stanwood Pier, *St. Paul's School, 1855-1934,* (New York: Charles Scribner's Sons, 1934), p. 3.

45. *Ibid.,* p. 1.

46. *Ibid.,* p. 1.

47. *Ibid.,* p. 14.

48. *Ibid.,* p. 8.

49. *Ibid.,* p. 17.

50. In the first hundred years of the school's history, some dozen members of the Wheeler family of Philadelphia have been at the school (almost continuously in the twentieth century there has been at least one member of the family at the school). See *Alumni Directory.*

51. Porter Sargent, *op. cit.,* p. 416.

52. *The Alonzo Potter Family,* (Concord, New Hampshire: The Rumford Press, privately printed, 1923). Also see *Alumni Directory.*

53. Alexander V. G. Allen, *Life and Letters of Phillips Brooks,* (New York: E. P. Dutton and Company, 1901), Volume II, p. 110.

54. *Alumni Horae,* (Autumn 1953), published by the Alumni Association of St. Paul's School.

55. *Alumni Directory,* 1956.

56. Alexander V. G. Allen, *op. cit.,* Vol. II, p. 110.

57. *Fortune,* January, 1936.

58. *Ibid.*

59. *Ibid.*

60. *Ibid.*

61. George Biddle, *An American Artist's Story,* (Boston: Little, Brown and Company, 1939), p. 66.

62. *Time,* Vol. LXII, No. 6, August 10, 1953.

63. See Frank D. Ashburn, *op. cit.*

64. George Biddle, *op. cit.,* p. 67.

65. Arthur Stanwood Pier, *op. cit.,* p. 60.

66. *Ibid.,* p. 181.

67. James Thayer Addison, *op. cit.,* p. 166, Italics mine.

68. Arthur Stanwood Pier, *op. cit.,* pp. 359-360.

69. *Royal Commission on Population,* (London: His Majesty's Station-

ery Office), p. 145.

70. Thomas Harrison Montgomery, *op. cit.*, p. 25.

71. Edward Potts Cheyney, *History of the University of Pennsylvania, 1740-1940*, (Philadelphia: University of Pennsylvania Press, 1940), pp. 17-53.

72. *Ibid.*, p. 28.

73. *Ibid.*, pp. 30-33.

74. Rufus M. Jones, *Haverford College*, (New York: The Macmillan Company, 1933).

75. Edward Potts Cheyney, *op. cit.*, p. 258.

76. *Ibid.*, p. 287.

77. Francis Newton Thorpe, *William Pepper*, (Philadelphia: J. B. Lippincott Company, 1904), p. 458.

78. *Ibid.*, p. 467.

79. *Ibid.*, p. 427.

80. These gifts to the University during Dr. Pepper's regime are discussed in Edward Potts Cheyney, *op. cit.*, Chapter 8, pp. 285-332.

81. The Harrison era of building is discussed in, *Ibid.*, pp. 332-359.

82. *Catalogue of the University of Pennsylvania*, (Philadelphia, 1903).

83. Edward Potts Cheyney, *op. cit.*, p. 377.

84. Quoted in Francis Newton Thorpe, *op. cit.*, p. 464.

85. Edward Potts Cheyney, *op. cit.*, p. 420.

86. *University of Pennsylvania, Directory of Officers Faculty Students Departments, 1940-1941*, (Philadelphia, 1940).

87. Joshua L. Chamberlain, Editor-in-Chief, *Universities and Their Sons*, University of Pennsylvania, (Boston: R. Herndon Company, 1901), p. 225.

88. *Bric-A-Brac*, Vol. LII, 1928, p. 31.

89. *The Groton School Address Book*, 1953.

90. Figures obtained from the Admissions Office, Princeton, New Jersey.

91. These figures were obtained from freshman class year-books in the stacks of the Firestone Library.

92. John P. Marquand, *The Late George Apley*, (New York: The Modern Library, 1940), pp. 216-17.

93. Cleveland Amory, *The Proper Bostonians*, (New York: E. P. Dutton & Co., Inc., 1947), p. 300.

94. *Ibid.*, p. 304.

95. Dixon Wecter, *The Saga of American Society*, (New York: Charles Scribner's Sons, 1937), p. 281.

96. *Ibid.*, pp. 284-285.

97. See the Ivy Club officers listed in the *Bric-A-Brac*, 1929, and compare with the *Social Register* for the same year.

98. George Biddle, *op. cit.*, pp. 81-82. George Biddle has some perceptive comments on the subtleties of stratification in extra-curricular activities during his day at Harvard: "Football and rowing were of course the *ne plus ultra*. About the baseball squad there was something a little—well you know. Very few Grotties went in for baseball at Harvard. The track team was quite all right and of course tennis, golf and soccer; but one hardly knew the fellows who played lacrosse or basketball; or for that matter the members of the Pierian Sodality; and never, never, never, the members of the wrestling or debating teams. They were probably Jews and one might just as well go to Columbia University." *Ibid.*, p. 82.

99. Arthur Stanwood Pier, *op. cit.*, p. 351.

100. Quoted in Dixon Wecter, *op. cit.*, p. 284.

101. For an interesting discussion of Booth Tarkington's days at Exeter and Princeton, see James Woodress, *Booth Tarkington*, (Philadelphia: J. B. Lippincott Company, 1955).

102. George Biddle, *op. cit.*, pp. 80-81.

103. See "The Rich Boy" in *The Stories of F. Scott Fitzgerald*, Edited with an introduction by Malcolm Cowley, (New York: Charles Scribner's Sons, 1951), pp. 177-208.

104. Quoted in Thomas Harrison Montgomery, *op. cit.*, p. 12.

Chapter XIII

SOCIAL CLUBS AND
THE CLASS STRUCTURE

1. W. Lloyd Warner defines an association as a "mechanism which helps place the members of a society

in a class hierarchy." It is "one of the foremost mechanisms of integration in Yankee City Society." W. Lloyd Warner and Paul S. Lunt, *The Social Life of a Modern Community,* (New Haven: Yale University Press, 1941), p. 301.

2. Crane Brinton, "Clubs," *Encyclopedia of the Social Sciences,* Vol. 3, (New York: The Macmillan Company, 1930), p. 575.

3. In "Yankee City," as in Philadelphia, those persons of high social class position are more likely to belong to associations than those of lower social position. Thus, within the upper-upper class, 72 per cent are members of associations, while 71 per cent of the lower upper, 64 per cent of the upper-middle, and 49 per cent of the lower-middle are members of associations. W. Lloyd Warner and Paul S. Lunt, *op. cit.,* p. 329.

Warner also found that, "both men and women of the upper-upper class have a significantly high membership in what are ordinarily called social clubs." *Ibid.,* p. 426.

4. In "Yankee City," "when the upper classes belong to exclusive clubs they do not join those with both men and women, but those with only men or only women. Associations in which both sexes are members also tend to be more 'democratic' and extend through several classes." Warner and Lunt, *op. cit.,* p. 350.

In this sense, the upper class in Philadelphia is very different from the "business class" in "Middletown" where the "woman makes the family's social status." Robert S. Lynd and Helen Merrell Lynd, *Middletown,* (New York: Harcourt, Brace and Company, 1929), p. 116.

5. Cleveland Amory, *The Proper Bostonians,* (New York: E. P. Dutton & Co., Inc., 1947), p. 358.

6. *From Max Weber: Essays in Sociology,* translated, edited and with an introduction by H. H. Gerth and C. Wright Mills, (New York: Oxford University Press, 1946), p. 311.

7. Bernard Darwin, *British Clubs,* (London: Collins, 1947), pp. 17-18.

8. Dixon Wecter, *The Saga of American Society,* (New York: Charles Scribner's Sons, 1937), p. 258.

9. *The Philadelphia Club, 1834-*

1934, (Philadelphia: Privately Printed, 1934), pp. 65-66.

10. Dixon Wecter, *op. cit.,* pp. 253-255.

11. *Ibid.,* p. 254n.

12. Frederick Lewis Allen, *The Lords of Creation,* (New York: Harper and Brothers, 1935), p. 99.

13. Sinclair Lewis, *Babbitt,* (New York: Harcourt, Brace and Company, 1922), pp. 54-55.

14. J. Thomas Scharf and Thompson Westcott, *History of Philadelphia,* 1609-1884, (Philadelphia: L. H. Everts & Co., 1884), Vol. II., p. 1096.

15. *Ibid.*

16. *Ibid.,* p. 1097.

"Social perspective" varies with position in the social structure. In Philadelphia, most persons outside the upper class view the Union League as *the* upper-class club. It is probably safe to say that 99 per cent of the people in Philadelphia have never heard of the Philadelphia or Rittenhouse Clubs. On the other hand, most upper-middle-class persons, at least, would know of, and have stereotyped, the Union League, Racquet, or Merion Cricket Clubs as upper-class strongholds.

W. Lloyd Warner found this same phenomenon in "Yankee City." He says: "Certain clubs, our interviews showed, were ranked at such extreme heights by people highly placed in the society that most of the lower classes did not even know of their existence." Warner and Lunt, *op. cit.,* p. 87.

17. *The Philadelphia Club, 1834-1934.*

18. *Ibid.* Philadelphia Club membership was compared to list of Assembly Manager in *The Philadelphia Assemblies,* edited by Joseph P. Sims, (Philadelphia: Privately Printed, 1948).

19. *The Philadelphia Club, 1834-1934.*

20. *Ibid.* Also inspection of the *Social Register.*

21. John P. Marquand, *The Late George Apley,* (New York: The Modern Library, 1940), p. 189.

22. *Rittenhouse Club,* Charter, By-Laws, Officers and Members, (Philadelphia: J. B. Lippincott Company, 1935).

23. Cleveland Amory, *op. cit.*, pp. 110-111.

In contrast to the Rittenhouse or even the Philadelphia Clubs, it is probably safe to say that the Acorn Club draws its members entirely from the upper class.

In "Yankee City," "The evidence from male and female membership in associations points to the women's acting more exclusively than the men. There is only one upper-upper association, a women's group." Warner and Lunt, *op. cit.*, p. 350.

24. Dixon Wecter, *op. cit.*, p. 272.
25. *Ibid.*, pp. 272-273.
26. *Ibid.*, p. 272.
27. George Birmingham, "The American at Home and in His Club," in *America in Perspective*, edited, with an Introduction and Notes, by Henry Steele Commager, (New York: The New American Library, 1947), p. 175.
28. John A. Lester, Editor, *A Century of Philadelphia Cricket*, (Philadelphia: University of Pennsylvania Press, 1951).
29. *Ibid.*, p. 15.
30. *Ibid.*, p. 10.
31. *Ibid.*, pp. 371-375. See the list of Philadelphia cricket clubs.
32. *Ibid.*, p. 135.
33. *Ibid.*, pp. 88-89.
34. *Ibid.*, p. 93.
35. *Ibid.*, p. 277.
36. *Ibid.*, pp. 342-359.
37. *A History of the Schuylkill Fishing Company of the State in Schuylkill*, (Philadelphia: Privately Printed, 1889), see Appendix, "Memoirs of the Glouster Fox Hunting Club," pp. 405-32.
38. *Ibid.*, p. 406.

Chapter XIV

A PRIMARY GROUP OF PRESTIGE AND POWER

1. Reinhold Neibuhr, *The Irony of American History*, (New York: Charles Scribner's Sons, 1952), pp. 12-13.
2. Frederick Lewis Allen, *The Great Pierpont Morgan*, (New York: Harper & Brothers, 1949), pp. 171-172.

Cleveland Amory provides an interesting example of the role of the exclusive men's club in the power structure in the following passage: "In 1941, when it became necessary for the Boston Symphony Orchestra to make a deal with James Caesar Petrillo, President Henry B. Cabot and Treasurer Richard C. Paine handled the negotiations with such delicate finesse that, although the Boston Symphony had fought Petrillo for years and was the last important organization to give in to him, the union changed its by-laws to meet Boston's demand that it be allowed to hire musicians outside the Boston area without permission from the local unions. It later appeared that the chief feature of these negotiations had been an exclusive dinner tendered Petrillo and his men at the Boston Harvard Club, and their welcome into the bosom of Boston Society and princely treatment by Mr. Cabot and Mr. Paine is generally credited with having had much to do with the unexpected amiability of Mr. Petrillo." Cleveland Amory, *The Proper Bostonians*, (New York: E. P. Dutton & Co., Inc., 1947), pp. 357-358.

3. Frederick Lewis Allen, *op. cit.*, pp. 174-175.
4. Biographical material on Thomas S. Gates obtained in *Who's Who* and obituary, Philadelphia *Evening Bulletin*, April 8, 1948.
5. Biographical material on Edward Hopkinson, Jr. obtained in *Who's Who*. Family background in *Universities and Their Sons, University of Pennsylvania*, (Boston: R. Herndon Company, 1901).
6. Biographical material on Benjamin Rush obtained in *Who's Who* and obituary, Philadelphia *Evening Bulletin*, April 26, 1948.
7. Biographical material on Leonard T. Beale obtained in *Who's Who*. Family background obtained in William Haynes, *Chemical Pioneers*, (New York: D. Van Nostrand Company, Inc., 1939), pp. 107-124.
8. Biographical material on Samuel Dexter Warriner obtained in *Who's Who* and obituary, New York *Times*, April 4, 1942.

9. Biographical material on John A. Stevenson obtained in *Who's Who* and obituary, Philadelphia *Inquirer*, September 1, 1949.

10. Biographical material on Nathan Hayward obtained in *Who's Who*.

11. Biographical material on C. Stevenson Newhall obtained in *Who's Who* and obituary, Philadelphia *Evening Bulletin*, December 15, 1950.

12. Biographical material on Joseph Wayne, Jr. obtained in *Who's Who* and obituary, Philadelphia *Evening Bulletin*, May 27, 1942.

13. Biographical material on Albert M. Greenfield obtained in *Who's Who*.

14. "The Bankers' Trust, with 19 branch offices, closed its doors . . ." Philadelphia *Evening Bulletin*, December 22, 1930.

15. Philadelphia *Evening Bulletin*, May 13, 1931.

16. *Ibid.*, May 12, 1931.

17. See "Russell W. Davenport: A Sketch by John Knox Jessup" in Russell W. Davenport, *The Dignity of Man*, (New York: Harper & Brothers, 1955), pp. 1-23. Also see references to his father, Russell W. Davenport, in Frank Barkley Copley, *Frederick W. Taylor*, (New York: Harper & Brothers, 1923), 2 volumes.
The threads of history are interesting. Russell W. Davenport, Senior, first came down to Philadelphia from New Haven with his friend, Charles A. Brinley, where they both worked at Midvale with Frederick W. Taylor. In 1940, Charles A. Brinley's son, Charles E. Brinley, was listed in both *Who's Who* and the Philadelphia *Social Register*. A graduate of Groton and Yale, he was president of the Baldwin Locomotive Works which owned The Midvale Company (see discussion of Baldwins and Midvale in Chapter VI).

18. Reprinted by special permission from the June 1936 issue of *Fortune Magazine;* copyrighted 1936 by Time, Inc.

Chapter XV

SUMMARY AND CONCLUSION

1. R. H. Tawney, *Equality,* (New York: Harcourt, Brace and Company, 1931), p. 61.

2. Quoted in John P. Mallan, "Roosevelt, Brooks Adams, and Lea: The Warrior Critique of the Business Civilization," *American Quarterly,* Vol. VIII, No. 3, (Fall 1956), p. 219.

3. Isaiah Berlin, "A Marvellous Decade (IV)," *Encounter,* Vol. VI, No. 5, (May 1956), p. 21.

4. A. C. Spectorsky, *The Exurbanites,* (Philadelphia: J. B. Lippincott Company, 1955).
William H. Whyte, Jr., *The Organization Man,* (New York: Simon and Schuster, 1956).

5. C. Wright Mills, *The Power Elite,* (New York: Oxford University Press, 1956).

Afterword

THE AMERICAN ARISTOCRAT AND OTHER-DIRECTION

1. David Riesman, in collaboration with Reuel Denney and Nathan Glazer, *The Lonely Crowd: A Study of the Changing American Character* (New Haven: Yale University Press, 1950), p. 301. (Italics mine.)

2. E. Digby Baltzell, "Rich Men in American Politics," *The Nation,* 186, No. 22 (May 31, 1958), 493–495.

3. See above, p. 58.

4. Andrew Hacker, "Liberal Democracy and Social Control," *American Political Science Review,* 51, No. 4 (December, 1957), p. 1015.

5. See below for a discussion of Riesman's equation of "tolerance" with other-direction.

6. The works of Lothrop Stoddard also played on the prevalent mood of Anglo-Saxon panic in America. In Volume 1, Number 1, March 3, 1923, of *Time,* interestingly enough, Charles Scribner's Sons took a full page to advertise Stoddard's books, which were called "An International Sensation." Down through the years, *Time* has continued to reflect middle-class American values.

7. That a prominent member of the upper class from another city, with all the right boarding school and col-

lege background, was at this very same time immediately taken into the club after taking over an executive position in another firm in the city did not help matters.

8. It is of passing interest to observe that a Proper Philadelphia lawyer's handling of my friend's legal and tax problems came to an end after the secondhand car business was sold, when it turned out that some sixty thousand dollars in cash profits had somehow not been reported.

9. Isolated instances of this pattern still exist. For example, the heir and president of one of Philadelphia's most ancient publishing houses, a business gentleman of the old school, never has asked his closest associate in the firm either home to dinner or to his club to lunch during more than thirty years of working together in the office.

10. See above, Chap. 9.

11. During an informal show of hands in the audience while talking to parent-teacher groups along the Main Line several years ago, it was interesting (especially for the audience) to see that two out of three of the parents had not lived in the community before the war.

12. Riesman, *op. cit.*, p. 56.

13. As an omen of change, perhaps, it is interesting that the one-man

and patriarchal nature of a number of the leading boarding schools came to an end just before, during, and immediately after the Second World War. Drury of St. Paul's, Peabody of Groton, Father Sill of Kent, and Boynton of Deerfield were among the great headmasters who died during this period. Institutionalization has replaced the personal touch today.

14. At Groton, this liberal trend has progressed even further. Negro students have been accepted since the war, and recently a member of the Jewish faith was added to the faculty.

15. In contrast to the past, the school's present effort to influence the main stream of American life is attested to by the fact that two of its most valued masters recently left the school to take important posts in the public school systems of two major cities in the Midwest.

16. S. M. Lipset, *Political Man* (Glencoe: The Free Press, 1960), p. 299.

17. Riesman, *op. cit.*, p. 177.

18. Among other reasons, the members of the American upper class during the New Deal days despised Roosevelt for his ethnic and racial tolerance and especially for his so-called philo-Semitism; and the bitter anti-Roosevelt story in those days often referred to "that man" as "Rosenfelt."

PERMISSIONS
AND ACKNOWLEDGMENTS

Grateful acknowledgment is made to the following publishers and individuals for permission to quote from copyrighted works:

The University of Pennsylvania Press for permission to quote from *A Century of Philadelphia Cricket* edited by John A. Lester, *History of The University of Pennsylvania, 1740-1940* by Edward Potts Cheyney, and *S. Weir Mitchell* by Ernest Earnest.

J. B. Lippincott Company for permission to quote from *Philadelphia Lawyer* by George Wharton Pepper.

Alfred A. Knopf, Inc. for permission to quote from *God and My Father* by Clarence Day, and *Democracy in America* by Alexis de Tocqueville.

Oxford University Press for permission to quote from *Max Weber: Essays in Sociology* edited and translated by H. H. Gerth and C. W. Mills, and *Quest for Community* by R. A. Nisbet.

Harper & Brothers for permission to quote from *The Lords of Creation* by Frederick Lewis Allen, and *Protestant Churches and Industrial America* by Henry F. May.

Greenberg Publisher for permission to quote from *Boies Penrose* by Robert Douglas Bowden.

The Viking Press, Inc. for permission to quote from *The Portable Veblen* edited by Max Lerner.

Charles Scribner's Sons for permission to quote from *The Saga of American Society* by Dixon Wector, *The Episcopal Church in the United States* by James Thayer Addison, *St. Paul's School, 1855-1934* by Arthur Stanwood Pier, and *The Self and the Dramas of History* by Reinhold Niebuhr.

Mr. George Biddle for permission to quote from *An American Artist's Story*.

Mr. Francis Biddle for permission to quote from *The Llanfear Pattern*.

Harvard University Press for permission to quote from *Soviet Politics* by Barrington Moore.

The University of Chicago Press for permission to quote from *The Gold Coast and the Slum* by Harvey Warren Zorbaugh.

Coward-McCann, Inc. for permission to quote from *Peabody of Groton* by Frank D. Ashburn.

G. P. Putnam's Sons for permission to quote from *Without Drums* by P. A. B. Widener, copyright 1940.

The University of North Carolina Press for permission to quote from *Meeting House and Counting House* by Frederick B. Tolles.

Appleton-Century-Crofts, Inc. for permission to quote from *The Study of Man* by Ralph Linton, copyright 1936 by D. Appleton-Century Co.

Harcourt, Brace and Company for permission to quote from *It's Not Done* by William C. Bullitt, and *Rebels and Gentlemen* by Carl and Jessica Bridenbaugh.

Basil Blackwell, Publisher for permission to quote from *L'Ancien Regime* by Alexis de Tocqueville.

Yale University Press for permission to quote from *Social System of the Modern Factory* by W. Lloyd Warner and J. O. Low.

New American Library, Inc. for permission to quote from *America in Perspective.*

Little, Brown and Company for permission to quote from *The Late George Apley* by John P. Marquand.

Mr. Nicholas B. Wainwright for permission to quote from *History of the First Troop Philadelphia City Cavalry, 1914-1948.*

The Philadelphia Contributorship for permission to quote from *A Philadelphia Story* by Nicholas B. Wainwright.

The Pennsylvania Railroad for permission to quote from *Centennial History of The Pennsylvania Railroad Company* by George H. Burgess and Miles C. Kennedy.

Index

QUADRANGLE PAPERBACKS

American History

James Truslow Adams. *Provincial Society, 1690-1763.* (QP403)
Frederick Lewis Allen. *The Lords of Creation.* (QP35)
Lewis Atherton. *Main Street on the Middle Border.* (QP36)
Thomas A. Bailey. *Woodrow Wilson and the Lost Peace.* (QP1)
Thomas A. Bailey. *Woodrow Wilson and the Great Betrayal.* (QP2)
Charles A. Beard. *The Idea of National Interest.* (QP27)
Carl L. Becker. *Everyman His Own Historian.* (QP33)
Barton J. Bernstein. *Politics and Policies of the Truman Administration.* (QP72)
Ray A. Billington. *The Protestant Crusade.* (QP12)
Allan G. Bogue. *From Prairie to Corn Belt.* (QP50)
Kenneth E. Boulding. *The Organizational Revolution.* (QP43)
Robert V. Bruce. *1877: Year of Violence.* (QP73)
Roger Burlingame. *Henry Ford.* (QP76)
Gerald M. Capers. *John C. Calhoun, Opportunist.* (QP70)
David M. Chalmers. *Hooded Americanism.* (QP51)
John Chamberlain. *Farewell to Reform.* (QP19)
Arthur C. Cole. *The Irrepressible Conflict, 1850-1865.* (QP407)
Alice Hamilton Cromie. *A Tour Guide to the Civil War.*
Robert D. Cross. *The Emergence of Liberal Catholicism in America.* (QP44)
Richard M. Dalfiume. *American Politics Since 1945.* (NYTimes Book, QP57)
Carl N. Degler. *The New Deal.* (NYTimes Book, QP74)
Chester McArthur Destler. *American Radicalism, 1865-1901.* (QP30)
Robert A. Divine. *American Foreign Policy Since 1945.* (NYTimes Book, QP58)
Robert A. Divine. *Causes and Consequences of World War II.* (QP63)
Robert A. Divine. *The Cuban Missile Crisis.* (QP86)
Robert A. Divine. *The Illusion of Neutrality.* (QP45)
Elisha P. Douglass. *Rebels and Democrats.* (QP26)
Melvyn Dubofsky. *American Labor Since the New Deal.* (NYTimes Book, QP87)
Arthur A. Ekirch, Jr. *Ideologies and Utopias.* (QP89)
Harold U. Faulkner. *The Quest for Social Justice, 1898-1914.* (QP411)
Carl Russell Fish. *The Rise of the Common Man, 1830-1850.* (QP406)
Felix Frankfurter. *The Commerce Clause.* (QP16)
Edwin Scott Gaustad. *The Great Awakening in New England.* (QP46)
Ray Ginger. *Altgeld's America.* (QP21)
Ray Ginger. *Modern American Cities.* (NYTimes Book, QP67)
Ray Ginger. *Six Days or Forever?* (QP68)
Evarts B. Greene. *The Revolutionary Generation, 1763-1790.* (QP404)
Gerald N. Grob. *Workers and Utopia.* (QP61)
Louis Hartz. *Economic Policy and Democratic Thought.* (QP52)
William B. Hesseltine. *Lincoln's Plan of Reconstruction.* (QP41)
Granville Hicks. *The Great Tradition.* (QP62)
Stanley P. Hirshson. *Farewell to the Bloody Shirt.* (QP53)
Dwight W. Hoover. *A Teacher's Guide to American Urban History.* (QP83)
Dwight W. Hoover. *Understanding Negro History.* (QP49)
Frederic C. Howe. *The Confessions of a Reformer.* (QP39)
Harold L. Ickes. *The Autobiography of a Curmudgeon.* (QP69)
William Loren Katz. *Teachers' Guide to American Negro History.* (QP210)
Burton Ira Kaufman. *Washington's Farewell Address.* (QP64)
Edward Chase Kirkland. *Dream and Thought in the Business Community, 1860-1900.* (QP11)
Edward Chase Kirkland. *Industry Comes of Age.* (QP42)
Herbert S. Klein. *Slavery in the Americas.* (QP84)
Adrienne Koch. *The Philosophy of Thomas Jefferson.* (QP17)
Gabriel Kolko. *The Triumph of Conservatism.* (QP40)
Aileen S. Kraditor. *Up from the Pedestal.* (QP77)
John Allen Krout and Dixon Ryan Fox. *The Completion of Independence, 1790-1830.* (QP405)
Walter LaFeber. *John Quincy Adams and American Continental Empire.* (QP23)
Lawrence H. Leder. *The Meaning of the American Revolution.* (NYTimes Book, QP66)
David E. Lilienthal. *TVA: Democracy on the March.* (QP28)

American History (continued)

Arthur S. Link. *Wilson the Diplomatist*. (QP18)
Huey P. Long. *Every Man a King*. (QP8)
Gene M. Lyons. *America: Purpose and Power*. (QP24)
Neill Macaulay. *The Sandino Affair*. (QP82)
Ernest R. May. *The World War and American Isolation, 1914-1917*. (QP29)
Henry F. May. *The End of American Innocence*. (QP9)
Thomas J. McCormick. *China Market*. (QP75)
August Meier and Elliott Rudwick. *Black Protest in the Sixties*. (NYTimes Book, QP78)
George E. Mowry. *The California Progressives*. (QP6)
Allan Nevins. *The Emergence of Modern America, 1865-1878*. (QP408)
William L. O'Neill. *American Society Since 1945*. (NYTimes Book, QP59)
William L. O'Neill. *Everyone Was Brave*. (QP88)
William L. O'Neill. *The Woman Movement*. (QP80)
Frank L. Owsley. *Plain Folk of the Old South*. (QP22)
Thomas G. Paterson. *Cold War Critics*. (QP85)
David Graham Phillips. *The Treason of the Senate*. (QP20)
Julius W. Pratt. *Expansionists of 1898*. (QP15)
Herbert I. Priestley. *The Coming of the White Man, 1492-1848*. (QP401)
C. Herman Pritchett. *The Roosevelt Court*. (QP71)
Moses Rischin. *The American Gospel of Success*. (QP54)
John P. Roche. *The Quest for the Dream*. (QP47)
Arthur Meier Schlesinger. *The Rise of the City, 1878-1898*. (QP410)
David A. Shannon. *The Socialist Party of America*. (QP38)
Andrew Sinclair. *The Available Man*. (QP60)
Preston W. Slosson. *The Great Crusade and After, 1914-1928*. (QP412)
June Sochen. *The Black Man and the American Dream*. (QP81)
John Spargo. *The Bitter Cry of the Children*. (QP55)
Bernard Sternsher. *Hitting Home*. (QP79)
Bernard Sternsher. *The Negro in Depression and War*. (QP65)
Ida M. Tarbell. *The Nationalizing of Business, 1878-1898*. (QP409)
Richard W. Van Alstyne. *The Rising American Empire*. (QP25)
Willard M. Wallace. *Appeal to Arms*. (QP10)
Norman Ware. *The Industrial Worker, 1840-1860*. (QP13)
Dixon Wecter. *The Age of the Great Depression, 1929-1941*. (QP413)
Albert K. Weinberg. *Manifest Destiny*. (QP3)
Bernard A. Weisberger. *They Gathered at the River*. (QP37)
Thomas J. Wertenbaker. *The First Americans, 1607-1690*. (QP402)
Robert H. Wiebe. *Businessmen and Reform*. (QP56)
William Appleman Williams. *The Contours of American History*. (QP34)
William Appleman Williams. *The Great Evasion*. (QP48)
Esmond Wright. *Causes and Consequences of the American Revolution*. (QP31)

European History

William Sheridan Allen. *The Nazi Seizure of Power*. (QP302)
Hans W. Gatzke. *European Diplomacy Between Two Wars, 1919-1939*. (QP351)
Nathanael Greene. *European Socialism Since World War I*. (NYTimes Book, QP309)
W. O. Henderson. *The Industrial Revolution in Europe*. (QP303)
Raul Hilberg. *The Destruction of the European Jews*. (QP301)
Raul Hilberg. *Documents of Destruction*. (QP311)
Richard N. Hunt. *German Social Democracy*. (QP306)
John F. Naylor. *Britain, 1919-1970*. (NYTimes Book, QP312)
Steven E. Ozment. *The Reformation in Medieval Perspective*. (QP350)
Percy Ernst Schramm. *Hitler: The Man and the Military Leader*. (QP308)
Telford Taylor. *Sword and Swastika*. (QP304)
John Weiss. *Nazis and Fascists in Europe, 1918-1945*. (NYTimes Book, QP305)

See our complete catalog for titles in Social Science *and* Philosophy.